BRITISH LIBRARIANSHIP AND INFORMATION WORK
1991–2000

BRITISH LIBRARIANSHIP AND INFORMATION WORK 1991–2000

Edited by
J. H. BOWMAN
University College London, UK

ASHGATE

Published by
Ashgate Publishing Limited
Gower House
Croft Road
Aldershot
Hampshire GU11 3HR
England

Ashgate Publishing Company
Suite 420
101 Cherry Street
Burlington, VT 05401-4405
USA

Ashgate website: http://www.ashgate.com

British Library Cataloguing in Publication Data
British librarianship and information work 1991–2000
   1. Libraries - Great Britain 2. Library science - Great
   Britain
   I. Bowman, J. H.
   027'.041'09049

ISSN 1752-556X

ISBN-10: 0 7546 4779 X
ISBN-13: 978 0 7546 4779 9

Printed and bound in Great Britain by Antony Rowe Ltd, Chippenham, Wiltshire.

Contents

Contributors

Stephen Adams, MRSC, CChem, MCLIP
Director, Magister Ltd, Reading

J. H. Bowman, MA, MA, PhD, MCLIP, FRSA
Lecturer in Library and Information Studies, School of Library, Archive & Information Studies, University College London

Phil Bradley
Internet Consultant

Vanda Broughton, MA, DipLib
Lecturer in Library and Information Studies, School of Library, Archive & Information Studies, University College London

David Butcher, BA, MCLIP
Editor, Refer

Douglas Dodds, BA, MCLIP, FRSA
Head of Central Services, Word & Image Department, Victoria & Albert Museum, London

Philippa Dolphin, MA, DipLib, MCLIP
formelry Librarian, Birkbeck University of London

Bob Duckett, MA, FCLIP
formerly Reference Librarian, Bradford

Peter Griffiths, BA, FCLIP
Head, Information Services Unit, Home Office

Frances Hendrix, JP, MBA, BA, FCLIP, MInstD
Chief Executive, Laser Foundation; formerly Director, LASER (London and South Eastern Library Region)

J. D. Hendry, MA, FCLIP, FSA
formerly County Heritage Services Officer, Cumbria County Council; President, Library Association, 1997–1998

Peter Hoare, MA, FSA, HonFCLIP
formerly Librarian, University of Nottingham

Marion Huckle, BSc, MCLIP
Head of Qualifications and Professional Development, CILIP

Grace L. Hudson, MA, MPhil, MIL, MCLIP
Deputy University Librarian (Academic Services), University of Bradford

Jane Inman, BA, DipLib, MCLIP
Technical Librarian, Warwickshire County Council

Ian Jamieson, FCLIP
Editor, The local studies librarian; *formerly Lecturer at University of Northumbria*

Ayub Khan, BA, FCLIP
Quality & Operations Manager, Warwickshire Libraries; formally Principal Project Officer, Library of Birmingham

Ian D. McGowan, BA, FRSA
Librarian, National Library of Scotland 1990–2002. Editor of Alexandria: the journal of national and international library and information issues

Bernard Naylor, MA, DipLib, MCLIP
Librarian, University of Southampton 1977–2000; Chair of the Executive, SCONUL 1986–1988; President, Library Association 2001–2002

Richard Nelsson
Information Manager, Guardian Newspapers Ltd; Chair-elect, Association of UK Media Librarians

David Nicholas, MPhil, PhD, MCLIP
Director, School of Library, Archive & Information Studies, University College London

Mary Nixon, BA, MA, DipLib, MCLIP
Librarian, Goldsmiths, University of London

Valerie Nurcombe, BA, MCLIP
Publications Secretary, SCOOP

Robert Parry, BA
Senior Research Fellow, Department of Geography, University of Reading, and formerly Curator of the University's Map Collection

John Pateman, MBA, DipLib, FCLIP
Head of Libraries, Lincolnshire County Council, 2003– ; Head of Libraries, Hackney 1995-1998; Head of Libraries, Merton 1998-2003

David Pearson, BA, DipLib, FCLIP
Director, University of London Research Library Services

Howard Picton, BA, MCLIP

Parliamentary Affairs Manager, Bank of England; Secretary, Standing Committee on Official Publications (SCOOP)

Chris Pond, OBE, MA, PhD, HonFCLIP, ACIPR
Head of Reference Services, Department of the Library, House of Commons

Scott Robertson, MA, MEd, DipLib, MCLIP
Head of Library Services, University of Chichester

Keith Sambrook, MA
formerly with Heinemann International

Elizabeth Shepherd, BA, MA, PhD, DMS, DAS, RMSA
Senior lecturer in Archives and Records Management, School of Library, Archive and Information Studies, University College London

Linda M. Smith, MCLIP
Publications Manager, Libraries and Learning Resources, Nottingham Trent University; Chair, Publicity and Public Relations Group, CILIP

Lucy A. Tedd, BSc, MCLIP
Lecturer, Department of Information Studies, University of Wales Aberystwyth; editor of Program: electronic library and information systems

Stella Thebridge, BA, DipLib, MCLIP
Young People's Librarian, Warwickshire Libraries

Pamela Thompson, BA, HonRCM
Chief Librarian, Royal College of Music, London

John Vincent
Networker, The Network tackling social exclusion in libraries, museums, archives and galleries; until 1996 a senior manager in the London Borough of Lambeth Library Service

Alison Walker, MA, BLitt, DipLib
Head, National Preservation Office

Margaret Watson, BA, MA, MCLIP
formerly Acting Head of Department, University of Northumbria; President, CILIP 2003–2004; Chair, CILIP's Qualifications Framework Steering Group

Preface

This volume stands as the latest of a long line. The first volume of *The year's work in librarianship* covered 1928 and was published in 1929. Coverage was international, and the intention was chiefly to provide a review of the literature rather than an account of events. With some disruption to the sequence during the Second World War, the annual volumes continued until v. 17, which covered 1950. From 1951 the plan changed, largely because of the inception of *Library science abstracts*: the intention became the recording of major trends and developments, though still with a focus on publications, and the volumes covered five years at a time, under the title *Five years' work in librarianship*. The first of these, for 1951–1955, was published in 1958. After three such compilations the focus changed again and the field was narrowed to Britain, the title becoming *British librarianship and information science*. From 1976–1980 onwards the book was divided into two volumes and was called *British librarianship and information work*. The five-yearly publication schedule continued and the last pair of volumes, covering 1986–1990, was published in 1993.

All those volumes were published by the Library Association. Its successor CILIP, however, did not wish to continue them, and it was therefore a great delight to find that Ashgate were willing to take them up. The title, despite the slight quaintness of *information work*, has been retained, to facilitate continuity.

In the spring of 2005 letters were sent out to potential contributors, and the response was very gratifying. A little over a year later most of the chapters were gathered in. Readers familiar with the previous volumes will have some expectations as to what should be in this one, and I hope will be pleased. However, inclusions have always varied from volume to volume and this one is no exception. Some subjects have been removed, or replaced with others – such as social inclusion, and the impact of the internet – which seemed more topical. Regrettably, a few authors found that when the time came, or indeed when it was long past, they were unable to furnish their contributions. There are therefore no chapters on children's services, industrial and commercial libraries, management, medical and health libraries, or multimedia, all of which had been originally agreed.

Contributors were given the same word limit as in the previous volumes, namely 7,500 words, but were encouraged to include as many bibliographic references as possible, so that readers may follow up topics that interest them. I have made no attempt to impose a uniform style on their writing, but I have tried to standardize spelling and have done my best to impose a uniform system of citation, though I have not tried to standardize every entry across all the chapters. I have agonized repeatedly over capital letters and italics and I know that I have not achieved total consistency. I have certainly not attempted to verify the references.

Contributors were asked to provide any post-nominal letters that thcy wanted included. Some specifically asked for such letters to be omitted, but this does not imply that they are lacking in qualifications.

It is perhaps worth referring here to a body which appears many times in these pages though it came into being only in the final year of this volume's coverage. In April 2000 an organization was formed which was fleetingly called the Museums, Libraries and Archives Council (MLAC). Within less than a month it had changed its name to Resource: The Council for Museums, Archives and Libraries, and remained so until February 2004 when it took again the name Museums, Libraries and Archives Council (now abbreviated as MLA). *Re:source* often appeared thus, with a colon, but I have taken the liberty of removing it whenever the name appears.

I should like to conclude by thanking my head of department, Professor David Nicholas, for his constant encouragement in this project, and by reiterating my thanks to all the contributors for providing material of such quality and for making it all such fun.

J.H.B.

1

National libraries

Ian D. McGowan

The story of national libraries in the United Kingdom in the 1990s is dominated to a great extent by the twin demands of providing suitable accommodation for the libraries' existing and future physical collections, and creating the structures necessary to exploit the opportunities made possible by the digital world – opportunities that by the end of the decade had encouraged these libraries to develop as hybrid libraries and to extend beyond the confines of their buildings as never before.

The financial climate of the decade was a significant factor in determining how the libraries went about meeting these demands, and their close relationship to central government could not fail to influence their strategic thinking.[1] Government initiatives such as the Citizen's Charter,[2] monitoring of performance against Code of Service Standards,[3] new approaches to staff management as well as reductions in staff numbers,[4] the market testing of operations, and the Private Finance Initiative all had an impact on what the libraries did and how they did it.

The British Library

In his introduction to the British Library's *Annual report* for 1991–92, the Chairman of the BL Board, Michael Saunders Watson, said: 'The period covered by this report has seen the British Library experiencing and successfully managing change on a scale which must surely be without precedent in the history of libraries.' This is a large claim, but surely no exaggeration and, as the decade progressed, one that could be repeated with justification each year as the saga of the new building at St Pancras unfolded.

Although it must not be forgotten that the British Library is so much more than its London operations, the significance of the St Pancras building, formally opened by the Queen on 25 June 1998, for its actual services and for the public perception of the Library can hardly be overstated. This is reflected in the strategy document *For scholarship, research and innovation*,[5] published in May 1993, which set out the Library's strategic objectives for the year 2000.[6] Four key areas are identified: satisfying users' needs, improving access, corporate collection development and corporate collection management. Much of this strategy depended on being able to bring together on a single site the various parts of the Library that had been absorbed administratively in 1973, but remained spread over 12 sites in London, serving such disparate constituencies as academic researchers in the humanities, industry and commerce.[7] Transferring some 1,000 staff from these different sites to St Pancras was seen as crucial for breaking down the cultural barriers that still existed between departments and at a practical level would reduce the staff time spent on travelling between sites. Improved services, for example faster book delivery times, would result from single site working, and the books and other library materials would benefit from being stored in better environmental conditions.[8]

By 1991 the Library was anticipating an early start to the transfer of books to the new building.[9] Although this was planned for July 1991, it had to be delayed after problems in the design and finish of bookshelves in the basement storage areas were discovered by the Library's staff during acceptance testing. The Library was at pains to point out that responsibility for the construction of the new building was not the Library's but rather was in the hands of government, in the shape of the Department of National Heritage (DNH), later the Department for Culture, Media and Sport (DCMS), and PSA Projects[10] – a distinction that was sometimes missed in the more sensational media accounts of the various problems in construction. With the privatization of PSA Projects, DCMS made changes to the management structure of the project, and a Steering Committee, with representatives from the Department and the Library, and a joint Project Office were established. The Library also appointed its own project director to guide it through the complex process of building handover and commissioning. Nevertheless, the Library still found itself having to try to plan for the occupation of the building and the introduction of services to the public in the absence of a firm date for the building's handover from the Department, under the spotlight of official scrutiny and in the face of public criticism.[11]

Further setbacks occurred when problems with the installation of electrical cabling and fire protection systems were discovered, and a programme of remedial works had to be devised. In the event the book move did not begin until December 1996. The formal handover to the Library took place on 1 July 1997, and the first services opened in the new Humanities Reading Room in November of the same year.[12] Initially it was necessary to limit reading room opening hours while the commissioning of plant was completed, but the popularity of the new facilities with readers was reflected in record usage and satisfaction rates achieved by March 1998. In spite of dire predictions by critics of the closure of reading rooms at Bloomsbury, such as the Regular Readers' Group, the speed with which the Library's users became accustomed to their new surroundings at St Pancras was shown by the fact that the North Library reading room in the British Museum building was soon deserted and closed a month before the scheduled date 'without notice or comment'. Through 1998 and 1999 reading rooms opened for rare books, maps, Oriental and India Office material, manuscripts, and science, technology and business,[13] leaving only the Newspaper Library and Boston Spa reading rooms not based at St Pancras. Facilities for the general public became available in April 1998 with the opening of the three exhibition galleries, conference centre, bookshop, restaurant and café.[14] A reader survey in January 2000 showed that 85% of readers rated the services and facilities as 'excellent' or 'good'. The general view of the public spaces was likewise positive, with particular praise for the quality of materials and finishes. The impressive spaces created by the architect, Professor Sir Colin St John Wilson, notably the entrance area and reading rooms, found wide favour.[15] Although funding for works of art to enhance the building was more limited than originally expected, the sponsorship of the Foundation for Sport and the Arts made it possible for the massive bronze of Isaac Newton by Sir Eduardo Paolozzi to be installed in the piazza – a new London landmark. Similarly private donations and a grant from the Arts Council of England Lottery Fund allowed the hanging of the spectacular 7 × 7m tapestry based on R. B. Kitaj's painting *If not, not* in the entrance hall.

By the time the move to St Pancras was complete, two and a half years after it began, some 12 million monographs had been transferred to the 300 km of new stacks, along with 20 million journal issues, not to mention the collections of manuscripts, maps, music, stamps, patents, sound recordings and other special materials such as seals. In all, 1,250 seats were provided in 11 reading rooms, and new hardware and software had been installed to allow the delivery of materials to the reading rooms.[16] The whole exercise was described, with a sense of pride and relief, by the then Chairman, Dr John Ashworth, as 'one of the largest and most complicated logistical exercises ever undertaken in peace time by a civil department of government'.

Somewhat overshadowed by St Pancras, but nonetheless essential for the Library's corporate collection strategy, was the development of the Library's northern arm at Boston Spa.[17] The addition of new buildings to the Boston Spa estate permitted the transfer firstly of 3.2 km of low use humanities and social sciences stock from London and subsequently a further 25 km of stock from the Woolwich book store to Boston Spa. In addition to moves of stock, the strategy of creating and maintaining a single collection on two main sites required the transfer of jobs from London to Boston Spa, and in the years 1991–94 staff in administration, computing, telecommunications, acquisitions processing and record creation were relocated on a voluntary basis to Yorkshire.

At the beginning of the decade, Boston Spa represented approximately half of the Library's operations in terms of staff numbers. Until the advent of the world wide web and the development of new forms of digital service delivery,[18] Boston Spa served the majority of the Library's remote users through its bibliographic services and the Document Supply Centre (DSC).[19] DCS experienced a steady growth in demand overall through the decade, with over 4 million requests being received by its end, although by then the impact of alternative methods and sources of document delivery was also beginning to be felt.[20] The success of document delivery and current awareness services such as *Patent Express*,[21] *Inside Information, Inside Conferences*, and *inside web*, particularly overseas, contributed significantly to the Library's ability, unique among national libraries, to generate almost one third of its income from its operations rather than from government grant-in-aid.[22] DSC had to adapt its methods of working as the number of requests received by electronic means increased from around 60% at the start of the decade to over 90% at its end. One innovation was the introduction of night shift working to allow the Library to respond quickly to requests from users in North America.

Experiments in electronic document delivery included a pilot scheme with the University of East Anglia using the Joint Academic Network (JANET), and trials involving members of the Research Libraries Group. The development of large-scale electronic document delivery services depended not only on the necessary technical infrastructure, but also on agreements with rights holders. Agreements were reached with the Association of American Publishers, in 1993, and the Copyright Licensing Agency, in 1995, on the payment of royalties or copyright fees for supplying photocopies through its fee-paid services, and building on the good relationships with publishers generated by these agreements it was possible also to reach agreement with a number of publishers on the use of digital data for document supply, for example with Elsevier Science in 1997. It was recognized that the new technology raised the possibility of competition between research libraries for the supply of documents in electronic form. A slight drop in UK demand was recorded in 1996–97, the first after a long period of expansion since 1973, which was explained by the financial pressures on academic libraries, the increased availability of abstracts online, and the Higher Education Funding Councils' electronic libraries programme (eLib) which included a number of pro-jects exploring cheaper options for electronic document supply. A joint working party of the British Library and the Consortium of University Research Libraries (CURL) concluded in 1996 that the collection policies of these institutions should nonetheless be complementary. A trial of the ARIEL electronic document delivery system began in September 1997 and the system was gradually extended so that by 2000 over 250,000 articles a year were being supplied using ARIEL.

The financial background
The general financial pressures experienced by public bodies in the 1990s, together with the particular financial demands of moving to the new St Pancras building, were reflected in the need to transfer resources from existing operational pro-grammes to fund the Library's highest priorities – St Pancras and the development of the digital library. By 1996 the Library was predicting staff cuts of 200 posts over the following four years, and as part of its financial planning the BL Board reluctantly asked Library management to investigate the option of charging for access to the reading rooms. Such a possibility predictably aroused a great deal of opposition, and following the General Election the incoming Secretary of State for Culture, Media and Sport added his voice to those encouraging the Library to consider other options. By 1998 the Board was able to confirm that it had no wish to, and would not, impose charges for access to the reading rooms. In March 1998 the Library launched BL2001,[23] a major change management programme, including a Strategic Review consultation paper sent to 8,000 users and other stakeholders. The priorities seen in the 1,500 responses were for free access,

collections and preservation rather than services, and the need for greater cooperation with other institutions. The Library's financial settlement in 1999 was better than expected and it was able to respond positively to the consultation by increasing spending on preservation by £1 million and on acquisitions by £3 million. Over £500,000 was spent on access to electronic products, including the ISI Web of Science. At the end of the decade the Library had established a Policy Unit to consider how the Library would react to predicted changes in patterns of publication which suggested that within a very few years 75% of books and 90% of scholarly journals would be available in digital form only.

The digital library
The development of the British Library as a digital library was seen as crucial for the realization of its strategic vision.[24] In the early 1990s the Library made clear its intention to become a centre for the capture, storage and transmission of electronic documents[25] and began to explore with publishers possible solutions to the problems posed by the exploitation of new digital technologies. In support of this, an Information Systems Strategy was produced, aimed at rationalizing the Library's systems for cataloguing, information retrieval and the production of bibliographic products.[26] Agreements with publishers for the right to use published materials in electronic format were supplemented by the Library's own first exercises in the creation of digital documents, such as the digitization of the manuscript of *Beowulf* and a heavily used microfilm collection of seventeenth- and eighteenth-century newspapers.[27] In 1998 the Library published *Towards the digital library*, describing the various initiatives that were being undertaken, noting that

> The goal of the Digital Library is much too important for failure even to be considered. The question is not whether the digital library should be developed, but how.[28]

The Information Systems Strategy called for a Corporate Bibliographic Programme. In 1997 the Library awarded a contract to Axis Resources under the principles of the government's Private Finance Initiative for the design, implementation and operation of the Programme based on AMICUS, a commercial package in use at the National Library of Canada.[29]

The provision of digital content took a step forward with the signing of agreements with Elsevier Science, which by 1999 allowed the Library to give networked access to over 900 of Elsevier's electronic journals and to use its Science Direct service as a source of document supply.

Seeking to accelerate the process of becoming a digital library, which inevitably was constrained by the financial resources available, the Library attempted to find partners under the Public Private Partnerships Programme with a view to enlisting some of the leading players in the fields of publishing and digital technologies to assist in taking forward the Library's vision. The process reached the stage where potential partners had been identified, but ultimately the search was unsuccessful, since as the Library explained, 'we found there was an unbridgeable gap between the Library's public service objectives and the commercial interests of our prospective partners'.

Although this particular outcome was disappointing, other aspects of the movement towards the digital library were undoubtedly successful. Access to the Library's catalogues via networks was promoted by the offer of free access to the online catalogues for universities and colleges through the Joint Academic Network (JANET). The online catalogues became a major component of the Library's initial world wide web service, Portico, which was launched in February 1995, and continued to represent some of its most heavily used and highly valued features as the Library's web-based services evolved.[30] The need for the conversion of catalogues in advance of the move to St Pancras imposed its own timetable, and the four-year programme to convert the main catalogue of printed books,[31] which saw the keyboarding and editing of more than 4 million records, was followed closely by programmes to convert the catalogue of printed music and the published map catalogue. Other major conversions included the catalogues of additions to the manuscripts, the National Sound Archive, and the Newspaper Library.

Collections

In the excitement over the move to St Pancras and the innovations brought about by the accelerating pace of technological change, it is easy to overlook the heart of the Library, which remained its unsurpassed collections.[32] While new methods of collection management and providing access to existing collections had to be embraced, and the concept of a single collection was developed,[33] leading to the cancellation of many duplicate journal subscriptions, the Library argued strongly for the financial resources for collection-building appropriate to a national institution of world standing. Substantial real terms cuts in the Library's acquisitions budget (approximately 35% in the years 1985–91) were partially restored in the early 1990s, but it was still necessary to call on external support for the purchase of the major items whose rightful home was in the national library. Fortunately, in spite of all difficulties, the Library was successful in buying the only complete copy of the first New Testament printed in English, the Tyndale New Testament, with around £1 million being raised through a public appeal. The Sherborne Missal, the great illuminated manuscript of the late Middle Ages, was acquired with the help of the National Heritage Memorial Fund and the arrangements for the acceptance of works of art in lieu of inheritance tax. The Library also secured the papers of John Evelyn[34] and Sir William Petty, and from more modern times purchased the archive of Kenneth Tynan and the manuscripts of the works of Sir Peter Maxwell Davis. The papers of Harold Pinter were also secured on indefinite loan.

The corporate collection development and collection management strategies identified in *For scholarship, research and innovation* called for improved selection, closer integration of acquisitions activities, increased cooperation with research libraries in the UK and overseas, and the exploitation of networking and digital technologies. Related initiatives included the centralization of UK 'grey literature' in a new National Reports Collection, and by 1996–97 the Library was able to announce 15% efficiency gains in acquisitions processing, and 20% efficiency gains in cataloguing as a result of merging activities previously carried out in London in a central unit at Boston Spa. The cancellation of duplicate journal titles demanded by the single collection policy had to be extended in 1997–98 as financial pressures mounted. As well as further cuts in duplicate high-usc journals, there were major cancellations of foreign journals and the purchasing of foreign-language scientific monographs virtually ceased. Budgets for the purchasing of foreign humanities monographs, rare books and manuscripts were also massively reduced. Approaches to mitigate the worst effects of such reductions included the signing in 1998 of a concordat with the University of London School of Oriental and African Studies aimed at covering cooperation on collection development as well as common access arrangements and the sharing of staff expertise.

The National Bibliographic Service
In 1991–92, the revenue from sales of the British National Bibliography on CD-ROM, launched in 1989, reached £1 million and the Library continued to report a shift by customers from printed to electronic access to the National Bibliographic Service.[35]

The Library was able to exceed regularly its target 'hit rate' of 80% for BNBMARC records, ascribing this to greater operational efficiency, the contracting out of the Cataloguing in Publication programme to a commercial supplier, and the positive outcome of the Copyright Libraries Shared Cataloguing Project.[36] This project allocated the responsibility for creating BNB records among the legal deposit libraries and was successful in improving both the currency and coverage of catalogue records for British books.

The historic impact of centralized cataloguing was undoubted,[37] but the new technologies were posing questions about future developments.[38] In 1997 the Library published a consultation paper on the future of the national bibliography, suggesting ways in which its scope and coverage could be widened through greater cooperation between the British Library and other agencies.[39]

Legal deposit
One fruitful area for collaboration was in the legal deposit of materials.[40] It had long been recognized that existing legal deposit legislation left some significant loopholes in the legal deposit, or 'copyright', libraries' efforts to acquire and preserve the published output of the nation.[41] Most significantly, legislation covered print material only.[42] The resulting gap in provision had always concerned the British Library, but the prospect of continuing this deficiency into a digital environment would be unacceptable. Consequently, in consultation with other legal deposit libraries and national repositories, the Library drew up a proposal for the extension of legal deposit for submission to the government. The proposal described the benefits of extended deposit, the disadvantages of maintaining the present system unchanged, likely costs to the deposit libraries, and the concerns of publishers, and was generally well received. The government, in one of its last acts

before the General Election of 1997, published a consultation document on the legal deposit of electronic publications, anticipating legislation in the following session of Parliament.[43] However, the election of a new government with its own legislative priorities meant that the timetable for extending deposit had to be extended.

In January 1998, the Secretary of State for Culture, Media and Sport set up a working group under the chairmanship of Sir Anthony Kenny, with representatives from the BL and other legal deposit libraries, the British Film Institute and the publishers, with a remit to advise on how an effective national archive of non-print material could be achieved, and on the feasibility of making deposited material available among the legal deposit libraries through a secure communications network. Additionally, the group was asked to consider the scope for greater cooperation among the legal deposit libraries with a view to improving the existing arrangements and minimizing the burden on publishers. The group's report, delivered in July 1998, confirmed that legal deposit was the only adequate system to ensure a comprehensive national published archive. The library representatives and the publishers had been unable to agree on recommendations for access to deposit material in a distributed model, and so the report reflected their differing views.[44] The Secretary of State accepted that the report made a convincing case for legislation to extend legal deposit to non-print materials, but asked that in the interim a code for the voluntary deposit of electronic materials should be devised and operated until legislation could be introduced.[45] These voluntary arrangements came into use in January 2000.

In all the discussions about the extension of legal deposit, government had been clear that the legal deposit libraries had to be able to demonstrate that their management of printed deposit was efficient and cost-effective. Through the 1990s, 'conventional' deposit of printed items continued to grow in step with the increase in the number of publications produced, and the legal deposit libraries looked to increased cooperation among themselves as one way to manage the increased workload without a corresponding increase in resources. A review of legal deposit by the then Deputy Chief Executive, Michael Smethurst, in 1996 coincided with moves to introduce a pilot scheme for sharing the intake of mass market leisure journals, and recommended further measures for sharing archival responsibilities, for example for Scottish and Welsh newspapers.

Cooperation

Although the Library was faced with very considerable internal changes and chal-lenges in the 1990s, nonetheless it also devoted significant resources to developing its outwards-facing activities, at home and abroad.[46] For example, at the start of the decade the Library became the first non-US member of the Research Libraries Group. It also played a leading role in establishing the Consortium of European Research Libraries[47] and developing the Consortium's database of pre-1830 printed books.[48] Other projects reflecting this desire to take an appropriate part in international librarianship included CoBRA, an EU-funded programme to develop research proposals on sharing bibliographic data internationally,[49] and the Conference of European National Librarians web server, Gabriel, originally hosted by the British Library, and providing a single point of access to information about European national libraries' collections and services. Relationships with libraries and other partners abroad were increasingly regularized through formal agreements, such as the Concordat with the British Council, already the Library's agent for document supply in a number of countries. In 1995 the Library signed a collaboration agreement with the Koninklijke Bibliotheek in the Netherlands to promote cooperation in a number of spheres, with an emphasis on information technology. This was followed in 1998 by a similar agreement with the National Library Board of Singapore, where a new Business Information Service based on *inside web* was concluded, and in 2000 by the Library joining the Fathom consortium, which hoped to establish the leading website for knowledge and education. A different aspect of the Library's international responsibilities was shown in its efforts to assist and encourage the development of libraries and librarianship in Eastern Europe. With the financial support of the Open Society Institute, the Library offered placements for Russian librarians, and entered into a 'special relationship' agreement with the National Library of Russia in St Petersburg to collaborate in a range of activities and exchanges. The Library also made a significant contribution to the work of the UNESCO Commission for the Rehabilitation of the Russian State Library in Moscow. Another example of the Library's engagement with Eastern Europe was the assistance given to the National Library of Sarajevo following the Dayton peace agreement in 1995.

The report of the Higher Education Joint Funding Councils' Libraries Review Group, chaired by Professor Sir Brian Follett, underlined the need, given continuing restrictions on funding, for closer cooperation among libraries supporting higher education in the United Kingdom, and in particular the importance of networking and rapid electronic document supply.[50] The Library's individual initiatives for cooperation, such as that with the University of Sheffield for collaboration on digitization, staff exchanges and the remote use of the Library's collections, were now accompanied by a more general discussion of how access to research collections could be enhanced. The Library's Chief Executive was appointed to the main implementation group for the Follett report, and working parties were set up jointly with the Consortium of University Research Libraries to consider the creation of a national bibliographic resource, a national approach to preservation and conservation, and a national approach to document supply and interlending.

The continuing importance of cooperation was seen in the responses to the Library's Strategic Review consultation paper issued in 1998. This confirmed the weight given by the Library's users and other stakeholders to collaboration among research libraries, and one consequence was the creation of the Library's Cooperation and Partnership Programme, which sought to stimulate, and importantly to fund, projects that developed such collaboration.[51] By the beginning of 2000 50 applications for funding had been received in the Programme's three main areas of collecting and access to library resources, preservation of resources for long-term access, and identifying and locating resources. In support of this work the Programme commissioned a study to create a high-level map of existing national and regional, cross-sectoral and cross-domain cooperative activity in these areas.

Research and development
From its creation in 1973, the British Library acted as one of the major funders of research and development in all aspects of library and information work,[52] and by 1991–92 it was spending some £1.4 million on research projects and awarding £1.3 million in new research grants.[53] The Research and Development Department was also responsible for the Library's Consultancy Services and administered the Public Library Development Incentive Scheme on behalf of government. In 1993 the Library issued a 5-year research plan, indicating its priority areas to be: information technology, the role of information in society, innovation in the provision and management of information services, and information policy and the economics of information. However, the government's decision to create a Library and Information Commission (LIC) made it necessary to clarify further the various responsibilities in the research field, and the new LIC assumed responsibility for research strategies and priorities, the European Library Plan and other international relations. The Research and Development Department then underwent a transformation to re-emerge in 1996 as the British Library Research and Innovation Centre (BLRIC) with an enhanced budget and core research programmes covering digital libraries, information retrieval, library and information management, the value and impact of libraries and information services, library cooperation, preservation, and providers and users of information. In 1998 the Department for Culture, Media and Sport issued a consultation document on the proposal to merge BLRIC's research funding activities with LIC, arguing that this would allow more effective coordination of research policy and programmes, and the merger duly went ahead.

Preservation
It is often the case that preservation and conservation are tempting targets for library administrators when financial pressures are felt. The British Library was no exception as the various financial crises of the 1990s were negotiated. Nevertheless, it was possible to make progress on several fronts, even as routine preservation activities were to some extent curtailed. The lurking time-bomb of acidic paper in library materials continued to tick. To address this problem, a paper-strengthening process was developed for the Library by the University of Surrey aimed at achieving the low-cost mass preservation of post-1850 materials printed on poor quality and acidic paper. A pilot plant was established by the Library's partner, Nordion International Inc to test the viability of the process, but by the end of the decade a totally satisfactory solution to the problem remained elusive.

An important administrative development was the transfer of staff of the Library's Conservation Bindery from industrial to non-industrial civil service grades. This change offered an improved career structure to the staff involved and made it easier to recruit and retain good trainees.

As well as the many in-house preservation activities undertaken by the Library, it also supported the National Preservation Office (NPO), which had been established as the UK forum for good practice in preservation and security in libraries and archives. In addition to its work in organizing conferences, seminars and workshops, providing advice and publishing guidance, the NPO managed the Mellon Microfilming Project on behalf of the Library. The Office organized the process of evaluating grant applications, making awards, and monitoring progress, thereby raising awareness of the importance of internationally recognized standards for preservation microfilming in the UK and Ireland. Until 1995–96, the NPO was almost entirely financed by the British Library, but it was then agreed that there were many benefits to be gained by the Office becoming an independent focus for preservation activities. At the same time, discussions with CURL and the legal deposit libraries on a national preservation strategy raised the possibility of a wider role for the NPO. An independent management committee was therefore established, and the NPO began to be funded jointly by the BL, CURL, the Public Record Office and the five other legal deposit libraries. The NPO's responsibilities would continue to include an information and referral service, the promotion of good practice, and coordinating and initiating research, but in 1996 the Office's stakeholders made an important strategic decision that the NPO was the appropriate body to take the lead in creating a national strategy for preservation digitization and digital archiving, guided by a representative Digital Archiving Working Group.[54]

The National Library of Wales
The National Assembly for Wales
The creation of a National Assembly for Wales, established by the Government of Wales Act 1998, must be seen as one of the most important landmarks in the development of the National Library of Wales in the 1990s. In anticipation of the transfer of powers, including the funding of the National Library of Wales, from the Secretary of State for Wales to the Assembly on 1 July 1999, the Library issued a consultation paper on its strategic priorities, *Choosing the future*, in February of that year. The responses to this consultation informed the first of the Library's corporate plans to be presented to the Assembly. The plan, published as *Access roads to learning*, as well as summarizing the Library's mission and functions, indicated its main strategic objectives, including a digitization programme, the 'Visitor Experience' project, points of presence outside the Library's home in Aberystwyth, and marketing and educational activities. The Assembly undertook a review of the Library – one of the first bodies to be scrutinized in this way – and its Reviewing Committee subsequently endorsed the Library's strategy and plans.

Accommodation

In addressing its accommodation requirements for the 1990s and beyond,[55] the Library was fortunate in having a certain amount of expansion space on its existing site in Aberystwyth.[56] Already in 1991 a five-floor storage building had been completed, allowing books stored off-site in temporary accommodation to be transferred back to the Library. Treasury approval to proceed with a new Third Building for the Library, again mainly for book storage, was given in September 1993 at an estimated cost of £11.5 million. The Third Building was completed early in 1996 and opened by the Queen on 31 May. The new facility was seen by the Library as securing its future for the next twenty-five years by providing storage over six floors for 112 km of book shelving, a floor of map storage, and eighteen cells for special materials, including one copper-clad cell for the storage of electronic materials. The collections, housed in controlled environmental conditions, were also safeguarded by state-of-the-art fire detection and control systems. The building also provided space for some sixty members of staff and a new computer suite.

Having secured this new storage, essential for the continually expanding collections of a legal deposit library, the Library turned its attention to the needs of visitors to its public areas. An ambitious project under the title 'The Visitor Experience' planned to provide a new lecture theatre, a relocated and upgraded restaurant, refurbished and extended exhibition areas, and improved reading room facilities. The proposals were to be successfully realized with the help of the Heritage Lottery Fund in the following decade.

The digital library

The Library began to consider the replacement of its existing computer system for printed books, URICA, at the start of the decade.[57] However, it was several years before the necessary operational and financial planning, including the decision to move from UKMARC to USMARC, resulted in the migration to the GEAC Advance system, which went live in October 1999. A feature of particular importance to the Library as a bilingual institution was the new bilingual online catalogue, GeoWeb. By this time, nearly 70% of the catalogue of printed books had been retro-converted, leading the Library to report significantly increased use of the pre-1986 collection. As the other national libraries rapidly discovered, the introduction of a web server in 1996 encouraged the use of the internet as an increasingly important means to showcase the Library's collections and provide wider access to them.

During the 1990s the Library also developed separate computer systems for the collections of non-print material and for cartographic information.[58] A Non-Print Material Management System was procured, although its implementation did not proceed as smoothly as anticipated. In common with the other legal deposit libraries, the National Library of Wales was faced with new problems in the long-term archiving of Ordnance Survey data. The large scale output of the Ordnance Survey in the shape of Survey Information on Microfilm (SIMS) ceased in 1996 as a result of the National Topographic Database becoming a completely digital database. The legal deposit libraries negotiated a short-term extension of the production of SIMS at a reduced frequency, and in 1999 agreement was reached with the Ordnance Survey for the annual deposit of the National Topographic Database in electronic format.[59] Free public access to view the data, but not to manipulate it, was secured by the agreement, subject to stringent security arrangements. Commercial users were required to reach their own service agreements with the Ordnance Survey.

Cooperation

The Library was no exception to the general increase through the 1990s in libraries' involvement in cooperative projects, such as NEWSPLAN,[60] the Mellon Microfilming Project, the Shared Cataloguing Project and the Copyright Libraries Working Group on Legal Deposit. Another important initiative was the creation of the Aberystwyth Centre for the Book in which the Library collaborated with the Welsh Books Council and the Department of Information and Library Studies in the University of Wales, Aberystwyth. Launched in March 1997, the Centre supported a programme of publications, lectures, exhibitions and other events celebrating and stimulating interest in the book in Wales. Similarly, in 1999 the Aberystwyth Centre for Archives and Records Research and Development resulted from a partnership with the Department of Library and Information Studies, with a remit to support the discipline of archives and records management through lectures and seminars, research projects, training activities and consultancies.

The Library took a central role in the discussions leading to the formation in 1997 of the Consortium of Welsh Library and Information Services (CWLIS), representing and giving a voice to the whole range of Welsh library and information services. The Library also provided the secretariat for the new body.

Collections

The ongoing work of describing and making accessible the Library's collections continued with the publication of guides and catalogues.[61]

Uniquely among the legal deposit libraries, the National Library of Wales functions as a Designated Archive for off-air recording of radio and television broadcasts. By 1995–96 the Library was recording over 4,000 television and 6,000 radio programmes of Welsh interest off-air, as well as receiving on tape the output of S4C. By the end of the decade, the long-term implications of the move to digital television and the expansion of free-to-air channels was beginning to influence the Library's planning for the Sound and Moving Image Collection and adding another imperative to the move to the creation of a digital library.

The Welsh Film and Television Archive worked from different premises but in close collaboration with the Library. By 2000 talks had begun with Sgrin: the Media Agency Wales, on the provision of a unified national collection, joining together the resources of the Film and Television Archive and the Library's Sound and Moving Image Collection.

The National Library of Scotland

The Scottish Parliament

Following the passing of the Scotland Act 1998, the first Scottish Parliament since 1707 took up its full legislative powers on 1 July 1999. One of its new responsibilities was for the National Library of Scotland (NLS), which had been funded previously through the Scottish Office. Like the National Library of Wales, the National Library of Scotland recognized that this new relationship made it opportune to examine its strategic priorities, and therefore issued a consultation paper *A national library for the 21st century* to solicit the views of users and other stakeholders. The key message emerging from this exercise was that new directions, such as the development of NLS as a hybrid library, must be complementary to the traditional services which were still highly valued by the Library's users.

Accommodation

Like the other national libraries, the National Library of Scotland devoted a great deal of time and money through the 1990s to securing the appropriate accommodation for its expanding collections, and ensuring that existing accommodation was fit for purpose. The £22 million contract for the second phase of the Library's new building in Edinburgh, the Causewayside Building, was let in March 1991, and the building was formally opened in May 1995. The building answered the Library's most pressing needs for book storage, but also provided more flexible space for staff and public use. This made it possible to relocate reading room and staff from the Library's George IV Bridge Building while that building was closed to the public for 18 months, undergoing a major programme of refurbishment. This programme, which stretched from 1994 to 1999 and cost over £12 million, was designed primarily to protect the building, its collections and occupants from fire. To this end, floors were strengthened, new fire escapes constructed, a water sprinkler system introduced, new air conditioning and other electrical and mechanical services installed, and reading rooms and the main entrance hall refurbished.

The digital library

During the 1990s the Library introduced a communications network using a high-speed fibre-optic cable to link its two main buildings, both in Edinburgh but a mile apart. On the basis of this network, which also extended to the University of Edinburgh, it was possible to work with the University on a joint procurement of a new computer system. The two institutions invited joint tenders, but evaluated the offered systems independently. Both selected the Voyager system from Endeavor Information Systems, and the new system was implemented in the autumn of 1999 on shared hardware. The system had the capability of integrating information about the Library's collections with digital versions of the collections themselves, and also provided a gateway to external information in digital form.

The successful exploitation of the new system demanded data to populate it.[62] Funding for the retrospective conversion of the catalogue of printed books had been secured in 1991, and by the end of the decade the conversion was complete, with only minor exceptions. By 1994 the Library was experimenting with the scanning and digitization of text and images, such as the Pont manuscript maps, the first detailed mapping of Scotland, dating from the end of the sixteenth century, and the Chepman and Myllar prints, the first works to be printed in Scotland. Funding from the New Opportunities Fund allowed the Library to accelerate the digitization of its own resources, while the Scottish Science Library,[63] a department of the National Library, pioneered the provision of public access to resources on the internet to supplement its collections in more traditional formats. The Map Library offered access to digital mapping from the Ordnance Survey. The Library's website began to host digital versions of Library exhibitions, and teaching resources designed for use in Scottish classrooms, for example a section of the site devoted to Sir Winston Churchill created jointly with the Churchill Archives Centre, Cambridge. The Library's website was increasingly seen as the primary means of access to bibliographical tools such as the *Bibliography of Scotland* and the *Bibliography of Scottish literature in translation*. By 2000 the Library's Inter-Library Services saw the rapid development of electronic document delivery as the preferred means of document supply.

Cooperation

The Library recognized that its role in the modern information world was not only to provide access for researchers to its rich collections through its reading rooms, although this remained an essential element of its mission. Engaging in and encouraging wider cooperation among information providers was increasingly important. Since the 1970s the Library's interlending operation had been one of the main vehicles for interaction with other library authorities. These relationships were strengthened by the creation in 1991 of the Scottish Library and Information Council (SLIC), which had grown from the Library and Information Services Committee (Scotland), a sub-committee of the Library's Board of Trustees. Around the same time, the Working Group on Library Cooperation, comprising the Scottish university libraries, the city libraries of Glasgow and Edinburgh and the National Library, was reborn as the Scottish Confederation of University and Research Libraries (SCURL) for which the National Library provided the secretariat.[64] SCURL's membership expanded through the decade as it undertook a series of projects aimed at ensuring that the collections of Scotland's major libraries were maintained in a coordinated way, and could be searched by scholars as if they were a single entity. The *Research Collections Online* project identified strong research collections in particular subject areas and maintained information about these collections online, while the Co-operative Academic Information Retrieval Network for Scotland (CAIRNS) allowed a simple means of cross-searching the online catalogues of the member libraries. Other projects addressed the feasibility of shared preservation responsibilities, the identification and mainte-nance of Scottish datasets,[65] cataloguing internet resources,[66] and the collating of information on journal holdings through the Scottish Academic Libraries Serials Information Service (SALSER). The Library worked closely with SLIC on a survey of collecting policies for Scottish material in local libraries and the resulting National Strategy for Scottish Materials was influential in the debate on how to achieve maximum coverage of Scottish material right across Scotland. The Scottish Newspapers Microfilming Unit, funded by the Mellon Microfilming Project and managed jointly by the National Library and SLIC, greatly expanded the capacity in Scotland for the microfilming of collections to international preservation standards.

Collections

In spite of the dominance of infrastructure developments in the decade, the Library was able to add to its existing collections some notable acquisitions, such as the literary manuscripts of Hugh MacDiarmid, the correspondence and papers of Muriel Spark, the archive of Sorley MacLean, the most distinguished Gaelic poet of the twentieth century, and the archive of the firm of Robert Stevenson and Sons, civil engineers. In a new approach to collection building, snapshots of the websites of the parties participating in the elections for the Scottish Parliament in May 1999 were harvested. Work continued on the description and history of the Library's collections and the services that maintained and supported them.[67]

A brief account such as this cannot hope to do justice to all the activities and services of the national libraries. Some of the gaps can be filled by reference to the libraries' own regular publications: The British Library *Annual report*, and the reports and newsletters of its various departments; The National Library of Wales *Annual report*, the Welsh Political Archive *Newsletter*, the *Journal of the National Library of Wales*, the Friends of the National Library of Wales *Newsletter*; The National Library of Scotland *Annual report*, *Quarto: newsletter of the National Library of Scotland*, *Folio: collections, research, events at the National Library of Scotland*. Joan de Beer's annual international survey of the literature on national libraries in *Alexandria* and the chapters on national libraries in the volumes of *Librarianship and information work worldwide* also include material of relevance to the national libraries of the United Kingdom.

Notes

1 Brynley Roberts, 'National library relations with government, financial and organizational structures', *Alexandria* **3** (1), 1991, 35–9.

2 Andy Stephens, 'National libraries and the Citizen's Charter' (guest editorial), *Alexandria* **8** (1), 1996, 1–2.

3 Ian McGowan, 'Measuring results of programmes', *Newsletter of the IFLA Section of National Libraries* Dec. 1998, 22–3.

4 Richard Huws, 'Training and career development at the National Library of Wales: some trends over 25 years', *Librarian career development* **3** (1), 1995, 14–18; Ian Malley, 'Preparing for the top: the British Library's policy-making and strategic management course', *Librarian career development* **1** (2), 1993, 25–7; A. O. Owen, 'Annual appraisals and performance related pay at the National Library of Wales', *Personnel training and education* **11** (1/2), 1995, 8–11.

5   British Library, *For scholarship, research and innovation: strategic objectives for the year 2000*. London: British Library, 1993.
6   Jim Craig, 'UBIS response to British Library Strategic Plan', *UBIS news* 2, 1993, 5–6; Kathleen Ladizesky, 'The British Library's strategic objectives for the year 2000', *Focus on international and comparative librarianship* **24** (2), 1993, 65–7; Andy Stephens and Marie Jackson, 'Working towards the millennium: the British Library's plans for the year 2000', *New library world* **97** (2), 1996, 33–7.
7   David Russon, 'The provision of information and library services to science and industry by national libraries with special reference to the British Library', *Alexandria* **3** (1), 1991, 57–67.
8   Alan Day, *The new British Library*. London: Library Association, 1994.
9   Ruth Coman, 'St Pancras: a focus for change at the British Library', *Aslib proceedings* **43** (4), 1991, 143–51; Graham Cranfield and Joe Helliwell, 'Use of a national library: a survey of readers in the humanities and social science reading rooms of the British Library', *Alexandria* **4** (3), 1992, 197–211; Derek Greenwood and John Shawyer, 'Moving the British Library – the book control system', *Aslib information* **21** (1), 1993, 28–31.
10   Alan Day, 'The British Library: the cost is counted', *Library Review* **45** (8), 1996, 6–16; Sir Anthony Kenny, *The British Library and the St Pancras Building*. London: British Library, 1994; Brian Lang and D. Kean, 'Batting for the British Library', *Bookseller* 4773, 13 June 1997, 26–8
11   Alan Day, 'The British Library 1973–1994: an outsider's view', *Alexandria* **7** (3), 1995, 139–154; Alan Day, 'Turning point for the British Library?' *Library review* **44** (2), 1995, 38–43; British Library Regular Readers' Group, *The great British Library disaster*. 2nd rev. ed. London: BLRRG, 1994.
12   Alan Day, 'I was there', *Library review* **47** (3), 1998, 79–82.
13   Beryl Leigh and Andrea Reid, 'The Science Reading Rooms of the British Library: the user community and patterns of use', *Alexandria* **7** (1), 1995, 61–70.
14   Alan Day, *Inside the British Library*. London: Library Association Publishing, 1998; Bart Smith, 'The new British Library: first anniversary', *New library world* **99** (7), 1998, 276–86.
15   Professor Sir Colin St John Wilson, *The design and construction of the British Library*. London: British Library, 1998.
16   Roger Butcher, 'The application of IT in the St Pancras Building of the British Library', *Alexandria* **7** (2), 1995, 83–96; Roger Butcher, 'An overview of British Library automation at St. Pancras', *Program* **27** (3), 1993, 281–92; Richard Foot, 'Automating the British Library – a case study in project implementation', *New library world* **99** (2), 1998, 69–71.
17   David Bradbury, 'British Library Document Supply Centre Strategy: the next ten years', *Interlending and document supply* **21** (3), 1993, 7–11; David Wood, 'Recent developments at the British Library Document Supply Centre', *Interlending and document supply* **20** (4), 1992, 159–61; David Wood, 'Recent developments at BLDSC', *Serials* **6** (1), 1993, 21–6.
18   Philip Barden, 'New technology at the British Library Document Supply Centre: developments and obstacles', *IATUL quarterly* **5** (2), 1991, 117–21; Andrew Braid, 'Electronic document delivery: a reality at last?', *Aslib proceedings* **45** (6), 1993, 161–6; Andrew Braid, 'Electronic document delivery: the dawn of a new age' in *Proceedings of the 7th Annual Computers in Libraries Conference, London, February 1993*. Westport, Conn.: Meckler, 1993, pp. 155–9.

19 Stella Pilling, 'From information to document: new developments at the British Library Document Supply Centre', *IATUL proceedings* new ser. **4**, 1995, 145–9; Stella Pilling, 'Putting the customer first: total quality and customer service at the British Library Document Supply Centre', *Interlending and document supply* **24** (2), 1996, 11–16.

20 Henry Heaney, 'National libraries and electronic document delivery', *Alexandria* **7** (3), 1995, 195–9.

21 Paul Blake, 'British Library's Patent Express adds jukebox system', *Information today* **10** (7), 1993, 36–7.

22 Susan Ashpitel, 'Patents online at the British Library', *Law librarian* **27** (2), 1996, 84–5.

23 David Stoker, 'Where does the British Library go from St. Pancras?', *Journal of librarianship and information science* **30** (3), 1998, 155–7.

24 Alice Prochaska, 'The British Library and its digital future as a research library', *Library review*, **47** (5/6), 1998, 311–16.

25 Stuart Ede, 'Strategic planning for the millennium: a national library perspective', *Information services and use* **13** (1), 1993, 25–34.

26 British Library, *Information systems strategy*. London: British Library, 1995.

27 Alan Day, 'Electronic library services: initiatives for access', *Information management report* 3, 1995, 14–17.

28 Leona Carpenter *et al.* (eds.), *Towards the digital library: the British Library's Initiatives for Access Programme*. London: British Library, 1998.

29 'British Library selects AMICUS software', *Program* **32** (1), 1998, 67–8.

30 Jan Ashton, 'Development of the British Library's OPAC 97: the value of a user-centred approach', *Program* **32** (1), 1998, 1–24; Roger Butcher, 'The British Library online catalogue', *Managing information* **1** (2), 1994, 41–3; Roger Butcher, 'Multi-lingual OPAC developments in the British Library', *Program* **27** (2), 1993, 165–71; Neil Smith and Jan Ashton, 'The British Library and Z39.50', *Vine* 97, 1995, 25–7.

31 Alan Danskin, 'The retrospective conversion of the British Library catalogue of printed books', *International cataloguing and bibliographic control* **26** (4), 1997, 90–1.

32 Robin Alston, *Handlist of unpublished finding aids to the London collections of the British Library*. London: British Library, 1991; Robin Alston and Brad Sabin Hill, *Books printed on vellum in the collections of the British Library compiled by R. C. Alston with a catalogue of Hebrew books compiled by Brad Sabin Hill*. London: British Library, 1996; Barry Bloomfield and Michael Smethurst, 'The view from the British Library' in *Collection management in academic libraries*, ed. Clare Jenkins, Mary Morley. Aldershot: Gower, 1991, pp. 259–81; Kenneth Gardner, *Descriptive catalogue of Japanese books in the British Library printed before 1700*. London: British Library, 1993; Anne Gilbert and Ilse Sternberg, 'The Printed Books photographic collection at the British Library', *IFLA journal* **21** (3), 1995, 191–4; Philip Harris (ed.), *The library of the British Museum: retrospective essays on the Department of Printed Books*. London: British Library, 1991; Stuart James, 'Moving the British Library', *Library review* **47** (3), 1998, 183–6; D. J. McTernan, *French Quebec: imprints in French from Quebec 1764–1990 in the British Library*. London: British Library, 1992–93. 2 vols.; David Paisey, *Catalogue of books printed in the German speaking countries and of German books printed in other countries from 1601 to 1700 now in the British Library*. London: British Library, 1994. 5 vols.; Andrew Phillips, 'Leaving the Reading Room: some personal reflections from within the British Library', *Alexandria* **5** (3), 1993, 201–14.

33 Clare Jenkins and Mary Morley (eds.), *Survival of the fittest? Collection management implications of the British Library Review of acquisition and retention policies.*

Loughborough: National Acquisitions Group, 1991.

34 Theodore Hofmann *et al.*, *John Evelyn in the British Library*. London: British Library, 1995; Theodore Hofmann *et al.*, 'John Evelyn's archive at the British Library', *Book collector* **44** (2), 1995, 147–209; Michael Hunter, 'The British Library and the library of John Evelyn: with a checklist of Evelyn books in the British Library's holdings', *Book collector*, **44** (2), 1995, 218–38.

35 Christopher Easingwood, 'Five years of NBS', *Select* (*National Bibliographic Service newsletter*) 13, 1994, 2–3; Steven Hall, 'National bibliographies on CD-ROM', *Alexandria* **9** (2), 1997, 143–54; Robert Smith, 'National bibliographies on CD-ROM: development of a common approach', *International cataloguing and bibliographic control* **23** (1), 1994, 15–18.

36 Ross Bourne, 'Shared cataloguing: the way forward', *New library world* **94** (3), 1993, 25–6; Copyright Libraries Shared Cataloguing Project Steering Group, *Shared Cataloguing: report to the principals of the six copyright libraries*. London: British Library National Bibliographic Service, 1993.

37 Andy Stephens, *The history of the British National Bibliography 1950–1973*. Boston Spa: British Library, 1994.

38 Ross Bourne, 'Legal deposit and bibliographic control' in *Legal deposit with special reference to the archiving of electronic materials: proceedings of a seminar organised by NORDINFO and the British Library (Research and Development Department) held at the Castle Hotel, Windsor, England, 27–29 October 1994*. Helsingfors: NORDINFO, 1995 (British Library R&D report; 6197), pp. 155–63; Ross Bourne, 'National bibliographies do they have a future?', *Alexandria* **5** (2), 1993, 99–110; Pat Oddy, 'The case for international cooperation in cataloguing: from copy cataloguing to multilingual subject access: experience within the British Library', *Program* **33** (1), 1999, 29–39.

39 A. Cunningham, 'New direction for the national bibliography', *Select* 21, 1997, 1–2; Cynthia McKinley and Peter Robinson (eds.), *The future of the national bibliography: proceedings of a seminar held in June 1997*. Boston Spa: British Library, 1997 (NBS occasional publications; 3).

40 Ian McGowan, 'Co-operation between legal deposit libraries in the United Kingdom and the Republic of Ireland', *Alexandria* **6** (1), 1994, 73–80.

41 Richard Christophers, 'Selection criteria for legal deposit: a view from the British Library' in *Legal deposit with special reference to the archiving of electronic materials*, pp. 39–47; Ann Clarke, 'The legal deposit of non-print publications' in *Legal deposit with special reference to the archiving of electronic materials*, pp. 13–19; David Haynes, 'Electronic publishing: an agenda for national libraries and publishers', *Alexandria* **11** (3), 1999, 167–79; Frederick Ratcliffe, 'Legal deposit: not a copyright issue – a cultural legacy for the future', *Logos* **2** (2), 1991, 82–9.

42 Peter Hoare, *Legal deposit of non-print material: an international overview, September–October 1995*. London: British Library Research and Development Department, 1996 (British Library R&D report; 6245); Peter Hoare, 'Legal deposit of electronic publications and other non-print material: an international overview', *Alexandria* **9** (1), 1997, 59–79.

43 Department of National Heritage, *Legal deposit of publications: a consultation paper*. London: DNH, Scottish Office, Welsh Office, Dept of Education, NI, 1997; Electronic Publishing Services, *The legal deposit of on-line databases*. London: British Library Research and Development Department, 1996 (British Library research and development report; 6244).

44 John Davies, 'Safe deposit: a UK publishing view', *Alexandria* **10** (2), 1998, 159–66.

45 J. Eric Davies and Adrienne Muir, 'Legal deposit of digital material in the UK: recent developments and the international context', *Alexandria* **12** (3), 2000, 151–66.

46 Michael Smethurst, 'The British Library and university libraries: a personal reflection upon co-operation between libraries serving scholarship and research', *Library review* **40** (2/3), 1991, 96–108.

47 'Consortium of European Research Libraries', *British Library news* 188, 1994, 1.

48 Michael Smethurst, 'The Consortium of European Research Libraries (CERL)', *Alexandria* **11** (3), 1999, 149–60.

49 Ross Bourne, 'Towards bibliographic cooperation amongst European national libraries', *LIBER quarterly* **8** (1), 1998, 106–9; Peter Dale, 'CoBRA+: a review, with a look to the future', *Alexandria* **11** (3), 1999, 161–6; Brian Lang, 'The exchange of bibliographic data across Europe', *Select* 14, 1994, 10–12.

50 Joint Funding Councils' Libraries Review Group, *Report.* Bristol: HEFCE, 1993. Chairman Sir Brian Follett. (The 'Follett report'.)

51 Stella Pilling, 'The British Library's co-operation and partnership programme', *Interlending and document supply* **28** (1), 2000, 38–9.

52 Brian Perry, 'The funding environment: the British Library Research and Development Department' in *Research policy in librarianship and information science,* ed. Colin Harris. London: Taylor Graham, 1991, pp. 11–20.

53 A. J. Meadows, *Innovation in information: twenty years of the British Library Research and Development Department.* East Grinstead: Bowker-Saur, 1994 (British Library research series).

54 Mary Feeney, 'Towards a national strategy for archiving digital materials', *Alexandria* **11** (2), 1999, 107–22; Tony Hendley, *The preservation of digital material.* London: British Library Research and Development Department, 1996 (British Library R&D report; 6242).

55 Lionel Madden, 'Llyfrgell Genedlaethol Cymru: the National Library of Wales', *Alexandria* **8** (1), 1996, 51–63; Lionel Madden, 'The National Library of Wales: the next twenty years' in *Celtic connections.* Hamilton: Scottish Library Association, 1996, pp. 97–102; Lionel Madden, 'The National Library of Wales and the future of the book' in *A nation and its books: a history of the book in Wales*, ed. Philip Henry Jones, Eiluned Rees. Aberystwyth: National Library of Wales in association with Aberystwyth Centre for the Book, 1998, pp. 399–405.

56 Daniel Huws, *The National Library of Wales: a history of the building.* Aberystwyth: National Library of Wales, 1994.

57 David Jeremiah, 'Investing your own reality: open systems at the National Library of Wales', *Aslib information* **21** (4), 1993, 161–2.

58 David Jeremiah, 'Procurement of a system to process non-print materials at the National Library of Wales', *Program* **32** (1), 1998, 49–54; Christopher Fleet, 'Early cartographic materials automation project, National Library of Wales, Aberystwyth', *Cartographiti: newsletter of the Map Curators' Group of the British Cartographic Society* 33, March 1993, 6–7; Christopher Fleet, 'Comparing automated map catalogue systems: a pilot study based on the National Library of Wales', *Program* **28** (3), 1994, 223–7.

59 Christopher Fleet, 'Ordnance Survey digital data in UK legal deposit libraries', *LIBER quarterly* **9** (2), 1999, 235–45.

60 Beti Jones, 'Newsplan Cymru: a progress report', *British Library Newspaper Library newsletter* 12, spring 1991, 4–6; Beti Jones, *Newsplan: report of the Newsplan project*

in Wales. London: British Library, 1994.

61 Robert Davies, *The tithe maps of Wales: a guide to the tithe maps and apportionments of Wales in the National Library of Wales*. Aberystwyth: National Library of Wales, 1999; Daniel Huws (ed.), *Guide to the Department of Manuscripts and Records: the National Library of Wales*. Aberystwyth: National Library of Wales, 1994; National Library of Wales, *The nation's heritage*. Aberystwyth: NLW, 1998; Gwyn Jenkins, 'The National Library of Wales: guardian of a nation's heritage', *Contemporary review* Sept. 1998, 140–4; Gwyn Jenkins, 'The Welsh Political Archive', *Contemporary record: the journal of contemporary British history* **7** (1), 1993, 174–80; J. Graham Jones, 'Liberal Party Archives at the National Library of Wales', *Journal of Liberal Democrat history* **26**, spring 2000, 26–31; Ceridwen Lloyd-Morgan, *Augustus John papers at the National Library of Wales*. Aberystwyth: National Library of Wales, 1996; Ceridwen Lloyd-Morgan, 'Medieval manuscripts at the National Library of Wales' in *Sources, exemplars, and copy-texts: influence and transmission*, ed. William Marx. Lampeter: Trivium, 1999, pp. 1–12; Glyn Parry, *A guide to the records of Great Sessions in Wales*. Aberystwyth: National Library of Wales, 1995; Hilary Peters, 'The Welsh probate records: research at the National Library of Wales', *Carmarthenshire antiquary* **35**, 1999, 105; Gwyn Walters, 'The National Library of Wales, the art of the book, and Welsh bibliography' in *A nation and its books*, ed. Jones and Rees, pp. 387–98.

62 Fred Guy, 'Record supply: experiences at the National Library of Scotland', *Catalogue & index* 108, 1993, 1, 4–6; Fred Guy, 'Developing the hybrid library: progress to date in the National Library of Scotland', *Electronic library* **18** (1), 2000, 40–50.

63 Antonia Bunch, 'The Scottish Science Library: a new national resource for Scotland', *Alexandria* **3** (3), 1991, 179–90; John Coll, 'Business information sources for Scotland', *Aslib information* **20** (5), 1992, 201–2; Morag Nisbet, 'The Scottish Science Library: its role in national provision', *Serials* **5** (3), 1992, 45–8.

64 Ann Matheson, 'Humanities information for Scotland' in *Information for Scotland II: proceedings of a conference organised by the Cataloguing and Indexing Group in Scotland with the Scottish Confederation of University and Research Libraries and held in the National Library of Scotland, Edinburgh, 29th March 1995*, ed. P. MacKillop. Edinburgh: CIGS, 1995, pp. 47–53; Ann Matheson, 'Libraries working together: a Scottish perspective', *Art libraries journal* **20** (1), 1995, 12–16.

65 Barbara Morris and Peter Burnhill, *Scottish Datasets Initiative: improving access to digital data on or about the land and people of Scotland*. 1998. Available at: <http://datalib.ed.ac.uk/projects/scotinit> (accessed 10/1/06).

66 Dennis Nicholson *et al.*, *Cataloguing the internet: CATRIONA feasibility study*. London: British Library Research and Development Department, 1995 (Library and information research report; 105).

67 Graham Hogg (ed.), *Special and named printed collections in the National Library of Scotland*. Edinburgh: National Library of Scotland, 1999; William A. Kelly, 'The German collections in the National Library of Scotland', *German Studies Library Group newsletter* 20, 1996, 2–11; Ann Matheson, 'Rare book security in the National Library of Scotland', *Rare books newsletter* 51, 1995, 42–51; *Mountaineering: catalogue of the Graham Brown and Lloyd collections in the National Library of Scotland*. Edinburgh: National Library of Scotland, 1994; Margaret Wilkes, 'He will do well in the beginning to provide a map – the National Library of Scotland map collection', *The map collector* **56**, autumn 1991, 2–7; Margaret Wilkes, 'Map memorabilia at the National Library of Scotland', *Cartomania* 25/26, 1992, 6–7.

2

Libraries and government

J. D. Hendry

Introduction
I have approached this from the stance of one who was closely involved in the process and relationship between central government, and public funded libraries as represented by the Library Association. The relationship with a Conservative government which had already been in office for twelve years, and had gone through the experience of Thatcherism, and that with a new Labour government in 1997, were markedly different. These are reflected in this theme. As a scholar in the field of library history, I believe this period was unique in the relations between government, the library profession and the Library Association. I have tried to reflect this objectively with the advantage of hindsight.

Public funded libraries of all kinds are amongst the longest established, traditional public services in Britain. The very different attitudes and values of a Conservative government (which had been in office since 1979) in the period 1991–1997, and that of the incoming Labour government in 1997 to 2001 should have marked a watershed in public funded library development, as a result of the Labour landslide victory of 1997.

Libraries in crisis
In public libraries in particular, the situation in 1991 was described in the *Library Association record* as that 'there were major reductions planned in the majority of Public Library Authorities in England'.[1] Some specific examples were:

- Derbyshire – closure of 11 libraries and cut in book fund of £900,000 (a total of £1.85 million)
- Manchester – cuts of 11.2% (£1,257,470), including loss of 80 posts
- Sheffield – all purchases of books and other materials to cease.

Much of the April 1991 issue of the *Record* was devoted 'the cuts'. Its editorial stated:

> Cuts in public and school library services have been over the last decade steadily eroding the whole information provision to most of the populace; they are now at the point when library and information services are mere shadows of the great educational

system envisaged by the enlightened Victorian philanthropists such as Carnegie ... the steady depreciation of resources by a number of measures, the latest of which is charge capping, has had a deleterious effect on public libraries, school libraries, academic and other libraries. Special and industrial libraries are also affected, whether indirectly via the interlending system or directly by dint of their employers being hit by recession, business rate or whatever.[2]

The details of this crisis were spelt out in a 'News' item in this issue. This report detailed a meeting between the Conservative government's Minister for Arts and Libraries (Timothy Renton) and a delegation from the Library Association:

> this meeting was devoted almost exclusively to the current crisis in public and school libraries. The Minister was told that the situation was of a quite different order from that in previous years. It was not now a case of a few isolated authorities making cuts but of virtually all authorities being obliged to close branches, cut book funds and sack staff. Mr Barnes [3] told the Minister that this must raise doubts as to whether authorities were meeting their obligations under the 1964 Act to provide a comprehensive and efficient service, and urged the Minister to use his powers of intervention.[4]

The report continued:

> After the meeting, George Cunningham[5] expressed deep disappointment with the Minister's response. '... I don't think we have yet persuaded the Minister that we really do have a crisis on our hands and that, given his legal responsibilities under the 1964 Act, he has a crisis on his hands which calls for urgent investigation and action.'[6]

On 20 February 1991 the Labour Peer, Lord Dormand, initiated a debate in the House of Lords, asking: 'What provision is being made for school libraries and the school library service in the light of the need for proper measures for the national curriculum.' His positive speech in support of the value of school libraries was supported by other peers such as Baroness David, the Earl of Stockton (former Conservative Prime Minister Harold Macmillan) and Baroness Blackstone (later to be Minister for the Arts in 2001).[7]

At the same period it was reported that the British Library was to lose 150 staff as part of a major cost-cutting exercise in the financial year 1991–92. Total BL cuts would amount to £3.5 million.[8]

The 'cuts', as they became known in the library profession, caused such great concern that the Library Association, for the first time in its history, set up a special officer team to address the situation.[9] An examination of the professional literature during all of the 20th century confirms that these were at least the worst reductions in expenditure facing libraries since the 1920s. It should also be appreciated that such cuts in the 1920s were in the midst of the Depression, and that there was no legislation in existence at that time, comparable to the Public Libraries and Museums Act of 1964.

The situation in university libraries, although not as difficult as that faced by the British Library, or public libraries, was also a concern. The *Times higher education supplement* reported an expected rise of 7% in students in the academic year 1991/92 compared to 1990/91.[10] University library expenditure had declined in real terms, in comparison to the overall growth in higher education expenditure. In the period 1983/85 to 1988/89 total university expenditure had grown by 41.8% while library expenditure had grown only by 28.6%. By 1990 library expenditure had hit an all time low as a percentage of total university expenditure, at 3.4%.[11] At the same period *LISU* found that Britain's university libraries were also unable to maintain their expenditure in real terms, on academic books and periodicals.[12]

By June 1991 the Library Association had taken at least one aspect of its campaign to Parliament. In a memorandum of evidence submitted to the Education, Science and Arts Committee of the House of Commons it stressed the central role of libraries in the education of 16–19 year olds. This evidence had three themes:

- the learning and skills curriculum
- learning resources
- information technology.

and pointed out that 'current provision in many areas fell short of what is required'.

The Minister for Arts annual report for 1990 was published in June 1991, and was was described by the Library Association as 'bland'. The Minister focused on 'use of resources', where he was concerned 'that Public Library Services did not have a disproportionate or unfair share of any reduction'; greater cooperation between libraries, particularly in areas such as legal deposit; and a concern that future trends would continue a decline in book purchases and a parallel decline in book issues.[13]

In parallel with this, in May 1991 the Labour Party launched a Charter for School Libraries. This urged:

- a school library in every school
- library to be opened throughout the day
- library to be adequately staffed
- books to be up to date and in good condition
- every education authority should have a School Library Service.

This Charter also highlighted a survey which found:

- only 50% of schools had self-contained, fully accessible libraries
- only 19% had chartered librarians
- only 24% had a published library policy
- 79% of schools had less than 10 books per pupil, while 22% had less than 5 books per pupil.

Despite all these difficulties the library profession at this period lobbied consistently, effectively and some times persuasively to influence government Ministers.

The Conservative government was then issuing proposals for 'local management of schools' (LMS), forcing local education authorities to delegate all but 15% of their budgets to schools. This was regarded by the library profession as being potentially very damaging to School Library Services.

As a result of these representations the Minister responsible for this process (Michael Fallon) stated that School Library Services were 'key central services' and that the 15% of the potential schools budget, which LEAs could retain centrally, was designed to provide for such services.[14]

In summary, the literature demonstrates that public funded libraries of all kinds were in real difficulty, as a result of central government policies over a number of years. This was particularly the case with public libraries, but applied to all types of libraries in the public sector, to varying degrees. What is apparent, however, is the robustness and effectiveness of the library profession's leadership at that time. Government ministers clearly listened on a regular basis, even if they did not always heed the profession's advice, while the use of Parliament and the media to highlight the plight of libraries was of a very high and consistent standard.

Two further reports by the British Library during 1991 demonstrated that academic research was being hampered by the failure of academic book budgets to keep pace with book and journal prices:

- 40% of researchers believed they were falling behind in their own subject
- 25% considered that research was less rigorous
- 45% thought research took more time
- 61% agreed that they were now less adventurous in their choice of research area.[15]

In parallel, the cuts in the BL budget had resulted in less support and back-up at a time when other academic libraries needed the BL's support to help make up for their own cuts.

Compulsory competitive tendering

During September 1991, the government announced the appointment of PA Consultants to undertake a feasibility study into the extension of compulsory competitive tendering (CCT) to white collar services in local government. This study was to include public libraries. Again, the Library Association produced a robust response.[16] It pointed out that in the few previous instances where CCT had been applied to particular aspects of public libraries such as bibliographical services, or video lending provision, these experiments had failed, as there was no profit margin for the private sector. It had made similar responses in 1988 when the government had produced a green paper, *Financing our public library services: four subjects for debate.*[17]

During April 1991, the government had issued green papers arising from a Ministerial Review of Local Government. The second of these, *Structure,* had implications for the future management and mobility of public libraries.[18] Again, the Association responded in a very sharp and focused way:

> We note that the consultation paper states that 'where a change to unitary authorities is proposed in an area there must be a proper justification for the upheaval and costs which are inevitably involved in reorganisations'. ... We believe that where a move to a unitary authority involves the dismantling and dispersal of an existing public library service, the result will be disruption in the short term, no guarantee of improved service in the long term, and an inevitable rise in costs.[19]

Relations between the library profession and government did not improve. The *Record* reported that at a national awards ceremony:

> The Minister (Tim Renton) declared his respect for the enthusiasm and commitment of professional librarians and claimed to care passionately about public libraries. *But he again talked about a few councils acting hurriedly, making ill-judged decisions, of not being able to protect the service from expenditure cuts, and of some branches having to be closed because of low use brought about by demographic change.* [my italics]

The *Record* commented that 'on a day devoted to celebrating achievement in public relations (the T. C. Farries Awards) it was rather ill-judged to rehearse arguments already rejected by his professional audience'.[20]

Government's view of public libraries in particular, and their relations with the profession in general, became even more strained when government published a Draft Statutory Instrument, *Libraries, the Library Charges (England and Wales) Regulations, 1991.*[21] The essence of this SI was to amend the Public Libraries and Museums Act of 1964 to permit charges to be made for any aspect of the public library service other than borrowing books or consulting them.

The political flurries continued apace, with the Labour Party publishing *Arts and the media: our cultural future*, in which they committed to a statutory responsibility for School Library Services.[22] In the same month a speech due to be delivered by the Minister to the Public Library Group Annual Conference, was instead given by his spokesman. Renton did not appear. The speech stated:

> Competitive tendering has an important role to play in using resources efficiently. ... we are considering the extension of compulsory competitive tendering into a number of local areas of local government ... including library services.

The *Record* continued:

> He modified his claim, and attempted to mollify his audience: 'I can accept that this cannot apply indiscriminately to all areas. There may be a case for the network of branch libraries, for example, to be excluded.'

The editor of the *Record* stated: 'The audience was appalled.'[23]

However, the Local Government Bill amending the Local Government Act of

1988 was placed before the House of Lords in December 1991, and was intended to reach the Commons by March/April 1992. It proposed:

- public library support services should be subject to CCT: acquisitions, cataloguing, book processing
- first contracts to be completed by October 1994
- duration of contracts to be between 4 and 6 years.

Although the Bill was an enabling one, in reality it allowed for a much wider tranche of services to be specified by the Secretary of State.

The Library Association's response was unequivocal: it was opposed to CCT. In the absence of successful examples of voluntary contracting out, it felt compulsion inappropriate, and that the exercise could be an expensive waste of resources. It was also opposed to direct services being contracted out.[24]

There was 'rather more heat than light and a good deal of bad temper' when the Commons debated the new Library Charges Regulations on 25 March 1991.[25] Much of this centred on the Minister's refusal to place an upper limit on reservation charges.

The profession continued its campaigning strategy. In order to influence both government and opposition parties, the Library Association produced a *Manifesto for libraries*, to follow up on the Association's 'Save our Libraries' campaign and, in particular, a highly successful 'Save our Libraries Day' at the Houses of Parliament on 27 February 1992.[26] The Association's strategy was to obtain the maximum media coverage, highlighting the plight of the public and school libraries in particular. Most of the quality dailies and Sundays carried major stories. There was extensive local and national media coverage, and Channel Four, *Newsroom South East* and *Blue Peter* (and many others) featured the 'Day' for television.

The crisis in public libraries, however, continued to deepen. The *Record* demonstrated that in England, of a response total of 70 out of 108 library authorities, 16 had standstill budgets planned and 31 faced cuts, on already depleted budgets. An example described by the *Record* as 'typical' was that of Newcastle City. Since 1979, opening hours had been reduced by 35%; mainstream staffing by 20%; bookfund cut by £170,000 in 1991, and a further £250,000 in 1992.

The evidence from 1991 demonstrated that many public funded libraries found their services at an all-time low, and that relations between the library profession and the Conservative government had never been worse. The government's proposals relating to CCT in public libraries, and the possible adverse effects on these same libraries if county library services were devolved to smaller unitary authorities and joint boards, also brought criticism from the local authority associations. The Chair of the Association of Metropolitan Authorities (AMA) remarked that the qualities that had made public libraries so popular could be jeopardised by CCT.[27] The Association of County Councils concurred, and also expressed concerns that proposals to devolve library services from the strategic county level would lead to fragmentation and higher costs.

Department of National Heritage

In May 1992 the country again returned a Conservative government to office, albeit with a much reduced majority. An early decision was to establish a new, substantial Department of National Heritage with a full ranking Cabinet Minister, David Mellor, who was a close friend of the Prime Minister. The new Ministry was to have responsibility for libraries, and also broadcasting, the arts, tourism, the national heritage and the film industry. This was welcomed by the library profession, the Association's Chief Executive commenting:

> The Association welcomes the fact that library responsibilities are now to be part of a full ministry with a Secretary of State in charge ... the department will have more clout in Whitehall and will be able to argue more strongly for the British Library and public libraries, and that it will have more influence *vis a vis* other government departments, such as Trade and Industry on copyright, and Education on school and university libraries, and the Scottish, Welsh and Northern Ireland Offices.[28]

However, there was no slowing down or stepping back from these controversial policies by government. Instead, 'the pace is hotting up', stated Prime Minister John Major, in a speech to the Adam Smith Institute, adding that in the 'next phase of Conservatism' he was going to 'chop down the Goliath of central and local government bureaucracy'.[29] Again, the evidence demonstrates that there was a clear philosophical difference between the Conservative government and the public sector library profession, the *Library Association record* editorially commenting:

> The core of librarians in the public sector still believe passionately in the traditions of public service and see the charges as no more than camouflage for cuts in resources. They cannot but feel angry, or saddened, by the tone of John Major's address which spoke of government, and some professions as being 'stiff' with an arrogance which assumes that people who ... are dependent on public services cannot be trusted with choice. [30]

In July 1992 the *Record* reported 'Civil Service libraries facing market testing'.[31] In Cumbria it reported on 'the dire state of school book provision examined', and in the same issue 'the rotten state of NHS information'.[32]

By September 1993 the National Heritage Junior Minister (Ian Sproat) was questioning both the continued existence of a free public library service and of the Net Book Agreement. This speech, at the Public Libraries Association Annual Conference, lasted 12 minutes. The Minister refused to take questions.[33]

By spring 1994, however, there was a sense that the Department of National Heritage, led by its new Secretary of State, Peter Brooke, was attempting to soften its attitude to public funded libraries. In March he announced a major review of public libraries. Current public library services in England and Wales would be examined, together with the working of the 1964 Public Libraries and Museums Act, and the changing environment in which libraries operated. In parallel Brooke appointed consultants to examine options for contracting out public library services, while further consultants were to carry out a review of School Library Services.[34] In April he issued a consultative document on a national commission dealing with cross-sector issues relating to different types of library services.[35]

This was welcomed by the Library Association, which had been lobbying for some twenty years for such an authoritative body to advise government on library and information issues.[36] Better news, and perhaps a better relationship between government and the library profession, began to emerge in 1995. The new Secretary of State at DNH (Stephen Dorrell) announced a further £46 million for the new British Library project, in order to allow building work to be completed and a hand-over of the building in the last quarter of 1996. The *Record* remarked that this news was 'as good as it has been for the library for a very long time'.[37] In the same issue the *Record* reported that the DNH feasibility study on contracting out public library services was unlikely to be recommended,[38] while in a speech in the Commons the Shadow National Heritage Secretary, Chris Smith, remarked on this study: '... a consultant's report has arrived ... which states that the library service is ripe for privatisation. ... the Opposition will resist root and branch any attempt ... to sell off our libraries ... .'[39]

Nevertheless the apparent war of attrition with the Library Association and many public library authorities on one side and government on the other continued:

> The Library Association is launching a major campaign to raise awareness of the threat to public libraries, in the continuing war over cuts in the government's grant to local authorities.[40]

This campaign was reported to have made a 'spectacular start', with extensive coverage on television, radio and the national press.[41]

Progress of a kind continued. Matthew Evans, Chair of Faber and Faber, was appointed Chair of the new Library and Information Commission, with agreed terms of reference.[42] On 16 May 1995 the Public Library Review was published by government.[43] There was to be no change envisaged in legislation; the core free service would continue; there were no recommendations to contract out services. This had taken much time and money – and not a little grief for the library profession – to recommend in essence, the status quo. It was described by Chris Heinitz, a member of the steering committee, as 'a damp squib'.[44] An editorial in the *Record* summarized the feelings of many in the profession at that time: 'there is still a feeling of being in limbo, with no clear direction yet as to where the public library service is going'.[45]

In the university library sphere, matters were much less contentious, and in many ways promised to be remarkably positive. Of the new financial resources for library and information services, resulting from the Follett report, Derek Law of King's College London remarked:

> The high burgeoning of resource will have a finite life of three to five years and is unlikely to be repeated in our professional lifetimes. There is a great opportunity to

experiment and innovate but with it goes a significant responsibility for the future of libraries and the profession.[46]

The new British Library project continued to struggle. The government and DNH (with yet another Secretary of State, Virginia Bottomley) had provided transitional funds for the move to the new library site. However, cuts in the BL's operational grant in subsequent years would mean, in the view of the BL's Chief Executive (Brian Lang), that 'current levels of service will not be tenable'.[47]

In her first statement on libraries, Mrs Bottomley described public libraries as 'a great British success story', but she was also adamant on the apparent advantage of involving 'the private sector more in providing library services'.[48]

Meanwhile there was reported 'uproar' in the House of Commons over government plans to privatize HMSO.[49] These resultant threats to privatize and contract out this range of public services led to the LA's Chief Executive to comment:

> All the experiments in contracting out have showed there is no real gain. The doctrinal insistence on continued experimentation does not take into account the drain on time and money that such experiments make on an already very stretched system.[50]

Despite these many difficulties and frustrations the library profession brought forward imaginative and forward-looking proposals for a nationwide Millennium Project. This was to be funded mainly by the National Lottery. Its aim was to create a national communications infrastructure to support and enable resource-sharing and service development between library authorities. This would provide access to the information highways in a friendly, apolitical, open door environment. However, this proposal was rejected by the Millennium Commission.[51]

Local government reorganization
In Scotland, local government moved to 32 unitary authorities, replacing the former two tiers of region and district. Yet government's funding reductions were leading to significant concerns on levels of service, 'forcing the first cuts for many years in Scottish libraries'.[52]

In Wales, reorganization of local government resulted in more, and in the main, smaller authorities (22, previously 13), 'while dilution and demotion seem to be the fate of public library departments'.[53] A response to the decline in library services and a parallel decline in the status and influence of librarians was a proposal 'to train and develop first class library managers who will become the future directors of huge multi-disciplinary departments, inside or outside the conventional framework of local government'. This was an attempt at a long-term professional strategy to address the declining status and influence of senior librarians in local authorities.

There was no response to those proposals for some eight more years, either within government or from the library profession.[54]

By September 1996 the *Record* reported further 'substantial' cuts in materials funds for public libraries. The LA had produced a thirteen-point Library Manifesto in the run-up to the general election.[55] Matthew Evans, Chair of the Library and Information Commission, intimated his concerns on how little libraries impinged on the consciousness of Ministers and civil servants. He also felt it was 'important to be nice to those in power ... if they are criticised too heavily they react badly'.[56]

Labour's spokesman on National Heritage, Jack Cunningham, was interviewed in some detail on Labour's plans for libraries, which he described as a 'precious resource'. Both in the library profession and in the professional literature there was a sense of change in the air. The Secretary of State for National Heritage announced in a Commons written reply: 'I ... have decided for the present not to introduce competitive tendering in the public library service on a compulsory basis.'

In a political sense the issue of public sector library funding, and in particular CCT, privatization of public and school libraries, were issues that had been 'kicked into the long grass' until the result of the general election was known. Public libraries' overriding difficulty was a significant lack of funding.

Labour government

In May 1997 a Labour government was elected with a landslide majority. The new Secretary of State, Chris Smith (for the new Department for Culture, Media and Sport) was regarded by many in the library profession as a long-standing sympathizer and friend to both public libraries and the arts. His Under-Secretary of State, Mark Fisher, was viewed similarly. Fisher's first statement on the new government's attitude to libraries was to see them 'develop into an outward-looking and proactive resource that both underpins our knowledge and information base and plays an active part in delivering wider social and economic benefits'.[57]

In July 1997 the Minister responsible for the Arts and Libraries (Mark Fisher) addressed the LA's UmbrelLA Conference in Manchester. This was a remarkable and quite spontaneous, warm and emotional occasion. I can see no similar description in the professional literature between 1877 and 2001. The following captures the emotionally charged atmosphere of the day:

> The new Government had, he said, a very different cultural agenda and libraries had a very important place in this. We see libraries as a cornerstone of the cultural community. We are essentially a literary culture and you are the custodians of that culture. You are the cultural welfare state and we are as proud of you as we are of the NHS'[58]

This upbeat message should be taken in tandem with the Audit Commission's *Due for renewal: a report on the library service.*[59] This gave an impression of a service in decline, lacking direction, costing more, failing to respond to the challenges of the new age of information. The report also opined that libraries lacked management information to inform strategic decisions.[60]

In October the brisk change of pace for libraries continued with the publication by the Library and Information Commission of *New library: the people's net-*

work.[61] Its principal recommendations were:

- a single UK-managed network to provide the core 'back bone' services
- standard connection to existing library networks
- central funding made available to encourage library authorities to upgrade their existing networks and access services where necessary.

The proposals in *New library* were confirmed by the then President of the Library Association, who challenged librarians to face up to the challenges of the information revolution:

> The whole public sector is now faced by an information revolution driven by the market forces of the private sector. A culture where information is regarded as a marketable commodity, where competitive tendering of services is the norm.[62]

At the launch of National Book Week in the House of Commons on 2 March 1997 Melvyn Bragg (author and broadcaster) remarked that since the election of May 1997 it was a great deal easier to be a fearless champion of libraries than had previously been the case. This was an accurate summing up of the feelings of much of the library profession at the end of 1997.[63]

During 1998 the Labour government brought forward the National Grid for Learning; the University for Industry; and the Public Library Network, as envisaged in *New library: the people's network*. There was real hope, in the words of Culture Secretary, Chris Smith, of a 'defining moment' for libraries.[64] A positive example was the government's intention to set aside lottery funding to train both public librarians and teachers in information and communications skills. A Freedom of Information white paper was also published in late 1997, and scrutinized during 1998.[65] The threat of CCT, which had caused real grief in many public funded libraries, was abandoned by government. Instead a Best Value (BV) pilot scheme was introduced.

The Labour government had given an election pledge that the projected and planned spending levels of the outgoing Conservative government in 1997 would be adhered to for two years. As a result, threatened and in many cases real cuts continued in 1998. The *Record* reported that:

> a huge public outcry has prevented the worst cuts this year. But the DCMS has sought clarification on the situation in three County Library Services (Oxfordshire, Shropshire and Nottinghamshire) after complaints that they are failing to offer a comprehensive and efficient library service.

Perhaps it was a sign of a change of political atmosphere in the country that many of the bleakest predictions did not materialize. The pace of change continued, with government requesting the Library and Information Commission to establish an Implementation Committee for a public libraries IT network. In parallel, the European Commission's DG XIII Electronic Publishing and Libraries Commission had drafted a green paper on the role of libraries in the information society. The assumptions in this paper were similar to and influenced by those of the UK's *New library: the people's network*.[66] These were quickly followed by a government green paper, *The learning age: a renaissance for a new Britain*, with wide-ranging implications for the library profession.[67]

On 25 June 1998 the Queen opened the new British Library building at St Pancras: 'the largest public building erected in Britain this century, and it is entirely fitting that it should be a library'.[68]

Better, more positive news continued from both central and local government. The local government white paper *Modern local government: in touch with the people* proposed scrapping the universal capping on local government spending, which had brought so much grief to public library services in the early 1990s.[69] In local government, Camden announced it was to drop a KPMG report, which had proposed the closure of eight libraries.[70] By November the British Library had announced it was ruling out charges for access to its reading rooms.[71]

In November 1998 the Queen's Speech heralded the white paper *Modern local government*, which promised Best Value criteria for libraries and the possibility of future National Standards.[72]

The Secretary of State (Chris Smith) also announced a public consultation, *New links for the lottery: proposals for the New Opportunities Fund*, with the possibility of libraries sharing in a £400 million fund to increase community access to ICT and community learning.

By April 1999 the *Record* editor was able to report that government investment in libraries was at an all-time high.[73] The details were confirmed in the same issue of the *Record*: up to £200 million from lottery sources, and the announcement by the Secretary of State for Education, David Blunkett, of a £400 million IT package and that school and public libraries and learning resources would benefit from this.[74] In March the government had heralded its intention 'to get tough on local authorities who could be failing in their obligation under the 1964 Act'.

Despite this, an assessment of the professional library literature from the spring of 1999 until early 2001 reveals a growing sense of a worsening relationship between government Ministers and the Library Association. In February 1999 the LA's Chief Executive – who had long-standing personal relationships with several Labour Ministers – resigned his post to move to IFLA. This resulted in a new appointment, which led in turn to a new editor of the *Record*, whose background was in the private sector of information science.

Conclusion
This period falls into two distinct parts. Between 1991 and 1997 and profession campaigned ceaselessly, and with great effect, to prevent an unsympathetic Conservative government from fundamentally undermining the public library service, locally and nationally. Between 1997 and 2001 a new Labour government worked closely with leaders of the profession to the extent that it could be reported that government investment in public libraries was at an all-time high. Yet the

following years were to prove disappointing, and the empathy with the government to be lost.

Notes

1 'Chargecapping: its effect on public library services', *Library Association record* **93** (1), 1991, 5.
2 Editorial, *Library Association record* **93** (4), 1991, 165.
3 Melvyn Barnes, then Chair of the Executive Committee, Library Association Council.
4 'Grim faces and straight talking as LA meets Renton', *Library Association record* **93** (4), 1991, 167.
5 George Cunningham, then Chief Executive of the Library Association.
6 *Library Association record* **93** (4), 1991, 167.
7 Hansard, 20 Feb. 1991, columns 624–50.
8 'Staff cuts planned at British Library', *Library Association record* **93** (4), 1991, 169.
9 Ibid.
10 'Union growths', *Times higher educational supplement* 8 Feb. 1991, 40.
11 Universities Funding Council, *University statistics 1988–89*. Cheltenham: Universities' Statistical Record, 1990.
12 MacDougall, Alan F., *Average prices of British academic books: July to December 1990*. Loughborough: Library and Information Statistics Unit, [1991].
13 *Report by the Minister for the Arts on library and information matters during 1990*. London: HMSO, 1991 (HC 353).
14 *Library Association record* **93** (7), 1991, 421.
15 Bob Erens, *Research libraries in transition: academic perceptions of recent developments in university and polytechnic libraries*. London: British Library Research and Development Department, 1991 (Library and information research report: 82); Helen Finch and Cathy North, *The research process: the library's contribution in times of restraint*. London: British Library Research and Development Department, 1991 (British Library research paper; 95).
16 Guy Daines, 'Tender trap reopens for public libraries', *Library Association record* **93** (9), 1991, 578.
17 Office of Arts and Libraries, *Financing our public library services: four subjects for debate: a consultative paper*. London: HMSO, 1988 (Cm 324).
18 Department of the Environment, *The structure of local government in England: a consultation paper*. London: DoE, 1991.
19 'Government plans may be "inefficient"', *Library Association record* **93** (9), 1991, 588–9.
20 'Renton repeats no crisis message', *Library Association record* **93** (9), 1991, 594–5.
21 *Library Charges (England and Wales) Regulations, 1991*. London: HMSO, 1991.
22 Labour Party, *Arts & media: our cultural future*. London: Labour Party, 1991.
23 'Minister plans review', *Library Association record* **93** (12), 1991, 787.
24 Ibid.
25 *Library Association record* **94** (1), 1992, 4.
26 *Library Association record* **94** (3), 1992, 150–1.
27 *Library Association record* **94** (3), 1992, 154.
28 'Welcome to the House of Fun', *Library Association record* **94** (5), 1992, 288–9.

29 'Contracting public services', *Library Association record* **94** (7), 1992, 430.
30 Ibid.
31 'Civil Service libraries facing market testing', *Library Association record* **94** (7), 1992, 433.
32 *Library Association record* **94** (10), 1992, 628, 642.
33 *Library Association record* **95** (11), 1993, 596–7.
34 'Minister's PL review takes off at last', *Library Association record* **96** (3), 1994, 116–17.
35 *Library Association record* **96** (4), 1994, 176–7.
36 Ibid.
37 *Library Association record* **97** (1), 1995, 4–5. See also **97** (12), 1995, 639.
38 *Library Association record* **97** (1), 1995, 6.
39 *Library Association record* **97** (1), 1995, 9.
40 'Campaign to raise cuts alarm', *Library Association record* **97** (3), 1995, 129.
41 'Cuts mounting in public service', *Library Association record* **97** (4), 1995, 189.
42 *Library Association record* **97** (3), 1995, 125; 'Year in review', **97** (12), 1995, 8.
43 Department of National Heritage, *Reading the future: a review of public libraries.* London: DNH, 1997.
44 *Library Association record* **97** (7), 1995, 376; 'Year in review', **97** (12), 1995, 12; and KPMG, *DNH study: contracting-out in public libraries.* [UK]: KPMG, 1995.
45 *Library Association record* **97** (8), 1995, 407. See also 421–4, 439, 639.
46 'Year in review', *Library Association record* **97** (12), 1995, 15.
47 'Relief gives way to renewed anxiety', *Library Association record* **98** (1), 1996, 3.
48 'Contracting out is ruled in', *Library Association record* **98** (2), 1996, 59.
49 Ibid.
50 Ibid.
51 *Library Association record* **98** (2), 1996, 85.
52 'Year one for Scottish unitaries', *Library Association record* **98** (4), 1996, 174.
53 'New authorities take shape', *Library Association record* **98** (1), 1996, 229.
54 Joe Hendry, 'On the fast track or the road to nowhere', *Library Association record* **98** (7), 1996, 356–7. See also Ford Partnership website: <http://fpmonline.co.uk>. Feb. 2005; Bob Usherwood et al., *Recruit, retain and lead: the public library workplace study.* [London]: Resource, 2001.
55 'Substantial cuts in materials funds', *Library Association record* **98** (9), 1996, 443.
56 *Library Association record* **98** (8), 1996, 396, 397.
57 *Library Association record* **99** (6), 1997, 291.
58 *Library Association record* **99** (8), 1997, 421.
59 Audit Commission, *Due for renewal: a report on the library service.* London: Audit Commission, 1997.
60 'A positive weapon for renewal?', *Library Association record* **99** (11), 1997, 580–1.
61 Library and Information Commission, *New library: the people's network.* London: LIC, 1997.
62 Joe Hendry, 'Bequeathing the future', *Library Association record* **99** (12), 1997, 652–4.
63 *Library Association record* **99** (12), 1997, 655.
64 *Library Association record* **100** (1), 1998, 1.
65 *Your right to know: the government's proposals for a Freedom of Information Act.* London: HMSO, 1997 (Cm 3818). See also 'White paper proposes radical change', *Library Association record* **100** (2), 1998, 62.

66 Anne Fisher and Rosalind Johnson, 'Making sense of European schemes', *Library Association record* **100** (5), 1998, 246–9.
67 *The learning age: a renaissance for a new Britain.* London: Stationery Office, 1998 (Cm 3790).
68 'Queen opens "remarkable" new building', *Library Association record* **100** (8), 1998, 391.
69 Department of the Environment, Transport and the Regions, *Modern local government: in touch with the people.* London: Stationery Office, 1998 (Cm 4014).
70 *Library Association record* **100** (9), 1998, 449.
71 *Library Association record* **100** (11), 1998, 567.
72 *Library Association record* **101** (3), 1999, 131.
73 *Library Association record* **101** (4), 1999, 193.
74 Usherwood *et al.*, *Recruit, retain and lead.*

3

From equal opportunities
to tackling social exclusion

John Vincent and John Pateman

Introduction

The decade 1991–2000 saw immense changes to the political and social fabric of the UK (broadly framed by the two General Elections of 1987 and 1997), and this chapter looks at how far these were reflected in the work of libraries: whilst there will be some coverage of libraries in general, it will focus primarily on public libraries. As institutions of the state, public libraries tend to reflect the dominant economic, social and political paradigms of the time. From 1991 to 1996, these can be characterized as income generation, business methods, inputs and outputs. From 1997 to 2000, there was a shift in emphasis towards social exclusion, joined-up working, impact and outcomes.

All change? Public library management strategies for the 1990s gave a good overview of public libraries at the start of the 1990s. Before looking forward to the coming decade, Margaret Kinnell Evans looked back and reminded readers that:

> The context for public library management in the last thirty years has been one of change, followed by yet more change – a context shared by all institutions in the public sector. … However, the pressures occasioned by structural changes, shifts in government policy, new funding arrangements, and at heart the move towards a more commercially oriented public library service, have placed tremendous demands on senior managers.[1]

So, change is a constant in local government, but the 1990s signalled a real departure from the previous development of public libraries, with a new focus on efficiency, economy and effectiveness. The backdrop for this was some significant retrenchment in service provision, which resulted from the 'capping' of the community charge in some authorities. Derbyshire, for example, announced the closure of 11 of its libraries and cut £900,000 from its book fund.[2]

As well as adopting new strategies and structures, public libraries also acquired a new culture:

Most significantly, the impact of LMS [Local Management of Schools] and CCT [Compulsive Competitive Tendering] is already changing the culture of library services, resulting in the need to reconcile moves towards a business oriented service philosophy with the concept of a free and 'comprehensive' public library service. Managers are having to balance centralist tendencies to privatisation, with the continuing local concern for adequate, publicly funded library services.[3]

The new focus on strategy and funding was also reflected in *Strategies in action: public library management and public expenditure constraints* which looked at the effect of spending cuts on public libraries.[4] The Thatcher period was driven by ideology and this was reflected in Office of Arts and Libraries reports which challenged the need for free public libraries and promoted business methods. These included reports on costing systems, income generation and performance indicators.[5] During the John Major years, there was less government scrutiny of libraries, apart from an emphasis on 'Back to basics' and the foundation of a national planning and assessment regime, as recommended by the *Review of the public library service in England and Wales.*[6] The biggest threat to libraries at this time came from the research into *Contracting out in public libraries.*[7]

As government interest in public library services waned, the vacuum was filled by organizations such as Comedia who produced a series of reports about libraries in the early 1990s.[8] Other external commentators included the Audit Commission and Insight Research.[9]

After 1997, the emphasis shifted away from meeting income targets and towards meeting community needs. There was a new breed of government reports on public libraries, with a focus on social outcomes, such as *Libraries for all: social inclusion in public libraries.*[10] The 1990s ended with some seminal research into the value and impact of public libraries and the publication of *Open to all? The public library and social exclusion.*[11] This report concluded that, while there were many examples of good practice, there were very few library services which were taking a totally holistic approach to tackling social exclusion. One notable exception was Leicester City Libraries who carried out a fundamental review of their services and published the outcome in *Achieving inclusion.*[12]

Despite this new focus on social outcomes, there was still a continuing emphasis on performance, cost and value, via, for example, Annual Library Plans, Standards, and Best Value.[13]

Background

It is not within the scope of this chapter to carry out a wholesale analysis of the broader social developments of the decade, but it is important to sketch in briefly some of the key background issues.

Following the Conservative election victory of 1987, the government began the process of a complete overhaul of public institutions, based primarily on the idea of public choice – and, closely allied to this, the drive towards privatization of public services and the establishment of internal markets (and business management techniques, such as performance measurement, customer care, and so on). This move also led to service users being thought of as 'customers', and, as Black and Muddiman suggest:

> Around 1990 ... it is arguable that the focus on the consumer began to take on a more serious character, signalled by John Major's inauguration of the 'Citizen's Charter' in 1991.[14]

At the same time there was a growing awareness of the increasing divide between the haves and the have-nots. For example:

- Real incomes between 1979 and 1995 showed a 38% rise in average incomes, a 62% increase in the wealthiest 10%, and a 17% decline in the incomes of the poorest 10%.
- The number of individuals living below 50% of average income more than doubled from 8% of the population to 19% between 1979 and 1994.
- The percentage of households without a working adult rose from 6.5% in 1977 to 19.1% in 1994.
- The proportion of those in workless households unemployed for three years or more increased from 45% to nearly 60% between 1992 and 1998.[15]

As Muddiman expressed it:

> The goals of social policy in most mid-twentieth century liberal democracies thus focused upon the amelioration of poverty and disadvantage through the provision of various kinds of relief, either in the form of cash benefits or public services providing benefit in kind.[16]

Concerns were growing too around the poor levels of literacy and numeracy in the UK.[17] Drawing on a survey by the Basic Skills Agency released in March 1998, the National Literacy Trust stated that:

> Tables compiled from simple reading and writing tests taken by more than 8000 adults across the country show that 16% of the population is functionally illiterate. London boroughs took four of the bottom five places for levels of literacy, with almost a quarter of adults in some areas unable to read parcel labels. ... The survey did not include those for whom English is not their first language.[18]

The Basic Skills Agency, in reporting a survey where respondents had to solve twelve numeracy tasks using only pen and paper, identified poor levels of numeracy:

> Overall, British respondents could only achieve an average of 7.9 correct answers out of the 12. All other nations surveyed achieved an average of 9 or more correct answers.[19]

However, there was also the realization that, whilst poverty was a critical issue, there was more to people's 'exclusion' than that alone. Within the European Commission particularly, the result of these social divides was seen as 'social exclusion'[20] (see, for example, work by Graham Room).[21] Social exclusion was also taken up by the Labour Party as part of its thinking around social justice, for example via the Commission on Social Justice which reported in 1994.[22] In the mid-1990s, a number of social analysts looked critically at 'the state we're in',[23] so that by the Election of 1997 there was a head of steam building around social justice, social inclusion and social exclusion.

Following the Labour Party's victory, they were quick to establish the Social Exclusion Unit (SEU) later the same year, with a brief to report on

> how to develop integrated and sustainable approaches to the problems of the worst housing estates, including crime, drugs, unemployment, community breakdown and bad schools etc.[24]

The SEU began to work at both a broad policy level (e.g., pursuing policies around Neighbourhood Renewal) and also by investigating and reporting on the needs of some high priority socially excluded groups (e.g., truancy and school exclusions; rough sleeping; young people who were not in education, employment or training; and teenage pregnancy).[25]

On Neighbourhood Renewal the SEU published a key report in 1998.[26] This set out the need for a national strategy, and one of its proposals was to establish 18 Policy Action Teams (PATs) to take forward this work around specific themes. The PATs drew on the government's earliest definition of social exclusion, which was quite broad and limited (and which continued in use well into the next decade):

> a shorthand term for what can happen when people or areas suffer from a combination of linked problems such as unemployment, poor skills, low incomes, poor housing, high crime, bad health and family breakdown.[27]

The importance of this definition is the flagging-up of social exclusion as 'a combination of linked problems'.

At the same time, work was developing in parallel across Wales, Scotland and Northern Ireland. Recognizing high levels of deprivation in a number of local authority areas, the Welsh Assembly established the 'People in Communities' programme[28] to target resources and also carried out a mapping exercise to chart the extent of social exclusion.[29] Following devolution, the Scottish Office and the Scottish Executive published their major strategy documents in 1999, laying out their social inclusion policies and social justice targets.[30]

In Northern Ireland, the 'Targeting Social Need' policy (which primarily aimed to redirect resources) was introduced in 1991, and was succeeded by the 'New

Targeting Social Need' programme in 1998; this aimed to tackle social need and social exclusion by targeting efforts and available resources within existing Departmental programmes towards people, groups and areas in greatest social need. In addition, the Irish National Anti-Poverty Strategy was published in 1997 as a major policy initiative to place the needs of the poor and socially excluded at the top of the national agenda in terms of government policy development and action.[31]

Some local authorities had responded to the social issues outlined above by developing anti-poverty strategies during the late 1980s and early 1990s, and much of the early work on social exclusion saw it as, basically, equating with poverty. However, deeper analysis (by writers such as Clive Miller) showed that, for example, there were people living below the poverty line, who were not socially excluded, and, at the same time, there were people living above the poverty line, who were excluded because of discrimination and other issues:

> It is clear that tackling material poverty, although essential, would not necessarily lead to the elimination of social exclusion. To ensure that exclusion is eliminated, interventions that are aimed at tackling material poverty must be matched with others that lead to a change in the excluding organisational and social behaviour of the rest of society, and of the alienated people who are involved in anti-social behaviour.[32]

Therefore, in talking about social exclusion, the focus is on the needs of groups and individuals who do not have access to services and facilities or to society's decision-making and/or power structures:

> There are excluders as well as victims of social exclusion, and these excluders include mainstream public services, such as health, housing and education.[33]

Taking this broader definition of social exclusion means that, for example, people who suffer direct or indirect discrimination (e.g., black and minority ethnic groups; lesbians, gay men, bisexuals and transgendered people; disabled people; people with mental health problems), those who may suffer from multiple disadvantage (e.g., children and young people, older people) and those who are frequently denied access to power (e.g., working-class people) need to be considered.

Probably the most significant event of the decade, partly because of its immediate tragic impact and partly because of its long-term consequences, was the murder of Stephen Lawrence in April 1993.[34] The positive outcomes of this tragedy included the Commission for Racial Equality's *Racial equality means quality*, the Macpherson report and the Race Relations (Amendment) Act 2000.[35] The Macpherson report identified, amongst its findings, that organizations in the UK were institutionally racist, and that this was why the public sector had failed to provide an adequate and appropriate service for black people.[36]

Gus John was very critical of the constant adoption of new policies to tackle the same problems ('The question is where was the agenda of valuing diversity long before any black person landed on these shores'),[37] and recent commentators[38] have also argued that, during the 1990s, there were a considerable number of shifts in race and equalities policy, including:

- multiculturalism
- 'municipal antiracism'[39] – which included the adoption of equal opportunity policies
- adoption of diversity policies, following the disappointment with equal opportunity policies, criticized for not tackling the root causes of racism (and other issues)
- cultural pluralism and social cohesion.[40]

Libraries in the 1990s

Although this chapter focuses on equal opportunities and social exclusion, it is important to see the impact on this strand of these wider matters, and so here is a very brief overview before we look at some of the major equalities developments.

Probably the best summary of the 'mood' in public libraries in the mid-1990s is that given by Evelyn Kerslake and Margaret Kinnell:

> Public libraries and public librarians have been charged with losing their sense of identity and purpose. The doubts hanging over public libraries fundamentally question their role, effectiveness, meaning and impact on the societies in which they work.[41]

With the changes in attitude (especially of the government) towards public services (as noted above), libraries strove to find their place in the new order of things, particularly in relation to access to funding.

> It is salutary to remember that for a decade people have been coming into library work in a context where local authority, public service provision is seen as low-status, poor and diminishing, and that in general during this period, the vital equality issues, especially regarding stock selection, have hardly been aired at all in the library press.[42]

Black and Muddiman argued too that the 'heritage vision'[43] was used as a means of criticizing and controlling public library developments, especially in relation to work with and in the wider community.[44] This 'vision' of a 'mythical, golden past'[45] was used, for example by Richard Luce (Minister for Arts 1985–1990) to argue that public libraries were over-extending themselves, and, as a result, he asked, were they not in danger of 'losing their identity and purpose by being all things to everybody'?[46] These arguments were used to develop the theme that public libraries needed to return to their 'core' functions – which implied, among other things, that anything not defined as 'core' (such as work in the community) was wasteful and unnecessary, and therefore under threat.

Right at the end of the 1980s, the government had signalled clearly that it was no longer prepared to see any expansion of public library provision via public expenditure, and, in its green paper, argued that the definition of the 'free' and 'basic' library service should be confined to the borrowing and reference use of print materials only – another emphasis on the 'core'.[47] What was particularly significant about this was that it signalled a change in the development of public libraries as a whole, a recognition that the UK had become a market-led environment, and that libraries were inextricably bound up in that. This trend continued with the publication of the Department of National Heritage's 'vision' for public libraries.[48]

One major result was that, during the 1990s, many library services began to focus almost entirely on the 'core' services, and to reduce – or stop altogether – work in the community. As Black and Muddiman say, 'by 1993, even Lambeth was serving only 350 groups compared with a high point of over 500 in the late 1970s'.[49]

At the same time, library managers began to adopt new managerial techniques and cultures, including:

- a resurgence of interest in management by objectives
- work to develop performance indicators
- the increasing use of computerized management information systems
- the development of financial devolution (with individual libraries in some authorities having their own cheque books) and specifying cost centres
- reorganizations along contractor/client lines
- a move to call users of library services 'customers'.[50]

The call by John Major's government for public libraries to go 'back to basics' was not universally accepted and some librarians baulked at turning their services into businesses:

> The commercial approach is not suitable for the services we offer. Commercial attitudes are based on a different kind of motivation. For the private sector the main aim is profit, not the provision of services to meet user needs, at least not those needs that are uneconomic to provide. Public services should not be organised or assessed in a way that assumes they simply mirror the private sector.[51]

All of these developments shifted the focus: meeting the needs of non-library users, working in the community to approach people on their own ground, and seeking out non-mainstream, community-published materials all took second place – or disappeared altogether.

Debate too raged about usage of public libraries: some claimed that the 'middle class myth of libraries is dead',[52] but other analysis showed that, for example, only some 33% of the population were active library users;[53] and that there were large differences in frequent library use between people in social classes C2, D and E (25%–26% of people) compared with 40% for classes AB and 30% for class C1,[54] although Alan Hasson[55] reported that a number of library services in Scotland 'adapted their services to the subculture of working class, young and often unemployed users'.[56] At this time, relatively little regard was paid to class issues, apart from work by John Pateman;[57] his summary of issues concerning public libraries and social class was published as one of the *Open to all?* working papers.[58]

There was also a growing volume of work looking at the impact that library services might have.[59] A few examples of major developments and initiatives (which related to equal opportunities work,[60] and which might be said to be the forerunners of work to tackle social exclusion) during the 1990s included:

- Bookstart schemes went national.[61]
- The growth in open learning (the provision of self-study packages in libraries): in 1996, about 10,000 different subjects were covered by open learning, and some 98 public library authorities in England, 30 in Scotland and 7 in Wales were making open learning provision.[62]
- Involvement by libraries in the National Year of Reading 1998/99.[63]
- Development of Family Reading and Family Literacy initiatives.[64]
- In October 1995, the Community Services Group of the Library Association ran a course, 'Less equal than others', which looked at library services for lesbians and gay men, the first time that an LA group had organized a course on this topic.[65]
- Growth of homework centres/study support, much of which was targeted at young people without other access to the internet and/or who needed special support.[66]
- Faced with worrying performance figures and a budget simply inefficient for their needs, some library services decided to ask their residents what they wanted for the library service – quality or quantity? The answer led to radical changes in places such as Hackney.[67]
- It was recognized that, in order to meet the new demands placed on library services, it was necessary to develop a more flexible workforce, combining both quality and equal opportunity perspectives.[68]
- It was also recognized that more innovative and inclusive approaches should be taken to stock selection.[69]

However, whilst there had been some work during the 1990s to develop standards for provision for some socially excluded groups,[70] there had been few in-depth investigations of library use by particular disadvantaged groups. A rare example was the work published in 1998, when Roach and Morrison produced a major report which focused on the 'social distance ... between the public library and ethnic minority communities', the 'lack of clear vision and leadership on ethnic diversity and racial equality matters', and the lack of account by public libraries for their 'progress in respect of race equality whilst current performance systems are largely colour-blind.'[71]

Amongst their recommendations were calls for:

- a clear strategic plan for public libraries

- greater integration and partnership between the public library service and related service providers
- a review of the ongoing training and professional development needs of public library staff in the light of changing demographic and social circumstances.

They also published a set of baselines for good practice, which some library authorities used to reassess their service provision.[72]

Another major shift in thinking that took place during this period was in relation to positive action[73] – which is defined by Reena Bhavnani and her colleagues as:

Offering special help to people who are disadvantaged because of prejudice, stereotyping and discrimination, in order that they may take full and equal advantage of opportunities in jobs, education, training, services, etc.[74]

Libraries had been working from the 1970s onwards to promote positive images (of young women, different faiths, black and ethnic minority people, for example) and to support this with stock selection policies based around equalities principles.[75]

However, critics of these policies equated them with censorship[76] and, to make matters worse, they were also labelled as 'political correctness':

Now that the loony left is no more, right-wing propagandists have had to find another vehicle with which to launch attacks on their 'progressive' enemies. The new bogey is 'political correctness' which is, of course, a close cousin of the loony left. It began last year with a spate of stories about barmy 'left-wing' activities – like the revising of Enid Blyton's books in order to expunge all traces of racism, classism, homophobia and sexism … As a result of the emphasising of these extremes, it is now taken for granted that 'political correctness' is undesirable …[77]

Despite some opposition to such sweeping generalizations (e.g., Trevor Phillips's 'Why political correctness is all about respect')[78] and arguments that 'this is challenging imagery, not hair-splitting',[79] nevertheless, as Rosemary Stones put it, there grew up 'a new social climate of ridicule and alienation around equalities issues which it has become socially acceptable to dismiss as "political correctness"'.[80]

All of this, allied with financial and political issues, found many library services in a state of uncertainty about major new directions. To take social inclusion policy and strategy as an example (and this will be covered in more depth in the next section):

By and large, public libraries are revealed as extremely uncertain about social inclusion policy and strategy, and … good practice and initiatives, whilst existing, are sporadic and uneven. Case studies reveal that public library authorities experience numerous problems in addressing social exclusion, ranging from the lack of coherent policy and strategy, through the limited abilities, attitudes and skills of their staff, to difficulties in both accessing and targeting sufficient materials and resources. The survey suggests that there are some exceptions to this pattern: a minority of [public library authorities] clearly are prioritising and mainstreaming librarianship for social inclusion. However, at the other extreme, the survey also suggests that there are perhaps a quarter of UK [public library authorities] who have little interest in or service development in the inclusion sphere at all.[81]

Libraries and social exclusion

The election of New Labour in 1997 and the creation of the Social Exclusion Unit opened up space for the discussion of issues concerning social exclusion and related matters such as poverty and racism. It also allowed the library debate on these issues to inform other agendas; the article, 'Public libraries' role in inclusion', for example, was published in *Anti poverty matters*, rather than a library journal.[82] Social class, the final taboo of many public librarians, could also be debated for the first time in many years in the professional press.[83]

There was a significant volume of activity in the library world during 1998 on social exclusion themes. The Arts Council's National Conference for the Promotion of Literature in Public Libraries, 'Reading for Life', in April 1998, for example, included a seminar on social exclusion as a key aspect of reading for life.[84] In October 1998 another event was held, this time an executive briefing by the Library Association London and Home Counties Branch, on Public Library Policy and Social Exclusion. Meanwhile, social exclusion was becoming a regular feature in the *Library Association record*.[85]

But the real explosion of activity started in 1999. An Action Planning Conference was organized in February: some early findings from the 'Public Library Policy and Social Exclusion' research project (the report of which would be published as *Open to all?* – see below) were unveiled at this event, and a decision was made to set up a Social Exclusion Action Planning Network which was launched in London and the south-east in May 1999 – the Network issued its first, draft newsletter in May 1999;[86] and social exclusion was addressed at the Library Association's Public Library Group conference in October 1999, where the Social Exclusion Action Planning Network was launched nationally.[87] Articles on social exclusion continued to appear in the professional press;[88] and a number of seminars and courses were organized (primarily involving members of the Public Library Policy team), including a training day for SHARE (the south-west London public libraries group) and contributions to the Library Association Yorkshire and Humberside Branch briefing, 'Social exclusion and public libraries'.[89]

The Policy Action Teams (PATs) (noted above) produced eighteen reports covering all the major government agenda items of the day, such as health, crime, school attainment, jobs, skills – and there were also PATs which looked at arts and sport (PAT 10) and information technology (PAT 15). The report of the latter did identify public libraries as potential 'public access points',[90] but not as central points of provision – however, these were the only mentions of libraries in all the eighteen reports.

Despite that unpromising start, the Department for Culture, Media and Sport (DCMS) established a working group that produced a consultation document, *Libraries for all*,[91] which identified the role that public libraries could take in tackling social exclusion (with case studies).[92] DCMS developed their work on social exclusion against the broad background definition noted above, and added:

> Social exclusion takes many forms. It can be direct or indirect, and can embrace both groups and individuals. Exclusion also has a geographical dimension embracing rural, urban and suburban areas alike.[93]

The report began by identifying some of the barriers which people face in trying to use libraries, and grouped these as:

- institutional
- personal and social
- related to perceptions and awareness
- environmental.

Its main recommendations were that:

- social inclusion should be mainstreamed as a policy priority within all library and information services
- library authorities should consider what specific services need to be tailored to meet the needs of minority groups and communities
- library authorities should consult and involve socially excluded groups in order to ascertain their needs and aspirations
- libraries should be located where there is a demand, but should build upon existing facilities and services wherever possible
- opening hours should be more flexible and tailored to reflect the needs and interests of the community
- library and information services should develop their role as community resource centres, providing access to communication as well as information
- library authorities should consider the possibilities of co-locating their facilities with other services provided by the local authority
- libraries should be the local learning place and champion of the independent learner
- libraries should be a major vehicle for providing affordable (or preferably free) access to ICT at local level
- library and information services should form partnerships with other learning organizations

- library authorities should consider whether some services aimed at socially excluded people might be more effectively delivered on a regional basis.

The report also encouraged libraries to adopt a strategy based on the following six-point plan:

- identify the people who are socially excluded and their distribution; engage with them and establish their needs
- assess and review current practice
- develop strategic objectives and prioritize resources
- develop the services, and train the library staff to provide them
- implement the services and publicize them
- evaluate success, review and improve.

The final results of the consultation were published in 2001.[94]

Meanwhile, interest in the topic in some quarters was growing, and CPI (Capital Planning Information Ltd) held one of their series of seminars on the topic, 'Social inclusion: where do libraries stand?', in 1999.[95]

However, at the same time, the appraisals of the Annual Library Plans[96] for 1998 and 1999 showed that there were still problems in taking on board social exclusion issues. (There was further evidence of concern in another Library and Information Commission report which stated that 'If even greater emphasis is to be placed on the Library as the lynch pin in the realisation of the Information Society, some concern is warranted that those currently excluded may remain so and, given the increasing importance of libraries' envisaged role, become even further disadvantaged because of this.')[97]

The 1998 appraisal concluded that:

> Social inclusion was scored poorly … we have found many individual initiatives that are clearly directed at one or more minority groups, but what seems to be lacking is a comprehensive review of social inclusion, from a library service standpoint, and a co-ordinated response.[98]

The 1999 appraisal included the following:

> 6.3.2   54 authorities were assessed as 'Good' in relation to social inclusion policies overall; 73 were assessed as 'Satisfactory'; 19 were assessed as 'Poor' and 3 were assessed as 'Inadequate' for this section …

> 6.3.4   Once again, it is surprising that so few authorities were assessed as 'Good' in relation to this policy area in view of the request from the DCMS to show how these policies were being taken into account in library planning. Of greatest concern is that the social inclusion dimension of access policies for the location and availability of libraries was considered by only 60 of the 149 authorities.

6.3.5   The low level of consideration of social inclusion relating to access policies is a matter of concern ...[99]

In 1998 the Library and Information Commission (which in April 2000 became Resource, The Council for Museums, Archives and Libraries) commissioned a research project, 'Public Library Policy and Social Exclusion', as part of its 'Value and Impact of Libraries' programme. The project was based at the School of Information Management, Leeds Metropolitan University, and was carried out between October 1998 and April 2000 in partnership with the London Borough of Merton Libraries, Sheffield Libraries, Archives and Information Services, and John Vincent. It had three main elements: researching and writing a set of working papers; a survey of all public library authorities in the UK; and eight case studies.

The report of the project, *Open to all?* was published by Resource in 2000.[100] Volume 1 contained the overview and conclusions of the research, and Volume 2 the survey, case studies and research methods. The working papers were published as the third volume and looked at both over-arching issues, for example:

- theories of social exclusion and the public library[101]
- public libraries and social class[102]
- user and community perceptions of public libraries[103]
- central and local government policies[104]
- the struggle against racial exclusion[105]
- ICT, social exclusion and public libraries;[106]

and provision for and issues facing certain groups, for example:

- provision for lesbians, gay men, bisexuals and transgendered people[107]
- social exclusion – an international perspective[108]
- public libraries, children and young people and social exclusion[109]
- women, public libraries and social exclusion[110]
- public libraries, disability and social exclusion.[111]

Some of these working papers were highly influential and were subsequently reprinted in a wide range of journals and publications.[112]

The report concluded 'that UK libraries have adopted only weak, voluntary and "take it or leave it" approaches to social inclusion. The core rationale of the public library movement continues to be based on the idea of developing universal access to a service which essentially reflects mainstream middle class, white and English values'.

Key consequences of this approach included:

- a continuing underutilization of public libraries by working-class people and other excluded social groups

- a lack of knowledge in the public library world about the needs and views of excluded 'non-users'
- the development in many public libraries of organizational, cultural and environmental barriers which effectively excluded many disadvantaged people.[113]

The project included a survey of UK public libraries, and findings included:

- only one-sixth of public library authorities (PLAs) approximated to a comprehensive model of good practice for social inclusion
- most PLAs (60%) had no comprehensive strategy and had uneven and intermittent activity
- ¼ of PLAs had little apparent strategy and service development
- only approximately ⅓ of PLAs comprehensively targeted disadvantaged neighbourhoods and social groups
- most PLAs had no consistent resource focus on exclusion, and this was sometimes very marginal
- many of the UK's most marginal and excluded people were not considered to be priorities in PLA strategy, service delivery and staffing. These included refugees, homeless people and travellers.

These findings were supported by the eight case studies (carried out across the UK), which found that there were:

- some successes in addressing social exclusion, most frequently linked to targeted initiatives employing community development, partnerships, and other proactive ways of working
- problems in developing an overall, PLA wide, policy framework with exclusion issues 'mainstreamed' only exceptionally
- a reluctance to adopt resourcing models that would consistently prioritize excluded communities or social groups
- limits on the ability of library staff to work with excluded people because of lack of skills and training and sometimes negative attitudes
- a tendency to suggest that any 'community' activity would automatically address exclusion and a tendency to consult with communities and excluded groups only sporadically
- a preoccupation with libraries as a 'passive' service which prioritized 'access' rather than with proactive and interventionist ways of working.[114]

The report also looked at the way that public libraries had responded to wider, government-initiated policy developments (such as Neighbourhood Renewal); to developments related to ICT (for example, the report of PAT 15 which included libraries in a range of possible locations or providers for deprived communities);[115] and to developments related to lifelong learning (e.g., the New Opportunities Fund proposals for community access to lifelong learning, which suggest public libraries as a delivery mechanism).[116]

The report noted that:

> In general, the response of the public library community to these policy developments has been to argue that the *modernisation* of the public library service, and in particular the creation of an electronic 'people's network', represents the best, and most cost effective way of developing a socially inclusive information society.[117] [their emphasis]

The government, however, had been cautious about accepting this advice: the report suggested that this was:

> clearly related to an uncertainty about the public library's capacity to deliver on social inclusion. Such uncertainties are supported by successive DCMS appraisals of English public library authority *Annual Library Plans*, which reveal lack of strategic planning and uneven and patchy activity.[118]

The report's conclusion was that public libraries needed to be more than modernized – they needed to be transformed 'to become much more proactive, interventionist and educative institutions, with a concern for social justice at their core'. The specific strategies for such a transformation were identified as:

- the mainstreaming of provision for socially excluded groups and communities and the establishment of standards of service and their monitoring
- the adoption of resourcing strategies to prioritize the needs of excluded people and communities
- a recasting of the role of library staff to encompass a more socially responsive and educative approach
- staffing policies and practices which would address exclusion, discrimination and prejudice
- targeting of excluded social groups and communities
- the development of community-based approaches to library provision, incorporating consultation with and partnership with local communities
- ICT and networking developments which would actively focus on the needs of excluded people
- a recasting of the image and identity of the public library to link it more closely with the cultures of excluded communities and social groups.[119]

On 10 July 2000, a pre-launch conference was held at the Library Association, attended by Cabinet Office Minister, Mo Mowlam (who had also contributed a foreword to the report).[120]

One of the concerns of the research team was to ensure that the findings of this project did not just get shelved. Every opportunity was therefore taken to present them to as wide an audience as possible: the findings were presented to the Library

Association Public Library Group Millennium Study Conference, 'Eye to the Future',[121] and were also disseminated in a wide range of journals and publications[122] and at professional events such as the Kent Arts and Libraries staff conference in November on 'Widening Participation and Public Access'.[123]

Work to build the Social Exclusion Action Planning Network[124] continued and in June 2000 it held its first conference, 'Public Libraries tackling Social Exclusion', which explored how public libraries could tackle social exclusion by interacting with Best Value, lifelong learning, and reader development.[125]

The second spin-off from *Open to all?* was the development of the Quality Leaders Project for Black Library and Information Workers, which aimed to enhance the role of black library staff whilst at the same time developing library services for the black community.[126]

Finally, although the focus in the 1990s was very much on public libraries – at least in the professional press – work was developed (particularly under the banner of 'widening participation') in academic libraries too.[127]

All change? – Borrowed time? – Open to all?

It is interesting to note that three major works on public libraries published between 1991 and 2000 all had question marks in their titles. This suggests that there are possibly more questions than answers when considering the role and purpose of public libraries. In 1991, Margaret Kinnell Evans asked the question *All change?* when she considered public library management strategies for the 1990s. The language she used was straight from the new lexicon of public sector management, with its emphasis on the operating environment, a planning culture, and the need to compete with other services, acquire funding and develop relationships with clients:

> The emphasis in recent studies of public librarianship has shifted towards environmental analysis as a means to strategic positioning of the public library in its increasingly competitive drive for funding – hence the impetus to developing marketing strategies, together with ever more sophisticated performance measures.[128]

There was an increasing concern for measuring the effectiveness of public libraries, as a means of 'proving' their value via performance indicators. There was also a shift to a wider range of funding sources – from local and central government, charging and other revenue-earning activities, and sponsorship – which meant that managers of public library services needed the kind of entrepreneurial skills seen in the business sector, such as business planning. One consequence of this new approach, compounded by diminished resources, was more targeting of services and the increased importance of a customer-driven approach to service development plus an emphasis on greater local cooperation and interdependence. In 1991, Evans ended her analysis of future library services by predicting that there would be 'further turbulence and change'.

Borrowed time? also looked at the future of public libraries in the UK and recommended that further research should be carried out into four priority areas:

- a fuller understanding of the economic impact of public libraries
- the social impact of public libraries
- the evaluation of the strategic buying power of public libraries in the commercial publishing and media markets
- developing more sophisticated performance indicators which would begin to measure some of the social, recreational and individual self-development functions of public libraries.[129]

Failure to address these issues would mean that the public library service would continue to live 'on borrowed time'.

Open to all? arrived at some far more radical conclusions:

Although we are convinced that the public library has the *potential* to play a key role in tackling social exclusion, we conclude that to *make a real difference* it will need not only to modernise its technical base, but to transform its fundamental purposes, policies, and priorities. Provision of 'access' to a mainly passive public library service is not, we believe, a strategy that will make a real impact on social exclusion in the contemporary UK. To make such an impact, we conclude that the public library will need to become a far more proactive and interventionist public institution, with a commitment to equality, education and social justice at its core. Only then, it seems to us, will marginalised and excluded communities be returned to the mainstream of the library world.

Only then will public libraries be truly open to all.[130]

The contrast in language and approaches between Margaret Kinnell Evans's 'a more commercially oriented public library service' and the *Open to all?* report's 'a far more proactive and interventionist public institution, with a commitment to equality, education and social justice at its core'[131] sums up some of the fundamental changes which took place in British librarianship and information work between 1991 and 2000. There was a shift from equal opportunities in 1991 to social exclusion in 2000. There was a further shift from social inclusion to community cohesion from 2001 to 2005 and this is considered in the next volume of this series.

Notes

1   Margaret Kinnell Evans, *All change? Public library management strategies for the 1990's*. London: Taylor Graham, 1991, p. 3.
2   *Library Association record* **92** (9), 1990, 613.
3   Evans, *All change?*
4   Tony Oulton, *Strategies in action: public library management and public expenditure constraints*. London: Library Association Publishing, 1991.

5   Office of Arts and Libraries, *A costing system for public libraries.* London: HMSO, 1987; Office of Arts and Libraries, *Financing our public library service: four subjects for debate.* London: HMSO, 1988; Office of Arts and Libraries, *Keys to success: performance indicators for public libraries.* London: HMSO, 1990.

6   *Review of the public library service in England and Wales for the Department of National Heritage.* London: Aslib, 1995.

7   *DNH study: contracting out in public libraries.* [London?]: KPMG, 1995.

8   *Out of hours: a study of economic, social and cultural life in twelve town centres in the UK.* London: Comedia, 1991; *Borrowed time? The future of public libraries in the UK.* Bourne Green: Comedia, 1993; Liz Greenhalgh, *Libraries in a world of cultural change.* London: UCL Press, 1995.

9   *Due for renewal.* London: Audit Commission, 1997; *Lending libraries: books and public service in a changing society.* [Welshpool]: Insight Research, 1998.

10   *Libraries for all: social inclusion in public libraries: policy guidance for local authorities in England.* London: Department for Culture, Media and Sport, 1999.

11   Dave Muddiman *et al., Open to all? The public library and social exclusion.* London: Resource, 2000. *Vol. 1: Overview and conclusions*; *Vol. 2: Survey, case studies and methods*; *Vol. 3: Working papers* (Library and Information Commission research reports; 84–86).

12   *Achieving inclusion ... review report 2000.* Leicester: Leicester City Council, 2000.

13   *Annual Library Plans.* London: Department for Culture, Media and Sport, 1998; *Comprehensive and efficient – standards for modern public libraries.* London: Department for Culture, Media and Sport, 2000; *Delivering best value in library and information services.* London: Library Association, 2000; David Streatfield, *Best value and better performance in libraries.* Twickenham: Information Management Associates, 2000 (Library and Information Commission research report; 52); and Angela Watson, *Best returns – best value guidance for library authorities.* London: Library Association, 2000.

14   Alistair Black and Dave Muddiman, *Understanding community librarianship: the public library in post-modern Britain.* Aldershot: Avebury, 1997, p. 96. Black and Muddiman also include a useful summary of these developments, especially in their chapter 5 'Community librarianship in retreat: the impact of the market'.

15   Taken from: Martin Dutch, 'Central and local government policies and social exclusion' in Dave Muddiman *et al., Open to all. Vol. 3: Working papers*, pp. 189–204, which cites the following: Peter Alcock, *Understanding poverty.* 2nd ed. Basingstoke: Macmillan, 1997; Carey Oppenheim (ed.), *An inclusive society: strategies for tackling poverty.* London: Institute for Public Policy Research, 1998; Paul Convery, 'Unemployment' in *Britain divided: the growth of social exclusion in the 1980s and 1990s*, ed. Alan Walker and Carol Walker. London: Child Poverty Action Group, 1997, pp. 170–97; Catherine Howarth *et al.* (eds.), *Monitoring poverty and social exclusion: Labour's inheritance.* [York]: Joseph Rowntree Foundation, 1998.

16   Dave Muddiman, 'Theories of social exclusion and the public library' in Muddiman *et al., Open to all? Vol. 3: Working papers*, p. 1.

17   For further information see John Vincent, 'Literacy, social exclusion and the public library' in Muddiman *et al., Open to all? Vol. 3: Working papers*, pp. 43–61.

18   'Adult literacy: literacy skills of adults', London: National Literacy Trust, 1998 [internet] (accessed 26/10/98).

19 *International numeracy survey: a comparison of the basic numeracy skills of adults 16–60 in seven countries*. London: Basic Skills Agency, 1997.

20 Social inclusion as a concept has been recognized in Europe since at least the 1970s, and there is a useful paper by Rob Atkinson, 'Combating social exclusion in Europe: the new urban policy challenge', *Urban studies* **37** (5–6), 2000, 1037–55, which looks at some of this background.

21 Graham Room *et al.*, *National policies to combat social exclusion*. Brussels: European Commission, 1992 (Second annual report of the EC Observatory on Policies to Combat Social Exclusion).

22 *Social justice: strategies for national renewal: the report of the Commission on Social Justice*. London: Vintage, 1994. Chairman Sir Gordon Borrie.

23 See for example: Will Hutton, *The state we're in*. London: Cape, 1995; Alan Walker and Carol Walker (eds.), *Britain divided: the growth of social exclusion in the 1980s and 1990s*. London: Child Poverty Action Group, 1997.

24 Social Exclusion Unit, *National strategy for neighbourhood renewal: Policy Action Team audit: a report by the Social Exclusion Unit*. London: Cabinet Office, 2001, p. 6.

25 Social Exclusion Unit, *Truancy and school exclusion*. London: TSO, 1998; *Rough sleeping*. London: TSO, 1998; *Bridging the gap: new opportunities for 16–18 year olds not in education, employment or training*. London: TSO, 1999; *Teenage pregnancy*. London: TSO, 1999.

26 *Bringing Britain together: a national strategy for neighbourhood renewal*. London: Social Exclusion Unit, 1998.

27 This one was taken from: Social Exclusion Unit, *Preventing social exclusion: a report*. London: Cabinet Office, 2001.

28 This was later to become the 'Communities First' programme. There is further information about these developments in, for example, *National Assembly for Wales annual report on social inclusion in Wales*. Cardiff: National Assembly for Wales, Community Regeneration and Social Inclusion Unit, 2001.

29 *Mapping social exclusion in Wales*. Cardiff: Welsh Office, Statistical Directorate, 1999.

30 *Social inclusion: opening the door to a better Scotland*. Edinburgh: Scottish Office, 1999; *Social justice: a Scotland where everyone matters*. Edinburgh, Scottish Executive, 1999.

31 *Measuring poverty and social exclusion in Northern Ireland*. Belfast: Northern Ireland Assembly, Research and Library Services, 2002 (Research paper; 42/02). Available at: <http://www.niassembly.gov.uk/io/research/4202.pdf> (accessed 11/11/05).

32 Clive Miller, *Managing for social cohesion*. London: Office for Public Management, 1999, p. 5.

33 S. Fitzpatrick, *Poverty and social inclusion in Glasgow* [discussion paper for the Glasgow Alliance Social Inclusion Inquiry]. [Glasgow]: 1999, quoted in: Mike Geddes, *Strategies for social inclusion: learning from the Scottish experience*. London: LGIU, 2000 (Local Authorities and Social Exclusion Network, research paper; 1), p. 7.

34 There is a valuable round-up of events, with a timeline, and a mass of links, at <http://news.bbc.co.uk/hi/english/static/stephen_lawrence/timeline.htm> (accessed 10/11/05).

35   *Racial equality means quality – standards for racial equality for local government.*
      London: Commission for Racial Equality, 1995; *Stephen Lawrence Inquiry: report of
      an inquiry by Sir William Macpherson of Cluny.* London: Home Office, 1999 (Cm
      4252–1).

36   Some examples, drawn from the Home Office, education, the police, health, etc, are
      outlined in Shiraz Durrani, 'Struggle against racial exclusion in public libraries: a
      fight for the rights of people' in Muddiman *et al., Open to all. Vol. 3: Working
      papers*, pp. 254–349.

37   Gus John, talk given at the conference 'The Significance of the Stephen Lawrence
      Inquiry for Public Libraries'. London and Home Counties Branch, the Library
      Association, in association with the Association of London Chief Librarians.
      Executive Briefing, 28 June 1999 (quoted in Durrani, 'Struggle against racial
      exclusion').

38   Reena Bhavnani, Heidi Safia Mirza and Veena Meetoo, *Tackling the roots of racism:
      lessons for success.* Bristol: Policy Press, 2005.

39   Paul Gilroy, 'The end of anti-racism' in *'Race', culture and difference*, ed. James
      Donald and Ali Rattansi. London: Sage/Open University, 1992 (cited in Bhavnani *et
      al., Tackling the roots of racism:* p. 118).

40   Runnymede Trust, *The future of multi-ethnic Britain: report of the Commission on the
      Future of Multi-ethnic Britain.* London: Profile, 2000. Chair Bhikhu Parekh.

41   Evelyn Kerslake and Margaret Kinnel [*sic* – i.e. Kinnell], *The social impact of public
      libraries: a literature review.* [London]: British Library Research and Innovation
      Centre, 1997, p. 1.

42   John Vincent, 'A broken heart?' *Assistant librarian* **86** (7), 1993, 99.

43   Black and Muddiman argued that 'community librarianship – and to a degree the
      public library's non-book and leisure-recreational functions which have so often been
      confused with that particular mode of service – has been subdued and has meta-
      morphosed, in part, due to the recent reverence for heritage displayed by British
      society, including the profession of public librarianship.' Black and Muddiman,
      Understanding community librarianship, p. 116.

44   Black and Muddiman, *Understanding community librarianship.*

45   Black and Muddiman, *Understanding community librarianship*, p. 118.

46   Richard Luce, 'Libraries: a ticket to civilization', *Independent* 27 Oct. 1993 (quoted in
      Black and Muddiman, *Understanding community librarianship*).

47   Office of Arts and Libraries, *Financing our public library service: four subjects for
      debate.* London: HMSO, 1988.

48   *Reading the future.* London: Department of National Heritage, 1997.

49   Black and Muddiman, *Understanding community librarianship,* p. 99.

50   List drawn from Black and Muddiman, *Understanding community librarianship*, pp.
      100–1.

51   John Pateman, 'Public libraries: let's get back to basics', *Library campaigner* 54,
      1996, 7–8.

52   House of Commons Culture, Media and Sport Committee, *Sixth report: public
      libraries.* London: HMSO, 2000, p. xiv.

53   *Borrowed time? The future of public libraries in the UK.* Bourne Green: Comedia,
      1993, p. 9.

54   *Review of the public library service in England and Wales for the Department of
      National Heritage.* London: Aslib, 1995.

55   Alan Hasson, 'Reaching out' in *Continuity and innovation in the public library: the development of a social institution*, ed. Margaret Kinnell and Paul Sturges. London: Library Association, 1996, pp. 148–66.

56   Dave Muddiman, 'Images of exclusion: user and community perceptions of the public library' in Muddiman *et al., Open to all? Vol. 3: Working papers*, pp. 179–88.

57   For example, John Pateman, 'A question of breeding', *Library Association record* **98** (7), 1996, 362–3.

58   John Pateman, 'Public libraries and social class' in Muddiman *et al., Open to all? Vol. 3: Working papers*, pp. 26–42.

59   Rebecca Linley and Bob Usherwood, *New measures for the new library: a social audit of public libraries*. [London?]: British Library, 1998 (Research & Innovation Centre report; 89).

60   An early-1990s summary was provided in: Helen Collins, *Equality matters: equal opportunities in the '90s: background and current issues*. London: Library Association, 1992.

61   See, for example: Debby Raven, 'Bookstart project goes national', *Library Association record* **101** (2), 1999, 78.

62   *Open learning in public libraries*. London: Department for Education and Employment, 1996; and *Open learning in public libraries: what you need to know*. London: Department for Education and Employment, 1996.

63   See, for example: *The role and contribution of library and information services to the National Year of Reading*. London: Library Association, 1998; and *Building a nation of readers: a review of the National Year of Reading*. London: Department for Education and Employment and National Literacy Trust, 2000. Executive summary available at: <http://www.nationalliteracytrust.org.uk/campaign/execsummary.html> (accessed 15/11/05).

64   See, for example: *The role and contribution of library and information services to the National Year of Reading*. London: Library Association, 1998.

65   The Association of Assistant Librarians, South-East Division (AAL SED) had previously organized sexuality awareness training for their committee (see Alistair Montgomery and Alison Behr, 'Significant others', *Assistant librarian* **81** (11), 1988, 164–8); and Alison Behr had also organized a course for AAL SED in 1990 on 'Section 28: 2 years on' (Alison Behr, 'Where are we now? Section 28: two years on' *Assistant librarian* **83** (9), 1990, 132–4).

66   See, for example: 'Homework clubs to get lottery funding', *Library Association record* **100** (3), 1998, 118; and *Homework help clubs*. London: London Borough of Southwark, 1998.

67   John Pateman, 'More or less in Hackney', *Library Association record* **98** (11), 1996, 582–3.

68   Anne Goulding and Evelyn Kerslake, *Developing the flexible library and information workforce: a quality and equal opportunities perspective*. London: British Library Research and Innovation Centre, 1996.

69   Shiraz Durrani, John Pateman and Naila Durrani, 'The Black and Minority Ethnic Stock Group (BSG) in Hackney Libraries', *Library review* **48** (1/2), 1999, 18–24.

70   For example: Domiciliary Services Group/London Housebound Services Group, *The Library Association guidelines for library services to people who are housebound*. London: Library Association, 1991; *Library and information services for visually impaired people: national guidelines – prepared for Share the Vision and the Library*

Association by Jean Machell. London: Library Association, 1996; and Roy Collis and Liz Boden (eds.), *The Library Association Public Libraries Group Guidelines for prison libraries*. 2nd ed. London: Library Association, 1997.

71   Patrick Roach and Marlene Morrison, *Public libraries, ethnic diversity and citizenship*. Warwick: University of Warwick Centre for Research in Ethnic Relations and Centre for Educational Development, Appraisal and Research, 1998 (British Library research and innovation report; 76).

72   Marlene Morrison and Patrick Roach, *Public libraries and ethnic diversity: a baseline for good practice*. Warwick: University of Warwick Centre for Research in Ethnic Relations, 1998 (British Library research and innovation report; 113).

73   Perhaps on purpose, critics of this work confuse positive action with positive discrimination, the treating of people more favourably on the grounds of race, nationality, religion, gender, etc. – which is illegal.

74   Bhavnani *et al.*, *Tackling the roots of racism*, p. 216.

75   See, for example: *Library service policy guidelines*. London: Lambeth Environmental Services, 1994; Ray Lonsdale, 'Collection development' in Judith Elkin and Ray Lonsdale, *Focus on the child: libraries, literacy and learning*. London: Library Association Publishing, 1996, pp. 133–58; and Judith Elkin, 'Children's libraries: current practice in action' in Elkin and Lonsdale, *Focus on the child*, pp. 193–222.

76   For example: Ian Malley, *Censorship and libraries*. London: Library Association, 1990 (Viewpoints in LIS; 5).

77   Terry Sanderson, 'Media Watch' column, *Gay times*, April 1993.

78   Trevor Phillips, 'Why political correctness is all about respect' (The Tuesday review), *The Independent*, 14 March 2000, 4.

79   *Reading for Life: the Arts Council's National Conference for the promotion of literature in public libraries*. London: Arts Council for England, 1998, p. 13.

80   Rosemary Stones, 'I din do nuttin … to Gregory Cool', *Books for keeps* 88, Sept. 1994, p. 5.

81   Muddiman *et al.*, *Open to all? Vol. 1: Overview and conclusions*, p. 40.

82   John Pateman, 'Public libraries' role in inclusion', *Anti poverty matters* **18**, 1998, 8–10.

83   John Pateman, 'Public libraries and social class', *Public library journal* **13** (5), 1998, 78–80.

84   *Reading for Life*, p. 18.

85   For example: John Pateman, 'Planning to tackle poverty', *Library Association record* **100** (9), 1998, 472.

86   *Public Libraries & Social Exclusion Action Planning Network newsletter* 1, May 1999.

87   John Vincent, 'Public Library Association Conference, 19–22 October 1999: edited version of the paper given by John Vincent, 21 October 1999', *Public Libraries & Social Exclusion Action Planning Network newsletter* 6, Oct.1999, 1–4.

88   For example: John Pateman, 'Public libraries and social exclusion', *Inside*, 1999, 6–7; John Vincent, 'Are your users just like you?', *Public library journal* **14** (4), 1999, 93–4; Dave Muddiman, 'Everyone on board?', *Public library journal* **14** (4), 1999, 96–7.

89   Taken from: John Vincent, 'Join up to tackle exclusion', *Public library journal* **15** (1), spring 2000, 23.

90 *Closing the digital divide: information and communication technologies in deprived areas: a report by Policy Action Team 15*. London: Department of Trade and Industry, 2000.

91 *Libraries for all*.

92 This proved to be a more useful and long-lasting approach than that adopted by the Library and Information Commission which produced a report (*Libraries: the essence of inclusion*. London: Library and Information Commission, 2000), the key message of which was 'stop investing in new institutions to do what libraries already can do – focus your investment'.

93 *Libraries for all*, p. 9.

94 *Libraries, museums, galleries and archives for all: co-operating across the sectors to tackle social exclusion*. London: Department for Culture, Media and Sport, 2001.

95 *Social inclusion: where do libraries stand? Proceedings of a seminar held at Stamford, Lincolnshire on 11th May 1999*. Bruton: Capital Planning Information, 1999.

96 Annual Library Plans were introduced in 1998, and every public library authority in England had to complete one; they included information about the library service, reviews of past performance, and strategies and targets for the current and future years.

97 Barbara Hull, *Barriers discouraging access to libraries as agents of life long learning*. London: Library and Information Commission, 2000 (Research report; 31).

98 *Appraisal of Annual Library Plans 1998*. London: Department for Culture, Media and Sport, 1999, p. 7.

99 *Appraisal of Annual Library Plans 1999 – progress and issues report*. London: Department for Culture, Media and Sport, 2000, pp. 19–20.

100 Muddiman *et al., Open to all? The public library and social exclusion*. London: Resource, 2000. *Vol. 1: Overview and conclusions*; *Vol. 2: Survey, case studies and methods*; *Vol. 3: Working papers* (Library and Information Commission research reports; 84–86).

101 Dave Muddiman, 'Theories of social exclusion and the public library' in Muddiman *et al., Open to all? Vol. 3: Working papers*, pp. 1–15.

102 John Pateman, 'Public libraries and social class' in Muddiman *et al., Open to all? Vol. 3: Working papers*, pp. 26–42.

103 Dave Muddiman, 'Images of exclusion: user and community perceptions of the public library' in Muddiman *et al., Open to all? Vol. 3: Working papers*, pp. 179–88.

104 Martin Dutch, 'Central and local government policies and social exclusion' in Muddiman *et al., Open to all? Vol. 3: Working papers*, pp. 189–204.

105 Shiraz Durrani, 'Struggle against racial exclusion in public libraries: a fight for the rights of people' in Muddiman *et al., Open to all? Vol. 3: Working papers*, pp. 254–349.

106 Martin Dutch and Dave Muddiman, 'Information and communication technologies, social exclusion and the public library' in Muddiman *et al., Open to all? Vol. 3: Working papers*, pp. 362–84.

107 John Vincent, 'Lesbians, bisexuals, gay men and transgendered people' in Muddiman *et al., Open to all? Vol. 3: Working papers*, pp. 62–86.

108 John Pateman, 'The state, communities and public libraries: their role in tackling social exclusion' in Muddiman *et al., Open to all? Vol. 3: Working papers*, pp. 111–43.

109   John Vincent, 'Public libraries, children and young people and social exclusion' in Muddiman *et al., Open to all? Vol. 3: Working papers*, pp. 144–78.

110   John Vincent and Rebecca Linley, 'Women, social exclusion and the public library' in Muddiman *et al., Open to all? Vol. 3: Working papers*, pp. 232–53.

111   Rebecca Linley, 'Public libraries, disability and social exclusion' in Muddiman *et al., Open to all? Vol. 3: Working papers*, pp. 205–31.

112   See, for example, the following articles by John Pateman: 'The state, communities and public libraries: their role in tackling social exclusion', *Focus on international and comparative librarianship* **30** (3), 1999, 139–47; 'Social exclusion: an international perspective on the role of the state, communities and public libraries in tackling social exclusion', *Journal of information science* **25** (6), 1999, 445–63; 'The state, communities and public libraries: their role in tackling social exclusion', *Link-up* **11** (1/2), March–June 1999, 10–16.

113   Muddiman *et al., Open to all? Vol. 1: Overview and conclusions*, p. viii.

114   Ibid., pp. ix–x.

115   *Closing the digital divide: information and communication technologies in deprived areas: a report by Policy Action team 15*. London: Department of Trade and Industry, 2000.

116   *Community access to lifelong learning: consultation paper England*. [London]: New Opportunities Fund, 1999.

117   Muddiman *et al., Open to all? Vol. 1: Overview and conclusions*, p. 39. These comments were made in the light of responses following the publication of *New library, the people's network*. London: Library and Information Commission, 1997.

118   Muddiman *et al., Open to all? Vol. 1: Overview and conclusions*, p. 39.

119   Ibid., p. x.

120   See <http://www.lmu.ac.uk/ies/dmudd/lib_conf.htm> (accessed 20/12/05).

121   John Pateman, 'Social exclusion: putting theory into practice', *Public library journal* **15** (2), summer 2000, 39–41.

122   See, for example: John Pateman, 'Working together to tackle social exclusion', *Assignation* **17** (2), Jan. 2000, 34–7; John Pateman, 'Are our libraries still a class act?', *Public library journal* **15** (3), autumn 2000, 81–2; John Pateman, 'Are public libraries a class act?', *Morning star*, 1 Sept. 2000.

123   The proceedings of this conference were subsequently produced as a resource pack: John Pateman, *Tackling social exclusion: a resource pack*. Maidstone: Kent County Council Arts and Libraries, 2000.

124   For example: John Vincent, 'Join up to tackle exclusion', *Public library journal* **15** (1), spring 2000, 23; John Vincent, 'The Social Exclusion Action Planning Network', *LASER link* autumn/winter 2000, 12–13.

125   *Public libraries tackling social exclusion: the Social Exclusion Action Planning Network Conference, 5 June 2000*. Exeter: Social Exclusion Action Planning Network, 2000.

126   See, for example: *A Quality Leaders Project for Black library and information workers: final report of research findings, feasibility study and proposals*. London: University of North London Management Research Centre, 2000; John Vincent, 'The Quality Leaders Project: conference report', *Information for social change* 11, summer 2000, 21–5, also available at:<http://www.seapn.org.uk/reports/qlp5.pdf> (accessed 20/12/05).

127   See, for example: *From elitism to inclusion: good practice in widening participation in higher education*. [London]: Committee of Vice-Chancellors and Principals, 1999; Margaret Noble and Pauline Lynn, 'Developing progression to learning: building progression pathways in the Tees Valley' in *Collaboration to widen participation in higher education*, ed. Liz Thomas, Michael Cooper and Jocey Quinn. Stoke-on-Trent: Trentham Books, 2002.

128   Evans, *All change?*

129   *Borrowed time? The future of public libraries in the UK*. Bourne Green: Comedia, 1993.

130   Muddiman *et al., Open to all? Vol. 1: Overview and conclusions*, p. 59.

131   Muddiman *et al., Open to all? Vol. 1: Overview and conclusions.*

4

Public libraries

Ayub Khan and Stella Thebridge

> Libraries have an almost unique opportunity to 'legitimise' a mass of cultural material and the interest of many publics.[1]

Public library activity in the 1990s was punctuated by three key reports which in different ways scrutinized the service and moved it into new directions. In terms of service development public library managers were to be held increasingly accountable both to the public they were seeking to serve and to their funders.

The 1993 report *Borrowed time?* described itself as a discussion paper rather than a definitive statement of where the public library was, yet it proved very useful in its description of the state of libraries at the time and the cultural influences upon them.[2] A number of working papers fed into the report, one of which outlined key themes as: traditions and functions; perceptions and uses; modern times.[3] Greenhalgh, quoted at the beginning of this chapter, examined the notion of the library as a physical place, while Landry addressed fundamental dilemmas for public librarians.[4] He posed some hypothetical questions to encourage discussion. For example, he asked for a definition of terms like 'knowledge' and 'public'. He asked: 'Is the library classless?'. He also said that the public library service 'tends to receive between 1.6% and 2.3% of the overall council budget'.[5] He asked what would happen if this were suddenly reduced to 0.6% or increased to 5.1%. Would an increase be a better way of spending than on education or leisure, for example? He urged public libraries to prove their case and find out their audience.

In a review of the report, Patrick Conway felt that no one could argue with its basic position and suggested that the Department of National Heritage (DNH) might do worse than use it as a starting point for its own review of libraries rather than starting again from the beginning.[6] However, the DNH in fact commissioned a review which became a weighty report published by Aslib in 1995.[7]

The research for the public libraries review was undertaken between March and December 1994. It identified four main purposes:

- providing for future generations
- the public library as a community asset

- facilities and services of direct benefit to people living or working in the area
- services to occasional users that have a 'contingency value'.

Thirteen core functions were also defined under the following broad headings:

- continuing or perpetual benefits (e.g., reading material, study space)
- sporadic or occasional benefits (reference, local information)
- social benefits (familiar, relaxing place).

Further recommendations, for example, for regional cooperation, for the merging of the Library and Information Commission and the Advisory Council on Libraries, and for the establishment of ICT links, were all taken up.

The third document to report in general terms on the state of public libraries was the 1997 Audit Commission's *Due for renewal*.[8] The first section is appropriately entitled 'The library service in the 1990s', and it gives an excellent introduction, with illustrations to the state of libraries, though commenting: 'although the library service is well regarded and well liked, there are signs that it is in gradual decline and may not be strongly placed to take up the challenges that are now facing it.'[9]

Its authors saw the main issues to be addressed as:

- declining usage
- reduced access
- increasing costs.

Other issues were identified as:

- partnerships
- the need to embrace ICT
- support for administrative functions.

The fourth chapter, on service planning, broke down costs into three dimensions:

- costs of each service (e.g., 'static lending')
- costs of activities (e.g., stock acquisition)
- traditional breakdown by 'subjective headings', i.e., employees, premises, supplies and services, transport, support services.

These reports bring us inevitably to the financial issues which would overshadow this decade for public library managers as they had consistently in earlier years.

Financial imperatives

> If the public library service had been stagnating during the 1980s, during the 1990s it began seriously to decline.[10]

Nick Moore, in a web-based history of public libraries, takes us neatly, if sombrely, into a decade of retrenchment in terms of expenditure on books, of staffing and of service points.

The financial decline is highlighted by John Sumsion writing in 1993 when he was head of the Library and Information Statistical Unit (LISU) at Loughborough University. He describes the nation's public libraries making the headlines in the autumn of 1992, when the Minister for Arts declined to meet the Library Association Chief Executive on what had been declared 'Libraries in Crisis' Day. The Minister had asserted that expenditure on public libraries in the UK over the decade had risen in real terms, keeping up with book prices. Chief librarians, however, could cite numerous instances of authorities where there were bookfund cuts, reduced opening hours and staff cuts. Both were correct, but coming at the situation from different perspectives and highlighting the real difficulty with statistics of interpreting and using them constructively to achieve change. John Sumsion went on to explain the developing role of LISU as a national centre 'to use statistics to clarify and publicise Libraries and Information Services'.[11]

Moore gives expenditure figures comparing the beginning of the decade with the middle years and the end. Overall expenditure fell in real terms by over 10%, with book and other material purchases falling during the decade by over 25%. He notes that staff expenditure remained generally constant (Table 1).

Table 1 Resource inputs 1990–2000 (England)[12]

	1990/91	1995/96	2000/01
Total expenditure (£ 000s)	579,946	641,251	730,894
Per 1,000 population	12,497	13,602	14,619
Expenditure on staff (£ 000s)	287,875	345,779	400,586
Per 1,000 population	6,203	7,335	8,013
Expenditure on materials (£ 000s)	95,940	107,269	99.301
Per 1,000 population	2,067	2,275	1,986

However, although the book expenditure rate fell by 25%, the rate of additions fell by only 15%. This implies that books were cheaper, but is probably explained by an increase in the proportion of paperback books purchased. This in turn had implications for stock maintenance as paperbacks are less durable. For the first time, therefore, the number of books in stock began to fall – by 13% over the decade. A student survey of paperback use in public libraries provides a helpful snapshot of users' views at this time and covers topics such as the paperback purchasing of different book categories, policy guidelines for paperbacks, the cataloguing of paperbacks, displaying fiction paperbacks, reinforcing and the shelf life of paperbacks.[13]

Returning to statistics for the 1990s, staff numbers fell by nearly 10% overall, and the proportion of qualified staff fell to 26% at the end of the century (Table 2).

Table 2 Staff, books and buildings 1990–2000 (England)

	1990/91	1995/96	2000/01
Total non-manual staff	21,848	20,820	19,936
Staff to population ratio	1:2,124	1:2,264	1:2,508
Proportion of qualified staff	30	28	26
Total books in stock (000s)	108,306	105,384	94,372
Annual additions to stock (000s)	10,877	9,528	9,185
Additions per 1,000 population	234	202	184
Stock replacement ratio	9.96	11.06	10.28
Service points open:			
More than 60 hours per week	21	9	19
30–59 hours per week	1,955	1,789	1,682
10–29 hours per week	1,178	1,315	1,331
Total open more than 10 hours per week	3,154	3,113	3,032

Book loans fell by nearly 30% and the average number of books borrowed per head declined during the decade to under 7 in 2000/01, maintaining a downward trend since a high point of 12 in 1980/81. Visits to public libraries also dropped by nearly 15%. Reference transactions increased in the first half of the decade, but fell back again in the second (Table 3).

Table 3 Use of libraries 1990–2000 (England)

	1990/91	1995/96	2000/01
Book loans (000s)	475,527	437,158	342,914
Loans per head of population	10.25	9.27	6.86
Reference transactions	45,462	52,548	50,051
Transactions per 1,000 population	980	1,115	1,001

Moore's research shows that the total expenditure for 2000/01 on the public library service per thousand population was no greater than it had been in 1985. He writes that while this is keeping pace with inflation it does not allow for any growth in quantity and quality of public services as the economy expands. In particular, the maintenance of staff numbers appears to have been at the expense of the quality of the staff, and this may have contributed to the decline in book issues.

Stock supply

A key financial influence on public libraries was in the area of stock supply, and this was the termination of the publishers' Net Book Agreement (NBA) in 1997. Frank Fishwick and Lindsey Muir of Cranfield University document the effect of the NBA's demise on library book-buying and note that the bargaining power of public libraries increased significantly after the end of the NBA.[14] However, increased discount opportunities were not used to increase book stocks. The authors perceive that book budgets fell by nearly 11% between 1995/96 and 1996/97 and that improved discounts were being used to cut spending rather than buy more books – a benefit to the authority (through meeting budget targets) rather than to the library service.[15]

Another sea change in stock supply was a move to 'supplier selection', a move seen by many professional librarians as striking at the heart of one of their areas of expertise. Hall *et al.* examined pilot schemes in Hertfordshire and Westminster in 1998 which were endeavouring to quantify the advantages and disadvantages of such a change to selection practice.[16]

Political spheres of influence

Government attempts to influence developments in local authorities centred on the requirement from 1998 for all local library authorities to submit annual plans. The Department for Culture, Media and Sport (DCMS) asked for standard information about each library service, including reviews of past performance and strategies and targets for the current and future years.

The concept of Best Value in local authority reviews meant that libraries too must demonstrate the quality of their service in meeting customer demand. However, Best Value did not establish itself fully until the year 2000.

Administrative changes were principally the change from a Conservative to a Labour government in 1997 and prior to that significant changes at local authority level with new unitary authorities and the division of some larger counties. In April 1996, 29 new unitary authorities were created in Scotland, 22 in Wales and 13 in England to replace some county and district councils. Further changes were made in April 1997 and April 1998. Each unitary authority automatically became a library authority.[17] Maureen Taylor writes in clear detail of the way that the break-up of Cleveland was achieved.[18] The effect on library services was in some cases the loss of the central large-scale library to another (often discrete) authority and the consequent loss of stock and facilities. The unitary authorities in their turn might have one large library and a very small number of branches, again bringing problems of scale, but in a different way to their neighbours. Many authorities immediately negotiated agreements to serve their public via reciprocal borrowing and stock acquisition agreements, in order to mitigate the effect on customers who could not reasonably be expected to understand new and seemingly inconsistent boundaries to their library service. Further deliberations in the professional press concentrate on the experience of Berkshire, Durham and Cleveland[19] and, in Ian Malley's case, show some valuable emerging joint arrangements for service delivery.[20]

Useful research was undertaken by Midwinter and McVicar for the British Library in the early 1990s. They analysed the relationship between the size of a library authority and its ability to deliver an efficient service. The fieldwork was conducted in 1992 and 1993 with 25 authorities. They contribute to the debate about reorganization and conclude: 'Reorganization is not a panacea for the ills of the public library service.'[21]

Ian Malley provides further information in a two-part investigation of authority reorganization in 1993.[22] In part one he lists the authorities as they were affected in five tranches. He notes the difference between this reorganization and that of 1974 because of other agents of change at the same time: 'compulsory competitive tendering, the enabling authority, quality assurance, performance indicators, etc.' In the second part he outlines the process for change and describes the enormous difficulties in accurately measuring costs and benefits of services such as libraries. The effects were researched by Sandra Parker and colleagues at the University of Northumbria in the LOGOPLUS project – investigating the impact of local government reorganization on public library users and staff.[23]

Further on into the decade Burton *et al.* at Comedia produced another report on the state of libraries, this time in the London boroughs, and this described a generally inadequate strategic leadership among library services as a whole.[24] Anne Fisher analysed ways in which libraries could respond to the new Labour government agenda through provision of community information, neutral space, voting locations, e-government, partnership working and Best Value.[25]

Towards the end of the decade, the government looked at the role of libraries in a regional context, as part of a general re-defining of the regions of the UK as regional cultural consortia and ultimately Regional Development Agencies (RDAs).[26]

In *Reading the future: the public libraries review*, published in February 1997, the government gave a clear signal that libraries would be funded to provide access to the internet.[27] This document was a product of the Conservative administration. Labour's shadow Secretary of State Jack Cunningham condemned it as doing 'little to address the very real problems that many public library services face'. He continued: 'Library closures, decreased opening hours and declining book stocks have been facts of life for local authority libraries for the last 18 years.' This point was echoed by Ross Shimmon who, while welcoming some of the recommendations, said 'The fundamental problem of funding remains unresolved'. However, the Labour party which took over in May 1997 followed the report's recommendations.

Other key points of the report were that the performance of public library services would be measured and evaluated by the Department of National Heritage and that authorities would be asked to 'consider alternative methods of service delivery, such as contracting out and the development of library trusts'.

The document stated that libraries would benefit from the money allocated to the 'IT for All' campaign but did not say in what way. The Library and Information Commission (LIC) was asked to report by July of that year on 'how public libraries can together respond to the challenge of new technology'.

Public Library Plans

From April 1998 each authority was asked to provide a Public Library Plan. Brendan Dwyer, a consultant speaking at a CPI conference in Stamford, Lincolnshire noted that the change of government had led to some confusion when plans were originally requested in 1997.[28] However, a surprisingly high 82 of the then 131 authorities submitted trial plans in 1997 following the *Reading the future* recommendations. The plan was to cover the indicators already required annually by the Audit Commission (issues, number of visits, expenditure – on materials and net – and stock per capita) plus a number of new indicators related to efficiency and access and usage. A clear summary of the process was given by Peter Beauchamp of the DCMS to a conference at Loughborough University devoted to public library plans.[29]

Librarians broadly welcomed the introduction of the plans and felt that they could link in with benchmarking processes that were already being developed across some authorities.

Other recommendations of *Reading the future*

The document also exhorted local authorities to consider devolving library services to independent trusts. Hounslow had already stated its intentions of becoming the first local authority to devolve its service in this way and proceeded to do so, becoming and remaining the only one.[30]

Reading the future also recommended that libraries should review their opening hours, if necessary opening more at evenings and weekends and closing during less busy periods. The use of volunteers was also recommended.

Quality issues in the public sector were high on the agenda in the 1990s. The 1980s were characterized by the emphasis placed by government upon the need to review all aspects of public service. The guiding principles of achieving greater public accountability and increased value for money in service provision signalled the start of a revolution that continued in the 1990s. Public librarians found themselves working in local authorities where a large proportion of services were subject to contracting out regulations. The move towards Local Management of Schools, and the impact that this had upon Schools' Library Service provision, sent powerful messages to public libraries as to what the future would hold for their service. Terms such as Total Quality Management, Citizen's Charter, ISO 9000 and BS 5750 were the language of the day in many local authorities.[31]

The key role of libraries in the information age

A report commissioned by the Department for Culture, Media and Sport and published by LIC in 1997 called for a radical overhaul of the public library system. The report, *New library: the people's network*, argued that public libraries, which had long been recognized as centres of knowledge and learning, should work to be at the heart of communications in the information society in order for the citizens of the UK to be competitive in the next millennium.[32]

The report, from a group under the chairmanship of Matthew Evans, chairman both of the Library and Information Commission and of the publishers Faber and Faber, demanded a central role for libraries in the government's lifelong learning programme – the National Grid for Learning. It identified three areas of interest:

- consumer – who this is and what he/she will expect
- content – what will be delivered
- training – preparing the library workforce to deliver ICT.

It recommended the formation of a 'Public Library Networking Agency'. It further recommended provision of a network across libraries, to provide free internet access and information.

The report suggested that funding for the initiative – £770 million over a period of seven years – should come from local and central government, private companies and the National Lottery. Partnerships with bodies like educational institutions, museums and business organizations, were encouraged.

Libraries would offer access to a wide range of information sources via the internet, and it was seen as crucial that technological developments and opportunities in rural areas should keep pace with those in urban areas.

The report also recommended that Britain's collections of rare books, paintings and artefacts be turned into digital records as a kind of technological 'Domesday Book' of the nation's heritage. This should give the general public access to databases of museums, galleries, the media, public services, and agencies in the voluntary and private sector from one location – the library.

This report went on to have a profound impact on public libraries into the next century. The proposed agency became the People's Network, a term which became common coinage for access to the internet in every public library in the land.

Reader development

The new Labour Government of 1997, buoyed up by a clear election victory and a wish to make dramatic changes, declared a new literacy strategy to improve reading standards. The first World Book Day was in 1998 and this contributed to the development of a National Year of Reading in 1998/99 with money made available for projects where partnership working could be demonstrated. Many libraries took up the challenge and successfully carried out a wide range of imaginative work with schools and commercial enterprises to move reading up the agenda.[33]

The National Year of Reading built on a growing move in public libraries in the 1990s to encourage not just literacy but a culture of reading. Back in 1993 Rachel Van Riel of 'Opening the Book' argued that librarians should demonstrate that they are 'proactive and educative in their approach to fiction.'[34] Here were the conscious beginnings of what was to become the reader development movement.

Van Riel observed that 'Reading is often seen as a passive activity, done by those who are fearful of the world and wish to retreat from it'. She encouraged librarians to consider their marketing of fiction stock, which she suggested was not done to the same extent as non-fiction. Librarians were encouraged to feel good both about reading in itself and about reading all kinds of literature. It is indicative of the situation in libraries that it took non-librarians like Van Riel to plead a cause which should be at the heart of our profession. She wrote: 'I came to libraries ten years ago from an arts and local publishing background. I was an immediate convert and have been a passionate advocate of the virtues of public libraries ever since.'[35]

Van Riel's work and vision is encapsulated in the proceedings of the 'Reading the future' conference of 1992.[36] Opening the Book continued to support public libraries in reader development initiatives and training. The 1990s ended triumphantly in this respect with the Branching Out project, an initiative of the Society of Chief Librarians, managed by Opening the Book. This was a three-year programme funded by the Arts Council and embedding work not just in public libraries (33 authorities) but with other partners like the National Library for the Blind and book suppliers. Its strength lay in its relatively long-term span of three years, in the training enshrined in the programme and in the careful evaluation of the programme throughout its life to ensure that its aims were achieved. The evaluators noted:

> those parties consulted after three years of participation reported a wide range of tangible, sustainable outcomes. It is significant that it was not just the practitioners but also the senior managers who gave examples of such outcomes.[37]

All parties consulted for the evaluation recognized that Branching Out had indeed made a significant contribution to cultural change and that it had demonstrated the value of reader development as a core activity in the public library sector.

A lasting legacy of the Branching Out programme was the Book Forager software, which became freely available as 'whichbook.net', enabling users to search for book titles to suit not just subjects but emotional moods.[38]

During the 1990s there were two occasions when National Libraries Week was promoted – in November of 1993 and 1997. Each time, public libraries took advantage of the opportunity to forge partnerships with other institutions to promote library services in general and reading in particular. Some saw it as a chance to survey non-users. Birmingham Public Libraries successfully presented a proposal to their local bookshop and received significant funds which they matched with funds from their own marketing fund and a local authority fund. The sizeable total (over £20,000) enabled them to organize over 200 events, attracting some 3,300 adults and 3,600 children. The funding enabled the production of high-quality promotional material including posters which were displayed throughout the city. Crucially there was a 7% increase in adult membership of the library and 27% in children joining. Two authorities summarized their participation in the 1993 week in the *Public library journal*, showing the value of long-term planning.[39]

Within public libraries, another national initiative was evolving – the Summer Reading Challenge. While the Library Association had coordinated 'one-off' summer reading schemes, an agency called LaunchPad (which in 2002 became part of the Reading Agency) took over organization of the programme on an annual basis, coordinating a theme and a programme which could be offered to young library users aged between 4 and 12 to read six books over the summer holidays. Later to become firmly established in most, if not all, library authorities, the success of the scheme lay in the realization in the 1990s that a professional product was required to encourage young people to participate in a reading programme and that a national initiative would enable hard-pressed and cash-strapped library authorities to participate most effectively.

Public libraries continued to seek ways to reach their 'non-users', often in partnership. One fruitful example of this was the 'Reaching Parents' programme, an initiative from LaunchPad where 'The Big Read' was established in 227 ASDA stores in May and June 1999. A research project by David Liddle and associates at Capital Planning Information for both the Arts Council and the Library Association brought up to date the partnerships between libraries and various arts organizations, not just in literature promotion, but across a range of visual and creative arts.[40] Meanwhile Davidson *et al.* looked specifically at reading partnerships.[41]

Teenagers continued to be a group that libraries wished to encourage, yet not always being sure of the best way to do so. One successful initiative was *Boox*.[42] This was a magazine for teenagers devoted to books, yet appealing to them visually, with a lot of related content from celebrities and a joke problem page. The magazine was piloted well with young people before reaching its final form and title. Above all, the teenagers themselves provided some of the content, creating that all-important sense of ownership.

Another way in which younger people were encouraged into libraries was through homework support. Public libraries had long offered this, but there was a concerted effort after 1995 across a number of authorities to provide homework clubs, helped by provision in many cases of start-up grants from the New Opportunities Fund.[43] Following work by the Princes Trust throughout the 1990s, a number of agencies – the DCMS and the Department for Education and Employment, the Library Association and the National Youth Agency – developed codes of practice to be used in secondary and primary schools and also in public libraries, the aim being to ensure consistency of study support.[44] This provided a helpful framework of ideas as well as benchmarks for varying degrees of good practice.

At the early end of the learning spectrum, the Bookstart programme was established in 1996 from a pilot project, quickly growing through commercial short-term sponsorship into a national scheme funded by the government. Although not run by public libraries as such, many services in fact became partners in their local scheme to give every baby a free book at a standard health check and encourage parents to introduce the sharing of books as early as possible in their child's life. Libraries were crucial in offering follow-up support, both in terms of reading material and activities in libraries.

In a climate of perceived decline in interest in books *per se*, the reader development movement and initiatives like Bookstart surely contributed to a counter-offensive on both literacy and declining fiction issues.

Open learning

Many public libraries in the early 1990s began to investigate the opportunities offered by the government initiative, 'Open Learning in Public Libraries'. The starting point for this service development was the white paper *People, jobs and opportunity* in which the government announced its plans for Training and Enterprise Councils (TECs) to establish partnerships with local libraries in order to make open learning material and supporting services available to the public.[45] Green provides a thorough description of the work of Staffordshire Libraries with Staffordshire TEC to establish three centres in libraries in the county.[46]

A special issue of the *Library Association record* was devoted to the topic of lifelong learning in 1998.[47] The government minister outlined the green paper on the subject and stressed the government's commitment to the integral role of public libraries in its lifelong learning strategy. Other contributors wrote about access to the new network services, about the work of the BBC and about a report called *Learning for the twenty-first century*.[48]

Chris Smith, the Culture Minister who proved an advocate for public libraries, referred to them as 'street-corner universities'. Broady-Preston and Cox analysed the extent to which they fulfilled this role and their potential for the future in a changed world where they needed to conform to private sector competitive models akin to the retail sector.[49]

Social inclusion

In the 1990s the Government placed a high priority on promoting social inclusion. DCMS provided libraries with clear guidelines to respond to the inclusion agenda, and to generate change. In his foreword to the guidelines, Chris Smith states:

A regenerated and pro-active library sector can help both individuals and communities to develop skills and confidence, and help improve social networking. The Government wants libraries to be at the very heart of the communities they serve.[50]

The research project *Open to all?* found that libraries mostly provided passive access to materials and resources, and that their service priorities and resourcing strategies favoured existing users rather than excluded or disadvantaged communities or groups.[51] The report recommended a number of strategies, including:

- mainstreaming provision for socially excluded groups and establishment of standards to monitor the provision
- prioritizing and targeting excluded groups
- staffing policies and practices to address exclusion, discrimination and prejudice
- development of a community-based approach to library provision
- adopting ICT and networking developments, which would actively focus on the needs of excluded groups.

The research also found that community development approaches worked more effectively when they were planned in partnership with other agencies and on a whole-authority basis. Case studies demonstrated the need for public library services to be offered outside the walls of their buildings.

Roach and Morrison of Warwick University questioned whether libraries stood at the heart of all local communities.[52] They conducted a postal audit of twelve authorities and case studies of four of these. They concluded that libraries needed to demonstrate that they had engaged all communities, including those that were hard to reach or marginalized. They wrote that, although libraries were based in the community, some did not give a sense of community ownership. Their research found that library objectives and standards rarely addressed racial equality issues because there were limited opportunities for ethnic minorities to influence service provision, and few library services had undertaken explicit research into the service needs of ethnic minority communities.

The Roach and Morrison research also found a lack of coherence in strategies to identify and track the changing needs of the community for library services. For example, data on ethnicity were being collected but not monitored. This applied as much to data on users as to data about the employment of library staff from ethnically diverse backgrounds. There was limited evidence of attempts to include ethnic communities in library consultations or planning. Roach and Morrison recommended that, in order to identify and improve their understanding of community needs, libraries needed to implement a range of actions, including consulting ethnic minority users and non-users to identify changing patterns and use, and to examine the underlying factors which influenced library use. They suggested that libraries needed to understand the use of other agencies, and establish better systems for dialogue with them. Libraries alone could not change the situation, but they appeared to be irrelevant to many from non-white communities. At the time of writing it appeared that many of Roach and Morrison's recommendations for national and local agendas had still not been taken up.

The reader might think that the 1990s represent unremitting gloom in a decade of financial cutbacks and an apparent inability to grasp the basics of an inclusive library service. Such a view would fail to do justice to the many examples of imaginative and innovative work carried out in a range of authorities, including new service developments and new buildings.

Libraries changing lives

François Matarasso examined projects submitted for the Holt-Jackson/LA Community Initiative Awards (from 1999 called 'Libraries Change Lives' Awards).[53] These were established in 1992, and every year three library projects were (and continue to be) shortlisted for the prize. Projects have to show measurable impact on their local community. Matarasso outlines how impact was shown in terms of personal development, social cohesion, community empowerment, local image and identity, imagination and creativity and health and well-being. His document gives useful summaries of each of the projects discussed, 18 in all.[54]

Towards the end of the 1990s, John Vincent followed up work on the *Open to all?* project by initiating a training programme for library staff on issues of social inclusion, as well as developing the 'Network', a web-based forum for interested individuals to share information and learn more of ways to tackle social exclusion.[55] His remit would go wider than libraries, reaching across the whole cultural and heritage sectors.

Other awards have offered authorities the chance to put forward their projects and showcase high quality initiatives. One such is the Public Relations and Publicity Awards, which celebrated ten years in 1994.[56]

1998 was the year the profession celebrated the centenary of the Library Association's Royal Charter. On 8 December HRH the Princess Royal presented Royal Charter Centenary Medals to members who exemplified the profession's achievements, and many of the recipients were public librarians. The centenary year was an opportunity to celebrate the value, and the values, of the library profession.

Buildings

Public library managers continued to be conscious of their library buildings, both in terms of their physical appearance and the inevitable need to re-examine opening hours or even closure.

New buildings and imaginative refurbishment of non-library buildings continued in this decade. For example, in 1999, the Public Library Building awards included for the first time a prize for small libraries (under 500m^2 of floorspace).

The winner was Bridport Library in Dorset, a refurbished building which had served as a private house, a fire station and a police station before being turned into a public library![57]

The destruction of Norwich Central Library in 1994, from a fire caused by an electrical fault, sent shockwaves through the public library community. The immediacy of the disaster is brought home in a short report of Hilary Hammond's talk to the Public Library Authorities' Conference just after the event: 'He was heard in stunned silence as he showed slide after slide of ashes.'[58]

But time brought a measure of good from the destruction, and the new library for Norwich would become a worthy successor for the new century. Furthermore, Hammond's exhortation to the conference delegates to 'put your catalogue in metal drawers' would soon seem quaintly outdated. The Norwich fire, while seeing the destruction of irreplaceable archives, did nevertheless move many managers to form a more coherent analysis of their disaster planning and prevention measures, often starting to work more closely with partners in the museum and archive sectors.

Jared Bryson and colleagues at Sheffield University investigated the impact of new library buildings at the beginning of the new century.[59] Most of these were 'millennium' buildings, but much of the planning was undertaken in the 1990s, particularly for Norwich and for Stratford (London Borough of Newham). The conclusion of their work was that libraries would continue to be vital as physical places, despite fears to the contrary, some years earlier, that all library services would be accessible at the click of a mouse from the customer's home or workplace. This research embeds the notion of public libraries as 'place', characterized by a surge in new building at the end of the 1990s.

Other researchers from Sheffield looked at the impact of library closures between 1986 and 1997. They did this in two separate pieces of research. The first looked quantitatively at the data, as the authors note:

> The early 1990s brought further hardship to library budgets as a result of rate-capping legislation. News of library closures was continuous and widespread and the most severe cutbacks were frequently charted in the headlines of the Record. [60]

Derbyshire, for example, closed eleven libraries in 1990. The authors go on to note that CIPFA statistics show that 'between 1986 and 1996 library service points open more than 60 hours a week in English authorities fell by 77% from 39 to just 9'.[61] They record that county libraries lost all their service points that were in this category. Libraries open between 45 and 59 hours per week also fell by 33%.

179 building-based services in 56 authorities closed – 5.5% of libraries which were open in 1986. They concluded that, in 1997, access was more limited than ten years previously in 9 out of 10 authorities in England and Wales, and that 88% of authorities had closed or reduced opening hours.[62]

This quantitative research was followed up by a qualitative study by Simmons *et al*.[63] During three months in 1998, information was gathered from 20 authorities which had closed libraries between 1991 and 1997. This included, for example, the criteria for closure and the effect on the public and on staff. It looked at whether there had been consultation and with whom. Above all, it endeavoured to highlight the experiences of the sample authorities as a way to offer help and pointers to others who might have to make this kind of difficult decision. The researchers concluded that forward planning for closures was essential as part of a whole-service strategy. They stressed that criteria for closure should be determined on a cooperative or inter-authority basis and noted:

> Consultation should be used as a tool for collecting evidence on which to base decisions rather than as a forum for negotiation after decisions have been made.[64]

Library usage

Changes in library usage were a feature of this decade, perhaps more than any other, with a distinctive shift from a book-based service to a range of services, which by the new millennium would see the installation of personal computers in every library in the land – whole banks of them in larger libraries. With increasing calls for accountability, managers needed effective ways to measure use, and one of the key developments was the CIPFA PLUS (Public Library User Survey) methodology. This was a partnership between librarians, piloting and advising on the system, and CIPFA statisticians, providing a robust methodology. The Department of National Heritage and the Audit Commission provided funding in 1992 for a pilot survey with 18 authorities which was carried out in April 1993.[65] The survey was refined and went on to offer a national survey for adult services, followed by a Children's PLUS and community PLUS. Public library managers consistently praised the methodology as a means of extracting useful and reliable data which could also be compared with 'family' groups of similar authorities or neighbouring services.[66]

Len England conducted several related pieces of research for Book Marketing Ltd looking at library usage in terms of book borrowing in 1992 and at the user perspective in 1994.[67] In the research on book borrowing, using data from 1991, he noted that two in five users had no library ticket. A third had a ticket which was used regularly. 16% of those who used libraries borrowed 50% of the books. It should be noted that this survey was just about borrowing books, not other uses of the library. He concluded that borrowers are 'not far from a cross-section of the population', but the elderly were a very important group. Library users were more likely to read a lot at home and to have more books in the home. What they read was not dissimilar from those who were not using libraries at all.

Len England was also responsible for the first volume of *Perspectives of public library use*, a large but handy collection of key statistics and research data from a variety of sources.[68] A second volume of *Perspectives* by Bohme and Spiller grouped data by subjects, for example, sources on user surveys, stock management, ICT.[69] Some are external research efforts (e.g., Reuben on paperback books, cited above), others are authorities' own work, for example, Hounslow's survey of Asian users and a survey of lapsed users from Sandwell. The volumes remain a useful resource.

A survey published in 1999 about usage of public libraries based on exit polls makes interesting reading.[70] One example is the opening sentence – 'Men and women use libraries about equally' – which is expanded as follows. Men and younger people use libraries more for information and to borrow non-fiction. They are more likely to buy books. Women, poorer people and older people use libraries more to borrow fiction. They are less likely to buy books. The authors conclude, as public library statistics themselves would probably confirm: 'Our research among lending libraries suggested "book issues down, library use up" as a summary of current change.'[71]

Research
The research climate in public libraries had traditionally been mixed. While many practitioners understood the need for research in order to improve practice, they could not justify 'blue sky' projects out of their funds, and outside sources of funding remained haphazard. Time was always a significant constraint. Yet the need for accountability meant that managers must be aware of research findings and not only keep and monitor statistics, but conduct adequate feasibility studies for new services. One useful source of funding at the time was the Public Library Development Incentive Scheme (PLDIS) which allowed for pump-priming of new developments. A review of the scheme recommended its continuation in some form, suggesting a sum of money and the need for a central choice between a large number of small-scale projects or a small number of large-scale ones.[72] It considered that the scheme had encouraged new initiatives and the development of partnerships. More importantly, projects were sustainable: 'nearly all the completed development projects started in the first three years of the Scheme continue to be viable'.[73] Sadly the scheme did not continue after 1992.

Goodall charted the research climate in public libraries through a review of articles in the *Public library journal,* and the British Library sponsored two major projects on the subject to encourage public library managers not only to undertake more research but to share their results and avoid re-inventing the wheel.[74] The first of the projects established the beginnings of a database of public library research, while the second specifically addressed the need for training, offering free courses in research skills in eight UK locations. Sadly, funding was not forthcoming to sustain it, so that although the need was perceived and the courses well-received, public librarians had to revert to more expensive options, and many could not embark on the road to research in the way that they would have liked, with sufficient trained personnel.

Prospects: a strategy for action was a consultation document from the LIC in 1997.[75] Sadly, library research in general suffered towards the end of the decade with the loss of the British Library Research and Innovation Centre. Their grant-funding powers were passed to the new Library and Information Commission, but when this was merged with the Museums and Galleries Commission, the research function changed. Such funding as there was tended to be awarded not for development projects or practitioner research but for work which informed the new body's own strategic and decision-making research needs.

It is sobering that, at the beginning of the decade, the *Borrowed time?* report had recommended an agency for libraries to include a research and development function, yet by the end of the decade this had disappeared.

Conclusion

Bob McKee, chief executive of the Library Association, speaking at the Public Library Authorities Conference in 1999, suggested that libraries had moved from feeling ignored by government, to having now to live up to some challenging expectations.[76] He cited rolling out the People's Network, surviving in a competitive culture, the need for research and the ability to achieve social inclusion as the challenges for the next few years, along with a workforce equipped to carry out the work. The end of the decade is perhaps neatly encapsulated in the IFLA/UNESCO guidelines for public libraries. These were billed as *not* prescriptive. They updated the previous guidelines of 1986 and were contained in a succinct but comprehensive document – a helpful pointer for public library practitioners in the new millennium.[77]

In a book entitled *Learning development,* one of the Comedia team, François Matarasso, encapsulated the major research of the 1990s on the social impact of public libraries.[78] He distilled it into a readable and thought-provoking summary under the following headings:

- renewing the library idea
- personal development
- community development
- local development agencies.

For each of these sections he showed how public libraries might contribute to the different types of people who are their public. There is a wonderful two-page summary of points at the beginning of the book which starts 'The research shows that effective library services can …', and thirty-three broad types of service are listed. This is an affirming book for the potential of public libraries. It should be on every library worker's bookshelf.

Notes

1   Liz Greenhalgh, *The public library as place*. Bournes Green: Comedia, 1993 (The future of public library services. Working paper; 2), p. 12.

2   *Borrowed time? The future of public libraries in the UK*. Bournes Green: Comedia, 1993.

3   *Key themes and issues of the study*. Bournes Green: Comedia, 1993 (The future of public library services. Working paper; 1).

4 Charles Landry, *Fundamental dilemmas for public libraries*. Bournes Green: Comedia, 1993 (The future of public library services. Working paper; 4)

5 Greenhalgh, *Public library as place*, p. 9.

6 Patrick Conway, 'Borrowed time? The future of public libraries in the United Kingdom: Patrick Conway reviews the Comedia report', *Public library journal* **8** (4), 1993, 101–2.

7 Aslib, *Review of the public library service in England and Wales for the Department of National Heritage: final report*. London: Aslib, 1995.

8 Audit Commission, *Due for renewal: a report on the library service*. London: Audit Commission, 1997.

9 Audit Commission, *Due for renewal*, p. 9.

10 Nick Moore, *Public library trends*. Acumen, 2003. Available at: <http://www.acumenuk.co.uk/papers/public_library_trends.php> (accessed 18/01/06).

11 John Sumsion, 'In search of the truth: library and information statistics', *Public library journal* **8** (3), 1993, 77–8.

12 This and the following two tables are based on tables in Moore, *Public library trends*, themselves compiled from CIPFA *public library statistics*. Reproduced by permission of Nick Moore.

13 Joan Reuben, *Paperbacks in public libraries*. Loughborough: LISU, 1999 (Occasional papers; 22).

14 Frank Fishwick and Lindsey Muir, 'The cost of cut-throat competition', *Library Association record* **100** (5), 1998, 244–5; Frank Fishwick, Sharon Fitzsimons and Lindsey Muir, *Effects of the abandonment of the Net Book Agreement: first interim research report*. London: Book Trust, 1997.

15 Lindsey Muir and Alex Douglas, 'Where now for the UK public library service?', *Library management* **22** (6/7), 2001, 266–71.

16 Christine Hall, Sue Valentine and Steve Fletcher, 'Into the age of supplier selection?', *Library Association record* **100** (9), 1998, 476–7.

17 *Key issues in the delivery of public library services: report of the LINC Standing Committee on Local Goverment Reorganisation*. Bruton: Library and Information Co-operation Council, 1996.

18 Maureen Taylor, 'Once upon a time in the north east of England', *Public library journal* **9** (6), 1994, 170–2.

19 Sandra Parker, 'Changing places', *Library Association record* **101** (2), 1999, 92; Debby Raven, 'Durham's delighted – but Cleveland is concerned', *Library Association record* **95** (7), 1993, 396; Debby Raven, 'Unitary status: good or bad?', *Library Association record* **101** (2), 1999, 90–1.

20 Ian Malley, 'Hands across the unitaries', *Library Association record* **98** (11), 1996, 576–7.

21 Arthur Midwinter and Murray McVicar, *The size and efficiency debate: public library authorities in a time of change*. London: Library Association, 1994 (British Library research and development report; 6143).

22 Ian Malley, 'The re-organization of public library services in England in the 1990s', *Public library journal* **8** (1), 1993, 9–10; Ian Malley, 'The local government review (2): the rules of the game', *Public library journal* **8** (2), 1993, 47–8, 50.

23 Sandra Parker, Linda Banwell and Moira Bent, 'Logoplus', *Public library journal* **12** (3), 1997, 49–52. A useful summary of the findings including a full list of related literature.

24 Chris Burton, Liz Greenhalgh and Ken Worpole, *London, library city: the public library service in London: a strategic review*. Bournes Green: Comedia, 1996.

25 Anne Fisher, 'Modernising local government', *Public library journal* **13** (2), 1998, 17–19.

26 Department for Culture, Media and Sport, *Libraries and the regions: a discussion paper*. London: DCMS, 1999.

27 Department of National Heritage, *Reading the future: a review of public libraries in England*. London: DNH, 1997.

28 Geoff Smith and Anne Sugg (eds.), *Strategic reviews of public library services: proceedings of a seminar held at Stamford, Lincolnshire in February 1998*. Bruton: Capital Planning Information, 1998.

29 David Spiller (ed.), *Public library plans: proceedings of a seminar held at Loughborough University 17–18 March 1998*. Loughborough: LISU, 1998 (LISU occasional papers; no. 19).

30 See Geoff Allen, 'Can you trust this model?', *Library Association record* **103** (12), 2001, 754–5; Linda Simpson, 'Can you spot the join?', *Public library journal* **15** (2), 2000, 47.

31 Eileen Milner, Margaret Kinnell and Bob Usherwood, 'Quality management: the public library debate', *Public library journal* **9** (6), 1994, 151–7.

32 *New library: the people's network*. London: Library and Information Commission, 1997.

33 *Public libraries and readers: building a creative nation*. [Leicester]: Reading Partnership, 2000.

34 Rachel van Riel, 'The case for fiction', *Public library journal* **8** (3), 1993, 81–2, 84.

35 van Riel, 'Case for fiction', p. 81.

36 Rachel van Riel (ed.), *Reading the future: a place for literature in public libraries*. London: Arts Council; Library Association, 1992. Unfortunately, this title was later appropriated by the DNH report of 1997, causing occasional confusion in the profession.

37 Briony Train and Judith Elkin, *Branching out: overview of evaluative findings*. Birmingham: Centre for Information Research, 2001.

38 <http://whichbook.net> (accessed 31/1/06).

39 Cathy Evans and Patricia Dunlop, 'National Library Week 1993: the Warwickshire experience', *Public library journal* **9** (1), 1994, 7–9.

40 David Liddle, Debbie Hicks and David Barton, *Public libraries and the arts: pathways to partnership*. London: Arts Council of England, 2000.

41 Jonathan Davidson, Debbie Hicks and Miranda McKearney, *The next issue: reading partnerships for libraries*. A report commissioned by the Library Association and the Arts Council of England, 1998.

42 Trish Botten, 'Boox', *Public library journal* **10** (6), 1995, 157–8.

43 Briony Train *et al.*, *The value and impact of homework clubs in public libraries*. London: Library and Information Commission, 2000 (LIC research report; 32).

44 *Study support: the code of practice for public libraries*. Glasgow: University of Strathclyde, Quality in Education Centre, 1999.

45 Department of Employment, *People, jobs and opportunity*. London: HMSO, 1992 (Cm 1810).

46 Andrew Green, 'Open & flexible learning opportunities', *Public library journal* **10** (5), 1995, 123–6.

47 'Lifelong learning', *Library Association record* **100** (10), 1998, 520–30, 532–3, 536.

48 National Advisory Group for Continuing Education and Lifelong Learning, *Learning for the twenty-first century: first report* .... [London]: The Group, 1997. Chair R. H. Fryer. Also available at: <http://www.lifelonglearning.co.uk/nagcell/> (accessed 3/2/06).

49 Judith Broady-Preston and Andrew Cox, 'The public library as street corner university: back to the future?', *New library world* **101** (4), 2000, 149–61.

50 Department for Culture, Media and Sport, *Libraries for all: social inclusion in public libraries: policy guidance for local authorities in England.* London: DCMS, 1999.

51 Dave Muddiman *et al.*, *Open to all? The public library and social exclusion.* London: Resource, 2000 (Library and Information Commission research reports; 84–86). Papers written 1998–2000 available on The Network website at: <http://www.seapn.org.uk/publication.html> (accessed 26/1/06).

52 Patrick Roach and Marlene Morrison, *Public libraries, ethnic diversity and citizenship.* London: British Library, 1998 (British Library Research and Innovation Centre report; 76).

53 François Matarasso, *Beyond book issues: the social potential of library projects.* Bournes Green: Comedia, 1998.

54 See also Philip Wark, 'Making a difference', *Library Association record* **101** (5), 1999, 288–9.

55 The Network: tackling social exclusion in libraries, museums, archives and galleries: <http://www.seapn.org.uk/> (accessed 26/1/06).

56 Alan White, 'Putting the name in the frame: ten years of the LA/T. C. Farries Public Relations and Publicity Awards', *Library Association record* **96** (5), 1994, 257–60.

57 Sarah Airey, 'Buildings for the millennium', *Library Association record* **101** (12), 1999, 711.

58 Rob Froud, 'The facts of life', *Public library journal* **9** (6), 1994, 181.

59 Jared Bryson, Bob Usherwood and Richard Proctor, *Libraries must also be buildings? New libraries impact study.* Sheffield: Centre for Public Libraries and Information in Society; University of Sheffield Dept of Information Studies, 2003. Also available at: <http://cplis.shef.ac.uk/publications.htm> (accessed 18/1/06).

60 Richard Proctor, Hazel Lee and Rachel Reilly, *Access to public libraries: the impact of opening hours reductions and closures 1986–1997.* Boston Spa: British Library, 1998 (British Library Research and Innovation Centre report; 90).

61 Proctor *et al.*, *Access to public libraries*, p. 3.

62 Proctor *et al.*, *Access to public libraries*, p. 95.

63 Sylvia Simmons and Richard Proctor, *People, politics and hard decisions: an investigation into the management of public library closures.* Boston Spa: British Library, 1999 (British Library research and innovation report; 132). Also available at: <http://cplis.shef.ac.uk/publications.htm> (accessed 18/1/06); Richard Proctor, 'People, politics and hard decisions', *Public library journal* **14** (1), 1999, 2–4.

64 Simmons and Proctor, *People, politics and hard decisions*, p. 32.

65 David Fuegi, 'Towards a national standard for a public library user survey', *Public library journal* **9** (2), 1994, 49–51.

66 Stella Thebridge and Clare Nankivell, *Working together and working smarter: a pragmatic approach to public library research.* Birmingham: University of Central England, 1999.

67 Len England, *Borrowing books: readership and library usage in great Britain.* London: Book Marketing, 1992 (BNB Research Fund report; 59); Len England, *The library user:*

the reading habits and attitudes of public library users in Great Britain. London: Book Marketing, 1994 (BNB Research Fund report; 68).

68 Len England, *Perspectives of public library use: a compendium of survey information.* Loughborough: LISU, 1995.

69 Steve Bohme and David Spiller, *Perspectives of public library use 2.* Loughborough: LISU, 1999.

70 *Usage of British public libraries: report on an exit survey.* London: Insight Research, 1999.

71 *Usage of British public libraries*, p. 8.

72 Roy Huse, *Public Library Development Incentive Scheme 1988–1992: a strategic evaluation. Report to the PLDIS Advisory Committee.* London: British Library, 1993 (PLDIS; 32).

73 Huse, *Public Library Development Incentive Scheme*, p. 26.

74 Deborah Goodall, '"It ain't what you do, it's the way that you do it": a review of public library research with special reference to methodology', *Public library journal* **11** (3), 1996, 69–76; Deborah Goodall, 'Public library research', *Public library journal* **13** (4), 1998, 49–55; John M. Pluse and Ray Prytherch, *Research in public libraries: final report of the project on research in public libraries.* London: British Library, 1996 (British Library research and innovation report; 8); Stella Thebridge, Clare Nankivell and Graham Matthews, *Developing research in public libraries.* [London]: Library and Information Commission, 1999 (LIC research report; 24).

75 Library and Information Commission, Research Committee, *Prospects: a strategy for action: library and information research, development and innovation in the UK.* London: LIC, 1997.

76 Bob McKee, 'Exit from the comfort zone', *Public library journal* **14** (4), 1999, 91–2.

77 Philip Gill, *Public library service: IFLA/UNESCO guidelines for development.* Munich: K. G. Saur, 2002.

78 François Matarasso, *Learning development: an introduction to the social impact of public libraries.* Bournes Green: Comedia, 1998.

5

University libraries

Bernard Naylor

The decade from 1991 to 2000 saw more dramatic changes in the university library sector than any comparable preceding period. There were four major causes of this, and they all interacted with one another. The first was the growth in student numbers, especially undergraduate and taught postgraduate. At the start of our period, there were no fewer than seven bodies involved in collecting different statistical information about tertiary education. It took the founding of the Higher Education Statistics Agency (HESA) in 1993 to bring this confusion to an end. HESA reported that in 1994/95 there were 830,000 full-time undergraduates and 128,000 full-time postgraduates.[1] By the year 2000, the comparable figures were 1,038,000 and 172,000. Many individual institutions can report at least a doubling of student numbers over the whole ten-year period. The second cause of change was the accelerating pace of the development of information technology, which showed no signs of stabilizing by the end of the period.

The third cause of change was the merger of the polytechnic and university sectors which took effect in 1994, following the Education Act of 1992. This created a fully unified system of higher education, with 35 'old' universities (including the University of London with eight major institutions and numerous smaller ones), 33 'new' universities (the former polytechnics) and 19 higher education colleges, some of which subsequently were also awarded the title of 'university'.[2] The Act also presaged some mergers between institutions, thereby further consolidating the system. Following the merging of the 'old' universities and the polytechnics, the Standing Conference of National and University Libraries (SCONUL) effected a merger with the Council of Polytechnic Librarians (COPOL). The special contribution brought to this merger by COPOL is excellently illustrated by their practical series of working papers, edited by Don Revill. Discounting those which date to the earlier period of the 1980s, the 1990s alone saw the appearance of papers on: development plans, general management concerns, in-house research, finance, rules and regulations, and staff development and appraisal.

All three of these change factors were driven from outside the libraries themselves, and the libraries' task was to assimilate the consequences and respond accordingly. In structuring their response, the libraries were guided – driven might not be an inappropriate word – by the outcome of the fourth factor, a special committee of investigation set up by the higher education funding authorities of the four home countries. Named, as is customary, after the chair of the committee, Professor (later Sir) Brian Follett, the Follett report will surely occupy a special place in the history of UK academic libraries for the foreseeable future.[3] With a broader focus than the Atkinson report of 1976[4] (which concentrated on capital provision) and a much more terse content than the Parry report of 1967,[5] the Follett report was not particularly remarkable for what it said. Many of its ideas were already present, more or less visibly, in the professional community of the time, which is not surprising since some of the outstanding representatives of that community were on the committee. Its central message was that, given changing modes of teaching and learning, the IT revolution and increased student numbers, the role played by libraries in universities had to become more prominent.[6] Its extraordinary impact was due to the amount of work which it inspired, and the amount of additional funding which that work brought into the library sector, the whole being progressed as a programme, guided by the 'Follett Implementation Group', and its sub-groups.[7] From the time of its publication in 1993, until the end of the period, the Follett report dominated the academic library scene.

A complementary role in prompting and steering change was played by the Joint Information Systems Committee (JISC). JISC was established on 1 April 1993, at the prompting of the Secretaries of State responsible for higher education in England, Scotland and Wales, but its reporting line was through the three funding bodies, the Higher Education Funding Council for England (HEFCE) and the corresponding bodies in Scotland (SHEFC) and Wales (HEFCW). The Department of Education for Northern Ireland (DENI) formally adhered to JISC in 1995. JISC's role was to explore a national dimension in the provision of electronic networking and specialized information services and to give leadership in bringing about developments for the benefit of the entire higher education sector. In performing these functions it was explicitly assuming tasks formerly carried out by the Information Systems Committee (ISC) of the Universities Funding Council (UFC) since 1990, the ISC itself being the successor to the Computer Board. This also constituted a role shift, the Computer Board having previously been heavily involved in funding large mainframe computer installations in the universities, a task which the development of the technology was making less important. For most of our period, JISC operated through four sub-committees, the Committee on Electronic Information (CEI) being the most important for our purposes. (Not the least of the distinguishing features of our period was its extreme fertility in the generation of acronyms.)

Finance
The squeeze on the higher education 'unit of resource' (the amount of money allocated per student to each institution by the funding authority), which was already well under way by the end of the 1980s, continued and was intensified by the inadequately compensated growth in student numbers. The merging of the two

sectors also sharpened the challenge to the old universities to demonstrate that their relatively generous provision, by comparison with the former polytechnics, was justified by results, and more particularly by their additional responsibilities for research. The effect of the financial squeeze on libraries was recognized by the Committee of Vice-Chancellors and Principals in their Press Release PR335 of 4 October 1993. This acknowledged that, while expenditure on university libraries had risen by 27% in cash terms in seven years, this represented a real-terms fall of 16% in relation to the Gross Domestic Product, and 23% when deflated by the specific deflators for university pay and prices (the UPPI or Universities Pay and Prices Index).

Apart from the general financial squeeze, the major change in the period for libraries was the increasing use of special funding, usually preceded by a bidding process. Libraries became familiar with the preparation of bids for funding under the programmes launched after the Follett report, and also with the accompanying factors, such as close monitoring of expenditure and outcomes, and greater use of staff on short-term contracts. By the end of the period, a whole new *modus operandi* had been put in place, and, though it still affected only a small proportion of any library's budget, it was increasingly important as a way in which innovations could be launched.

Another important development during the period was the growing transparency adopted by funding bodies and funded institutions as to the basis for and application of their funding. An essential element in this was progress towards the harmonization of unit costs between the 'old' universities and the former polytechnics. As this advanced, institutions became clearer about the basis for their funds. In any given discipline, each student, whether undergraduate or postgraduate, was considered to be funded at a basic rate which varied according to the subject and the level, but not (following a process of convergence) according to the institution. On top of this, individual institutions received funding for research, based on the periodic 'Research Assessment Exercise'. (There was also some 'special factor funding', that in respect of the two academic copyright libraries being the most important for the purposes of this article.) It was assumed that the cost of administration and academic support services (such as libraries) was rolled up into the student and research costs. Institutions were not under any obligation to distribute money according to the algorithm by which the allocation from the funding council had been determined. However, teaching departments not surprisingly raised questions about the distribution of 'their' money, and exercised close scrutiny over any funds allocated to administrative or academic support services.[8] In the most extreme cases, institutions made teaching departments the holders of the purse-strings and gave them power to 'buy' (or not to buy) administrative, computing or library services in an internal institutional economy. Since this was happening in a period of growing financial stringency, the budgets of service departments came under acute pressure in some institutions, and intervention from the centre of the institution was sometimes required to ensure that essential services were not destabilized.[9]

Within and beyond the library walls

In 1976 the Atkinson report, which was widely regarded as an attempt to curb the growth of libraries, had ushered in a period of massive investment in new library buildings, as those institutions perceived to be under-provided were helped to make good the deficit. After the Follett report, the investment was similarly large, amounting to £140 million. But the manner of the investment reflected the spirit of the time. The age of pure largesse from the centre had been superseded by a requirement for institutions themselves to input large sums if they wanted some investment by the funding council. Nevertheless ninety-six institutions benefited.[10] One commentator argued that this large investment was essentially propping up the technology of the past.[11] However, most libraries made significant efforts to satisfy the increasing demand for terminals, initially for access to catalogues and locally mounted data services, and later for the growing number of national services and for general access to the world wide web. The provision of terminal clusters took the library service beyond its own walls and required collaboration with other providers, especially computing services.

The theme of convergence of the library, the computing service, and other technology-led learning support services continued to be a feature. However, no dominant pattern emerged, with individual institutions choosing their own way from among a number of optional models, and possibly changing their minds more than once in the period. A new element in the convergence picture was provided by the concept of the 'campus-wide information service' (CWIS) made possible by the development of access technologies.[12] The question of whether this service should be managed by the information specialists (the librarians) or the technologists (in the computing service) was, for a time, a focal point of the general convergence debate.

Books and services for taught students

Book prices were relatively stable over the period. The main pressure on book collections arose from the increase in student numbers, and various strategies were invoked. The growing practice of placing photocopies of articles and chapters of books in short loan collections came under close scrutiny from copyright owners, who joined together in seeking recompense from libraries for the use of copyright materials. Collectively, they were represented by the Copyright Licensing Agency (CLA), which had been founded in 1982. During the 1990s, the CLA periodically negotiated a 'blanket licence' with higher education authorities which allowed participating institutions certain photocopying permissions in return for licence payments. The use of photocopiers was also monitored on a sampling basis, and institutions became used to taking it in turns to accommodate the sampling. At the same time, the licence was limited in usefulness because it covered only those publishers in membership of CLA, and this meant, among other things, the exclusion of foreign publications.

Another feature of the period was the wish of some libraries to create or acquire electronic copies of required articles or book chapters, by which means they hoped to be able to solve the problem of large numbers of students wanting simultaneous access to the same material for coursework purposes.[13] The HERON Project was an attempt to use technology to provide access to materials required for taught courses.[14] It also embraced the issue of copyright clearance for electronic content, something on which the CLA had been reluctant to strike a deal in the earlier stages of their negotiations with institutions.

Another and different look at the problem of increased student numbers took the form of pressure on library opening hours. It was suggested that if libraries were open longer hours, use of the premises and their collections could be more evenly spread out, and sheer pressure would encourage some students to make use of the libraries at times previously thought unacceptable. The most extreme result of this was the institution of seven days a week, twenty-four hours a day (24/7) opening in some institutions. Normally it was only a part of the library which operated such generous opening hours, possibly the short loan collection, or a cluster of PC terminals, or even a completely unresourced (except for tables and chairs!) study room. It is doubtful whether this had more than a marginal effect on the pattern of use of libraries; students who preferred to work 'normal office hours' mostly continued to do so. The Flowers Review, which *inter alia* proposed to enhance the exploitation of universities' fixed assets by introducing a 'fourth term' in the summer vacation, can be seen as another attempt to address the student numbers problem.[15] Library commentators made it clear that this would create serious operational problems for libraries which had long used the summer vacations to catch up on essential administrative and reorganization tasks.

Changes in the teaching role were investigated by a special committee set up by the government and chaired by Sir Ron Dearing.[16] The importance of their report for academic librarians lay in the fact that it assumed that one way to deal with greater student numbers and the declining unit of resource was to make more use of education technology. This was inevitably and rightly seen by librarians as implying an expansion of 'resource-based learning', and hence an increase in library use and in the demands on library staff to provide more support for the learning process.[17] In accordance with the report's recommendations, an Institute of Learning and Teaching in Higher Education (ILTHE) was created, which was charged with fostering the professional expertise which the teaching function in higher education required. The question for library staff was whether their own role should be seen as entitling them to membership of the proposed Institute and, if so, how such membership would fit alongside their more traditional professional allegiances. Their case rested partly on whether instruction, or guidance, in the use of the internet and its information content should be provided by the library, with its specialists in internet use, or the teaching departments, which had the overall responsibility for the teaching process itself.

A particular effort was made to facilitate inter-institutional library use. Most institutions had customarily been helpful in admitting researchers, both staff and senior postgraduates from other institutions. UK Libraries Plus was an attempt to extend this helpfulness to the undergraduate level, for part-time and distance-learning students.[18] It can be seen as a sensible extension of the SCONUL Vacation Reading Scheme, but it broke new ground in attempting to minimize the bureaucracy involved in inter-library use. It would be right to see it, originally, as an initiative coming mainly from the former polytechnic sector, but it was also notable for the speed with which other institutions with different traditions accepted the rationale behind the innovation and themselves joined the scheme.

Periodicals and research services

A general atmosphere of financial restraint pervaded the beginning of the period.[19] Various efforts were made to try to mitigate the impact of rising journal costs. Following the Follett report, a Pilot Site Licence Initiative (PSLI) was launched by the four higher education funding bodies in 1995 and ran until 1997. The aim was to address two problems: the spiral of increasing prices for academic journals, leading to cancelled subscriptions and further price rises, and the restrictive effect of copyright laws on the copying and distribution of journal content, both problems having been identified in the Follett report. Under the Initiative, the funding bodies entered into agreements with Academic Press, Blackwell Publishers, Blackwell Science and Institute of Physics Publishing. During 1996 and 1997 these publishers offered their printed journals at discounted prices to universities and colleges throughout the UK, and provided licences which allowed generous permissions for copying. In addition, an extensive range of electronic material was made available. The price discounts were made possible by pump-priming funds provided by the funding bodies. The initiative was formally evaluated by the Commonwealth Higher Education Management Service.[20]

PSLI was followed by the National Electronic Site Licence Initiative (NESLI), which began delivering services in January 1999. Reflecting technological progress since the foundation of PSLI, NESLI was explicitly aimed at the delivery of journal content in electronic form. It was jointly managed by the periodicals agent, Swets and Zeitlinger, and University of Manchester Computing, through its specialist datasets service, MIDAS. Unlike PSLI, NESLI was seen as a project which would expand in scope as the managers pursued and concluded negotiations with the various journal publishers. Nor was there any subvention from the funding bodies. Pursuing the objective of electronic access brought to light some complications of UK VAT legislation, which, depending on the interpretation of the law, could have some adverse implications for the use of the technology.[21] An important achievement of the NESLI managing agents was the creation of a model licence for use in negotiating agreements with publishers.[22] The progress achieved by PSLI and NESLI was reviewed at the end of the period by Hitchcock and others.[23]

There were at least three other initiatives targeted at different aspects of the periodicals problem. The Scholarly Publishing and Academic Resources Coalition (SPARC) was launched by the United States Association of Research Libraries

(ARL) in 1997 and sought to enhance awareness of scholarly communication issues, and to advocate fundamental changes in the system and culture of scholarly communication.[24] Three US research specialists, Paul Ginsparg (Los Alamos National Laboratory), Stevan Harnad (Princeton University, and later Southampton University) and Andrew Odlyzko (Bell Telephone Laboratories), proposed access to non-commercial article repositories as a substitute for the stranglehold which they saw journals as exercising over research library budgets.[25] JSTOR, another US initiative which, like SPARC, was open to membership from other countries, sought to ease the increasing demand for adequate stack space for the long runs of back files of scholarly journals by converting back issues into electronic formats that would allow savings in space and improve access to the journal content.[26]

Meanwhile, some publishers were themselves exploring electronic access and investigating ways in which they could maintain their income and customer base while exploiting the technology, Elsevier, for example, trialling its TULIP electronic access system in the United States.[27] A policy was also developed by some publishers of offering customers electronic access to all the titles on their list, provided that no paper subscriptions were cancelled. By the end of the decade, Elsevier was signing up UK libraries to deals which involved some curtailment of inflationary increases (though these were still well above general levels of inflation), and a three-year contract, in return for 'no cancellations' undertakings (applicable to Elsevier titles only) by the libraries. Signatory libraries also got access to the whole of the Elsevier electronic periodical content, in return for the continuation of their existing subscriptions.[28]

Special collections
One of the most dramatic consequences of the Follett report was the fillip given to that Cinderella of many academic libraries, the Special Collections Department. The Follett report itself acknowledged that there might well be extensive collections across the whole system which were seriously under-exploited because they were not sufficiently well publicized, and possibly not even in a fit state for regular use. A Non-Formula Funding programme (NFF) was therefore launched devoted partly to the cataloguing of special collections, including manuscript collections, and also to the acceleration of conservation work.[29] It was followed by the Research Support Libraries Programme (RSLP).[30] RSLP provided additional support for libraries with humanities and social science collections, to enable them to improve information about, and access to, materials through retrospective conversion, improved indexing, cataloguing and conservation. RSLP also promoted collaborative collection management projects (in any subject area), the object of which was to document the collective research potential of holdings in certain fields spread across a number of institutions.[31] Although the selection of content was regarded as important, an additional objective was the encouragement given to libraries to work together more closely. In both programmes, NFF and RSLP, libraries were bidding for the available funds by proposing projects which

would make information about their collections more widely available. Any cataloguing information created was to be made available electronically across the higher education system. Numerous additional cataloguing posts were created, albeit on a fixed term basis.

Preservation continued to be a comparatively under-resourced activity. The most obvious area of progress was in the drafting of disaster plans, but there was a general impression that pressure from funding constraints and increased student numbers was compelling libraries to focus their attention elsewhere.[32] However, some conservation work was funded as part of the NFF programme, and was targeted at making accessible collections which were having to be withheld from use because of their fragile condition. The immediate consequence was a sudden increase in temporary conservation posts which appeared at one point to be overstraining the market of available candidates. For a time, the recruitment of qualified conservators, as of archivist cataloguers, became difficult because of the demand. Given a proper opportunity to undertake conservation work, many libraries came to realize how expensive and labour-intensive such work is, and to appreciate the need for special laboratory facilities to carry out the work to a reasonable standard. Some consideration was given to the possibility of establishing a smaller number of specialized centres which could take in conservation work from libraries unable to afford their own facilities. However, the additional national investment in conservation was short-lived and it was quickly clear that no new centre would have sufficient guarantee of a steady flow of conservation work to allow long-term investment in the necessary facilities and staff. In due course, the special funding of NFF and RSLP projects, and the fixed term contracts, came to an end, though the temporary funding left a more permanent mark, in the emergence of a larger number of experienced staff, the completion of specific cataloguing and conservation tasks, and the general fillip given to this area of library work.

As an accompaniment to the investment in NFF and RSLP, a Committee chaired by Professor Michael Anderson looked at possibilities for collaboration in the provision of research material, and produced a report.[33] A special study of the use of libraries by members of institutions other than the parent institution was also carried out, by Coopers and Lybrand.[34] One of the most important outcomes was the institution of a system of special recurrent payments to libraries which were found to be giving library access to researchers from other institutions. The payments were based on recorded levels of use.[35]

Library users' changing perceptions prompted by these developments in research provision were demonstrated in two volumes by Erens who based his findings on an investigation by questionnaire.[36]

Cataloguing and access to collection information
Early on in the period, it was noted that 73 university library catalogues were available over JANET, though, in almost all instances, the catalogue would remain incomplete, awaiting further retrospective conversion of records.[37] The main

impact on cataloguing in the period resulted from the NFF and RSLP initiatives which followed the Follett report. Undoubtedly, significant cataloguing and listing arrears (the latter in respect of manuscripts) were dealt with. It was an important aspect of these programmes that the records created should be in electronic form and therefore available over the internet, the aim being to facilitate inter-library use both of records and of materials.

The CURL database grew during this period and became enmeshed in the post-Follett arrangements. CURL being a consortium of the largest and richest (in terms of holdings) academic research libraries in the country, a database of those holdings would be of great value.[38] A special injection of funds was made available after the Follett report was published, on condition that the records were made available (as COPAC) to the entire higher education community and not just to those institutions whose libraries were in membership of CURL.[39] The relationship between the funding source and the largest libraries was undoubtedly mutually advantageous. However, it inevitably raised questions as to the distinctness of the CURL member libraries as a group. To what extent could they retain their identity, exclusivity even, while in receipt of a subvention from such a general funding source?[40] In the light of the potential afforded by technological advances, there was also a revival of a more general interest in union catalogues. JISC/RSLP and the British Library's Co-operation and Partnership Programme found a common interest in this theme and promoted a study which took place in this period though the report appeared a little later.[41]

The problem of the retrospective conversion of catalogues to machine-readable form continued to be real throughout the decade. The Follett report had recommended an investigation into the cost of general conversion of catalogues. The idea of a general programme was greeted with less enthusiasm by those libraries which had done the most to tackle the problem themselves. On the other hand, it was appreciated that converting the catalogues of the really large libraries would make many more records available over the internet and this was seen as a clear benefit for all libraries. A study was therefore conducted by a steering group chaired by Bernard Naylor, and with Philip Bryant as principal investigator.[42] However, the funding powers decided that the cost was too great, especially as funding for post-Follett report programmes was regarded as already largely committed. By the end of the decade, the familiar process of slow attrition continued to be the principal way of addressing the problem, and meant that, for some libraries, the completion of retrospective conversion was likely to be a long way in the future.

One of the aids towards enhanced inter-institutional use of collections was thought to lie in an improved and more consistent approach to collection description. The approach which attracted most attention during the period was the Conspectus methodology, which originated in the United States.[43] There was some controversy about the efficacy of the methodology, one critic describing it as 'a bushelful of best guesses'. The most coordinated attempt to implement the approach in the UK occurred among the academic and research libraries of

Scotland.[44] Some individual institutions also adopted the methodology in the knowledge that it was the most developed approach to the problem and therefore more likely to be adopted in due course elsewhere than any other.[45]

Electronic services

The general progress in the technology made it inevitable that the 1990s would be a period of intensive growth in the provision of electronic services. Three factors accentuated this, the role played by JISC, the eLib programme and the emergence of the world wide web.[46]

Founded in 1993, JISC grew increasingly important, in the 1990s, in the negotiation of deals for the provision of electronic materials and services. In this, it was building on the success of BIDS which was announced in the 1980s but was inaugurated in 1991 whereupon it quickly became a routine aspect of service. Initially BIDS consisted of two products of the Institute of Scientific Information, Science Citation Index and the Social Sciences Citation Index. It was seized upon by many libraries as the answer to a difficult problem: how to provide library users with more access to computerized bibliographic searching without exposing the library to runaway costs.

In the expansion of electronic services, JISC and its Committee on Electronic Information played a growing role. At a practical level, the number of service options for which it negotiated or prompted the negotiation of contracts for possible take-up by individual libraries grew continually. Various approaches were used. Sometimes, JISC actually funded the production and delivery of content. Sometimes, externally produced content was acquired and then delivered with a JISC interface or with the publisher's own interface. Sometimes, negotiated access to the publisher's own site was the preferred route, and sometimes it was left to individual institutions to deliver content which JISC had created.[47] An ancillary requirement for these various services, which had frequently been negotiated with firm restrictions placed on accessibility and use, was the development of user authentication technology, and this was met by the ATHENS national authentication service. By the year 2000, 70 services were using ATHENS user authentication and there were 700,000 ATHENS users in 300 institutions. The standard was also taken up by commercial providers offering ATHENS-compliant facilities.[48]

As has been implied, the development of electronic services under the aegis of JISC was administratively complex. One important step was a diversification of possible suppliers of data services, with the addition of MIMAS (based at the University of Manchester Computing Service) and EDINA (based at Edinburgh University Computing Service). In 1998, the BIDS service itself was taken over by the newly-founded Ingenta, a private company providing information and data services to higher education and other clients. During the period, there was a steady development of the purchaser/provider split which characterized many areas of British life in the 1990s, with JISC or CHEST (the Combined Higher Education Software Team) acting as the purchaser/initiator in negotiating deals with information and data suppliers, and then franchising bodies such as MIMAS, EDINA or Ingenta to run the data service. In service terms, it made it possible for the library to act as information mediator in the way it had long done with books and periodicals, paying the 'subscription' cost on behalf of the institution in return for a right of access, free at the point of use, by all its members. This model became increasingly pervasive during the period.

At the strategic level, JISC developed the concept of the Distributed National Electronic Resource (DNER) and the Resource Discovery Network (RDN). The RDN consisted of a series of faculty-based electronic subject gateways.[49] The DNER was described in 1999 as containing over fifty high-quality electronic datasets available for subscription to academic institutions and hundreds of other datasets available free of charge.[50] DNER and RDN were concepts in the sense that they were not offered, fully-fledged, to higher education institutions. To some extent, they provided a theoretical and strategic framework for some developments already launched. Equally, they provided a framework within which the rationale of newly negotiated deals could be presented.[51]

A scenario was therefore emerging in which, to some extent, all the libraries in the sector would constitute a part of a national service. They would be offering their local users a greater or lesser selection of the resources negotiated centrally by JISC and CHEST and would be able to make some use of the resources of other libraries to make up for their own inadequacies. However, this development was taking place in a climate of increasing competition (rather than collaboration) between institutions, competition for research funds, competition for the 'best' academic staff and so on. It would be unrealistic to portray the period as one in which mutual interdependence between university libraries triumphed and more selfish or self-reliant modes of operation took a back seat. The larger libraries naturally felt some concern that the resources they had carefully built up for the benefit of their own institution would be opened to those of less well endowed places. They felt that the advantages for which they had worked might be lost and their own users would suffer from pressure on their resources from members of other institutions.

The second factor was the eLib programme, launched following the publication of the Follett report.[52] eLib eventually became a three stage exercise. The first two stages were extremely diverse. They featured a budget of £15 million and were put together very quickly after the publication of the Follett report, considering the complex picture of provision which eventually emerged. There were over 60 projects, involving at least as many libraries. This large number of projects did spread very widely the opportunities for gaining experience. The aim of each project was the creation of a viable service, and the drafting of an 'exit strategy' became an essential feature of most. Evaluation, both formative and summative, was a feature of the whole programme, as was dissemination, both nationally and for the individual projects.[53] Projects can be grouped under a number of headings: electronic journals, pre-prints and digitization (aimed at research); electronic short-loan and on-line publishing (targeting the needs of taught students); access to networked resources (subject gateways); electronic document delivery; and training and awareness.[54] However, there were also some drawbacks. A number of projects did find themselves tackling the same problems (for example, copyright clearance) in parallel and with inadequate resources, some of which might better have been tackled from the centre right from the start. There was a failure to link with expenditure being disbursed elsewhere in the higher education system, for example, on the Teaching and Learning Technology Programme (TLTP). One analyst also speculated whether eLib consumed a disproportionate amount of money, some of which might have been better spent elsewhere (for example, on retrospective conversion of catalogues).[55]

The third stage of eLib was a more targeted programme. One area explored was that of 'clumps', the intention of which was to improve access to the catalogues of the countries' major libraries, especially on a regional basis.[56] Another theme was the development of examples of the 'hybrid library', that is, a library in which electronic and traditional print-on-paper services would exist side by side, in what was hoped would be a seamless and coherent provision.[57] The study of hybrid libraries included IMPEL2, an investigation into the impact of the hybrid library on the organization and staff of the libraries themselves.[58]

The third factor in this period of intensive growth was the emergence of the world wide web as the pre-eminent technology for access to information. Initially appearing at a time when there appeared to be other competing technologies (such as GOPHER, VERONICA and WAIS), it rapidly proved itself superior to them all. Although many institutions had embarked on establishing locally managed CD-ROM based networks in order to make datasets available to their users, the web quickly made such initiatives obsolescent.[59] As an enabling technology, the world wide web can be regarded as a background matter, notwithstanding its great importance. However, the timing of its emergence was providential. At the time, the Follett Implementation Group for Information Technology (FIGIT) was awarding its first round of eLib grants. A number of project proposers quickly saw the potential of the world wide web, and adjusted their plans accordingly. There is no doubt that if the ambitious first stage of the eLib programme had been launched a year earlier, much effort would have been wasted in using rapidly superseded and less effective networking solutions.

The increasing emphasis on electronic services brought into focus some points of pressure between the Publishers Association (representing copyright owners) and the universities.[60] These eventually came to be addressed in a series of working parties which were set up jointly by the Publishers Association and JISC. The work covered three areas. In 1997, a Clearance Mechanisms Working Party produced a supporting study *Copyright clearance and digitisation in UK higher education*, which explored the distinction between electrocopying and digitization proper. The Working Party followed this up, in the same year, with *Charging mechanism for digitized texts,* which examined pricing models. A second Working Party, which reported in 1998, dealt with fair dealing in an electronic environment. It concentrated on fair dealing for research and private study and did not consider (for example) fair dealing for criticism and review. The third Working Party explored the options for model licences for possible use by individual publishers. Their conclusions were unveiled early in 1999.[61]

With the advance of technology came a growing interest in the conservation of digital content, and this inspired the CEDARS (CURL Exemplars in Digital ARchives) project, which was funded in 1998 as part of the eLib-3 programme.[62] Continuing interest in this topic, not least with the encouragement of JISC,[63] led to the establishment of the Digital Preservation Coalition, which brought together interested parties in an alliance seen as of crucial importance for future work in this area.[64]

Planning and performance

Libraries have traditionally been organizations devoted to the administration of the *status quo*. Change has been the exception rather than the rule. Over the period, the pace and extent of change in academic libraries steadily increased, and with it there came a change in the role to be performed, especially by the senior managers. In effect, the language of managerialism, which had previously played only a small part in the vocabulary, became much more pervasive.[65] For example, it became much more common for libraries to adopt mission statements, and to write strategic plans, in effect programmes for the achievement of essential changes. This theme was taken up at national level. In December 1995 HEFCE published *Guidelines for developing an information strategy*,[66] and looked increasingly for evidence that institutions and their component parts were taking planning seriously.

At the beginning of the decade, higher education libraries were already taking some steps towards monitoring performance.[67] SCONUL had an Advisory Committee on Performance Indicators and the terminology of 'inputs', 'outputs' and 'outcomes' was becoming commonplace, especially among those most closely involved. By the year 2000, the idea that libraries had to be accountable for what they delivered in return for the money invested in them was firmly installed. A historic emphasis on collecting data about stock, and a more recent interest in data on resourcing, were both being superseded by an emphasis on processes, and, more importantly on outputs, reflecting a genuine change in the predominant managerial philosophy.[68] This switch in emphasis towards 'processes' and 'outcomes' reflected the fact that libraries were increasingly being demand-driven rather than producer-driven.[69] But the pressure for this change of emphasis had come from several different quarters.

Individual institutions were instituting their own processes for the assessment of the performance of teaching departments. Inevitably and rightly, this review process spread to non-teaching departments, and the library was among those chosen to undergo review. Another intra-institutional possibility was the negotiation of service level agreements between the library and individual teaching departments. The impetus for such agreements was probably derived from the 'charter movement' initiated by the Major government of that period, which had inspired the creation of a 'charter for higher education'.[70] A national programme for the review of teaching departments was also established and quickly made library provision for each subject a matter for its attention. This programme can be seen as a direct descendant of the programmes of review, to which teaching departments in the polytechnic sector operating under the Council for National Academic Awards (CNAA) had long been accustomed. Nevertheless, its beginnings were controversial for libraries because there appeared in most instances to be little or no understanding of library matters among the subject specialists carrying out reviews. A HEFCE prompt sheet for assessors was said to contain only one point which explicitly applied to the library, as a learning support service.[71] Surreptitious visits from review panel members and arbitrary checks were frequently experienced until the libraries themselves cried 'foul' and proposed a systematic method of review.[72] At the same time, the library necessarily found itself involved with almost every subject review and hence acquired a great deal of experience in how to deal with them.[73] Whereas any given teaching department might expect to be reviewed every five years or so, the library underwent partial review several times each year and, in many instances, library staff proved to be a valuable source of experience for teaching colleagues.

The Follett Committee had also proposed a review of performance indicators for higher education libraries and this was in due course conducted by a committee chaired by Kevin Ellard.[74] It resulted in the definition of a 'basket' of indicators intended to serve as an objective way of measuring the performance of academic libraries though it had to be recognized that, since academic communities themselves differed so widely, different measures would be more important for different institutions. Another view on performance indicators for higher education libraries was offered by Barton and Blagden.[75] It is also worth noting, by the end of the period, an increased interest in 'bench-marking' as a form of performance appraisal.[76]

The review of a whole library service was also complemented by a range of measures for the review of library staff, especially senior staff. The Follett Committee itself had had a sub-group devoted to 'human resource management and staffing issues' and a separate report was issued following an investigation by a consultant.[77] The report was discussed at length by a selection of contributors in a special section of the *British journal of academic librarianship*.[78] Fielden himself later reviewed progress with regard to the recommendations of his report and the general environment in which they were being considered for implementation.[79] A number of institutions instituted formal systems of staff appraisal during the period, after the funding authorities had found themselves obliged by government to ensure that institutions had systems of staff appraisal in place in return for a salary settlement reached in 1987. By 1993, appraisal of academically-related staff in libraries was regarded as 'well-established' by one commentator, and 'well-received by most staff ... as a means of reviewing and communicating feedback on performance, setting personal objectives, and aiding training and development programmes'.[80]

A major factor in promoting interworking among library staffs was the creation of a wide range of email lists and similar discussion groups, together with bulletin boards devoted to library issues.[81] By the end of the decade there were many instances of library staff who came to know colleagues very well through internet communications and discussions without ever meeting them face to face.

Conclusion

On one occasion, when presenting the work of his committee to an audience, Professor Follett was heard to remark that, although his report did presage major changes in academic libraries, these would take considerable time to occur. He expressed the view that, by the year 2000, libraries would not be very different from how they were observed by his committee less then ten years before. To some extent, events bore him out. Many library users continued to use their libraries in the same old way; books and periodicals continued to find their way on to shelves, and library staff mediated them to users in the way they had done for decades or even centuries. However, alongside these familiar features, many new services, especially electronic services, were growing up, showing much more growth potential than their traditional precursors, and competing strongly for a share of available resources. Even more important, among library staff, there had, for many, been major changes, both in the way they worked and the way they looked at the organization they served. From being a service strongly devoted to administering continuity, university libraries had also come to terms with accepting and managing change, and this was to feature prominently in the years to come.

Notes

There is an immense amount of source material on what went on during this tumultuous period. It is worth mentioning that, as the list of references witnesses, UK academic libraries were particularly well served by 'their own journal', the *British journal of academic librarianship*, later the *New review of academic librarianship*, which played an important role as a channel of information and discussion about the wide-ranging changes under way.

1 *Higher education digest* **23**, 1995.
2 Christopher Hunt, 'Academic library planning in the United Kingdom', *British journal of academic librarianship* **8** (1), 1993, 3–16.
3 Joint Funding Councils' Libraries Review Group, *Report*. Bristol: HEFCE, 1993. Chairman Sir Brian Follett. (The 'Follett report'.) For a summary of the report see *British journal of academic librarianship* **9** (1/2), 1994, 3–10.
4 University Grants Committee, *Capital provision for university libraries: a report of a working party under the chairmanship of Professor R. Atkinson*. London: HMSO, 1976. (The 'Atkinson report'.)
5 University Grants Committee, *Report of the Committee on Libraries (Chairman: Dr Thomas Parry)*. London: HMSO, 1967. (The 'Parry report'.)
6 Adrian Peasgood, 'Follett and some prevailing winds', *British journal of academic librarianship* **9** (1/2), 1994, 39–47.

7   Higher Education Funding Council for England, [Circular 17/94]. Bristol: HEFCE, 1994. ('This circular announces the Council's decisions on the recommendations of the Joint Funding Councils' Libraries Review Group report and how these will be implemented.')

8   Elizabeth Lyon *et al.*, *Impact of devolved budgeting on library and information services in universities in the UK*. London: British Library, 1998 (Research and innovation report; 138).

9   John Stirling, 'Devolved budgeting', *British journal of academic librarianship* **7** (1), 1992, 1–8.

10 Andrew McDonald, 'Space planning and management' in *Resource management in academic libraries*, ed. David Baker. London: Library Association, 1997, pp. 189–206.

11 Annette Howarth, 'The Follett report: a computer services perspective', *British journal of academic librarianship* **9** (1/2), 1994, 97–104.

12 Louise Rothnie, 'Campus wide information system development at three UK universities', *Vine* 93, 1993, 18–30.

13 Adrienne Muir and Charles Oppenheim, 'Electrocopying, the Publishers Association and academic libraries', *Journal of librarianship and information science* **25** (4), 1993, 175–86.

14 David McMenemy, 'Expanding access to learning materials in higher education', *Information management and technology* **32** (4), 1999, 169–72.

15 Committee of Enquiry into the Organization of the Academic Year, *The review of the academic year: a report ... prepared for the Committee of Vice-Chancellors and Principals*. Bristol: HEFCE, 1993. Chairman Lord Flowers.

16 National Committee of Inquiry into Higher Education, *Higher education in the learning society*. London: HMSO, 1997. Chair Sir Ron Dearing. (The 'Dearing report'.)

17 Patrick Noon, 'Libraries and the Dearing report', *SCONUL newsletter* 15, 1998, 32–6; Roddie Shepherd, 'All you need to know about Dearing', *Library Association record* **99** (9), 1997, 480–2.

18 Catherine Edwards, Joan M. Day and Graham Walton, 'eLib's IMPEL2 project: organisational structures and responses to change in academic libraries', *New review of academic librarianship* **4**, 1998, 53–70.

19 Helen Finch and Cathy North, *The research process: the library's contribution in times of restraint*. London: British Library, 1991 (British Library research paper; 95).

20 *Report on Phase 1 of the evaluation of the UK Pilot Site Licence Initiative*. Bristol: HEFCE, 1997. HEFCE Ref. M3/97; *Evaluation of the UK Pilot Site Licence Initiative-Phase II*. Bristol: HEFCE, 1998. (Report 98/22).

21 Charles Oppenheim, 'An agenda for action to achieve the information society in the UK', *Journal of information science* **22** (6), 1996, 407–21.

22 For the model licence see: <http://www.headline.ac.uk/publications/n-licence.html> (accessed 27/1/06). Note: at the time of writing this licence had been superseded by an updated version.

23 Steven Hitchcock, Leslie Carr and Wendy Hall, 'Web journals publishing: a UK perspective', *Serials* **10** (3), 1997, 285–99.

24 For SPARC see <http://www.arl.org.sparc> (accessed 27/1/06).

25 Ann S. Okerson and James J. O'Donnell (eds.), *Scholarly journals at the crossroads: a subversive proposal for electronic publishing*. Washington: Association of Research Libraries, 1995.

26 For JSTOR see <http://www.jstor.org> (accessed 27/1/06); Lynne Brindley and K. M. Guthrie, 'JSTOR and the Joint Information Systems Committee: an international collaboration', *Serials* **11** (1), 1998, 41–5.

27 Marthyn Borghuis, 'Tulip final report', *Information services and use* **17** (1), 1997, 74–6.

28 Bernard Naylor, 'Whose side are we on?', *Newsletter on serials pricing issues* 245, 2000, available from: <http://www.lib.unc.edu/prices/2000/2000-245.html> (accessed 30/1/06).

29 Higher Education Funding Council for England, [Circular 5/95]. Bristol: HEFCE, 1995. ('This circular announces allocations of 1994–95 non-recurring non-formula funding for research collections in the humanities.')

30 Ronald Milne, 'Joined up libraries', *Library Association record* **101** (8), 1999, 472–3.

31 For example: Simon Brackenbury and Simon de Montfalcon, 'Great Britain and Northern Ireland', *Journal of government information* **27** (6), 2000, 831–41.

32 Paul Eden, John Feather and Graham Matthews, 'Preservation policies and conservation in British academic libraries in 1993: a survey', *British journal of academic librarianship* **8** (2), 1993, 65–88.

33 Joint Funding Councils Libraries Review, *Report of the group on a national/regional strategy for library provision for researchers.* Bristol: HEFCE, 1995. (The 'Anderson report'); *Library provision for researchers: proceedings of the Anderson report seminar, Cranfield University, 10 and 11 December 1996.* Bruton: LINC, 1997.

34 Coopers and Lybrand, *Funding Councils study of the level and costs of use of higher education libraries by external researchers.* [Bristol: HEFCE], 1997; Ronald Milne and Gillian Davenport, 'The Research Support Libraries Programme access survey', *New review of academic librarianship* **5**, 1999, 23–39.

35 Michael Anderson, 'Access to research collections in the UK: the Anderson report updated', *Library review* **47** (5/6), 1998, 262–6.

36 Bob Erens, *Research libraries in transition.* London: British Library, 1991 (Library and information research report; 82); Bob Erens, *Modernizing research libraries: the effect of recent developments in university libraries on the research process.* London: Bowker-Saur, 1996.

37 Peter Brophy, 'Networking in British academic libraries', *British journal of academic librarianship* **8** (1), 1993, 49–60.

38 For CURL see: <http://www.curl.ac.uk> (accessed 27/1/06).

39 Reginald Carr, 'Research collections in the digital age: the role of CURL', *Library review* **47** (5/6), 1998, 277–81; Shirley Anne Cousins, 'COPAC: the new national OPAC service based on the CURL database', *Program* **31** (1), 1997, 1–21.

40 Bernard Naylor, 'Follett and upward mobility', *British journal of academic librarianship* **9** (1/2), 1994, 30–8.

41 Peter Stubley, Rob Bull and Tony Kidd, *Feasibility study for a national union catalogue: final report.* Bristol: JISC, 2001; Peter Stubley, Rob Bull and Tony Kidd, 'The UK national union catalogue feasibility study. Part 1: Creation of a conceptual model', *New review of information and library research* **7**, 2001, 5–25; 'Part 2: Observations and user testing of physical and virtual models', *New review of information and library research* **7**, 2001, 27–45.

42 Philip Bryant, Ann Chapman and Bernard Naylor, *Retrospective conversion of library catalogues in institutions of higher education in the United Kingdom: a study of the justification for a national programme.* Bath: University of Bath, 1995.

43 G. N. Olson and B. M. Allen, *Cooperative collection management: the conspectus approach*. New York; London: Neal-Schuman, 1994.

44 Ann Matheson, 'The Conspectus experience', *Journal of librarianship* **22** (3), 1990, 171–82.

45 J. Russell, 'Collection profiling', *SCONUL newsletter* 16, 1999, 26–30.

46 Joint Funding Councils' Libraries Review Group, Information Technology Sub-Committee, *Libraries and IT: working papers of the Information Technology Sub-Committee of the HEFCs' Libraries Review*. Bath: UKOLN, 1993.

47 Stephen Pinfield, 'The relationship between national and international electronic library developments in the UK: an overview', *New review of academic librarianship* **6**, 2000, 3–20.

48 Pinfield, *op. cit.*

49 Justine Kitchen and Simon Jennings, 'The Resource Discovery Network: www.rdn.ac.uk', *New review of information networking* **6**, 2000, 157–75.

50 Alicia Wise, 'A distributed national electronic resource for UK higher and further education institutions', *New review of academic librarianship* **5**, 1999, 1–6.

51 Lorcan Dempsey and Rosemary Russell, *National resource discovery workshop: organising access to printed scholarly material*. Bath: UKOLN, 1996.

52 Joint Information Systems Committee (of the Higher Education Funding Councils), *Electronic libraries programme*. 3rd ed. Bristol: HEFCE, 1996.

53 Tavistock Institute, *Evaluation of the Electronic Libraries Programme. Policy mapping study: the set-up, operation and content of the Electronic Libraries Programme*. London: Tavistock Institute, 1996.

54 Andrew Green, 'Towards the digital library: how relevant is eLib to practitioners?', *New review of academic librarianship,* **3**, 1997, 39–48.

55 Green, *op. cit.*

56 Jan Wilkinson, 'Introduction', *New review of academic librarianship* **4**, 1998, 1–2.

57 *New review of academic librarianship* **4**, 1998. (Whole issue devoted to the proceedings of a workship on hybrid libraries held at the University of Leeds.)

58 Edwards *et al.*, 'eLib's IMPEL2 project'.

59 Barbara Stratton, 'The transiency of CD-ROM? A reappraisal for the 1990s', *Journal of librarianship and information science* **26** (3), 1994, 157–64.

60 Joint Information Systems Committee, *Papers on copyright issues in the electronic library*. Bristol: JISC, 1995.

61 For the text of these documents see <http://www.ukoln.ac.uk/services/elib/papers/pa/> (accessed 27/1/06); Charles Oppenheim, 'JISC/Publishers' Association work on developing guidelines for copyright issues in the electronic environment' in *Digital library: challenges and solutions for the new millenium. Proceedings of an international conference held in Bologna, Italy, June 1999,* ed. Pauline Connolly and Denis Reidy. Boston Spa: IFLA, 2000, pp. 39–43.

62 Kelly Russell, 'Digital preservation and the Cedars project experience', *New review of academic librarianship* **6**, 2000, 139–54.

63 *Electronic libraries programme, Long-term preservation of electronic materials: a JISC/British Library workshop.* London: British Library, 1996 (British Library R & D report; 6238); David Haynes and David Streatfield, 'Who will preserve electronic publications?', *Serials* **10** (3), 1997, 345–51.

64 Neil Beagrie, 'The JISC Digital Preservation Focus and the Digital Preservation Coalition', *New review of academic librarianship* **6**, 2000, 257–67.

65 Shirley Chambers and David Perrow, *Project management tools and techniques in UK university libraries*. London: British Library, 1998 (Research and innovation report; 119).

66 Joint Information Systems Committee, *Guidelines for developing an information strategy*. Bristol: HEFCE, 1995; Michael Breaks, 'Information systems strategies', *British journal of academic librarianship* **6** (2), 1991, 65–70.

67 Council of Polytechnic Librarians, *Final report on the COPOL Performance Indicators Experimental Project 1989 to 1992*. Brighton: COPOL, [1993]; Standing Conference of National and University Libraries, *Performance indicators for university libraries: a practical guide*. London: SCONUL, 1992.

68 Ian Winkworth, 'Into the House of Mirrors: performance measurement in academic libraries', *British journal of academic librarianship* **8** (1), 1993, 17–33.

69 Christopher Hunt, 'Academic library planning in the United Kingdom', *British journal of academic librarianship* **8** (1), 1993, 3–16.

70 Don Revill and Geoffrey Ford, *Working papers on service level agreements*. London: SCONUL, 1994; Geoffrey Ford, 'Service level agreements', *New review of academic librarianship* **2**, 1996, 49–59.

71 Winkworth, 'Into the House of Mirrors'.; Graham Bulpitt, 'A new university view', *British journal of academic librarianship* **9** (1/2), 1994, 48–59.

72 Jean Sykes, *SCONUL briefing paper: aide-mémoire for assessors when evaluating library and computing* services. London: SCONUL, 1996.

73 Richard Battersby, 'Teaching quality assessment: the role of the subject librarian', *Library review* **45** (5), 1996, 26–33.

74 Joint Funding Councils' Ad-hoc Group on Performance Indicators for Libraries, *The effective academic library: a framework for evaluating the performance of UK academic libraries. A consultative report to the HEFCE, SHEFC, HEFCW and DENI*. Bristol: HEFCE, 1995. (Chair Kevin Ellard.)

75 Jane Barton and John Blagden, *Academic library effectiveness: a comparative approach*. London: British Library, 1998 (Research and innovation report; 120).

76 Alistair Paterson, 'Common measures: 94 Group libraries and benchmarking', *SCONUL newsletter* **14**, 1998, 22–3.

77 John Fielden Consultancy, *Supporting expansion: a report on human resource management in academic libraries for the Joint Funding Councils Libraries Review Group*. Bristol: HEFCE, 1993.

78 *British journal of academic librarianship* **9** (3), 1994.

79 John Fielden, 'The Fielden report three years on', *BUOPOLIS* 2, 1997, 1–3.

80 Andrew Green, 'A survey of staff appraisal in university libraries', *British journal of academic librarianship* **8** (3), 1993, 193–209.

81 Peter Brophy, 'Networking in British academic libraries', *British journal of academic librarianship* **8** (1), 1993, 49–60.

6

Colleges of higher education

Scott Robertson

Background

Presenting a paper at the joint conference of the Education Librarians Group and Librarians of Institutes and Schools of Education in July 1988, Alec Ross, then Director of the School of Education at the University of Lancaster, predicted the future contribution that would be made by the Colleges of Higher Education in the next decade.[1] Because of the College of Education background from which many originated, and the diversification from the monotechnic role that was already happening, he felt that these institutions were in a strong position to tackle the challenges posed by a declining population of teenagers, the need for widening access, particularly to mature post-experience students, and the necessity to develop vocational routes in addition to teacher education (e.g., social work, nursing). Ross recognized that the greater emphasis on teaching and learning, on providing a supportive and caring experience, and on flexibility of provision, would lend itself to the new HE environment:

> The institutions which will thrive in the rest of the century are those which are responsive to new demands, not only in terms of clientele but also in terms of content. …'more of the same' will not do as a way of expanding higher education.

Ross also predicted the demise of the binary system, expressing his view that a system of two separate streams of funding was wasteful when all HE institutions were actually teaching similar level courses.

By the end of the 1980s the HE Colleges had become a fully established part of the HE sector, funded by the Polytechnics and Colleges Funding Council, represented by the Standing Conference of Principals (as opposed to the Committee of Vice Chancellors and Principals for the universities and later for the former polytechnics), with their teaching standards monitored by the CNAA (Council for National Academic Awards). Their academic provision was predominantly at HE level. The institutions fell into two fairly distinct types: general colleges largely from the college of education tradition with a mixed background of public sector and Church funding; and specialist colleges of art, music, drama, etc. The emphasis of each was more on teaching and learning, although there were certainly pockets of important research.

In 1992 when the separate funding councils for universities and polytechnics and councils were abandoned and the HE funding councils for England, Scotland and Wales were created, there were 23 general colleges and 26 specialist colleges included within the remit of HEFCE, the English council. By 1996 a total of 66 HE colleges were listed by Brennan and Ramsden in their statistical report on the diversity of higher education in the UK.[2]

During the 1990s, the demise of the CNAA forced the colleges to seek alliances with universities for the accreditation of their degrees. The unification of the sector under one funding council; the renaming of polytechnics; the development of new and changing methods of external quality assurance; the impact of research assessment exercises; the expansion of student numbers; and developments in widening access and lifelong learning all created a constantly changing environment for the whole of the sector to operate within. This scenario was complicated and challenged by another external factor – the rapid developments in IT and their impact on learning, teaching and research and the availability of scholarly material.

By 2000 the HE landscape had changed considerably. Some colleges had gained university status, several others had sought and gained independent degree awarding powers, others had merged with or been absorbed by universities. At the end of the turbulent decade, the colleges had a more universally understood role as a significant part of the HE sector; generally smaller than universities, with one or two notable exceptions; predominantly teaching-led institutions; and with a reputation for high-level student support, both academic and pastoral, as a result of the higher proportion of non-traditional students they brought into the sector.

Libraries/learning resources

In his conference paper, Ross also anticipated some of the changes that would affect libraries in the HE colleges and the influence that librarians should have on learning provision:

> Resourcing (and this is where Librarians and Directors of Resources would have a strong say) would focus less on the personal research needs of the staff ... and more on the learning needs of the students. The balance of expenditure would alter from periodicals towards software, from single copies of advanced monographs to multiple copies of teaching texts, from book to non-book materials, from shelves to work-centres and – for part-time students are important in this – from day-time to evening provision.[3]

Certainly some trends are predicted here that have applied to most of the HE sector, but perhaps more so to colleges and the former polytechnics. Indeed, to some extent, this scenario was already unfolding in the colleges. Because, in most instances, the colleges were relatively small institutions, the library senior managers tended to have a wider area of responsibility; indeed the concept of service convergence was already in existence, commonly under the banner of 'learning resources'. The constitution of these merged services varied, but usually included media services and reprographics alongside library services, and sometimes areas as diverse as educational development, careers, archives, galleries, museums and television production. Although IT services occasionally featured, this wave of convergence pre-dated the common 1990s convergence between library and IT services.[4] In some institutions any IT infrastructure development was in its infancy.

The phrase 'learning resources' did denote a more active relationship with the core learning function, which represented a different focus from some traditional university libraries where the principal role was the development of research collections. 'Learning resources' was also symbolic of the broader area of responsibility held by those charged with library management. These post-holders were often members of senior management teams, of core academic planning and decision-making committees, and would sometimes play an active role in the processes of validation, review and monitoring of academic programmes. Most, but not all, of these heads of learning resources were librarians, but were not eligible to join the two established national professional representative organizations for university and polytechnic librarians, SCONUL (Standing Conference of National and University Libraries) and COPOL (Committee of Polytechnic Librarians), which then merged in 1993.

The Higher Education Colleges Learning Resources Group (HCLRG)

In 1990 a group of twelve heads of learning resources from the north of England, who had started to meet as an informal self-help group, established themselves formally as the PCFC Learning Resources Group. At the same time a similar group from a consortium of nine HE colleges across the south of England, the Midlands and Wales started to meet for mutual support. The PCFC had agreed to the existence of the northern group as an official representative group and they consequently organized a meeting in London to which all college heads of learning resources in England and Wales were invited. This brought together 31 interested people in July 1991 to discuss mutual areas of interest and experience and start the planning of future amalgamation.

Inspired by the northern group's example, a Southern PCFC Learning Resources Group was formed with a committee and a regular newsletter. At its very first full membership meeting, the committee was encouraged to form a merged national group, but also to contact SCONUL and COPOL to propose full amalgamation within the new non-binary world now funded by the newly established national HE funding bodies.

Representatives of the two committees duly met in the London College of Printing in May and planned a two-day national conference at a geographically central venue, Harper Adams College in Shropshire, where a mandate would be sought to set up a foundation committee of three members from each group.

So the first annual residential conference was held with 26 delegates and Nigel Brown, the Finance Director of the new funding council, as keynote speaker. The delegates agreed the mandate and a formal constitution. Officers were elected and committee roles agreed at the subsequent foundation committee meeting. An appropriate geographical balance was achieved with equal members from north and south. An annual subscription fee of £25 was set.

Throughout the group's existence, the national committee met regularly. The personnel changed and the committee grew from a membership of 6 eventually to 12. The balance of membership was maintained with a Welsh representative being added as well as representation from specialist colleges. Observers were invited from the Library Association and SCONUL in later years and committee members were also represented on various SCONUL and LA committees.

Advocacy

The Group committee felt that one of its most important activities was advocacy. Consequently responses to policy papers were written and selective lobbying took place to present the case for the college sector. Right from the start the committee involved itself in the great flurry of activity surrounding the Follett Committee's deliberations (see below).[5] Responses were written to all the consultation and HCLRG lobbied hard for more college representation on the various sub-committees. A special meeting was held with the then Vice-Principal of King Alfred's College, the only college representative within the core Follett Committee.

The group's chair and secretary actually took part as observers in the joint SCONUL/COPOL discussions which led to the formation of the new SCONUL. As a result of the HE reorganization of 1992 and the emergence of the former polytechnics as new universities, there was no longer any reason for COPOL and SCONUL to be separate organizations. At that stage the inclusion of the HE colleges as full members was perceived as a step too far for the then SCONUL membership. However, important links were made which proved to be the first steps towards the future full integration of all HE institutions into SCONUL. Members of HCLRG were co-opted on to several SCONUL standing committees; associate membership was introduced for those colleges who were approaching university status in terms of size and breadth of subjects; and a strong association between the two organizations was forged.

Both HEFCE and the Standing Conference of Principals (SCOP) accepted the representative role of the group and the Library Association (LA) declared HCLRG to be an organization in association. The group also had observer status on the LA's Academic Sub-committee in its various guises.

An important development for HCLRG was the compilation of national HE College statistics for publication in line with SCONUL and in liaison with the Libraries and Information Statistics Unit at Loughborough. Publication started in 1994 and for the rest of the decade there was an annual set of library statistics for HE colleges which afforded useful comparisons for LISU and featured in HESA studies of trends across the sector.

The HCLRG annual conferences were relatively small with the number of delegates varying from 26 to 33 (out of a total membership of between 40 and 46), but highly successful in terms of relevance and quality of speakers and themes, attracting delegates from universities and the FE sector. Stimulating papers were presented by many notable people on highly significant issues of the day. Apart from Nigel Brown at the outset of HEFCE, Brian Fender was invited to speak immediately after his appointment as Chief Executive. Mike Fitzgerald of Thames Valley University, Annie Grant from the Teacher Training Agency and Gerry Taggart from HEFCE were other notable speakers, as well as several figures from the Library and IT worlds.

Throughout its existence HCLRG took the initiative on several occasions and communicated with the decision-makers, particularly HEFCE, to present its views on current issues. Response documents were sent to the Follett Committee, the Anderson Committee, the Higher Education Quality Council, the Quality Assurance Agency for Higher Education, Ofsted (the Office for Standards in Education), the Institute for Learning and Teaching in Higher Education, the Joint Information Systems Committee (JISC), and SCOP. The group's intention was always to ensure that the powers that be recognize the diversity within the sector; that the HE sector did not wholly consist of large, research-led universities; and that economies of scale often disadvantaged the smaller institutions who were undertaking equally valuable teaching and research work, albeit on a smaller scale. This lobbying activity paid dividends, and contributed to the general awareness within JISC, for instance, that banded payments based on student numbers had to be part of their negotiated terms with publishers and database suppliers.

On a couple of occasions initiatives were taken that almost had significant repercussions across the whole of higher education. Firstly in 1995 members of the committee negotiated with the HEFCE Auditor to carry out, with HEFCE funding, a Value For Money study in the management of learning resources in HE colleges. With the full support of the funding council, the HCLRG committee formed itself into a steering group for the project, wrote a tender document, sought competitors for the project, selected Touche Ross, and then worked with them to plan a sample survey of four colleges and a rationale and strategy for representative consultation on which the published report and recommendations would be made. The results were reported in HEFCE's *VFM news* as being helpful indicators for an extended survey of the whole sector, and only political events and changes in personnel and focus within HEFCE at the time prevented this report being the benchmark for a wider study.

Similarly, a joint initiative from the SCONUL Joint Working Group on Quality, largely at the urging of the HCLRG group, to work with Ofsted to create an aide-memoire for Ofsted inspections of Initial Teacher Education, actually led to a joint survey of good practice for library and IT support for teacher education, involving visits by combined Ofsted/SCONUL/HCLRG/UCISA teams to four universities and three colleges. The subsequent report might have had more influence in the conduct of future inspections, had there not been a major reorganization of the Teacher Education division of Ofsted at the time.

A significant step in the strengthening of the alliance with SCONUL came in 1998 when the then Chair of HCLRG was invited to be an observer on the SCONUL Executive. HCLRG members had played active roles in several of SCONUL standing committees, but this took the developing cooperation between the two organizations to a more formal level with evident recognition from SCONUL that a strategic alliance was important for the representation of the whole HE sector.

As an inevitable development of the close relationship a historic, unanimous vote took place at the 2000 SCONUL AGM to include the HE Colleges within SCONUL. Once this had been achieved, there was no longer any reason for HCLRG to exist, as members were then able to be an even more effective lobbying force within SCONUL, which now represented the whole sector's librarians and heads of learning resources and information services.[6]

The Follett report
Although the HCLRG activity was important to the development and public awareness of the HE College libraries and learning resources in the 1990s, more needs to be said about the impact of external forces and trends on the operation of these services. What were the principal external influences – political, economic, cultural and technological – that drove changes to the learning support environment in HE colleges? They were, in the main, the same drivers that affected university libraries. Major changes certainly did take place as soon as the binary system was abandoned. The new funding councils for England, Wales and Scotland became much more inclusive in their approach and language. HEIs (higher education institutions) became the common parlance for describing the institutions included in the sector. Regional groupings of HEIs included the colleges as equal members.

It is rare indeed for a major government agency report on HE to concentrate on library provision, but that is what happened in 1993, when the joint funding councils commissioned Sir Brian Follett to chair a group to review libraries and related provision in HE, taking into account the planned expansion of the sector, the impact of IT and the possibilities of greater cooperation.[7] The review's practical remit included operational and space requirements and funding. The Review Group included several librarians, but only one senior academic from an HE college. Responses to the report from the Library Association and HCLRG did express disappointment at the lack of college representation, and the omission was remedied by the inclusion of college librarians in some of the follow-up groups.

A useful account of the college view on Follett can be found in Jenkinson.[8] She points out the paradox that some of the changes proposed to the provision of library services and resources in converged centres were already familiar to most colleges where, for economic and strategic reasons, integrated management and provision of facilities had already happened. Similarly Follett's emphasis on access to research resources rather than investing in research holdings was already a familiar approach, although Jenkinson also expressed the hope that the colleges would not be ignored in the move to establish arts and humanities research collections.

The proposals for closer involvement by library and learning resource managers in general decision-making, and for closer liaison between library and teaching staff were welcomed by Jenkinson, and she points out again that, in smaller institutions, this was likely to be already happening. However, she warns of the effect of the economies of scale on the levels of staffing able to perform the liaison effectively.

The proposed inclusion of library provision in quality assessment activity was also welcomed and Jenkinson indicated that HCLRG had already proposed names of college librarians who were prepared to act as consultants or inspectors in the new QA processes. The article was also positive about the stated intention to establish a generic set of performance indicators building on the work of SCONUL and HCLRG.

An interesting comment made by Jenkinson was a criticism that Follett failed to take account of the changes taking place in the area of teacher education which were likely to have a significant impact on several colleges and universities. It is certainly the case that the subsequent development of the Teaching Training Agency and its separate funding system for this area of HE and the arrival of Ofsted with its separate inspection and quality standards regime would create complications for the sector, affecting significantly a number of colleges where teacher education remained a large proportion of their learning and teaching activity.

The final point in the article suggests that the Follett report had given college library and learning resource managers a script on which to base their plans for future developments. This was certainly the case for those colleges who, along with several universities, used the content of the report as an argument for successful bids for the two tranches of funding resulting from Follett to enable the construction of new library buildings or extensions. Perhaps one of the most far-reaching aspects of the Follett report was the actual provision of two sums of funding council money to be spent on improving library/learning centre accommodation across the UK. Several colleges were able to take part in this initiative, resulting in centres that merged IT with library provision more than ever before, creating a more integrated, converged learning environment.

IT developments

Many colleges began the decade with an under-developed IT facility. However by 2000 the IT infrastructure had grown enormously and computer technology had transformed the means of communication, file storage and maintenance of student records, access to information and literature, and methods of learning and teaching.

The situation at University College Chichester may be illustrative of the development in several colleges. In 1990 the Learning Resources Unit of the West Sussex Institute of Higher Education operated a small suite of RM Nimbus computers at each of its two campuses with dial-up access to JANET, managed by the Media Services team. There was no central IT infrastructure or department, merely a few stand-alone computers in some academic departments. By the end of the decade, a converged Information Services department managed the college network and supported all the administrative computing systems, as well as over 200 student open access PCs available for 90 hours a week and a computer on every staff desk. The college had moved from student-centred low-level provision, to the creation of a technically driven IT department responsible for developing the whole infrastructure, to an integrated department with technical systems technicians and user support staff working alongside librarians and library assistants.

During the 1990s the IT revolution had brought huge changes to college libraries: to library/learning resources centre design with the need for centrally available computer suites to be available on evenings and weekends with technical support; to the provision of online catalogues, bibliographical databases and other web-based information with support and training; to more flexible resource-based modes of learning with electronically linked distance learners; and to the role of librarians who had to manage the provision, access, training and support for effective use of the electronic information by students and staff. The development of the Windows operating system led to the adoption of the PC as a standard piece of equipment for all, and the increasing potential of the MS Office software was fully exploited for its presentation and administrative potential. The rapid expansion of the World Wide web in the 1990s provided easy access to online information from a huge variety of sources. With the Joint Academic Network already in existence providing a fast, good quality conduit for this communication and information potential, the HE sector enthusiastically embraced this new technology, channelling resources into IT staffing, infrastructure and equipment, spurred on by funding initiatives such as Follett.

Libraries and learning resources centres became a focus for much of this development and the IT revolution had a huge impact on aspects such as the management of loans and the catalogue, the nature of the study environment, the presentation of resources and the opening up of access to further sources of published information with all the additional skills training this necessitated.

The extent to which an HEI embraced this technology and embedded it into its activity depended on several factors, but most importantly for colleges, economy of scale had a significant bearing. With a funding allocation based on student numbers and research activity, most colleges took longer to be able to fund the IT infrastructure (not totally disadvantageous, as rapid changes in technology sometimes meant that a slightly later investment could obtain a better value product) and could not afford the staffing levels, higher level systems, or subscriptions to digital information, that many of the larger institutions could. Several colleges for instance did not initially invest in the larger, more sophisticated library management computer systems because of the ongoing cost, which often necessitated a later switch in supplier and system in the volatile world of LMS supply. The centrally funded 'electronic library' initiatives that emerged from the Follett proposals did enable all institutions to take advantage of free or inexpensive subject-based information gateways to electronic sources of scholarly information, but later publisher-based licences to access comprehensive or selective journal contents directly, proved to be too expensive and not selective enough for the smaller HE libraries. The extent to which libraries and learning resources centres could introduce computer technology into their student-centred environment was also limited by the available funds.

Another difference in approach between HE colleges and certainly some of the large research-centred universities in the adoption of IT into libraries in the early 1990s was the emphasis on learning and the proactive involvement of the library and learning resources staff in the learning process. The IT revolution offered a new set of powerful tools to be utilized in the delivery and support of teaching programmes. The college network enabled multiple access to learning materials, to improved methods of presentation and illustration of tutors' and students' work and to sources of supplementary material created elsewhere. This potential was grasped and exploited and librarians were involved in the training of research and navigation skills to facilitate its effective utilization as a central facility.

Kam Patel described how the London Institute, an unusually large member of the HE college fraternity at the time, was investing hugely in IT systems particularly to transform teaching, learning, research and communication.[9] William Stubbs, the rector of the Institute, which had five art and design colleges in central London, was quoted: 'Computers are proving themselves to be very powerful in helping us move away from learning programmes that are didactic towards a model that is more student-centred.'

Traditional universities with a more faculty-centred organization often concentrated more on the power of IT to extend the subject-based collections and enhance the quality of access to the bibliographical record.

Both approaches fed into the electronic library developments and the work of JISC, the Joint Information Systems Committee of the funding councils. However, the bulk of this activity tended to concentrate on the research-led areas in which the larger institutions expressed an interest. JISC projects necessitated the involvement of library and IT staff in the HEIs in their development. Because of the economy of scale in staffing, that generally meant that only the larger universities had the staff numbers to lend to these activities. The many JISC committees spawned a large number of such information-mapping and digitization projects with a plethora of acronyms which made up the Distributed National Electronic Resource, based on many research-led university initiatives, which nonetheless opened up a considerable number of specialist library resources for all scholars.

Peters, reporting on a 1998 JISC library strategy workshop for SCONUL, expressed a concern that the NESLI scheme for licensed access to electronic journals might have an up-front charge that was beyond the means of smaller institutions.[10] But she was also encouraged by the work of a separate JISC working group on charging for dataset access which had produced a tiered charging structure which 'was felt to be fair, predictable, simple and well-defined, and intended to encourage use'. She continues:

> As a member of a small Higher Education Institution, I can only applaud the work of the group – many of us should now be able to benefit from services for which we have been 'paying' via JISC top-slicing for years, but with no hope of affording flat rate subscriptions.

By 1998 the message from the colleges and smaller universities was percolating through and the era of the banded subscription based on student numbers was beginning.

Converged services

It was clear that the dramatic increase in the role of IT in HE was having a considerable impact on the way the central support services had to operate in the late 1990s. There were varying degrees of convergence of library and IT departments – some operated separately under a common management structure, others converged the student/user IT services with the library service, and a few went for full operational integration. There are a few published accounts of how this was being managed in some HE colleges during the decade.

Sykes and Gerrard in 1997 compared the approaches taken by Liverpool John Moores University and Roehampton Institute.[11] Roehampton had adopted a radical 'bottom-up model' where library assistants became learning services assistants and were trained in basic IT skills so that a certain level of technical support for the computer suites in the libraries was offered. This service quality focus and multi-skilled approach helped to deal with the recognized cultural differences that often existed between library and IT staff, and 'the presence of (non-technical) support staff led to a dramatic increase in take-up of computer facilities, particularly among mature students'. User feedback indicated that co-locating information services and technology in a seamless way was appreciated.

The aims of convergence, according to the authors, were efficiency, greater customer focus and the development of new kinds of information services. Their conclusion was that this form of operational convergence 'is likely to be an appropriate strategy for similar teaching-led, modestly funded, multi-site institutions. ... It is less easy, perhaps, to extend this generalisation to longer-established libraries with superior levels funding and a greater commitment to research.'

A different approach to the management of an even more diverse range of learner-centred services is described by Connor.[12] At the North East Wales Institute of Higher Education, an integrated Information and Student Services department was formed in response to the demands of increased participation and a diverse student population, and to the inclusion of more life skills in the curriculum. This mix of library, IT, media, reprographics and other services normally managed outside the realm of learning or information services (careers, counselling, health care etc.) was also influenced by government recommendations on lifelong learning.[13]

The principal emphasis in Connor's account was the importance of the integrated department's central proactive role in the academic life of the Institute, in planning, staff development and quality assurance, at a time when innovative student-centred approaches to learning were being developed:

> A transition from contact-intensive teaching to supported, resource-based, student-centred learning is taking place … with information technology being exploited to support staff and students and to provide alternative strategies.

Connor also alluded to the need to provide a 'facilitating environment', for the diverse student population to which Ross referred. 'Such a diverse student population necessitates innovative user education on behalf of library and information services, recognizing different levels of educational background and confidence amongst students.' Franchised students in remote locations were also mentioned, as well as having to negotiate service levels with the student 'customers'. Indeed the department consisted of a 'Customer Services Team' and an 'Academic Services Team', both of which were trained to be multi-skilled, and they had a direct impact on the college curriculum through the delivery and support of a compulsory Transferable Skills module.

Connor concluded by listing challenges and opportunities for all HE library and information services. These included playing a strategic role in institutional development; being proactive in good practice and initiatives in teaching and learning; monitoring services and responding to feedback; forming partnerships with other information providers and with academic staff and students; developing networked resources; and creating a rich, diverse and accessible educational environment for all.

It could be argued that at least some of the earlier approaches to such a broad and pervasive role for the library and associated services in Higher Education occurred in the colleges because of the aspects of size and central involvement in the learning process.

Organizationally, the third example from the literature took the concept a stage further by the creation of a separate faculty devoted to learning and information services. Les Watson, the then Dean of the Faculty of Learning and Information Services at Cheltenham and Gloucester College of Higher Education, wrote in 1999 of the faculty focusing on learning 'as it views this as the key activity of the institution, and indeed of any university.'[14] The Faculty strategic plan referred to the 'centrality of knowledge creation and learning development to the business of the College' and to learning as 'the core of all College activities'. His philosophy was based on the premise that library and information services were actively supporting learning as much as lecturers, referring to Charles Handy's comment that in the new world of easy access to information through IT, traditional didactic approaches to lecturing are much less valid.

The Faculty was simply structured into three converged units providing 'backoffice, frontoffice, and a research and development function'. The first was responsible for the provision of technical and bibliographical resources, the second for integrated access and support to all library and computer services and the third had an active educational development role. Watson also noted that the faculty had been responsible for 80 learning projects and had led the process of acquiring an online learning environment for the college. The development of virtual learning environment systems was driven by the work of such activists in learning-centred HE and enabled by the continuing march of information technology.

These accounts of innovative approaches to library and information services were indicative of what was happening in learning-led HE institutions, in response to the demands of new groups of learners, to a need for more skills-based training and to the rapidly emerging possibilities of information technology, in fact many of the trends that Alec Ross had spotted in 1988. An accompanying factor was the HE management pressure to increase staff–student ratios as the recruitment of lecturing staff did not keep pace with the substantial increase in student numbers and new courses. Although the contact hours for individual lecturers were rising during the decade, the contact hours received by students seemed to be reducing. All of this led to greater expectations of independent learning and an active role for the learning resources centres and libraries.

Subject librarians

A key figure in enabling this to be managed effectively for students was the subject librarian, who worked closely with the academic staff to build and manage appropriate resource collections to support the course needs; who prepared course-related training materials; and who delivered skills training to student groups and provided students and staff with advice on information retrieval. These providers of subject-based services had been a feature of many university and college libraries since the 1970s, but their acceptance by faculties and academic departments as useful allies in the successful delivery of their courses through more effective exploitation of the emerging variety of resources and the provision of useful skills training blossomed in the 1990s in many HEIs, particularly those whose principal focus was on learning and teaching. In more research-led universities, the subject librarian's main driver was more the development of the research collections, in print and online. Indeed, in his literature review on the role of the subject librarian, Gaston concluded that 'the role that subject librarians perform has evolved from subject-based collection development into subject-based user support'.[15]

In Gaston's view from surveying the literature, the Follett report seemed to be the watershed.

In summary, prior to the Follett report subject librarians seem to have been employed on the basis of their subject specialist knowledge and were involved in: liaison, collection development, reference enquiries, user education, the compilation of bibliographies and cataloguing and classification.

Later he adds: 'Comparison with role descriptions of subject librarians prior to the Follett Report suggests that involvement in teaching and the impact of IT have significantly changed the job description of subject librarians.'

Gaston begins to define the factors which led to the change in the role when he refers to the Dearing Report and the studies which it commissioned. The role of the lecturer had been affected by the growth of IT, changes in delivery of courses and 'the enterprise culture'. Consequently librarians generally were 'becoming more like academics by mimicking their teaching function (educating students in learning skills) rather than their research function (the development of subject specialist knowledge)'.

He compares the views of Heseltine, who perceived no future in subject teams in libraries, but only in the delivery of end-user services on a functional, institution-wide basis, with those of Heery and Morgan, who described the subject-based approach as the best way of 'integrating the work of libraries into the educational process'; and with Pinfield, who claimed that the subject librarian's role had continued to develop, utilizing IT, focusing more on 'proactive liaison with users and information skills training'. Gaston then finds Reid's opinion helpful, that 'subject knowledge' has become less important than 'subject responsibility'.

He concludes by pinpointing the concept of 'liaison' and its user focus as being more significant than subject knowledge by the end of the 1990s, associated with a pedagogy based more on generic skills rather than on subject specific knowledge. In Gaston's experience, the reality of subject librarianship involved a combination of the two, as the function might be to deliver the generic skills, but only in the context of the subject and as a means of enabling the students to gain more subject knowledge.

However, the significance of the use of information skills had risen to prominence in the library world by the end of the decade. SCONUL formed a task force in 1998 (led by an HE college librarian) to prepare a statement on the topic. It produced an Information Skills model which was discussed and adopted widely. Indeed several HEIs, such as Cheltenham and Gloucester, established such information skills courses as an essential part of the institutional curriculum.

The flourishing of subject librarians, or indeed tutor librarians, in more learning-centred, skills-based institutions, responsible for the delivery of 'information and library skills' was also the subject of some accounts of learning support activity for HE level students in colleges in the FE sector. Davies and Murdoch described the role of tutor librarians at Norwich City College and the contributions they made to some degree level courses.[16] As a result of their input, course assignments had become more research oriented, the topics more broadly based and changes had been made to the delivery and learning style of the courses.

Having Tutor Librarians means that the library has now become the focus of learning. It is actually the focus and source of some very useful and central information, and this kind of development has led to a tremendous improvement in the quality of assessed work which is produced by students.

The authors expressed concern that this resource-centred approach placed a great deal of pressure on the library, where the level of funding might not be able to sustain access to the breadth of resources that it demanded. This may be part of the reason why, in HE, the skills-driven approach has been usually contained within the confines of a limited discipline-defined area of subject knowledge as concluded by Gaston, rather than the pursuit of information skills as a core transferable skill. Confusion with information technology skills did not help, as the latter became universally seen as essential for all. However, there is plenty of evidence of the significant impact made during the 1990s by the subject librarian role on approaches to learning and on the structure of library services, particularly in HE colleges and polytechnics, and in support of HE courses in FE.[17]

The Dearing report and lifelong learning

Where the early part of the decade in HE libraries was dominated by Follett and the relatively unfettered expansion of student numbers, the end of the decade became influenced by the somewhat contradictory focus of the incoming New Labour government on lifelong learning opportunities; widening participation in learning to under-represented disadvantaged groups; the development of different modes of learning made possible by technological change; and, surprisingly, the movement towards self-funded students who then became more demanding customers of HE as a result.

The Dearing report in 1997, entitled *Higher education in the learning society*, and the Government green paper, *The learning age*, set the lifelong learning agenda, perceiving higher education as an important stage in a community-wide learning network.[18] This message was somewhat undermined by the New Labour decision to turn students into tuition fee-paying customers and, in doing so, set academic libraries a considerable challenge in a rapidly changing technological and diverse HE world as the millennium approached. The development of community-based electronic learning networks; the establishment of university and HE college-controlled regional area networks; the encouragement of collaboration between sectors, most notably HE and FE; and the exploitation of advanced computer software to create multi-media learning material that could be delivered everywhere, seemed to make a global, cooperative world of learning tantalizingly possible. Inspired by the continuing success of the Open University and perhaps influenced by the enthusiasm in the FE sector for an open learning approach, many HE colleges and new universities committed themselves to a more integrated approach to resource-based learning, where libraries, and in particular subject librarians, had a major role to play in its facilitation. Set against this, the demands of the fee-paying student customers were influencing course designers to continue with more traditional teaching methods so that the value of their course could be measured in lecturer contact hours.

The rich and diverse world of university sector education and indeed the library's role was further complicated by the Research Assessment Exercise and its drive to reward high level research publication. To support this richly rewarding contest, the larger libraries of the more traditional research-led universities were encouraged by their faculties to build specialist collections and provide access to large electronic databases, rather than concentrating their energies primarily on an integrated, active learning and teaching partnership with the lecturing staff.

So by the end of the decade, HE sector libraries had to balance all those functions in response to the internal and external influences, which they did in a variety of ways, depending on the nature of the institution. Universities and colleges had to compete and collaborate. No matter how fiercely competitive the institutional leadership was, the librarians were always good at collaboration, none more so than the smaller college libraries. In 1998 Roddie Shepherd, then Professional Advisor to the Library Association on Higher and Further Education, wrote a brief piece on the HE Library of the 21st century, where he described the HE context at the end of the decade in terms of national policy issues, including lifelong learning, widening participation (the need to draw in the non-traditional students), collaboration, the technological drive and the focus on learning.[19] Within this context HE libraries would have to operate successfully in a number of ways. They would have to be collaborative within and beyond the sector, for resources, for access (actual and virtual), for staff development and shared expertise; be networked to lifelong learning and research infrastructures; provide multi-media learning materials to support independent, remote, flexible learners with a variety of learning styles; be integrated with the learning and teaching processes; and be open and accessible to a variety of on-campus and electronic users.

The HE world described by Shepherd could be seen as an extension of the predictions of Ross, and the library characteristics, with their emphasis on the active role of the library in the learning process, participation in regional networks and exploitation of information technology and related skills to open up access to a broader constituency of students, chimed in with developments in college libraries, developments that helped to add a new dimension to the HE library world and led to their acceptance into the university library fold.

In the same way that the funding councils and their information service offshoot (JISC) became more inclusive, so the university library world understood and accepted the significance of HE college libraries, helped by the parallel work undertaken by HCLRG, and welcomed them into SCONUL membership. The major developments and influences of the decade, social, political and technological, encouraged diversity on the one hand and a unified academic network on the other. Advances in accessible research resources driven by the major research universities brought specialist materials closer to the students and staff of smaller HE colleges, and the integration of the library, particularly the active role of the subject librarians, typical of HE colleges and many former polytechnics, also influenced the whole sector to extend the library's role in supporting the variety of approaches to learning enabled by technological developments.

At the start of the 1990s the expansion of HE was seen in terms of increasing diversity of courses, students and institutions. Subsequently the government's unification of the sector and the ever-changing measures to manage the sector and impose quality assurance systems actually encouraged homogeneity.[20] All HEIs had to be drawn into the Research Assessment Exercise with varied success and all universities were influenced by the changes in approaches to learning largely introduced by the colleges and former polytechnics. Although the accumulation of special research collections, actual and digital, was still a major priority for several university libraries, the active contribution that many converged learning resources and learning support departments made to the student experience in HE colleges also influenced the way all university library services perceived and undertook their role.

Notes

1 Alec Ross, 'Higher education in the 1990s: the contribution of the colleges of higher education': paper presented at the Education Librarians Group/Librarians of Institutes and Schools of Education Annual Study Conference, Lancaster, 8–10 July 1988.

2 John Brennan and Brian Ramsden, 'Diversity in UK higher education: a statistical view' in *UK higher education in the 1990s: diversity: too much or too little?* Milton Keynes: Open University Quality Support Centre, 1996, pp. 2–15.

3 Ross, 'Higher education in the 1990s'.

4 Scott Robertson, 'Learning resources in colleges of higher education: a qualitative study', *Learning resources journal* **5** (1), 1989, 16–19.

5 Joint Funding Councils' Libraries Review Group, *Report*. Bristol: HEFCE, 1993. Chairman Sir Brian Follett. (The 'Follett report'.)

6 A slightly more detailed account of the history of the group can be found in Scott Robertson, 'Higher Education Colleges Learning Resources Group 1990–2001: a brief history of an effective organisation', *SCONUL newsletter* 25, spring 2002, 93–7.

7 Joint Funding Councils' Libraries Review Group, *Report*.

8 Ruth Jenkinson, 'The Follett report: a view from the colleges and institutes', *British journal of academic librarianship* **9** (1/2), 1994, 60–7.

9 Kam Patel, 'The networked campus', *Times higher educational supplement* 27 August 1999, 6.

10 Janet Peters, 'JISC Library Strategy Workshop: Manchester Conference Centre 30 April/1 May 1998', *SCONUL newsletter* 14, autumn 1998, 67–70.

11 Phil Sykes and Sarah Gerrard, 'Operational convergence at Roehampton Institute London and Liverpool John Moores University', *New review of academic librarianship* **3**, 1997, 67–85.

12 Clare M. Connor, 'The challenge of diversity: managing information and student services at the North East Wales Institute of Higher Education', *COFHE bulletin* 84, summer 1998, 1–6.

13 National Committee of Inquiry into Higher Education, *Higher education in the learning society: the report of the National Committee of Inquiry into Higher Education*. London: The Committee, 1997. Chairman Sir Ron Dearing. (The 'Dearing report'); Department for Education and Employment, *The learning age: a renaissance for a new Britain*. London: HMSO, 1998 (Cm 3790).

14 Les Watson, 'Partnerships for learning at Cheltenham and Gloucester College of Higher Education', *Relay* 48, 1999, 10–11.

15 Richard Gaston, 'The changing role of the subject librarian, with a particular focus on UK developments, examined through a review of the literature', *New review of academic librarianship* 7, 2001, 19–36.

16 Bryn Davies and Anne Murdoch, 'Tutor librarians: creating a climate for change', *Education libraries journal* 34 (1), 1991, 9–14.

17 Gaston, 'Changing role'.

18 See note 13.

19 Roddie Shepherd, 'The HE library of the 21st century', *NATFHE Library Section newsletter* spring 1998, 4–7.

20 Martin Trow, 'Comparative Reflections on diversity in British Higher Education' in *UK higher education in the 1990s: diversity: too much or too little?* Milton Keynes: Open University Quality Support Centre, 1996, pp. 16–23.

7

Government information services and libraries

Peter Griffiths

Introduction

The decade from 1991 to 2000 was significant for government libraries and librarians, as it was for central government generally, for a number of reasons. In political terms the decade began with the departure of Margaret Thatcher as Prime Minister in November 1990, just a few weeks before this survey begins, and is marked by the historic Labour election victory in May 1997 – but with hindsight, and whatever we predicted at the time, this event may be less of a landmark in terms of government libraries than it was in terms of politics itself. The civil service is, of course, politically neutral (which means that the opinions expressed in this survey are those of the author alone, and do not reflect any official position), but the forces that direct it and shape it are nonetheless influenced by the politics of the ruling party. A number of the shaping forces and high priorities in government libraries were, as we shall shortly see, driven by the need to deal with policies intended to address management issues in the civil service; but as librarians became more adept at handling policy issues (often for their own survival) so they became more adept too at identifying the opportunities that the new policies offered.

Key themes

The key themes of the decade reflect earlier concerns described in previous surveys in this series, but often with a new emphasis or political driver. Thus the lack of awareness of government libraries described by Wormald and Burge and the new financial initiatives such as 'Next Steps' referred to by Pantry could be seen as joint precursors of the market testing programme that involved a number of departmental libraries in the early 1990s.[1] The entrepreneurial spirit described by Pantry underlay the early leadership by librarians in the emergence of internet-based services, particularly the world wide web, and the widening involvement of librarians in a range of information-based services and activities, not just the management and operation of libraries.

The service ethic

Among the policies that John Major's government will be noted for is the development of a strong citizen-centric service ethic. The blueprint for the policy was the Citizen's Charter programme, launched in July 1991 with a white paper by the Prime Minister saying that it would 'find better ways of converting money into better services'.[2] The Citizen's Charter programme focused on a number of areas which were not aimed directly at government libraries, local or central: but these issues were of sufficient importance either to affect libraries' policies or else to create a new climate which brought services such as libraries to sometimes uncomfortable prominence when assessing the value of internally provided services. The principles of public service promoted by the programme included the publication and adoption of service standards, consumer choice, audit, published complaint management procedures, accessibility and scrutiny. The programme led to a number of other initiatives: the Charter Mark, first awarded in 1992, was not given directly to any central department libraries, but was awarded to some government agency libraries within the healthcare sector in the late 1990s. Central department libraries were however affected by the programme of market testing that derived from the principles of the Citizen's Charter, with a number of departments putting their libraries through full tests and a number of others undertaking reviews, sometimes repeated at intervals, before concluding that a full test was not required. Lawes presented the case as seen by TFPL in 1994, arguing for the involvement of specialist bidders such as TFPL from a survey identifying other non-specialist contenders such as facilities managers, storage companies and management consultants.[3] She highlighted the importance of service quality issues and the importance of the specification in ensuring this quality, and considered the likely effects on the profession and on librarians' careers. Whilst not all her concerns proved to be irresoluble, Lawes rightly drew attention to the changes in management style that were needed to cope with the integration and management of contract and temporary staff, especially within the traditional civil service human resources systems. No fully detailed account of market testing in government libraries has been published, although Burge presented an overview of events and an assessment of the outcomes at IFLA in 1998.[4] Snowley examined the use of market testing using case studies to date at the 1994 annual conference of the UK Serials Group.[5] Other papers and publications by Grimwood-Jones, Lawes and Foreman (editor), as well as the proceedings of the 1991 HERTIS conference which included contributions from central government, and the Capital Planning 1992 seminar, the Office of Public Service and Science guide to market testing and the somewhat americanized overview in Woodsworth and Williams all add information, as do examples in Pantry and Griffiths' guide to service level agreements, a tool that came into widespread use following market testing in government libraries.[6]

Some departmental libraries went through market tests, either actual or as paper exercises, more than once. The Department of Health put its library through a full exercise although the 'authority', as the department's representative issuing the invitation to tender is called, chose to exclude external contractors from applying to provide management, reader services or cataloguing, but also to exclude the existing library service from bidding to provide publications ordering (in a library where the norm had been for library staff to obtain publications directly from suppliers). External consultancy was provided to support the staff in the production of their bid, and a particular issue was that (given the lack of library expertise among those preparing the invitation to tender) the head of the library service had to be co-opted on to the authority's team during the production of the specification before he was then released to take part in his team's development of the response. This was managed by a period of purdah during which the consultants worked with the library team and the head of service worked with the specification team. Although it did not undergo formal market testing the Home Office Library was assessed in 1993 and 1996 in a form of 'shadow testing' which concluded that the market was insufficiently strong to warrant the investment in a full test. Other tests included EMIC, the Department of the Environment and the Department of Transport, and the Ordnance Survey, most of which are described by Burge.[7] Full proposals were produced by the Department of Health and Department of the Environment Libraries for their respective departments although these contained commercial details and were not published. Lapworth described the EMIC test in more detail at the 1995 Circle of State Librarians annual conference, where Maclachlan took a wider view of the scene following the first wave of tests.[8] She identified a number of changes in the client base as other services that had drawn upon library services were themselves outsourced, but there was also a growing awareness of the importance of information, expansion of IT networks, and management change, all of which would lead to changing roles for library and information professionals.

The Charter programme continued beyond the 1997 election, with health sector libraries taking a notable part, and the new government's policy is contained in Service First.[9] New elements in the revised programme such as an additional focus on quality and the creation of quality networks influenced the thinking of departmental librarians and the work of the Committee of Departmental Librarians.

Evidence-based policy making
The early 1990s were notable in the healthcare sector for the emphasis placed on the use of information and in particular the use of evidence to evaluate clinical interventions and other medical practices. Following Cochrane's early work on the concept and development of systematic reviews, the approval of funding by Peckham in early 1992 and the foundation of the Cochrane Centre in Oxford later that year drew attention to the ability of information science to make a positive contribution to the quality of life.[10] The British Library took this forward by organizing a seminar in 1992 championed by the then Minister Baroness Cumberlege (and thus now known as the first Cumberlege seminar) to debate the future of healthcare library services.[11] The NHS regional librarians group, working with (among others) the Department of Health Library, organized a second seminar

in 1993 (usually known, unsurprisingly, as 'Cumberlege 2') on the theme 'Managing the knowledge base of healthcare'.[12] Reforms were at the same time taking place in the structure of the NHS which included, from January 1995, an NHS Libraries Adviser located in the Department of Health. Work in the NHS, particularly that led by Booth, eventually led to wider recognition of the value of systematic reviews and evidence assessment as tools to support policy making in a variety of government contexts.[13] In work that would eventually reach the mainstream of policy making in the early 21st century, Westcott carried out a study for the Cabinet Office's Centre for Management and Policy Studies (CMPS) on behalf of the Committee of Departmental Librarians, looking at how policy developers could be encouraged to make greater use of verifiable and independent evidence during policy making and how government libraries could work together to support this.[14] The recommendations of the study were gradually implemented from 2000 onwards. Lewis provides an overview of the involvement of librarians in this work and indicates how their work leads on to later developments such as the Electronic Library for Government and the various inter-departmental thesauri (of which the Integrated Public Sector Vocabulary is the current manifestation).[15]

Expanding roles for librarians: the internet and beyond
Maclachlan drew attention to the changing roles of librarians following from government reforms and policies in the first part of the 1990s.[16] These, combined with the technical revolution that brought the internet from being an almost closed, academic, military and specialist network towards its later ubiquity, had a profound effect on the opportunities for government librarians. The posting of librarians to work in client teams outside the library where their skills could improve the output of an administrative or policy section (generally known as outbedding) had been going on for some years.[17] The second half of the 1990s saw a rather different approach with libraries and librarians taking on wider responsibilities in response to new opportunities. The rapid development of the world wide web and intranets, coupled with the lack of departmental staff able to combine the librarian's skills in systems and information, gave librarians in a number of departments effective control of the development of websites and intranets, or at least made them prominent partners.

One result was that in a number of departments libraries emerged from their traditional grouping with support services and aligned themselves more closely with other functions – sometimes moving between them as political fortunes changed. Some common models emerged, with three predominant arrangements: the traditional link between libraries and records management within a support services framework; libraries within the information technology function; and libraries within communications (and therefore with such functions as press offices, marketing, and the growing field of internal communications). Examples of each of these types were respectively the Foreign and Commonwealth Office, the Department of Health, and the Home Office, where Griffiths explained the rationale for the changes following the creation of the Communication Directorate in 1995.[18] However, even where the traditional links remained, members of other professional groups (particularly the Government Information and Communication Service, later known as the Government Communication Network) encountered librarians from other departments working in their environment, and were thus led to consider further how their own librarians might contribute more widely to the organization. This ultimately led (after 2000) to a number of librarians becoming members of GICS in addition to their library and information professional qualification.

Library automation, indexing and thesauri

Automated management systems continued to be important for government libraries. A number of librarians specialized to a greater or lesser degree in systems and in a number of departments there were posts whose responsibilities included the management and operation of an automated system. The range of systems installed became smaller, reflecting changes in the market, and the withdrawal of the INTERLIB II system using the BLAISE/LOCAS service provided by the British Library National Bibliographic Service. Thus for example the Equilibrium system installed at the Home Office was replaced by Unicorn, which also replaced the Department of Health's system based on an implementation of Status over the office information system.[19] Allum describes the history of INTERLIB and its subsequent replacements at the Department of Education, whilst Scott Cree reviewed the position later in the decade, by which time around half of the departments surveyed had opted for Unicorn, with the remainder using five other systems between them.[20] A specialist system, MODMAP, was installed at the Ministry of Defence Map Library to automate its card catalogue but was reported to have encountered problems due to poor computer performance.[21] Similar exercises were undertaken to convert data at the Home Office and at the Department of the Environment following the change to integrated automated systems and the need to import records originally held in the INTERLIB collaborative cataloguing systems.[22]

Information asset registers

The publication of a white paper on the future management of Crown copyright in March 1999 was expected following the 1998 green paper *Crown copyright in the information age.*[23] Less expected was the inclusion of a complete chapter proposing the introduction of an information asset register system along the lines of the Government Information Locator Service (GILS) in the United States and the Canadian equivalent Info Source.[24] This proposal reflected work that HMSO had been doing with departmental libraries since November 1998. It was intended to provide access to government information in a way that complemented and supplemented department websites, and allowed users to navigate by broad subject without needing to know departmental responsibilities in order to do so. The HMSO website would include the full IAR service, later named Inforoute, and allow users a means of accessing information that could not be easily traced on departmental websites; data sets and other unpublished information resources; and materials in a range of formats.[25] There was some imprecision about the overlap with published materials – it was not intended to duplicate existing bibliographic records – and there was some initial confusion whether to include for example documents that were indexed in Chadwyck-Healey's *Catalogue of official publications not published by the Stationery Office* or included in BOPCAS, the *British official publications current awareness service* based on the Ford Collection of British Official Publications at Southampton University. One important result of the project which came to fruition during the next five-year survey period was the proposal that it would benefit from the establishment of a cross-departmental thesaurus. As it was, the project was a major example of the implementation of an extensive metadata structure, based on the Dublin Core.

The role and purpose of government libraries, and the effect on the careers of government librarians

The 1990s were, as has been widely noted, a decade of great and often continuous change. Government librarians, like many others, were increasingly concerned about their role and its future.

One aspect, to which discussion returned at intervals, was the role of departmental libraries. Pressure on resources and the need to define the purpose of libraries more closely in order to support market testing exercises had led to some departments restricting the services they made available to the general public. Departments also found it more difficult to justify holding long runs of historic materials in the face of the need for services to support current policy and business. Humphrey drew attention to this issue through the Information Services Group of the Library Association, and a debate followed, but it was not conclusive and the issue was to resurface some years later.[26]

Pantry's paper on special libraries at an Aslib conference in 1997 encapsulated many of the points that she had made to the Committee of Departmental Librarians (CDL) some years previously and contributed to the Circle of State Librarians' journal, and which remained under discussion into the new century.[27] Government libraries along with the special library sector were being affected by their declining ability to attract and reward good candidates with a combination of worthwhile salaries, flexible working patterns and making available opportunities such as sabbaticals. The range of abilities required to identify, present and validate information, coupled with marketing, technological, training and political skills, was an increasingly difficult combination to attract and retain. CDL began to address a number of the most pressing issues, such as the need to develop new competencies which were presented in May 1998 (and were in use until updated competencies were adopted in October 2005 to align with the Professional Skills in Government initiative).[28]

Hunter reported on the results of a survey of career patterns of librarians in the Ministry of Defence that she had undertaken in 1992.[29] This was a comprehensive examination of 73 staff, covering their career choices, qualifications, mobility, job satisfaction and future career plans. In retrospect the additional comments made by respondents have considerable interest, particularly their concerns about future career opportunities and patterns, remuneration, promotion and reward, and issues about civil service perceptions. Having commented on training and development opportunities for government librarians in 1991, Burge took Hunter's pilot work at MOD forward by compiling a more comprehensive volume that surveyed the whole Librarian Class.[30]

As noted at other points in this review, there were concerns that the growth of end-user access and the internet would lead departments to conclude that they could reduce the number of librarians employed. Allen argued at the 1996 Online meeting that other roles were emerging, notably that of trainer to the end-user as disintermediation became more widespread.[31] Whilst agreeing with Allen's premise, Griffiths argued at the following year's meeting that there were signs of information professionals repositioning themselves by undertaking work of higher value that could not be undertaken by automated systems or by end-users at their computers.[32] By the 1999 Online conference there was sufficient experience at the Home Office for him to present a case study of the effect of providing access to the world wide web, and of the changes in the way that Units within the Office published information.[33]

Earlier in this chapter it was noted that the trend to evidence-based policy making began in the healthcare libraries sector and was then taken up by the mainstream. Similarly, the search for measures of activity and effectiveness other than pure transaction counting began in the healthcare sector. Marshall presented work based on her work in Canada and the United States by invitation of the British Library in March 1993, demonstrating a methodology which measured the impact of library services rather than the volume of transactions.[34] A study in the Canadian financial sector showed 84% of 299 respondents saying that information contributed to better informed decision-making, and 97% of 208 returns among the American physicians saying that the information provided in the survey improved the quality of decision-making. Following this the British Library Research and Development Department commissioned sector studies to test the methodology, including one in the government libraries sector. Although it focused on information use rather than library use, the study was carried out by library and information consultants (TFPL) and involved three government departments. The results were complex and informative, with the recommendations of the research including the further development of Marshall's methodology, further study of the decision-making process in government departments, and the development of toolkits.[35] Government information and library services were recommended to develop structured networks of internal resources, to develop the role of information and library professionals to include facilitation, advice, and the assessment of needs and information resources, and to structure themselves to support decision-making processes. A related study by Grieves is useful in highlighting the differences between the decision-making process in government in the 1990s and those in five other sectors surveyed as part of the BLR&DD study, and for putting the results of the Winterman study in context.[36]

Government librarians in the wider arena

During the 1990s government librarians became involved in a wide range of activities beyond the management of departmental libraries themselves. One particular development, the Knowledge Network, is discussed below, but librarians were adept at identifying broader initiatives in which they could become involved, and where they could make the case for the involvement of information professionals.

In 1996 the Government published its white paper on training and development for civil servants.[37] Its ministerial foreword, by the then Chancellor of the Duchy of Lancaster, Roger Freeman, summarized the message of the paper by saying:

> This white paper looks to departments and agencies to provide the support, where it is needed, so you can develop a greater professionalism in carrying out your work, and a wider knowledge and awareness of your work area. In return, you are expected to commit yourself to a programme of continuous development.

Librarians could see their obvious role in supporting this objective, and at the November 1996 conference of the Circle of State Librarians the Chancellor gave the keynote address.[38] He emphasized the need to set the day's proceedings in the context of the development and training programme. The skills and awareness thread of the white paper considered the role of specialists (section 3.2), saying: '... action is needed in pursuit of ... a much greater emphasis on the use and development of civil servants with specialist expertise in, of in-depth experience of, particular areas, complementing more generalist management skills – and, conversely, on the flexible use of specialists in wider roles'. In the Minister's words:

> you have particular expertise to offer departments and agencies, both about how to acquire the right sort of information and how to ensure that the right people have access to it. This is critical to the effective operation of our organizations. We must all look at how we can best benefit from this type of expertise across departments and agencies.

Whilst the outcomes in departmental terms were not perhaps as instantaneous and enthusiastic as librarians might have wished, occasions such as this marked the growing profile of librarianship and its increased visibility at Ministerial and senior levels.

By the end of the decade, government librarians were involved in a wide range of information-related work, and in the development of knowledge management strategies in a number of departments and agencies (which would mostly come to fruition in the following quinquennium – see for example Cotterill and Chisholm's description of work at the Department of Trade and Industry).[39]

Information superhighways, the Knowledge Network, intranets and the internet

In 1994 Kable, the public sector informatics research and publishing organization, issued *Wired Whitehall 1999*, which described a fictitious future state of affairs in government information technology and systems, projected from the policies in force at the time of writing (at the original suggestion of Antony Jay, one of the authors of *Yes, Minister,* and with the sponsorship of BT, Hoskyns and Ernst & Young).[40] The report identified key issues that might need to be addressed in the creation of an information society at the turn of the millennium. It caught the imagination of many at the time and it was a focus of discussion on the potential role of librarians and other information specialists, as were three official papers setting out the potential of the internet – the information superhighway as it was often referred to at the time. CCTA (which originally stood for the Central Computing and Telecommunications Agency, although by this time it was known only by its initials, followed by the strapline 'The Government Centre for Information Systems') issued two reports, one in 1994 – *Information super-highways: opportunities for public sector applications in the UK: a government consultative report* – and *Information superhighways* in 1995.[41] The second report included a report from several COGs (Collaborative Open Groups) which had been set up by CCTA to stimulate discussion of significant issues concerning the information superhighway and its use by UK government. Among these was a Library COG, newly formed in 1995, which had identified several issues of concern to libraries including cooperation, resource-sharing, promotion and marketing, and the increasing scope and availability of information – although at this stage the latter point was welcomed for the ability to serve remote patrons with a range of up-to-date, accurate and authoritative content, without the thought (discussed above) that patrons might opt for self-service when the sheer volume of available content became too tempting to leave to the librarians as intermediaries.

The issues identified as having particular relevance in the context of CCTA's work were intellectual property and copyright; the 'information divide' between the information rich and poor; network literacy, and following from this through the concept then known in the United States as 'civic networking' to the responsibility for making government information available in electronic form; and the opening up of networks such as SuperJANET to secure the widest possible participation in the development of those systems that were already capable of becoming true 'information superhighways'. The reader may care to reflect on whether this list would be greatly different after the passage of more than a decade. The third paper, *Our information age*, set out the vision of the 1997 Labour government for the use of electronic information in society, as well as setting ambitious targets for the adoption of electronic technology by government for achievement by 2002 (for the first tranche) and 2008 (later shortened to 2005).[42] Although government librarians working within libraries were perhaps more excited by their prospective involvement than by their actual participation, those librarians working on websites and in policy areas found themselves involved and sometimes responsible for the development of services that would go towards meeting the targets. Some indeed found themselves involved in other related initiatives such as the Department of Trade and Industry's work on the development of a knowledge economy, set out in *Our competitive future*.[43] In some departments librarians were involved not only in general websites but in the creation of sites dedicated to particular government initiatives or campaigns, such as explaining the introduction of the Crime and Disorder Act.[44]

Modernising government set out an agenda for bringing government up to date.[45] Once again, there was an emphasis on information and information technology, with government librarians being interested in the potential for bringing information as far into the mainstream as technology.

There were various reasons for believing that information would be valued more highly and that librarians would have a role to play in this change. One was the Knowledge Network, which was based in the Cabinet Office in the Office of the e-Envoy and provided a number of applications that allowed groups to organize information resources on an inter-departmental basis. It supported them with the basic facets of knowledge management such as the ability to share and retrieve information on government policies. Thus for the first time it became possible to look for information about policies relating to a single topic which are shared among several departments. (For example, government responsibilities for children's issues are or have been shared by the Department for Education and Skills, the Home Office, the Department of Health, and others.)

Underlying the Knowledge Network was a suite of applications written in Lotus Notes, reflecting their origin in the Department of Health which made extensive use of this software. The original intention was to emulate the use made of information retrieval techniques by the Labour Party in the run-up to the 1997 election; as described by Joe McCrea, the special adviser who piloted its creation in a 2002 interview, it was

> a system which would deliver the modern, rapid and accurate service that I and Frank [Dobson, the then Minister of Health] needed. It was called MINT (Ministerial Information Networking Technology). It brought together in one electronic space all the key information I needed (press releases, speeches, policy briefings, media transcripts, rebuttals, parliamentary transcripts etc). It was available 24/7 and offline via laptop.[46]

In several departments key roles were taken by librarians, who were credited with the ability to identify relevant information, manage its lifecycle and ensure its authenticity, and to organize it so that key users such as Ministers and senior policy-makers could both find it and rely on it. McCrea outlined the rationale of MINT in a speech to the 1999 Circle of State Librarians conference whilst Parry brought the story up to date in 2000.[47]

Websites and intranets
Government librarians applied their skills to other emerging areas of information

management, notably the management of their departments' websites and later their intranets. Their interest in the use of the internet as an information resource, which became far stronger with the development of the world wide web, led to an interest in the creation and editing of websites and pages. The CCTA encouraged departments to make use of the new medium from an early date (in for example the *Information superhighway* documents cited earlier in this section) and provided a dial-up service, GT-Net, which made use of the Government Telecommunication Network (GTN) to provide departments with simple access. This service was later extended to provide hosting facilities for departmental websites, with a basic service that was initially offered free of charge on the assumption that websites would only need updating once every six months! Bishop reported on a survey of CDL members undertaken in 1997 by the committee's IT Working Group, which already reported that ten departments had migrated from the CCTA service to their own server.[48] The drive to expand government websites was accelerated by the work programme of the Labour government following the 1997 election, and the Government Direct programme with its initiative of placing guidelines, regulations and forms on departmental websites.

Bishop's survey showed greater involvement of librarians in external website management than in intranets, where only one department reported that an information professional was involved in site architecture, and two others that senior library staff members were on the intranet project team. Resourcing was seen as a key difficulty, with other services being reduced or cancelled in some cases to provide additional staff for work on the internet. It was already apparent that the use of external consultants was growing in this area, and that the work of the webmaster was becoming aligned with corporate strategy and marketing, reflecting the growing recognition that a web presence was an important element of the department's image. A follow-up survey in 1999 showed that the use of the internet for browsing had rapidly become established in the intervening two years, with the introduction of the Government Secure Intranet (GSI) being credited with changing departmental attitudes to browsing.[49] But one result of this was the growth of end-user searching, which had implications for the future role of departmental librarians. By 1999, all departments had websites, and 68% reported no library input to web publishing, even indexing and information management being managed by other staff such as IT managers. The authors of the 1999 survey noted the contrast between the academic sector, where websites were often the responsibility of the library, and government, where the marketing and publicity function generally had control. The greatest change was in the development of intranets, which were present in 90% of the respondents' departments compared with only 35% two years earlier. Libraries had a far greater role in managing intranets, being responsible for them in around one-third of the sample. The authors also looked at the early growth of knowledge management, and the role of intranets, and considered information retrieval and the role of metadata in making this more effective. They indicated a number of likely developments, particularly improved interoperability, the promotion of metadata standards, and a pan-government thesaurus. They also proposed that library and information professionals would need to look beyond their traditional boundaries, or risk marginalization: and that they should market their skills whilst responding to the growth in demand for end-user searching.

The wider picture in the development of government websites, including those in which librarians were involved, is reflected in a number of documents, of which perhaps the most useful is *Government on the web*, though even this would soon seem surprisingly dated in places ('an active website [is one where] static inform-ation and the agency's home page are regularly reviewed, revised and re-presented once every six months at least' – extract from the executive summary).[50]

Librarians involved themselves with the web for a number of reasons but their motives were generally associated with the view (embodied in the open government initiative originally contained in the so-called Croham Directive of 1977) that information of public interest should be made easily available, an idea that underlay the 1996 House of Lords Science and Technology Committee paper *Information society*, which included a call for all such documents to be made available in electronic format free of charge.[51] This and other aspects of electronic publication were considered by Lampard, who also drew attention to developments such as the MAFF helpline (which was managed by a librarian) and fax-based services such as HSE's Autofax and the ONS's Statfax.[52] A further white paper on open government was issued in 1993, with a new voluntary code of practice for departments following in 1994 (revised in 1997) which remained in place until the Freedom of Information Act 2000 came into force in January 2005.[53]

The Public Record Office recognized early on that the archiving of websites was neither systematic nor thorough, and came to an agreement with the providers of the Internet Archive ('Wayback Machine') website to download and archive a number of key government department and agency sites. It became possible for researchers to access these either through the Internet Archive site itself or through the relevant page of the National Archives website.[54] Nevertheless, until the electronic record was far more complete – for all types of paper, not just websites – it would remain a problem for researchers discovering which department was responsible for a particular subject at a given date, and therefore where to look for departmental publications on that topic.

At the end of the review period, CDL members were formulating plans for services to the entire GSI community and were planning the creation of a electronic library for government (ELG). Latham describes CDL's requirements for the site, and provides further information about librarians' work on depart-mental intranets and on the creation of a GSI community of interest as well as the ELG itself.[55]

Departmental changes and library services

There were inevitably changes in the structure of government departments during the review period. The Department of Trade and Industry saw a number of minor changes that adjusted its responsibilities, or moved various functions into agencies.

Its library services made the necessary changes, so that for example the DTI continued to provide a service in the newly separated Department of National Heritage following the 1992 election, and absorbed the library and information requirements of the former Energy department.

One of the greatest changes made during the Conservative administration was the restructuring of departments which took place in July 1995. This included the dissolution of the Employment Department and the consolidation of the majority of its work into the Department for Education (to become the Department for Education and Employment), requiring the merger of the departmental library to become the DfEE Library.

Under the Labour administration the manner of change became somewhat different. Rather than departments being abolished or merged, responsibilities were transferred from one department to another, so that both remained in business but with different responsibilities. This gave librarians a rather different issue to deal with, namely ensuring that relevant publications were available in the library of the department assuming responsibility whilst also maintaining a complete archive of departmental publications in the exporting department. As noted earlier, this leaves the issue of recording the policy responsibilities of each department at a given time, so that researchers know where the relevant departmental publications can be found.

New libraries and services were however created. Even though the Department of Health and Social Security had been divided into two departments in July 1988, the DSS continued to receive its library service from the DH until well into the 1990s, and the two also shared a legal service and legal library. The services were eventually divided in 1996 when a separate Department of Social Security Library was launched in March as the first new central government departmental library in a decade.[56] Across London, the Office of National Statistics was formed in April 1996 by combining the Central Statistical Office and the Office for Population, Censuses and Surveys, bringing together their respective library services.[57] A new library was created in Pimlico, based on the OPCS collection and the CSO library continued in Newport, Gwent. The new combined library services opened in January 1997.

Changes also took place in the agencies that supported central departments, or had been created from them as part of 'Next Steps'. The combination in 1996 of the National Rivers Authority, Her Majesty's Inspector of Pollution, and the Waste Authority into the Environment Agency created the scope for the creation of a new library service.[58]

The devolved legislatures in Wales and Scotland came into being at the end of the survey period, requiring the development of the Welsh and Scottish Office libraries into more comprehensive services to support the new executive structures that supported them; these changes were briefly described by Coburn.[59] In Northern Ireland a professional government library service was developed during the early part of the 1990s, and Porter (who played a major role in their development) set out the role of government libraries as well as describing the position in Northern Ireland.[60]

Conclusion

The period 1991–2000 was one of considerable upheaval, and many central government librarians undoubtedly felt threatened by the events and developments that took place at that time. With the benefit of hindsight, the picture is more optimistic than would have seemed likely. By the end of the decade, librarians had become involved in a wide range of information-related activities across their departments. They had improved their management skills, partly because of the way that they had reacted to the market testing initiatives and had become more aware of both cost and value. The long-recognized skill of many librarians in dealing with specialist technical issues as systems managers had paid a rich dividend by opening up opportunities in the field of intranets and departmental internet sites. Librarians had moved into mainstream policy areas with activities such as their contribution to the Knowledge Network and the developing work on the Policy Hub and the beginnings of evidence-based work in central government.

The account of the next five years will show how many of these opportunities were further consolidated, and how the pace of change showed no sign of slowing.

Notes

1   J. H. Wormald, 'Government and public authority libraries' in *British librarianship and information work 1976–1980*, ed. L. J. Taylor. London: Library Association, 1983, v. 2, pp. 1–9; J. H. Wormald and Suzanne Burge, 'Government libraries' in *British librarianship and information work 1981–1985*, ed. David W. Bromley and Angela M. Allott. London: Library Association, 1988, v. 2, pp. 1–8; Efficiency Unit, *Improving management in government: the next steps*. London: HMSO, 1988. Also known as the Ibbs report after its principal author Sir Robin Ibbs. The Next steps initiative is conveniently summarized in *The evolution of the United Kingdom civil service 1848–1997*, section 6, available at:
     <http://www.civilservice.gov.uk/the_uk_civil_service/history_of_the_civil_service/evol ution_of_the_civil_service/06.asp> (accessed 21/1/06); Sheila Pantry, 1993, 'Government information services and libraries' in *British librarianship and information work, 1986–1990*, ed. David W. Bromley and Angela M. Allott. London, Library Association, 1993, v. 2, pp. 1–9.
2   *The citizen's charter: raising the standard.* London: HMSO, 1991. (Cm. 1599); John Major, quoted in
     <http://news.bbc.co.uk/onthisday/hi/dates/stories/july/22/newsid_2516000/2516139.stm > (accessed 21/1/06).
3   Ann Lawes, 'Contracting out', *New library world* **95** (4), 1994, 8–12.
4   Suzanne Burge, 'Much pain, little gain: privatisation and UK government libraries', *Inspel* **33** (1), 1999, 10–19. Paper presented at the 64th IFLA Conference, Amsterdam, August 1998 and available at <http://www.ifla.org/IV/ifla64/187-139e.htm> (accessed 21/1/06).
5   Ian Snowley, 'Managing the market', *Serials* **7** (2), 1994, 129–32.

6 Diana Grimwood-Jones, 'Contracting out in the public sector: issues and implications', *Library management* **17** (1), 1996, 11–17; Ann Lawes, 'Contracting out library and information services', *Inform* March 1994, 2–3; Lewis Foreman (ed.), *Market testing and after: effective library and information services in the '90s.* London: HMSO, 1994; *Contracting out: the information business, key issue '91 ; based on the papers given at a one day conference on contracting out of library and information services ..., held at Hatfield Polytechnic on 11th September 1991.* Hatfield: University of Hertfordshire Press, 1992; Maggie Ashcroft (ed.), *Piloting competitive tendering: proceedings of a seminar held in Stamford, Lincolnshire on 27 October 1993.* Stamford: Capital Planning Information, 1993; Office of Public Service and Science, *The Government's guide to market testing.* London: HMSO, 1993; Anne Woodsworth and James F. Williams (eds.), *Managing the economics of owning, leasing and contracting out information services.* Aldershot: Ashgate, 1993; Sheila Pantry and Peter Griffiths, *The complete guide to preparing and implementing service level agreements.* 2nd ed. London: Library Association, 2001.

7 Burge, 'Much pain, little gain'.

8 Andrew Lapworth, 'Partnerships & market planning: a case study of the DTI's Export Market Information Centre (EMIC)' in *Who needs libraries? Challenges for the 90s*, ed. Lewis Foreman. London: HMSO, 1995, pp. 29–37 (special issue of *State librarian* **42** (2), 1994/95); Liz MacLachlan, 'Government libraries after market testing: the way forward' in *Who needs libraries?* ed. Foreman, pp. 21–7.

9 Cabinet Office, *Service first: the new charter programme.* London: Cabinet Office, 1998.

10 For a full chronology and list of key publications see <http://www.cochrane.org/docs/cchronol.htm> (accessed 21/1/06).

11 Michael Carmel, 'Thriving amid chaos: health care and library services in the 1990s', *New library world* **96** (3), 1995, 28–34; Mary Feeney (ed.), *Health care information in the UK: report of a seminar held on 1st July 1992 at the King's Fund Centre, London.* London: British Library, 1992 (British Library R & D report; 6089). Chaired by Baroness Cumberlege.

12 *Managing the knowledge base of healthcare: report of a seminar held on 22nd October 1993 at the King's Fund Centre, London chaired by Baroness Cumberlege.* London: British Library, 1993 (British Library R & D report; 6133); Alan Beevers, *Managing the knowledge base of healthcare: follow up survey.* London: British Library, 1995 (R & D report; 6182).

13 For example A. Booth and B. Madge, 'Finding the evidence' in *Evidence-based healthcare: a practical guide for therapists*, ed. Tracy J. Bury, Judy M. Mead. London: Butterworth Heinemann, 1998; A. Booth and A. J. O'Rourke, 'Searching for evidence: principles and practice', *Evidence-based medicine* **4** (5), 1999, 133–6.

14 Sue Westcott, 'Modernising government: the cataloguing and indexing contribution', *Catalogue & index* 138, winter 2000, 1–3; Sue Westcott, *Linking up the knowledge: report to Centre for Management and Policy studies for the Knowledge Pools Resource Centre project.* London: [Committee of Departmental Librarians?], 2000.

15 Karen Lewis, 'When is a resource centre not a resource centre', *State librarian* summer/autumn 2001, 25–30. Also available at <http://www.nglis.org.uk/summer-autumn2001.pdf> (accessed 21/1/06).

16 MacLachlan, 'Government libraries after market testing'.

17 See for example Janet Driels, editorial on outbedding of librarians, *State librarian* **34** (3), Nov. 1986, 32.

18 Peter Griffiths, 'Creating communication: blending two traditions of information at the UK Home Office', *Electronic library* **15** (3), 1997, 215–20.

19 Martin Callow, 'Equilibrium at the Home Office', *Vine* 82, 1991, 26–8; Martin Callow, 'OPAC at the Home Office using Equilibrium', *Vine* 84, 1991, 4–10; John Scott Cree, 'Unicorn at the Department of Health', *Catalogue & index* 119, spring 1996, 6–8; John Scott Cree, 'Implementing UNICORN at the UK Department of Health', *Program* **30** (3), 1996, 279–84.

20 D. Allum, 'Getting the best out of automated retrieval' in *Computers in libraries international 1991: proceedings of the Fifth Annual Conference on Computers in Libraries, London, February 1991*. Westport; London: Meckler, 1991, pp. 120–3; John Scott Cree, 'The development of automated systems in government libraries in the UK', *State librarian* autumn 1998, 23–40.

21 Murray Parkin, 'MODMAP: the automation of the UK Ministry of Defence Map Library card catalogue', *European research libraries cooperation* **3** (1), 1993, 67–75.

22 John Scott Cree, 'Data conversion and migration at the libraries of the Home Office and the Department of the Environment', *Catalogue & index* 126, winter 1997, 1–5.

23 Cabinet Office, *The future management of Crown copyright*. London: HMSO, 1999 (Cm 4300); Cabinet Office, *Crown copyright in the information age*. London: HMSO, 1998 (Cm 3819).

24 *Government information locator service*. Washington, D.C.: U.S.G.P.O.: <http://www.access.gpo.gov/su_docs/gils/> (accessed 21/1/06): for a history of GILS see <http://www.access.gpo.gov/su_docs/gils/gils-eval/html/ch2.html> which forms part of an evaluation report of the service: <http://www.infosource.gc.ca (accessed 21/1/06).

25 The prototype and production versions can be seen on the Internet Archive by following links from <http://web.archive.org/web/> and searching <http://www.hmso.gov.uk/inforoute/>; and later <http://web.archive.org/web/> searching <http://www.inforoute.hmso.gov.uk>.

26 Fran Humphrey, 'Fragmentation of government sources of information', *Refer* **10** (3), 1994, 14–15.

27 Sheila Pantry, 'Whither the information profession? Challenges and opportunities: the cultivation of information professionals for the new millennium', *Aslib proceedings* **49** (6), 1997, 170–2; Sheila Pantry, 'Government library and information service: where is it going?', *State librarian* **39** (2), 1991, 23.

28 Committee of Departmental Librarians, 'CDL Compentencies Framework, by the CDL Competencies Working Group', *State librarian* summer 1999, 55–60.

29 Catriona Hunter, 'Career patterns of librarians in government libraries', *Librarian career development* **4** (1), 1996, 5–12.

30 Suzanne Burge, 'Training in government libraries', *Government libraries journal* **1** (3), 1991, 6–9; Suzanne Burge, *Broken down by grade and sex: the career development of government librarians*. London: Library Association Government Libraries Group, 1995.

31 G. Allen, 'Disintermediation: a disaster or discipline?' in *Online Information 96*, ed. D. I. Raitt. Oxford: Learned Information, 1996, pp. 29–32.

32 Peter Griffiths, 'When push comes to shove: reintermediation, or the welcome return of the information professional' in *Online Information 97: proceedings, 21st International Online Information Meeting*. Oxford: Learned Information, 1997.

33 Peter Griffiths, 'End-users, gurus and information experts: business roles of an LIS in supporting web users on an office network' in *Online Information 99: proceedings, 23rd International Online Information Meeting.* Oxford: Learned Information, 1999.

34 J. Marshall, *The impact of information services on decision making: some lesions from the financial and healthcare sectors.* London: British Library Research and Development Department, 1993. (Information policy briefings; 1).

35 Vivienne Winterman, Christine Smith, Angela Abell, 'Impact of information on decision making in government departments', *Library management* **19** (2), 1998, 110–32.

36 Maureen Grieves, 'The impact of information use on decision making: studies in five sectors – introduction, summary and conclusions', *Library management* **19** (2), 1998, 78–85.

37 Chancellor of the Duchy of Lancaster, *Development and training for civil servants: a framework for action.* London, HMSO, 1996.

38 Chancellor of the Duchy of Lancaster, 'Keynote address by the Chancellor of the Duchy at the Circle of State Librarians Conference, Monday 4 November, 1996'. Unpublished.

39 Alison Cotterill and Alex Chisholm, 'A very civil approach to DTI's future', *Library Association record* **101** (10), 1999, 588.

40 Michael Cross *et al.*, *Wired Whitehall 1999.* London: Kable, 1994. See the invitation to potential contributors from William Heath, then at Kable, which remains in the archive at BUBL: <http://www.bubl.ac.uk///archive/subject/politics/whiteh13.htm> (accessed 21/1/06).

41 CCTA, *Information superhighways: opportunities for public sector applications in the UK: a government consultative report.* London: CCTA, 1994; CCTA, *CCTA report on information superhighways.* Norwich: CCTA, 1995.

42 Cabinet Office, *Our information age: the Government's vision.* London: Stationery Office, 1998.

43 Department of Trade and Industry, *Our competitive future: building the knowledge driven economy.* London: DTI, 1998. Available at <http://www.dti.gov.uk/comp/competitive/main.htm> (accessed 21/1/06).

44 Peter Griffiths *et al.*, 'Getting in on the Act: the Home Office, the Crime & Disorder Act and the internet', *Computers and law* **9** (4), 1998, 10–11.

45 Cabinet Office, *Modernising government.* London: HMSO, 1999 (Cm 4310). Available at <http://archive.cabinetoffice.gov.uk/moderngov/download/modgov.pdf> (accessed 21/1/06).

46 Helen Baxter, *Interview with Joe McCrea – Government Innovator of the Year 2002.* Knowledgeboard, 2002. Available at <http://www.knowledgeboard.com/cgi-bin/item.cgi?id=2098> (accessed 9/2/06).

47 Joe McCrea, 'Speech given to the annual conference of the Circle of State Librarians February 1999', *State librarian* summer 1999, 9–13; Jan Parry, 'CHIP (the Comprehensive Health Information Project)', *State librarian* summer 2000, 58–62.

48 Rebecca Bishop, 'Internet in CDL library and information services', *State librarian* summer 1999, 41–52.

49 Maewyn Cumming and Lucy Cuthbertson, 'Wired in Whitehall: a survey of internet and intranet use in government', *Aslib proceedings* **53** (1), 2001, 32–8.

50 National Audit Office, *Government on the web: a report by the Comptroller and Auditor General.* London: Stationery Office, 1999 (HC 87, session 1999–2000). Available at <http://www.nao.org.uk/publications/nao_reports/990087es.pdf> (accessed 21/1/06).

51 House of Lords, Science and Technology Committee (1996). *Agenda for action in the UK: information society, 5th report.* London: HMSO, 1996 (HL 77, session 1996–97).

52 Liz Lampard, 'Government departments: developments in the delivery of information', *Business information review* **14** (4), 1997, 179–83.

53 Cabinet Office, *Open government: white paper.* London: HMSO, 1993 (Cm 2290); Duchy of Lancaster, *Open government: code of practice on access to government information: guidance on interpretation.* London: The Duchy, 1994. 2nd ed., 1997. The 1997 edition, marked 'second edition (1997)', scanned by agreement with the Department for Constitutional Affairs, is available at the Campaign for Freedom of Information website: <http://www.cfoi.org.uk/pdf/copguidance.pdf> (accessed 21/1/06). Electronic transcription also available on DCA website: <http://www.dca.gov.uk/foi/ogcode981.htm> (accessed 21/1/06).

54 Internet Archive: <http://www.archive.org> (accessed 21/1/06); <http://www.nationalarchives.gov.uk/preservation/webarchive/> (accessed 21/1/06).

55 Stephen Latham, 'Intranets: a UK government perspective', *66th IFLA Council and General Conference, Jerusalem, Israel, 13–18 August, 2000.* Paper available at <www.ifla.org/IV/ifla66/papers/002-131e.htm> (accessed 21/1/06).

56 Heicke Dieckmann and Graham Monk, 'Managing Information at the Department of Social Security', *Managing information* **4** (3), 1997, 20–2; Shaunagh Robertson, 'A new service for the DSS', *Library Association record* **98** (5), 1996, 258–9; Shaunagh Robertson, 'The DSS launches a new information and library service', *Assignation* **13** (4), 1996, 14–18.

57 John Birch *et al.*, 'Managing Information discovers official statistics', *Managing information* **4** (4), 1997, 27–30; John Birch, 'Government statistics? The answer's at NSILS!', *Assignation* **14** (3), 1997, 24–7.

58 Graham Coult, 'Managing Information @ the Environment Agency', *Managing information* **6** (3), 1999, 24–6.

59 Andrew Coburn, 'Standing Committee on Official Publications: report on May meeting', *Catalogue & index* 135, spring 2000, 3–4.

60 Kirby Porter, 'Libraries and the management of information in the Northern Ireland Civil Service', *An leabharlann* **11** (1), 1994, 5–11.

8

Learned, professional and independent libraries

Mary Nixon

Methodology

Initial attempts to gather information about the libraries of learned societies and professional associations in the 1990s suggested that the '90s might well be the new 1960s – those who were there at the time seemed to remember remarkably little about them. A literature search revealed, as Peter Hoey found in 1991, 'if sorely pressed staff have found time to publish in open literature, this has tended to be in in-house journals or in those with small circulations which are not covered by abstracting services'.[1] To augment the available articles, a questionnaire was sent to 150 learned, professional and independent libraries, of which some 20% responded.[2] This comparatively small and self-selected sample was extremely varied: staff numbers ranged from one to over 60, date of foundation (where known) from the early sixteenth century to 1998, subject matter from engineering to theology and marketing to dogs. It included libraries of learned societies, professional organizations, an abbey, and Inns of Court as well as some independent libraries. Where percentages are given in the following article, they are based on the results of this survey, with the proviso that they may illustrate trends but cannot be treated as in any way statistically accurate. Where no bibliographic reference is cited, information has come from the answers to the questionnaire.

Background

The 1990s began in recession and ended in the steadiest economic period for decades, and the situation of these libraries to some extent reflects this. Learned, professional and independent libraries are largely dependent on the subscriptions of their members and several were in difficulties in the early '90s; later in the decade, however, the situation appears to have improved in libraries as in the wider world. Other external circumstances also had an effect: at the beginning of the decade the publication of the second edition of BS5454 probably provided the impetus for a number of new storage areas and strong rooms for historic collections and archives,[3] and the onward march of information technology both increased costs and improved services in all but a handful of these libraries. The introduction of automated library management systems and the retrospective conversion of library catalogues occupied an inordinate amount of staff time over the period.

Activities

Bernard Nurse, in an article on the archives of learned societies, drew a possible distinction between learned and professional libraries:

> Learned societies are characterized by their purpose, which is to promote understanding of a particular branch of knowledge ... In theory they can be distinguished from ... professional associations, which exist primarily to promote the interests of their members. [4]

This description of the Library of the Institute of Chartered Accountants, helpfully provided in their answer to the questionnaire (see above), gives a picture of a large professional library in the 1990s, which demonstrates Nurse's thesis:

> Throughout this period ... the Library's role was to collect extensively all publications on UK accounting, auditing and taxation; international and English language speaking countries accountancy publications are also acquired, though not so comprehensively. The print and digital collection extends to every subject that is required by a chartered accountant in his or her work so that the full range of their business activities can be supported.
>
> Though primarily in the UK, our users are spread throughout the world (about 16,000 work abroad) so the service is designed to deliver information remotely, using a range of channels.

However, as Nurse suggests, the distinction between learned and professional libraries is not always clear-cut in practice, as the following list of facilities offered by the Royal Society of Chemistry shows:

- expert staff
- enquiry service (technical, business, patent and bibliographic)
- web, online and CD-ROM data and literature searching facilities
- document delivery
- largest collection of information in the UK specifically in the field of chemistry
- 700 current periodical titles, 20,000 monographs and reference books
- classical 16th–19th century literary works on alchemy and chemistry
- portraits and photographs of distinguished chemists
- society archives research service and artefacts collection
- open access reference and reading room in central London. [5]

The Library of the Inner Temple, too, served both functions:

> Apart from its legal collections, which cover the UK and the Commonwealth, it houses a

large rare books collection encompassing many subjects as well as law, and a major collection of manuscripts (legal and non-legal) dating from the 12th to the 20th century. This is regularly used by scholars based in the UK and around the world.

One of the libraries in the sample, the Advocates Library, had the privilege of legal deposit of law materials in Scotland, which again suggests a mingling of the learned and the professional. In fact, of the libraries in the sample, over two-thirds had responsibility for archives and a number had a professional archivist on the staff. Several were also custodians of portraits, artefacts, photographs and other materials, although only the Library and Museum of the United Grand Lodge actually included the museum function in its title. The collections of the English Heritage Library range from deeds of EH's properties to training videos. Perhaps surprisingly, only the Institute of Actuaries and Faculty of Actuaries Library admitted to responsibility for records management; seminars were organized by the Goethe Institut Library and the Médiathèque of the Institut Français du Royaume Uni, and the staff of Westminster Abbey Library undertook editorial work on the Abbey's publications, including concert programme notes and publicity material. The Library and Information Services of the Royal Society (whose remit included modern and rare books, archives and manuscripts, portraits, artefacts, and current information services) was also responsible for managing the elections to Fellowship of the Society until the late '90s. The Information Services of the Royal College of Obstetricians and Gynaecologists included the library, archives, museum and college website, while the Inner Temple Library staff included the network administrator for the entire organization, having been the first department to have a website. The Institute of Chartered Accountants Library was also ahead of the game when it came to IT, having introduced the internet to the organization and seconded a member of staff to build the Institute's first website.

Arrivals, departures, changes and moves
While many of these libraries had existed for centuries, new ones continued to be founded in response to new needs; even membership organizations may succumb to external pressure to create specialist information centres, such as the 'international canine resource centre' of the Kennel Club, founded 1986.[6] In 1991 an appeal was launched to establish a specialist housing library, the Harry Simpson Memorial Library, to commemorate the former Director of Housing at the GLC and first Director General of the Northern Ireland Housing Executive.[7] This opened in 1998, the year in which the Institute of Direct Marketing set up its Knowledge Centre.

On the other hand, the library of the Royal Commonwealth Society was threatened with dispersal until saved by a gift of £3 million and transferred to a safe new home at the University of Cambridge Library.[8] Sion College Library was split up, its pre-1851 works going to Lambeth Palace Library, while post-1850 material went to King's College London.[9] Two other libraries that were under threat in the early 1990s were the Royal Asiatic Society Library, whose librarian ruefully wrote that 'Its strength, and sometimes its weakness, is that it has always been entirely independent of outside sources of money',[10] and the Chatham House Library of the Royal Institute of International Affairs, whose pre-1950 collections were transferred to the British Library of Political and Economic Science at the LSE with the assistance of the Burton tailoring family.[11]

In an ecumenical move, the Catholic Central Library was rehoused at the Anglican-owned St Pancras Church House,[12] while BLISS, long subsumed into the British Library, became one of the first collections to move into its new building – a move that was not without its detractors.[13] The Women Artists' Slide Library changed its name to the Women's Art Library and moved from its accommodation in Fulham Palace to a temporary home in Central St Martin's College.[14] The Lindley Library of the Royal Horticultural Society was threatened with a move to the Society's Wisley site in 1995, but a prolonged and vociferous campaign ensured that the projected move did not go ahead.[15]

Collections

Possibly the largest collection acquired by any of these libraries in the 1990s was that of 35,000 books from Sion College to Lambeth Palace Library, which also acquired a not insubstantial collection from the Industrial Christian Fellowship. The archives of the GMB union and its precursors were given to the Working Class Movement Library, and the Institut Français received a donation of video films and documentaries from the French Foreign Ministry. The Geological Society acquired two large map collections from BP in 1998 and RTZ in 1999, while the Women's Art Library was presented with 5,000 files on European women artists by Danish Cultural Information Centre.[16] The Royal Botanic Gardens Kew acquired the Michael Hoog collection of *Tulipa* drawings by Mary Grierson at auction in 1992 and in 1994 a printer's proof set of Sir Joseph Banks's *Florilegium*, a massive work that had to wait 150 years for publication. At the British Geological Survey, regional offices in Aberystwyth, London and Newcastle closed and their library stock was transferred to the remaining libraries in Keyworth and Edinburgh, while at English Heritage the Library was amalgamated with libraries formerly held by the Department of National Heritage's Conservation Unit and the London Division of the Conservation Department of English Heritage, doubling the size of the library. The resultant duplication allowed the library to keep two copies of many items, one for reference and one for loan.

Of the libraries that reduced their collections, the hardest hit was Chatham House, where serious retrenchment led to the relinquishing of UN deposit library and European Documentation Centre status. Two deposited collections, those of the Avicultural Society and the British Herpetological Society, were removed from the Linnean Society Library. The Inner Temple and Institution of Electrical Engineers Libraries both rationalized their collections, the former by selling some non-legal and foreign material, the latter by disposing of runs of journals in peripheral subjects. The Royal Asiatic Society sold the Farquhar Collection on natural history, collected by an early nineteenth-century Resident of Malacca, which was returned to Singapore in 1994 and was given to the Singapore History Museum in 1996.[17] The Linen Hall Library, having sold off a collection of works by Burns in 1994, was forced to buy it back in 1995 because of fears that the Library was ignoring the Scottish heritage of Ulster.[18]

Funding

As mentioned above, most of the libraries under consideration are funded by their members, either directly from subscriptions or through other activities of the parent body, such as publishing or events management. The near collapse of the RIBA Companies, along with a drop in subscriptions, led to serious cuts in staff and services being considered at the British Architectural Library.[19] In the end, the crisis was averted in part through the decision to start charging non-members both for enquiries and access. The National Library for the Blind lost a £100,000 grant in 1991, which forced it for the first time to engage in substantial fundraising. The Institute of Race Relations Library found that prudent management was no help when it lost its funding from the London Boroughs' Grants Scheme on the grounds that it had a contingency fund.[20] The Feminist Library, originally funded by the Greater London Council, was threatened by a rent rise, but saved thanks to a grant from Southwark Borough Council.[21]

Of those libraries that responded to the questionnaire, half reported no change in their funding (apart from inflation), a quarter reported that funding fell in the decade, while for another quarter it rose; of those, the Inner Temple and Lincoln's Inn Libraries received additional funding from their parent bodies, to cover the serious increase in the price of law books. Chetham's Library, Lambeth Palace Library and the Royal Society Library attributed the rise to grants and income for special projects. The Geological Society Library reported some additional income from bequests, though its funding from the Society remained stable. A number of professional libraries began to augment their income by charging non-members for use or members for premium services.

The Library of the Institute of Chartered Accountants in England and Wales is funded by the Chartered Accountants' Trust for Education & Research, one of the Institute's charitable trusts, the Library and Museum of the United Grand Lodge acquired charitable status in 1996, which enabled it to access specific grant funding from its parent body, but the Chartered Institute of Marketing wistfully reported that 'We have had some funds from the CIM Charitable Trust but they do not favour me any more'. The Wiener Library and Lambeth Palace Library were among those with Friends' organizations.

Understandably, many in the sector were keen to obtain external funding; the newly-formed Historic Libraries Forum was not slow to investigate this, holding a conference on 'Alternative sources of library funding'.[22] Not all was plain sailing, however: the Lord Coutanche Library of the Société Jersiaise was one of those whose budget fell in 1990s but could not afford to employ a full-time fundraiser. Several libraries received grants from the Pilgrim Trust and the National Monuments Conservation Trust, the British Library having ceased to offer its own grants for cataloguing and conservation after its move to St Pancras.[23] The Society of Antiquaries Library raised £50,000 from these two plus the Getty and Marc Fitch Funds, while Lambeth Place Library launched an appeal for £180,000 to cover the costs of computerization and the London Library also had an appeal to celebrate its 150th anniversary.[24] The Royal Society Library obtained a private donation of £275,000 for the Raymond and Beverly Sackler Archive Resource, which provided biographical information on Fellows of the Society since its foundation in 1660.[25] The Women's Art Library received funding from the Gulbenkian Foundation and the Arts Council to pay a full-time librarian for a year.

The arrival on the scene of the Heritage Lottery Fund opened up new opportunities. By 1997 5% of applications to the Fund were from archives and special libraries and 5% of its funding was going to them.[26] Early beneficiaries included Chetham's Library (£1.8 million), York Minster, and the National Poetry Library.[27] The Linen Hall Library obtained two grants, the first to purchase an additional building, and the second of £1.8 million for improving facilities, computerization, cataloguing and conservation. The same sum was contributed to a £4 million project for the Lindley Library that included major building works, complete recataloguing and the creation of a digital library; leaving over £2 million to be raised from other sources.[28] Other major cataloguing projects were funded at the Working Class Movement Library and the Society of Genealogists, and the Royal Society of Arts received over £650,000 to 'transform [its] archive into a significant research resource'.[29] The British Architectural Library, while failing to get a large grant, managed to obtain a number of small ones, mainly for purchases for its Drawings Collection.[30]

Buildings

Apart from the major lottery-funded projects mentioned above, two-thirds of the libraries in the sample had undertaken building work in the '90s. At least half of these had new storage for archives, manuscripts, rare books or other valuable materials, the Médiathèque of the Institut Français was refurbished (and reported a subsequent increase in users) and the enlargement and refurbishment of the English Heritage Library included a new strong room, a climate-controlled rare books room and a microforms room. At Lambeth Palace Library, a new manuscripts strong room and reading room were created from the old ones, increasing user spaces, and a new seminar room and conservation studio were also created. The British Dental Association Library acquired a multimedia room and the Zoological Society of London Library an art store. A building was bought and refurbished to provide additional storage for the Advocates' Library, while the Inner Temple Library lost some storage space, an alternative but smaller space being provided elsewhere on the premises. At the Institute of Chartered Accountants additional office space was created within the library's public area, thereby reducing reader places.

The Fawcett Library, the world's first women's library, was threatened but saved by a £4.2 million grant from the Heritage Lottery Fund, which enabled it to move to a new purpose-built building.[31] On the other hand, the British Architectural Library was forced to abandon its ambitious plans to rehouse some of its collections in the Roundhouse, when the Heritage Lottery Fund, initially encouraging, withdrew its support for the plan.[32]

Staff

As mentioned above, the size of the libraries varied considerably, but the majority had a staff of fewer than 10, so even small changes made a considerable difference. At the Royal Asiatic Society, for example, the retirement of one member of staff halved the complement, although the survivor was the first professional librarian in the Society's 150-year history, faced with the task of 'turning what is in many respects a nineteenth-century library into a late-twentieth century or even twenty-first century one'. The Society of Genealogists also appointed its first professional librarian, a mere 80 years after its foundation in 1911.[33] While five libraries in the survey stated that their staff had been reduced – in the case of Chatham House from 15 to 5.5 – three times as many reported an increase. The picture is not always clear; at the Chartered Institute of Marketing Information and Library Service, staffing rose after 1991 and then reduced as a result of redundancies in 1995, while at the Royal Society Library the permanent staff increased by one in 1995 and fell again three years later, when the same post was made redundant, but at the same time two additional temporary staff were engaged in project work. Volunteers were used in half the libraries in the sample, and of those only the Linnean Society and the Royal Society reported a decrease in their numbers over the period. Their contributions included indexing slides in the photographs collection at the British Architectural Library and adding to the Wiener Library's collection of cuttings from the European press, dating back to 1933.[34]

Access and use

Of the sample, four libraries restricted access to their own members, although in the case of the Goethe Institut Library, where charges were introduced in 1999, anyone could join for a modest £20 annual subscription. The Institute of Chartered Accountants and the Royal College of Surgeons of Edinburgh required external users to have a reference from a member, a requirement that was dropped by the Royal Society by 1995. The others were all open to the public, although terms varied: most required an appointment (often on the grounds of lack of reader spaces), some required a letter of introduction. Lambeth Palace Library abandoned its earlier ban on undergraduates but like several others started registering and issuing tickets to readers. Six of the respondents made a charge for external users, as did a number of other libraries, with the charges ranging widely; the British Standards Institution Library charged £25 for half a day in 1997[35] while the British Architectural Library charged £90 a year (half price for students).

Librarians' definitions of 'users' varied according to whether they were looking at visitors, remote users, individuals or instances of use. However, of the survey sample, 5 stated that there had been no change, 6 that user numbers were down, and 17 that they were up. At English Heritage, where the library was opened for the first time to the public, use rose fivefold, at the Royal Botanic Gardens Kew it was up by 50% and at Lambeth Palace Library visitors were up by 30%, despite the fact that use by family historians was much reduced. The Royal Society of Chemistry had 500 enquiries a month, including requests for document delivery in 1991, and 1,200 a month for document delivery alone by 2000.[36] As ever, the picture is far from simple; at the Institution of Electrical Engineers loans and photocopy requests rose and then fell again, at Chatham House Library successive cuts led to reductions in users with numbers then gradually rising again, at the British Architectural Library too use fell sharply when charges were introduced and then started rising again. At the Royal Asiatic Society user numbers fell when the library became closed access, while the Chartered Institute of Marketing saw visitors fall but had no way of gauging whether remote use had risen or fallen.

Computers and the internet
In the year 2000, of the 31 libraries in the sample, 29 had email, 28 had a website and 27 had some form of computerized catalogue, although of the last, 11 were not available on the web and 12 were incomplete. Although a number of libraries had had some form of computer catalogue in the 1980s, systems became both more common and more complex in the 1990s. The Royal Society of Chemistry was early in the field; by 1991 its networked system incorporated cataloguing, circulation, periodicals and acquisitions modules, an OPAC and a CD-ROM player and it needed a separate package to support its current awareness service.[37] Many different systems were in use: DataTrek at the Royal Society of Chemistry and the Institute of Chartered Accountants, Inmagic at the Royal College of Veterinary Surgeons, Libertas at the British Geological Survey, TINLib at Lincoln's Inn, CALM 2000 at the Harry Simpson Memorial Library, CAIRS at the Institution of Mechanical Engineers, the Institution of Electrical Engineers and the Chartered Insurance Institute.[38] In 1991 the Royal Botanic Gardens Kew Library and Archives became the second library outside North America to install Sirsi's Unicorn, which was also favoured by the Library and Lumley Study Centre of the Royal College of Surgeons of England.[39] By the end of the decade old systems were being replaced with more modern ones; the Institute of Personnel Management replaced BookshelF (first implemented there in 1986) with Genesis in 1994.[40] Ironically, the National Meteorological Library, which had a computerized catalogue as early as 1972, still did not have its catalogue online in 2000.

The British Architectural Library, like some others, had begun its computerization using text retrieval software, and created a sophisticated integrated catalogue and index for its various collections, inadvertently setting up problems when the time came to change to a conventional library system (Unicorn) in the middle of the decade. By 1998 new archive management systems were being developed, such as CALM 2000 for archives, used by the Royal Society (which also changed its LMS from CAIRS to CALM), and AdLib, used by the Royal College of Physicians. At the second meeting of the Historic Libraries Forum, there was a presentation on the development of 'a PC-based rare-book cataloguer's work-station' with the National Trust.[41]

Publications

One of the features of learned and professional libraries is the range of services they provide; in many cases they hold the leading collection in the UK on their subject and are therefore well-placed to produce authoritative bibliographies and other products. The British Architectural Library was remarkably active in this field in the 1990s, publishing a guide to its manuscripts and archives, a bio-graphical dictionary of Victorian architects and starting the publication of its five-volume catalogue of early printed books, in addition to producing picture books based on its photographs collection, a CD-ROM version of its long-running *Architectural publications index* and a CD-ROM of images from its collections.[42] 'Producing publications of relevance to members became a major priority in the development of the information service' at the Institution of Mechanical Engineers and by 1991 there were: a monthly materials bulletin; information packs; source-books; bibliographies, reading lists, and a current awareness bulletin *Green engineering*. The Linnean Society published a booklet on the handling of archives and papers of naturalists.[43] The Society of Antiquaries also published a catalogue of its manuscripts, and the Scottish Poetry Library a supplement to its catalogue of books, while the Linen Hall Library published a bibliography of its unique Northern Ireland Political Collection.[44] The London Library celebrated its 150th anniversary by publishing its history.[45] The Royal Society Library also published its history and a guide to its manuscripts and archives and also collaborated with the British Library's then Science Reference and Information Service and the Science Policy Research Unit at the University of Sussex to produce an index to science policy material on CD-ROM.[46] The National Institute for Social Work Library also moved from being 'a traditional academic special library to a database publisher'.[47] The Wellcome Institute created a videodisc of its iconographic collections (fortunately this was available via JANET).[48] At the beginning of the decade, the catalogues of the libraries of the Royal Shakespeare Theatre and Shakespeare Birthplace Trust were published jointly on microfiche, a format that seemed quaintly old-fashioned ten years later.

Services

The relentless onward march of technology is illustrated by the services introduced in the 1990s; microform reader/printers were installed in several libraries at the beginning of the period, along with facilities (either networked or stand-alone) for using CD-ROMS and access to online services, before the internet began to make even these redundant. The Institute of Chartered Accountants Library, which subscribed to Dialog, Datastar and Reuters, among others, later withdrew them as increased use of the internet meant that they were little used. The Institute also introduced online company information services and withdrew its searching of newspaper articles and legal cases. Specialist information services were withdrawn at the Institution of Electrical Engineers (where a bibliographic abstracting service was introduced) and the Royal Society and the press cuttings service at Chatham House Library was also withdrawn. At the same time, more current awareness services could be provided online, such as that at the Geological Society.

The major new service provided by the majority of libraries in the sample was, as mentioned above, putting their catalogue online. This led to new possibilities for collaboration: the four Inns of Court agreed cataloguing standards and reconfigured their catalogues so that they could all be held on the Inner Temple Library server and accessed by all barristers. The British Geological Survey Library moved its catalogue from Libertas in 2000 and records from its new Geoweb catalogue were contributed to the Geosearch database. The Scott Polar Research Institute contributed its catalogue records to the Cold Regions Bibliography Project and also added multimedia to its catalogue so that records of manuscripts, photographs, paintings and artefacts could also be searched.[49] Another library which created a multimedia catalogue was the Wellcome Institute's Medical Film and Video Library.[50] At the end of the decade, a number of the libraries, including a consortium of scientific learned societies, contributed their archive catalogues to the A2A project, but participation in collaborative partnerships was limited as several major initiatives were sector-specific; for example, the Research Support Libraries Programme was funded by the higher education funding councils and the Royal College of Physicians of Edinburgh had to fund its own participation in an RSLP project.[51]

As it became easier to find references to articles, document delivery assumed an ever-increasing importance. The Institute of Chartered Accountants set up a document delivery service in 1995, charging £3.50 to members and £7 to non-members. At the Institution of Electrical Engineers increased demand led to automation of the inter-library loan system – and to finding convenient ways to pay for quicker services; some libraries began to take credit cards and the Institution of Mechanical Engineers also offered vouchers and deposit accounts. Improved services could also generate income: at the Royal Society of Chemistry over three years the learned and professional society library gradually became a business centre, with charges for information services, electronic resources used to answer business and technical enquiries, and emphasis placed on marketing and promotion.[52] The British Architectural Library set up an Information Centre with premium phone lines for members as well as external enquiries, and charged for carrying out research. The British Institute of International and Comparative Law had access to a full-text database, the Council of Europe Human Rights Database, as early as 1991, and these became more common as the decade progressed.[53]

Nonetheless, by the end of the decade, none of the libraries was abandoning print as a medium; 'the majority of collections are still in print and will remain so until electronic archiving is secure and well-established', according to Nigel Lees of the Royal Society of Chemistry in 2000.[54]

At Westminster Abbey, concerns over conservation and health and safety led to the cessation of regular open days in the Old Library (a medieval chamber with seventeenth-century bookcases), which were replaced with groups visits by appointment. The Royal Society also included tours of the building in its services, introducing charges as a way of lessening demand.

Marketing

Learned and professional libraries were often in an invidious situation: 'Often we form part of an organization most of whose activities are directed towards objectives different from ours.'[55] This was not necessarily a bad thing – at the Kennel Club, for example, library staff had more freedom and more responsibility than others on the same grade – but it meant that libraries might be insular and needed to 'sell' themselves to management as well as to their users. Marketing, like charging, became more important in the '90s. The Chartered Institute of Bankers' Library opened in the evenings during National Libraries Week in 1993,[56] the Royal Society of Chemistry went so far as to appoint a Senior Marketing Officer in 1994, while as early as 1991 at the Institution of Mechanical Engineers 'Information Services staff regularly attend major trade exhibitions ... to demonstrate computer searches and sell the services to as wide a market as possible'.[57] The National Library for the Blind also developed logos and leaflets and attended relevant events to market its services.

Conservation

Only a few libraries in the sector seem to have had major conservation projects in the 1990s, perhaps because so much effort went into automation and retrospective cataloguing or because funding for this activity was hard to come by. Nevertheless, the Linen Hall Library's Lottery funding included the conservation of 30,000 books; the Herbarium of James Edward Smith, first president of the Linnean Society of London was conserved by the Conservation Centre of the National Museums and Galleries on Merseyside[58] and in 1995 Lambeth Palace Library finally completed the repair and rebinding of its war-damaged stock, 40 years after the project began.

Collaboration

Although many of the libraries covered by this chapter are small, they collaborate with each other and sometimes with libraries from other sectors in a large number of specialized groups. The Association of British Theological and Philosophical Libraries, the Cathedral Librarians Group, the Construction Information Group, and the Forum for the History of Science, Technology and Medicine are just a few of the numerous groups which meet to exchange ideas in a more or less formal manner, sometimes publish newsletters or guidelines, perhaps provide training, and generally give each other advice and support. The Historic Libraries Forum was founded in 1993 and had seventy representatives at its first meeting.[59] The Society of Antiquaries found a different means of collaboration by becoming an Associate of the University of London School of Advanced Study.

Conclusion
'Reading of real, live (often recurring) events and issues (for instance, inadequate finance, lack of storage space, conservation concerns, accuracy and updating of catalogues, loan regulations, moving the library) ... it struck me that little today is totally new'; thus Graham Matthews, reviewing the 330-year history of the Royal Society Library and Archives.[60] While all these things still concerned learned and professional libraries in the 1990s, information technology had a profound effect on their services and opened up new possibilities for them and their users.

Notes
1   Peter Hoey, 'Learned, professional and other independent libraries' in *British Librarianship and information work 1985–1990*, ed. David W. Bromley, Angela M. Allott. London: Library Association, 1993, v. 2, pp. 10–26.
2   Peter Dale and Paul Wilson, *Guide to libraries and information services in government departments and other organisations*. London: British Library, 2004; Keith W. Reynard, *Aslib directory of information services in the United Kingdom*. 12th ed. London: Europa, 2002.
3   British Standards Institution, *British Standard recommendations for storage and exhibition of archival documents*. London: British Standards Institution, 1989.
4   Bernard Nurse, 'The archives of learned societies', *Journal of the Society of Archivists* **17** (2), 1996, 195–200.
5   Peter Hoey, 'Marketing the Library and Information Centre at the Royal Society of Chemistry', *Managing information* **6** (7), 1999, 47–9.
6   Teresa E. Slowick, 'The Kennel Club Library', *Aslib information* **19** (2), 1991, 83–4.
7   Lyndsey Rees-Jones, 'Housing benefits', *Library Association record* **101** (12), 1998, 646.
8   'Commonwealth Library saved with £3 million gifts', **95** (6), 1993, 329; T. Barringer, 'The rise, fall and rising again of the Royal Commonwealth Society Library', *SALG newsletter* 41, 1994, 15–22.
9   'Sion College faces further dilemma', *Library Association record* **98** (2), 1996, 61.
10 M. J. Pollack, 'The library of the Royal Asiatic Society and its collections relating to Southeast Asia', *Libraries and culture* **33** (3), 1998, 306–16.
11 'Burton donation suits LSE collections', *Library Association record* **95** (10), 538.
12 'Services at St Pancras', *Library Association record* **99** (11), 1997, 475.
13 Anthony Croghan, 'Plans for BLISS material' (letter), *Library Association record* **99** (6), 1997, 310.
14 Debby Raven, 'Filling in the missing picture of women's art', *Library Association record* **95** (10), 1993, 564–5.
15 'Replanting postponed', *Library Association record* **97** (5), 1995, 195.
16 'Women's art post funded', *Library Association record* **96** (3), 1994, 129.
17 Antiques of the Orient, *New products,* 2000, <http://www.aoto.com.sg/newprod1.htm> (accessed 14/01/06).
18 'Linen Hall buys back Burns', *Library Association record* **97** (5), 1995, 258.
19 'Cuts "disaster" for architects' collection', *Library Association record* **94** (1), 1992, 1.
20 Debby Raven, 'Unique race library in funding dilemma', *Library Association record* **94** (7), 1992, 434.
21 'Feminist books threatened', *Library Association record* **94** (4), 1992, 236; Debby Raven, 'Feminist collection is saved', *Library Association record* **95** (7), 1993, 385.

22 Peter Hoare, 'Funding history', *Library Association record* **99** (10), 1997, 556.

23 *Library Association record* **101** (3), 1998, 143.

24 'Lambeth Palace plans to automate', *Library Association record* **96** (8), 1994, 406.

25 Mary Nixon, 'The Raymond and Beverly Sackler Archive Resource at the Royal Society: a work in progress', *Notes and records of the Royal Society* **53** (2), 1999, 183–6.

26 *Library Association record* **99** (6), 1997, 304.

27 Fergus Wilde, 'Chetham's Library Manchester 1653–2003', *Local historian* **33** (4), 2003, 221–5; 'The year in review', *Library Association record* **99** (1), 1997, 19.

28 'Improved access nets lottery sum', *Library Association record* **101** (1), 1999, 10.

29 'Cataloguing the winners', *Library Association record* **98** (11), 1996, 549; J. Addis-Smith, 'The society's library catalogue project', *Computers in genealogy* **6** (7), 1998, 308–17; Prue Leith, 'Winning ways with Heritage', *Library Association record* **99** (9), 1997, 464.

30 Heritage Lottery Fund, *Annual report and accounts*. London: National Heritage Memorial Fund, 1997, 1998, 1999, 2002.

31 'National library of women', *Library Association record* **101** (7), 1999, 341.

32 'National architecture library', *Library Association record* **98** (4), 1996, 185; 'RIBA plan turned down by NHMF', *Library Association record* **98** (9), 1996, 437.

33 *Library Association record* **93** (5), 279.

34 Julie Woodland, 'Preserving the pages of tragedy', *Library Association record* **101** (7), 1999, 410.

35 Heike Dieckmann and Mary Yates, 'Managing information at the British Standards Institution', *Managing information* **4** (9), 1997, 22–3.

36 Peter Hoey, 'The Library today', *Chemistry in Britain* **27** (2), 1991, 153–4; Nigel Lees, 'Spotlight on SLA members: an interview with Nigel Lees', *Information outlook* **4** (9), 2000, 32–7.

37 Peter Hoey, 'The Data Trek automated library management system in the Library of the Royal Society of Chemistry', *Program* **26** (1), 1992, 19–28; S. Brown, 'TRIP supports current awareness from the RSC', *TIP applications* **8** (4), 1994, 6–8.

38 S. Brown, 'Data Trek for Chartered Accountants', *C and L applications* **7** (5/6), 1993/4, 2–4; J. Harris, 'INMAGIC Plus inter-library loans system at the RCVS', *Vine* 96, 1994, 24–9; Guy Holborn, 'Using TINLib for cataloguing at Lincoln's Inn', *Law librarian* **21** (2), 1990, 67–9; Annette Watts, 'Computerisation at the Institution of Mechanical Engineers', *Aslib information* **19** (5), 1991, 175–6; G. Bennett and J. Tomlinson, 'Inter-library loans management with CAIRS at the Institution of Electrical Engineers', *Vine* 96, 1994, 19–23; R. Cunnew, 'The analytic OPAC: incorporating a journal index in an online catalogue using CAIRS and AACR2', *Catalogue & index* 118, 1995, 1–5.

39 Sylvia Fitzgerald and John Flanagan, 'Unicorn at Kew: computerising the Library and Archives at the Royal Botanic Gardens, Kew', *Program* **27** (4), 1993, 331–40; Sylvia Fitzgerald and John Flanagan, 'Unicorn in the special library', *Library hi tech* **48**, 1994, 42; 'Special libraries choose Sirsi's Unicorn', *Library Association record* **98** (2), *Library technology* supplement.

40 Janice Jones, 'Personnel services', *Assistant librarian* **87** (7), 1994, 105–6.

41 Bob Duckett, 'Historic collections preservation', *Library Association record* **96** (1), 1994, 54.

42 Angela Mace, *Architecture in manuscript, 1601–1996: guide to the British Architectural Library Manuscripts and Archives Collection*. London: Mansell, 1998; Alison Felstead, Jonathan Franklin, and Leslie Pinfield (eds.), *Directory of British architects 1834–1900*. London: Mansell, 1995; Paul Nash *et al.*, *Early printed books 1478–1840: a catalogue of the British Architectural Library's Early Imprints Collection*. Munich: K. G. Saur,

1994–2003; Robert Elwall, *Building a better tomorrow: architecture of the 1950s.* London: Wiley, 2000; Robert Elwall, *Eric de Maré: images from the photographs collection of the Royal Institute of British Architects.* London: RIBA Publications, 2000; Robert Elwall, *John Maltby: images from the photographs collection of the Royal Institute of British Architects.* London: RIBA Publications, 2000; *Architectural publications index.* London: RIBA Publications, 1972–   ; *APId. Architectural publications index on disc.* London: RIBA Publications. 1995– ; *Architecture & design illustrated: images from the British Architectural Library, Royal Institute of British Architects.* Sheffield: Image Resource, 1997.

43 Jacqui Ollerton, 'Marketing services to mechanical engineers', *Aslib information* **19** (2), 1991, 44–5; Linnean Society, *Preserving the archives of nature: a guide for the owners of papers on nature conservation.* London: Linnean Society, 1994.

44 Pamela J. Willetts, *Catalogue of the manuscripts in the Society of Antiquaries of London.* Woodbridge: Boydell & Brewer, 2000; Scottish Poetry Library, *Catalogue of the Lending Collection. Supplement no. 1.* Edinburgh: Scottish Poetry Library, 1991; 'NI politics', *Library Association record* **97** (4), 1995, 186; John Gray, 'Documenting civil conflict: the case of the Linen Hall Library, Belfast' in *Disaster and after: the practicalities of information services in times of war and other catastrophes. Proceedings of an international conference sponsored by IGLA (the International Group of the Library Association), University of Bristol, UK, 4–6 September 1998*, ed. Paul Sturges and Diana Rosenberg. London: Taylor Graham, 1999, pp. 91–106.

45 John Wells, *Rude words: a discursive history of the London Library.* London: Macmillan, 1991.

46 Marie Boas Hall, *The Library and Archives of the Royal Society, 1660–1990.* London: Royal Society, 1992; Keith Moore and Mary Sampson, *A guide to the archives and manuscripts of the Royal Society.* London: Royal Society, 1995; *Science technology and innovation on CD-ROM.* London: British Library, 1999– .

47 M. Watson, 'Publishing a CD-ROM database in house: a case study', *Managing information* **1** (11/12), 1994, 24, 26–7.

48 'Wellcome sights now on JANET', *Library Association record* **96** (5), 1994, 248.

49 H. Shibata, 'Collaborating with the Cold Regions Bibliography Project: the SPRI experience' in *Electronic information and publications: looking to the electronic future let's not forget the archival past. Proceedings of the 24th Annual Conference of the International Association of Aquatic and Marine Science Libraries and Information Centers and the 17th Polar Libraries Colloquy, Reykjavik, Iceland, 20–25 September 1998*, ed. James W. Markham, Andrea L. Dude, Martha Andrews. Fort Pierie, Fla.: AMSLIC, 1999, pp. 211–17; W. Mills, 'SPRILIB Multimedia: new databases at the Scott Polar Research Institute' in *Electronic information and publications* (same), pp. 167–70.

50 Rebecca Davies, 'Development of an online catalogue for a specialised multimedia library', *Multimedia information and technology* **24** (3), 1998, 175–8.

51 Ronald Milne, 'The collaborative imperative', *Library Association record* **102** (11), 2000, 634.

52 Nigel Lees, 'The changing role of a professional society library', *Electronic library* **15** (4), 1997, 305–10.

53 Mary Foster, 'The British Institute of International and Comparative Law Library and Information Services', *Law librarian* **25** (1), 1994, 43–4.

54 'Spotlight on SLA members: an interview with Nigel Lees', *Information outlook* **4** (9), 2000, 32–7.

55 Christopher Hilton and Sue Gold, 'Selling the medicine show', *Library Association record* **99** (6), 1997, 320–2.

56 'Institute library banking on success', *Library Association record* **95** (12), 1993, 677.
57 Jacqui Ollerton, 'The Information and Library Service of the Institution of Mechanical Engineers', *Library Association record* **93** (1/2), 1991, 66.
58 A. Hillcoat-Imanishi, 'The Smith herbarium conservation project', *Paper conservation news* 93, 2000, 8–9.
59 'Dynamic life of historic libraries', *Library Association record* **95** (2), 1993, 118.
60 Graham Matthews, 'Royal history', *Library Association record* **95** (6), 1993, 355.

9

Library history

Peter Hoare

Theory and practice

This survey is perhaps rather different in scope from some others in this volume. It is not so much a record of professional activity within libraries or information establishments, rather an account of writing on the history of libraries (and information) in Great Britain and Ireland, whether by librarians or not, and of more general studies of the topic by British writers in the field. It aims to include, under the topical headings which follow, the major works and a representative sample of other publications, without claiming to be comprehensive in its coverage. (Private libraries and book-collecting are deliberately treated less fully than the history of institutional libraries.)

The ten years covered by this survey saw many changes in the practice and scope of 'library history' (to use the term which has been most used in the past) – indeed, it began to be questioned as a distinct discipline, or at least one to be constrained within its old borders. Two developments in particular expanded its field of study:

- The rapid growth of 'book history' on an international scale, evidenced for example by the success of SHARP, the Society for the History of Authorship, Reading and Publishing, whose conferences have provided a forum for many library historians in a wider context, and whose annual *Book history* has included many contributions from British writers.[1]
- The expanding interest in 'information' as a crucial element of the library world – with its own history as a legitimate addition to traditional library-history concerns. This was put forward by Black in a key paper which led to a thought-provoking riposte by Davis and Aho on the role of library history and to further developments in the philosophy of the discipline.[2]

In both these areas historical research is undertaken by many outside the library profession as well as within it – but this has always been true of library history itself. Historical studies are not a part of the normal professional activity of most workers in the LIS world, and the subject has less prominence in professional curricula than it once did, as shown by a survey reported at the 1999 UmbrelLA conference.[3] (The earliest formal education for librarianship, in the early decades of the 20th century, was also studied by Webber: at that time the history of libraries was more prominent, if less scholarly, than it is today.)[4]

Within the Library Association, the focus was the work of the Library History Group (LHG), thirty years old at the beginning of the period under review and continuing to develop in new ways. (Its attempts to maintain a position as the 'historical conscience' of the Library Association were not always very successful.) It maintained an interest in the raw material of history in the shape of the Library Association's archives, which for many years were not given a high priority by the LA, and it showed the way by having its own archives properly sorted and deposited in Aberystwyth in 2000.[5] The history of the LA itself was not neglected.[6]

Its journal *Library history* changed format in 1998, moving to a subscription base which allowed expansion and a more handsome appearance; in consequence its newsletter also expanded as a free service to its members. In its new commercial guise the journal continued the tradition of providing a focused scholarly outlet for research which had been its aim since its foundation in 1967. Unfortunately the LHG was unable to find a successor to Denis Keeling, who had compiled the *British library history: bibliography* on its behalf for more than a quarter of a century – the volume covering 1962–1968 appeared in 1967, while the sixth and last volume of this most valuable work was published in 1991.[7] (The present survey is in no way intended to replace Keeling's bibliography: it is both much more selective and lacks the invaluable critical comments that made the bibliography such a pleasure to read. The lack of later coverage has however undoubtedly made this survey more difficult to compile.)

Other LHG initiatives included proposals for a library museum,[8] which at the time of writing was still awaited, and for directories of historic library buildings (a suggestion which bore fruit after the period covered here) or indeed of historic libraries themselves, supplementing the invaluable *Directory of rare book and special collections* published by its sister Rare Books Group but recognizing that library history is not co-terminous with rare books.[9] Important reference books in the LHG's area include the American *Encyclopedia of library history* (with many British entries) and the *International encyclopedia of information and library science*, which includes a number of useful historical entries.[10] An oral history project to compile an electronic archive of reminiscences was initiated by the LHG in 2000, under the title 'The profession's memory'. The Group was quick to offer support to the plan put forward by Cambridge University Press, on the initiative of Robin Alston, for a standard history of libraries in Britain and Ireland to complement the *Cambridge history of the book*,[11] and members of the LHG became major contributors (as editors and authors) to this work.[12] Various seminars and conference papers stemmed from the Cambridge project and it will clearly fill a long-felt need for a comprehensive history of libraries in this country. Alston's own major contribution to the field, in the shape of a web-mounted database of libraries up to 1850, was started in 1991 and was to be used by many researchers, as was his handlist of manuscript catalogues in the British Library.[13] Alston also initiated a series of postgraduate library history seminars at the University of London in 1998, setting the subject in the context of other historical research.

Similar projects aiming to publish histories of the book (and libraries) in Scotland and Ireland began but no publications emerged. For Wales, however, the appearance of *A nation and its books* in 1998 provided a fine overview, with chapters on country house libraries, miners' institutes and public and academic libraries in addition to broader studies.[14] For many parts of England the continuing publication of the *Victoria county history* provided references to libraries of all sorts, particularly those associated with particular towns or even villages.[15]

In 1996, with the sponsorship of MCB University Press, the LHG established an annual prize for the best essay in library history published in the UK in the previous year. The winners of the prize often came from outside the boundaries of professional publishing, illustrating again how library history is by no means solely a 'professional' concern in the narrow sense. In the same year the Group published its own substantial collection of essays as a festschrift for William Munford, the main progenitor of the LHG itself. This included biographical contributions on Munford but also a wide range of articles in areas of interest to Dr Munford.[16]

Through its own programme of meetings, through its sponsorship of several Anglo–German conferences on library history jointly with the Herzog August Bibliothek in Wolfenbüttel, and most particularly through its active involvement in the Library Association's biennial 'Under One UmbrelLA' conferences which began in 1991, the LHG strove to present a historical view to a wider audience. In 2000 it took up the challenge of celebrating 150 years of public libraries with an international seminar at Croydon under the title 'From people's university to people's library' (but the LHG was not itself responsible for the issue of a fifty pence piece marking the sesquicentenary). Its members and officers were also involved with the IFLA Round Table on Library History, and with various initiatives in the United States such as the celebration of the Library of Congress's bicentenary in 2000. The output from some of these activities is recorded below.

Other conferences not directly involving the LHG but supported by its members included those on 'Gendering library history' held at Loughborough University in 1999, and on 'Lost libraries' held in Cambridge in 2000.[17] These, like the parallel series of annual conferences on book history organised by Myers and Harris and by the British Book Trade Seminar, have given library historians a wider audience and, in their published proceedings, provided a great deal of important material for further research.[18] The conference on 'Material cultures' organized by the Edinburgh Centre for the History of the Book in 2000, like other book history seminars, was another important outlet. A further source for library history from outside the profession was to be the Reading Experience Database 1450–1945, established at the Open University in 1996 (and more recently the recipient of major research council funding).[19]

The LHG was also the moving spirit behind the establishment of the Historic Libraries Forum, which began with a single meeting in November 1992 and continued to grow as a meeting place for all those associated with 'historic libraries' however defined – and to provide opportunities for the sharing of experience (not solely on historical topics).[20] Other bodies concerned with the Forum were the Association of Independent Libraries, again with a historical focus,[21] and the Association of Cathedral Libraries and Archives, representing some of the most ancient libraries in the country.

Medieval libraries

The significance of libraries, particularly monastic libraries, in the culture of the Middle Ages has long been recognized, and scholarly effort has been recognized more widely in this field, perhaps, than for later library history. The publication of major source material in the *Corpus of British medieval library catalogues* under the auspices of the British Academy and the British Library, which began in 1990 with K. W. Humphreys on the friars' libraries, continued apace. In 1991 came an edition of the *Registrum Anglie,* the 14th-century Franciscan 'union catalogue', and in the following year a collection of Cistercian, Gilbertine and Premonstratensian library catalogues.[22] These were followed by catalogues from smaller Benedictine and Augustinian houses and from Dover Priory; in 2000 came Carley's work on Henry VIII's libraries.[23]

Many other medieval libraries, not all monastic, were studied, many of them in vol. 3 of the *Cambridge history of the book* or in *Books and collectors 1200–1700,* the important festschrift for A. G. Watson, or like Lovatt's valuable paper on a 15th-century Carthusian's library, in journals well outside the LIS field.[24] Others appeared as monographs, for example on Salisbury Cathedral, Syon Abbey, Reading Abbey, or on the reading of Cistercian nuns.[25] Several works considered the dispersal of the monastic libraries in the sixteenth century, a topic studied in relation both to the original owners and to those who acquired the books after the dissolution of the monasteries.[26] A useful summary is given in Ramsay's paper to the 2000 conference on 'Lost libraries'.[27] Some studies of the later fate of the books are also mentioned under 'Academic libraries' and 'Ecclesiastical libraries', below, and the dispersal is reflected in the many collections described in the *PLRE* series.[28]

National libraries

Early moves towards a national library centred on the Cottonian library, which had as its basis a remarkable collection of manuscripts and early documents. Its history was studied in a number of articles by Tite and others, and notably in the collection of essays edited by Wright.[29] Another important collection, made by George Thomason in the 17th century, had a complicated history until it reached the British Museum under George III.[30]

The establishment of the British Library in 1973 and the move of its London activities to the new St Pancras site occasioned important studies of the British

Museum Library, notably Harris's comprehensive history of its first 220 years of existence, and the earlier volume of essays edited by him dealing with the Department of Printed Books, which gives a number of insights on particular aspects such as legal deposit.[31] Sternberg, a contributor to that volume, also published articles on legal deposit and relationships with the colonies up to the incorporation of the India Office Library and records into the British Library.[32] Willison considered the European context of the British Museum's role in its earlier years, while others studied different international aspects of the library.[33] The catalogue of the British Museum Library is itself an important historical artefact, and was the subject of a number of studies such as King's chapter in Harris's collection of essays and elsewhere.[34] After the establishment of the British Library it also took over the national bibliography, now old enough to have its own history (for the pre-BL period).[35]

A parallel to the national library in archives terms, the Public Record Office (from 2003 part of the National Archives) also has a long history, which Cantwell's books examined not least in comparison with the British Museum.[36] The British Library's own archives (including those of the British Museum) also received attention.[37]

Other national libraries in the British Isles were studied in various ways: the forerunner of the National Library of Scotland by Kelly, and the National Library of Wales in chapters in its own publication on the Welsh book world.[38] A volume on the treasures of the National Library of Ireland was edited by Kissane, and its history studied by Long in two articles.[39]

Public libraries

The British public library has always been a prominent feature in these reviews of library history writing. Two influential books by Black transformed the scene, with an emphasis on motivation and social role which had not always been so developed in the past.[40] Black also wrote many articles on special aspects of the public library world, again developing new methods of research and interpretation.[41]

Local studies include a centenary pamphlet on Chiswick and a study of the Bishopsgate Institute, where closed access continued until 1941.[42] Studies reflecting earlier forms of public library before rate support was possible include an overview of early libraries in Leicester, and a detailed analysis of the donation book from the old library in Norwich.[43] The library founded by Robert Baikie in Kirkwall, on Orkney, survives in the town museum; its history and contents were assessed by Armstrong.[44]

The biography of prominent librarians can be a useful resource for the historian, a notable example being Harrison's account of his life's work in public libraries.[45] Somewhat similarly the LHG's tribute volume to W. A. Munford included several articles on the public libraries he had worked in, in Ilford, Dover and Cambridge;[46] the same volume also has an account of the early years of Portsmouth by Ollé, and a more general historical survey of public library use by

Sturges, who also wrote (with Barr) on the role of fiction in 19th-century libraries.[47]

The pattern of public (and other) libraries in Britain affected policies for libraries in the British Zone of Occupation in Germany after 1945.[48] The public library scene in Wales was covered in two chapters of *A nation and its books*.[49] Ó hAodha publicized an important study of rural libraries in Ireland from the early 20th century, while Dublin's unusual situation, with no central library, was studied by Kennedy.[50]

Particular aspects of library provision also attracted attention, such as reference services, women's reading rooms, and the needs of those in air-raid shelters in war-time.[51] The phenomenon of libraries discarding old stock is not a new one, nor restricted to public libraries, but these attracted special scorn in West's controversial polemic.[52] This contrasts with the positive view of a hundred years of public library development which had been put forward by the Library Association in 1950.[53]

Subscription and circulating libraries

Subscription libraries, seen as a dying breed a decade earlier, enjoyed a resurrection, partly through the foundation of the Association of Independent Libraries.[54] Several published accounts of their history, often to mark anniversaries. Examples are the Highgate Literary and Scientific Institution in London, the Liverpool Athenaeum, Newcastle 'Lit and Phil', with its bicentenary lectures complementing its earlier history;[55] Nottingham Subscription Library (including the longer history of its building) and the Guildford Institute, rescued from closure by the intervention of the local university.[56] The Leeds Library issued an update of its classic history and was also the subject of two essays, on the library in 1817 and the Foreign Circulating Library of 1779–1814, by Elaine Robinson and Alice Hamilton.[57] The Portico Library in Manchester would not mark its bicentenary until 2006, but its history was well described by Brooks and Haworth.[58]

The London Library celebrated its 150th anniversary in 1991 with an 'informal history' not by a library historian but by the actor John Wells, who also studied the early librarians.[59] The library's administration in its earliest years was dealt with in considerable detail by Baker, using access to archival material not readily accessible elsewhere.[60]

Libraries no longer extant were also studied, for example by Hoare on a short-lived subscription library at St Martin in the Fields in London,[61] and Manley on a longer-lived Yorkshire book club in Sedbergh;[62] other book clubs in Dalton (Lancashire) and Wadebridge (Cornwall) were described by Boddy and Swanton.[63] Despite the name, the 'circulating-library society' in Kilkenny was similar to subscription libraries, as Legge makes clear in her account of its activities.[64]

The libraries of the working classes formed a particular type of subscription library (most now vanished). Crawford places them in the context of self-development.[65] Everitt's study of the cooperative movement and its libraries was based on her Ph.D. thesis, while Baggs's article compared them to mechanics' institutes;[66] Baggs also provided a chapter on Welsh miners' libraries for the history of the book in Wales.[67]

The commercial lending library and its influence on publishing were studied by Skelton-Foord and Hiley among others, and in Day's pamphlet on the North-East of England.[68] Manley deals with them more generally and draws on his extensive documentation of the phenomenon.[69]

Academic libraries

The Bodleian Library at Oxford published an attractive historical survey (though only up to 1700) by Rogers, and Barber surveyed the buildings of a whole range of libraries in Oxford.[70] Carley examined the sources of one of the Bodleian's early benefactions,[71] and the early acquisitions of Trinity College library were discussed by Coates, together with notes on later developments.[72] A variety of libraries in 18th-century Oxford, not only in the colleges, was described by Morgan, and John Radcliffe, one of the great benefactors of the university, together with his foundations the Radcliffe Camera and Science Library, was the subject of a substantial study by Guest.[73] Bengtson studied the way in which donations were recorded in college libraries.[74]

Cambridge University Library also celebrated its major collections (up to the late 20th century) with an attractive volume of scholarly essays on different topics, complementing earlier formal histories of the library.[75] Andrew Perne (d. 1591) was a notable librarian of the University Library and his anniversary was commemorated in an important collection of essays.[76] A detailed analysis and transcription of a catalogue of the library from his time by Leedham-Green and McKitterick is also valuable for its evidence of the arrangement and of the stock itself, while a study by Hall of the library's 19th–20th century catalogue is useful for comparison with other libraries.[77] Trinity College Cambridge has one of the most remarkable college libraries, designed by Sir Christopher Wren; the building and the collections were fully documented in a handsome tercentenary publication.[78] Its neighbour Trinity Hall published a more modest history of its library, while Gonville & Caius College took over the Cockerell building originally erected for the University Library and published an informative booklet recording the history of the building.[79] The library of the late 16th-century foundation of Sidney Sussex College was also studied.[80]

English provincial universities were also studied historically, most notably Birmingham with a 'centennial history'.[81] Two articles by Morrish study aspects of Leeds University Library, and one by Dyson examines the war-time history of Hull University College's library;[82] a further article by Priestman considers the later Librarian of Hull, Philip Larkin, especially in his relationship with Oxford.[83]

The ancient Scottish university libraries, too, continued to be studied, for example three centuries of librarians at Glasgow, and from Aberdeen both a study of an early catalogue and a concise historical guide.[84] The library of Trinity College Dublin, which celebrated its quatercentenary in 1992, is studied in a valuable collection of essays, covering the collections and the buildings as well as the librarians.[85] The Catholic college at Maynooth, two hundred years old and part of the National University, like other libraries produced a volume on its treasures, also documenting its history.[86]

Ecclesiastical libraries

Several English cathedrals published histories, many of which include a section on the cathedral library, for example Canterbury, Chichester, Exeter, and Hereford.[87] David Pearson's article on 17th-century bishops and their libraries is complemented by studies of individual bishops such as Thomas Cranmer, John Cosin, and William Sancroft.[88] Matteson continued his study of Archbishop William King's collections (completed after the period under review) with a closer consideration of what survives in Cashel cathedral library.[89] The fate of other historic Irish libraries, the Protestant diocesan libraries mostly dating from the 18th century, were discussed by Connolly at the 'Lost libraries' conference in 2000.[90] The troubled 20th-century history of Sion College and its library, a major resource for Anglican clergy in London, was studied by Huelin in a study continuing an earlier history.[91]

Special libraries

Scholarly works on two major specialist libraries are Menhennet's history of the House of Commons library, and Hall's study of the library and archives of the Royal Society over 300 years;[92] an early special collection within the Royal Society is discussed by Peck.[93] Jenkinson explains the use of libraries in Scottish medical societies over two centuries, and Symons provides a useful account of the Wellcome Historical Medical Library in his history of its parent body.[94] Black's investigation of a northern chocolate company gives a valuable insight into information and library provision in the earlier 20th century.[95]

Hoare's paper on a European information society, from the late 17th century onwards, is concerned with special libraries and the information world in modern times.[96] A further expansion of the special library area, also illustrating the development of information history, is presented in a paper by Richards on use of enemy technical information in war-time, and by Black and Brunt's studies of information activity in commercial enterprises and in Britain's intelligence agency.[97]

Finally, though hardly a special library in the usual sense, the role of the prison library is an important element in penology, and is studied in Fyfe's monograph on the topic.[98]

Notes

1   *Book history* **1** (1998) and annually thereafter; published for SHARP by Pennsylvania State University Press. A good survey of developments in book history and library history is given in David McKitterick, 'Books, libraries and society: the past ever with us', *Libraries and culture* **27** (3), 1992, 231–51. Cf. also Nicolas Barker's 1986–87

Clark Lectures, published as *A potencie of life: books in society*. London: British Library, 1993), notably 'Libraries and the mind of man', pp. 179–94.

2   Alistair Black, 'Information and modernity: the history of information and the eclipse of library history', *Library history* **14** (1), 1998, 39–45; cf. also his 'Lost worlds of culture: Victorian libraries, history and prospects for a history of information', *Journal of Victorian culture* **2** (1), 1997, 124–41; Donald G. Davis and Jon Arvid Aho, 'Whither library history? A critical essay on Black's model for the future of library history, with some additional options', *Library history* **17** (1), 2001, 21–37 (with a response from Black, 37–9); Alistair Black, 'New methodologies in library history: a manifesto for the "new" library history', *Library history* **11**, 1995, 76–85, and – with a less theoretical view – K. C. Harrison, 'Why library history?', *Library review* **43** (8), 1994, 9–13.

3   Alistair Black and John Crawford, 'The identity of library and information history: an audit of library and information history teaching and research in departments and schools of library and information studies in Britain and Ireland', *Library history* **17** (2), 2001, 127–31. Cf. also R. C. Alston, 'Library history: a place in the education of librarians?', *Library history* **9** (1/2), 1991, 37–51.

4   Nigel Webber, 'The first library school in the United Kingdom: the London School of Economics, 1900–1919', *Library history* **12** (1996), 142–54.

5   Graham Jefcoate, 'Library Association branch and group archives: a report on a study carried out by the Library History and Rare Books Groups, with guidelines on practice and a checklist of records reported', *Library history* **9** (5/6), 215–24.

6   Elizabeth Hanson, 'Conference proceedings as disseminators of new knowledge: the Library Association and British public libraries, 1878–1882', *Library history* **12**, 1996, 93–105; K. A. Manley, 'The official library journal wars of the 1870s and '80s', *Library history* **12**, 1996, 106–17.

7   Denis F. Keeling (ed.), *British library history: bibliography 1985–1988*. Winchester: St Paul's Bibliographies, 1991.

8   R. P. Sturges, 'Towards a museum of librarianship', *Library history* **9** (1/2), 1991, 76–80.

9   *A directory of rare book and special collections in the United Kingdom and the Republic of Ireland*. 2nd ed., ed. B. C. Bloomfield. London: Library Association, 1997. This is itself a valuable source of historical information on the libraries included (and on those incorporated in them).

10 Wayne A. Wiegand and Donald G. Davis (eds.), *Encyclopedia of library history*. New York: Garland, 1994; John Feather and Paul Sturges (eds.), *International encyclopedia of information and library science*. London: Routledge, 1997.

11 *The Cambridge history of the book in Britain*. Cambridge: Cambridge University Press. The first volume to appear was *Vol. 3: 1400–1557*, ed. Lotte Hellinga and J. B. Trapp, 1999.

12 *The Cambridge history of libraries in Britain and Ireland*. Cambridge: Cambridge University Press (forthcoming at time of writing). To span 1500 years of British and Irish library history: Vol. 1, ed. Teresa Webber and Elisabeth Leedham-Green, from the sixth century to c. 1650; Vol. 2, ed. Mandelbrote and Keith Manley, 1650–1850; Vol. 3, ed. Alistair Black and Peter Hoare, covering the years 1850–2000. A great deal of library history activity in the period under review was in preparation for this work.

13 'Library history: the British Isles to 1850' <http://www.r-alston.co.uk> (accessed 21/2/06; database to be transferred to the Institute of English Studies in the School of Advanced Studies of the University of London); R. C. Alston, *Handlist of library*

catalogues and lists of books and manuscripts in the British Library Department of Manuscripts. London: Bibliographical Society, 1991.

14 Philip Henry Jones and Eiluned Rees (eds.), *A nation and its books: a history of the book in Wales*. Aberystwyth: National Library of Wales, 1998.

15 Formally known as the *Victoria history of the counties of England*. An example is D. A. Crowley (ed.), *A history of the county of Wiltshire. Vol. 14*. Oxford: Oxford University Press for the Institute of Historical Research, 1991, which has references to various libraries in Malmesbury.

16 K. A. Manley (ed.), *Careering along with books: studies in the history of British public libraries and librarianship in honour of the 85th birthday of Dr William A. Munford*. London: Library History Group, 1996. This also formed *Library history* **12**.

17 Evelyn Kerslake and Nickianne Moody (eds.), *Gendering library history*. Liverpool: John Moores University, 2000; James Raven (ed.), *Lost libraries: the destruction of great book collections since antiquity*. Basingstoke: Palgrave Macmillan, 2004.

18 Examples of the book trade history conferences: Robin Myers and Michael Harris (eds.), *Property of a gentleman: the formation, organisation and dispersal of the private library 1620–1920*. Winchester: St Paul's Bibliographies, 1991; *Antiquaries, book collectors and the circles of learning*. Winchester: St Paul's Bibliographies, 1994. Both these, like others in the series, include important contributions on book-collecting as well as on institutional libraries. For an example of the Book Trade Seminars see Peter Isaac and Barry McKay (eds.), *The reach of print: making, selling and using books*. Winchester: St Paul's Bibliographies, 1998.

19 'The Reading Experience database 1450–1945' <www.open.ac.uk/Arts/RED/> (accessed 21/2/06).

20 Historic Libraries Forum: <www.historiclibrariesforum.org.uk> (accessed 21/2/06).

21 Association of Independent Libraries: <www.independentlibraries.co.uk> (accessed 21/2/06).

22 Richard H. Rouse and Mary A. Rouse (eds.), *Registrum Anglie de libris doctorum et auctorum ueterum*. London: British Library, 1991; David N. Bell (ed.), *The libraries of the Cistercians, Gilbertines and Premonstratensians*. London: British Library, 1992.

23 R. Sharpe *et al.* (eds.), *English Benedictine libraries: the shorter catalogues*. London: British Library, 1996; Teresa Webber and A. G. Watson (eds.), *The libraries of the Augustinian canons*. London: British Library, 1998; William P. Stoneman (ed.), *Dover Priory*. London: British Library, 1999; James P. Carley (ed.), *The libraries of King Henry VIII*. London: British Library, 2000. The series continues.

24 James P. Carley and Colin G. C. Tite (eds.), *Books and collectors 1200–1700: essays presented to Andrew Watson*. London: British Library, 1997; Roger Lovatt, 'The library of John Blacman and contemporary Carthusian spirituality', *Journal of ecclesiastical history* **43** (2), 1992, 195–230.

25 Teresa Webber, *Scribes and scholars at Salisbury Cathedral c. 1075–c. 1125*. Oxford: University Press, 1992; Christopher de Hamel, *Syon Abbey: the library of the Bridgettine nuns and their peregrinations after the Reformation*. London: Roxburghe Club, 1991; Alan Coates, *English medieval books: the Reading Abbey collections from foundation to dispersal*. Oxford: Clarendon Press, 1999; David N. Bell, *What nuns read: books and libraries in medieval English nunneries*. Kalamazoo, Mich.: Cistercian Publications, 1995.

26 See for example: David N. Bell, 'Monastic libraries: 1400–1557' in *The Cambridge history of the book in Britain,* v. 3, pp. 229–54; James P. Carley, 'John Leland and the

contents of English pre-dissolution libraries: the Cambridge friars', *Transactions of the Cambridge Bibliographical Society* **9** (1), 1986, 90–100; Christopher de Hamel on Christ Church Canterbury in *Books and collectors 1200–1700*, ed. Carley and Tite, pp. 263–79; R. I. Page's 1990 Sandars lectures at Cambridge, published as *Matthew Parker and his books*. Kalamazoo: Medieval Institute, 1993.

27 Nigel Ramsay, '"The manuscripts flew about like butterflies": the break-up of English libraries in the 16th century', in *Lost libraries*, ed. Raven, pp. 125–44.

28 Robert J. Fehrenbach and Elisabeth Leedham-Green (eds.), *Private libraries in Renaissance England: a collection of Tudor and early Stuart book-lists. Vol. 1: PLRE 1–4*. Binghamton, N.Y.: Medieval Texts and Studies, 1992.

29 For example Colin G. C. Tite, '"Lost or stolen or strayed": a survey of manuscripts formerly in the Cotton library', *British Library journal* **18** (2), 1992, 107–47; James P. Carley and Colin G. C. Tite, 'Sir Robert Cotton as collector of manuscripts and the question of dismemberment', *The library* 6th ser. **14** (2), 1992, 94–9; C. J. Wright (ed.), *Sir Robert Cotton as collector: essays on an early Stuart courtier and his legacy*. London: British Library, 1997.

30 David Stoker, 'George Thomason's intractable legacy, 1644–1762', *The library* 6th ser. **14** (4), 1992, 337–56.

31 P. R. Harris, *A history of the British Museum Library 1753–1973*. London: British Library, 1998; P. R. Harris (ed.), *The library of the British Museum: retrospective essays on the Department of Printed Books*. London: British Library, 1991.

32 Ilse Sternberg, 'The British Museum Library and colonial copyright deposit', *British Library journal* **17** (1), 1991, 61–82, and 'The British Museum Library and the India Office', *British Library journal* **17** (2), 1991, 151–66.

33 Ian Willison, 'The development of the British National library to 1837 in its European context', *Library history* **12**, 1996, 31–48; also his 'Legal deposit: a provisional perspective', *Publishing history* **45** (1), 1999, 5–45; Robert Henderson, 'Russian political émigrés and the British Museum Library', *Library history* **9** (1/2), 1991, 59–68; Peter Hoare, 'A Russian librarian's view of European libraries in 1859: V. I. Sobol'ščikov's Grand Tour', *IFLA journal* **17** (4), 1991, 349–57; also his 'Sobol'shchikov and the modern European library in 1859', *Library history* **14** (1), 1997, 47–53; David Paisey, 'Selective universality? The development of the British Museum's collections of German books in the 19th century', *Library history* **14** (2), 1998, 133–141.

34 Alec Hyatt King, 'The traditional maintenance of the General Catalogue of Printed Books' in *The library of the British Museum*, ed. Harris, pp. 165–99; Barbara McCrimmon, 'Ellis v. Panizzi: an unequal cataloging contest', *Libraries and culture* **27** (2), 1992, 177–91; and her 'Reverend Richard Garnett and the Ninety-One Rules', *Library history* **10** (1994), 45–50.

35 Andy Stephens, *The history of the British National Bibliography 1950–1973: a catalogue of achievement*. London: British Library, 1994.

36 John D. Cantwell, *The Public Record Office 1838–1958*. London: HMSO, 1991; and *The Public Record Office 1959–1969*. Richmond: PRO, 2000.

37 Andrew Griffin, 'Preserving an archive of the British Library', *Library history* **9** (1/2), 1991, 52–8.

38 W. A. Kelly, *The library of Lord George Douglas (ca. 1667/8–1693?): an early donation to the Advocates Library*. Cambridge: LP Publications, 1997; Gwyn Walters, 'The National Library of Wales, the art of the book, and Welsh bibliography', and

Lionel Madden, 'The National Library of Wales and the future of the book' in *A nation and its books*, ed. Jones and Rees, pp. 387–98 and 399–405.

39 Noel Kissane (ed.), *Treasures from the National Library of Ireland*. Drogheda: Boyne Valley Honey Co., 1994; Gerard Long, 'The foundation of the National Library of Ireland, 1836–1877', *Long Room* **36**, 1991, 41–8, and his 'The National Library of Ireland', in *The heritage of Ireland*, ed. Neil Buttimer *et al.* Cork: Collins Press, 2000, pp. 305–12.

40 Alistair Black, *A new history of the English public library: social and intellectual contexts, 1850–1914*. London: Leicester University Press, 1996; and *The public library in Britain, 1914–2000*. London: British Library, 2000.

41 Alistair Black, 'Libraries for the many: the philosophical roots of the early public library movement', *Library history* **9** (1/2), 1991, 27–36; 'Representations of the public library in Victorian and Edwardian fiction: assessing the semiological approach' in *Bibliotheken in der literarischen Darstellung / Libraries in literature*, ed. Peter Vodosek and Graham Jefcoate. Wiesbaden: Harrassowitz, 1999, pp.151–66; and 'Skeleton in the cupboard: social class and the public library through 150 years', *Library history* **14** (1), 1998, 37–43.

42 Carolyn Hammond, *Chiswick Library: one hundred years of service to the community*. London: Hounslow Leisure Services, 1991; David Webb and Alison Carpenter, *Bishopsgate Foundation centenary volume*. London: Bishopsgate Foundation, 1991.

43 Joyce Lee, 'From chains to freedom: libraries in Leicester from the Middle Ages to the opening of the free library', in *Aspects of Leicester: discovering local history*, ed. John Hinks. Barnsley: Wharncliffe, 2000, pp. 105–14; Joy Tilley, *A catalogue of the donations made to Norwich City Library 1608–1656*. Cambridge: LP Publications, 2000.

44 Katherine A. Armstrong, 'The Baikie Library at Tankerness House Museum, Kirkwall, Orkney', *Library review* **40** (1), 1991, 37–44.

45 K. C. Harrison, *A librarian's odyssey: episodes of autobiography*. Eastbourne: The author, 2000.

46 Denis F. Keeling, '"All sky and turnips": William Munford's Ilford interlude'; J. F. Hannavy, 'Dover Public Library 1934–1945: William Munford as first librarian'; and Brian D. Hutchin, 'Cambridge Borough Library, 1945–1953: the Munford years', *Library history* **12**, 1996, 224–31, 232–45, 246–52.

47 James G. Ollé, 'Portsmouth Public Libraries: the first fifty years', *Library history* **12**, 1996, 201–15; Paul Sturges, 'The public library and its readers 1850–1900', *Library history* **12**, 1996, 183–200; Paul Sturges and Alison Barr, '"The fiction nuisance" in 19th-century British public libraries', *Journal of librarianship and information science* **24** (1), 1992, 23–32.

48 Peter Hoare, 'Hungry for reading: libraries in the British Zone of Occupation' in *The cultural legacy of the British Occupation in Germany*, ed. Alan Bance. Stuttgart: Hans-Dieter Heinz, 1997.

49 Philip Henry Jones, 'Welsh public libraries to 1914', and G. I. Evans, 'Welsh public libraries 1914–1994' in *A nation and its books*, ed. Jones and Rees, pp. 277–86 and 287–95.

50 Micheál Ó hAodha, 'Irish rural libraries: glimpses of the past', *Library history* **16** (1), 2000, 49–56; Máire Kennedy, 'Civic pride versus financial pressure: financing the Dublin public library service, 1884–1920', *Library history* **9** (3/4), 1992, 83–96.

51 Bob Duckett, 'Paradise Lost? The retreat from reference', *Library review* **41** (1), 1992, 4–24; Lindy Moore, 'The provision of women's reading rooms in public libraries', *Library history* **9** (5/6), 1993, 190–202; Dale C. Russell, '"Our special province": providing a library service for London's public shelters, 1940–1942', *Library history* **13**, 1997, 3–15.

52 W. J. West, *The strange rise of semi-literate England: the dissolution of the libraries*. London: Duckworth, 1991.

53 Graham Jefcoate, 'Democracy at work: the Library Association's "Centenary assessment" of 1950', *Library history* **15** (2), 1999, 99–111.

54 Geoffrey Forster, 'Libraries for the few: the members of the Association of Independent Libraries and their archives', *Library history* **9** (1/2), 1991, 15–26.

55 *Heart of a London village: the Highgate Literary and Scientific Institution 1939–1990*. London: Historical Publications, 1991; Neville Carrick and Edward L. Ashton, *The Athenaeum Liverpool, 1797–1997*. Liverpool: Athenaeum, 1997; *Bicentenary lectures 1993*. Newcastle-upon-Tyne: Literary and Philosophical Society, 1994, complementing Charles Parish's *The history of the Literary & Philosophical Society of Newcastle upon Tyne. Vol. 2: 1896–1989*, published in 1990.

56 Rosalys T. Coope and Jane Y. Corbett (eds.), *Bromley House 1752–1991: four essays celebrating the 175th anniversary of Nottingham Subscription Library*. Nottingham: Nottingham Subscription Library, 1991; Russell Chamberlin, *Survival: the rise, fall and rise of the Guildford Institute of the University of Surrey*. Guildford: University of Surrey, 1997.

57 Frank Beckwith, *The Leeds Library 1768–1968; with a new preface by Dennis Cox*. Leeds: Leeds Library, 1994; Geoffrey Forster *et al.*, *'A very good public library': early years of the Leeds Library*. Wylam: Allenholme Press for the History of the Book Trade in the North, 1991.

58 Ann Brooks and Bryan Howarth, *Portico Library: a history*. Lancaster: Carnegie Publishing, 2000.

59 John Wells, *Rude words: a discursive history of the London Library*. London: Macmillan, 1991; and 'Some previous librarians' in *Founders and followers: literary lectures given on the occasion of the 150th anniversary*. London: Sinclair-Stevenson, 1992, pp. 149–74.

60 William Baker, *The early history of the London Library*. Lewiston, N.Y.: Edwin Mellen Press, 1991.

61 Peter Hoare, 'St Martin's Subscription Library, Westminster, 1839–1852: an overlooked library and its links with Edward Edwards', *Library history* **12**, 1996, 62–76.

62 K. A. Manley, 'Rural reading in north-west England: the Sedbergh Book Club 1728–1928', *Book history* **2**, 1999, 78–95.

63 Ernest H. Boddy, 'The Dalton Book Club: a brief history'; and M. J. Swanton, 'A dividing book club of the 1840s: Wadebridge, Cornwall', *Library history* **9** (3/4), 1992, 97–105 and 106–121.

64 Marie-Louise Legg, 'The Kilkenny Circulating-Library Society and the growth of reading rooms in 19th-century Ireland' in *The experience of reading: Irish historical perspectives*, ed. Bernadette Cunningham and Máire Kennedy. Dublin: Rare Books Group of Library Association of Ireland, 1999, pp. 109–23.

65 John C. Crawford, 'The ideology of mutual improvement in Scottish working class libraries', *Library history* **12**, 1996, 49–61.

66 Jean Everitt, 'Co-operative societies and their libraries', *Library history* **15** (1), 1998, 33–40; Christopher M. Baggs, 'The libraries of the co-operative movement: a forgotten episode', *Journal of librarianship and information science* **23** (2), 1991, 87–96.

67 Christopher M. Baggs, 'The Miners' Institute libraries of South Wales' in *A nation and its books*, ed. Jones and Rees, pp. 297–306.

68 Christopher Skelton-Foord, 'To buy or to borrow? Circulating libraries and novel reading in Britain 1778–1828', *Library review* **47** (7/8), 1998, 341–7; Nicholas Hiley, '"Can't you find me something nasty?" Circulating libraries and literary censorship in Britain from the 1890s to the 1910s', in *Censorship and the control of print in England and France 1600–1910*, ed. Robin Myers and Michael Harris. Winchester: St Paul's Bibliographies, 1992, pp. 123–47; John C. Day, *The circulating library in the Northeast*. Newcastle: History of the Book Trade in the North, 1994.

69 K. A. Manley, 'Booksellers, peruke-makers, and rabbit merchants: the growth of circulating libraries in the 18th century' in *Libraries and the book trade: the formation of collections from the 16th to the 20th century*, ed. Robin Myers, Michael Harris and Giles Mandelbrote. Winchester: St Paul's Bibliographies, 2000.

70 David Rogers, *The Bodleian Library and its treasures, 1320–1700*. London: Aidan Ellis, 1991; Giles Barber, *Arks for learning: a short history of Oxford library buildings*. Oxford: Oxford Bibliographical Society, 1995.

71 James P. Carley, 'Sir Thomas Bodley's library and its acquisitions: an edition of the Nottingham benefaction of 1604', in *Books and collectors 1200–1700*, ed. Carley and Tite, pp. 357–86.

72 Alan Coates, 'The old library of Trinity College, Oxford', *Bodleian Library record* **13** (4), 1991, 466–78.

73 Paul Morgan, 'Oxford college libraries in the 18th century', *Bodleian Library record* **14** (3), 1992, 228–36; Ivor Guest, *Dr John Radcliffe and his Trust*. Oxford: Radcliffe Trust, 1991.

74 Jonathan B. Bengtson, 'Benefaction registers in Oxford college libraries', *Library history* **16** (2), 2000, 143–52.

75 Peter Fox (ed.), *Cambridge University Library: its great collections*. Cambridge: University Library, 1998.

76 David McKitterick (ed.), *Andrew Perne quatercentenary studies*. Cambridge: Cambridge Bibliographical Society, 1991.

77 Elisabeth Leedham-Green and David McKitterick, 'A catalogue of Cambridge University Library in 1583' in *Books and collectors 1200–1700*, ed. Carley and Tite, pp. 153–235; J. J. Hall, 'The guard-book catalogue of Cambridge University Library', *Library history* **13**, 1997, 39–56.

78 David McKitterick (ed.), *The making of the Wren Library*. Cambridge: University Press, 1995.

79 Lavinia Hutton, *Trinity Hall: the story of the library*. Cambridge: Trinity Hall, 2000; *Caius and Cockerell: the transformation of a library*. Cambridge: Gonville & Caius College, 1997.

80 Nicholas Rogers, 'The early history of Sidney Sussex college library' in *Sidney Sussex College, Cambridge: historical essays*, ed. D. E. D. Beales and H. B. Nisbet. Woodbridge: Boydell Press, 1996, pp. 75–88.

81 James Thompson, *A centennial history of the library of the University of Birmingham 1880–1985*. Birmingham: University of Birmingham, 2000.

82 P. S. Morrish, 'Fanny Juliet Passavant (1849–1944): a Leeds librarian', *Library history*

12, 1996, 126–41; and 'Dichotomy and status: Leeds university librarianship to 1934', *History of universities* **15**, 1997/99, 227–59; Brian Dyson, 'In the line of fire: the library of Hull University College during World War II', *Library history* **15** (2), 1999, 113–23.

83 Judith Priestman,'Philip Larkin and the Bodleian Library', *Bodleian Library record* **14** (1), 1991, 33–66.

84 Peter Hoare, 'The librarians of Glasgow University over 350 years: 1641–1991', *Library review* **40** (2/3), 1991, 27–43; Iain Beavan, 'Marischal College, Aberdeen, and its earliest library catalogue: a reassessment', *Bibliotheck* **22**, 1997, 4–19; Colin A. McLaren, *Rare and fair: a visitor's history of Aberdeen University Library*. Aberdeen: University Library, 1995.

85 Vincent Kinane and Anne Walsh (eds.), *Essays on the history of Trinity College Dublin*. Dublin: Four Courts Press, 2000.

86 Agnes Neligan (ed.), *Maynooth library treasures: from the library of St Patrick's College*. Dublin: Royal Irish Academy, 1995.

87 Nigel Ramsay, 'The cathedral archives and library' in *A history of Canterbury Cathedral, 598–1982*, ed. Patrick Collinson, Nigel Ramsay and Margaret Sparks. Oxford: University Press, 1995, pp. 341–407; Mary Hobbs, 'The cathedral library' in *Chichester Cathedral: an historical survey*, ed. Mary Hobbs. Chichester: Phillimore, 1994, pp. 171–88; A. M. Erskine, 'Library and archives' in *Exeter cathedral: a celebration*, ed. Michael Swanton. Crediton: Dean and Chapter, 1991, pp. 193–201; Joan Williams, 'The library' in *Hereford Cathedral: a history*, ed. Gerald Aylmer and John Tiller. London: Hambledon, 2000, pp. 511–35.

88 David Pearson, 'The libraries of English bishops, 1600–40', *The library* 6th ser. **14** (3), 1992, 221–57; David G. Selwyn, *Thomas Cranmer's library*. Oxford: Oxford Bibliographical Society, 1994; and his 'Thomas Cranmer and the dispersal of medieval libraries' in *Books and collectors 1200–1700*, ed. Carley and Tite, pp. 81–94; A. I. Doyle, 'John Cosin (1595–1672) as a library maker', *Book collector* **40** (3), 1991, 335–57; Helen Carron, 'William Sancroft (1617–93): a 17th-century collector and his library', *The library* 7th ser. **1** (1), 2000, 290–307.

89 Robert S. Matteson, 'Archbishop William King and the conception of his library', *The library* 6th ser. **13** (3), 1991, 238–54.

90 Margaret Connolly, 'A plague of books: the dispersal and disappearance of the diocesan libraries of the Church of Ireland' in *Lost libraries*, ed. Raven, pp. 197–218.

91 Gordon Huelin, *Sion College and its library*. London: Sion College, 1992.

92 David Menhennet, *The House of Commons library: a history*. London: HMSO, 1991; Marie Boas Hall, *The library and archives of the Royal Society 1660–1990*. London: Royal Society, 1992.

93 L. L. Peck, 'Uncovering the Arundel Library at the Royal Society: changing meanings of science and the fate of the Norfolk donation', *Notes and records of the Royal Society of London* **52**, 1998, 3–24.

94 Jacqueline Jenkinson, 'The role of medical societies in the rise of the Scottish medical profession 1730–1939', *Social history of medicine* **4** (2), 1991, 253–75; John Symons, *Wellcome Institute for the History of Medicine: a short history*. London: Wellcome Trust, 1992.

95 Alistair Black, 'Information, paternalism and cocoa: "confectionery" Fordism, northern innovation and library provision at Rowntree of York before the Second World War', *Library history* **10**, 1994, 51–70.

96 Peter Hoare, 'The development of a European information society', *Library review* **47** (7/8), 1998, 377–82.

97 Pamela Spence Richards, 'The quest for enemy scientific information 1939–1945: information history as part of library history', *Library history* **9** (1/2) 1991, 5–14; Alistair Black and Rodney Brunt, 'Information management in business, libraries and British military intelligence: towards a history of information management', *Journal of documentation* **55** (4), 1999, 361–74; and their 'MI5, 1909–1945: an information management perspective', *Journal of information science* **26** (3), 2000, 185–97.

98 Janet Fyfe, *Books behind bars: the role of books, reading and libraries in British prison reform, 1701–1911*. Westport, Conn.: Greenwood Press, 1992.

10

Rare book librarianship and historical bibliography

David Pearson

Rare book librarianship is that branch of the profession which is concerned with the custodianship and exploitation of collections which are accorded special treatment on such grounds as age, fragility, value or rarity – typically, early printed books (libraries usually define a chronological boundary somewhere in the nineteenth century), but possibly also including manuscripts or valuable modern books (e.g. private press material, or artists' books). These collections commonly exist within larger libraries whose traffic is predominantly focused on their general, modern collections, although their special collections may be regarded as a significant element in their overall profile. Many of the trends affecting librarianship as a whole therefore apply to rare book librarianship, but it has an identifiable development path of its own centred on the ways in which such collections are treated differently from other library materials, by way of cataloguing, collection management and use. Rare book librarianship – everything to do with the professional management of rare books in libraries, however 'rare books' are defined – is not the same as historical bibliography, although the two are traditionally closely linked. The latter term is here taken to embrace that range of activities around the study of early printed books and manuscripts which leads to the dissemination of knowledge about book history, through publications or other means. Rare book librarians of necessity play an important facilitating role in the development of historical bibliography, and they may be actively involved themselves as researchers and authors in this field.

Associations and societies
Professional associations, learned societies and other special interest groups continued to play an important role throughout the decade in co-ordinating activities across all these areas. As regards rare book librarianship, the Library Association Rare Books Group provided the primary focus for discussing and developing professional issues; its membership rose steadily during the decade, from 1025 in 1990 to 1199 in 2000, and its *Newsletter* (issues 39–64 published 1991–2000) provided regular updates on events, conferences, exhibitions, projects,

new publications and other matters.[1] The Bibliographical Society, the main UK learned society for promotion of study around book history, marked its centenary in 1992 with the publication of *The book encompassed*, a series of essays summarising developments in historical bibliography during the second half of the twentieth century, and by launching a Centenary Appeal whose success enabled the Society to introduce a new series of annual grants to support bibliographical research.[2] Its regular activities (publishing *The library* and occasional monographs, and organizing lectures) were supplemented by the similar doings of regional bibliographical societies, particularly those of Cambridge, Oxford and Edinburgh, and through the work of other more focused groups such as the Printing Historical Society or the Book Trade History Group. The Historic Libraries Forum was formed in 1992, with the aim of providing support targeted at small and independent libraries with important special collections; SHARP, the Society for the History of Authorship, Reading and Publishing, was founded in 1991 as an international venture, with the initial impetus based in the USA but significantly supported by British scholars with an interest in the growing switch in emphasis from textual bibliography towards study of the dissemination and reception of books.[3]

Short-title catalogues

The creation of an authoritative national bibliography, listing every traceable item printed in the English-speaking world from the beginning of printing to the end of the hand-press era, was one of the defining achievements of Anglo-American historical bibliography in the twentieth century. 1991 saw the publication by the Bibliographical Society of the third and final volume of the revised version of *A short-title catalogue of books printed in England, Scotland, and Ireland ... 1475–1640*, a cornerstone of English bibliography commonly known simply as *STC*.[4] Pollard and Redgrave's original 1926 edition was extensively revised in a process begun by W. A. Jackson and F. S. Ferguson, completed by Katharine Pantzer, leading to the new work published in 1976–91; the third volume comprised indexes and appendices. It has always been recognised that the companion bibliography for 1641–1700, originally compiled by Donald Wing and published in three volumes 1945–51, is equally indispensable but less reliable; the revised edition of volume one issued by Wing in 1972 was not an improvement, and it was the publication in 1994 of a new revised version of this volume, edited by John Morrison, Carolyn Nelson and Matthew Seccombe, that properly concluded the creation of the second edition (volumes 2 and 3 were issued in 1982 and 1988).[5] In 1996, the whole bibliography was issued on CD-ROM.[6]

The eighteenth century had begun to be dealt with in similarly comprehensive fashion with the creation of the *Eighteenth-century short title catalogue* (*ESTC*), which began life at the British Library in 1977. This was created from the start as an automated file, although its first published product was the 1983 microfiche covering 145,000 books held in the British Library; a second microfiche, containing twice as many records and incorporating the holdings of many libraries, was issued in 1990, but this was followed by a CD-ROM version in 1992.[7] The major development for *ESTC* during the 1990s, planned from 1987 onwards but only publicly visible in the online file from 1994, was its transformation from the *Eighteenth-century short title catalogue* to the *English short-title catalogue*, by expanding to take in the whole handpress period, 1475–1800. Records for books from *STC* and Wing were incorporated by various means, including the import of records from elsewhere, with much of the developmental work led by the North American office under the direction of Henry Snyder.[8] A further CD-ROM was published in 1998, containing records for over 375,000 items.[9] By the end of the decade the *ESTC* file was increasingly established as the principal bibliographical reference point for pre-1801 English books, although the means of its creation and the size of the file meant that it inevitably had some rough edges, a cause of occasional sniping and skirmishes within the circles of bibliographical debate.[10]

Its sister bibliography *ISTC* – the *Incunabula short-title catalogue*, building up a union catalogue of holdings of pre-1500 imprints not only in the UK, but across Europe and further afield – continued to be developed at the British Library and by the beginning of the decade held records for nearly 25,000 discrete editions.[11] A CD-ROM version, including images of selected pages from the books, was published in 1994, with a second edition in 1998.[12] Another major electronic database of early printed books was created through the formation in 1992 of CERL, the Consortium of European Research Libraries.[13] This was an initiative to bring together major research libraries from across Europe and create a union catalogue of rare book records, partly to create a resource discovery tool, and partly to create a source of records for shared cataloguing. The idea was led in the UK initially from the British Library, particularly through the support of Michael Smethurst, then Director-General; the US-based Research Libraries Group was something of a model. The actual gathering and editing of files began in 1994, and a public interface to the *Hand press book database*, covering imprints down to 1830, went live in 1997. The Consortium included members from numerous European countries, typically national libraries and big university libraries; it had established a stable *modus operandi* by the end of the decade, with 35 full members and 21 associate members.

Other catalogues
The rise of these great databases, and the growing trend to provide all kinds of catalogue access electronically, inevitably led to decline in the publication of the kinds of printed catalogues which had previously been important not only as finding aids but also as bibliographical reference works. The tradition was however still alive in the 1990s; David Paisey's five-volume *Catalogue of books printed in the German-speaking countries ... 1601 to 1700 now in the British Library* (1994) was the fruit of many years of patient and authoritative scholarship.[14] The decade also saw the publication of the penultimate volume of the Wellcome catalogue of pre-1850 imprints, covering authors M–R (1995).[15]

A union catalogue which had long been in preparation and which came to published completion during the 1990s was the *Cathedral libraries catalogue*. The project to compile a listing of all pre-1701 books in Anglican cathedrals in England and Wales began in 1943, the brainchild of Margaret Hands; its history thereafter was long and intermittent but a first volume was issued in 1984, covering English imprints. Volume two, published in 1998, covered continental books and was a much more substantial production, with full catalogue entries where volume one had relied only on citations to *STC* and Wing numbers.[16] The *CLC* opened up the contents of an important, though easily overlooked, sector in the overall picture of national holdings of early printed books and was brought to completion under the editorship of David Shaw, whose pioneering work in applying automated cataloguing methodologies to rare books work was an important factor in making it possible.

Cataloguing

Cataloguing was a significant professional issue for rare book librarians generally during the 1990s, as a number of developments took place around standards and the move from manual to automated platforms. The situation at the beginning of the decade was summarised in *Rare book cataloguing in the British Isles*, a British Library-funded survey by Ann Lennon and David Pearson, published in 1991.[17] By this time most libraries of any size were running automated library management systems and catalogue access for current materials had moved from cards or sheaf catalogues to OPACs, but rare books tended to be at the end of the queue as far as the overall transition process was concerned. The 1991 report found that only 6% of 125 libraries surveyed held all their records for early printed books in automated format, and in 47% of cases all records were still manual. Many libraries had sizeable backlogs of rare books which were not catalogued at all; only 34% of the sample could report that all their holdings were catalogued in some form. There was a considerable diversity of practice regarding the standards in use; *AACR2* was generally predominant but local codes and British Museum rules still featured, and there was dissatisfaction over the limitations of the MARC format for handling the special requirements of rare books work, such as accurate transcription and copy-specific information. Library systems were typically not geared towards accommodating the indexing and searching of this kind of data and the result was a wide variety of workarounds in different libraries, inventing or adapting MARC fields to cope, and inputting data which could not always be retrieved.

One direct outcome of the survey was the establishment of a Rare Books Group-sponsored working party, chaired by Ross Bourne of the National Bibliographic Service, to review provision for rare books cataloguing within the framework of UKMARC. A set of new fields, based on ones then used by USMARC, was recommended in 1992 and formally adopted laer that year; they included designated fields for recording provenance, binding, genre headings and fingerprints.[18] These fields were gradually taken up by the professional community during the years that followed, encouraged by a series of Rare Books Group training events. In 1997 the Group issued a set of *Guidelines for the cataloguing of rare books*, giving examples of the use of the fields according to optional levels of cataloguing detail.[19] UK rare book cataloguing became increasingly standardised around *AACR2* and UKMARC, but commonly enhanced by reference to one of three specialised codes, two of which were issued in revised editions in 1991: *Descriptive cataloguing of rare books*, the Library of Congress code, and *International standard description of older books (antiquarian)* (*ISBD(A)*), the code issued by IFLA. The third code, the *ESTC* rules, dated from 1984.

Retroconversion was also a cataloguing challenge during the decade, as many libraries contained significant rare book collections which were not the top priority when it came to turning card catalogues into online ones; more current holdings inevitably took precedence. Libraries were sometimes able to find local resources to tackle this – work on converting the pre-1920 card catalogue of the Bodleian Library, subsequently published on CD-ROM, began in 1992, funded by a special grant from the University – but typically needed to look to external grant-giving sources to underwrite such work.[20] The 1993 Follett report was a help in this respect; although concerned with academic library provision generally, its recognition of the special support needs of research collections in the humanities and the subsequent creation of a non-formula funding stream by the Higher Education Funding Councils led to a number of major initiatives in this area.[21] Rare books in the university libraries of Aberdeen, Birmingham, Cambridge, Durham, Manchester and elsewhere came to be retroconverted; the Early Printed Book Project in Oxford, automating the union catalogue of early imprints across the Oxford colleges, began in 1995 under this funding umbrella.[22]

The next major injection of new funding into higher education, the result of the 1995 Anderson Report, was the Research Support Libraries Programme (RSLP), which disbursed over £11 million in project funding between 1999 and 2002.[23] RSLP was less sympathetic to retroconversion pure and simple, and preferred collaborative discipline-focused projects aimed at opening up researcher access to a wealth of material in particular subject fields through electronic means, including the creation of subject portals and collection-mapping exercises. A number of grants did nevertheless include significant elements of retroconversion, such as the Birmingham-hosted projects around nineteenth-century pamphlets, and nineteenth- and twentieth-century church history. The Oxford Early Imprints Project also managed to continue its activities through RSLP funding. The RSLP programme supported a host of other initiatives to open up knowledge of rare book collections in various ways, as well as some web portals dedicated to book historical studies (BOOKHAD created a union catalogue of resources on book history and design, AIM25 gave unified access to archive holdings across London, and the Palaeography project sought to create a focal point for online collaborative work as well as for the dissemination of information on resources).[24]

Catalogues allow researchers to find resources at item level but it is also helpful to have information at collection level, and to have an overview of the holdings and strengths of particular libraries. The *Directory of rare book and special collections in the United Kingdom and the Republic of Ireland*, produced by the Rare Books Group under the editorship of Moelwyn Williams, had been published in 1984 and was quickly recognised as a unique and valuable guide which filled a gap in the literature. It was not, however, above criticism and its reliance on a network of volunteers to gather data meant that a number of libraries and geographical areas were covered either poorly or not at all. The need for a second edition was soon recognised and after some false starts this task was taken up in earnest by Barry Bloomfield in 1991 when he became Chairman of the Rare Books Group. With financial support from the Leverhulme Foundation, he undertook the comprehensive revision of the work, contacting libraries systematically for new or updated entries, and the new edition was published in 1997.[25] With summary descriptions of the early printed book collections in over 1200 libraries across the UK and Ireland, large and small, this has continued to be a indispensable reference work.

Collections

Rare book collections are not, or should not, be static things and acquisitions work is a regular component of the professional activity of many rare book librarians, depending on the sums available from the parent body. Many books and manuscripts found new institutional homes in special collections departments during the 1990s, fuelled by the equally regular activities of book dealers, auction houses and private collectors. There were obvious high spots, like the British Library's 1994 purchase of the Bristol Baptist College copy of Tyndale's 1526 New Testament (£1 million), or its purchase four years later of the Sherborne Missal, one of the most famous and spectacular English illuminated medieval manuscripts (£6 million), but a roll call of interesting acquisitions across the country would be a long list.[26] There were some *causes celèbres* representing the other side of the coin, the selling of books by libraries in order to raise money, which generated much more negative publicity. Two cases which attracted a degree of national attention were those of Edinburgh University in 1991, over the sale of Gould and Audubon plate books, and Keele University in 1999, when it was revealed that a collection of early mathematical books had been sold.[27] A library whose financial circumstances forced a more radical approach was Sion College in London, a seventeenth-century foundation with a number of important collections as well as the legacy of having been a copyright deposit library from 1710 to 1836. A happier outcome was achieved here by transferring all the pre-1850 books (about 35,000 volumes), together with 30,000 pamphlets, to Lambeth Palace Library, while the later imprints were taken in by King's College London.[28]

Funding

Rare books work is particularly dependent on grants from charitable bodies, national agencies or private donors to fund all kinds of activities, including acquisitions, cataloguing, conservation, equipment and buildings. The important role of the special funding streams created by the Higher Education Funding

Councils during the 1990s has already been mentioned; other bodies, such as the Friends of the National Libraries, the Museums and Galleries Commission Purchase Grant Fund, the National Heritage Memorial Fund and the Pilgrim Trust continued to dispense bounty to help with exceptional purchases and other work which could not otherwise be supported. An important new source which became available from 1994 onwards was the Heritage Lottery Fund, whose very first grant was the somewhat controversial £12.5 million awarded towards the purchase of the Churchill Papers for Churchill College, Cambridge.[29] By 1999 the Fund could report that over £67 million had been allocated to libraries and archives, although this was only about 5% of the total sum of £1.18 billion which had been disbursed.[30] The library and archive grants covered a range of activities, not all including rare book or heritage collections, but there were numerous awards which did. The British Library's purchase of the Sherborne Missal, mentioned above, was underwritten by the HLF to the tune of £4,125,000, and the BL also received £358,000 from the Fund around the same time to automate its catalogues of western manuscripts. In 1996 Chetham's Library in Manchester was awarded £1.8 million to carry out a range of beneficial work, including new facilities as well as cataloguing, and in 1997 the National Art Library received £1 million for a major recataloguing programme, including its important early collections.[31] Despite these positive results the feeling of the HLF's Archives and Libraries Policy Advisor at the end of the decade was that libraries were not benefiting from the Fund's potential as much as they might, and the Rare Books Group organized a series of regional workshops in 1999 to raise awareness and offer practical guidance in presenting projects.

Publications
Much new work was published across the broad spectrum of historical bibliography throughout the decade, in monographs and journal articles. The broad trend in this field towards the end of the twentieth century was one of moving away from an emphasis on textual and enumerative bibliography towards a greater interest in the social impact of books, as revealed by the study of their distribution, ownership and use – the ongoing evolution of historical bibliography, as a discipline, into the history of the book. One symbol of this was the establishment in 1995 of the UK's first MA course in the History of the Book, at the Centre for English Studies in the University of London; another was the appearance in 1999 of a volume of *The Cambridge history of the book in Britain*, covering the period 1400–1557.[32] This was the third volume in a projected series of seven, but the first to be published, the fruits of an ambitious long-term publishing programme which began in the 1980s. The project set a trend which inspired similar ventures in other countries both within and beyond the British Isles, and *A nation and its books: a history of the book in Wales* was published in 1998.[33]

Another major multi-volume study, focusing on one particular publishing centre but very much concerned with understanding its activities in the broader historical, economic and social context, was David McKitterick's *History of*

Cambridge University Press, whose first two volumes (out of three) were published in 1992 and 1998.[34] The importance of printed outputs in shaping cultural history, and the ways in which that happened in the early modern period, were central themes in Adrian Johns' *The nature of the book* (1998), a substantial and generally well-received study by a British author then based in America.[35] Other books of the 1990s concerned with printing and publishing history included one by Vincent Kinane on Dublin University Press and Christine Ferdinand's *Benjamin Collins and the provincial newspaper trade in the eighteenth century.*[36]

In harmony with that growing interest in the ownership and use of books, a number of useful studies of individual private libraries appeared; examples are David Selwyn's *Library of Thomas Cranmer* (1996), David and Mary Norton's *David Hume library* (1996), *Richard III's books*, by Anne Sutton and Livia Visser-Fuchs (1997), and *Sir Robert Cotton as collector* (1997), edited by Christopher Wright.[37] Kevin Sharpe's *Reading revolutions* (2000) looked at the historical insights to be gained from a detailed study of the marginalia and commonplace books of a member of the English gentry during the Civil War period.[38] An Anglo-American project to edit and publish early owners' book lists, focusing initially on Oxford probate inventories of the sixteenth and seventeenth centuries, was *Private libraries in Renaissance England*, whose first volume was published in 1992; four more volumes were published, 1993–98.[39] The UK editor of this project, Elisabeth Leedham-Green, also launched a separate series of occasional monographs, *Libri pertinentes*, as a vehicle to publish various kinds of early lists of books in private or institutional ownership; six volumes were issued between 1992 and 2000.[40] David Pearson's *Provenance research in book history: a handbook* (1994) was aimed at both helping and fostering this developing area of interest, by providing an overview of the kinds of evidence of previous ownership found in books, and ways of identifying it.[41] In parallel with this growing body of work on provenance and private libraries, the history of reading also gathered pace as an academic discipline, spurred on by the publication in 1996 of Alberto Manguel's book with that title.[42] A *Reading experience database*, to record and bring together evidence of early reading practice, was launched in 1994.[43]

Bookbinding studies were advanced through the 1992 publication of Howard Nixon's 1979 Lyell Lectures, edited by Mirjam Foot and issued under their joint authorship as *The history of decorated bookbinding in England.*[44] A fourth, revised edition of Bernard Middleton's seminal *History of English craft bookbinding technique* appeared in 1996, while understanding of structural aspects of bindings was developed by Nicholas Pickwoad in several essays, most notably 'Onward and downward: how binders coped with the printing press before 1800', published in 1994.[45] Nineteenth-century bookbinding history benefited from Maurice Packer's *Bookbinders of Victorian London* (1992), and an important article by Esther Potter on 'The London bookbinding trade: from craft to industry', in *The library* in 1993.[46] Early Oxford bookbinding was surveyed afresh by David Pearson in *Oxford bookbinding 1500–1640* (2000), building on the earlier work of Neil Ker.[47] In line with broader trends in bibliographical studies, bookbinding historians towards the end of the century were increasingly moving away from traditional emphases on fine and decorated bindings, and an art-historical type of approach to the subject, to look at the various lessons to be learned from bindings of all kinds, and to see the evidence presented by bindings as one part of the book-historical whole. This was a central theme of Mirjam Foot's 1997 Panizzi Lectures, *The history of bookbinding as a mirror of society*.[48]

Manuscripts

Manuscript researchers were served not only by developments in catalogue automation but also by advances in some important reference series, most notably Neil Ker's authoritative survey of *Medieval manuscripts in British libraries*, whose fourth and final volume, posthumously completed by Alan Piper, appeared in 1992.[49] Kathleen Scott's *Later gothic manuscripts 1390–1490* (1996) was the final volume in the Harvey Miller series, *A survey of manuscripts illuminated in the British Isles*, which began in 1977; the *Index of English literary manuscripts*, another project whose work began in the 1970s, saw a further nineteenth-century volume issued in 1993.[50] A new series which began publication under the aegis of the British Library was the *Corpus of British medieval library catalogues*; the *Registrum Anglie*, edited by R. H. and M. A. Rouse, appeared in 1991 and six further volumes had been issued by 2000.[51] Among monographs in manuscript studies of the 1990s one might mention the second, revised edition of Christopher de Hamel's very successful *History of illuminated manuscripts* (1994), and Henry Woudhuysen's study of later manuscript culture, *Sir Philip Sidney and the circulation of manuscripts* (1996).[52]

Conferences

The annual conference on the history of the book trade which began in 1979, organized under the auspices of Birkbeck College, University of London by Robin Myers, Michael Harris and (latterly) Giles Mandelbrote, continued to flourish throughout the decade, producing a series of published volumes of essays which cumulatively amount to a significant and valued body of work.[53] The parallel series of annual British Book Trade Seminars, focusing primarily on provincial book trade history in association with the British Book Trade Index project (run by Peter Isaac) began to be formally published on a similarly regular basis as the *Print networks* series from 1997 onwards, although some earlier proceedings from these conferences had been published less uniformly.[54]

Historic houses

Rare book collections are found not only in national, academic and ecclesiastical collections; it has long been recognized that the many historic houses around the UK have important and diverse holdings, although they are generally less well known and not always easy to access. The combined libraries of the National Trust constitute a major asset, with over 150 collections running to hundreds of thousands of books of all periods. The 1999 publication of Nicolas Barker's

Treasures from the libraries of National Trust country houses, in conjunction with a major exhibition at the Grolier Club in New York, was welcome not only as a new window on some of their more remarkable books, but also because it marked a substantial funding injection from the Royal Oak Foundation, making it possible to endow a new librarian's post for the Trust.[55] This increase in the professional complement within the Trust ensured a significant increase in activity, in cataloguing and publicity for the libraries, in the years which followed.

New technology

The transformational power of new technology is surely the key theme affecting all developments in librarianship in the 1990s, and rare books librarianship is no exception to this. Although the internet has a history going back to the 1960s, with the steady development thereafter of computer networks, it is widely recognized that the launch of the World Wide Web in 1991 was the catalyst that led to massive expansion in the transmission of every kind of information electronically. Many of the developments in cataloguing and retroconversion described above were spurred on by the increasing interconnectivity brought about by the evolution of the internet, as it became easier to search catalogues remotely via web interfaces.

Electronic catalogues, and online bibliographies like *ESTC*, deal in metadata about books and other kinds of information resources, but not in the texts themselves. Digital technology allows us to make a step change in this regard by scanning or keying in texts so that it is not only metadata, but also a full-text facsimile of the original item that is transmitted electronically. Like the internet, this process has a longer history than might at first be thought – Project Gutenberg, converting out-of-copyright printed texts into freely available eBooks, began in 1971 – but the momentum increased greatly towards the end of the century.[56] Rare books are by their nature scarce, fragile, and consultable in libraries under special conditions; digital facsimiles have the potential to make them much more easily accessible, in a more user-friendly way than the microfilm surrogates of the preceding generation.

Digitization

The 1990s saw a variety of projects springing up around the digitizing of rare books; the period was initially one of experimentation, looking at what was possible, what the benefits were, and what the business models should be, leading to the emergence by the end of the decade of some large and firmly-rooted products which would point the way to the future. In 1993 the British Library began its Electronic Beowulf project, producing high-quality digital facsimiles of every page of the *Beowulf* manuscript, using the technology to reveal pieces of text which had previously been illegible.[57] Selected pages were subsequently mounted on the internet and the entire file was published on CD-ROM.[58] A different approach to the application of digital technology to early books, also pioneered by the British Library, was their *Turning the pages* project, launched in 1998, which allowed exhibition gallery visitors to see selected treasures in digital versions whose pages could literally be turned by running a finger across the page.[59]

Digitization presented libraries with a number of challenges, not only concerning technical standards, modes of delivery and long-term preservation of electronic media, but also in relation to the funding of such initiatives. Investment in equipment and expertise could not easily be found from within normal operating budgets, and various kinds of special funding had to be sought. At Oxford, a project to produce high quality digital facsimiles of early medieval manuscripts from several Oxford libraries, Early Manuscripts at Oxford University, ran from 1995 to 2000, funded by HEFCE through its post-Follett non-formula funding stream; Aberdeen University Library was able to use the same source to fund the digitization of its medieval Bestiary manuscript.[60] Another Oxford project, to digitize ephemera from the John Johnson Collection, found money from the JISC Image Digitization Initiative.[61] Oxford was also involved in a collaborative venture with several other university libraries (Birmingham, Leeds and Manchester) who successfully bid to the eLib Programme in 1996 to run a pilot project around the digitization of eighteenth- and nineteenth-century printed journals, the internet Library of Early Journals.[62] When the British Library made a full-text facsimile of the Gutenberg Bible available on its website in 2000 it immediately attracted considerable interest, with almost a million hits on those web pages during the first six months, but the project was only made possible by partnership funding from Keio University in Japan.[63]

The major large-scale development in this area was made not by a library but by a commercial publisher, who had both the resources to invest and access to ready-made raw material. University Microfilms International (in the 1990s part of the Bell and Howell Company, subsequently renamed ProQuest) included among their products microfilm facsimiles of early English printed books, with almost complete coverage for the period down to 1700 (i.e. that covered by the two major bibliographies, *STC* and Wing). These could easily be digitized, without needing recourse to the original books, and in 1998 Bell and Howell launched *Early English books online*, an electronic database with a search interface provided, which initially gave access to over 90,000 titles in full-text facsimile, although the number steadily grew as more material was added.[64] The database was searchable at keyword in title level but not keyword in text, and the Universities of Michigan and Oxford led the way in forming the Text Creation Partnership, a consortium of libraries working with ProQuest to key in selected *STC* and Wing books so that the texts were fully searchable at this level.[65]

EEBO was a transformational step forward in bringing access to rare books into the digital age, although the six-figure price tag facing any library wishing to buy the product was a daunting barrier. It created a model for applying the potential of digital technology to early printed books in both a technical and a business sense which came to be copied in the years that followed; the longer-term impact on rare book librarianship is yet to be worked out. If comprehensive full-text access to the documentary printed heritage is available, and rare books are no longer rare as regards obtaining copies of the texts, how does that affect our approach to the printed originals? How should that affect cataloguing practice at local and union level: do previously held beliefs about the importance of detailed title transcriptions, or of locating individual copies in different libraries, need to change? How should databases like *ESTC*, in which public funding has been so heavily invested, respond or adapt when new generation electronic resources offer a one-stop shop not only to the metadata, but also to the full texts? These kinds of questions were increasingly taking shape as the decade came to its close, but it would be wrong to suggest that there was any consensus as to what the answers might be. There was, rather, a framework of debate emerging, as the potential of new technology became clearer, which would increasingly challenge traditional beliefs of rare book librarians and call for them to engage positively with the issues. The impact and pace of change continued to gather momentum into the first decade of the new century; in this respect, of course, rare book librarianship was no different from librarianship as a whole, where every aspect of the profession was undergoing radical review.

Notes

1 *Rare books newsletter* 39–64, April 1991–spring/summer 2000. Membership figures taken from the Group's annual reports, *Newsletter* 40, 1991, 17 and *Newsletter* 65, 2001, 33.

2 Peter Davison (ed.), *The book encompassed: studies in twentieth-century bibliography.* Cambridge: Cambridge University Press, 1992; B. C. Bloomfield, 'The Bibliographical Society Centenary Appeal Sub-Committee: final report', *The library* 6th ser. **18** (4), 1996, 376–80.

3 Bob Duckett, 'Historic Libraries Forum', *Rare books newsletter* 43, March 1993, 21–3; Society for the History of Authorship, Reading and Publishing, Introduction <http://www.sharpweb.org/intro.html> (accessed 9/05).

4 Katharine F. Pantzer, *A short-title catalogue of books printed in England, Scotland, & Ireland and of English books printed abroad 1475–1640. ... Vol. 3: A printers' & publishers' index: other indexes & appendices.* London: Bibliographical Society, 1991.

5 Donald Wing, *Short-title catalogue of books printed in England, Scotland, Ireland ... 1641–1700*, 2nd ed., newly revised and enlarged, ed. John J. Morrison *et al.* New York: Modern Language Association of America, 1994.

6 Donald Wing, *Wing short-title catalogue, 1641–1700.* Alexandria: Chadwyck–Healey, 1996.

7 *ESTC on CD–ROM.* London: British Library, 1992.

8 Henry L. Snyder, 'A history of the ESTC in North America', in *The English short-title catalogue: past, present, future,* ed. Henry L. Snyder and Michael S. Smith. New York: AMS Press, 2003, 105–54, pp.130–5. The progress of the ESTC project is also recorded in its newsletter *Factotum* (issues 33–40 published March 1991–December 1995).

9 *English short title catalogue 1473–1800.* London: British Library, 1998.

10 See letter from Peter Blayney, and reply by Henry Snyder and M. J. Crump, in *The library* 7th ser. **1** (1), March 2000, 72–7.

11 Lotte Hellinga, 'Incunabula Short Title Catalogue', *Rare books newsletter* 37/38, Nov. 1990, 29–32.

12 *The illustrated ISTC on CD-ROM.* Reading: Primary Source Media, 1996; 2nd ed., 1998.

13 Consortium of European Research Libraries <http://www.cerl.org> (accessed 9/05).

14 D. L. Paisey, *Catalogue of books printed in the German-speaking countries and of German books printed in other countries from 1601 to 1700 now in the British Library.* London: British Library, 1994.

15 H. J. M. Symons and H. R. Denham, *A catalogue of printed books in the Wellcome Historical Medical Library. IV: Books printed from 1641 to 1850, M–R.* London: Wellcome Institute for the History of Medicine, 1995.

16 David J. Shaw (editor-in-chief), *The cathedral libraries catalogue. Vol. 2: Books printed on the continent of Europe before 1701 in the libraries of the Anglican cathedrals of England and Wales.* London: British Library; Bibliographical Society, 1998.

17 Ann Lennon and David Pearson, *Rare book cataloguing in the British Isles.* London: British Library, 1991 (British Library research paper; 94).

18 'UKMARC revision for rare books: a progress report', *Rare books newsletter* 41/42, March 1992, 24–6.

19 Brian Hillyard and David Pearson, *Guidelines for the cataloguing of rare books.* London: Library Association Rare Books Group, 1997; 2nd rev. ed., 1999.

20 'News', *Rare books newsletter* 44, July 1993, 19–20.

21 Joint Funding Councils' Libraries Review Group, *Report.* Bristol: HEFCE, 1993. Chairman Sir Brian Follett.

22 *Accessing our humanities research collections: a guide to specialised collections for humanities researchers.* London: JISC, 1997.

23 Research Support Libraries Programme <http://www.rslp.ac.uk> (accessed 9/05); Michael Anderson (chairman), *Report of the group on a national/regional strategy for library provision for researchers.* Edinburgh: SHEFC, 1995.

24 Details of all these RSLP-funded projects will be found at <http://www.rslp.ac.uk/projects> (accessed 9/05).

25 B. C. Bloomfield (ed.), with the assistance of Karen Potts, *A directory of rare book and special collections in the United Kingdom and the Republic of Ireland.* 2nd ed. London: Library Association Publishing, 1997. See also Barry Bloomfield, 'Where are they now? Some reflections on the *Directory*, *Rare books newsletter*' 58, spring 1998, 37–50.

26 'Recent acquisitions', *Rare books newsletter* 47, July 1994, 21–2; 59, summer 1998, 26–7.

27 'Edinburgh University sells one of the earliest subscription copies of Audubon's *The Birds of America* at Christie's, New York', *Times*, 25 April 1992, p. 6; David McKitterick, 'The Keele affair', *Book collector* **48** (2), 1999, 202–7, and 'News and comment', *Book collector* **49** (1), 2000, 91–2.

28 Richard Palmer, 'Sion College Library', *Rare books newsletter* 55, spring 1997, 42–5.

29 'Lottery cash pays for Churchill's £12.5m papers', *The Times*, 27 April 1995, p.1. The sale sparked an ongoing controversy which can be traced through the newspapers of the time.

30 Stephen Green, 'Taking a gamble: rare books and the Heritage Lottery Fund', *Rare books newsletter* 60, winter 1998, 43–7.

31 Details of HLF grants can be found on their website, www.hlf.org.uk (accessed 9/05).

32 'News', *Rare books newsletter* 48, Nov. 1994, 22; Lotte Hellinga and J. B. Trapp (eds.), *The Cambridge history of the book in Britain. Vol. 3: 1400–1557*. Cambridge: Cambridge University Press, 1999.

33 Philip Henry Jones and Eiluned Rees (eds.), *A nation and its books: a history of the book in Wales*. Aberystwyth: National Library of Wales, 1998.

34 David McKitterick, *A history of Cambridge University Press. Vol. 1: Printing and the book trade in Cambridge 1534–1698* and *Vol. 2: Scholarship and commerce 1698–1872*. Cambridge: Cambridge University Press, 1992, 1998.

35 Adrian Johns, *The nature of the book: print and knowledge in the making*. Chicago: University of Chicago Press, 1998.

36 Vincent Kinane, *A history of the Dublin University Press, 1734–1976*. Dublin: Gill & Macmillan, 1994; Christine Ferdinand, *Benjamin Collins and the provincial newspaper trade in the eighteenth century*. Oxford: Clarendon Press, 1997.

37 David G. Selwyn, *The library of Thomas Cranmer*. Oxford: Oxford Bibliographical Society, 1996 (Oxford Bibliographical Society publications, 3rd ser.; 1). David Fate Norton and Mary J. Norton, *The David Hume library*. Edinburgh: Edinburgh Bibliographical Society, 1996. Anne F. Sutton and Livia Visser-Fuchs, *Richard III's books*. Stroud: Sutton Publishing, 1997. C. J. Wright (ed.), *Sir Robert Cotton as collector: essays on an early Stuart courtier and his legacy*. London: British Library, 1997.

38 Kevin Sharpe, *Reading revolutions: the politics of reading in early modern England*. New Haven: Yale University Press, 2000.

39 R. J. Fehrenbach and E. S. Leedham-Green, *Private libraries in renaissance England:a collection and catalogue of Tudor and Stuart book lists. Vols 1–5*. New York: Medieval and renaissance texts and studies, 1992–98. See also E. S. Leedham-Green, '*Private libraries in renaissance England*: a progress report', *Papers of the Bibliographical Society of America* **91** (4), 1997, 563–72.

40 The volumes in this series are: 1. Alain Wijffels, *Late sixteenth-century lists of law books at Merton College*, 1992; 2. Christian Coppens, *Reading in exile: the libraries of John Ramridge (d. 1568), Thomas Harding (d. 1572) and Henry Joliffe (c. 1573)*, 1993; 3. Sachiko Kusukawa, *A Wittenberg University Library catalogue of 1536*, 1995; 4. Owen Morris, *The 'chymick bookes' of Sir Owen Wynne of Gwydir*, 1997; 5. W. A. Kelly, *The library of Lord George Douglas (ca. 1667/8?–1693?)*, 1997; 6. Joy Tilley, *A catalogue of the donations made to Norwich City Library 1608–1656*, 2000. All published: Cambridge: LP Publications.

41 David Pearson, *Provenance research in book history: a handbook*. London: British Library, 1994. Repr. with a new introduction, 1998.

42 Alberto Manguel, *A history of reading*. London: HarperCollins, 1996.

43 Simon Eliot, 'The Reading Experience Database: or, what are we to do about the history of reading?', *Rare books newsletter* 48, Nov. 1994, 30–5.

44 Howard M. Nixon and Mirjam M. Foot, *The history of decorated bookbinding in England*. Oxford: Clarendon Press, 1992.

45 Bernard C. Middleton, *A history of English craft bookbinding technique*. 4th rev. edn. New Castle: Oak Knoll Press, 1996; Nicholas Pickwoad, 'Onward and downward: how binders coped with the printing press before 1800', in *A millennium of the book*, ed. Robin Myers and Michael Harris. Winchester: St Paul's Bibliographies, 1994, 61–106.

46 Maurice Packer, *Bookbinders of Victorian London*. London: British Library, 1991; Esther Potter, 'The London bookbinding trade: from craft to industry', *The library* 6th ser. **15** (4), 1993, 259–80.

47 David Pearson, *Oxford bookbinding 1500–1640*. Oxford: Oxford Bibliographical Society, 2000 (Oxford Bibliographical Society publications, 3rd ser.; 3).

48 Mirjam M. Foot, *The history of bookbinding as a mirror of society*. London: British Library, 1998.

49 N. R. Ker and A. J. Piper, *Medieval manuscripts in British libraries. 4: Paisley–York*. Oxford: Clarendon Press, 1992.

50 Kathleen L. Scott, *Later gothic manuscripts 1390–1490*. London: Harvey Miller, 1996; Barbara Rosenbaum (ed.), *Index of English literary manuscripts. Vol. 4: 1800–1900. Part 3: Landor–Patmore*. London: Mansell, 1993.

51 The volumes are: 1. K. W. Humphreys (ed.), *The friars' libraries*, 1996; 2. R. H. and M. A. Rouse (eds.), *The Registrum Anglie*, 1991; 3. David N. Bell (ed.), *The libraries of the Cistercians, Gilbertines and Premonstratensians*, 1992; 4. R. Sharpe *et al.* (eds.), *English Benedictine libraries: the shorter catalogues*, 1995; 5. William P. Stoneman (ed.), *Dover Priory*, 1999; 6. T. Webber and A. G. Watson (eds.), *The libraries of the Augustinian Canons*, 2000; J. P. Carley (ed.), *The libraries of King Henry VIII*, 2000. All published: London: British Library.

52 Christopher de Hamel, *A history of illuminated manuscripts*. 2nd rev. ed. London: Phaidon, 1994; H. R. Woudhuysen, *Sir Philip Sidney and the circulation of manuscripts, 1558–1640*. Oxford: Clarendon Press, 1996.

53 Titles published during the decade: *Property of a gentleman*, 1991; *Censorship and the control of print in England and France 1600–1910*, 1992; *Serials and their readers 1620–1914*, 1993; *A millennium of the book*, 1994; *A genius for letters: booksellers and bookselling*, 1995; *Antiquaries, book collectors and the circles of learning*, 1996; *The Stationers' Company and the book trade 1550–1990*, 1997; *Medicine, mortality and the book trade*, 1998; *Journeys through the market: travel, travellers and the book trade*, 1999; *Libraries and the book trade*, 2000. All edited by Robin Myers and Michael Harris, published: Winchester: St Paul's Bibliographies (except volume for 2000, published: New Castle, Del.: Oak Knoll).

54 *Images and texts*, 1997; *The reach of print*, 1998; *The human face of the book trade*, 1999; *The mighty engine: the printing press and its impact*, 2000. All edited by Peter Isaac and Barry McKay, published: Winchester: St Paul's Bibliographies.

55 Nicolas Barker, *Treasures from the libraries of National Trust country houses*. New York: Royal Oak Foundation and the Grolier Club, 1999.

56 <http://www.gutenberg.org> (accessed 9/05).

57 <http://www.bl.uk/onlinegallery/themes/englishlit/beowulf.html> (accessed 9/05).

58 Kevin Kiernan (ed.), *Electronic Beowulf*. London: British Library, 1999.

59 *The British Library 26th annual report, 1998–99*, 15; see also <http://www.bl.uk/onlinegallery/ttp/digitisation6.html> (accessed 9/05).

60 <http://image.ox.ac.uk/static/aboutproject.html> (accessed 9/05); <http://www.adbn.ac.uk/bestiary> (accessed 9/05); see also I. Beavan, M. Arnott and C. McLaren, 'Text and illustration: the digitisation of a medieval manuscript', *Computers and the humanities* **31** (1), 1977, 61–71.

61 <http://www.odl.ox.ac.uk/collections/johnson.htm> (accessed 9/05).

62 <http://www.odl.ox.ac.uk/collections/journals.htm> (accessed 9/05).

63 <http://www.bl.uk/treasures/gutenberg/homepage.html> (accessed 9/05).

64 <http://eebo.chadwyck.com/about/about.htm> (accessed 9/05).

65 <http://www.lib.umich.edu/tcp/eebo/> (accessed 9/05).

11

Art libraries

Douglas Dodds

Introduction

Previous surveys in this series highlighted a number of major themes that concerned art libraries and art librarians in earlier decades. In the most recent volume,
Beth Houghton discussed the nature of art documentation and the role of the art
library in Britain, then went on to describe the work of the Art Libraries Society
and other organizations in the UK and elsewhere. In earlier volumes, Ruth Kamen
argued that art libraries were different from libraries in other areas and Philip
Pacey also emphasized their uniqueness. All of them drew attention to the special
role of visual material, the importance of cooperation, the need for better bibliographic control, and the impact of new technology.[1]

Of course, many of these same themes persisted throughout the 1990s too, but
the growth of the internet seemed to provide real opportunities to deal with at least
some of the outstanding issues. At the same time it generated new challenges that
could not necessarily be resolved all at once, or straightaway. This report examines
the role of ARLIS and other societies, then looks at the activities of individual art
libraries and other organizations that were actively engaged in attempting to provide access to art-related information, within the overall context of changing priorities, real competition for resources and a significant increase in access to online
sources.

ARLIS/UK & Ireland

Any account of British art librarianship in the 1990s must start by acknowledging
the central role of the Art Libraries Society (ARLIS), the professional organization
for individuals and institutions involved in providing information about the visual
arts. ARLIS was founded in 1969, and subsequently became ARLIS/UK & Eire in
order to distinguish it from the other national or regional art library societies that
were established later. In 1993 the Society changed its name again, to ARLIS/UK
& Ireland, becoming an educational charity in 1995. Throughout the remainder of
this chapter, ARLIS is used as a convenient abbreviation for ARLIS/UK & Ireland.

The Society's activities continued to be overseen by a Council, elected
annually. Much of the practical work was (and still is) undertaken by a number of
committees and working parties, including those for cataloguing, education,

national coordination and visual resources. ARLIS members organized a wide range of conferences, seminars, workshops and study visits, all of which contributed to the professional development of art librarians. The Society also produced a range of publications, including the *Art libraries journal* (*ALJ*), the *ARLIS news-sheet* and an *Annual directory*. Under the editorship of Philip Pacey, then Gillian Varley from 1997 onwards, the *ALJ* maintained its position as a prime source of information about developments in art librarianship. As such, it represents essential reading for the period under review. A special issue was published to coincide with the Society's 25th anniversary conference in 1994, providing a useful overview of ARLIS and its achievements.[2] The *News-sheet* provided practical information about the activities of the Society and its members, plus developments of interest elsewhere. The *Directory* set out the ARLIS constitution, listing members and subscribers. In addition, an ARLIS website was established in February 1997 and was initially hosted by the National Art Library at the Victoria and Albert Museum.[3] The ARLIS archives for the period are also held in the V&A's Archive of Art and Design (AAD).[4]

In practice, all of the Society's activities depended on the voluntary contributions of members, with or without the support of their employers. An attempt to establish a national network for collecting exhibition catalogues, for example, was in danger of foundering through a lack of resources and a perceived reluctance to commit to acquiring material that might be of little or no interest to many readers.[5] In 1991, however, ARLIS obtained a modest grant that enabled it to embark upon an ambitious project to establish an all-embracing Library and Information Plan (LIP) for the art, design and architecture subject areas. A number of geographical LIPs were in the process of being implemented at the time, but subject-based 'sectoral' plans had yet to be created. Further funding was obtained, and a steering committee was assembled to oversee the production of a report by the consultant Lawrence Brandes. The group was chaired by the V&A's Director, Elizabeth Esteve-Coll, who had formerly been Chief Librarian of the NAL. The Visual Arts Library and Information Plan (VALIP) was published in 1993 and contained a number of substantive recommendations. In particular, the report proposed that VALIP should be concerned with collecting, documenting and providing access to published and unpublished material in the visual arts, including exhibition catalogues, serials, trade literature, slide collections and auction house sale catalogues. In addition, the consultant recommended that finance should be sought and a paid manager should be appointed to support the aims of the initiative.[6] An executive committee was then established to take the proposals forward, but a bid for the necessary funding was ultimately unsuccessful. As the project head, Ian Monie, explained, subsequent changes in national policy and personnel were less than supportive and VALIP was eventually disbanded in 1997.[7]

Despite this apparent setback, ARLIS nevertheless managed to make real progress in many of the areas highlighted by the report. A paid administrator, Sonia French, had been appointed in 1990 and was able to absorb some of the day-to-day burden of running the organization. This helped to free up the time of

ARLIS members, who were thus in a better position to press ahead with a range of practical cooperative activities.[8] In addition, individual libraries demonstrated a willingness to become more involved in supporting collaborative projects that would be of real benefit to librarians and the public alike. Perhaps the most notable example was the Union List of Art and Design Periodicals, which had last been produced during the mid-1980s, in hard copy and on microfiche. By the early 1990s, though, the momentum had decreased and the Union List needed to be re-established in a new format. By a happy coincidence, the National Art Library was engaged in a project to create online records for all of its serials at the time. In 1991 the Library offered to host a new edition based upon its own holdings, which would form the single largest collection to be included in the database. The work was initially undertaken by NAL staff and volunteers, who created brief records from the information supplied by participating libraries. The database grew throughout the decade, and by 1999 the online system contained some 26,000 location records for 14,000 serial titles held in more than 60 libraries throughout the UK and Ireland.

Nevertheless, it was clear that the service needed to continue to evolve, not least because of developments outside the art library sector. Early in the year 2000, the Victoria & Albert Museum (V&A) and ARLIS submitted a proposal to the British Library's Co-operation and Partnership Programme, with the aim of enhancing the bibliographic records, adding the holdings of additional libraries and creating an online *Directory of art resources* that would be linked to the serials database. A printed directory had been published by ARLIS in 1993, but there was a clear need to have information about the libraries available online too.[9] In addition, it was felt that the collection-mapping aspects of the project would be of real value for future collaborative collection management and/or collection development initiatives. Financial support came from both the British Library and the Research Support Libraries Programme (RSLP), with the V&A providing substantial funding in kind. The project started in September 2000 and was due to last for two years. A new interface to the serials database was launched in the autumn, and the *Directory* followed later.[10]

Other local, national and international groups

In addition to pursuing its own initiatives, ARLIS also maintained or developed close links with a number of regional, national and international groups. The Society's National Co-ordination committee included representatives from Leeds Art Libraries in Co-operation (LALIC), the Association for the Visual Arts in Ireland (AVAIL) and the Scottish Visual Arts Group (SVAG). LALIC was one of the few groups that operated locally, meeting regularly and producing a union list of journals held by member institutions.[11] In the public library sector and elsewhere, art specialists were increasingly being replaced by humanities librarians or more generic posts that covered a much broader range of duties. As a result, fewer public libraries were able to hold on to extensive art-related collections and Bristol, for example, explored the possibility of disposing of some of its art publications. In response to growing concerns about material being discarded, the National Co-ordination Committee produced guidelines for dealing with stock disposal.[12] Those public libraries that did manage to retain an interest in the subject area were obliged to make the best use of the resources that were available locally.[13]

The Association for the Visual Arts in Ireland (AVAIL) was established in 1992, in order to provide a forum for visual arts professionals throughout the island. The organization's aims were to provide a communications network for the provision and exchange of visual arts information, and to ensure the preservation and conservation of all Irish visual arts material. AVAIL also retained close links with ARLIS/UK & Ireland, which held its annual conference in Dublin in 1995.[14] The *Art libraries journal* subsequently devoted an entire issue to activities on both sides of the border.[15] One of the projects highlighted was the Planning Architecture Design Database Ireland (PADDI), the development of which began in the early 1990s. The database was originally known as IDEAL, and was a joint venture of the Architecture and Planning Libraries of Queen's University Belfast and University College Dublin. In addition to being one of the most memorable acronyms of the decade, PADDI promised to provide comprehensive access to bibliographic references on all aspects of the built environment in Ireland.[16]

The Scottish Visual Arts Group (SVAG) was established in 1994. The group evolved from the Union Catalogue of Art Books in Libraries in Scotland (UCABLIS), itself a development of the Union Catalogue of Art Books in Edinburgh Libraries (UCABEL). A proposal to establish SVAG was made at an UCABLIS event in 1993, and the first full meeting was held in June of the following year. Members met twice a year thereafter, at various locations throughout the country. The group was made up of academic and public libraries, museums, galleries and other institutions concerned with the promotion and documentation of the visual arts in Scotland. SVAG's aims were to maximize the opportunities for cooperation in Scottish institutions; to promote collections and services; to act as a lobbying body; and to provide links to local visual art groups and UK-wide initiatives. The group's outputs during the 1990s included a report on photographic literature in Scotland,[17] a directory of members and a survey of holdings of artists' books. By the end of the decade, widespread access to other online sources of information about art books and periodicals meant that the future of the UCABLIS database was under review.[18]

ARLIS also maintained links with equivalent organizations in other countries, as well as with the IFLA Section of Art Libraries, which acted as a focal point for art librarians worldwide. In 1992, for example, ARLIS organized a major international conference on behalf of the IFLA Section, entitled 'The art book: from Vasari to videodisc', held in London and Oxford. Under the chairmanship of Jan van der Wateren the Art Libraries Section produced a updated glossary of terms for art librarians and also maintained an international directory of art libraries, hosted by Vassar College in the USA.[19]

The British Library, the National Art Library, the Tate and other national collections

Throughout the decade, many of the major libraries that held substantial art-related collections participated in a variety of formal and informal discussions that touched upon collection development, collection management or other collaborative initiatives that would benefit the libraries and their users. The British Library Standing Committee on Art Documentation, a subject-specific advisory committee of the BL established in 1985, was one forum and the University of London Library Committee on the History of Art was another. However, the overlap between the various groups was apparent, and the BL committee was suspended for some years before being finally disbanded. In any event, the BL played an active part in the ARLIS National Co-ordination Committee, which also included the Tate, the National Art Library and the British Architectural Library among its permanent members.

Jan van der Wateren, the NAL's Chief Librarian throughout the decade, has described how the largest art library in the UK moved from isolation to active involvement in ARLIS and the wider library community.[20] The Library published a comprehensive collection development policy in 1993, describing the categories of material to be collected and placing them in the context of other public and non-public collections in London and elsewhere.[21] The NAL's emphasis on the need to guarantee long-term access to the material was vindicated when the Design Museum library, for example, closed its doors to the public in 1994. As described above, the systematic acquisition of exhibition catalogues had long been a concern of ARLIS, and various collaborative approaches had been explored without real success.[22] However, in a ground-breaking but little-publicized agreement in 1996, the British Library agreed to deposit many of its newly-acquired exhibition catalogues at the NAL. The bilateral agreement covered any catalogues with less than 60 pages, published by any UK museum or gallery except the British Museum, the V&A and the BL itself. The NAL's holdings were certainly more comprehensive as a result, and duplication of effort was reduced.[23] In a separate initiative, the British Library also deposited a major collection of book jackets at the V&A's Archive of Art & Design.

Individual institutions continued to work to provide better access to their collections and expertise. The NAL had started to automate its activities in the late 1980s, somewhat later than various comparable institutions. In the pre-internet age, the catalogue was initially made available via a dial-up modem.[24] All recent acquisitions were included in the online system, but the UK's largest art library was faced with a huge task to transfer all its older records too. Although various retrocon projects were undertaken in the early 1990s, it was clear that the work could only be completed in a realistic time-scale if additional external resources were obtained. The UK's National Lottery was launched in the mid-1990s and the NAL was one of the first libraries to benefit on a large scale, obtaining a £1 million grant to convert all its older catalogues by 2003. By the end of the decade the Library had around 600,000 records in machine-readable form.[25]

Despite the growth in online access and electronic publishing, libraries continued to acquire – and produce – printed materials. A bibliography and chronology of V&A publications and exhibitions won the Library Association's Besterman medal in 1998.[26] The British Architectural Library commenced publication of a printed catalogue of its early architectural publications.[27] Physical art libraries continued to grow at an alarming – or, some might say, reassuring – rate. The National Art Library, for example, needed some 170 metres of additional shelving every year. Much like the British Library until it moved out of the British Museum, the NAL occupied valuable space at the very heart of the V&A. The Library was an ever-expanding physical manifestation of the Museum's accumulated knowledge but, somewhat inconveniently, it also restricted public circulation around the centre of the V&A at first-floor level. The architect Harry Faulkner-Brown carried out a feasibility study that considered a range of options, and a detailed investment appraisal was prepared in 1995. Various other proposals to create more space at South Kensington had also been examined by the time the Rolls Estate, the former Public Record Office building, became available in 1998. The V&A gave serious consideration to moving the Library to Chancery Lane, but this would have required major capital investment and additional running costs. King's College subsequently acquired the site and the NAL remained in South Kensington, within its parent institution and with its space issues only partly resolved.

The Tate Library and Archive collections also suffered from severe storage problems. The book collections were located in the rotunda at the front of the Tate Gallery, with additional book stacks elsewhere on the Millbank site. A lack of suitable accommodation made it difficult to open up the library to a broader range of readers, and the catalogue was not yet available externally. As a result, the collections remained somewhat less accessible than those of the NAL, for example. However, a feasibility study confirmed that the library and archive collections could be relocated on the lower floor of the Millbank building that became known as Tate Britain, in an area that had previously been used for storing works of art. Planning for the new study centre began in 2000, and the Tate set about raising the necessary funds to complete the work.[28]

Elsewhere, the British Architectural Library at the Royal Institute of British Architects (RIBA) struggled with similar space constraints, but an attempt to move its collections to the Roundhouse ultimately came to nothing. Instead, an application entitled *Architecture for all* was submitted to the Heritage Lottery Fund in August 2000, with the aim of re-housing the RIBA's drawings, manuscripts and archives collections in the V&A's Henry Cole Wing. Whether or not the bid succeeded, the RIBA Library's book collections were due to remain at the Institute's headquarters in Portland Place.[29]

The Drewe case

Security was also an issue, albeit in a somewhat unexpected way. The Tate, the V&A and the Institute of Contemporary Arts (ICA) were among a number of institutions that found themselves caught up in a high-profile scam that had far-reaching implications for the art world and for major art libraries too. The prime mover was a con-man known as John Drewe, who employed a struggling artist, John Myatt, to create fake paintings that were then sold to unsuspecting buyers in the UK and abroad. The pictures themselves were less remarkable than the elaborate techniques that Drewe employed to persuade potential clients that they were indeed genuine. In a subversion of the usual practice of stealing from libraries, Drewe managed to smuggle fabricated documents into both the Tate and the National Art Library, thus establishing false provenances for the paintings. He then brought at least one potential purchaser into the NAL to see the fake entry in the falsified exhibition catalogue. Drewe's activities continued until the mid-1990s when his estranged partner finally contacted the police. Myatt was arrested in September 1995, and Drewe's house was raided in April 1996. The trial finally began in September 1998 and lasted until February 1999. Myatt cooperated with the police and was sentenced to one year in prison, but released after 4 months. Drewe was found guilty of conspiracy to defraud, forgery, theft and 'using a false instrument with intent'. He was sentenced to six years in prison, and served two. The case received extensive publicity at the time, and continued to feature in university art history courses relating to the history of fakes and forgeries. The rights to an article by Peter Landesman were acquired by MGM, who planned to produce a film based upon events.[30] The motion picture had not yet materialized at the time of writing but the ramifications for major art libraries were potentially significant. In effect, the credibility of at least some of their rare or unique source materials had been brought into question. The NAL subsequently undertook a fundamental review of its security procedures, and public access to the collections was subject to greater invigilation as a result. The Tate's archivist at the time, Jennifer Booth, has also described her involvement in the case.[31]

From slide libraries to electronic libraries
The impact of the Copyright, Designs and Patents Act of 1988 was still being absorbed by slide librarians well into the 1990s, since the Act prohibited the creation of unauthorized slides from published material. As a result, members of the ARLIS Visual Resources Committee, the Association of Curators of Art and Design Images (ACADI), the Association of Art Historians (AAH) and other interested parties were all involved in exploring ways of continuing to produce slides legally. After much debate and some unhappiness, a licensing scheme was finally introduced, to be administered by the Design and Artists Copyright Society (DACS). Five slide libraries had already signed up by June 1995, and others followed soon after. A revised scheme was introduced in 1997, and there were 88 members by 1999.[32]

In an article published in 1994, Lorcan Dempsey and Ann Lennon described the rapid growth of the internet and the creation of the world wide web, then went on to list some of the most useful art resources available online.[33] Very few of the art-specific sites they cited were based in the UK, but an increasing number of British institutions were certainly becoming interested in exploiting the potential of the new technology and this was already starting to have an impact on future planning. In an earlier volume of this series, Philip Pacey noted that the V&A's National Art Slide Library was 'under serious threat' as long ago as the early 1980s.[34] By 1991 the Museum had decided to transfer the collection to Leicester Polytechnic which, it was felt, was better placed to rationalize and exploit the material. As part of a nationwide drive to expand access to higher education, the Polytechnic became De Montfort University in 1992, under the terms of the Further and Higher Education Act. Other 'new' universities with significant art and design collections – and substantial slide libraries – included those at Brighton, Coventry, Middlesex and Manchester Metropolitan. By then the National Art Slide Library contained an estimated 150,000 images and seemed to offer the prospect of providing an online service that might ultimately replace the individual slide libraries in each institution. However, many of the pictures were of poor quality, inadequately documented or required copyright clearance.[35] Nevertheless, some of them were subsequently digitized and made available via the Higher Education Library for Image eXchange (HELIX), a project managed by De Montfort University and funded by the Joint Information Systems Committee (JISC). Other partners included the Hulton Getty Picture Collection and St Andrews University Library. However, a truly national image service still seemed some way away when the project ended in April 1998.

The V&A and De Montfort also participated in the Electronic Library Image Service for Europe (ELISE), a research project that was part-funded by the European Union. Other ELISE partners with art-related collections included Radio Telefís Éireann, the Hunt Museum in Limerick and the Université Libre de Bruxelles, in Belgium. ELISE I started in Feb 1993 and ran for two years. The aim was to model a facility that would provide access to the full-colour image banks and the supporting metadata held by the partners in the various locations. ELISE II commenced in 1996 and ran for three years, contributing to the development of new methods and standards where necessary. In particular, the project attempted to use the emerging Z39.50 standard to make the digital images available through a distributed network, rather than storing them all in a single database. Libraries had been using Z39.50 for some years, but ELISE was one of the first European projects to attempt to implement it for image searching. The project also explored the use of controlled vocabularies such as the Art and Architecture Thesaurus (AAT), plus an experimental technique known as Query By Image Content (QBIC), which promised to facilitate the retrieval of images by their colour, shape, texture or other characteristics. By 1999 it was clear that a combination of text- and image-based retrieval was likely to be more successful that querying by image content alone.[36]

With the growth of the internet, an increasing number of other organizations also sought to make their collections or knowledge available online. Although firms such as Emmett Publishing continued to produce microform collections of rare or unique material, it was clear that the future lay elsewhere. Whilst major reference works continued to be appear in printed format, the shift towards electronic publishing became increasingly evident in both the commercial and the public sector. One of the landmark works of the decade, *The dictionary of art*, was first published in hard copy then became available online some years later.[37] The establishment of the Scottish Cultural Resources Access Network (SCRAN) was approved in principle in 1995, at a total cost of some £15 million, half of which came from the Millennium Commission. SCRAN's mission was to 'build a networked multimedia resource base for the study and celebration of human history and material culture in Scotland'.[38] Two contributors, the V&A and the National Museums of Scotland, also participated in the Art Museum Image Consortium (AMICO), a not-for-profit organization established in North America in 1997. AMICO's members created a digital resource known as the AMICO Library, which was made available through various distributors including H. W. Wilson and the Research Libraries Group (RLG). The service was aimed at universities, colleges, public libraries, schools, and museums themselves. By 1999 AMICO contained images of more than 50,000 works of art. However, as Trant, Bearman and Richmond have noted, librarians were concerned (and continued to be at the time of writing) about maintaining access to digital collections, since the long-term future of such services was by no means assured.[39]

ADAM and VADS

The increasing proliferation of digital resources demanded new ways of locating, preserving and exploiting the material. The Art, Design, Architecture and Media (ADAM) information gateway, established in 1995, was one of a number of projects that attempted to address some of these issues. Funded by the Electronic Libraries (eLib) Programme, ADAM was conceived as a subject-based information gateway to quality-assured art resources on the Internet. ADAM's subject areas included fine art, design, architecture, the applied arts, film, television, photography, animation, art theory, museum studies and conservation. The lead partner was the Surrey Institute of Art and Design, whilst others involved included the University of Northumbria, Glasgow School of Art and the National Art Library, plus Birkbeck College, Coventry University, Middlesex University, the Tate and Winchester School of Art. ADAM aimed to employ the most appropriate standards for cataloguing and information retrieval, thus relieving the burden for individual art libraries. Although the project was highly innovative and succeeded in cataloguing relevant resources to a high standard, it was nevertheless unable to attract sufficient resources to continue indefinitely. Sadly, the funding expired at the end of 1998 and the service was wound down as a result. The ADAM database remained available for some years, but there was no immediate successor to fill the gap.[40]

Instead, the Resource Discovery Network (RDN) commissioned the Consortium of Academic Libraries in Manchester (CALIM) to investigate the need for a new service provider to support the needs of those working in the creative arts and industries. By then, 'hubs' had started to replace 'information gateways' as the label of choice. The consultancy work started in December 1999 and was completed in 2000.[41] In the meantime, the next best thing was the (then) London

Institute's highly regarded *i page*, the flagship of its Library and Learning Resources department. The 'i' stood for 'inspiration, information, images…'. The site was assembled by a project team of six staff during the first half of 1999, and proved to be an instant success within and outside the Institute.[42] Other art libraries followed suit, but the Institute's pages were particularly elegant and easy to use.

The Surrey Institute also hosted the Visual Arts Data Service (VADS), one of a number of subject-specific centres that operated under the aegis of the Arts and Humanities Data Service (AHDS). The AHDS had been created in 1995 and VADS followed in 1997, with the aim of providing data archiving facilities, data delivery channels and advice to the visual arts community, notably those involved in fine arts, applied arts, design, crafts and architecture. VADS staff proceeded to acquire digital collections that might otherwise have been neglected or lost, and then documented them in the VADS Catalogue. The owners retained all rights to the original material, which was made freely available for educational use. Like ADAM, VADS was heavily involved in the development of appropriate standards such as Dublin Core metadata, the subject of a VADS workshop in Edinburgh in 1997.[43]

Archival material
The establishment of VADS coincided with a number of institutional upheavals that could have resulted in the dispersal or loss of valuable printed or electronic information. In 1993, for example, the Design Council was subject to an extensive review that led to major changes in its role. The organization's slide collection was deposited at Manchester Metropolitan University in 1995, and the Design Council Archive was transferred to the University of Brighton. Some 2,800 images from the slide collection were subsequently digitized as part of the JISC Image Digitisation Initiative (JIDI) from 1997 to 1999, and a further 6,300 images were created via a Research Support Libraries Programme (RSLP) project that started in 1999. In a separate initiative, individual issues of *Design magazine* from 1965 onwards were scanned and indexed by the then London College of Printing's Digitisation In Art and Design (DIAD) project, which had to grapple with the complex copyright issues that arose. Although each of the institutions made its own digital collections available directly, all of the Design Council material could also be searched via the VADS catalogue, which acted as an aggregating service.

Elsewhere, the V&A's Archive of Art and Design (AAD) acquired a number of significant archives, including those of Habitat, the Crafts Council and the Arts Council of Great Britain. The increasing quantity of material held in various repositories made it all the more important that the contents should be properly documented in a standard format. The V&A adopted Encoded Archival Description (EAD), an XML standard that provided a structured method of listing the contents of individual archive groups, and some of the Museum's holdings were subsequently incorporated in RLG's archival database. In the UK, the need for a comprehensive guide to publicly accessible papers relating to artists and designers had been recognized for many years. The idea of an Artists' Papers

Register had been proposed by the Association of Art Historians in the mid-1980s, and a pilot project covering the west of Scotland had been undertaken in 1987. This established the framework, but further expansion was inhibited by a lack of resources. In 1996, however, Leeds University Library and the Henry Moore Foundation managed to fund a project officer with responsibility for identifying and recording material held in Scotland and the north of England. The following year, the Getty Grant Program, Birmingham University Library and the Barber Institute of Fine Arts funded a second post, with responsibility for surveying Wales and the south of England. Although London, Northern Ireland and Eire were not covered at the time, the Artists' Papers Register was well-established by the end of the decade as an essential source for locating primary material on individual painters, sculptors, designers, craftspeople and other individuals and organizations involved in art and design activities.[44]

International developments
The Research Libraries Group (RLG), based in California, provided a significant focus for art libraries throughout the English-speaking world, and many institutions participated in the activities of its Art and Architecture Group. RLG's bibliographic database, RLIN, was a prime source of information about art publications in general, plus exhibition catalogues and auction house sale catalogues in particular. By 1997 the organization's unique SCIPIO database contained some 200,000 bibliographic records for sale catalogues held by member institutions.[45] The Art and Architecture Group also explored the possibility of creating a Shared Histories of Exhibitions Database (SHED), but this ultimately came to nothing. However, RLG did establish a working relationship with the Getty Information Institute, another major provider of invaluable resources for the art documentation community. The Getty's Art and Architecture Thesaurus (AAT) was widely acknowledged to be a major achievement when it was first published in hard copy. The Getty Art History Information Program (AHIP) subsequently launched its own website in 1995, providing information about its various projects, including AAT, the Union List of Artist Names (ULAN) and the Thesaurus of Geographic Names (TGN). The Getty-controlled vocabularies were subsequently utilized in many databases and online services.[46]

Conclusion
Throughout the 1990s, art libraries – and art librarians – sought to acquire, organize and provide access to an ever-increasing range of art-related information, whether in printed or digital form. Local, national and international collaboration provided the best means of achieving the desired results with the resources available, and by the end of the decade real progress had been made in many areas. As ever, much remained to be done but the activities that were undertaken certainly helped to provide a useful framework for any initiatives that might follow in subsequent years.

Notes

1   Philip Pacey, 'Art libraries' in *British librarianship and information work 1976–1980*, ed. L. J. Taylor. London: Library Association, 1983, v. 2, pp. 44–8; Ruth H. Kamen, 'Art libraries' in *British librarianship and information work 1981–1985*, ed. David M. Bromley and Angela M. Allott. London: Library Association, 1988, v. 2, pp. 44–52; Beth Houghton, 'Art libraries' in *British librarianship and information work 1986–1990*, ed. David M. Bromley and Angela M. Allott. London: Library Association, 1993, v. 2, pp. 58–70.

2   See, for example, Gillian Varley, 'Making the vision work', *Art libraries journal* **19** (3), 1994, 13–17.

3   The original ARLIS website was at <http://arlis.nal.vam.ac.uk>, and early pages can still be seen via the Internet Archive at <http://www.archive.org>. The current pages are at: <http://www.arlis.org.uk> (accessed 6/5/06).

4   ARLIS/UK & Ireland, Records, 1968–2002. V&A AAD/1989/3.

5   Beth Houghton and Gillian Varley, 'A local approach to national collecting: a UK feasibility study for the co-operative collection of exhibition catalogues', *Art libraries journal* **14** (1), 1989, 38; Gaye Smith and Lotta Jackson, *ARLIS/UK & Eire national collecting network for art exhibition catalogues*. London: British Library, 1990.

6   *A library and information plan for the visual arts*. [Bromsgrove]: ARLIS/UK & Ireland, 1993 (British Library R&D report; 6111).

7   Ian Monie, 'The Visual Arts Library and Information Plan (VALIP): history of a campaign', *Art libraries journal* **22** (3), 1997, 26–32.

8   Beth Houghton, 'Bottom up: a UK approach to art library co-operation', *Art libraries journal* **24** (4), 1998, 9–17.

9   Gillian Varley, *Art & design documentation in the UK and Ireland : a directory of resources*. [England]: ARLIS/UK & Ireland, 1993.

10 Douglas Dodds & Aileen Cook, 'The National Art Library, ARLIS/UK and Ireland and the Union list of art, architecture and design periodicals', *Serials librarian* **32** (3/4), 1997, 127–37; Miranda Stead, 'Love's labours – : creation of a union list of art, architecture and design serials', *Art libraries journal* **27** (1), 2001, 36–9. Initially available through the NAL's website at <http://www.nal.vam.ac.uk/ulist/>, the service was subsequently re-branded as ARLIS.NET. It remains available at: <http://www.arlis.net> (accessed 6/5/06).

11 The LALIC union list is available via the Leeds city council website at: <http://www.leeds.gov.uk> (accessed 6/5/06).

12 ARLIS/UK and Ireland, *Guidelines on stock disposal*. [England]: ARLIS/UK & Ireland, 2000.

13 Amanda Duffy, 'Visual arts provision in public libraries: threats and opportunities', *Art libraries journal* **24** (1), 1999, 11–15.

14 Elizabeth Kirwan, 'The Association for the Visual Arts in Ireland (AVAIL)', *Art libraries journal* **20** (1), 1995, 7–11.

15 'Special issue: the visual arts and architecture in Ireland', *Art libraries journal* **25** (3), 2000, 3–44.

16 Karen Latimer, 'The Irishness of Irish architectural information provision: the PADDI database', *Art libraries journal* **25** (3), 2000, 25–8. The database is available at: <http://www.paddi.net> (accessed 6/5/06).

Art libraries 195

17 Scottish Visual Arts Group, Photography Working Party, *Report on photographic literature in Scotland*. [Edinburgh]: SVAG, 1996.
18 Hilary Williamson, 'The Scottish Visual Arts Group', *Art libraries journal* **28** (3), 2003, 11–14.
19 IFLA Section of Art Libraries, *Multilingual glossary for art librarians*. 2nd rev. ed. Munich; London: K. G. Saur, 1996; The IFLA Directory is available at: <http://artlibrary.vassar.edu/ifla-idal/> (accessed 6/5/06).
20 Jan van der Wateren, 'British art librarianship today and tomorrow', *Art libraries journal* **19** (3), 1994, 20–6; Jan van der Wateren, 'National library provision for art in the United Kingdom: the role of the National Art Library', *Alexandria* **6** (3), 1994, 173–92.
21 Jan van der Wateren and Rowan Watson (eds.), *The National Art Library: a policy for the development of the collections*. London: National Art Library, Victoria and Albert Museum, 1993. The full text of the policy was also available online until it was superseded by a new version.
22 Gaye Smith and Lotta Jackson, *ARLIS/UK and Eire national collecting network for art exhibition catalogues: a feasibility study*. London: British Library, 1990.
23 Christine Love Rodgers, 'New initiatives to solve old problems: collecting exhibition catalogues at the National Art Library,' *Art libraries journal* **24** (2), 1999, 8–11.
24 Douglas Dodds, 'Documentation systems in Britain's National Art Library', *Art libraries journal* **18** (4), 1993, 15–23; Douglas Dodds, 'Computer applications in the National Art Library', *Computers and the history of art* **3** (2), 1993, 15–25.
25 Douglas Dodds, 'Raising the funds and delivering the goods: the National Art Library Heritage Project', *MDA information* **5** (1), 2000, 67–70.
26 Elizabeth James, *The Victoria and Albert Museum: a bibliography and exhibition chronology, 1852–1996*. London: Fitzroy Dearborn in association with the Victoria and Albert Museum, 1998.
27 Nicholas Savage *et al*., *Early printed books, 1478–1840: catalogue of the British Architectural Library Early Imprints Collection*. London: Bowker-Saur, 1994–2003.
28 Beth Houghton, 'The Hyman Kreitman Research Centre for the Tate Library and Archive', *Art libraries journal* **27** (4), 2002, 19–24.
29 Mark Haworth-Booth and Michael Snodin, 'Architecture for all: the Royal Institute of British Architects and the Victoria and Albert Museum', *Art libraries journal* **26** (2), 2001, 5–8.
30 Peter Landesman, 'A 20th-century master scam', *New York times magazine* 18 July 1999. Full text available at: <http://www.nytimes.com/library/magazine/home/19990718mag-art-forger.html> (accessed 6/5/06).
31 Jennifer Booth, 'Dr Drewe: a cautionary tale', *Art libraries journal* **28** (2), 2003, 14–17.
32 Jenny Godfrey, 'The DACS slide collection licensing scheme', *Art libraries journal* **26** (4), 2001, 10–17; Nigel Llewellyn, 'Slide libraries: the copyright law', *AAH bulletin* 52, 1994, 2. See also subsequent issues of the bulletin.
33 Lorcan Dempsey and Ann Lennon, 'Art and the internet: some notes on resources and trends', *Art libraries journal* **19** (4), 1994, 10–15.
34 Pacey, 'Art libraries', 47.
35 'Leicester move upsets slide library users: London-based National Art Slide Library to close for 18 months', *Museums journal* **92**, March 1992, 10.

36 Douglas Dodds, 'Integrating access to distributed images: the Electronic Library Image Service for Europe (ELISE) Project', *Art libraries journal* **24** (1), 1999, 40–2.

37 Jane Turner (ed.), *The dictionary of art*. New York: Grove; London: Macmillan, 1996. Sometimes called *The Macmillan dictionary of art*, it subsequently became known as *The Grove dictionary of art*, and is available online at: <http://www.groveart.com> (accessed 6/5/06).

38 Bruce Royan, 'The art of partnership: a Scottish case study', *Art libraries journal* **28** (3), 2003, 15–21. The SCRAN web site is at: <http://www.scran.ac.uk> (accessed 6/5/06).

39 Jennifer Trant, Kelly Richmond, David Bearman, 'Open concepts: museum digital documentation for education through the Amico Library,' *Art libraries journal* **27** (3), 2002, 30–42.

40 Tony Gill and Catherine Grout, 'Finding and preserving visual arts resources on the internet', *Art libraries journal* **22** (3), 1997, 19–25. Although no longer updated, the ADAM site remains available at: <http://www.adam.ac.uk> (accessed 6/5/06).

41 Georgina Porter, 'The Resource Discovery Network creative arts and industries consultancy,' *Art libraries journal* **26** (3), 2001, 14–17.

42 Liz Lawes and Jessica Crilly, 'The London Institute's *i page*: creating and maintaining an academic gateway website', *Art libraries journal* **27** (1), 2002, 31–5. The Institute subsequently became the University of the Arts London. Parts of the original *i page* service can still be seen at <http://www.arts.ac.uk/library/> (accessed 6/5/06).

43 Phill Purdy, 'Visual Arts Data Service: not just a pretty face', *Art libraries journal* **27** (3), 2002, 13–17. The service was subsequently re-branded as AHDS Visual Arts, but the website remained at <http://vads.ahds.ac.uk/> (accessed 6/5/06).

44 David Tomkins, 'Creating the Artists' Papers Register,' *Art libraries journal* **24** (2), 1999, 16–21. The Register itself is at: <http://www.apr.ac.uk> (accessed 6/5/2006).

45 Katharine Martinez, 'The Research Libraries Group: new initiatives to improve access to art and architecture information', *Art libraries journal* **23** (1), 1998, 30–7.

46 Toni Petersen *et al.*, *Art & architecture thesaurus*. 2nd ed. New York; Oxford: Oxford University Press, 1994; Toni Petersen and Patricia J. Barnett (eds.), *Guide to indexing and cataloging with the Art and architecture thesaurus*. New York; Oxford: Oxford University Press, 1994. The current address for the vocabularies is: <http://www.getty.edu/research/conducting_research/vocabularies/> (accessed 6/5/06).

12

Music libraries

Pamela Thompson

Introduction

The varied range of music libraries in the UK makes a coherent overview in any period challenging. Music libraries exist in the national and university libraries, in conservatoires, in schools, in the public library sector in a bewildering variety of small and large guises, in broadcasting, in music publishers' archives in the commercial sector, in specialist composers' archives, in ecclesiastical establishments and in the homes of musicians whose collections are sometimes surprisingly extensive and accessible. This leaves music libraries open to an equally wide variety of influences and trends, whether in local government, national government, education, technological developments or cooperative ventures. The decade of the 1990s is memorable for an accelerating impact in all of these fields.

It is also memorable as a period of structural change, whether in national government departments, in local government which underwent far-reaching restructuring, in library and information representative bodies, in education, or in funding streams for library development. Technological developments brought perhaps the most overwhelming changes, whether through the migration of recordings from vinyl to compact disc, through the building of electronic communications and networks, through digitization projects, and, more simply, through the provision of computers in public libraries.[1] In 1991, many music libraries lacked even one computer for staff, many music catalogues remained to an unfortunate extent manual, largely on account of the complexity and subsequent cost of music cataloguing, and the notion of computers for library users, not only in the public library sector, was for many a distant dream.

While the trends and developments may be broad, in a relatively small subject area the issues involved in them are likely to be closely focused and the personalities taking work forward relatively small in number, even in so international and disparate a field as music. This is compounded in the case of music libraries by the existence of IAML (the International Association of Music Libraries, Archives and Documentation Centres) and in the United Kingdom by its national branch, an organization which attempts to bring together the differing strands of the profession and represent its interests.[2] It is perhaps indicative of its success, or at least of its determination in this, that a high proportion of the literature relating to music library developments in the 1990s, as at other times, emanated from IAML, and that its members' collective memory inevitably informs an account of those times.

They will be remembered as a time of opportunity and achievement overall and of a paradoxical decline in specialist services and provision, often accompanied by a whirlwind of activity with high and low points in equal measure.

Decline of specialist music services

Moves away from specialist library provision had begun well before the decade under consideration, as training for library and information gradually began to favour a more generalist and managerial approach and as funding for libraries in all sectors was stretched. This trend was exacerbated in the 1990s by continuing budgetary constraints, but also by the introduction of new structures, a greater demand for time-consuming and expensive accountability, and by new patterns of working driven by computer use and the development of multimedia resources.[3]

Exact figures on reductions in music library posts in the period are difficult to compute, despite IAML's best efforts at the time to record them through a network of regional reporters and advisers, coordinated by Liz Hart. Her analysis of the difficulties clarifies the complexities of the situation:

> There are going to be times when music – and music libraries – are accorded such a low priority that the pressure is on if not to abolish the service totally (which has certainly happened) at least to reduce it substantially. The funding may be cut and/or charges imposed: hours of opening may be restricted; staff may be asked to take on unrelated areas of work, or their numbers will be decreased, or the music specialist is redeployed to other duties; music or audiovisual services may be absorbed into the general service during a restructuring process. The means are various, depending on circumstances and the type of library – academic, public, special – involved.[4]

In universities, the main trend was for the creation of 'liaison librarian' posts, with music becoming only a part of the former music librarian's responsibilities, but the decline in specialist posts was also accelerated by the closure of some university music departments or by budgets devolved from libraries to music departments.[5] By the time that HEFCE published quality assessment subject overview reports of music in 1994/95, a clear reduction in specialist music posts was evident – and 'a strong correlation between the employment of a specialist music librarian and good overall stocks and services'.[6]

In the public library sector, more radical events left their mark. In 1991 the government announced a thorough-going review of local government, in which a radical overhaul of local authorities was proposed.[7] The potential impact of this on libraries could only be speculative, but the dangers for music libraries in particular were obvious, as a multitude of small authorities might well not have the resources to support adequate music provision, and music collections built up by county libraries could well be dispersed, staff expertise lost and users' access to music materials substantially reduced. IAML responded to the consultation papers, stressing the value of music libraries in the community and encouraging 'the development of voluntary and informal arrangements for the sharing of costs, staff and facilities between library authorities ... and the idea of more formal statutory joint arrangements for the provision of sets of performance material'.[8]

In the following few years, the effects of local government restructuring did indeed make their mark, with a number of county music libraries split up and others forced into not always appropriate cooperative arrangements.[9] For the music library community this was compounded by ongoing reductions in many municipal music library services, the London boroughs being especially seriously affected.[10] At the same time other major municipal music libraries (in Manchester, Liverpool, Glasgow, Westminster and Bristol, for example), many of them key suppliers to the music community at large and to smaller music libraries, were likewise affected by cuts in funding and services. By March 1993, calls for a national strategy for music library services based on centres of excellence including the British Library and other major providers were becoming extraordinarily clear, with the debate actually reaching Parliament:

> Robert Key (Under-Secretary of State, Department of National Heritage: I shall certainly consider how national co-operation to meet users' needs can best be enhanced. My Department is already jointly funding a study for a library and information plan for music. This study is investigating the provision of music scores and music information across the country ... It will produce an action plan for improvements in services.[11]

It was in this somewhat overheated atmosphere that the action plan appeared.

Music library planning

While the concept of library and information planning on a regional or local basis was already well established by the beginning of the 1990s,[12] the idea of national plans for subject areas was still emerging. With encouragement and a little funding from the Library and Information Co-operation Council (LINC), in 1991 IAML(UK) submitted a formal proposal to various funding bodies for an 18-month study to produce a library and information plan for music services in the UK and the Republic of Ireland. By the autumn of 1992, funding had been secured from LINC, the British Library Research and Development Department, the ERMULI Trust and the Office of Arts and Libraries, a representative steering group from all sectors had been established and an information consultant, Royston Brown, and a project officer, Susi Woodhouse, had been appointed.[13] Research was undertaken in 400 detailed questionnaires, with every music library and library authority in the UK and Ireland covered, and by a series of 27 visits and meetings undertaken by the project team. The work was concentrated on the supply of printed music, the area in which the most pressing need for a way forward was perceived, although this left many other elements in music provision, such as recordings, literature and archives earmarked for further study.

The *Library and information plan for music* (Music LIP) was published in the summer of 1993.[14] It represented the fullest ever analysis of the issues surrounding music libraries ever undertaken and contained 53 recommendations, the major ones centred on cooperation, fugitive material, meeting users' needs, standards of provision, staffing, education and training, data control, inter-library lending, strategies for a national music library, and funding for the future.[15] The report's most telling conclusion was that few of the recommendations could be achieved without a coordinated structure and funding to support it. Its launch and subsequent reception were encouraging, but, in a period of retrenchment, funding was elusive.[16] A Music LIP Development Group continued to press for progress, but disappointment was hard to dispel, not least as other subject plans developed and LIPs were gaining acceptance as models for the future.[17] Only in retrospect can an objective assessment of the plan's value be made. As the 1990s progressed and a number of funding opportunities emerged, the existence of a published plan and its recommendations were to provide vital evidence of music libraries' needs and could be used in support of applications for further developments.

Cooperative ventures and funding opportunities
Late in 1993, the Follett report on libraries in the higher education sector ushered in a more positive climate for libraries in the sector with recommendations which included the top-slicing of funding from the education budget to achieve radical progress in modernization.[18] Modernization, particularly in the areas of automation and the retrospective conversion of catalogues, was exactly what many music libraries, not least some in the conservatoires, had long sought in vain. Funding for special collections in the humanities enabled work to begin and sowed the seeds for further collaboration.

Another result of the Follett report was the establishment of the Joint Information Systems Committee (JISC) which was to encourage programmes relating to information technology.[19] JISC's direction was further influenced by the 1995 Anderson report on library provision for researchers which recommended the development of networks of libraries.[20] JISC established an electronic libraries programme (eLib) to develop digital and electronic networks and services.

Still relatively technologically backward, the nine UK music conservatoire libraries were perhaps surprising applicants to this programme. They formed a consortium Music Libraries Online (MLO) to test the possibilities for a web-based virtual union catalogue of their music holdings, using the Z39.50 retrieval protocol, and received funding from JISC to develop it, the only subject-based and nationwide 'clumps' project to gain support.[21] The project was unique in demonstrating that the technology could produce good results on a subject basis, and was expanded to include four university music libraries, two public music libraries and the British Music Information Centre.[22]

The Anderson report also encouraged the birth of another funding programme in 1998 to enhance access to collections, the Research Support Libraries Programme (RSLP), with a stream dedicated to the retrospective conversion of catalogues – and this time music was specifically identified as being a subject area in need of development.[23] A consortium of fourteen music libraries in universities and conservatoires, with secondary partners including the British Library, was hastily created and the *Ensemble* consortium achieved RSLP funding.[24] Its aim was 'to effect swift retrospective conversion of music catalogues by using the good offices of CURL [the Consortium of University Research Libraries], sharing all records free of charge and reducing the cost of one record to £4.00, considerably less than the prevailing £6.00–£8.00'.[25] The *Ensemble* project provided an invaluable boost to the academic music libraries which participated; at the beginning of the project they were estimated to hold 1,131,000 music titles without a record in electronic form, rare evidence of the scale of the backlogs not uncommon in the music library sector as a whole.[26]

While academic music libraries were offered unprecedented opportunities in this era, the public music library sector, throughout the decade both invigorated and weighed down by responsibilities emanating from public library review and the People's Network initiative to bring computers to their users (often finding their collections displaced to accommodate the equipment), did nonetheless discover that new funding streams for partnership and cooperation projects became available for them.[27]

Music found a champion in Project EARL, funded by the British Library, the Library Association and its own partners, which aimed to bring the benefits of networked computer systems to its libraries. The Public Library Development Incentive Scheme (PLDIS) assisted the development of Project BARM (Building a Regional Music Resource) in 1994, which, centred within Berkshire Cultural Services, was intended as an initial stage in cooperative automated access to printed music resources in the South East region, an important aim at a time when public music library catalogues were often not networked, often not automated and often of varying standards.[28] Local government reorganization, alas, brought about its demise.

PLDIS did, however, enable a project of more permanent value and considerable potential. The inter-library lending of performance sets was a recurring theme in the 1990s (see below). It was also a perennial headache, with no integrated national catalogue of vocal sets available, even in printed form, and many regional catalogues out of date and out of print. Access to sets for choirs depended on determined users, an informal network of music librarians sourcing material by phone around the country, and fast working with performances and rehearsals fixed. Music is ever time- and place-sensitive. In 1995 the West Midlands Regional Library System applied successfully to PLDIS for funding to develop a regional catalogue of vocal sets, using MARC and *AACR2* standards, as a pilot for a possible national catalogue.[29] It exaggerates only a little to say that a star was born. By the time of the publication of the catalogue in 1997, other regions had also been spurred into action.[30] The East Midlands published their catalogue and some other regions took encouraging interest.[31] Malcolm Jones, happily then recently retired and even more happily willing to work voluntarily, found a new mission in life: to begin to gather all available data from all the regions. Support for the work was near universal, but funding for real development took rather longer to achieve.

In 1999, the British Library Co-operation and Partnership Fund (BLCPF) provided the long-awaited opportunity. A successful application was made by IAML(UK) for a new project *Encore!*, to produce a single catalogue of both orchestral and vocal sets through collection mapping, data collection (in electronic form where possible), data conversion to acceptable standards, a great deal of input, and eventually on online union catalogue of all performance material.[32] The catalogue was launched two years later on time.

Over the same period, IAML(UK) had been developing plans for a further online resource, this time a guide to music materials in libraries, museums and archives, and had undertaken preliminary research. Emboldened by the success of *Encore!*, the branch made a further bid to the British Library late in 2000 for *Cecilia*. *Cecilia* was to be a pioneering 'online directory of institutions holding collections of music materials, providing a web-based tool enabling enquirers to search descriptions in collections in music using free-text and structured keywords', covering every kind of music and acting as an online gateway to music resources in the UK and Ireland.[33] Its development and launch belong to a later decade.

Documentation and standards

While the outcomes of many of the projects already mentioned sit firmly in the category of documentation, there were other equally significant publishing and documentation ventures in the 1990s which warrant mention.

1992 saw the publication of *Cecilia*'s forerunner, *Music in British libraries* by Barbara Penney, a volume slimmer in purpose than *Cecilia*, but fulfilling a much-needed role in documenting the extent of British music collections.[34] IAML(UK) itself collected and published statistics on music libraries from 1984 to 1999, providing snapshots of annual changes in provision but, as dedicated music library posts declined, the availability of librarians to submit returns increased, and the anticipated comprehensiveness and usefulness of the surveys faded.[35]

Over the same period, the promotion of public library music standards was a perennial concern, with opportunities constantly taken to persuade of their importance. As an example, they featured prominently in the 1993 Music LIP, but were still a serious concern in 1999, when, in the consultation on public library standards, IAML submitted a detailed response, laying out recommended standards for the provision of music scores, performance sets and music sound recordings related to size of population, and went further: 'These standards are fundamental to provision of music in libraries. In addition to stock, however, the most important standard should be with regard to knowledgeable staff ...'.[36]

A standard of a different and fundamental nature finally emerged in 1992: the International Standard Music Number, an internationally accepted standard for the identification and control of printed music materials. It was the brainchild of a

British music retailer, Alan Pope, and two British music librarians, Malcolm Jones and Malcolm Lewis, and had taken nine years to come to fruition and gain official acceptance, 'arguably the most important initiative yet undertaken by the United Kingdom Branch of IAML'.[37] Further developments in its international acceptance and use proved necessary, but by the end of the decade it had been embraced by music publishers around Europe and beyond, if not quite universally.

Another major publication on which music librarians collaborated, under the determined leadership of John Wagstaff, although this time only for six years, was the second edition of *The British union catalogue of music periodicals*, the comprehensive coverage of which marked it out as 'a landmark of musico-bibliographic literature', to quote Roger Taylor in the preface to the work.[38]

The decade also saw a notable increase in the availability of music library catalogues on CD-ROM, pre-dating their subsequent availability on the web. *CPM plus*, the British Library's catalogue of printed music to 1990, published in 1993, represented a fine step forward for researching both British and foreign printed music.[39] 1995 saw the publication on CD-ROM for the first time of RISM's music manuscripts database, another long-awaited development by music researchers.[40] *RILM*, the international inventory of music literature,[41] was issued on CD-ROM for the first time in 1993, as was the music catalogue of the Library of Congress. These are but a few examples among many, not all British in origin, but all of crucial importance for music libraries and their users.

Inter-library lending

The *Encore!* project already mentioned did much to improve the inter-library lending of performance sets, but in fact the inter-library lending of music was a primary and seemingly insoluble consideration throughout the 1990s. It dominated much of the Music LIP and consumed large quantities of music librarians' time, both in achieving the loans and debating the issues.

The inter-library loan of single scores was in theory enormously aided by the existence of the extensive music collections at the British Library Document Supply Centre. In practice, its lack of any published catalogue provoked repeated calls for improvement, as, without knowledge of holdings, the service was constantly perceived as under-used and under threat. The issue was key at a time when few music library catalogues were published and when even those that were or were available in regional or university systems contained only a relatively small proportion of printed music titles.

But arrangements for the loan of performance sets were equally contentious, not least because of the volume of material held and loaned. Conservative estimates in the late 1990s put the holdings of sets across the UK as over 16,000 orchestral sets and 50,000 sets of vocal music, or around 1,500,000 individual scores, a very considerable cultural resource offering an unsung underpinning of amateur music-making. Two surveys offered a snapshot of loan activities. The first in September and October 1997, conducted by IAML(UK), found that in the two months surveyed and the 23 public libraries which participated, 6,000 sets were loaned, comprising 136,000 individual scores.[42] Set interloan statistics recorded by CONARLS also showed that in 1996/97 17,095 loans were made. A survey in Birmingham Central Library undertaken between January and December 2000 registered 884 borrowers 'in person' at the music library, only 50% of whom were from Birmingham. They borrowed 19,088 vocal scores.[43]

The problems inherent in sets interlending are too diverse to summarize, but are centred on an inequality of holdings and provision, the cost of sets, charges imposed for loans, whether to other libraries or to individual borrowers, and a lack of specialist staff experienced in handling complicated materials.[44] Barriers to cooperation abounded, and resolute attempts by CONARLS and LIPLINC and IAML(UK) failed to find a universal solution, but did establish a voucher scheme which assisted in ironing out some inequities. Paradoxically, the emergence of the data in *Encore!*, while easing beyond measure the tracing of sets, only served to highlight those inequities, revealing in stark detail those authorities with a good collection of sets, those who subsidized others, and those who offered no service whatsoever to their local music community.

Education and training
The impact of the demise in specialist training for subject specialists from the early 1980s onwards took time to be recognized. It was only a decade later, as the supply of those with relevant qualifications and experience declined, that the real effects were felt. Increasingly, music libraries had to train their own staff in the mysteries of the profession, or band together under the auspices of IAML to offer courses. The IAML committee charged with this set about devising a course aimed at non-specialist staff. The result was 'Music for the terrified', a one-day course offered to public libraries around the country at low cost and almost invariably run by IAML members in their free time.[45] Further courses followed: '40 copies of Messiah, please', to unravel the mysteries of sets interlending, and 'Advanced reference sources for music librarians'.[46]

The lack of professional training continued, however, to be problematic. Approaches to UK schools of library and information studies with offers of free short modules rarely brought a response beyond 'too specialist' or 'insufficient demand from students', that is until 1995 when the Music Libraries Trust (MLT) offered to seek funds to sponsor a lectureship.[47] A positive response came from the Open Learning Unit at Aberystwyth's Department of Information and Library Studies, with the suggestion of modules in music librarianship to add to their course. Funds were gained from the Britten-Pears Foundation and an author for the modules was found in Ian Ledsham, formerly music librarian at the University of Birmingham. The first module was delivered to students in January 1998, the second some months later, and both were enthusiastically received.[48] The funding agreement obtained by MLT had a supplementary strand: the production of a stand-alone version of the course on interactive CD-ROM with accompanying printed texts. This, also undertaken by Ian Ledsham, was published in 2000.[49]

Audio-visual developments

Only a brief overview of matters as they affected music libraries is included here. The overwhelming and determining feature of the period was the gradual demise of collections of vinyl recordings and tapes, frequently disposed of with sometimes scant regard for their value, to be overtaken rapidly by the inclusion of compact discs and videos in libraries of all types.[50]

Enthusiasm for the new format was tempered by increasing concerns relating to record rental right in the wake of the 1988 Copyright, Designs and Patents Act. Negotiations between the British Phonographic Industry, the Library Association and IAML(UK) throughout the early 1990s finally resulted in 1994 with an agreement on a three-month holdback period for recordings acquired by libraries.

Given the durability of the new formats, compared with the fragility of earlier ones, it was perhaps surprising that the inter-library lending of CDs was not seized upon overnight as an invaluable addition to services. Even by the end of the decade, no scheme had been initiated, despite tentative suggestions, the overriding suspicion being that the income generated by audio-visual loans and often self-financing collections might be hampering cooperative endeavour.

The major, largely successful foray into audio-visual lending, the GLASS scheme (Greater London Audio Specialization Scheme), also underwent several reviews in the 1990s as financial constraints and newer, more popular considerations took hold. Some authorities withdrew from the scheme, while others failed to cover the areas allotted to them.[51] By 1995/96, the decline in the success of the scheme had become more serious, sparking reports on its effectiveness and a working party on its future which culminated in a GLASS performance report which was eventually ratified by the Association of London Chief Librarians.[52] In future the scheme would attempt to be comprehensive, but would be request-driven.

As the decade progressed, so too did the technology in both sound carriers and the internet, enabling potentially a greater sharing of resources. An early experiment in this field from 1993 to 1996 was Project Jukebox, supported by the European Library Plan, in which the UK National Sound Archive participated. Its aim was to set up and test a pilot system for online access to recordings, even in the most remote areas. The project's final report revealed a multitude of factors considered and tested and emphasized the value of the project, but acknowledged that the speed of change was such that its findings would soon be superseded.[53]

Outreach work

The 1990s were the post-communist decade, the period when contacts with Central and Eastern Europe eased and more mutual assistance became possible. IAML's international outreach programme found a number of enthusiastic supporters in the UK, with a number of libraries supplying materials to those starved for decades of western publications, and participants from a wide array of countries (Albania, Bulgaria, Croatia, Czech Republic, Estonia, Moldova, Slovakia and Tajikistan, to name but a few) welcomed to IAML(UK)'s annual study weekends, and study visits organized for individual librarians. Underpinning these activities were a number of fact-finding expeditions to learn what was most needed, most notably those to Albania, Macedonia and the Balkans, undertaken by the intrepid Roger Taylor, which resulted in endless pursuits of funding to establish, amongst other endeavours, an Albanian Music Information Centre.[54] Further visits by others followed – to Russia,[55] Lithuania, Estonia, Croatia[56] and Hungary, frequently funded by the travellers themselves, but invaluable for the contacts made, the exchange of materials and expertise enabled, and the professional colleagues encountered.

Postscript

In a fitting end to a decade of fruitful activity, music librarians from the UK came together in 2000 in Edinburgh to host the international conference of IAML, with over 400 delegates in residence.[57] It served as an appropriate reminder that music libraries have an international dimension, an international language in music and an international family bound by similar difficulties but, most of all, similar aspirations.

Notes

1   Julie Crawley, 'Information technology and music libraries' in *Music librarianship in the United Kingdom*, ed. Richard Turbet. Aldershot: Ashgate, 2003, pp. 141–171.

2   International Association of Music Libraries, Archives and Documentation Centres: <http://www.iaml.info> (accessed 30/1/06); IAML (UK & Ireland): <http://www.iaml-uk-irl.org> (accessed 30/1/06).

3   Special Libraries Association, Special Committee on Competencies for Special Librarians, *Competencies for special librarians of the 21st century*, ed. B. M. Spiegelman. Washington: SLA, 1996.

4   Liz Hart, 'You don't know what you've got till it's gone: the UK Branch's response to reductions in music library services', *Fontes artis musicae* **38** (3), 1991, 188–91.

5   Malcolm Lewis, 'Cuts, catalogues and standards: a report on the annual meeting of academic music librarians', *Brio* **29** (2), 1992, 89–91.

6   Higher Education Funding Council England, *QAA subject overviews* (June 2003): <http://www.qaa.ac.uk/revreps/subrec/All/go_15_95.htm>; Pamela Thompson and Malcolm Lewis, *Access to music: music libraries and archives in the United Kingdom and Ireland*. London: IAML (UK & Ireland), 2003.

7   Department of the Environment, *The structure of local government in England: a consultation paper*. London: DoE, 1991; Welsh Office, *The structure of local government in Wales: a consultation paper*. London: Welsh Office, 1991; Scottish Office, *The structure of local government in Scotland ... a consultation paper*. Edinburgh: Scottish Office, 1991.

8   Malcolm Lewis, 'The restructuring of local government in Great Britain', *Brio* **28** (2), 1991, 65–70.

9   Chris Muncy, 'Breaking up is hard to do: the effects of local government re-organisation on music library services in the UK'. IAML international conference paper, Edinburgh, 2000.

10 Roger Taylor, 'National report: United Kingdom branch (IAML UK): 1996', *Fontes artis musicae* **44** (1), 105–6.

11 Hansard, 26 March 1993, col. 728.

12 Office of Arts and Libraries, *The future development of library and information services – progress through planning and partnership: report of the Library and Information Services Council*. London: HMSO, 1986.

13 Pamela Thompson, 'Larks ascending: co-operation in music libraries – the last 50 years' in *Music librarianship in the United Kingdom*, ed. Turbet, pp. 172–99.

14 IAML (UK), *Library and information plan for music: written statement*, ed. Susi Woodhouse. Hove: IAML(UK), 1993.

15 Lewis Foreman (ed.), *Lost and only sometimes found*. Upminster: British Music Society, 1992.

16 Pamela Thompson, 'Dance to the music of the information plan', *Library Association record* **97** (7), 1994, 353–5.

17 Susi Woodhouse and Pamela Thompson, 'Towards a Music LIP', *Fontes artis musicae* **41**(4), 1994, 313–39; IAML(UK), *Forty-second annual report, 1994*. London: IAML(UK), 1994; LIPLINC, *LIPs – the way forward: 1994 conference papers*. Sheffield: LIPLINC, 1994.

18 Joint Funding Councils' Libraries Review Group, *Report*. Bristol: HEFCE, 1993. Chairman Sir Brian Follett. (The 'Follett report'.)

19 JISC: <http://www.jisc.ac.uk> (accessed 30/01/06).

20 Pat Wressell & Associates, *Library service provision for researchers:. proceedings of the Anderson Report Seminar, Cranfield University, 10–11 December 1996*. Bruton: LINC, 1997.

21 Music Libraries Online: <http://www.musiconline.ac.uk> (accessed 30/1/06); Kate Sloss and Celia Duffy, 'Music library online' *Brio* **35** (1), 1998, 9–13.

22 Katherine Hogg, 'Music libraries online: a virtual union catalogue for music', *Fontes artis musicae* **47** (1), 2000, 14–21; Marion Hogg, 'Music libraries online', *Brio* **37** (2), 2000, 18–23.

23 Research Support Libraries Programme: <http://www.rslp.ac.uk> (accessed 30/1/06).

24 Ensemble: <http://www.is.bham.ac.uk/ensemble> (accessed 30/1/06).

25 Pamela Thompson and Malcolm Lewis, *Access to music*. London: IAML(UK), 2003, p. 25.

26 Pamela Thompson, 'Ensemble, a vision for music cataloguing cooperation', *Brio* **37** (2), 2000, 24–8.

27 The People's Network: <http://www.ukoln.ac.uk/services/lic/newlibrary/full.html> (accessed 30/1/06).

28 Chris Muncy and Kay Chambers, 'Building a regional music resource', *Brio* **34** (1), 1997, 19–22; Susi Woodhouse, 'Project BARM – a rationale', *Brio* **34** (1), 1997, 23–5.

29 Malcolm Jones and John Gough, 'Greater than the sum of its parts: towards a national service for music performance material' in *Music librarianship in the United Kingdom*, ed. Turbet, pp. 209–19.

30 Malcolm Jones, *Vocal sets in West Midlands libraries*. Birmingham: West Midlands Regional Library Services, 1997.

31 A. Helen Mason (ed.), *Music for choirs*. 2nd ed. Matlock: East Midlands Regional Library System, 1997.

32 Encore!: <http://webhotel.mikromarc.no/encore> (accessed 30/1/06).

33 Paul Andrews, 'Cecilia: towards a map of the music resource of the UK and Ireland' in *Music librarianship in the United Kingdom*, ed. Turbet, pp. 200–8; Cecilia: <http://www.cecilia-uk.org> (accessed 30/1/06).

34 Barbara Penney, *Music in British libraries: a directory of resources*. 4th ed. London: Library Association, 1992.

35 Christopher Bornet, *Annual survey of music libraries*. London: IAML(UK), 1992, 1993; Adrian Dover, *Annual survey of music libraries. No. 11*. Birmingham: IAML(UK), 1997.

36 IAML(UK), Response to consultation on public library standards, in IAML(UK) archive.

37 Malcolm Lewis, 'The International Standard Music Number', *Brio* **29** (2), 1992, 78–82.

38 John Wagstaff (ed.), *The British union catalogue of music periodicals*. 2nd ed. Aldershot: Ashgate, 1998.

39 *CPM plus*. London: Bowker-Saur, 1993.

40 *RISM – Répertoire international des sources musicales*: <http://stub.uni-frankfurt.de/> (accessed 30/1/06); RISM details: <http://www.iaml.info/drupal/en/joint_projects> (accessed 30/1/06).

41 *Répertoire international de la littérature musicale (RILM)*: <http://www.rilm.org> (accessed 30/1/06).

42 Roger Taylor (ed.), *IAML(UK) sets survey: sets of music and drama on loan during September/October 1997*. London: IAML(UK), 1998.

43 Malcolm Jones and John Gough, 'Greater than the sum of its parts: towards a national service for music performance material' in *Music librarianship in the United Kingdom*, ed. Turbet, pp. 209–19.

44 Malcolm Lewis, 'Music interlending: some notes and a lot of issues', *FIL [Forum for Interlending] newsletter*, 1998.

45 Liz Hart and Ruth Hellen, 'Music for the terrified: basic music courses for library staff', *Fontes artis musicae* **47** (1), 2000, 22–3.

46 *IAML(UK) annual report*. London: IAML (UK), 1999, 2000.

47 Music Libraries Trust: <http://www.iaml.info/iaml-uk-irl/mlt/aboutmlt.html> (accessed 30/1/06).

48 Ian Ledsham, 'Who needs music librarians anyway? From FQM to OLU', *Brio* **35** (1), 1998, 3–8.

49 Ian Ledsham, *Music librarianship: the comprehensive guide to music librarianship*. Aberystwyth: Open Learning Unit, Department of Information and Library Studies, University of Aberystwyth, 2000.

50 Lewis Foreman, *Information sources in music*. Munich: Saur, 2003.

51 Peter Griffiths, 'I don't mind if I do: topping up GLASS', *Audiovisual librarian* **19** (2), 1993, 126–8.

52 Daniel Williams, 'Making GLASS visible: the effectiveness and future of the Greater London Audio Specialization Scheme', *Brio* **33** (1), 1996, 3–10; Frank Daniels and Robert Tucker, *Report of the working party on the future of GLASS*. 1995.

53 Jukebox final report: <http://www.sb.aau.dk/Jukebox/finalrep.html#5.1> (accessed 30/1/06).

54 Roger Taylor, 'International outreach: fireworks of the 1990s?' in *Music librarianship in the United Kingdom*, ed. Turbet, pp. 220–35.

55 Pamela Thompson, 'Mimoletnosti/visions fugitives: a fleeting look at Russian music libraries', *Brio* **35** (2), 1998, 101–4.

56 Margaret Brandram, 'Margaret Brandram, music libraries and Croatia', *IAML(UK) newsletter* 31 and 32, 1996 and 1997.
57 IAML conference: <http://www.iaml-uk-irl.org/edinburgh_2000/conf2000.htm> (accessed 30/1/06).

13

News libraries

Richard Nelsson

The approaching tidal wave of change prophesied by Geoffrey Whatmore in the 1976–1980 volume in this series finally came crashing down on newspaper libraries in the early 1990s. Practices that had been in operation for over fifty years were destroyed, collections dumped and scores of jobs were lost. By the end of the decade, developments in online information and the internet had totally changed both the nature and size of the news information profession.[1]

For the purposes of this overview, the term 'newspaper library' will mean a library that exists to support a newspaper's production rather than a collection of newspapers in a library. It will not cover newspaper preservation issues such as the progress of the NEWSPLAN programme, nor will it deal with picture libraries. As many broadcasting organizations, most notably the BBC, boasted similar types of information units, these are also included. In this context, the term media librarian and newspaper librarian will be interchangeable. The phrase Fleet Street will be used to refer collectively to British national newspapers, despite the fact that by 1991 almost of all them had left their traditional home in London's EC4.[2]

In the final pages of his chapter in the volume covering 1986–1990 Geoffrey Hamilton looked at the growing influence of online full-text databases in the late 1980s.[3] However, at the beginning of the next decade technology had yet to make any real impact on the majority of regional and national newspaper libraries. Many still consisted of cuttings collections managed by experienced, but non-professional, staff. A good example of such a library was that of Mirror Group Newspapers (MGN) which included the *Daily* and *Sunday mirror* titles as well as *The European*.

Housed in a large windowless office, the library consisted of row upon row of filing cabinets, each containing folders full of cuttings and photographs, plus a small reference section. The service was operated by a staff of around 40 between the hours of 6.00 a.m. and 3.00 a.m. Early each morning, the day's newspapers and magazines would be marked – that is, each story would be assigned a name of a particular file from the library index. The paper would then be cut up and an average of 1,600 cuttings filed away each day. Newspaper libraries up and down the land were run along similar lines.[4] The majority of queries would be answered using the relevant cuttings file. Towards the end of the afternoon, as deadlines approached, there would be a manic atmosphere as phones rang, users shouted out their requests and librarians literally ran around looking for material.

This manual system worked efficiently enough but management had been looking to automate the operation for years and the office was littered with the debris of failed systems. In 1980 Questicon was introduced (a fiche of the cutting was mechanically retrieved and then displayed on a VDU) but before long it crashed resulting in 18 months' worth of archive being lost. By the late 1980s they were ready to try again with OPAL, an optical disc system, but this was eventually abandoned in 1991.[5]

The latest nod towards the future was a PC linked up to the online, full-text database FT Profile that was usually operated by one of a couple of the recently recruited library school graduates. Change was on its way and within four years the library was fully automated, employing only a handful of staff.

The Association of UK Media Librarians

No discussion of newspaper libraries in the 1990s can be made without reference to the Association of UK Media Librarians (AUKML). Most of the major news librarianship figures of the era were either members, gave papers at the annual conferences or wrote for *Deadline*, the association's quarterly newsletter.[6]

Formed in 1986, the aim of the group was to create a network of information professionals in the print and broadcasting industries, as up until this point there had been no organized body to represent them. With the growth in online information and the perceived threat to jobs, informal links had begun to be made between individual librarians. However, it was a networking lunch hosted by David Nicholas, senior lecturer at the Polytechnic of North London, that proved to be the catalyst in bringing most of the London-based librarians together in the summer of 1986. Nicholas had been in contact with a range of people working in the media as part of a British Library-funded study into online information.[7] The lunch provided the impetus for the new group with Sarah Adair, librarian at London Weekend Television (LWT), assuming a leading role. The inaugural meeting took place on 12 November 1986.[8]

At the same time, the National Association of Newspaper Librarians (NANL) had been formed independently to represent the views of regional librarians. Led by Peter Chapman, chief librarian at the *Northern echo*, the group soon had a membership of at least 30 that were meeting regularly. With similar aims the two groups formally merged on 7 March 1988. The AUKML name was retained and *Deadline* became the newsletter for the new group.[9]

Online information and end-user access

In 1986, Rupert Murdoch's conversion of a warehouse in Wapping to new technology, so that journalists could input copy directly on screen, revolutionized the newspaper industry.[10] However, while the new editorial and production processes had been widely adopted by both the national and regional press during the latter half of the 1980s, automation had had little impact – with a few exceptions – on newspaper libraries. In 1986, David Nicholas *et al.* concluded that this was due to the fact that online provision was still inadequate and existing information-seeking methods and sources were well liked.[11] Moves to look for information outside of the traditional cuttings collection had been inhibited by 'Union problems, management hostility and the librarians' natural conservatism'.[12]

Not all media librarians were conservative and a new breed emerged in the 1980s that saw online's potential as a valuable research tool.[13] In 1986, Justin Arundale, librarian at the newly launched tabloid, *Today*, took the decision to use Datasolve's *World reporter* rather than cuttings and a couple of years later at the *Independent* he made sure that librarians had a 'suite' of databases at their fingertips.[14] The *Guardian* was the first British newspaper to go online with searching initially only carried out by librarians.[15] Meanwhile, a few regional newspapers were in the vanguard of the online information revolution. At the Wolverhampton-based *Express and Star*, Steve Torrington had been involved in setting up the UK's first electronic library in 1985,[16] while at the *Northern echo*, Peter Chapman was confident enough in his electronic sources to take the bold step of ceasing to take cuttings in 1988.

At the same time, Express Newspapers and MGN had invested in OPAL, an optical storage system that presented the image of a cutting on the screen. Keith Beard, chief librarian at the *Express* explained that journalists preferred this as 'They wanted to see the headlines, how a story is placed on a page, that was the boldness of the print'.[17] There was certainly some truth in this, at least for those working on tabloids, and it was the reason why some newspaper librarians were reluctant to get rid of their cuttings collections. However, the survey carried out by David Nicholas had shown that most journalists were more interested in the actual content rather than in the layout. On a practical level, the primitive OPAL system did not incorporate full-text searching and in effect just gave users a facsimile of their own newspaper. It was also very labour-intensive. The Mirror Group abandoned OPAL in 1991 but the *Express* carried on using it until 1993.

In January 1991, *Deadline* published a detailed article by David Stoker, senior lecturer at the University of Wales Aberystwyth, setting out all of the options for automating newspapers.[18] By the end of 1992 it was becoming hard to ignore online information as every British national broadsheet plus *Today* was available online. Management at many newspapers was giving journalists access to *World reporter*, in part because concerns about the cost had been tempered by the large royalty cheques newspapers were receiving from the online vendors. These in turn were increasingly targeting 'intermediaries as a "conduit" to the end-user market'.

This created a major dilemma for many media librarians.[19] The traditional media library fiercely guarded its collection – at MGN users were not allowed to search the shelves themselves – but now users could bypass them by searching online via ATEX terminals at their desks. The well-rehearsed arguments about online leading to job losses seemed to be coming true. There were also professional concerns that roles were being undermined and questions about the quality of end-user searching.

Two schools of thought emerged about end-user access. One, led persuasively by the *Independent* and backed by a number of tabloids plus (at the time) the BBC argued that end-user searching was not cost-effective: journalists searched for information already paid for on the shelves, their searching was crude and ineffective, they had little source knowledge and so looked in the wrong places. Finally, they had no idea of the true price of the information.[20]

However, others – the *Guardian*, News International (the *Times*, *Sunday times*, *Today*, the *Sun* and *News of the world*) and the *Financial times* (*FT*) took the view that journalists were sufficiently adept at information-seeking to manage on their own (at least for simple searches).[21]

In what was once called Fleet Street, every possible online set-up was being used. At the *Independent* only librarians were searching, at the Telegraph Group only journalists, while the *Observer* was an online-free environment. Each position was backed up by anecdotal evidence but the one voice usually missing from the debate was that of the users. In 1992, David Nicholas, now at London's City University, undertook a study to try and throw some light on this.

The survey on the searching behaviour of nearly 100 *Guardian* journalists and librarians was carried out in respect of FT Profile which had been available to both for nearly ten years. The breakdown in online usage was found to be around 50% each. Evidence though showed that the vast majority of journalists preferred librarians to search for them and they were not interested in getting to grips with the finer points of Boolean searching. The conclusion was that 'high volume end-use does not spell the end of the online intermediary'. In fact high volumes of end-use had led to a rise in library searching. Journalists searching for themselves as part of a wider online strategy in which the information professional was engaged seemed to be working.[22]

Of course this was just one paper. At News International, Richard Withey was pursuing a policy of which 'direct access to data by journalists is part of our long-term strategy for information services'. While the library – staffed in part by professionals – was still answering hundreds of queries each week,[23] they had also been working on the technology to give journalists direct menu-driven access to Nexis as well as providing information via an internal database.[24] The ultimate aim here was 'to put librarians on to the editorial floors, with computers around them … the library will shrink and become in effect a core activity providing information from other sources that are not suitable for editorial searching'.[25]

At this stage in the early 1990s, the feared job losses did not materialize. If nothing else, the increased expenditure incurred by online at least showed an interest in information activity by management. A change in the charging for online information from the amount of time spent searching to the amount downloaded also benefited the libraries. Journalists were big browsers spending a lot of time online whereas librarians were more specific; in short librarians' searches cost less, thus librarians spent less. A side-effect of this was that it encouraged the maintenance of the print library as online became the index for the cuttings.[26]

Despite this, there was unease amongst some about the amounts being spent searching external databases and the dominance of FT Profile. To reduce this reliance, papers, most notably News International, had been capturing their own data to create their own in-house archives. The next step was to start exchanging this data.

Fleet Street Data Exchange

The Fleet Street Data Exchange is a lasting testament to the warming of relations between newspaper librarians that began during mid-1980s. It works by each newspaper group exchanging an electronic version of their full news content with each other. Each party then has its own database thus enabling it to search across all the (contributing) national newspapers – ostensibly cost-free. This is not a shared database but shared data and other newspapers do not have access to each other's libraries. It began in 1991 and by the end of the decade most of the UK national press was swapping data.

The idea for the exchange came from Steve Torrington, library manager at Associated Newspapers and Richard Withey, editorial services manager at News International. Both were relative newcomers to the world of newspaper libraries. Torrington was a former journalist who had become interested in automating libraries and after setting up the UK's first electronic library at the Wolverhampton-based *Express and Star*, had moved on to a similar, if much larger, role at Associated. Withey had been Head of Information Services for the British Institute of Management.[27] In October 1990 Torrington met with Withey to explore the possibility of freely exchanging published electronic data between the two libraries.[28] Both publishing houses had been building up full-text databases of their own material; in the case of News International from the mid-1980s and at Associated, librarians had been adding subject index references to each record.[29] The driving force was the cost of having to pay to access published stories (often their own material) from commercial databases such as FT Profile as at the time charging was usually per line downloaded which could lead to huge bills. The aim was:

> To provide the broad sweep of coverage at little or no ongoing cost to any contributing organization. For a fraction of the price of commercial databases, libraries could set up their own database system, swap data with other publishers and provide an electronic library adapted to meet their own particular needs.[30]

With some deft footwork they managed to convince their respective managements about the idea and the exchange began in 1991. The arrangement proved to be successful and in 1993 the Telegraph Group joined, followed by the *Independent* in 1995. The Guardian/Observer (the *Guardian* bought the *Observer* in 1993) did not follow suit mainly because, as the first newspaper to go online, they had a very good deal with FT Profile. This meant that the cost of searching other sources was greatly reduced and so the exchange would have been of little use given the lack of sources. *Guardian* chief librarian Helen Martin also felt that users would benefit more from access to online databases 'that plug us into the outside world instead of focusing on our own archives'.[31] This view was based in part on the results of the City University study which had suggested that journalists were more interested in searching a selection of papers rather than just their own publications. The *Guardian* joined the exchange in 1998 when it was felt useful to do so.[32]

One of the reasons for the success of the exchange was that the agreement was not subject to a formal contractual arrangement – it continued only while beneficial to both parties. The fact that it was a librarian's idea and has been managed and maintained by librarians (with some IT help) also contributed to its success.

From its early years there was a view that the exchange should eventually be centrally hosted. That is, as Richard Withey put it in 1993, 'the decision will come that we shouldn't really all be housing each other's data, we should house it centrally'. This was resisted by some librarians and never materialized.[33] Also resisted at this time was the creation of a single, central Fleet Street library that would serve all the national titles. There were a number of management meetings in Fleet Street to discuss the idea and in 1997, Roy Greenslade, a former *Daily mirror* editor and media commentator, made a forceful plea on the pages of *Deadline* for all media libraries to get together and pool their archives. This plan though failed to take into account the fact that a good news library was one where the librarians understood the unique needs of their particular users, essential when working on exclusives and investigations. A centralized library would destroy this relationship.[34]

CD-ROM

CD-ROMs had been used by the information industry for some time but it was not until the autumn of 1990 that a number of British publishers announced the availability of their products via a disc. Reasons for this included the fact that 'newspaper text represents a very generalist, somewhat disorganized and extremely voluminous information resource'.[35] The first to appear was the *Northern echo* and Peter Chapman was heavily involved with the development and production.[36] Most of the broadsheets soon followed with their own discs.

Compared with the costs of online, CD-ROMs offered a cheap alternative to searching a paper's archive and they found great favour with public and academic librarians. However, their lack of currency and the fact that only one source could be viewed at a time meant that media information professionals didn't wholeheartedly embrace them. As the pages of *Deadline* testified, though, there was a great deal of interest in reference products such as *Britannica* and *Hansard* and the 1993 AUKML conference featured a long session on evaluating these new products.

A year later and the conference, that barometer of all the latest developments, had turned its attention to the amazing possibilities of multi-media. It was around this time, though, that people were starting to take note of something even more exciting, the internet.

The internet

Although the internet had been around since the late 1960s, until the early 1990s it was a world largely inhabited by a relatively small group of scientists and academics. With one or two exceptions, media librarians were too preoccupied with the potential of online and CD-ROM to be interested in the 'high-level cocktail-party conversation' of electronic bulletin boards.[37]

All that began to change in 1992 when articles, initially from the US, started to appear about the internet's great potential as a research tool. Barbara Semonche, the respected library director from the University of Carolina's School of Journalism, talked about the rich resources to be explored,[38] while there was plenty of advice in library journals about how to get connected. Similar articles began to appear on the technology pages of British newspapers and interest really began to be aroused with the news of the arrival of the world wide web in late 1993.[39] This coincided with the 17th Online Exhibition conference which featured a series of lectures about the internet.[40] A few months later an article in *Deadline* left AUKML members in no doubt about the unlimited potential of this new source.[41]

A handful of forward-thinking librarians realized that, like the introduction of online a few years previously, they had to be at the forefront of the revolution and ahead of end-users. The Guardian/Observer library had had a modem connection since April 1993 and a year later all members of staff were being trained in how to search the internet. Progress was steady but slow until it got its own ISDN link in 1997. From there use accelerated and the department began to position itself as the place for internet expertise on the paper.[42] A similar situation was developing at the Scottish Media Group where the Research Library began promoting the use of the web from the mid-1990s.[43] Meanwhile at News International Gertrud Erbach, the online and research librarian, was given the task of finding out as much as possible about the internet.

At the BBC, news librarian Annabel Colley was carving out a niche for herself as the resident internet expert. As well as using it in her research role on *Panorama*, she was giving everything from one-to-one tuition to seminars for hundreds of journalists.[44] There was a strong media librarian presence at NetMedia 97, the media and the internet conference held in London.[45]

With the growth in all of this internet-related activity, David Nicholas once again turned his attention to information provision in the media with a British Library-funded study into the media and the internet. A lack of data and research of 'very dubious quality' fuelled the desire to find what sort of web use was really going on in British newsrooms.[46]

Around 250 interviews were carried out with journalists and librarians at a number of publications although the situation at the Guardian/Observer was investigated in some detail. The results showed that use was patchy and there was some suspicion as to the worth of the internet. An interesting fact was that it was often older journalists or subject specialists, as well as new media journalists, who used the internet the most. For librarians, the internet provided an opportunity for raising their profile through end-user training, doing difficult searches and evaluating the authenticity of websites.[47] Optimistically the study noted that 'the more information there is, the more filtering by professional staff is needed'.[48]

At last it seemed that the media librarians' role was being secured. However, the research project had barely been published when events began to overtake the findings. In 1998, the Guardian/Observer went live with its Mac-based editorial system QPS which provided desktop access to the web for all editorial staff. Email use exploded and journalist began to search themselves. The system was adopted by many other newspapers.[49]

This was a watershed moment for the profession. After all, journalists could now search for everything – not just traditional online – from their desktops, so why the need for the librarian? The familiar questions began to be asked about the need for the intermediary and the carefully argued position about leaving the searching to the qualified information professional could be seen as protectionist and out of touch. For some, one of the answers to this came in the shape of an intranet. This was the vehicle they could use to market themselves as the navigators through the uncharted waters of the internet.

Intranets
At first, newspaper librarians developed their intranets either as gateways to in-house databases or as guides to the greater internet. News International adopted the former. By the end of 1996, librarians, with some IT help, had begun to develop an intranet with the aim of giving users access to the editorial database, allowing them to search without much need for training. Information compiled by the library such as a list of IRA attacks in mainland Britain was also added and Edse-web (Editorial Services Web) was launched in July 1997.[50] The Guardian/Observer was also developing an intranet during this period but without any help from the IT department. Here the concern was exclusively about useful and reliable websites for reporters and again, information compiled by the library.[51] This concept was hardly new though as since the late 1980s the library had offered information via lib-wir, the library's own section on the old ATEX system.[52] North of the border, Ian Watson's Information & Research team developed an intranet at the *Glasgow herald*.[53]

Intranets were the hot topic amongst newspaper libraries in 1998 with at least five papers having developed one.[54] At the annual conference in November of that year Phil Bradley talked about how to set up an intranet with limited resources.

One information service that certainly was not working with limited resources was that at the BBC. Launched in May 2000, Research Central was a one-stop research site, accessible to all BBC employees via Gateway, the BBC's intranet. This was a portal for external sites and in-house such as book and film catalogues. The project, led by Kate Arnold, an Information & Archives manager, began in October 1999.[55] With the full backing of BBC management, the team (composed of BBC librarians and an external designer) had the time and resources to visit newspaper intranets both in the UK and US as well as conduct user surveys at the BBC.[56]

However, a study in 1999 suggested that finding out what exactly users wanted from an intranet was something that few media libraries had done. While there had been much enthusiasm for intranets, there was little apart from anecdotal evidence to suggest how successful they had been. Of course these intranets were the first generation and would no doubt be refined in the next millennium.[57]

Computer-assisted reporting
Another development in the wake of the internet was computer-assisted reporting (CAR). American news librarians had been talking about this since the early 1990s and word soon spread across the Atlantic.[58] For some, CAR was simply another way of describing the use of the internet and databases to find information. A more in-depth interpretation was the marrying of electronic data such as crime figures and voting registrations to generate original story ideas. It could also involve creating staff-developed databases. On American newspapers, librarians and journalists had worked together on a number of successful stories. The NetMedia97 conference featured several talks and workshops about the possibilities of CAR and the key role that news librarians could play in such programmes.[59]

Of course much was dependent on getting raw data via US Freedom of Information laws. Undeterred by the lack of such legislation in the UK, a number of media librarians did begin CAR projects. At the Guardian/Observer, a relational database of election and social statistics material was built in 1997 and while it did not quite succeed as originally intended, it did form the backbone of *The Guardian election guide 1997*.[60] At the BBC, Annabel Colley was using her CAR skills on groundbreaking *Panorama* programmes.[61]

Media libraries in broadcasting: the BBC
Broadcasting libraries faced the same challenges as their newspaper colleagues, as Michelle McKeown, Librarian at LWT, described at the 1993 AUKML conference.[62] However, nowhere was the wave of change felt more than at the BBC.

At the beginning of the decade there were two distinct types of libraries: the traditional reference library and news information. The first category also included services such as sheet music and gramophone collections and was staffed by people with professional library qualifications. The news information units were the cuttings collections and although some staff were qualified, a keen interest in the news was seen as the most important attribute.[63]

In 1991 the three main News Information departments, Broadcasting House, Bush House and TV Centre, employed around 80 people in total. While there was duplication of content, each served a distinct customer base.[64]

All this began to change in April 1993 with the introduction of 'Producer Choice', which established an internal market inside the BBC. The corporation's 23,000 staff were divided into 8,500 'buyers' – the producers, and 14,500 'sellers' such as camera crews and librarians. To justify their jobs, the librarians, competing with outside suppliers, had to do enough business with the producers.[65]

For the first year this worked as it was supposed to, with users accessing and paying for library services. But then they began to look for cheaper options which led to the sometimes ridiculous situation whereby it was cheaper to buy a CD or book from a shop than borrow it from the library.[66] Instead of paying news information for cuttings, journalists resorted to trying to get them free from other media libraries. This brought into question the old tradition of newspaper libraries helping each other out.[67]

There was more change in the summer of 1997 when it was decided to merge all the libraries to form Information & Archives (I&A). There would no longer be a distinction between cuttings, reference or picture libraries and all staff were expected to do a variety of roles. All managers had to apply for the posts, jobs were lost and some, especially former reference staff, found it hard to adapt.

At the same time, information such as the library catalogues began to be delivered electronically to BBC staff throughout the UK. In 1999 News Information Online (NEON) was launched, which gave desktop access to over 80 titles and was free at the point of use. It was an overnight success but use of I&A dropped by 50%. In 2000, it was announced that charges would be abandoned but in most areas it was too late as users had got used to going elsewhere. Other developments included the launch in May 2000 of Research Central, the one-stop research portal (see above).

From the 1980s, a unique feature of the BBC had been the secondment of librarians to individual programmes. These information researchers acted as a link between library resources and the programmes. In the 1990s they became permanent placements, such as Annabel Colley at *Panorama*. Echoing the trend at some newspapers, the nature of the work became much more journalistic.[68]

Regional newspaper libraries
From the mid 1980s onwards, a number of regional titles (taken to include Scottish national papers) had been early adopters of online and subsequent technological developments. The *Express and Star* was the first paper to ditch cuttings and use electronic information in 1985, while at the *Northern echo* Peter Chapman had introduced practices that would be later taken up by many of the nationals. In 1990 the paper employed six professional librarians whose roles ranged from an information researcher to managing the database.[69] A decade later the information researcher was the only post left, the rest being carried out by other departments. Reasons for this decline included the company passing through various stages of ownership and the fact that journalists were doing much of their research themselves.[70] An in-depth study of English regional libraries was carried out in 1992.[71]

In Scotland, Pat Baird introduced technology at the *Daily record* library in 1991 and was one of the first people to start talking about the whole concept of re-selling information.[72] Two years later she claimed that the only way for the profession to survive was to keep up with technological advances and diversify.[73] By 1994 the *Herald* in Glasgow had stopped taking cuttings and introduced a range of databases and the internet.[74] Soon the intranet had been developed so that staff could now concentrate on the management of information.

Regional librarians were instrumental in the early success of AUKML and remained an active force within the group at least until the mid-1990s. They always had a strong presence at the annual conferences, often organizing them, as Christine Cole did at Birmingham in 1994. Other developments included Western Media Publishing's decision to digitize three-quarters of a million cuttings in 1998.[75]

From the middle of the decade jobs began to be lost from regional libraries. Typical of this was the *Nottingham evening post* where a staff of six that had included two professionals was reduced to a few assistants in 1996. However, two years later new owners realizing that a mistake had been made appointed Elena Hayward as Librarian. At this point there was not even a computer in the department but eventually she had convinced management to equip it with electronic resources and the department had internet access before journalists on the paper.[76] Efforts were still being made by AUKML members in the regions to meet but tiny budgets often meant that they could not afford to attend the conferences or meetings.

The professional newspaper librarian
While the most obvious developments through the decade were technological, it was perhaps changes in personnel that were the most dramatic. In the past, libraries like that at the *Daily mirror* had been run by 'large teams of willing, experienced but largely untrained library staff some of whom were appointed as a result of union practices',[77] or to put it bluntly, 'they were dumping grounds for those who might otherwise be made redundant'.[78]

The new breed of library manager realized that if they were to survive they would have to employ staff able to deal with new technology as well as work with young computer-literate journalists. This was not to suggest they were anti-union, but in the future 'post, rather than prior-entry, union membership would have to be encouraged'.[79] The *Guardian* began to employ only staff with postgraduate qualifications and Fleet Street libraries were soon filling their ranks with qualified staff. A number introduced pre-library school graduate trainee schemes and in 1996 AUKML started to sponsor an open day for people thinking of entering the industry. Links were made with library schools with some introducing news librarianship courses.[80]

This was not to denigrate the non-professional, and moves were made in 1993 to introduce National Vocational Qualifications (NVQ) for older, experienced staff.[81] *Daily mail* librarian George Johnson kept the old style viewpoint alive on the back pages of *Deadline*.

With all of this change, it might have seemed a logical step for AUKML to join one of the professional library associations, but this was always rejected as it was felt that open membership would weaken the lobbying power of the group. Despite informal links being made over the years, the issue was still being debated at the end of the decade.[82]

Justin Arundale had always been (at least in the early years of the decade) one of the most vocal proponents of the new professional. His model was that the news librarian should be 'pro-active, dynamic and entrepreneurial', working with their journalistic colleagues as partners and always looking forward. While few would disagree with this there was always a divergence of views as to what the exactly the librarian should be doing in the digital age.[83]

As far back as 1992, Richard Withey had seen, with the advancement of technology, the sweeping away of the traditional intermediary, with information going straight to the journalist. Librarians would be responsible for the processing of this.[84] In the wake of desktop access to the internet this appeared to be coming true. Most libraries were spending considerable amounts of time archiving their material for the data exchange and online hosts, while journalists were being encouraged by management to search themselves. Some libraries had very little, if any, contact with their users. There was resistance though in some quarters to the media library only having an archive function. Instead they should become proactive research units.

This view was articulated most persuasively by Nora Paul, library director of the Poynter Institute of Media Studies in Florida. Armed with their unique skills, librarians could make sense of the morass of information, build intranets, help with CAR projects and train their users. Instead of being in a remote part of the building, as newspaper libraries so often were, staff should be sitting in the newsrooms and where they contributed to editorial content they should be given a byline.[85]

These ideas had been around for a while but from the mid-1990s they began to be put into practice and formalized within organizations. At the *Financial times* there had always been a couple of specialist researchers in the library but from 1996 the number was increased while at *Time* magazine the distinction between librarian and journalist was becoming blurred as the former took on more research work. At the Guardian/Observer, staff were working alongside specialist reporters on big investigations and being credited in the papers when they produced original work.

To reflect this new role and to signal a break from the image of the old cuttings collections, a number of newspaper libraries changed their names. At the BBC the service became Information & Archives, the Guardian/Observer's library became Research & Information, the *FT*'s became Editorial Information Services while at *Herald* the name chosen was Information & Research.[86] Certainly there was a growing confidence in the profession. Links were made with the American Special Libraries Association's News Division,[87] AUKML launched a website in 1997 and a listserv soon after.

Throughout the decade David Nicholas had been shouting from the sidelines, primarily to tell people to find out what their users really wanted. These documented surveys were essential but *Deadline* had regularly solicited and challenged the views of prominent journalists.[88] An obsession with status – common to all areas of librarianship but particularly pronounced in the media – led inevitably to the question of salaries and in 1998, AUKML conducted a salary survey amongst its members.[89] The idea was that this could then be used as a basis for negotiations with respective managements.

For some organizations, though, the pace of change had been so quick that newspaper executives did not always understand the new information environment and the idea of the 'research' library was met with disdain. The prevailing view more often than not seemed to be, as media commentator Robin Hunt put it to AUKML delegates at the 1997 conference, that new search tools such as Ask Jeeves were well on the way to making the librarian and information professional redundant. Many jobs were lost, especially in the regions and most of the nationals saw their numbers decline. The library at the *Independent* more or less disappeared when the Mirror Group bought the paper in 1994 and the staffing levels at the BBC had been greatly reduced.

Hunt though later changed his mind arguing that information managers had become 'databases of experience rather than information ... [they] bring value beyond measure, or any intelligent agent to, an organization. They bring non-artificial intelligence'.[90] As publishers developed their websites, Julie Rombotham described ways in which librarians with indexing skills were getting involved with information architecture, structuring the data that drove sites.[91]

In truth, the newspaper library left standing in 2000 was something of a 'transitional or hybrid library'. Users had access to all manner of online services from their desktops but the fact remained that there was still a need for the central resource managed by skilled information professionals. Staffing levels may have been reduced, but whether they were involved in producing intranets, training or in-depth research, there was a recognition of the real value that the intermediary brought to journalism. After the turbulent past few years, the profession was confident in its role as part of the editorial process but apprehensive at what the next wave of digital technology in the new millennium might bring.[92]

Notes

1   Geoffrey Whatmore, 'News libraries and newspaper collections' in *British librarianship and information work 1976–1980*, ed. L. J. Taylor. London: Library Association, 1982, v. 2, pp. 37–48.

2   NEWSPLAN: <www.bl.uk/collections/nplan.html> (accessed 31/1/06).

3   Geoffrey Hamilton, 'Newspapers and newspaper libraries' in *British Librarianship and Information Work 1986–1990*, ed. David Bromley and Angela M. Allott. London: Library Association, 1993, v. 2, pp. 41–57.

4   Steve Torrington, speech to Aslib, 14 June 1991.

5   Bernard Willams, 'Press cuttings automation at the *Daily mirror*', *Information media and technology* **21** (5), 1989, 216–18.

6   AUKML: <www.aukml.org.uk> (accessed 31/1/06).

7   David Nicholas, Kevin Harris and Gertrud Erbach, *Online searching: its impact on information users*. London: Mansell, 1987 (British Library R & D report; 5944).

8   Mark Noades, 'One year on – ', *AUKML newsletter* **1** (1), Nov. 1987.

9   Belinda Fisher, 'Editor's note', *Deadline: quarterly journal of the Association of UK Media Librarians* **2** (2), April 1988.

10 'Wapping: 10 years on', *Guardian*, 8 Jan. 1996.

11 David Nicholas *et al.*, *Online searching*.

12 David Nicholas and Kevin Connolly, 'Information technology developments in the newspaper industry and the future of the librarian', *Library Association record* **89** (10), 1987, 530–3.

13 Helen Martin, 'End of an era', *Deadline* **15** (4), Oct. 1990.

14 J. Arundale and G. Erbach, 'The Library of the *Independent*: A case study in the introduction of information technology in a newspaper library' in *Online Information 88: 12th International Online Information Meeting, London, 6–8 December 1988: proceedings*. Oxford: Learned Information, [1989], v. 2, pp. 575–9.

Datasolve Information Online was launched in 1982 providing a full-text news database for journalists and researchers. The original product, World Reporter, consisted of just the BBC summary of world broadcasts. Over the next four years various newspapers were added, the first being the *Guardian* in 1984. It became FT Profile when acquired by the Financial Times Group in 1987. Reuters Textline, started in 1984, was also used in newsrooms. Nexis, which dominated the US market, began to be increasingly used owing to its huge range of sources. Nexis bought FTProfile in January 2000. See Justin Arundale, 'Databases seek soft options in a war of words', *Independent* 3 June 1990. Atex was a pioneering system of networked machines adopted by newspapers because it offered a very robust set of editing tools. 'Atex messaging' was credited as a major predecessor of email.

15 Kevin Jackson, 'Online Information at the *Guardian*: an interview with Harold Jackson', *Library Association record* **88** (11), 1986, 541–3.

16 Steve Torrington, speech to Aslib, 14 June 1991.

17 Andrew Lycett, 'Battle of the hi-tech libraries', *Times* 21 June 1989.

18 David Stoker, 'Options for the automation of newspaper libraries', *Deadline* **5** (1), Feb. 1991.

19 Richard Poynder, 'Online vendors' strategies for reaching the end-user: FT Profile', *Online review* **16** (3), 1992, 147–55.

20 Justin Arundale, 'The importance of information management' in *Information sources for the press and broadcast media*, ed. Selwyn Eagle. London: Bowker-Saur, 1991, pp. 37–49.

21 David Nicholas and Helen Martin, 'Should journalists search themselves (and what happens when they do?)', *Online Information 93: 17th International Online Information Meeting: proceedings, London 7–9 December 1993*, ed. David I. Raitt and Ben Jeapes. Oxford: Learned Information, 1993, pp. 227–34.

22 Helen Martin and David Nicholas, 'End-users coming of age? Six years of end-user searching at the *Guardian*', *Online and CD-Rom review* **17** (2), 1993, 83–90.

23 Gertrud Erbach, Lynda Iley and Hugh Porter, 'Discover: news and current affairs information', *Managing information* **3** (10), 1996, 27–30.

24 Richard Withey, 'Library lecturer found on the moon', *Library Association record* **95** (2), 1993, 104.

25 Roland Stanbridge, 'Journalists begin to embrace online databases', *Information world review* Dec. 1992, 46–8.

26 David Nicholas and Kevin Connolly, 'Big browsers are watching you', *Library Association record* **95** (1), 1993, 34–5.

27 Steve Torrington, 'Seven years of electronic libraries', speech to Newstec conference, 1993.
28 Private letter from Richard Withey to Steve Torrington, 5 Oct. 1990.
29 Richard Withey, 'The news information industry and the media library in the 21st century' in *Information sources for the press and broadcast media*, ed. Sarah Adair. 2nd ed. London: Bowker-Saur, 1999, pp. 71–84.
30 Torrington, 'Seven years'.
31 David Nicholas and Keven Connolly, 'To cut or not to cut – and who does the cutting?', *Library Association record* **95** (2), 1993, 104–5.
32 Roland Stanbridge, 'Online usage by the British news media: a brief survey', unpublished seminar paper at the Department of Journalism, Media and Communication (JMK), Stockholm University, Jan. 1993.
33 Withey, 'Library lecturer found on the moon'.
34 Roy Greenslade, 'Breeding bad habits', *Deadline* **11** (1), Jan. 1997.
35 Justin Arundale, 'Newspapers on CD-Rom: the European perspective' in *12th National On-line Meeting: proceedings, 1991: New York, May 7–9, 1991*, ed. Martha E. Williams. Medford, N.J.: Learned Information, 1991.
36 Peter Chapman, 'Practical experience: CD-Rom publishing', *AUKML conference proceedings*, June 1995.
37 Beverly T. Watkins, 'Seeking tools of the future', *Chronicle of higher education* 37, Nov. 1991.
38 Barbara P. Semonche, 'Computer-assisted journalism: an overview' in *News media libraries: a management handbook*, ed. Barbara P. Semonche. Westport, Conn.: Greenwood Press, 1993, pp. 265–316.
39 Joe Levy, 'The world in a web', *Guardian* 11 Nov. 1993.
40 Ian Watson, 'The internet: bizarre information world or world information bazaar?', in *Online Information 93*, ed. Raitt and Jeapes, pp. 465–76.
41 Gertrud Erbach, 'The internet: what's in it for us?', *Deadline* **9** (2), July 1994.
42 Helen Martin, 'Internet use at the *Guardian* and the *Observer*: a case study' in *Information sources for the press and broadcast media*, ed. Adair. 2nd ed., pp. 91–104.
43 Ian Watson, 'Professionals and neophytes: contrasting approaches to the web', *Business information review* **17** (3), 2000, 125–9.
44 Annabel Colley, 'From gopher to guru: the changing role of a BBC Television programme information researcher' in *Information sources for the press and broadcast media*, ed. Adair. 2nd ed., pp. 38–70.
45 *NetMedia 97: the media and the internet conference proceedings*, July 1997.
46 David Nicholas *et al.*, *The media and the internet: final report of the British Library funded research project The changing information environment: the impact of the internet on information seeking behaviour in the media*. London; Aslib, 1998 (British Library research and innovation report; 110).
47 David Nicholas *et al.*, 'Journalists and the internet: how they use it, what they think of it' in *NetMedia 98: conference proceedings*, 1998.
48 Peter Williams and David Nicholas, 'The Net, the journalist and the news libber: a case study of the changing information environment', *Deadline* **13** (3), 1998.
49 Helen Martin, 'The Guardian/Observer: information developments since 1998', *Aslib proceedings* **53** (5), 2001, 161–6.
50 Gertrud Erbach and Lynda Iley, 'The News International newspaper's intranet experience: a case study', *Aslib proceedings* **51** (1), 1999, 30–4.

51 Martin, 'Internet use at the *Guardian* and the *Observer*'.
52 Lucinda Convert-Vail, 'News libraries in the European Community' in *News media libraries*, ed. Semonche, pp. 83–130.
53 Ian Watson, 'The development of an intranet at Scottish Media Newspapers' in *Handbook of information management*, ed. Alison Scammell. London; Aslib, 1997.
54 Jackie Drennan, 'The introduction of intranets into the UK newspaper industry', MA dissertation, City University, 1998.
55 Susan Pryce, 'BBC intranet', *Deadline* **15** (3), July 2000.
56 'BBC staff portal', *Library Association record* **103** (6), 2001, 353.
57 Jackie Drennan, 'The introduction of intranets into the newspaper industry', *Aslib proceedings* **51** (8), 1989, 269–74.
58 Barbara P. Semonche, 'Computer-assisted journalism: an overview' in *News media libraries*, ed. Semonche; Richard Nelsson, 'Pass notes: computer-assisted reporting', *Deadline* **8** (4), Dec. 1993.
59 *NetMedia97: conference proceedings*.
60 Helen Martin, 'The changing information environment in the media', *Aslib proceedings* **51** (3), 1999, 91–6.
61 Annabel Colley, 'BBC Panorama information research' in *Super searchers in the news: the online secrets of journalists and news researchers*, ed. Reva Basch. Medford, N.J. : Information Today, 2000.
62 Michelle McKeown, 'Broadcasting libraries in a brave new world', *AUKML conference proceedings*, 1993.
63 David Stoker, 'Library support for features beyond news and current affairs: an account of the BBC Reference Library service' in *Information sources for the press and broadcast media*, ed. Eagle, pp. 78–96.
64 Margaret Katny, 'Online information systems and newspaper cuttings at the BBC World Service Information Research Unit', *Deadline* **9** (2), July 1994.
65 Frances Tait, 'Information doesn't come free anymore!', *Deadline* **7** (3), July 1993.
66 Paul McCann, 'BBC staff shop for archive material', *Independent* 22 Oct. 1997.
67 'Mediafile', *Guardian* 16 Aug. 1993.
68 Colley, 'From gopher to guru'.
69 Catharine Edwards, 'Working with journalists at the *Northern echo*', *AUKML conference proceedings*, 1991.
70 Peter Chapman, 'Change and the changing face of a regional newspaper library 1990–2000', *Aslib proceedings* **53** (2), 2001, 55–7.
71 Julia Kent, 'An examination of libraries and Information units operating within regional newspapers in England today', MA dissertation, Manchester Metropolitan University, 1993.
72 Pat Baird, 'A freshman's view of media librarianship', *AUKML conference proceedings*, 1991.
73 Pat Baird, 'Media librarianship: where is the profession going?', *AUKML conference proceedings*, 1993.
74 Ian Watson, 'Caledonian newspapers: a profile', *Deadline* **9** (3), Oct. 1994.
75 Tim Owen, 'Digital clippings save costs for regional newspaper', *Information world review* April 1998.
76 Personal communication from Elena Hayward.

77 Richard Withey and Elizabeth Huggett, 'Fleet Street's second revolution: online technology in information gathering for newspapers' in *Information sources for the press and broadcast media*, ed. Eagle, pp. 124–56.
78 Baird, 'Freshman's view'.
79 Martin, 'Changing information environment'.
80 David Nicholas, 'Education and training of media librarians', *AUKML conference proceedings*, 1991.
81 Justin Arundale, 'NVQs – what's in it for us?', *Deadline* **7** (3), July 1993.
82 Fiona Tennyson, 'So what's the LA got to do with AUKML?', *Deadline* **14** (2), June 1999.
83 Arundale, 'Importance of information management'.
84 'Do we need libraries and librarians?', *AUKML conference proceedings*, 1992.
85 Nora Paul, 'Media libraries and new media', *NetMedia97: conference proceedings*, London, 1997; Nora Paul, 'The changing role of the news librarian' in *Information sources for the press and broadcast media*, ed. Adair, pp. 85–90.
86 Ian Watson, 'Hanging on to their coat-tails', *AUKML conference proceedings*, 1996.
87 Special Libraries Association News Division: <www.ibiblio.org/slanews/> (accessed 31/1/06).
88 Melanie Phillips, 'Cutting comment', *Deadline* **8** (4), Dec. 1993.
89 Lesley Phillips, 'Salaries & conditions survey'. Issued by AUKML, Oct. 1998.
90 Robin Hunt, 'News information and value', *Aslib proceedings* **50** (8), 1998, 215–20.
91 Julie Rowbotham, 'Librarians – architects of the future?', *Aslib proceedings* **51** (2), 1999, 59–62.
92 Withey, 'News information industry'.

14

Map libraries

Robert Parry

While spatial data in digital form became increasingly important to the UK economy, map libraries continued to be under severe financial and political pressure. Owing to funding constraints affecting both purchasing and staffing levels, most libraries were unable to adopt a very high profile in promoting and servicing the digital revolution. Nevertheless, the decade was marked by the growing and inevitable impact of the computer on map library management, by the fast-growing effects of the internet and world wide web on networking and access to information, and by developments in digital archiving and the electronic distribution of maps and spatial data.

Copyright issues and intellectual property rights also became significant points of concern to map libraries, particularly with respect to library access to digital data and the hard line taken by organizations such as Ordnance Survey and the British Geological Survey over free public access and the raster scanning of maps.

The decade saw the appointment of new heads of several of the legal deposit map libraries, and sadly, in 1995, the passing of the doyen of former map librarians, Dr Helen Wallis.[1]

Organizations, funding and staffing

The principal map libraries set up for public access remained the six legal deposit libraries, namely the British Library Map Library, the National Libraries of Scotland and Wales, and the university libraries of Cambridge, Oxford and Trinity College Dublin. In addition substantial map collections continued to flourish at the Royal Geographical Society (which afforded public access during this period)[2] and the Ministry of Defence (for internal use). Much smaller, but significant, collections usually focused on contemporary maps were to be found in most universities and some other higher education institutions (HEIs).[3] Maps also formed an important part of the archives of county record offices and some of the larger public libraries, and there were also a few specialized map collections, such as those of the Guildhall Library, the Imperial War Museum and the National Maritime Museum. Significant collections, mainly for internal use, were held by some government and commercial mapmakers, and by research organizations.

Staffing as well as resourcing continued to be a problem in many map libraries, as HEIs and other bodies cut back on funding. Some collections had to restrict their opening hours owing to reductions in staffing, a policy which in turn had a negative effect on map library usage. Full-time map librarian posts were lost from the National History Museum and the National Maritime Museum as well as from several vulnerable smaller university collections.

Some collections benefited from improved accommodation. A major move took place for the British Library Map Library (BLML) and the India Office Records Map Collection which relocated in 1998 to the new British Library building at St Pancras, and extensions and/or refurbishments were provided at the National Libraries of Wales and Scotland, the Hydrographic Office at Taunton, and the Public Record Office at Kew. The map library of the School of Geography, University of Leeds, moved to improved, refurbished accommodation.[4]

Education, training and networking
Irrespective of their academic backgrounds, for most map library staff, the special (and evolving) skills required to curate a map collection continued to be self-taught with the aid of guides such as Larsgaard's *Map librarianship: an introduction*,[5] and through contact and shared experiences with others in the profession. In this connection, the development of internet list-servers was of particular importance during this decade, as was also the arrangement of occasional in-service training courses.

Formed as a special interest group of the British Cartographic Society (BCS), the Map Curators' Group (MCG) continued to provide the focus for map library interests, and to be the lead organization in arranging courses and seminars.[6] The annual Map Curators' Workshops, normally held as a pre-meeting before the BCS Annual Symposium each September, were well supported and put on lively and well-attended programmes. Map library interests also featured in the 'Edinburgh 3-Day Event' arranged by the BCS and the Charles Close Society in association with the National Library of Scotland,[7] while map curators living in or near the Midlands were able to benefit from the popular 'Midmap' meetings arranged by Joan Chibnall. Throughout the decade, *Cartographiti*, the newsletter of the MCG, continued its quarterly publication schedule, grew in volume and stature, and remained the principal printed source of news on developments in UK map libraries.[8]

Matters of concern to map libraries continued to be discussed at meetings of the British and Irish Committee for Map Information and Cataloguing Systems (BRICMICS), originally established in 1984 as a consultative committee of Ordnance Survey, but subsequently adopting a broader remit, with a sub-committee, BRICMICS/OS, serving as one of the seven OS Consultative Committees. A summary by its secretary, Anne Taylor, of the committee's deliberations began to reach a wider audience during the decade through the pages of *Cartographiti*.

Founded in 1989, the Association for Geographic Information (AGI) became an important player in the field of digital cartography. Although at first serving mainly the interests of government departments, utility companies and commercial enterprises concerned with geographical information and GI science, it took a lead in such issues as the development of a national transfer format for digital data and metadata standards, which were also of importance for map libraries.[9]

In the international arena, British map curators played an educational role in the programmes and activities of the Section of Geography and Map Libraries of the International Federation of Library Associations and Institutions (IFLA), in the conferences of the *Groupe de cartothécaires de LIBER*, and in the conferences of the International Cartographic Association (ICA) and the International Map Collectors' Society (IMCoS). The first two organizations were concerned especially with the establishment of standards for the automation of cataloguing systems, retrospective catalogue conversion, and digital archiving. Numerous conference papers by members of the British map librarian community were published in *LIBER quarterly* or *INSPEL* (an official journal of IFLA).[10] Both journals devoted whole issues to papers on map librarianship.[11]

Britain was host to meetings of several international cartographic organizations, including the ICA at Bournemouth in 1991, and IMCoS in 1991 and 1998. British map curators were involved with the international map exhibition at the ICA conference in Bournemouth in 1991, in which Ordnance Survey also mounted a special exhibition to mark its bicentenary.[12]

Manuals, periodicals and resource publications
A number of fundamental resources to help in running map libraries were published during the decade. Larsgaard's standard book on map librarianship was published in its third (and final) edition in 1998 and, although orientated towards American collections, remained the best guide to the principles and practices of the profession.[13] A more detailed multi-authored handbook on cataloguing and classification appeared in 2000.[14]

Internationally, *Bibliographia cartographica: documentation of cartographic literature* continued to provide an annual listing of new literature on the broader realm of cartography, and included a specific section on map collections.[15]

Under the auspices of IFLA, new editions of the *World directory of map collections* were published in 1993 and 2000, while in 1995 the British Cartographic Society published the third edition of *A directory of UK map collections*.[16] This was updated and placed on the BCS website in 2000 but not issued in printed form.

The decade also saw new editions of *Who's who in the history of cartography*, the ninth edition appearing in 1998 and listing 630 people in 45 countries engaged in research in early cartography.[17]

An exhaustive sourcing and evaluation of UK map publishers and their products, *Mapping the UK*, was provided by Perkins and Parry, who also completed a much expanded and revised second edition of their standard work on world mapping, *World mapping today*.[18]

Other valuable reference books included Richard Oliver's *Ordnance Survey maps: a concise guide for historians*, and *Historians' guide to early British maps*, edited by Helen Wallis and Anita McConnell, which provides a directory of collections holding significant early mapping.[19] Sarah Bendall provided a greatly enlarged second edition of Peter Eden's *Dictionary of land surveyors and local mapmakers of Great Britain and Ireland 1530–1850*.[20]

Although there is no UK academic journal devoted specifically to research relating to map libraries, papers by or of interest to map curators were published in *The cartographic journal*, principal organ of the BCS, and in the *Bulletin of the Society of Cartographers*, the latter also carrying a substantial review section on cartographic books, maps and atlases.

The map collector, first published in 1977, also continued to provide news and articles of interest to map curators, but unfortunately ceased publication in 1995. It was effectively replaced by the launch the same year of *Mercator's world*, with its former editor becoming a consulting editor to the new publication. Thus although published in the United States, this heavily illustrated magazine continued to feature some articles relating to UK map libraries, and news about people in the map world.

Imago mundi, published annually by the British Library Map Library, remained the main organ for research publication in the history of cartography, and was also notable for its reviews of new literature in the history of cartography and for its detailed bibliographic section.[21] The International Map Collectors' Society also published its own journal for members, *IMCoS journal*.[22]

The ambitious *History of cartography project*, initiated by Brian Harley (who died in 1991) and by David Woodward at the University of Wisconsin, continued slowly to bear its fruits, with three substantial books, together comprising Volume 2, published during the decade.[23]

Ordnance Survey consultative papers began to appear on the Ordnance Survey website, and provided a valuable means of tracking fast-moving developments in this primary mapping organization.[24]

During the decade a variety of carto-bibliographies were published of which only a selection will be mentioned here. Particularly welcome were the third volume of Hodson's valuable bibliographies of county atlases, and a fourth volume in the Public Record Office series of maps and plans in the PRO.[25] John Moore, map librarian at the University of Glasgow, produced a second edition of his *The historical cartography of Scotland*, Roger Kain and Richard Oliver produced a catalogue of tithe mapping for England and Wales, while Robert Davies (National Library of Wales) authored a guide to tithe maps of Wales held in the National Library of Wales, and Margaret Wilkes (National Library of Scotland) a booklet *The Scot and his maps*.[26] A substantial and beautifully illustrated volume cataloguing the globes in the National Maritime Museum was published under the authorship of Elly Dekker, while Ralph Hyde authored a book on the ward maps of London.[27] Additionally a number of carto-bibliographies of individual counties were published by a diversity of authors and publishers.[28]

The Charles Close Society continued to publish a valuable series of detailed studies of individual Ordnance Survey map series, each including a sheet by sheet listing of editions and revisions, and providing a useful resource and check-list for map libraries.[29] The Society also published two volumes of sheet index maps to early Ordnance Survey map series, while other Ordnance Survey listings were produced by Nigel James at the Bodleian Library.[30]

Online resources

One of the most significant developments of the decade was the establishment of list-servers enabling map librarians with internet access to communicate and exchange messages with a wide diversity of list subscribers. An email list-server for map librarians, MAPS-L, was launched in the United States in 1991, and many UK map librarians participated in its use throughout the 1990s. However, in 1993 LIS-BRICMICS was also launched, initially to serve that committee but then, recognizing its value to the whole UK map library community, it was renamed LIS-MAPS.[31] Other list-servers were launched about this time, including MAPHIST, for those interested in the history of cartography,[32] and the USA-based Gis4lib for issues relating to Geographic Information Systems and libraries. The Society of Cartographers (formerly Society of University Cartographers) also carried many items of relevance to map libraries on its list-server Carto-SoC.[33]

During the 1990s, numerous other online resources became available to map libraries, and by the end of the decade map curators had a huge range of websites as well as email list-servers at their disposal. Many national and commercial mapping organizations had developed comprehensive websites, sometimes with online purchasing facilities, while major dealers had begun to put their stock catalogues on the web. *Oddens' bookmarks*, which was started in 1995 by the curator of the Map Library of the Faculty of GeoSciences at Utrecht University, soon became the premier site for finding web-based information on anything cartographic.[34] This began as a local resource for users of the Utrecht map library, but developed into a classified list, searchable by subject, country, category or a combination of these. Conversion to a database structure in 1999 made adding links much easier than it had been before. By 2000 more than 12,000 links had been created. It became important for map curators to become familiar with useful websites, and libraries began to construct their own home pages with links to favoured sites.

Acquisitions

Apart from the legal deposit libraries, most map libraries continued to depend heavily on donations and exchanges to build their collections. Some began to make use of LIS-MAPS to advertise disposals, a practice which had become well-established among American map libraries using MAPS-L.

The break-up of the Soviet Union from 1989 had far-reaching effects on the availability of modern topographic maps published by the USSR during the Cold War period (and which approached a world-wide cover), and by the neighbouring former Soviet bloc countries. Among these effects was the establishment of marketing outlets for this mapping in both Europe and the United States, and several major libraries in the UK began, within budget limitations, to build partial collections of these maps. In order to share information and to discourage unnecessary overlap in purchasing, Francis Herbert of the Royal Geographical Society collected and compiled regular summaries of these acquisitions for *Cartographiti*. An indirect effect was the appearance of many new commercial or privatized cartographic companies in Eastern Europe, issuing a wealth of quality public and tourism-orientated maps where before there had been a dearth. A further effect was the redistribution by the UK Ministry of Defence Map Library of older and now superseded East European maps to many university map libraries.

The legal deposit libraries acquired a number of valuable collections. The British Library acquired the papers of William Petty (1623–1687) which included manuscript maps from the famous Down Survey of Ireland. The National Library of Scotland received the Bartholomew archive (donated by HarperCollins with their move from Edinburgh to Glasgow), collections of maps from the Royal Scottish Geographical Society (including the Wade Collection of military maps and plans of the Highlands of Scotland from the period 1724–35), and also received the Royal Society of Edinburgh's residual map collection with much 19th-century topographic and geological mapping of Europe and Asia. The Scottish Record Office acquired substantial collections of plans resulting from de-nationalization of the rail and coal mining industries. A large collection of charts and atlases was transferred from the Admiralty Library to the Hydrographic Office Archive at Taunton.

Digital maps
With their limited resources, many map libraries were slow or reluctant to engage with the digital revolution, but by the end of the decade there was little choice but to try to come to terms with the proliferation of maps in new digital formats. Many thematic maps ceased to be published in printed form, while conversely a wealth of new spatially encoded thematic data became available digitally. Consequently a variety of formats, both digital and analogue, became possible: digital data structured and packaged in different ways became available on CD-ROM and increasingly online; Ordnance Survey offered a print-on-demand service for large-scale maps, and maps which were site-centred or customized in other ways also became an option. As Ordnance Survey large-scale mapping became wholly digital and subject to continuous update, concepts of 'map edition' and of map series with fixed format sheets, traditionally important fields in map cataloguing, began to lose their relevance. Meanwhile, users began to find online alternatives to library hard-copy material.

The early years of the decade saw the production of many commercial map and mapping packages on CD-ROM. Of particular interest to map libraries were the increasingly sophisticated, and cheaply priced, route navigation packages, and a variety of 'electronic atlases'. The complete UK census data for 1991 were also released on CD-ROM complete with digitized enumeration districts' boundaries and choropleth mapping software.[35] Such developments signalled a move from libraries being simply the providers of ready-made maps, to resource centres for the supply and management of digital data in a computer environment – users of map libraries could now create their own thematic maps from digital data, but often this necessitated some measure of help from hard-pressed map library staff.[36] Indeed some users began to expect libraries to supply a full digital mapping service.

Thus the decade was marked by a growing concern about how map libraries were to adapt to the increasing availability of maps in a more elusive digital format, and the attendant problems of acquisition, storage, delivery to library users, copyright, cataloguing and conservation. A major issue concerned the new skills which were required to handle data in digital form: should map curators become fully trained GIS practitioners, or should they, as Perkins queried, 'leave it to the labs'?[37] The route followed would depend to a large extent on the institutional framework within which the map library operated and its specialisms. For example, a map library attached to a geography department using GIS for research would experience different curatorial demands from a county record office.

Most UK map libraries depend heavily on Ordnance Survey mapping as a mainstay of their holdings. This includes not only the topographic series mapping at scales of 1 : 50,000 and 1 : 25,000 (and to a lesser extent 1 : 10,000), which continued to be issued in paper form, but also the larger scaled planimetric mapping of urban areas (at 1 : 1,250 scale) and cultivated rural areas (at 1 : 2,500 scale). These latter, so-called 'basic scale' maps (including also 1 : 10,000 basic scale mapping of mountain and moorland areas) had been subject to a vector digitizing programme by OS since 1972, and capture of the entire archive of some 230,000 large-scale map sheets was completed in 1995. A consequence of this was that Ordnance Survey ceased to provide regular printed editions of these maps. Instead they could be plotted on demand, generally on paper of inferior quality and which retailed at a high price (the so-called *Superplan* service). Alternatively, the digital data themselves could be licensed, but again at a price which was unaffordable to map libraries. In short it became practically impossible from the early 1990s for map libraries to maintain the currency of their large scale OS map holdings.

A particularly important issue concerned the need to ensure that digital 'snapshots' of the national digital archive were captured and conserved at regular intervals, given that the archive was now held by OS as a master database, under continuous revision and with no publication of regular printed editions. This was especially a problem for the legal deposit libraries, as there was no provision in law for the deposit of non-print materials with these libraries.[38] Moreover it was not only a case of maintaining currency, but also of archiving 'the future history of the landscape'. In 1992 a seminar with this name was held at the Royal Society, which sought to investigate the demand for historical map data.[39] Subsequently a questionnaire survey confirmed the extent and interests of the user community of historic OS mapping.[40]

For the legal deposit libraries, an agreement was initially reached with Ordnance Survey for large scale mapping to be deposited in microform for five years beginning 1990 (later extended to 1999), but microforms were also due to be phased out. After protracted negotiations, an agreement was signed in 1997 by the British Library on behalf of all six legal deposit libraries for a copy of the National Topographic Database (i.e., the *ca.* 230,000 digitized basic scale maps) to be deposited with them annually. It remained for the copyright libraries to select and adapt suitable hardware and software to manage the data for public access. BRICMICS set up a working group to consider the options, and a customized version of MapInfo was subsequently developed.[41]

This of course provided no solution for non-legal deposit libraries such as those in HEIs, many of which had requirements for contemporary OS mapping for both teaching and research, and for using the maps in a digital as well as an analogue form.[42] So of equal significance was the award in 1996 of a grant under the Electronic Libraries Programme (eLib) from the Joint Information Services Committee (JISC) to Edina, Edinburgh University's Data Library 'to identify and assess appropriate service models by which staff and students in HEIs may gain cost effective and timely access to Ordnance Survey digital map data'. The proposal for this project evolved from concerns initially investigated in Scotland by the Data Library under its director, Peter Burnhill, as to how universities might access Ordnance Survey digital data.[43] The so-called Digimap programme ran from 1996 until 2000, and involved user trials at six university sites, chosen to provide a cross-section of the map library services available in HEIs.[44] The project proved highly successful, and parallel talks undertaken by JISC with OS led to an agreement to provide a national subscription service to HEIs for access to OS digital data, with Edina (with support from MIMAS – see below) winning the bid to provide the service. Digimap went online to over 40 subscribing institutions in 2000. Although not invariably administered through libraries, the availability of OS digital maps to staff and students was bound to raise the profile of digital mapping and GIS throughout these institutions, and in many instances to present an enhanced role for map librarians. During the years of the pilot demonstrator service, many presentations and papers were given by Edina staff and by trial site representatives.[45]

Before launching the Digimap service to map users in British HEIs, the Edinburgh Data Library had already been hosting online access to national digital census and postcode boundary files through a service called UKBORDERS, and to OS *Strategi* (1 : 250,000 scale topographic) vector data. Towards the end of the decade the JISC-supported data centre MIMAS (formerly called MIDAS) at Manchester Computing began to offer census data download facilities to subscribers in HEIs.[46]

These developments marked a migration of digital map data from CD-ROM to online access and a move away from what had been a local map library's function to a nationally centralized facility. It may have signalled the beginnings of a trend towards a diminishing role for map libraries in disseminating map data to the user, and indeed doubts and concerns about the future of map libraries began to surface as the decade progressed.

Automating map libraries

Few meetings and seminars convened for map curators avoided discussion of the issues of map library automation and of problems arising from the appearance of maps in digital format and on new distribution media.[47] Most of the annual Map Curators' Workshops held as pre-meetings to the BCS Annual Technical Symposia covered such themes.[48] The falling costs of computing and the move from centralized mainframes to powerful networked PCs with user-friendly interfaces began to make automated map cataloguing feasible for both large and small map libraries.

Essentially, automation focused mainly on two issues: *how* to do it (what software to use, what cataloguing standards to adopt, record storage and access), and *doing* it (e.g., retrospective conversion of card catalogues, cooperative cataloguing projects).

Several national libraries undertook major retrospective conversion projects during the decade, and began to automate their cataloguing procedures, but there was no standard procedure. Among the first was the National Library of Wales which began a pilot project 1992 to automate its catalogue of early cartographic materials. Also beginning in 1992, the British Library Map Library engaged a third party to convert and render in a simplified UKMARC format the sixteen volumes of its pre-1974 catalogue records, and the three published volumes of manuscript map records. The catalogue was published on CD-ROM in 1999, together with the post-1974 cartographic materials file (current to 1997), which had already been made available online via BLAISE, the British Library's Automated Information Service.[49] The full catalogue was also put on to the library's OPAC. Other national libraries, together with the Public Record Office and Scottish Record Office, also moved towards automating their catalogues, while the British Geological Survey undertook conversion of its map catalogue into its LIBERTAS library management system, with sophisticated graphical and search facilities, and subsequently made the catalogue available on the web.[50]

The Ministry of Defence Map Library continued its MODMAP programme of retrospective data capture, begun in 1989, for the 750,000 or so map sheets in its collection. Forty contract staff were employed to undertake this massive task. This sheet-level cataloguing included capturing sheet corner coordinates to enable the production of graphical sheet indexes, and retrieval of records by coordinates.[51] The retrospective data capture was completed in 1996, and subsequently the system was migrated from a mainframe to a Windows NT environment as MODMAP2. This new version offered a much improved and more user-friendly interface and enabled the production of high quality graphic indexes of map series. There were plans to market both software and metadata.

Collaboration in the retrospective conversion of card catalogue records of overseas mapping was facilitated by a three-year project beginning in 1999, funded by the Research Support Libraries Programme and dubbed *Mapping the world: collaborative support for overseas mapping*. Led by the Bodleian Library, Oxford, it involved six other libraries, with each creating MARC-format records for a particular geographical region. The records were to be added to the CURL (Consortium of University Research Libraries) database, and to COPAC, the free-access online catalogue of the CURL libraries.[52]

Discussions were underway at the end of the decade on the feasibility of cooperation among the legal deposit libraries in cataloguing the maps deposited under copyright. There was also talk about MODMAP supplying relevant catalogue data to libraries which received copies of their superseded maps.

Many small collections developed their own home-grown computer cataloguing or recording systems using PCs or Apple Macs. The University of Leicester Department of Geography, for example, developed an on-screen cataloguing system for series-level records,[53] while others catalogued using proprietary database software such as Cardbox™ for Windows.

Research projects
A rather fine distinction can be made between research projects in map librarianship and special projects concerned with moving a collection into the digital era by, for example, digitizing its map catalogue or scanning some of the maps in the collection for storage on CD-ROM or display on the web.

At the beginning of the decade, the University of Manchester undertook with its *All about maps project*, funded by the British Library Research and Development Department, to explore the potential for record sharing, and ways to improve the ease and quality of constructing carto-bibliographic records, and gave special attention to the (in)appropriateness of MARC standards for map cataloguing.[54] The project included extensive computer cataloguing of holdings in the University's collections.

In 1996, the National Library of Scotland, in association with the Royal Commission on the Ancient and Historical Monuments of Scotland and several Scottish universities, initiated *Project Pont*, a five-year multidisciplinary research project to coordinate research on Timothy Pont and his manuscript maps of Scotland created towards the end of the 16th century. An important feature of this project was the digital scanning of all these manuscript maps,[55] but the project also included numerous seminars and field forays, and culminated in the publication of a book *The nation survey'd* and the establishment of a website with access to the scanned maps.[56] A further Scottish project was launched in 1999 following the award of a grant to the University of Edinburgh by the Research Support Libraries Programme, and was due to run for three years. *Charting the nation: preserving and widening access to maps of Scotland and associated archives, 1590–1740* aimed to capture high quality digital images of manuscript and printed maps from this time period and place them on a new website.[57]

Much research was done not *by* map librarians but with implications *for* map librarians. Thus the *Great Britain Historical GIS Project* initiated in 1993 set out to construct a database of digitized historic administrative boundaries of Britain to which statistical data of the relative time periods could be plotted. A related project was begun in 1998 by Roger Kain and Richard Oliver at Exeter University to reconstruct and prepare a digital version of pre-1850 parishes of England and Wales.

Individual research in the British Library and elsewhere was stimulated through the award of Helen Wallis Fellowships, initiated in 1999, and by J. B. Harley Research Fellowships in the History of Cartography established in 1994. The Godfrey Award was introduced in 1994 to be given annually by Alan Godfrey maps in association with the BCS to 'a librarian who has, in the opinion of the judges, furthered the use, appreciation and understanding of maps in an exceptional way'.

Exhibitions, public education and outreach
The most obvious ways to promote public awareness and understanding of maps (and indirectly the use of maps in libraries) is through exhibitions, public lectures, external courses, and the media, and the map library community made noteworthy use of all these during the course of the decade.

Most national libraries held major exhibitions from time to time, some accompanied by catalogues or books.[58] Mention has been made of the 1991 map exhibition for the ICA conference at Bournemouth, which included a special exhibit marking the Ordnance Survey bicentenary, and which was open to the general public. Bicentenary exhibitions were also held at other locations, including the RGS with an exhibit by the Charles Close Society featuring the history of the one-inch map series, accompanied by a useful catalogue.[59] In 1995, the Hydrographic Office also celebrated its bicentenary, and an exhibition with an associated publication was held at the Bodleian Library, Oxford.[60]

By the end of the decade most national map libraries, and some university ones, had created their own websites, and some had begun to add scanned maps from their collections.[61]

Map libraries received prominent media exposure through a six-programme television series entitled *Tales from the map room* broadcast in 1993 on BBC2, in which staff at the British Library Map Library were closely involved. An accompanying book of the same title, edited by Peter Barber (of the BLML) and Chris Board, was also published.[62] Radio also featured maps and mapping, including three half-hour programmes broadcast by BBC Radio Scotland, which included contributions from map librarians.

1991 saw the initiation of a series of winter meetings at the Warburg Institute in London entitled 'Maps and society: a seminar in the history of cartography', while the Bodleian Library Oxford also established a series of 'Seminars in cartography'.

Other issues

The issue of copyright in relation to educational use was much discussed during this period. Negotiations on the interpretation of the 1988 Copyright Act resulted in OS issuing a new guidance leaflet *Copyright 3: Digital map data.*[63] A voluntary agreement was also reached on permissible paper-based copying from in-copyright OS maps. Changes were made in 1996 to the duration of copyright giving protection of 70 years beyond the lifetime of the author. This affects many maps, though not those – like Ordnance Survey – under Crown copyright, which continued to last for 50 years from publication.[64]

Particular concerns were raised through the growing availability of the means to digitize and re-model copyrighted paper maps. Many map library users, particularly in universities, now wished to use maps for research within a computerized geographical information system. Many such operations were essentially the digital equivalent of processes which in earlier days would have been done with paper maps using, for example, tracing paper and pencil. But in many cases the digital equivalent, which involved scanning or vector digitizing paper maps, was seen as an infringement of copyright. The British Geological Survey also issued cautionary advice on digital copying of its maps.

A further controversy arose with the availability of topographic maps from the former Soviet Union (discussed above), which included cover of western countries including the UK. Because these maps were not copyrighted, many commercial publishers saw them as a way to obtain copyright-free source material. However, Ordnance Survey maintained that as the Soviet mapmakers appeared to have copied OS material in compiling their own military maps of Great Britain, they represented an infringement of British Crown copyright, and demanded that these maps should be removed from the market. This view was circulated as a statement at the BCS symposium in 1997. As noted above, many major map libraries had been acquiring Soviet mapping (though not necessarily of Great Britain) and have continued to do so. The issue remained unresolved.

Occasionally, exceptional and sometimes unexpected demands are put upon the nation's map libraries, and the decade was marked especially by two examples of this. In 1993, new arrangements for managing European farm subsidy schemes via the Common Agricultural Policy resulted in UK farmers queuing at the national map libraries to ascertain parcel numbers and hectares of their fields as shown on Ordnance Survey 1 : 2,500 scale maps (but not shown on the digitally produced *Superplans*). The second resulted from the proposal under the 1990 Environmental Protection Act that local authorities should produce and maintain a Register of Potentially Contaminated Land. Although the proposal was eventually withdrawn, planning regulations still required property developers to undertake careful investigation of the history of brownfield sites before new building commenced; in the early 1990s there was a substantial growth in the number of consultancies doing this work, and this began to put a huge pressures on the OS historic archive in both national and, to a lesser extent, local collections.[65] These incidents serve to remind us of the importance of the role of map libraries in continuing to maintain both a current and historical archive of topographic and planimetric mapping of the country.

At the end of the decade, however, the biggest issue remained the extent to which map librarians should re-skill themselves to handle digital spatial data. Should they limit their role to access and advice, or should they follow the trend established in North America towards providing a full digital mapping service? This debate would continue to be played out in the years to come.

Acknowledgements

In compiling this report, the author acknowledges his extensive use of the news of map library developments reported in *Cartographiti*, and is indebted to its editors and numerous contributors. He is also beholden to the authors (Dr Andrew Tatham and Mr Nick Millea) of the excellent biennial *National progress reports* to the Groupe des Cartothécaires de LIBER.

Notes

1   Dr Helen Wallis, former curator of the British Library Map Library, and founder and first convener of the Map Curators' group, passed away on 7 February 1995. A celebration of her life and work, 'The globe my world', was held at the Royal Geographical Society in May 1975 and a further celebratory seminar was held at St Hugh's College, Oxford, in 1997.
    New appointments were made at the British Library Map Library (Peter Barber) with the retirement of Tony Campbell, the National Library of Scotland (Diana Webster) with the retirement of Margaret Wilkes, the University of Cambridge (Anne Taylor) with the retirement of Roger Fairclough, and the Bodleian Library Oxford (Nick Millea) with the retirement of Betty Fathers.

2   Following termination of the government grant which had ensured free public access to its map collection, the Royal Geographical Society instituted a daily charge in 2000 to non-Fellows for access to its map collection and other holdings.

3   An analysis of the map libraries in UK academic institutions, based on the third edition of the *Directory of UK map collections*, was made by John Moore in 'The new millennium and the university map collection: a view from the sidelines?', *Cartographiti* **59**, 1999, 16–23.

4   Anne Tillotson, 'On the move: the University of Leeds Map Library', *Cartographiti* **38**, 1994, 7–10.

5   Mary A. Larsgaard, *Map librarianship: an introduction*, 3rd ed. Englewood, Colo.: Libraries Unlimited, 1998.

6   'Opening up the map collection', a seminar organized by the Library Association and the Map Curators' Group, was held at the Bodleian Library in December 1995, and a further seminar aimed at people working in archives and local studies at Hampshire Record Office in February 1997. 'Digital maps and damaged maps: the reality of working with public map collections', a seminar organized by the Society of Archivists and the MCG, held at Birmingham Central Library, November 1998. 'Maps and plans investigated', Society of Archivists' training day held at the Public Records Office, December 1999. 'Preservation of maps and plans', Society of Archivists' training day

held at the PRO, December 2000. A workshop, 'New initiatives in map library automation', was held in September 1992 at the headquarters of the British Geological Survey arranged in cooperation with the *All about maps* project at the University of Manchester.

7   The 3-Day event was held in 1992 and revived after a lapse of six years in 1998.

8   *Cartographiti*, the newsletter of the Map Curators' Group of the British Cartographic Society, distributed free of charge to interested members of the BCS, or on subscription to non-members.

9   The Association for Geographic Information was founded in 1989 to represent interests of users and providers of geographical information. See <http://www.agi.org.uk> (accessed 31/1/06).

10   Many of the papers published in *LIBER quarterly* have been placed on the web by Jan Smits at a website of the Koninklijke Bibliotheek, The Netherlands: <http://liber-maps.kb.nl/intro.htm>; *INSPEL: international journal of special libraries*. Available at <http://forge.fh-potsdam.de/~IFLA/INSPEL/> (accessed 31/1/06).

11   *INSPEL* **28** (1), 1994 was devoted to retro-conversion of map catalogues, *INSPEL* **30** (2), 1996 to preservation of maps and spatial data. *LIBER quarterly* published the papers given at the biennial conferences of the Groupe de Cartothécaires.

12   Of particular value to map libraries are the catalogues of these exhibitions, e.g., Mary A. Lowenthal (ed.), *Mapping exhibitions catalogue.* International Cartographic Association 15th Conference and 9th General Assembly, Bournemouth, 23 September–1 October, 1991. The OS bicentenary was also marked by the publication of an illustrated history of OS: Tim Owen and Elaine Pilbeam, *Ordnance Survey: map makers to Britain since 1791.* London: HMSO, 1992.

13   Larsgaard, *Map librarianship.*

14   Paige G. Andrew and Mary Lynette Larsgaard (eds.), *Maps and related cartographic materials: cataloging, classification and bibliographic control.* Binghamton, N.Y.: Haworth Information Press, 2000. Also published as *Cataloging and classification quarterly* **27**, 1999.

15   Lothar Zögner (ed.), *Bibliographia cartographica: international documentation of cartographic literature.* Munich: Saur.

16   Lorraine Dubreuil (ed.), *World directory of map collections*, 3rd ed. Munich: Saur, 1993; Olivier Loiseaux (ed.), *World directory of map collections.* 4th ed. Munich: Saur, 2000; Joan Chibnall (ed.), *A directory of UK map collections*, 3rd ed. London: British Cartographic Society, 1995 (Map Curators' Group publication; no. 4).

17   Mary A. Lowenthal (ed.), *Who's who in the history of cartography: the international guide to the subject.* 9th ed. Tring: Map Collector Publications, 1998. Part 1 'What's what?' provides a guide to literature, lectures, conferences, research fellowships and grants, while Part 2 'Who's who?' lists researchers and their interests.

18   Christopher R. Perkins and Robert B. Parry, *Mapping the UK: maps and spatial data for the 21st century*, 1996. East Grinstead: Bowker-Saur, 1996; Robert B. Parry and Christopher R. Perkins, *World mapping today*, 2nd ed. East Grinstead: Bowker-Saur, 2000.

19   Richard Oliver, *Ordnance Survey maps: a concise guide for historians.* London: Charles Close Society, 1993. A companion guide to Irish Ordnance Survey maps with much information on mainland activities is J. H. Andrews, *History in the Ordnance map: an introduction for Irish readers*, 2nd ed. Kerry, Newtown: David Archer, 1993. Helen Wallis and Anita McConnell (eds.), *Historians' guide to early British maps: a guide to*

the location of pre-1900 maps of the British Isles preserved in the United Kingdom and Ireland. London: Royal Historical Society, 1994 (Royal Historical Society guides and handbooks; 18).

20 Sarah Bendall (ed.), *Dictionary of land surveyors and local mapmakers of Great Britain and Ireland 1530–1850*. 2 vols. London: British Library, 1997.

21 *Imago mundi*, ed. Catherine Delano Smith, with reviews edited by Paul Ferguson and bibliography compiled by Francis Herbert.

22 IMCoS: <http://www.IMCoS.org/> (accessed 31/1/06).

23 J. Brian Harley and David Woodward (eds.), *The history of cartography*. Chicago; London: University of Chicago Press. *Vol. 2, Book 1: Cartography in prehistoric, ancient and medieval Europe and the Mediterranean*, 1992; *Vol. 2, Book 2: Cartography in the traditional Islamic and South Asian societies*, 1994; *Vol. 2, Book 3: Cartography in the traditional African, American, Arctic, Australian and Pacific societies*, 1998. Website for the History of Cartography Project at <http://www.geography.wisc.edu/histcart/> (accessed 31/1/06).

24 Ordnance Survey: <http://www.ordnancesurvey.co.uk/> (accessed 31/1/06).

25 Donald Hodson, *County atlases of the British Isles. Vol. 3: Atlases published 1764 to 1800 and their subsequent editions*. London: British Library, 1997. This was third in a series of carto-bibliographies providing detailed reconstruction of the publication history of all county atlases published after 1703; Geraldine Beech (ed.), *Maps and plans in the Public Record Office. Vol. 4: Europe and Turkey*. London: Stationery Office, 1998.

26 John Moore, *The historical cartography of Scotland*. 2nd ed. Aberdeen: University of Aberdeen, Dept of Geography, 1991 (O'Dell memorial monograph; 24); also: John N. Moore, *The maps of Glasgow: a history and cartobibliography to 1865*. Glasgow: University Library, 1996; Roger Kain and Richard Oliver, *The tithe maps of England and Wales: a cartographic analysis and county by county catalogue*. Cambridge: Cambridge University Press, 1995; Robert Davies, *The tithe maps of Wales: a guide to the tithe maps and apportionments of Wales in the National Library of Wales*. Aberystwyth: National Library of Wales, 1999; Margaret Wilkes, *The Scot and his maps*. Motherwell: Scottish Library Association, 1991.

27 Elly Decker, *Globes at Greenwich: a catalogue of the globes and armillary spheres in the National Maritime Museum, Greenwich*. Oxford: Oxford University Press; Greenwich: National Maritime Museum, 1999; Ralph Hyde, *Ward maps of the City of London*. London: London Topographic Society, 1999.

28 These include: Kit Batten and Francis Bennett, *The printed maps of Devon: county maps 1575–1837*. Tiverton: Devon Books, 1996; Eugene Burden, *Printed maps of Berkshire 1574–1900. Part 1: county maps; Part 2: Town plans*. Ascot: Privately published, 1996; John Chandler (ed.), *Printed maps of Wiltshire 1787–1844*. Trowbridge: Wiltsgire Record Society, 1998; John Higham, *The antique county maps of Cumberland*. Carlisle: Bookcase, 1997; Keith Needell, *Printed maps of Somersetshire 1575–1860*. 2nd ed. Muswell Hill: Privately published, 1995.

29 Richard Oliver, *A guide to the Ordnance Survey one-inch Seventh Series*, 1991; Roger Hellyer, *The 'Ten-mile' maps of the Ordnance Surveys*, 1992; Yolande Hodson, *Popular maps: the Ordnance Survey Popular Edition one-inch maps of England and Wales, 1919–1926*, 1999; Richard Oliver, *A guide to the Ordnance Survey one-inch Popular Edition, Scotland*, 2000; Richard Oliver, *A guide to the Ordnance Survey one-inch New Popular Edition*, 2000; Richard Oliver, *A guide to the Ordnance Survey one-inch Fifth Edition*, 2000. All published: London: Charles Close Society.

30 *Ordnance Survey: indexes to the 1:2500 and 6 inch maps: Scotland.* Kerry, Newtown: David Archer, 1993; Roger Hellyer, *Ordnance Survey small scale maps: indexes 1801– 1998.* Kerry, Newtown: David Archer, 1999; Nigel N. James, *A list of Ordnance Survey District Special and Tourist maps 1861–1939.* Oxford: Bodleian Library, 1993 (Map Room maplist; no. 1); and *A list of the Ordnance Survey catalogues, publication reports and other publications.* Oxford: Bodleian Library, 1993 (Map Room maplist; no. 2).

31 LIS-MAPS, 'a forum for issues related to map & spatial data librarianship. Topics can be broad ranging including acquisition, cataloguing, information retrieval, management of metadata, relationship to Geographical Information Systems and conservation': <http://www.jiscmail.ac.uk/lists/LIS-MAPS.html> (accessed 31/1/06).

32 Accessible at <http://www.maphist.nl/> (accessed 31/1/06). See also the website *Map history/History of cartography*: <http://www.maphistory.info/>. This is maintained by Tony Campbell, former map librarian of the BLML, and contains an enormous amount of information and numerous links.

33 Accessible at <http://www.soc.org.uk/cartosoc/index.html> (accessed 31/1/06).

34 Roelof P. Oddens, 'Four years of Oddens' Bookmarks: the fascinating world of maps and mapping', *LIBER quarterly* **10** (4), 2000, 480-4.

35 In 1994, the publishers Chadwyck-Healey, Cambridge, issued the complete 1991 census data together with digitized enumeration district boundaries as a set of eight CD-ROMs packaged with Supermap software and a user manual. A more limited version, *SCAMP CD* by Claymore Services, included AA digital mapping to provide a reference base for displaying census data.

36 For a more detailed discussion of new map formats and their implication for map libraries, see Christopher R. Perkins, 'Map acquisition' in *World mapping today*, ed. Robert B. Parry and Christopher R. Perkins. 2nd ed. East Grinstead: Bowker-Saur, 2000; Christopher R. Perkins: 'Quality in map librarianship and documentation in the GIS age', *Cartographic journal* **31**, 1994, 93–9.

37 Christopher R. Perkins, 'Leave it to the labs? Options for the future of map and spatial data collections', *LIBER quarterly* **5**, 1995, 312–29. For another view of the map curator's role in the digital age, see also Tony Campbell, 'Where are map libraries heading? Some route maps for the digital future', *LIBER quarterly* **10**, 2000, 489–98.

38 A 'code of practice' for voluntary deposit of non-print publications became effective in January 2000, but only applied to offline publications.

39 'The future history of our landscape', seminar held at the Royal Society on 16 October, 1992. Proceedings published as Christopher Board and Peter Lawrence (eds.), *Recording our changing landscape: the proceedings of a seminar on the future history of our landscape.* London: Royal Society; British Academy, 1994. See also David Fairbairn, 'The future history of our landscape', *Cartographic journal* **30** (1), 1993, 62– 7.

40 Results of the follow-up questionnaire survey, undertaken by Tony Campbell, on the uses made of early OS maps were reported in *Ordnance Survey information paper* 12/1994, 'Future history of our landscape'.

41 Christopher Fleet, 'Ordnance Survey digital data in UK Legal Deposit Libraries', *LIBER quarterly* **9**, 1999, 235–43.

42 For a librarian's view see Graham Steele, 'The acquisition of maps in digital form in an academic library', *Cartographic journal* **30** (1), 1993, 57–61.

43 Peter Burnhill, 'The Data Library model: networked access to digital resources' in *Proceedings of the British Cartographic Society 31st Annual Technical Symposium*, 1994.

44 Originally funded for two years, the project was extended to 2000. The six trial sites were at Edinburgh University Library, Aberdeen University Library, Glasgow University Library, Newcastle University Library, the Map Library at the Bodleian Library, Oxford, and the Map Library at the University of Reading Department of Geography.

45 Annual progress and usage reports were issued for limited circulation, numerous conference presentations made, and a number of papers published, e.g.: Peter Burnhill, David Ferro and Alistair Towers, 'Digimap: national online access to Ordnance Survey digital map data', *Proceedings of the British Cartographic Society 33rd Annual Technical Symposium and Map Curators' Group Workshop*, 1996, 8–14; Barbara Morris, David Medyckyj-Scott and Peter Burnhill, 'EDINA Digimap: new developments in the internet mapping and data service for the UK higher education community', *LIBER quarterly* **10** (4), 2000, 445-53; David Medyckyj-Scott and Barbara Morris, 'The virtual map library: providing access to OS digital map data via the WWW for the Higher Education Community', AGI 97; Hugh Buchanan, 'EDINA Digimap maps higher education', *SoC Bulletin* **33** (1), 1999, 23–6.

46 CASWEB provided a service for downloading 1981 and 1991 small area census statistics, while DESCARTES provided an online visualization tool for combining data with digital boundaries to create choropleth maps.

47 An overview of the broader functions of automation in map libraries may be found in: Christopher Fleet, 'The role of computer technology in the future map library', *LIBER quarterly* **8** (2), 1998, 136-45.

48 For example, 'Cards, catalogues and computers–where next?', MCG Workshop, Southampton, 5 September 1991; 'Digital cartographic information: the map curator's challenge', MCG Workshop, Aberdeen, 10 September 1992; 'Curating a world of change', MCG Workshop, Swansea, 9 September 1993; 'Digital mapping and the CD-ROM', MCG Workshop, Manchester, 8 September 1994.

49 *The British Library map catalogue*, CD-ROM. Reading: Primary Resource Media for British Library, 1999. For background information on the project see: Tony Campbell, 'Retroconversion of the British Library's map catalogues: the art of the possible', *European research libraries cooperation* **3**, 1993, 1–6; Tony Campbell, 'Conversion of the British Library's map catalogues: the keys to success', *INSPEL* **28** (1), 1994, 67–79.

50 Other cataloguing projects included a three-year project to catalogue the Todhunter Allen Collection at the Bodleian Library by Paula Dryburgh, and the cataloguing of maps in the Royal Library at Windsor by Yolande Hodson.

51 Murray Parkin, 'MODMAP: the automation of the UK Ministry of Defence Map Library card catalogue', *European research libraries cooperation* **3**, 1997, 67–75; Sue Antonell, 'MODMAP: post-retrospective data capture developments', *Proceedings, British Cartographic Society 34th Annual Symposium, Lecicester*. London: BCS, 1997; Sue Antonelli, 'Breaking with conventions: what does digital spatial data require?' *LIBER Quarterly* **9** (2), 1999, 149–61.

52 The libraries involved were at the universities of Oxford (Bodleian), Cambridge, Edinburgh, Manchester, Imperial College London, and the University of London Library at Senate House. A website was established at:
<http://www.bodley.ox.ac.uk/mapworld/index.html> (accessed 31/1/06).

53 Suzanne Mawdsley, 'The design and implementation of a computerized map library cataloguing system', *Bulletin of the Society of University Cartographers* **26** (2), 1992, 13–16.

54 Christopher R. Perkins, E. McAdam and Phil Guest, 'All about maps: establishing a CARTO-NET based map data base.' *Bulletin of the Society of University Cartographers* **21**, 1992, 88–9; Chris Perkins and Philip Guest, *Operationalizing a sheet-based cartographic information retrieval system.* [London]: British Library, 1993 (BLR&DD report; no. 6114).

55 Jeffrey C. Stone, 'Project Pont', *Bulletin of the Society of Cartographers* **31** (2), 1997, 11–12. Website at: <www.nls.uk/collections/maps/subjectinfo/projectpont1.html> (accessed 31/1/06).

56 Ian C. Cunningham (ed.), *The nation survey'd: essays on late sixteenth-century Scotland as depicted by Timothy Pont.* Edinburgh: Tuckwell Press in association with the National Library of Scotland, 2001.

57 Website at: <http://www.chartingthenation.lib.ed.ac.uk> (accessed 31/1/06). The project was coordinated by the Department of Geography but involved the University's library and nine other national or higher education libraries.

58 Peter Whitfield, *The mapping of the heavens.* London: British Library, 1995. Also by Peter Whitfield: *The image of the world: twenty centuries of world maps.* London: British Library, 1994; *The charting of the oceans: ten centuries of maritime maps.* London: British Library, 1996; *New Found Lands: maps in the history of exploration.* London: British Library, 1998.

59 Yolande Hodson (ed.), *An inch to the mile: the Ordnance Survey one-inch map 1805–1974.* London: Charles Close Society, 1991.

60 *All at sea: the story of navigation charts: an exhibition to celebrate two hundred years of the Hydrographic Office.* Oxford: Bodleian Library, 1995. The exhibition attracted more than 12,000 visitors.

61 The Bodleian Library launched its website in 1995: <http://www.bodley.ox.ac.uk/guides/maps/> and the National Library of Scotland in 1996: <http://www.nls.uk> (accessed 31/1/06).

62 Peter Barber and Christopher Board (eds.), *Tales from the map room: fact and fiction about maps and their makers.* London: BBC Books, 1993.

63 Ordnance Survey, *Copyright 3: Digital map data.* Southampton: Ordnance Survey, 1997.

64 Derek Earnshaw, 'Intellectual property and the Ordnance Survey', *Bulletin of the Society of Cartographers* **32** (2), 1998, 1–4.

65 A full explanation of these developments is given by B. M. Rideout in *Cartographiti* **38**, July 1994, 11–13. The pressure on libraries was subsequently relieved by the capture in raster format of the entire OS large-scale historic archive through a joint venture between OS and by the Landmark® Information Group.

15

Local studies

Ian Jamieson

During the decade, local history and family history continued to flourish, with more and more people getting involved. This showed itself in increasing numbers of courses and the continuing popularity of local history societies, where members, at the least, came together to hear about aspects of their local areas and some, usually the minority, carried out research for instance using census reports. Numbers of these societies established periodicals, and the contents of these were made known to a wider audience in listings in *The local history magazine* and *The local historian*. Older local antiquarian societies and record societies continued their publications, but often reported financial problems. The academic sector increased the number of courses they ran, at either certificate or diploma level, while local authority courses remained highly popular. In addition the media – television and in particular local radio – presented many programmes on local and family history. All of these activities, as well as much greater amounts of work on local history in schools and colleges, increased the demand on local studies collections and record offices or, increasingly, local studies centres which combined the two, sometimes with the addition of the local museum as well. Whatever the background to information need, the place of first resort is likely to be the public library local collection, as this is where most material is likely to be, and where help is available to users. Thus this chapter concentrates on collections in the public sector and their development over the decade: although there are local collections in academic libraries and societies they do not appear to have been written up to any great extent and certainly the academic world makes up a considerable proportion of local studies collection users.

The profession

The main body for local studies librarians continued to be the Library Association Local Studies Group, which by 2000 was reported to have over 1,600 members. Through its regional branches and its periodical *The local studies librarian* it keeps those working in local studies in touch with each other and offers guidance in the form of courses and conferences. Most of its members are not in fact designated local studies librarians, but people for example working in branch libraries where answering enquiries on local history topics is only part of their job. The Group is very aware of this and regional subgroups, set up where there is evidence of demand, and sufficient members to support one, have always run meetings and day schools, though by the end of the period there was some evidence that, as libraries had had to cut back, members found it difficult to obtain funding and even leave to attend such gatherings, even though they were clearly educational. By 2000 there were five subgroups: London and Home Counties, Midlands and Anglia, North West, Scotland and Wales. In addition a representative of the Local Studies Panel of the Library and Information Services Council (Northern Ireland) attended committee meetings to represent members in the province. Most of them published newsletters or journals, the most substantial being that from Scotland. *The local studies librarian* continued to be the main channel of communication for all Group members, carrying substantial articles as well as official items, news and reviews. The Group also supported the UmbrelLA weekend schools from their inception by presenting programmes at each one.

As part of its services to the profession the Local Studies Group had issued *Guidelines for local studies libraries* in 1990.[1] This continued to sell well, but with so many developments in IT it became clear that it needed to be revised and a working party developed a draft version. This was presented to members and to the Library Association for discussion and by 2000 the revised *Guidelines* were almost ready for publication.

Education for local studies librarians was well established by 1990. At a formal level several library schools including Birmingham, Newcastle and the University of Wales Aberystwyth offered options as part of their full-time undergraduate and postgraduate courses. However, with changes in direction in education to a more purely academic approach, and increasing emphasis on general library management and IT, these options gradually disappeared: Newcastle for example, which had had a full three-year option, discontinued this in 1996. Education for local studies librarians continued for example at Aberystwyth, where the distance learning degree course included a local studies option which was still on offer in 2000. Education became much less formal, with day schools and workshops on specific topics being organized by LSG and its subgroups, sometimes jointly with bodies such as the Youth Libraries Group.

Apart from courses specifically for librarians, many librarians realized the need for better subject knowledge, and therefore took advantage of the many local and family history courses available across the country. Levels ranged from certificates through first degrees and postgraduate diplomas to Masters' degrees, by either attendance, distance learning or the internet. The Open University, for example, offered a course on local history, and an article on the course, and the experiences of three of its librarian students, was published,[2] while the Oxford University Department for Continuing Education established a diploma in local history via the internet in 1999.

The other source of information, of course, is the literature. Books, however, were thin on the ground, mainly perhaps because of the wide range of subjects covered in *A manual of local studies librarianship* (1987), each accompanied by a substantial bibliography. A follow-up volume was published in 1991 under the title *Local studies collections*.[3] The aim of this second volume was to consolidate and develop some of the topics dealt with in the previous work – for instance considering the implications of more recent trends in information technology, preservation and conservation, as well as offering advice and guidance on the practicalities of maintaining diverse material. Forms of material were given individual chapters and the importance of creating a viable collection of local history in even small branch libraries was stressed. A problem with this type of comprehensive work is that inevitably there are major developments particularly in areas such as information technology – for instance computer indexing and desktop publishing – but even so the basic volumes became the standard work on local studies librarianship for several years. Another work intended for librarians was a very much revised edition of *Genealogy for librarians*, the bibliography of which alone runs to 28 pages.[4]

Local studies librarians are not only interested in their own services, or not even those across Britain, with whom they can cooperate, but increasingly look further afield still: at one of the Local Studies Group's sessions at UmbrelLA 1991 one of the speakers was Assumpta Bailac, a Catalan librarian, who talked about local studies in her region, including a survey.[5] The Group in fact established relations with several countries, mainly in eastern Europe: these tended initially to be reactive rather than proactive when local studies librarians from abroad made approaches to the Group directly, or via Library Association headquarters. By 2000, for instance, liaison was maintained with Hungary, Romania and Latvia. Of these the links with Hungary were the most formal, the Group having signed an Accord in 1995: following this agreement Hungarian librarians visited Britain and British local studies librarians attended and presented papers at the Hungarian local studies conferences. By then, too, the Local Studies Group had published an international policy statement.[6] A visit from a Russian librarian and one from Australia took place, and there was an article by Michael Dewe based on a long visit to Australia.[7] Various individual librarians or authorities, too, made arrangements or agreements with libraries in other countries, one example being the 'Hampshire Accorde' between Hampshire County Library and Normandy, whereby exchange visits were made and information exchanged. Although this was a library service-wide agreement, the local studies collection took a full part.[8] There was also a relationship between Devon and Calvados, and Ian Maxted, the Devon Local Studies Librarian, in the course of an article on his experiences of twinning, listed other authorities in the South West twinned with North West France.[9] There was also a contribution on French regional and local history by Alain Girard from Caen, presented at a meeting of the Local Studies London and Home Counties subgroup in 1993.[10]

One of the features of librarianship over the years has been the establishment of awards for librarians or library authorities. The Local Studies Group's McCulla Award for outstanding work in local studies librarianship continued throughout the period, as did the Alan Ball Awards for local history publications by libraries.

Local studies librarians, however, were successful in more general awards: among others Mike Spick of Sheffield became the Public Library Entrepreneur of the Year in 2000 for the publication of a CD-ROM on Sheffield history.[11] Frank Manders of Newcastle won an award in the 'Publications for sale' category in the Library Association/T. C. Farries Publications and Publicity Awards, 1991 and in the same year Durham County Library won the 'special event' category for one of its community exhibitions.

Employment was another topic which concerned librarians throughout the period. Doubts were expressed about the possible effect on public library services of local government restructuring as soon as the first white paper was issued: the fear was that local studies librarians could in effect be downgraded in new smaller unitary authorities. Archivists also opposed the proposals.[12] On the other hand, it was reported in 1993 that Dumbarton District Libraries had expanded their local collection staff from one to three following the identification of the subject as an area of growing interest to the public. Concerns about staffing, however, continued to be expressed by local studies librarians right through the decade. On a more mundane level, Morris Garratt looked at advertisements for local studies posts and their effectiveness in giving sufficient information for potential candidates even to consider applying.[13]

The community
Librarians continued to look at the communities they served in order to make sure that they were providing the right kind of service. Bob Usherwood, in an article describing research at Sheffield University, found that local studies libraries were important to the communities surveyed (in Newcastle upon Tyne and Somerset) and many points were raised during focus group discussions with users and by library staff – many quotations were given.[14]

Despite the specific examples, this was a general piece of research, but librarians also realized the importance of looking at their own communities and enquirers to help them see how they could provide the best service possible. Surveys at Bolton, an urban service, and Derbyshire, which had many rural libraries, found many of the results were similar.[15] While Bolton achieved an 84% response rate, with 260 returns, Derbyshire had an 82% response rate, with 666 returns from three libraries. In both, family historians made up the largest proportion of users, but there was also good use by students shown in both. Opening hours, old or insufficient equipment and parking were the main matters of complaint in both. At a different level the British Library Newspaper Library at Colindale carried out a user survey which quantified for the first time the use of the collections made by family and local historians, a surprisingly high 32%.

At a more specific level, libraries were interested in various identifiable groups and how best to make provision for them: examples included the disabled, children and ethnic minority groups. Libraries had more contact with the school world as more children came in as a result of the National Curriculum, where for the first time all primary schools had to teach local history and all children in Key Stage 2 had to undertake projects. This had obvious implications for local studies services as more demands were made on them and many teachers realized the need for help in preparation for this kind of work. Not all teachers were familiar with local history sources, and some librarians managed to find time to visit schools or accept school class visits. The School Library Association was aware of the need for information and Andrew Blizzard of Birmingham Public Library wrote a pamphlet for teachers.[16] To help teachers, too, Lancashire Polytechnic and Lancashire public library joined forces to provide a series of joint INSET courses for local teachers.[17] In Scotland, where there had also been changes in National and Higher grade examinations, similar problems existed as this affected demand on collections too. Edinburgh City Libraries introduced new user education schemes for children,[18] and a day school in Perth on 'working with younger children' highlighted problems of dealing with local research, and also gave an example of how a specific library ran educational visits to the library.[19]

Ethnic minorities by now were clearly part of the British population, but librarians at least seemed to know little about their life in Britain, how they had adjusted or their family way of life. Local studies librarians therefore consciously began to find out about the experiences of individuals, usually by using oral history techniques. Tameside local studies library, having established an annual series of Family History Awards, used the 1995 competition to ask entrants to produce an oral history interview with someone who had come from another country: awards were made for tapes from immigrants from Yugoslavia, Penang and India. The aim was not only to acquire information which could be added to the local collection stock, but to encourage other people who had come to the area from other countries to tape their reminiscences and to deposit copies at the library for the benefit of future researchers.

At a more general level, Sheila Cooke produced an article on serving a multicultural community, using the local studies library at Nottingham as an example.[20] There was, too, a workshop at a Local Studies Group Midlands and Anglia Branch day school in 1999 which considered the whole question of equal opportunities and local studies, it being felt important to look at some of the special problems encountered by particular client groups in accessing local studies materials.[21] While it covered ethnic minorities and school children and older students, it also considered the housebound and the visually and physically handicapped and looked at the barriers and some solutions for each client group.

Information sources
There are two kinds of information sources which libraries need to acquire – those which help users carry out research, and bibliographic sources which provide both staff and users with keys to the literature. Numerous examples of the former were published in keeping with the needs of increasing numbers of users. Related directly to libraries, Diana Winterbotham, a librarian, and Alan Crosby, a local historian, produced a most useful work covering the use of local collections and the materials they hold, as well as a chapter on the thorny subject of copyright.[22] A

major general encyclopedia was issued by Oxford University Press. It included some 2000 A–Z articles, ranging from a few lines to several pages and giving many sources for further information.[23] It proved most useful to local historians and indeed produced a smaller spin-off.[24] However, while the new work was based on material collected for the larger one, its aim was different: it was an aid to amateurs, and was intended to be a handbook which could be taken to libraries and record offices or used for quick reference at home. It contained about 1,500 entries, together with various lists and an essay on using records in family history research.

There are many general works on the importance of local history and 'how to do it': some are more useful than others and older works have not necessarily been superseded. Their arrangement varies: for example, among others published during the nineties Kate Tiller provided a general introduction to English local history, arranged by period: this, while more academic than some works of its kind, was well worth reading.[25] Another useful introduction, intended to get local historians started and to keep them going was a helpfully written work by James Griffin and Tim Lomas.[26] An introduction for Ireland also appeared: it consisted of essays by Irish local historians discussing what local history is and how research projects should be approached, giving practical help and advice for both beginners and experienced local historians, and is useful for those outside Ireland as well.[27] A general work introducing archives was issued by the National Council for Archives.[28]

Apart from the general introductions, there were many examples of material dealing with specific aspects of local historical materials: many of them, such as *Dating old photographs*,[29] are helpful to librarians themselves as well as to their users. The publisher of the latter, the Federation of Family History Societies, continued to be a prolific publisher of material useful to local historians, and introduced a series of 'Basic facts about …' or 'Approaches to …' pamphlets, including such topics as *Sources for local history in the home* and *Keeping your family records*, and a basic introduction to Latin for local historians.[30] As another example, oral history became an interest with local historians, who realized that this was a way of acquiring information about relatively recent events, particularly those unlikely to be recorded any other way, and several works appeared on importance and techniques: these, too, were of value to both librarians and the public.[31]

There were thus many works to which librarians could refer enquirers for guidance. Keys to the literature were also numerous, published by societies, commercial publishers or libraries, and were useful to librarians and users alike: many were cooperative publications. There were too many of these, covering individual periods, places, topics or types of material, to cite examples, but lists or reviews can be found in local history and professional library journals. One of the topics, however, which is raised by enquirers after the research has been completed is how to get it published. There have been several suitable publications over the years, but one which was up to date and, while it did not forget the researching and writing aspects, concentrated on the use of the home computer, whether it was for self-publishing or for submission to a publisher, was written by Bob Trubshaw, himself both a local historian and a small publisher.[32]

Organization and administration

The most important aspect of organization and administration in libraries during the decade was the reorganization of local government in both England and Wales and in Scotland. As mentioned earlier, in England the first white paper was published at the beginning of the decade and attracted immediate concern among librarians: a note in the *Local studies librarian* dealt briefly with the Library Association's response,[33] and doubts continued to be expressed by local studies librarians. Here the problems were related to the geographical changes which they felt could seriously affect collections. The reorganization, when implemented from 1996, made big changes in many boundaries: some counties disappeared altogether, while most others lost areas to new unitary district councils, some of which had themselves been independent county borough councils before the changes of 1974. The local authority picture was therefore largely of smaller councils, which therefore had smaller incomes. The real worry was the effect on local studies services at both collection and administrative levels. Since 1974 the counties in particular had made great strides in the provision of local studies services, providing central collections and district collections in larger centres of population, and many had appointed a designated county local studies librarian for the first time. In most places there had not been a large transfer of stock, particularly where there were large collections in former boroughs: in effect one of these sometimes became the main county collection. However, amalgamating and improving services was one thing: demerging and downsizing was another, and worries were expressed about fragmentation of county central collections and the ability of smaller new authorities to maintain a full local studies service.

In the light of these boundary changes the Library Association Local Studies Group issued a short 'guidance statement' about local studies collections, intended to remind authorities of the importance to the community of these collections, and it was hoped that it would be used as a basis for policy decisions by individual authorities.[34] One of the new authorities which did so was Telford and Wrekin Council, which organized a major spend on local studies material to ensure that all its service points had a relevant local studies collection, with a local studies manual for each service point: close relationships were maintained with Shropshire Heritage Services, which was still responsible for certain services.[35] On the whole, however, there was not as much upheaval as had been feared by some. One of the main problems from the local studies service point of view was that, as before 1974, and in the light of general problems of funding, smaller authorities were unable to appoint a dedicated local studies librarian, settling instead for a post which combined reference and local studies. This was unfortunate, for while populations were smaller, demands on local studies by schools and colleges and local and family historians were increasing everywhere. Similar problems were affecting archivists, but by and large these seem to have been settled amicably, with varying patterns of provision. Reorganization in Wales and Scotland likewise involved changes in boundaries as they moved to unitary authorities in 1996.

Funding, in fact, was a major factor underlying most local studies service provision. Throughout the 1990s local government was under severe pressure to cut costs and libraries were not immune. The local studies service was seen in many authorities to be an easy option compared, for instance, with lending and children's services, despite the fact that demand was steadily increasing. Most librarians fought hard for their services, and the topic was mentioned regularly at meetings and conferences as well as occasionally in the local press. However, because it was a local matter, it was not generally written up as a whole, though there was a report on cuts in the North West of England: although the survey was small it did suggest that cuts were clearly being made.[36] Over half the libraries reported reductions in staffing and half that opening hours had been reduced. The main areas felt to be affected were seen to be enquiry work, stock work and promotional work and the acquisition of stock.

A second major administrative factor was the accelerating move towards local studies centres, mainly combining local studies and archives, but sometimes other bodies as well: this both fitted in with increasing demands by people who needed to use both, thus providing improved user convenience, and was also intended to reduce costs. The main problem lay in the differing systems of control and sometimes differing philosophies of preservation and exploitation. However, it gradually became accepted that it would be useful to enquirers to have a 'one-stop shop' to consult the increasingly wide range of materials available. There were problems with differing emphases in education and training and in some authorities archivists and local studies librarians rarely met. Where the services came together it did not necessarily mean that they completely merged: in Lancashire, for example, where the local studies library moved into the record office building – a move partly due to local government reorganization, some parts of the county having become independent district councils – the local studies library maintained its own workroom. One of the new local studies centres, where relevant material was brought together from various departments and locations, was the new Centre for Oxfordshire Studies, housed in an underused part of Oxford Central Library which, as it was adjacent to the existing local studies library, was a convenient answer.[37] In London, Camden opened the new Local Studies and Archives Centre in Holborn library, replacing the existing collections at Hampstead and Holborn, thus making it possible for the first time since the formation of the London Borough of Camden in 1974 for users to find all material in one place. Leicestershire brought its archives and local history collections together, and the magnificent new Surrey Local History Centre opened in 1998 at a cost of £6.5 million.[38] Even within individual authorities a centre could be established: in Devon the North Devon Local History Centre was established in Barnstaple, bringing together the collections of the North Devon Local History Library, the North Devon Record Office and the North Devon Athenaeum, a long-established private organization.[39] At an even more local level, Horley library in Surrey opened a local studies centre in

1997 when library staff realized that it was the natural focus for people's passionate interest in their family history and the locality. As an example of a local initiative, the centre received a good deal of publicity in the press, professional and otherwise.[40] Working in partnership with the local history society, part of the library was set aside for local history activities where weekly advice sessions staffed by volunteers were offered. The enterprise won the 1997 LA/Holt Jackson Community Initiative Award. This initiative was, of course, separate from the main Surrey Local Studies Centre.

Disaster planning was another topic of wide concern: though it was largely a matter for the library service as a whole, local studies collections, because so much of their stock was unique or irreplaceable, had to be particularly considered in such plans. The Norfolk Collection in Norwich central library was largely destroyed in the disastrous fire of 1994, as was the important local studies catalogue: as was said at the time, '150 years of scholarship went up in smoke'. The insurance company, however, made funds available for both catalogue and stock: in fact the main problem was acquiring replacement stock because so much of it was rare or irreplaceable, though there were many donations from the public or other organizations. By 2000 rebuilding work was still in progress. The Norwich fire may have been an accident, but a further example of a disaster was deliberate, when the Linen Hall Library in Belfast, home to major local collections, suffered a firebomb attack in 1994. A further relevant point is that many older local works would be considered 'rare books' *per se*, and that therefore plans needed to be put in place.[41] A day school particularly intended for local studies librarians was, by coincidence, in preparation at the time of the Norwich fire and was held in November 1994.[42]

Yet another administrative aspect, which hitherto had affected local collections relatively little, was copyright. The Copyright, Designs and Patents Act 1988, and later regulations, together with new EU directives, did lead to problems. The general increase in length of copyright and regulations on technically 'unpublished' materials gave cause for concern. Whether allowing access to material constituted publication, and how that might affect the collection, was one problem to add to the existing ones of tracing authors and minor or private publishers of works which might or might not be out of print, as well as questions related to audio-visual material There were general books which gave some answers, but these often suggested that case law would be needed to clarify situations.[43] By the end of the decade some of these problems were still awaiting clarification. Copyright in electronic publications became a matter for real concern, but this was something for the library world as a whole to deal with.

During the decade information technology in its various forms underpinned more and more developments in local studies libraries. It might be for reproduction of material, management of stock or exploitation of collections. Though computerization of catalogues for example was being done in the 1980s, other aspects of IT came into their own: the National Library of Scotland, for instance, moved publication of its *Bibliography of Scotland* from paper to CD-ROM, allowing it to keep it up to date. Librarians seemed to show most interest in the internet and digitization, allied often with such activities as oral history. Meanwhile, NEWSPLAN continued to use microfilm for newspapers on the grounds of conservation, though part of their 1998 Lottery award was to look at digitization of newspapers for permanent use. NEWSPLAN's survey of newspapers was completed, and they received a grant of £5 million from the Lottery fund toward the microfilming of 3,500 'most at risk' fragile local and regional newspapers dating from 1800 to 1950. The Scottish Newspapers Microfilming Unit was set up in 1994, with funding from the Mellon Microfilm Foundation to produce archival quality microfilms of Scottish newspapers.[44] Some newspapers, such as the (Glasgow) *Herald*, however, were producing their own files on CD.[45] In Scotland, too, the Scottish Cultural Resources Network (SCRAN) had been set up as a Millennium-funded project to build a networked multimedia resource base for Scottish history. While largely archive and museum-based, some libraries took advantage of the grants available to input sources: Edinburgh, for example, produced a project on 'A hundred years of the Royal Mile'.[46]

Most libraries, however, were equally interested in database technology, digitization of materials and the internet. The 'People's Network' report, while concerned with libraries as a whole, laid heavy emphasis on local studies, saying that community history and community identity should be one of the principal strands of the project: this would allow the most isolated library to provide access to local and global material.[47] This meant, of course, that huge amounts of material would need to be digitized, an exceedingly costly process and one beyond most libraries, even with the aid of grants. Even before the report, however, examples had been reported from early in the decade onward: for instance, Gateshead produced an interactive CD for schools. Durham County Council produced in 1995 the *Durham record*, an interactive database of digitized materials – photographs, maps and site records – available offline in various sites in the county.[48] Many libraries used the internet to make material available to readers from outside as well as for their own customers. Websites, whether part of the authority's website or free-standing, varied widely in their content from a simple guide to the department and its collections to large amounts of stock: photographs were particularly popular. Tameside, for example, went on to the internet in 1999: the site included details of the main collections and services, but the *Tameside bibliography* remained in printed form only. Knowsley, which went on the web in 1997, was surprised by the number of external enquiries the site generated.[49] Including these, in its first two years of operation it had over a million successful hits, the millionth being from Australia. Many libraries wished to digitize all of their stock, but in an era of cuts the cost was prohibitive: however, many took advantage of Lottery awards for specific projects. It is difficult to know how many of these there were, as many were only publicized locally by means of guides to the library or by press releases to local organizations and publications. However, David Parry, in an important report on digitization, in reviewing the situation attempted to list those libraries where projects had been completed or were under way or under consideration.[50] He pointed out that the majority of projects that he identified and described, over 100 altogether, were in the local studies field; the most popular materials for digitization were photographs.

Digitization is such a major field that it can be mentioned only briefly here: most local studies librarians were simply coming to terms with it regarding the systems and methodology which were becoming available, and were developing uses both internally and for the benefit of enquirers locally and worldwide.

The Heritage Lottery Fund was in many ways closely linked to IT as it provided funds which helped libraries carry out projects they had identified, thus allowing them to provide services which could not be afforded otherwise – this is one of the conditions of receiving an award. Librarians, however, did find that preparing a proposal could take a good deal of time; and even though the conditions had been carefully studied and guidelines followed there was no certainty that an award would be made. One of the features was that there had to be matched funding, although that could often include, for example, notional costs for volunteer work or benefits in kind. Awards varied greatly in amount. In 1998, for instance, the National Monuments Record was awarded £3.09 million to produce some 360,000 photographs of all listed buildings and make them available on the internet. NEWSPLAN was awarded £5 million to microfilm newspapers and to provide microfilm readers to libraries and in 1998 the Linen Hall Library, Belfast, following an earlier grant of £255,000, received over £1.8 million to improve facilities for staff and readers, to computerize catalogues of key collections and to repair some 30,000 books. Surrey Local History Centre received £2.4 million from the Fund toward its cost. Many awards, however, were on a smaller scale: Bury received £39,245 for its Digital Archive Project to allow the Borough's collection of local historic photographs to be conserved and scanned into a computer database, while Redbridge received £39,400 to catalogue the library's collection of photographs, maps and drawings and to make them more available by using computers. Other examples of awards are mentioned elsewhere in this chapter. Another opportunity for awards came through the Public Library Development Incentive Scheme, operated by the Department for National Heritage: both the Gateshead CD-I and the *Durham record* received awards under this scheme.

Promotion and exploitation
There is no value in assembling and organizing a collection unless it is known about and used. The local studies collection is often said to be the communal memory and also an instrument for 'lifelong learning', as envisaged by government. Thus libraries ought to be trying to attract people, both to learn about their area or family, and to contribute to that memory.

The first aspect of this is to make known the existence and scope of the service, and this calls for good public relations outside the library itself. Local studies librarians are not on the whole good at advertising their services, although during the period this was becoming recognized, with some more dynamic librarians doing a great deal with the press in the way of news items, books for review and even regular articles or photographs of the past. Mike Petty gave a description of his personal approach to promotion in Cambridgeshire, while Elizabeth Melrose gave a more general overview.[51] Other openings are to send publicity to schools, local societies, and local magazines. As Sheila Cooke put it, we must blow our own trumpets![52] We could then hope that at least people would know of our existence and come to us for their information as a place of first resort.

As librarians became more aware of the need to 'sell' their services, exploitation within the collection became more important, and guides to the local studies collection in general, and to parts of it, became more generally available. Increasingly these were put on the internet – the Devon local studies catalogue, for instance, was put on the internet in 1997. Devon also produced a local studies newsletter which, while intended mainly for internal circulation as it included lists of material so that branch librarians could select material, carried increasing amounts of professional news and was available to outside enquirers.

Exhibitions have for long been a prime means of publicizing collections and appealing for donations. Most are relatively small-scale, although they can be important to the community – for instance one in Chester-le-Street about the now defunct local sweet factory – but it became apparent that cooperation between libraries could help make a larger impact. The best example of this was Scotland's National Libraries Week, by now organized by LocScot. There was a theme for each year, with a day school in advance, so that librarians could get ideas from each other. The majority of libraries took part, and national publicity helped to attract visitors. Events during the Week went further than just exhibitions, including such things as talks, local competitions and town walks. At regional level, the local studies librarians in the north-east of England organized a local history week in 2000 as part of the millennium celebrations, the theme being photographs. Again a joint poster was produced and appeals were made to the public to donate photographs. Within individual local authorities, weeks could be organized. Devon, for instance, ran a Devon Heritage Week in September 1997 which, while centred on Exeter Central library, included talks, exhibitions and village trails across the county, and Kirkcaldy in Scotland ran one over three weeks, offering various kinds of activity.[53]

A different kind of publicity, particularly to ethnic minorities, was embodied in the Birmingham History Van, which was specially painted and travelled round the city, being available both to discuss local history in communities and to gather material – it carried mobile equipment which allowed the digital capture of photographs where the owners were not willing to give or lend them permanently to the central library.[54] Schools were also seen as one of the target groups. Yet another enterprise was West Lothian's promotional video, introducing the local studies service to the public and to schools, though it was not available for purchase.[55]

As libraries continue to find, publishing is an excellent way of publicizing and making use of local collections, and acquiring new material not otherwise available as well as hopefully creating income. In most areas there are local publishers, but these are often very small and do not necessarily advertise generally, while many private publishers hardly advertise at all. There is thus an opening for public libraries to exploit the field. Some libraries have been publishing substantial books for years: the Alan Ball Awards were set up to encourage better standards all round, and the winners were (and continue to be) reported annually in *The local studies librarian*. Many are also reported or reviewed in local newspapers – again good publicity. One of the consistently successful publishers was Northamptonshire, which received a special Millennium award in 2000 for the greatest number of titles given Ball awards. Another major publisher was Newcastle City Libraries, who were able to employ a full-time publishing assistant and maintain a strong backlist. Design and typesetting were done in-house. They also commissioned local authors and sold through local bookshops (with a trade discount) as well as in City Council outlets and experimented with joint publication.[56] At the other end of the scale a branch librarian in Worcester described how he published a substantial book of local reminiscences, most of it due to his own voluntary work, and the problems he encountered.[57] At a Midlands and Anglia subgroup day school, staff from Nottinghamshire, Derbyshire and Leicestershire described their publications programmes – all were very different in approach and type of production, but all saw their role as exploiting their collections. Ian Reid discussed the practicalities and problems of publishing local material, using Midlothian as an example,[58] while an example of a more specific approach was Clwyd's venture into publishing via facsimile reproductions of out-of-print local works, on a minimum advance subscription base, so that costs were covered before printing began – thus each copy made a profit for the library service.[59]

Conclusion

During the 1990s local studies librarianship continued to develop, with increasing demand, against a background of local government reorganization and financial problems. It was helped by the increasing sophistication of information technology, using in particular digitization and the internet: this helped libraries to exploit and conserve their own stock, to improve their services by accessing material from outside, and in return making their own material available to a wider readership. However, this was sometimes seen to have its own disadvantages: some librarians and some local historians felt that with increasing reliance on information technology by both management and the local authority, together with cuts in staff, the personal element was being diminished, with a loss of reader/librarian interface and the ability to identify precisely readers' needs through detailed user interviews. Cutbacks concerned staff, too, in view of local demands in the light of the government's 'lifelong learning' initiatives and remembering how high a place was placed on local studies in the 'People's Network' report.

At the end of the decade, though, local studies libraries were still seen as a success story by the public, and librarians were aware of, and were trying to deal with, more clients using a more diverse range of sources. The internet was of great value and was seen as a major way forward. The major problems continued to be time and cost: librarians were very aware of what they would like to do to improve their services against these constraints.

Acknowledgements

Although there were some articles about local collections in the general library press during the period, and various news items, most material appears in the two specialist journals. However, a great deal of useful information is only reported in press releases, annual reports and library newsletters, and at professional meetings and conferences. Papers from the latter are not often published, though reports may be given in journals, and one of the values of these events is interpersonal communication. Grateful acknowledgement is made to all who have supplied information.

Notes

There are two main sources for professional information about local studies librarianship – *The local studies librarian* (Vol. 1 no. 1, 1982–) and *LOCSCOT* (Vol. 1 no. 1, 1981–). The former is the journal of the Local Studies Group of the Library Association, while *LOCSCOT* is the magazine of its Scottish branch. These are the only national journals on the subject, and carry specialist articles, news items and reviews of relevant literature. There is an index to vols. 1–15 of *The local studies librarian*, and it is abstracted in *Library and information science abstracts*. The British Association for Local History is also helpful, producing various publications which are useful to the local historian and the librarian. Its journal, *The local historian*, also carries numerous reviews and listings of material and *Local studies news* has short articles and comments, together with news items relating to libraries, record offices and museums. *Local history magazine* (No. 1, 1984–) has always been supportive of libraries and their services, and carries news items, articles, and reviews and notices of books.

1   Library Association, Local Studies Group, *Local studies libraries: Library Association guidelines for local studies provision in public libraries*. London: Library Association, 1990.
2   Michael Drake, 'Doing local studies: a new course from the Open University', *Local atudies librarian* **14** (1), 1995, 6–7: 'DA301 – studying family and community history: some comments', *Local studies librarian* **14** (1), 1995, 8–10.
3   Michael Dewe (ed.), *A manual of local studies librarianship*. Aldershot: Gower, 1987; Michael Dewe (ed.), *Local studies collections: a manual. Vol. 2*. Aldershot: Gower, 1991.
4   Richard Harvey, *Genealogy for librarians*. 2nd ed. London: Library Association, 1992.
5   Assumpta Bailac, 'Local studies in Catalonia, Spain', *Local studies librarian* **11** (1), 1992, 18–24.
6   'Library Association Local Studies Group International policy,' *Local studies librarian* **12** (2), 1993, 23–4.
7   Michael Dewe, 'Local studies libraries and librarianship in Australia', *Local studies librarian* **12** (1), 1993, 2–7.

8   Philippa Stevens, 'Entente cordiale in Hampshire', *Local studies librarian* **10** (1) 1991, 8–10; 'Entente cordiale in Hampshire – Mark II', *Local studies librarian* **12** (1), 1993, 16.

9   Ian Maxted, 'Remember Waterloo: how to sabotage your library's twinning programme', *Local studies librarian* **13** (1), 1994, 10–16.

10 Alain Girard, 'Local and regional studies in French libraries', *Local studies librarian* **12** (2), 1993, 2–11.

11 Mike Spick, 'Entrepreneurship and the Sheffield Time Machine', *Local studies librarian* **19** (2), 2000, 5–6.

12 'A new structure for local government?', *Local studies librarian* **10** (2), 1991, 16.

13 Morris Garratt, 'Vacancies and the prospective candidate: some personal observations', *Local studies librarian* **18** (1), 1999, 15–17.

14 Bob Usherwood, 'The social impact of local studies services', *Local studies librarian* **18** (1), 1999, 2–6. Local studies was exemplified from a general report on social audit techniques. The full report was issued by Sheffield University Department of Information Studies as: Rebecca Linley and Bob Usherwood, *New measures for the new library: a social audit of public libraries.* [London]: British Library, 1998 (British Library Research and Innovation Centre report; 89).

15 Kevin Campbell and Barry Mills, 'Bolton Archives and Local Studies: a customer survey', *Local studies librarian* **14** (1), 1995, 10–12: Christina Matkin and Ruth Gordon, 'Consulting the customers: a survey of local studies library users in Derby and Derbyshire', *Local studies librarian* **19** (1), 2000, 2–5.

16 Andrew Blizzard, *A sense of place: local studies and the school library.* Swindon: School Library Association, 1991.

17 Geoffrey Timmins, 'Local history teaching and the National Curriculum: implications for the library service', *Local studies librarian* **11** (2), 1992, 16–18.

18 Andrew Bethune, 'Working with schools: the experience of Edinburgh City Libraries', *LOCSCOT* **2** (9), 1991, 15–17.

19 Jan McLaughlin, 'Work with younger children', *LOCSCOT* **3** (6), 1995/6, 8–9.

20 Sheila Cooke, 'Local studies and the multicultural community', *Local studies librarian* **11** (2), 1992, 2–5.

21 Joan Bray, 'Equal opportunities and local studies', *Local studies librarian* **19** (1), 2000, 6–9.

22 Diana Winterbotham and Alan Crosby, *The local studies library: a handbook for local historians.* Salisbury: British Association for Local History, 1998.

23 David Hey (ed.), *The Oxford companion to local and family history.* Oxford: Oxford University Press, 1996.

24 David Hey (ed.), *The Oxford dictionary of local and family history.* Oxford: Oxford University Press, 1997.

25 Kate Tiller, *English local history: an introduction.* Stroud: Sutton, 1992.

26 James Griffin and Tim Lomas, *Exploring local history.* London: Hodder, 1997.

27 Raymond Gillespie and Myrtle Hill (eds.), *Doing Irish local history: pursuit and practice.* Belfast: Institute of Irish Studies, 1998.

28 Christopher Kitching, *Archives: the very essence of our heritage.* Chichester: Phillimore for the National Council on Archives, 1996.

29 Robert Pols, *Dating old photographs.* 2nd ed. Birmingham: Federation of Family History Societies, 1995.

30 The Federation of Family History Societies is of much wider interest to local historians than its name suggests, in that many of its publications are very important sources for the general public, and are worth stocking by local studies libraries.

31 Stephen Caunce, *Oral history and the local historian*. Harlow: Longman, 1994; Ken Howarth, *Oral history: a handbook*. Stroud: Sutton, 1998.

32 Bob Trubshaw, *How to write and publish local history*. Loughborough: Heart of Albion Press, 1999.

33 'A new structure for local government?'.

34 Library Association. Local Studies Group, 'Local government reorganization and local studies', Local studies librarian **15** (1), 1996, 19.

35 Marilyn Higson, 'Local studies in Telford and Wrekin', *Local history magazine* 72, 1999, 7.

36 Alice Lock, 'Spending cuts in local studies libraries: a survey in the North West', *Local studies librarian* **14** (2), 1995, 18–21.

37 Malcolm Graham, 'Local studies: a new approach', *Public library journal* **7** (3), 1992, 65–8.

38 David Robinson, 'Surrey's new history centre', *Local history magazine* 70, 1998, 23–6.

39 Mark Lawrence, 'North Devon Local Studies Centre, Barnstaple', *Local studies librarian* **10** (2), 1991, 3–7.

40 For instance, *Library Association record* **99** (9), 1997, 487 and **99** (12), 1997, 660 and *Local history magazine* 64, 1997, 7 give useful information.

41 Ian Maxted, 'Local studies libraries as rare book collections', *Local studies librarian* **17** (1), 1998, 3–7.

42 Philippa Stevens, 'Preparing for disasters in archives, libraries and museums', *Local studies librarian* **14** (1), 1995, 14–16.

43 Graham Cornish, *Copyright: interpreting the law for libraries, archives and information services*. 2nd ed. London: Library Association, 1997; Sandy Norman, *Copyright in public libraries*. 4th ed. London: Library Association, 1999; Sandy Norman, 'The effect of the extended term of protection', *Local studies librarian* **15** (1), 1996, 14–15.

44 John Lauder, 'Preserving newspapers', *LOCSCOT* 3 (5), 1995, 4–6.

45 Ian Watson, 'The *Herald* on CD Rom', *LOCSCOT* 3 (7), 1997, 14–15.

46 Anne Nix, 'SCRAN', *LOCSCOT* 3 (8), 1998, 5–7.

47 *New library: the people's network*. London: Library and Information Commission, 1997; 'Library report gives community history a high profile', *Local history magazine* 63, 1997, 4–5. The latter article picks out local history elements mentioned in the report.

48 Iain Watson, 'The *Durham record*', *Local studies librarian* **15** (2), 1996, 2–6. The full report on the project appeared as Public Library Development Incentive Scheme (PLDIS) report no. 47, British Library, 1996.

49 Peter Marchant and Eileen Hume, 'Visiting Knowsley's past', *Library Association record* **100** (9), 1998, 468–9.

50 David Parry, *Virtually new: creating the digital collection*. London: Library and Information Commission, 1998.

51 Mike Petty, 'Wake up to your potential for promotion!', *Local studies librarian* **13** (1), 1994, 17–24; Elizabeth Melrose, 'Marketing the local studies collection: some observations', *Local studies librarian* **18** (2), 1999, 11–15.

52 Sheila Cooke, 'With the éclat of a proverb: or blow your own trumpet!', *Local studies librarian* **10** (1), 1991, 3–4.

53 Janet Klak, 'How to age ten years in three weeks!', *LOCSCOT* 3 (3), 1993, 4–5.

54 Patrick Baird and Richard Allbutt, 'The Birmingham history van', *Local studies librarian* **13** (1), 1994, 33–4.

55 M. Sybil Calderwood, 'A video in seven weeks? The West Lothian experience', *LOCSCOT* **2** (10), 1991, 12–13. Also reprinted in *Local studies librarian* **11** (2), 1992, 13–15.

56 Anna Flowers, 'Local history publishing at Newcastle Libraries and Information Service', *Local studies librarian* **18** (1), 1999, 7–9.

57 Philip M. Adams, 'Library publishing on a shoestring', *Local studies librarian* **18** (1), 1999, 10–12.

58 Alan Reid, 'Publish and be damned', *Scottish libraries* **10** (2), 1996, 20–1.

59 Alan Watkin, 'Welsh publisher that's sewn up its local market', *Library Association record* **95** (3), 1993, 170–1.

16

Archives

Elizabeth Shepherd

The 1990s were years of significant change in the archival domain.[1] Major legislative changes were introduced, although no new national archives Act emerged. For the first time a coherent policy framework for the whole domain (national, local and specialist archives) developed. The Public Record Office (PRO) went through a major restructuring and change of status, followed by the appointment of the first female Keeper. Local government archives, which had provided a safety net of services across England and Wales for seventy years, faced the loss of their historic administrative units, the counties, but embraced collaborative initiatives which brought about improved standards in many areas of professional work. Business and specialist archives, in particular university archives, were recognized as innovative parts of the domain. By 2000, archives and records management services were part of a varied and vibrant profession, engaging with users and offering many new remote (online) services.

Legislative and policy framework

In 1991 the Department of the Environment published a consultation paper on the structure of local government in England, which proposed a review of local government structures, based on the premise that unitary authorities were the ideal model: 'a single tier should reduce bureaucracy, improve the co-ordination of services, increase quality and reduce costs'.[2] The Local Government Act 1992 did not require local authorities to provide archives services. It set up a Local Government Commission for England which considered structural, electoral and boundary changes in each area, a task which took several years to complete. Government advice on archives was set out in 1995 in *Guidance on the care, preservation and management of records*.[3] This addressed current records and archives and stated that 'services should continue to be provided to at least the same standard following reorganization' (s 1.2). The *Guidance* asserted that automatic archive powers would be extended to new unitary authorities (s 3.2) and that successor authorities could not split up archive collections (s 4.2). This still left uncertainty over areas where there was a hybrid solution (i.e., the continuation of an existing authority and the establishment of a new one for part of the old county area). Guidance on joint arrangements (s 6) indicated that 'building on the infrastructure of the existing repositories' was preferable, thus giving some protection to existing local archives services.

No single national pattern of local government emerged and the archives profession realized that this meant that it needed to lobby both nationally and locally to ensure that the needs of archives services were met.[4] The Society of Archivists (SoA) took the lead in coordinating the profession's responses to reorganization. It developed strong political contacts, met with ministers, peers and MPs, and officials in government departments and involved the membership regionally and locally as well as nationally.[5] The SoA followed the roving Local Government Commission, seeking to influence its work in each locality. It continued lobbying and giving support locally until 1998.[6]

The loss of the link between county councils and county archives services based on historic county boundaries led to some destabilization of local archives and funding problems. However, in spite of fears at the time that the reorganization would result in poorer archives services, in practice, partly as a result of the determination and hard work of many county archivists, local archives emerged reasonably unscathed from the reorganization. By 2000, the new unitary authorities created as a result of the review had mostly settled into joint arrangements to maintain existing archives services. Increasingly, local archives looked to regional and national structures and to professional networks to provide stability and leadership. In *Archives at the millennium* the Royal Commission on Historical Manuscripts (HMC) pointed the way to regional or 'strategic' repositories serving larger areas and providing specialist services.[7]

Archives in the European Union
The advent of the single European market under the Maastricht Treaty on European Union in 1993 provided a transition from a community of member states to a closer union. An EU Experts Group on archives was formed in 1991 to look at areas of coordination, including appraisal, conservation, access to traditional archives and computerized records, legislation, training and qualifications and professional networks.[8] The resulting report made recommendations which tended to reflect the position of the national archives (e.g., the Public Record Office) and not, perhaps, of the wider profession.[9] Nevertheless in the longer term UK archives benefited from EU initiatives, especially in the management of digital records and technological innovation, through initiatives such as the DLM-Forum, which started in 1994.[10]

Information policy legislation
The development of data protection and freedom of information legislation in the UK was largely driven by European Directives. The second Data Protection Act 1998 (which came into force between 1998 and 2007)[11] maintained the duty on those holding personal data to comply with data protection principles and to allow data subjects access to the data. The most significant feature of the new Act was that the data protection regime was extended to manual records.[12] Data protection

applied only to living subjects, so more directly affected records managers responsible for records containing current personal data. However, archivists were concerned in the late 1990s that the use of personal data in research and statistical analysis would be significantly restricted by the new Act: in the event, the limited exemptions (s 33) enabled most historical work to be undertaken satisfactorily. The Data Protection Act was the first part of information policy legislation in the UK.

The second piece of information policy legislation was the Freedom of Information Act 2000.[13] In 1993 a white paper on open government appeared, after a long campaign by organizations such as the Campaign for Freedom of Information.[14] The white paper was the beginning of an 'open government' initiative which extended access to official information. A *Code of practice on access to government information* was published in 1994 and provided a significant improvement in public access to government information, both explanatory information and also information about policies, actions and decisions in response to specific requests.[15] The *Code* did not have statutory force but it provided a benchmark for access to government archives and records. Tens of thousands of public records, which had been subject to extended closure beyond 30 years, were re-reviewed and subsequently released.

A Labour government white paper, *Your right to know,* was followed by a Bill in 1999.[16] The Freedom of Information Act 2000 created new statutory rights of access to government information and extended the range of public authorities for the purposes of the Act. As well as central government departments, local government, police authorities, schools, colleges and universities came within the legislation. Public authorities had to produce publication schemes which set out the classes of information to be made available and the manner in which it would be published. The Act also established a new Information Commissioner.

In response to the information policy legislation, most public sector bodies appointed data protection and freedom of information officers, and established systems to monitor the progress of information requests. Often, though not always, responsibility for information policy was delegated to records managers and archivists in public bodies. Where the information policy role was separate, records managers nevertheless had a significant contribution to make to enable organizations to identify relevant records, organize them appropriately and make information available to requestors. Information policy legislation raised the profile of records managers, in particular, and resulted in the establishment of many new records management posts.[17]

Policy leadership
Ministerial responsibility for archives and records management services was scattered. The PRO was part of the Lord Chancellor's Department, the HMC had been transferred to the Department of National Heritage, local government archives were within the Department of the Environment, university archives fell within the Department for Education, and so on. The lack of a single departmental home for archives was a growing concern. Central and local government archives

faced new challenges and were struggling to respond effectively. Local archives had few common objectives and disagreed about priorities. The profession lacked information about its strengths and weaknesses and its ability to manage its resources. Key individuals began to see a valuable national role in leading the profession. Local individual initiative gave way to a broader perspective. The advent of the National Council on Archives (NCA) led to a new approach to political engagement. NCA provided local and specialist archivists with access to national archival organizations (HMC, PRO) which were, in any case, more disposed to be open. Individuals with political experience (including successive chairmen David Vaisey and Alice Prochaska and Keepers, Michael Roper and Sarah Tyacke) and those seeking to institute change (chairmen Victor Gray and Nicholas Kingsley) came together at NCA meetings. Through them the profession learnt greater political astuteness and developed new ways of working, including much greater representation of users. NCA provided an environment in which archivists could develop their skills and learn to engage with those outside the profession with one voice. Proactive political engagement became a normal activity for the profession, which established mechanisms for identifying and responding to government reports, draft legislation and regulations. Archivists recognized the effectiveness of joint action and the need to inform and engage the whole profession.

A national archives policy

In the early 1990s the professional bodies made further progress towards a national archives policy, as recommended in *Yesterday's future*.[18] The SoA produced a discussion paper in 1994, *The outline of a national policy on archives*.[19] It recommended a comprehensive network of public archive repositories, each with a centrally approved acquisition policy, alongside private archives where appropriate; legislation for local authority records; centres of technical excellence to provide support for records with special characteristics; a single government department to regulate standards and archival policy; and a public education programme on archives. The paper acknowledged that additional resources would be needed, but failed to say where these would come from.

Although criticized at the time as flawed and limited, it was an excellent catalyst for action. A Liaison Group brought together Archives Council Wales, the Association of County Archivists, the British Records Association, the Business Archives Council, NCA, and SoA, chaired by Michael Roper, recently retired Keeper of Public Records, to publish a further statement, *A national archives policy for the United Kingdom*.[20] It was aimed at government policy-makers as well as at the profession and set out 12 principles to 'guide a national archives policy' (part 1), an implementation programme (part 2), and detailed discussion of the background (part 3). The 'principles' brought together the key issues from previous discussions, recommending a single 'reference point for government policy in respect of archival issues' (principle 1), a nationwide network of public sector and private sector archival services (principle 2), external funding to stimulate improvement and reinforce existing centres of excellence (principle 3), legislation requiring public bodies to manage their records and archives (4, 5), proper resources and access for archives (6, 7), coordinated acquisition (8), and professional education, training and methodology development (10–12).

The *National archives policy* endorsed the work of the NCA, especially in coordinating policy and representing users as well as professionals, even though it was not the government body envisaged by earlier reports (part 2, s 1.3). Other achievements were also made, such as the development of standards (part 2, ss 6.1–9.2), and the completion of the network of regional film and sound archives (part 2, s 2.4) but many recommendations, such as those relating to legislation and funding, did not happen immediately.

Scotland and Wales

Although originally intended as an archives policy for the UK, dissension from Scotland, and later Wales, led to the development and publication of an Archives Policy for Scotland and one for Wales.[21] These statements adopted, with amendments, the principles of the original *Policy*. In Scotland, draft archives legislation for public authorities in Scotland emerged, although no parliamentary time was allocated.[22] The Wales statement recommended 'A National Record Office for Wales' (principle 3.1) and the Government of Wales Act 1998 provided for a Public Record Office of Wales. Meanwhile the PRO continued to keep Welsh public records.[23]

The *National archives policy* was widely discussed within the professional bodies but was never fully endorsed by the profession as the way forward.[24] However, in spite of some criticism by professionals, it remained an authoritative statement and resulted in some progress in government action on archives. The achievement of the policy statement was largely due to the willingness of the professional bodies to act cooperatively, strongly encouraged by the NCA. The statement gave an impression of clarity of vision and unity of voice. It proved to be the first of a series of significant documents which informed government about the priorities of the profession and enabled action to be taken.

Government policy on archives

One of the *National archives policy* recommendations was a 'national inter-departmental archives committee' to bring together the national archives and the ministries with archival responsibilities (part 2, s 1.2). The heads of the UK national archives institutions met informally from time to time to discuss matters of common concern.[25] The Inter-Departmental Archives Committee was formally established in 1996 to coordinate archives policy matters within government in the UK and to consider archives policy and legislation issues and to speak on UK government archive interests to the European Union.[26] The Committee was asked to prepare a national archives policy, to look at regional structures and review the legislative basis for archives services. The *Government policy on archives* formed the government's response to the profession's *National archives policy* and provided a comprehensive statement on the way in which archives could contribute to key government policy objectives on modernizing government, social inclusion and improving access to information.[27] It raised awareness of the value of archives and sought ways to deliver services more effectively. The policy addressed access to archives, educational uses of archives, improved compliance by public archives institutions with best practice for current records and archives, developing skills in managing electronic data, encouraging cross-sectoral work and incentives for private organizations and individuals to care for their records well.

Resource: The Council for Museums, Archives and Libraries

In 1997 the Department for Culture, Media and Sport (DCMS) commissioned the Library and Information Commission to report on public library provision in the 21st century. The resulting reports, *New library: the people's network* and *Building the new library network*, brought significant government financial support to develop public libraries to support lifelong learning and provide networked resources in libraries.[28] In 1998 DCMS undertook a detailed review of its cultural activities and spending in a consultation document, *A new approach to investment in culture*.[29] There was universal dismay in archival circles because the review made hardly any reference to archives. DCMS set out its initial conclusions in a further document, *A new cultural framework*, in which the idea of a Museums and Libraries Council (to replace the Museums and Galleries Commission and the Library and Information Commission) was expanded to encompass archives.[30] Regional Archive Councils were proposed. As part of the review, Chris Smith, then Minister for Culture, commissioned a report from a group of senior professionals to advise on the formation of a new Museums, Libraries and Archives Council (MLAC). The MLAC Design Group recommended that a Council should be established as a strategic policy body which would provide leadership to the sector and focus on cross-domain issues. The Group believed that the advent of MLAC offered 'a major opportunity to promote the development of the sector'.[31] Further consultation on the role and work of MLAC was undertaken in early 2000.[32] MLAC was positioned as a strategic body, not a service delivery body, so the executive functions inherited from the Museums and Galleries Commission were mainly transferred elsewhere. A governing Board with representatives from museums, libraries and archives, education and the creative industries was established: Victor Gray, Director of Rothschild Archive, was the archival representative, although Lola Young, Professor of Cultural Studies at Middlesex University, had strong archival interests. MLAC became operational in April 2000 with initial funding from the DCMS of £19.5 million. Shortly afterwards it was renamed Resource: The Council for Museums, Archives and Libraries.

Resource took up the cause of archives with enthusiasm, recognizing that 'though smaller in scale than either libraries or museums, the archives domain needs to be given specific help in order for it to fulfil its potential'.[33] One of the weaknesses of the Resource approach was its cultural focus. Its sponsor department, DCMS, and the predominance of museums in the sector, made it difficult for Resource to do more than acknowledge that libraries and archives often had a dual objective. Resource took the view that work on information policy and records management could be left to other bodies, and that it would focus on cultural services. Resource's priorities also reflected the government agenda on social inclusion and education and lifelong learning and it became a cultural policy body for government.

The role of the regions
The trend towards regionalization, following Scottish devolution and the establishment of the Welsh Assembly and regional government offices, was reflected in the archives domain. Regional Development Agencies were established in 1998 and Regional Cultural Consortiums the following year. Regional structures for archives were proposed in the MLAC Design Group *Report* to mirror the existing Area Museum Councils (established between 1959 and 1965)[34] and regional library services. DCMS asked the NCA to 'develop regional arrangements which will address strategic issues for the archives sector'.[35] NCA recognized that given the increasing weight accorded by government to regional views and strategies 'the absence of bodies in the archive field capable of contributing an authoritative archival perspective to cultural debate in each of the regions was likely to prove a significant disadvantage'.[36] During 1999, shadow Regional Archive Councils were established to mirror the eight Regional Development Agency areas: London was added later. The RACs quickly gained 'parity of esteem' with their sister bodies for libraries and museums, although funding varied greatly between the three domains.[37] A new post of Regional Development Officer for Archives was set up with funding from the SoA and the PRO.[38] Regions played an important part in 'delivering and monitoring government policy' regionally and 'ensuring that such policy is informed by local circumstance'.[39]

In summary, during the decade the legislative and policy framework for archives and records management services in the public sector changed significantly. Building on national archives policy statements promulgated by the profession itself, government responded with a government policy on archives. A new government agency (Resource) which included archives as part of the cultural policy spectrum was established and began to develop regional and national frameworks for service improvements. Information policy legislation, specifically data protection and freedom of information, led to an improvement in the profile of records management in the public sector and provided a counterbalance to the cultural orientation for archives. In spite of discussions about ministerial responsibility for archives, they had no single departmental home: the PRO remained with the Lord Chancellor and the HMC within the DCMS. The weaknesses of the existing archival legislation continued, with local government services relying on the permissive Local Government (Records) Act 1962 and the PRO on the now outdated Public Records Act 1958, and little progress was made towards new comprehensive legislation for archives and records management services.

National archival institutions
Royal Commission on Historical Manuscripts
During the 1990s, the Royal Commission on Historical Manuscripts (HMC) was located in Quality Court, Chancery Lane, premises which it had occupied since 1959. The main functions of the HMC also remained constant, providing central government support and guidance for local and private archives. In 1991, the HMC had a budget of over £800,000 and a staff of 23: by 2000 it had grown to over £1 million and 26 staff.[40] It focused on providing support to private owners and on supplying information to users, especially about 'the whereabouts and nature of manuscripts of all kinds, that are of value for the study of the nation's history'.[41] Catalogues and other finding aids received from local record offices were filed and indexed in the National Register of Archives (NRA) and were made available in the public searchroom. Computerization of the NRA indexes (business, subject, personal, and the repository file) was extended and online public access to the indexes provided.[42] The NRA celebrated its 50th anniversary in 1995, when it was still one of only a handful of similar national archival information systems in the world. The staff of the HMC became specialists in description and retrieval and contributed to professional standards developments through the International Council on Archives (leading to the publication of the *International Standard Archival Description (General)* in 1994) and NCA's *Rules for the construction of personal, place and corporate names*.[43] Publication series continued, including *Guides to sources for British history* and the penultimate volumes in the great series of reports on private papers.[44]

As well as information provision and publishing activities, HMC carried out advisory functions. HMC advised government on appropriate places of deposit for historical manuscripts accepted in lieu of capital taxation. HMC provided guidance to local record offices through its inspection programme (originally begun to enable it to carry out its manorial and tithe responsibilities) which was supported by the publication of *A standard for record repositories* in 1990, giving advice on policies, administration, services, storage and preservation.[45] The National Manuscripts Conservation Trust, an independent charitable trust supported by HMC, raised funds for conservation, reboxing and repair projects in local, university and specialist archives. HMC also monitored the sale of manuscripts in salerooms.

HMC published a major review of the state of archive care and use, following large-scale consultation in 1998/99, *Archives at the millennium*.[46] In surveying the 'archival health' of the nation, the report identified strengths including a steady overall growth in provision, greater numbers of records in safe custody, a rise in reader numbers, improvements in storage accommodation, better access to information about archives and a greater 'sense of community among those who deliver archive services'.[47] Set against these were problems including continuing unevenness of provision of archives services, lack of public awareness of the value of archives both among potential users and among funders and decision-makers, shortfalls in funding and changes in governing administrative structures. Issues for the future included information technology, digitization, the impact of freedom of information (FoI) legislation, finding new sources of funding, the increasing importance of the views of users and the proposals for the Council for Museums, Libraries and Archives. The report made a number of recommendations. More strongly than in previous HMC reports, *Archives at the millennium* recommended 'legislation to make the provision of archive services by local authorities ... a mandatory responsibility', together with a long-term obligation to fund services at an appropriate level. It called for the reimbursement of local places of deposit for their care of public records. The report supported the development of records management services to secure FoI. It set out funding priorities for national archival networks, preservation activities including improved buildings and digitization, elimination of cataloguing backlogs in order to make archives available for use and tackling the problems of digital records. Underpinning these was a continuing need for training in both new and traditional skills.

Public Record Office

Under Michael Roper, Keeper from 1988 to 1992, the PRO finally accepted its role as a leader for the UK archival profession. It participated in the affairs of national and international archival associations, it adopted innovative approaches to archival automation through a centralized Records Information System and a plan to establish a machine-readable data archive using optical disk, it sought publicity for its activities and mounted regular exhibitions, it had a state-of-the-art repository at Kew and served 170,000 readers annually with over 400 staff.[48] Within government it provided advice and training in records management, including its Departmental Record Officers' conference.[49] A new repository at Kew was planned and commercial and electronic publications were considered.[50]

A major preoccupation for Roper was the Next Steps 'efficiency scrutiny'. In 1988 the Conservative administration had initiated *Next steps – improving management in government* and the PRO was considered a candidate for one of the new executive agencies.[51] Part of the process was an 'efficiency scrutiny' of the PRO which took place in 1990. It looked at the functions, management and organization of the PRO. In 1991 the scrutiny report proposed that the PRO should become an executive agency with greater freedom to manage its affairs from April 1992, headed by a chief executive and Keeper.[52] It also recommended a single grading structure for curatorial and administrative staff, longer opening hours, more competitive reprographic services, building an extension at Kew for the records from Chancery Lane, retaining a central London reading room and continuing free access to public records (although this was reviewed in 1993).[53] Most of the report's 127 recommendations were accepted and acted upon.[54] In April 1992 the PRO became an executive agency under its new Keeper, Sarah Tyacke. Mrs Tyacke was the first female Keeper to be appointed in the UK.

In the decade following agency status for the PRO, Mrs Tyacke established a new approach to the national archives. Internally, the introduction of new management and strategic planning systems and a total reorganization of the office's structure and staffing provided the flexibility and strong leadership needed to adapt to new challenges and to become a more responsive organization.[55] Public access and consultation became a priority: regular reader satisfaction surveys were introduced,[56] internet services began in 1995,[57] and in 1997 the Family Records Centre was opened in Clerkenwell with the Office for National Statistics to provide access to microfilm of censuses, wills and the indexes of births, marriages and deaths.[58] These changes were reflected in the make-up of the Advisory Council, which appointed a 'senior archivist ... to provide an independent professional view' and non-academic users.[59]

The major building project at Kew led, by December 1996, to the removal of the PRO to Kew and the closure of the Chancery Lane building.[60] The new building provided much improved storage and outstanding conservation facilities. Reader services were significantly extended with enlarged reading rooms, a new shop and restaurant and a schools visit room. Innovative use of internet-delivered services, including digitized documents, archival catalogues (Archives Direct), and the education service, the Learning Curve, gradually revolutionized services to users.[61]

Mrs Tyacke was well aware of the need for the PRO to engage with government. She highlighted the role it could play in the implementation of FoI (initially in the release of records and later in effective records management services)[62] and as a leader for electronic government and digital records initiatives.[63] Digital archives projects were finally implemented at the PRO for datasets and office documents in 1997.[64] Part of the PRO's 'modernizing government' agenda was a shift from supervising selection of records in departments to leadership in the management of current and non-current records across government.[65] In 1998 the PRO's first acquisition policy was published following widespread consultation, and operational selection policies across themes and historical periods were introduced to guide selection.[66]

The PRO also became an effective leader for the archival profession. It invested in the development of new techniques for archival description, establishing a methodology for retrospective conversion of catalogues, helping to develop Encoded Archival Description and to train UK archivists in its use, and playing a role on the NCA's Network Policy Committee.[67] It hosted the Access to Archives project (A2A) which sought to build a network of online catalogues for regional, local and specialist archives across the UK.[68] The PRO developed a methodology for mapping the archival resources of the UK and contributed to the development of standards which underpinned its archive inspection services. The PRO was finally moving towards a national archives service model.

Local government and specialist archives
Bidding culture
New sources of funding opened up to archives in the 1990s. University and local authority archives, in common with most public services, were increasingly subject to the 'bidding culture' (i.e., competitive bidding for the allocation of public resources).[69] Among the new funds available was the Heritage Lottery Fund (HLF)

which made its first grants in 1994. The National Heritage Act 1997 gave wider powers to the Trustees of the National Heritage Memorial Fund to award grants for projects which helped to secure or improve access to heritage collections which were of public benefit. This led to an increased emphasis on outreach and access by archives and on cross-domain work and provided a new source of funds for projects. HLF bids were complex to construct and involved lengthy consultation and preparation: many archivists were unused to the bidding culture.[70] By 1996 only 18 bids had been made to the HLF by archives, of which only two had been successful.[71] NCA convened a seminar on archives and the HLF in 1997, which proposed a Heritage Lottery Adviser post to offer support and advice to archivists preparing bids to the HLF.[72] The post, which had no counterpart in the library or museum domains, was jointly established with the SoA and PRO. The Adviser ran workshops, advised on draft bids and maintained close links with HLF personnel. By 2000 the majority of archives (68%) had been involved in one or more bids for external funds.[73] Several major capital projects were funded by HLF and almost all of the bids made under the cataloguing project phases, Access to Archives (A2A), were successful.

NCA's millennial statement, *British archives: the way forward*,[74] was prepared as guidance to the HLF, but actually helped to shape the agenda for the development of UK archives services. The report set out a vision of digital access and wider use of archives. Its four main recommendations were widening access through an electronic network, improving availability by eroding cataloguing backlogs, improving preservation through new buildings and refurbishment, and conservation projects. Controversially, the report made indicative funding allocations placing the highest priority (30% of funds) on digital networks for archives and less on traditional conservation and preservation activities. In fact, traditional concerns were strongly represented within the report while the focus on access and use appealed to government priorities.

National Archives Network
Developing standards for aspects of professional practice in archives was a significant feature of the 1990s. University archivists saw the value of standards in helping them to adapt to the bidding culture.[75] The SoA Professional Methodology Panel developed nationally agreed approaches in the early 1990s.[76] NCA established a group on information technology standards and archival description in 1991, which made recommendations on name authority controls and archival authority records.[77] NCA's report, *Archives on-line* (1998), provided a framework for national action towards an electronic archival information network.[78] Its vision was a series of projects in different parts of the domain which together would form a gateway National Archives Network (NAN). Steered by Nicholas Kingsley, the NCA facilitated agreements on standards, coordinated bids and developed a national strategy for the retrospective conversion of archival catalogues.[79]

Several strands developed in parallel. A consortium of universities developed a model for the networking of collection level records, the National Networking

Demonstrator Project.[80] The Higher Education Archives Hub included over 50 university archives.[81] A second strand, Access to Archives (A2A), arose from the experience of the PRO in developing its online catalogues.[82] A consortium of employers (PRO, HMC, British Library) and professional bodies (Association of Chief Archivists in Local Government, SoA, NCA) bid for funds through the Treasury's Invest to Save Budget, complemented by regional and thematic bids funded by HLF. Infrastructure development funds were secured in 2000 and 13 bids in A2A phase 1 were made to the HLF.[83] Further strands were added to the NAN by AIM25 (Archives in the M25 area), SCAN (Scottish Archive Network) and ANW (Archive Network Wales).

Local archives in the 1990s
Local government offered employment for over half the archives workforce: in 1992 all but one shire county (Avon) had a record office and some shire districts had archive powers. A series of surveys carried out by the HMC, NCA and PRO in 1984, 1992, 1996 and 1998 enabled trends in local archives services to be mapped over time.[84] These revealed an impending crisis in local archives. Staffing grew by 36% between 1984 and 1992 but reader numbers rose by 59%.[85] The typical county record office in 1992 had 16.4 staff (including six archivists and two conservators), very different from the one or two staff of the 1940s: however, in boroughs and elsewhere, one-person offices were still common. Local authority archives were hampered by the loss of the historic links between county councils and local record offices as the pattern of local government administration altered, causing disruption and uncertainty. Their focus on historical public services over records management services to their employing authority resulted in neglect of information policy values.

Most county record offices held far more private and public archives than official records of the council, which raised the question of why county councils should continue to fund the services. By 1992, 23% of holdings were records of the parent body and its predecessors, 26% other local authority and public records, and 51% private records.[86] 24% of repositories were full, in spite of over 40 new buildings or extensions since 1984[87] and many archives fell short of British Standard benchmarks.[88] Local record offices offered secure storage for unique archives often on loan from their owners, and yet in many cases the archives were either full or the storage had obvious deficiencies. Was it luck that so few disasters and losses occurred?[89]

The parent departments for archives had shifted: in 1968, 30 of 35 county archivists reported to the clerk of the council but by 1992 only 15 still did so. Another 15 were in leisure or library departments, four were independent and one in an education department. This represented a major shift away from central legal and administrative functions for the county towards cultural and leisure objectives, a probably inevitable consequence of the focus on acquisition and public services rather than records management. Even by 1992 only half of repositories offered records management services to the authority, making them vulnerable to funding cuts and loss of status in times of organizational change.[90]

The introduction of the National Curriculum for schools under the Education Reform Act 1988 promoted the use of original source material but only 20% of offices had a dedicated education officer by 1992, probably because the Act did not provide any new resources.[91] On the contrary, as budgets were increasingly devolved from the local education authority to schools, subventions to central services such as archival education were lost.

Increasingly archives had outreach policies and well planned outreach programmes, such as those in Nottinghamshire, Kent and Gwynedd in Wales.[92] As well as the traditional talks, exhibitions and publications, many regularly used newspapers, local radio and television to reach their audiences. Fifteen counties had 'Friends' organizations, run independently of the archive, which organized visits, talks, meetings and fund-raising events and coordinated volunteers. New outreach activities included history fairs, road shows, open days, local history days, children's clubs and family history surgeries.

To a large extent local archivists failed to prepare for the impact of automation on records, perhaps believing that the problem could be ignored until the records reached the archives in 30 years' time. As a result, although three-quarters of archives held non-traditional media (film, video, audio, digital) in 1992, only 12% had specialist storage and 19% suitable consultation facilities.

The state of local authority archives was comprehensively mapped in 1998 in *Our shared past*, which identified funding priorities for the Heritage Lottery Fund.[93] The findings confirmed that local archives services needed serious solutions. Although local record offices were providing for 463,000 visitors a year, who consulted over two million documents or copies, pressure on front-line services had led to a reduction of effort in traditional areas such as cataloguing. Few offices had recent collection-level descriptions. IT made data exchange possible at a lower cost but record offices had backlogs of cataloguing which might take months or even years to complete. Local archives lagged behind libraries in the use of IT and lacked both technical hardware and staff skills. *Our shared past* recommended linking local archives into information networks, so that archival resources could be properly shared and exploited, an idea that was redeveloped in the NCA report *Archives on-line*.

Regional solutions were suggested for electronic records, since 98% of local archives had no arrangements for the digital records of their employing authority or for deposited records. There was now 'an urgent need for local authorities to review their strategy with regard to records management', especially for digital records. Local archives services were most often linked with libraries, museums and other cultural departments, but subsumed within them archives were gradually losing chief officer status.[94] The overall picture was of great unevenness of provision, with some offices acting as centres of excellence and others struggling with inadequate staffing and premises. A 'fully effective system for co-ordinating our national archives, both central and local' was needed more than ever.[95]

Specialist repositories

The diversity of archival institutions grew in the last decade of the 20th century.[96] Specialist repositories made up a significant, and dynamic, minority of archives by 2000. At least ten sub-divisions, based on a mixture of subject specializations (medical and scientific, film and sound) and organizational type (businesses, universities and schools, charities, historic houses, professional and learned bodies, religious institutions, museums and galleries and national repositories) could be identified.[97]

University archives departments were indirectly funded by the Department for Education via the funding councils as part of the university function: there were about 30 in 1990.[98] They tended to be small departments within large institutions and often held the institution's own records and archives together with research-related collections of either local or national significance. A joint report by SoA and SCONUL on the role and resources of university archives services led NCA to recommend a survey of polytechnics and further education colleges and to hold a forum on university archives.[99] Many university archives still had inadequate storage and few professional archives staff, and the care of their own records often fell below that accorded to special collections. Following Sir Brian Follett's review of university library and special collection provision, university archives gained access to new funds under a funding council programme for research collections in university libraries for projects including conservation and cataloguing.[100] About £50 million was distributed between 1994 and 1999 and archives 'proved remarkably successful in making their case for funding and ... accounted for very nearly half of all the projects supported'.[101] University archivists led the way in the development of networking technology, regional information hubs and use of Encoded Archival Description (EAD).[102]

Libraries, museums and galleries, both nationally and locally, held many archives at the end of the 20th century. Typically their archives included public records held locally (e.g., of museums as government institutions), records of their artefact collections and subject-based archives relating to their museum collections.[103] Examples include the National Railway Museum Research Centre which held technical, engineering and scientific archives from British Railways and its predecessor private companies, business and technical archives from the British railway supply industry and the archives of significant individuals and organizations related to the railway industry, including the national archive of railway oral history.[104] The Archive of Art and Design at the Victoria and Albert Museum collected the archives of individuals, associations and companies involved in any stage of the art and design process, including collections of artists and designers, in British 20th century design and also held the records of the museum as an institution.[105] The *Code of practice on archives* for museums helped to promote good practice and archival standards.[106] In addition, the national libraries continued to hold significant archival and manuscript collections: at the British Library, for example, archives could be found in the manuscript collections, sound archive, Oriental and India Office, and music collections.

Business archives were an important part of the archival scene: many business records (especially those of defunct companies) were held in public archives, such as the Guildhall Library in London, while increasing numbers of companies employed in-house archives expertise. The number of business archivists grew in the 1980s and 1990s and a mark of their maturity and significance was the first UK textbook on business archives, coordinated by the Business Archives Council and published in 1991.[107] In addition, several surveys of the development of business sectors and their records were carried out.[108] Business archives, in common with much of the rest of the archives domain, often struggled for funds, competing with departments that had a more immediate effect on the company's profitability and yet not eligible for public funding sources. Some business archives carved out innovative approaches to their structure and funding, for example the establishment of a charitable trust for the archives, separate from the commercial business. Multinational corporation archives and those of international organizations posed new issues about the interpretation of provenance and levels of description, as well as where the archives should be held, who should be given access and for what purpose.

Conclusion
In the 1990s, the professional community, spurred by new ways of working in specialist archives, led by the vision and enthusiasm of a new generation of senior local archivists and inspired by the new leadership of the PRO, began to work towards national objectives which resulted in significant changes in archives and records management. The development of a national archives policy by the professional bodies and the government response set archives as cultural services in a new direction. NCA published an advocacy text, *Archives: the very essence of our heritage*, published in time for the ICA Congress in Beijing in 1996.[109] Information policy legislation was strengthened by new data protection and FoI Acts, which in turn required improvements in the records management capabilities of public sector bodies. However, new archives and records legislation was not promulgated and the multiplicity of ministerial responsibilities for archives was not resolved or simplified.

The national archival institutions, HMC and PRO, developed a greater role in leadership for the professional community, in spite of having limited legislative obligations. The change of status of the PRO to an executive agency and appointment of a new Keeper enabled a major shift in central activity towards leadership, innovation and responsiveness to stakeholder needs. Local government archives services experienced great threats to their future, as non-statutory services, in an era of local government reorganization. Yet by the end of the 1990s, new funding streams, notably from HLF, resulted in improvements in buildings and preservation, as well as the establishment of national archives information networks, the widespread adoption of descriptive standards and the development of new services through harnessing internet technologies. Specialist, university and business archives established their place within the spectrum of the archival domain and led the way in areas of professional practice (e.g., EAD) and organizational structure (e.g., trusts). Uniquely British contributions to professional practice, such as the electronic National Archive Network, resulted.

The emergence in 2000 of a new policy body for the cultural sector, Resource, encouraged archivists to work strategically and to take account of regional and national perspectives and provided the possibility of coherent cross-domain working with museums and libraries. Whether that promise was fulfilled in the early 2000s is a story for another occasion.

Notes

1   This chapter mainly deals with England and the UK as a whole. The pattern of archival developments in Wales, Scotland and Northern Ireland is significantly different from England and it is not possible to cover them here in detail.

2   Elizabeth Shepherd, 'Local government review – England'. Papers on local government review read at Society of Archivists AGM, Birmingham Central Library, Birmingham, 28 April 1992; and 'Local government review at the AGM', *Society of Archivists Newsletter* **61**, 1992, 5.

3   Department of National Heritage, *Guidance on the care, preservation and management of records following changes arising from the Local Government Act 1992*. London: DNH, 1995.

4   National Council on Archives, Society of Archivists, Association of County Archivists, *Challenge or threat? England's archive heritage and the future of local government*. [UK]: National Council on Archives, 1992.

5   Society of Archivists, *Annual report 1990–91, year book 1991–92*, np: SoA, 1991, 8–9. Society of Archivists, *Annual report 1992*, 6.

6   Society of Archivists, *Annual report 1998*, 13.

7   Royal Commission on Historical Manuscripts, *Archives at the millennium: the twenty eighth report of the Royal Commission on Historical Manuscripts 1991–1999* London: Stationery Office, 1999.

8   European Commission, *Archives in the European Union*. Luxembourg: Office of Official Publications of the European Communities, 1994.

9   Minutes of Council 20 Nov. 1991, Top copy minutes 1988–97, NCA 1, National Council on Archives archive, Birmingham City Archives.

10   Dlm-forum on electronic records: <http://www.dlmforum.eu.org> (accessed 1/8/02).

11   *Data Protection Act 1998*. 46&47 Eliz. 2, c. 29. London: Stationery Office, 1998.

12   Public Record Office, *Data Protection Act 1998: a guide for records managers and archivists*. Richmond: PRO, 2000.

13   *Freedom of Information Act 2000*. 48&49 Eliz. 2, c. 36. London: Stationery Office, 2000.

14   Chancellor of the Duchy of Lancaster, *Open government*. London: HMSO, 1993 (Cm 2290).

15   *Code of practice on access to government information* London: Stationery Office, 1994; 2nd ed., 1997.

16   *Your right to know: the government's proposals for a Freedom of Information Act* London: Stationery Office, 1997 (Cm 3818); *Freedom of Information Act: consultation on draft legislation*. London: Stationery Office, 1999 (Cm 4355).

17   Susan J. Davies and Mary Ellis, 'Employment trends in the archive domain 1993–2001', *Journal of the Society of Archivists* **24** (1), 2003, 15–24.

18   Association of County Archivists, *Yesterday's future: a national policy for our archive heritage.* Newcastle upon Tyne: ACA, 1983.

19   Society of Archivists, *The outline of a national policy on archives: a discussion paper.* [UK]: SoA, 1994.

20   National Archives Policy Liaison Group, *A national archives policy for the United Kingdom: a statement prepared by the National Archives Policy Liaison Group.* [UK]: National Archives Policy Liaison Group, 1995.

21   Scottish National Archives Policy Working Group, *A Scottish national archives policy.* [UK]: The Group, 1998; Archives Council Wales, *A national archives and records policy for Wales.* Aberystwyth: ACW, 2001.

22   Scottish Records Advisory Council, *Proposed Scottish national archive legislation 1999*, at: <http://www.dundee.ac.uk/archives/snal/htm> (accessed 21/7/99).

23   Public Record Office, *National Assembly for Wales/PRO memorandum of understanding*, at: <http://www.pro.gov.uk/recordsmanagement/NAWPROMoU/Contents.htm> (accessed 21/5/03).

24   Council minutes, 22 Nov. 1995, NCA 1, National Council on Archives archive, Birmingham City Archives; Victor Gray, 'National archives policy', *Society of Archivists Newsletter* 81, 1995, 1, 4.

25   Informal meetings began before 1992: email from David Leitch, TNA, to the author, 15/3/04.

26   Council minutes 23 April 1996, NCA 1, National Council on Archives archive, Birmingham City Archives.

27   Lord Chancellor's Department, *Government policy on archives.* London: Stationery Office, 1999 (Cm 4516).

28   Library and Information Commission, *New library: the people's network.* London: LIC, 1997.

29   Department for Culture, Media and Sport, *The comprehensive spending review: a new approach to investment in culture.* London: DCMS, 1998.

30   Department for Culture, Media and Sport, *The departmental spending review: a new cultural framework.* London: DCMS, 1998.

31   Department for Culture, Media and Sport, *The establishment of a Museums, Libraries and Archives Council: report of the Design Group.* London: DCMS, 1999.

32   Museums, Libraries and Archives Council, *Consultation on the work of the new Museums, Libraries and Archives Council.* London: MLAC, 2000.

33   Resource, The Council for Museums, Archives and Libraries, *Developing the 21st century archive: an action plan for United Kingdom archives.* London: VIP Print, 2001, 5.

34   Rosemary Ewles, 'Archive of the Committee of Area Museum Councils', *ARC: Archives and records management* 171, 2003, 17.

35   Department for Culture, Media and Sport, *Departmental spending review*, 1998.

36   National Council on Archives, *Review of the year 1999/2000.* Cheltenham: National Council on Archives, 2000, 3.

37   Victor Gray, 'The English regions: the archival dimension', *Journal of the Society of Archivists* **21** (2), 2000, 149–57.

38   Victor Gray, 'Strategic development, cross-domain working and regional structures' in *Proceedings of Archives in the regions: future priorities*. Cheltenham: National Council on Archives, 2002, pp. 5–8.

39   Katie Norgrove, 'A seat at the table: the development of the English Regional Archive Councils', *Journal of the Society of Archivists* **22** (1), 2001, 27.

40   Royal Commission on Historical Manuscripts, *Annual review 1991–1992*. London: HMSO, 1992; *Annual review 1999–2000* . London: HMSO, 2000.

41   Royal Commission on Historical Manuscripts, *Annual review 1997–1998*. London: Stationery Office, 1998, 1.

42   Dick Sargent, *The National Register of Archives: an international perspective: essays in celebration of the fiftieth anniversary of the NRA*. London: Institute of Historical Research, 1995.

43   International Council on Archives, *International standard for archival description (general)*. Ottawa: International Council on Archives, 1994; 2nd ed., 2000; National Council on Archives, *Rules for the construction of personal, place and corporate names*. Chippenham: NCA, 1997.

44   Royal Commission on Historical Manuscripts, *Records of British business and industry, 1760–1914. Textiles and leather*. London: HMSO, 1990 (Guides to sources for British history; 8); Royal Commission on Historical Manuscripts, *Records of British business and industry, 1760–1914. Metal processing and engineering*. London: HMSO, 1994 (Guides to sources for British history; 9); Royal Commission on Historical Manuscripts, *Principal family and estate collections*, London: HMSO, 1996 (Guides to sources for British history; 10); G. Dyfnallt Owen and Sonia P Anderson (eds.), *Manuscripts of the Marquess of Downshire. Vol. VI: Papers of William Trumbull the elder, 1616–1618* .London: HMSO, 1995 (Reports and calendars series; 75).

45   Royal Commission on Historical Manuscripts, *A standard for record repositories on constitution and finance, staff, acquisitions and access*. London: HMSO, 1990; 2nd ed., 1997.

46   Royal Commission on Historical Manuscripts, *Archives at the millennium*.

47   Royal Commission on Historical Manuscripts, *Archives at the millennium*, 5–6.

48   Public Record Office, *Annual report of the Keeper of Public Records on the work of the Public Record Office and the Report of the Advisory Council on Public Records (34th report 1992–93)*. London: HMSO, 1993, 16.

49   PRO, *31st report 1989–90*, 6.

50   PRO, *32nd report 1990–91*, 3.

51   PRO, *30th report 1988–89*, 3.

52   PRO, *32nd report 1990–91*, 3–4.

53   PRO, *36th report 1994–95*, 29.

54   A proposed change of title, to The National Archives, was rejected: PRO, *32nd report 1990–91*, 4.

55   PRO, *34th report 1992–93*, 9–10.

56   PRO, *34th report 1992–93*, 17.

57   PRO, *37th report 1995–95*, v.

58   PRO, *38th report 1996–97*, v.

59   PRO, *33rd report 1991–92*, 40.

60   Chancery Lane building re-opened in 2002 as the library for King's College, London.

61   PRO, *40th report 1998–99*, vi, 3.

62   PRO, *34th report 1992–93*, 7; *35th report 1993–94*, 7; *40th report 1998–99*, 20.
63   PRO, *35th report 1993–94*, 5; *36th report 1994–95*, 26; *37th report 1995–96*, vi; *38th report 1996–97*, 9.
64   PRO, *38th report 1996–97*, 10.
65   PRO, *39th report 1997–98*, 19.
66   PRO, *39th report 1997–98*, 18.
67   PRO, *39th report 1997–98*, 28; *40th report 1998–99*, 3–5.
68   PRO, *40th report 1998–99*, 6.
69   Sandra Parker *et al.*, *The bidding culture and local government: effect on the development of public libraries, archives and museums*. Newcastle upon Tyne: Resource, 2001, 5.
70   Society of Archivists, *Annual report 2001*, 35–6.
71   Council minutes, 13 Nov. 1996, NCA 1, National Council on Archives archive, Birmingham City Archives.
72   Council minutes, 15 April 1997, NCA 1, National Council on Archives archive, Birmingham City Archives.
73   Parker *et al.*, *Bidding culture*, 25–6.
74   National Council on Archives, *British archives: the way forward*. [UK]: National Council on Archives, 2000.
75   Patricia Methven, 'Performance measurement and standards', *Journal of the Society of Archivists* **11**, 1990, 78–84.
76   Patricia Methven *et al.*, *Measuring performance*. London: Society of Archivists, 1993 (Best practice guideline; 1).
77   Council minutes, 8 Nov. 1989, 7 Nov. 1990, 22 May 1991, 20 Nov. 1991, 20 April 1994, 26 April 1995, NCA 1, National Council on Archives archive, Birmingham City Archives; Peter Gillman, *National name authority file: a report to the National Council on Archives*. London: British Library, 1998 (Research and innovation report; 91).
78   National Council on Archives, *Archives on-line: the establishment of a United Kingdom archival network*. [UK]: NCA, 1998.
79   National Council on Archives, *Review of the year 2000/2001*. Cheltenham: National Council on Archives, 2001, 18–19.
80   D. Kay and I. Ibbottson, *National networking demonstrator project: technical consultant's report*. Fretwell-Downing Informatics, 1998.
81   Amanda Hill, 'Bringing archives online through the Archives Hub', *Journal of the Society of Archivists* **23** (2), 2002, 239–48.
82   Sarah Flynn, Matthew Hillyard and Bill Stockting, 'A2A: the development of a strand in the national archives network', *Journal of the Society of Archivists* **22** (2), 2001, 177–91.
83   NCA, *Review 2001/2002*, 10–11.
84   Brian S. Smith, 'Record repositories in 1984', *Journal of the Society of Archivists* **8**, 1986, 1–16; Heather Forbes, *Local authority archive services 1992*. London: HMSO, 1993; Heather Forbes and Rosemary Dunhill, 'Survey of local authority archive services: 1996 update', *Journal of the Society of Archivists* **18**, 1997, 37–57; Archival Mapping Project Board, *Our shared past: an archival Domesday for England*. Richmond: Public Record Office, 1998.
85   Forbes, *Local authority services*, 2–3.
86   Ibid., 6.

87 Ibid., 4–5.
88 British Standards Institution, *Recommendations for the storage and exhibition of archival documents*. 2nd ed. London: BSI, 1989 (BS 5454:1977).
89 An exception was the fire which destroyed Norwich City Library and local archives building in 1995. See Jean Kennedy, 'Norfolk Record Office fire: an initial report', *Journal of the Society of Archivists*, **16**, 1995, 3–6.
90 Forbes, *Local authority services*, 8–9.
91 Ibid., 21–3.
92 Ibid., 24–7.
93 Archival Mapping Project Board, *Our shared past*. See also National Archives of Scotland, *An archival account of Scotland: public and private sector archives in Scotland*. Edinburgh: National Archives of Scotland, 2000; Archives Council Wales, *Archival mapping project for Wales*. Aberystwyth: Archives Council Wales, 2001.
94 HMC, *Archives at the millennium*, 36–43.
95 Rosemary C. Dunhill, 'The National Council on Archives: its role in professional thinking and development', *Journal of the Society of Archivists* **11**, 1990, 34.
96 HMC, *Archives at the millennium*, 46–8.
97 Society of Archivists, *The missing link: specialist repositories in England: a map of development and funding needs*. London: Society of Archivists; British Library, 2002, 7–9.
98 Royal Commission on Historical Manuscripts, *The twenty seventh report 1982–1991*. London: HMSO, 1992, 26.
99 Council minutes, 29 April 1992, 18 Nov. 1992, 3 Nov. 1993, NCA 1, National Council on Archives archive, Birmingham City Archives.
100 Joint Funding Council Libraries Review Group, *Report*. London: Higher Education Funding Council for England, 1993. Chairman Sir Brian Follett. (The 'Follett report').
101 HMC, *Archives at the millennium*, 47.
102 Willpower Information, *Survey of needs-consultancy report* Joint Information Systems Committee (JISC) Archives Sub-Committee of the Non-Formula Funding of Specialized Research Collections Initiative, 1998.
103 HMC, *Archives at the millennium*, 49–53.
104 National Railway Museum Research Centre, at: <http://www.nrm.org.uk/home/menu.asp> (accessed 23/3/2006).
105 Victoria and Albert Museum, Archive of Art and Design, at: <http://www.vam.ac.uk/resources/archives/aad/> (accessed 23/3/2006).
106 Standing Conference on Archives and Museums, *Code of practice on archives*. London: SCAM, 1990; revised 1996, 2003.
107 Alison Turton (ed.), *Managing business archives*. Oxford: Butterworth Heinemann, 1991.
108 Surveys of railway industry records, the pharmaceutical industry and veterinary medicine were reported in: Business Archives Council, *Annual report 1998*. London: BAC, 1998, 7–9.
109 Christopher Kitching, *Archives: the very essence of our heritage*. Chichester: Phillimore & National Council on Archives, 1996.

17

British and European Union official publications

Howard Picton, Chris Pond, Valerie Nurcombe, David Butcher,
Jane Inman, Grace L. Hudson

UK OFFICIAL PUBLISHING
Howard Picton

Overview

The nineties saw significant changes to official publishing. In the early years digital publishing increased in the form of CD-ROMs and online databases. By 2000, the internet was the dominant digital form. However, in the rush to load content many websites ignored navigation and access suffered accordingly. The decade was punctuated by the loss of the UK government publisher, HMSO, privatized in 1996. These events sum up the themes of the decade: the transition to the web; the move to digital publishing either in place of, or in tandem with, print, and the move from the official publisher (although it never had a monopoly) to private publishers.[1]

Another trend, overlaying these technological and bureaucratic changes, was the gradual opening up of access to official information. This was the first time that government had recognized the right of the citizen to both published and unpublished information. Previously, governments had instituted information management initiatives on official information (for example, the move to charge for data under Mrs Thatcher) but these were for reasons other than to increase access. However, the Major government laid down principles of access for the citizen, albeit in non-statutory form. By the end of the decade a Freedom of Information (FOI) Act was in place if not in force.

However, it would be true to say that the essential problems of official publishing did not change even though the format did.

Government information policy

The period saw government begin to address the question of an information policy. Allan argued that prior to this there had been no attempt at a coherent policy[2] and he reviewed the issue with the advent of the web in 1997.[3] The Major administration published an 'open government' white paper in 1993 and introduced the *Code of practice on access to government information* in April 1994 (revised, February 1997).[4] A green paper on the electronic delivery of government services followed in 1996.[5] The House of Lords Select Committee on Science and Technology produced its own contribution to the debate on electronic information (to which the government responded) in the same year.[6] In December 1997, the new Blair government published a green paper on proposals for an FOI Bill.[7] The draft Bill was published in May 1999 and, much altered, received royal assent in 2000.[8] The Data Protection Act 1998 came fully into force in March 2000.[9] A *Modernising government* white paper was published in 1999 and an e-government strategy followed.[10] The National Audit Office reviewed government progress in use of the web,[11] and the Treasury produced a study on the knowledge economy in 2000 which set a goal that all government services must be capable of being delivered electronically by 2005.[12] A consultation paper on Crown copyright appeared in 1998 and in 1999 the Cabinet Office issued a white paper on the future management of Crown copyright.[13] This paper, together with the government's spending review, 2000, laid the foundations for the development of Information Asset Registers, registers of information assets held by government organizations.[14]

Government created the Office for National Statistics (ONS) in 1996 (from a merger of the Central Statistics Office and the Office of Population Censuses and Surveys), and established the Statistics Commission in June 2000.[15] A green paper on statistics appeared in 1998 and a white paper in 1999.[16]

Privatization of HMSO
The Standing Committee on Official Publications (SCOOP) met the government's consultants to express its concerns in 1993.[17] A Cabinet Office press release announced the possible privatization in September 1995,[18] HMSO was privatized on 30 September 1996, and became The Stationery Office (TSO) on 1 October.[19] The Public Accounts Committee examined the sale.[20] Most of the business became TSO but a small residuary body, still known as HMSO, remained within government to undertake various functions that could not be transferred, including the administration of the Public Library Subsidy, the 50% discount given to public libraries on core official publications.[21] Changes to this scheme subsequent to the privatization were detailed in *Refer* and by Rowell.[22]

CD-ROM and the internet
The appearance of several CD-ROMs allowed easier and greater access to official information and offered an alternative to print.[23] For example, the *Civil Service yearbook* appeared on CD-ROM in 1993. HMSO and Context Limited issued *Statutory Instruments CD* (*SICD*) in 1991. Version 2 was released in 1992 and covered the full text of statutory instruments from January 1987 and bibliographic references to those published by HMSO, 1980–90. The House of Commons *Hansard* on CD-ROM was published in 1992 and offered the full text from session

1988/89.[24] The House of Lords *Hansard* followed in 1994. Context published *Justis Parliament* (the CD-ROM version of Parliament's POLIS database) in 1994[25] and *Justis UK statutes* in 1999.

The new order, in the form of the internet, appeared in the mid-nineties with the first official websites in 1995. The Foreign and Commonwealth Office site went live in May and Parliament's in December. The first attempt at a UK government portal, open.gov, also appeared that year.[26] Government produced *Guidelines for government websites* in 2000.[27] Jellinek wrote a guide to government websites.[28]

The concept, indeed the development, of an online database, the *Statute law database*, that would hold both current and historic texts of legislation, continued over the entire decade without being published. A decision to cease work on the long-running printed *Statutes in force* and to transfer resources to the development of the online database was announced in June 1993.[29] In 1998, *Refer* reported that the database was fully revised to 1992. The story may be traced in the regular 'SCOOP news' columns in *Refer*.

Bibliographic control
Digital versions of print bibliographic products appeared at this time. The Chadwyck-Healey *Catalogue of British official publications not published by HMSO* (*CoBOP*) issued CD-ROM versions both for the 1990s and retrospectively for the 1980s. *CoBoP* also combined with the HMSO listings to produce *UK official publications* (*UKOP*) on CD-ROM, introduced in 1990; this increased in frequency from four to six issues per year in 1996. *UKOP online* was launched in April 1998, comprising an archive CD-ROM and online access to monthly updates.[30] HMSO's bibliographic database appeared as a file on DIALOG in the early nineties but later was withdrawn owing to lack of use.

The Ford Collection of British Official Publications at Southampton University set up *New UK official publications online* (*NUKOP online*) in 1995 and offered a free trial. In 1998, *NUKOP* was re-launched as *British official publications current awareness service* (*BOPCAS*)[31] and Brackenbury reviewed developments in 1999.[32]

In 1995, HMSO loaded on to its website its subject catalogues and the contents and digests of selected Acts.[33]

Following HMSO privatization, TSO chose to maintain its predecessor's high bibliographic standards. In 1998, *Refer* reported that TSO was terminating *TSO in print* microfiche and that it would be publishing *subject* rather than *sectional* lists.[34] In January 2000, TSO launched a new-look *Daily list* and added a 'weekly abstracts' section in July.

While HMSO was not perfect, the alternatives were sometimes problematic and the move away from publishing with HMSO/TSO was of concern to the library profession.[35] Two cases in particular highlighted aspects of the problem, HSE Books,[36] and the changes to the *Business monitor* series (see below).

PARLIAMENTARY INFORMATION WORK AND LIBRARIANSHIP
Chris Pond
(*Parliamentary copyright, House of Commons, 2005*)

Introduction

This section is divided into two parts – the development of parliamentary information sources available to the public and the profession, and the progress of and changes in the House of Commons (and to some extent the House of Lords) Libraries, as being the main sources of information organized for parliamentarians. *It represents the author's own views, and not necessarily those of the House of Commons or its Library.*[37]

Parliamentary information sources

In 1991, the provision of material by Parliament was almost wholly in print form. The exceptions to this were the POLIS system, which had been inaugurated in 1979 (but which was not widely available outside Parliament), and the issue (from 1978) of public information by the House of Commons Public Information Office (PIO) through the Prestel viewdata service.[38] Apart from the PIO's telephone service, which by 1991 was answering 120,000 calls a year, Parliament relied for its external issue of documentation and information upon printed material, which with a few exceptions was controlled and executed by HMSO, a government trading fund, whose principal concern was increasingly not the more effective dissemination of material, but the protection of its revenue sources and cash flow. In this, parliamentary and statutory publications played a big part.

The theme of the 1990s was in large measure the repatriation to Parliament of the control of its own publications, and thus of its information-issuing policy, which had effectively been under the direction of HMSO since the 19th century.

A catalyst for this, in retrospect, and somewhat perversely, was the decision of HMSO (jointly with Chadwyck-Healey) in 1991–92 to issue Hansard on CD-ROM, then a relatively new technology. Various parts of the Library were using CD-ROM technology already, for instance, for newspapers, as an alternative to the clumsy and never-popular microforms. But it was seen by HMSO as a premium, leading-edge technology, into which Hansard, generated since 1988 by computer typesetting, could fit neatly and cheaply. It would also generate significant revenue; the first advertisement of this service in the annual catalogues was in 1994. HMSO had intended to charge the two Houses, and their Members, commercial rates for access to this information, which parliamentary staff and public money had generated, and of which Members and Parliament were likely to be the main customers. It may be said that this episode set alarm bells in Parliament ringing, and the opportunity was taken at the time of HMSO privatization in 1996 to restore to the two Houses full control of their own publishing activity.[39] The right of the citizen to economic access to parliamentary outputs took shape with the work of Electronic Publishing Group (see below).

Publications on the web

The two Houses had realized the potential of electronic publishing as early as 1978, when their Information Offices became information providers to the Prestel viewdata service. The infinitely greater possibilities offered by the internet had become apparent by about 1992. The URL <www.parliament.uk> was registered on 10 July 1995 and a website inaugurated over the following year. Certain Public Information Office publications (and parts of the *Weekly information bulletin*) had been presented via HMSO on the internet from the end of 1994, but without doubt, the seminal event in the greater availability of parliamentary documentation in this decade was the report of the Electronic Publishing Group in February 1996. The Group had been set up by the Commons Board of Management the previous year. In the context of received thinking of the early 1990s, its recommendations were far-reaching, and the salient recommendation that 'the full text of parliamentary publications be published free of charge on the internet', was revolutionary[40] – 'if anyone had suggested in 1990 that Acts, SIs, Select Committee reports ... would be available electronically and free of charge, he or she would quickly have been despatched to some bibliographical Bedlam'.[41] The recommendations of the group were actioned incrementally over the period 1996–1999 and by the end of the decade a practically complete library of parliamentary publications was available free on the <www.parliament.uk> website.

POLIS, the House of Commons Library's information database, which had started in 1979, was made available in an intranet browser version in 1999. This was to be carried over into the public internet site just into the new decade. From July 1998, Early Day Motions and their signatories had been available on the internet.

Locata

The *Locata* service of 1997 was developed by the software house, Infernet, and the House of Commons Public Information Office. This was a system to identify the constituency in which an address fell. It was built on technology developed in relation to the 1997 General Election campaign. It was intended at first to replace manual searching in the PIO itself, but was soon delivered over the intranet and internet. The system relieved the Library of some 15,000 enquiries a year.

The House of Commons Library

Accommodation

The Library moved its research service and ancillary staff to newly converted accommodation at 1 Derby Gate in May and June 1991. This much larger building facilitated an expansion of staff and resources. In March 1992, a new central reserve stock for the Library, the Lords Library, and the Record Office, was opened underneath the Queen Elizabeth Conference Centre.

Staff

Despite general retrenchment in the public service, staff in the HC Library grew from 140 in 1990 to 198 in 1999.[42] In the early 1990s, the bar on people in the librarian grades being promoted to research and other specialized grades was removed. From 1999, the requirement for certain postholders in the Library to possess library qualifications was gradually removed, as a recognition that segregation led to demarcation problems and blocks in career development, and that disciplines other than librarianship could provide the competencies necessary.[43]

Computerization

The first personal computers, mainly for statistical work, had appeared in the Library about 1987. By 1995 PCs were on the desks of almost every member of staff and, as well as dealing with office functions, were used for accessing internet information, as well as many more specific electronic sources of information, home-grown or bought in. The overall impact was substantially to increase the quality, timeliness, efficiency and utility of the Library's work. One colleague, returning to work in late 1997 after a five-year career break, reported that IT '... has left me with the odd impression of inhabiting two parallel but different time zones ... the nature of the work itself has changed little, [but] the methods of working have undergone something of a revolution'.[44]

This was facilitated by the Parliamentary Data and Video Network (PDVN). The PDVN came about following a debate in the House on 30 June 1994 which endorsed recommendations of the Information Committee[45] to create a permanent network, following a pilot service which had been in operation from 1992. By 1999 some 2,600 individuals in the House of Commons were connected: 188 MPs, nearly 1,200 Members' staff and more than 1,200 staff of the House. 148 Peers, 41 Peers' staff and 184 staff of the House of Lords were also connected.[46] User self-service was an aim of the last years of the 1990s.[47]

Research

A reorganization of the research service took place in January 1994. The provision of general and statistical economic briefing was integrated by the creation of a single new Economic Policy and Statistics Section, and there was a reallocation of staff and subjects elsewhere to maintain coherent and effective research teams of a readily manageable size. A Parliament & Constitution Centre was inaugurated in 1999 to promote cooperative working throughout the Department on these key issues.

Internal databases

Management information was greatly improved by the introduction between 1993 and 1995 of a computerized Enquiries database which allowed for the first time department-wide recording and tracing of Members' research enquiries, to provide more and better information than previously, on the volume, source, subjects and speed of turnover of enquiry work. This was carried on a variation of BASIS, which also supplied the POLIS platform.[48] A new European Scrutiny Database was implemented in the spring of 1999. It greatly improved access to detailed inform- ation concerning the scrutiny of draft European legislation and other proposals in a database that was compatible with POLIS.

External databases

Electronicization of the delivery of press material was still being considered. In the meantime, press cutting and filing continued manually as it had since the 1960s. It was thought that commercial databases were too broad-brush for the Library, and especially its researchers, who needed to be able to isolate articles with significant content to the exclusion of less important material. They were also thought to be much too expensive and the currency of some of them was doubted. An optical disk press cuttings system was seriously considered, but rejected on copyright and feasibility grounds. The eventual result of this need was the Press Comment Database, a home-grown system, with material being selected by practitioners in the Reference and Reader Services and International Affairs and Defence Sections. This was inaugurated in 1998, with access via the intranet.

POLIS

In 1994, the third version of POLIS was to be delivered through the fledgling network, in order to encourage Members needing access to POLIS to use the PDVN. In the run-up to POLIS III, 1992–93, there were over 100 registered dial- up accounts for Members and their staff, used mostly by staff. It was when a browser-driven version of POLIS was developed in March 1999 that the POLIS became available to all network users.

The e-library

In 1999, the new parliamentary building, Portcullis House, was completed.[49] The Department here inaugurated what was called the e-library; a training area for IT, plus a bank of eight PCs in cyber café style. These became very popular, not so much with Members, but with staff. They certainly popularized electronic searching.

Research papers on the net

In 1998, the Library's published papers – Research papers – were made available via the internet. In part, this was a response to pressures on staff time in despatching these documents to an ever-growing mailing list – not this time of Members, who simply picked up their copies in the Library, but outside collaborators, academics, researchers, and other parliamentary libraries. The burden of despatching hard copy had become oppressive, so the solution adopted was to present the documents on the internet and allow people to use them at will. In fact, this was a significant milestone in making information about current parlia- mentary activity better known on a worldwide basis, such that the texts received

420,000 hits in the first year of reliable statistics, 2001/02 (by 2004/05 this had risen to 887,000).[50]

The Lords Library

Many of the developments that affected the Commons Library had their counterpart in the Lords. Networking the CD-ROM collection on the PDVN was one area where the Lords led. In retrospect, this was an intermediate technology, but it did much to popularize electronic searching. The Lords Library had always placed more emphasis on its catalogue than did the Commons; it was presented in electronic form, complete, and accessible to all users, by 1995.

GOVERNMENT DEPARTMENTS AND AGENCIES
Valerie Nurcombe

Butcher summarized the main types of central government publishing from a wide range of departments, agencies and other bodies in 1991.[51] The annual *Civil Service yearbook* recorded changes affecting government departments, including the many changes of name after the 1997 General Election. The establishment of thirty executive agencies under the 'Next Steps' initiative by 1990, rising to 105 by 2000, marked a significant change in the management of government.[52] Each carried out specific functions for their sponsoring department and many were important publishers. Changes to the wider range of public bodies were recorded in the annual *Public bodies*, which listed almost 2000 executive, advisory and other official bodies in 1991.[53]

Changes of name and departmental responsibilities caused difficulty for anyone working with official publications. The Office of Arts and Libraries, the Department of National Heritage and the Department for Culture, Media and Sport were successively responsible for libraries in the 1990s. Goodier summarized responsibilities for environmental matters in 1993.[54] There were many agencies and official bodies in this sphere with varying status and lifespans, such as: Nature Conservancy Council (until 1991), Countryside Commission (Countryside Agency from April 1999), Ordnance Survey, English Heritage, Forestry Commission, Building Research Establishment (privatized 1997) and HM Inspectorate of Pollution. These bodies published directly, or used commercial publishers or HMSO/TSO according to the nature of the item.

Several factors increased the fragmentation of publishing by departments and agencies. HMSO became a trading fund in 1986 and had to tender for departmental publishing contracts, which it did not always win. HMSO lost many publications, including Department of Energy, Cabinet Office[55] and Audit Commission titles,[56] and Health & Safety Executive publications.[57] Market testing led to the transfer of several key publications, such as *British business* and *Employment gazette*, to the private sector.[58] The move to more open government encouraged publishing by government organizations of all types and in all ways, including many free publications outside the scope of HMSO/TSO.[59] Some publications from government departments were hard to obtain or became restricted to particular groups, such as DTI export publications.[60] SCOOP was concerned at the increase in non-HMSO published titles and the consequent decline in standards of publishing; it issued guidance in 1992 that temporarily improved bibliographic coverage and standards of bibliographic content.[61] The most significant change was the growth of electronic publishing by official publishers, first on CD-ROM or floppy disk and later on the internet.

Only a limited amount of government information was available electronically in 1990. Several databases from government departments were available from online hosts such as Dialog, DataStar, ESA-IRS and FT Profile. Prestel contained over 10,000 pages of government information aimed at the wider public. The number of CD-ROM products grew substantially. HMSO had already begun publishing topic-based CD-ROMs such as OSH (mainly Department of Health and Health and Safety Executive) and Fire. CD-ROM compilations, such as the PLATO database of poisonous plants, and searchable texts of standard printed works like the *British pharmacopeia*, were seen as the way forward. Some departments issued CD-ROMs without using TSO, such as the Department of the Environment's reference work on housing.[62]

Government use of the internet developed from 1995 when the Treasury made the budget and circulars available. Departments like the Ministry of Agriculture, Fisheries and Food (MAFF) embraced the internet as a means of getting advice to their public (though most of it was available in print as well). The open government site <www.open.gov.uk> was a portal providing access to government websites from 1995. By 2000 many government departments and agencies published partly on the web and partly in print; websites such as that of the Countryside Agency offered some titles in PDF format and the rest in print, but without an online ordering facility. Some older, but still current, publications were available in PDF format on the web. TSO publications for departments still tended to be mainly in hard copy and were rarely found on departmental websites, most of which included only their own publishing output.

Archiving of web content began to be considered as, for the first time, it was realized some publications no longer appeared in print. SCOOP expressed fears that some internet publications could disappear from mid-1996.[63] A consultation paper appeared in 1997 from the Department of National Heritage but no action had been taken by 2000.[64]

Statistics

Most major statistical publications such as *Annual abstract of statistics* or *Social trends* remained with HMSO/TSO. The new Office for National Statistics (ONS)[65] reviewed many statistical series. The *General household survey* appeared less regularly and the 2000 survey was redesigned.[66] ONS produced a useful *Guide to official statistics* in 1996 and a revised edition in 2000.[67] Many government departments continued to produce and publish their own statistics.[68]

The Rayner reviews in the 1980s had cut back statistical publishing, especially social statistics, but business statistics were also affected. Some quarterly *Business monitors* became annual in 1990, although still HMSO publications.[69] By 1995 the publishing contract was awarded to Taylor Nelson and costs for the renamed *UK markets* (91 annual and 34 quarterly reports) doubled. ONS moved the *Business monitors* back to TSO,[70] but transferred them to their own publishing unit at Newport in April 1998.[71]

The issue of the 1991 Census on CD-ROM was described as a 'unique opportunity' in official publishing[72] but this was published by Chadwyck-Healey, who had also issued a 1981 Census CD-ROM in 1992 (HMSO still produced the printed volumes). This new style of presentation was a challenge for libraries in making them available to their public.

Tracking publications

Government publishing remained fragmented with organizations publishing some items through HMSO/TSO and some themselves (both priced and free). HMSO publications were listed daily, monthly and annually as well as in UKOP. Until the mid-1990s HMSO issued Sectional Lists covering its own and occasionally some non-HMSO publications from departments and agencies. They were replaced by subject lists from TSO but lost their prominence as efficient retrieval tools.[73] For libraries the HMSO/TSO Selective Subscription Service was a good way of ensuring a collection of the major official publications. Changes after HMSO became a trading fund, and especially after privatization, meant its output was increasingly parliamentary and statutory and less inclusive of central government publications.

Many departments continued to produce their own printed lists of publications, but these faded as the internet developed and few survived by 2000. DTI admitted that in 1994 their list was not comprehensive when they set up their Publications Unit to list and distribute everything.[74] There was a catalogue and order points, but by 2000 these had gone owing to economies. Publications lists on the internet were not necessarily complete and none included older relevant publications. Some government websites listed publications in one location, but in others they were scattered. The SIGLE database provided access to some government report literature and other 'grey' literature. UKOP was the only listing of all items from the government no matter who had published them, although many departmental items were known to be missed. An analysis of its central departmental content between 1980 and 2000 showed that 90% of the items were not published by HMSO/TSO.[75]

The decade was one of constant change influenced mainly by market forces and by the attempts to realize the opportunities of the new internet. The movements of statistical publishing showed this most clearly. SCOOP began a series of seminars in 1988, with published proceedings, which formed the main resource for coverage of official publications in the nineties.[76]

DEVOLUTION AND THE DEVOLVED ADMINISTRATIONS
David Butcher

Devolution in the late 1990s led to a significant expansion of official publishing, with new elected bodies in Scotland, Wales and Northern Ireland. The Labour Party's proposals for devolution were set out in its 1997 election manifesto.[77] White papers were published in July 1997[78] and referendums held in Scotland and Wales in September. Legislation in 1998 set the framework for devolution, specifying the powers and responsibilities of the new bodies and those reserved to the Westminster Parliament.[79] The Cabinet Office issued a series of *Devolution guidance notes* in 2000 providing advice on the working arrangements between the UK government and the devolved administrations.[80]

Scotland
The first Scottish Parliament (SP) since 1707 was elected in May 1999 and received its powers on 1 July. It had a single chamber with 129 members (MSPs), elected for a four-year term. The new SP had powers to pass primary as well secondary legislation and to vary the rate of taxation. The full Parliament normally met for one-and-a-half days each week, but much work was carried out by committees. These conducted inquiries, considered Bills in detail, scrutinized the work of the Scottish Executive, and could also suggest new legislation. Eight mandatory committees were appointed as well as a similar number of subject committees that considered such matters as equal opportunities, rural development and transport and environment. The Scottish Executive was the devolved government of Scotland, responsible for the government departments and spending. It was led by the First Minister, with around twenty ministers and law officers chosen from the party with a majority of seats in the SP.

Parliamentary publishing was quite similar to the Westminster model with a daily *Business bulletin*, a weekly digest of *What's happening in the Scottish Parliament*, verbatim *Official reports* of proceedings in the full Parliament and in committees and a *Written answers report*.[81] Bills and Explanatory Notes were published separately, as were Acts of the Scottish Parliament and their Explanatory Notes. The Scottish Parliament website was the principal source for proceedings and other documents.[82] The full text of Acts and their Explanatory Notes, as well as Scottish Statutory Instruments, were on the Scotland Legislation website.[83] The Stationery Office was awarded the contract for the main hard copy publications. These were included in the *Daily list* and the bibliography of *Scottish Parliamentary and statutory publications* (which also covered documents not published by TSO).[84] The Partner Library network was set up 'in each of the 73 constituencies to act as a focus for information about the Parliament at a local level'.[85] These were public library service points that could receive sets of printed SP publications and make them available to the public. Staff at the SP Information Centre also provided an enquiry support service to Partner Libraries.

Wales

Wales was offered a devolved assembly rather than a parliament, with no powers to make primary legislation. The sixty members of the National Assembly for Wales (NAfW) were elected in May 1999 and served for a four-year term. The Assembly received its powers in July 1999. It could develop and implement policy in a wide range of areas such as education, health, the environment, planning and transport.[86] The Assembly met in two half-day plenary sessions a week and in committees. Several types of committees were appointed: standing committees included those on audit, equality of opportunity, European affairs, legislation and standards of conduct; subject committees for education, agriculture, economic development, health and local government; and four regional committees that represented the interests of their localities. Executive powers were exercised by a Cabinet comprising the First Secretary and eight Assembly Secretaries with responsibility for individual subject areas.

Two significant differences between NAfW and devolved bodies elsewhere were that proceedings and most publications were bilingual and its decision (partly on cost grounds) to publish most of its information only electronically.[87] The Assembly *Record of proceedings* was the principal publication; it appeared in two versions: a 24-hour edition with contributions in the language used by each speaker; and a fully bilingual edition within five working days. There was a greater delay in producing bilingual editions of committee minutes, reports and papers. Each committee had its own page on the NAfW website where its papers were listed by subject. An *Annual list of National Assembly for Wales publications* was published for 1999 and monthly lists began in 2000.[88] The Wales Information Link was launched in May 2000 with public libraries in each constituency providing internet access and printouts of web screens of Assembly publications.[89]

Northern Ireland

Northern Ireland had its own parliament with full legislative powers from its creation in 1921 until 1973. A Northern Ireland Assembly was set up in 1973 but collapsed within a year and subsequently the province was mainly ruled directly from Westminster.[90] An Assembly was set up in 1982 but was dissolved in 1986. A new Northern Ireland Assembly (NIA) was elected in June 1998, following the Belfast Agreement.[91] This met from July 1998 and had 108 members, but did not receive full legislative and executive powers until December 1999, when a government was formed. This was headed by a First Minister and Deputy First Minister, with ten ministers drawn from the four largest parties.

Proceedings of the NIA were recorded in the *Official report* from July 1998. The Assembly considered bills and passed its first five Acts in 2000, despite being suspended from February to May.[92] Eleven reports were published directly by the Assembly prior to receiving devolved powers, but subsequent reports and the *Official report* were printed by TSO and included in the *Daily list*. Several committees were established and their minutes, evidence and reports were, like the

Official report, made available in full text on the Assembly's website and printed by TSO.[93]

The English regions
Devolution did not progress as far in the English regions as in Scotland, Wales and Northern Ireland. Several bodies were created during the 1990s and a White Paper on regional government was issued in 1997.[94] The Government Offices for the Regions were established in 1994 to coordinate the activities of government departments in each region and to work with regional partners. Eight Regional Development Agencies were established in April 1999 to promote economic development and regeneration.[95] Regional Chambers were set up at the same time; they were consultative bodies comprising councillors from local authorities and representatives from other sectors in the region.

London was the only region to have its own government and elected assembly, following a White Paper in 1998 and legislation in 1999.[96] The Greater London Authority was established in April 2000 with responsibility for planning, economic development, transport, policing, fire and emergency services, culture, environment and health.[97] The London Assembly was elected in May 2000 with 25 members to scrutinize the work of the Mayor and discuss issues affecting London. Records of meetings of the Assembly and its committees, scrutiny reports and other papers were made available on the Assembly website.[98]

LOCAL AUTHORITY PUBLISHING[99]
Jane Inman

In the 1986–1990 volume of *British librarianship and information work* two tools were listed as recording the output of local authorities. These were ACOMPLINE,[100] published by the London Research Centre and SIGLE (System for Information on Grey Literature in Europe) developed by the British Library.

ACOMPLINE was described in 1990 as the 'practical national database centre for local authority publications' and along with the complementary database URBALINE covered all aspects of social and urban policy. Both databases were maintained by the London Research Centre Library which became the Research Library of the Greater London Authority (GLA) in 2000 with the formation of the GLA.

SIGLE covered non-conventional or grey literature issued informally throughout the European Union (EU) member countries and was begun in 1980. It had an inclusion policy which meant that it only collected local authority publications selectively. The British Library (BL) was the largest contributor to SIGLE; all the BL records related to material held by the Document Supply Centre and these appeared in the British Library's Integrated Catalogue.

SCOOP (the Standing Committee on Official Publishing), part of the Information Services Group (ISG) of the Library Association, held regular meetings throughout this period and encouraged good practice in the dissemination of official information. The journal of the ISG, *Refer*, carried a regular column describing the work of SCOOP and is a useful source of information on the topic. SCOOP had issued its *Guidelines on the preparation of local authority publications*[101] in 1989 and these continued to be the main source of information on this topic for local authorities. A third edition of SCOOP's guide to *Local authority information sources* was published in 1992.[102]

ALGIS (the Affiliation of Local Government Information Specialists) was established as an informal group in 1988 and in 1991 was accepted as a Special Interest Group of the Institute of Information Scientists. Its objectives were 'to raise awareness of the potential and actual benefits of the work of information specialists within local government' and 'to improve the effectiveness of inform-ation specialists within local government'. ALGIS, whose members included researchers, information scientists and librarians, aimed to act as a network for the exchange of ideas through meetings, events and a regular newsletter.[103]

The British Library's Official Publications and Social Sciences Reading Room was finally open in the new British Library building in St Pancras at the end of June 1999. The service was operated by the Social Policy Information Service (SPIS) which had been established in 1996. With a new building to work from SPIS was able to offer the kind of service it had been set up to deliver, providing improved access to the British Library's social sciences collection and assisting in the dissemination of current research results to practitioners and policy makers.[104] The major change to local authority information during this period was in the use of the web. During the 1990s there was increasing use of information technology, the internet and email by local government and by the end of the decade many local authorities were publishing material online via the world wide web.

SOCITM (the Society of Council Information Technology Managers), founded in 1986, had been producing annual reviews of IT trends in local government from its inception. In 1999 SOCITM published its first review of local authority websites, *Well-connected? A snapshot of local authority web sites.*[105] It found that 75% of authorities had websites. By the time the next survey was published this had risen to 95%.[106]

Bedfordshire County Council's Local Government Information Service pro-duced a briefing note on *The internet and local authorities* in 1995 in which it developed a SWOT analysis of the internet as a publishing tool as well as describing and defining the web and related technology.[107] In 1999 the London Research Centre published a report called *London local government in the information society.*[108] This looked at the progress made by London Boroughs in developing their use of information and communication technology. It showed that in 1997 only 19 boroughs had a website of any sort but that by 1999 every London borough was represented on the web and use of email amongst staff in the London Boroughs had increased over the same period by 32%.

A further development in the dissemination of local authority information was the creation in 1992 of LGCNet, a web-based news and information service produced by the publishers of the *Local government chronicle* magazine.[109] This subscription service provided current awareness on all aspects of local government and gradually built into an archive of information.

The end of the decade saw the Freedom of Information Act passed.[110] The Advisory Group on Openness in the Public Sector (AGOPS) published its final report in 1999.[111] The group had been established in March 1999 to advise the Home Secretary on developing a culture of openness in the public sector and on the implementation of the Freedom of Information Act generally. The report recommended a publicity campaign to make the public and public sector employees aware of the implications of the Act, increasing the publication of information through publication schemes and encouraging use of the legislation. The Home Office was charged with creating a culture of openness before the legislation came into force.

EUROPEAN UNION
Grace L. Hudson

Provision of European Union (EU) information was marked most notably by the increasing move to electronic dissemination, initially through command language dial-up services, later using CD-ROM format and more recently via the internet. Alongside the technical changes a number of key policy developments in Europe had a major impact on both the range and content of the information as well as the information providers themselves.

The completion of the Single Market by 1992,[112] the adoption of the Treaty on European Union (Maastricht Treaty)[113] – introducing new legal terminology – and later the Treaty of Amsterdam,[114] together with the creation of the euro[115] produced a wealth of related information. As well as key official publications[116] a number of valuable secondary sources[117] sought to record and explain the changes. The UK held the Presidency of the EU twice in the decade, in the latter half of 1992 and during the first half of 1998, raising the profile of EU affairs in the UK. The initial rejection of the Maastricht Treaty in the Danish referendum and the 'petit oui' of the French vote sent shock waves through the European Communities, providing the impetus to review the information and communications strategy.[118] The conclusions of the Council meetings in Lisbon and Edinburgh in 1992,[119] and the Birmingham Declaration[120] which called for a more informed debate, introduced a new vocabulary – subsidiarity,[121] openness and transparency[122] – and the determination to improve communication and information dissemination. The De Clercq report reviewing existing practice was followed by a number of Commission communications and reports to develop a new policy.[123] The Pex report later re-examined the situation.[124] Practical examples were proposals for simplification and codification of legislation, greater use of discussion documents (green papers) to be published in the *COM series*, decentralization of information work, more user-friendly and accessible databases, improved coordination of the network, the publication of a directory of relays, reorganization of DG X, a one-stop shop approach to information provision, and the recommendation to allow public access to documents. A code of practice on access to documents was produced,[125] followed by a formal proposal for a regulation.[126] Gradually evidence emerged of other recommended initiatives being implemented.[127]

In the UK the Commission London Office organized a conference of EU information providers at Stoke Rochford in 1993, to consider how to coordinate information provision here.[128] Gallup surveys for the European Commission investigated how people found EU information and highlighted the value of strengthening provision via the public library system.[129] A follow-up initiative of the Local Government International Bureau brought together local authorities and the EC London Office. The Federation of Local Authority Chief Librarians (FOLACL) committed themselves to working in partnership with the EC London Office and in 1994 the new Public Information Relays (PIRs) were launched, offering a three-tier approach from basic provision in branch libraries to more in-depth support in major reference libraries.[130] Free publications and training were provided, with an agreement for discounts on priced titles. Previously the EC Offices had dealt directly with the public but their role altered as information provision was devolved more to the relays and there was a formal name change to Representation of the Commission in the UK. A conference in January 1995 was the genesis of the UK Network of European Relays.[131] Printed directories[132] were later supplemented by the launch of the website which provided regional contact details and an intranet.[133]

In 1991 the European Information Association (EIA) was launched.[134] It grew out of the professional organization, the Association of EDC Librarians, but had a wider remit to include all organizations with an interest in EC information. It offered training and publications to support information providers through the European maze.[135] That same year the commercial consultancy and conference organizer Relay Europe was established.[136] It ran the mobile unit which toured the country, taking EC information to the regions and arranged delivery of a programme of training to the new PIRs, which were later re-launched in 1999 as European Public Information Centres (EPICs). The European Documentation Centres (EDCs),[137] Euro Info Centres (EICs)[138] and the PIRs were joined by three other official relays: the Carrefours for rural information,[139] the Value Relays[140] (later renamed Innovation Relay Centres) and specifically in the UK at the instigation of the Representation of the EC, the European Reference Centres for Schools and Colleges.[141] Though the number of networks was proliferating, each was aimed at a very specific audience. EDCs were required to sign an agreement with the Commission and were evaluated twice by questionnaire. Training seminars in Brussels,[142] annual meetings of national representatives and an exchange programme were introduced for EDCs as part of the Commission's plan to encourage networking.[143] After reorganization of DG X, EDCs came under the unit responsible for the Commission Libraries, which to many felt a better fit.[144]

No reduction in numbers resulted in the UK from the evaluation or the reflection paper, which reconsidered the role of EDCs.[145]

The most significant development of the decade was the explosion in electronic provision of information, and the free accessibility of increasingly user-friendly sources, many of them offering the full text of documents. The Europa website was launched in 1995 in a small way but its usage grew exponentially and by 2000 it contained more than 1.5 million documents.[146] The reorganization of Directorates General and the decision to move to descriptive titles rather than numbers following the election of the new Commission in 1999 required major changes to the structure of the site.

In 1992 DG XXIII selected Aslib as one of the National Awareness Partners under the IMPACT II programme to work with ECHO in raising awareness of the availability and use of online services.[147] ECHO acted also as a pilot for new databases, some of which ultimately became fully-fledged resources and migrated to other hosts. The suite of CORDIS R+D databases for example was made freely available on its own server. ECHO closed in 1998 when it was considered to have achieved its purpose. TED, the key database on public tenders and the exception to ECHO's free availability policy, continued as the responsibility of EUR-OP (formerly OOPEC), finally becoming freely available in 1999.[148]

The important Bangemann report and resulting action plan were concerned chiefly with the 'information superhighway' infrastructure, but there was other evidence of the impact of the information policy recommendations.[149] Database training was decentralized and the EIA, working jointly with EDIT, and Admiral Training were the successful bidders for the Eurobases tender in the UK. The EIA delivered courses directly for Eurobases and later on behalf of the national gateway Context Ltd when Eurobases established local gateways to supply helpdesk support and invoicing.[150] Simpler database interfaces were developed. A menu-driven version of the legal database CELEX, and then later a web interface, was produced, dispensing with the complex Mistral command language.[151]

Like ECHO, Eurobases also closed at the end of 1998. The RAPID press releases database had already moved to the web, but other Eurobases sources were either merged or completely revamped.[152] EUR-OP retained responsibility for CELEX. APC was relaunched on the web as Pre-Lex, monitoring the legislative process, but SCAD was closed with some content being transferred to ECLAS, the catalogue of the Commission Libraries. CELEX continued to hold information about national implementing measures,[153] and with the availability of the full text of Statutory Instruments on the HMSO website direct access to UK measures transposing Directives became easier. The EUDOR electronic archive and document delivery service was developed, containing most of the full text of the *Official journal* of the European Communities. While CELEX remained a subscription service, a new free legal portal, EUR-Lex, was established, initially with the last 20 days of the *Official journal L* and *C*;[154] links to EUDOR, the treaties and the Court of Justice site for case law from 1997; and consolidated legislation. Though limited at first, it quickly expanded but decisions about charging for some material remained under discussion. The Council opened a public register of documents in 1999[155] and the European Parliament made its OEIL database available. The CELEX User Group, later renamed the Eurobases User Group and then the EU Databases User Group, monitored database provision and lobbied for improvements.[156]

Publication of some items in the *Official journal C series* was moved to a new *OJ CE* series produced only in electronic format. A new hybrid CD-ROM of the *Official journal* provided PDF files of the full text with links to Europa for updates.[157] The *Debates of the European Parliament* ceased in print in 1999, being produced instead on the internet or on CD-ROM. Distribution of the printed version of the *Official journal* was withdrawn from EDCs in 2000, although print remained the legally authentic text in the UK. The Eurotext project created a database of digitized key documents for academic use, available on the web and on CD-ROM.[158]

Significant cuts were made in the distribution of the printed Eurostat statistical publications to the information relays, resulting in major gaps in collections. Although concern was expressed, there was no redress and the cost to purchase was prohibitive for most of the official networks. With the exception of the limited but free EUROCRON database and the later publication of some free data on the internet, the provision of statistical information remained an issue throughout the period.[159] Eurostat Index continued to be a useful way in to the content.[160] When the Data Shop Network was established for the dissemination of Eurostat data, r.cade joined the Office for National Statistics in the UK as one of the two official providers.[161] Arrangements were made to allow academic access to the data via r.cade but the agreements were complex and unsatisfactory. Free distribution to EDCs of the Eudorstat CD-ROM also proved disappointing due to technical problems. HMSO, later TSO, remained the UK agent for the purchase of both Eurostat and other official publications of the EU.

On the commercial front, the field was highly competitive with Context, Ellis Publications, ILI and Technical Indexes offering versions of the CELEX database, and generally SCAD as well.[162] CELEX was also accessible through DataStar, LexisNexis and FT Profile, while the Norwegian company Lovdata was the first to produce a web version. Chadwyck-Healey launched Eurocat CD-ROM, a bibliographic catalogue of publications. The DTI Spearhead database on the Single Market remained extremely useful and was included in some commercial CD-ROMs as well as through online hosts such as FT Profile. All providers sought to add value to the official sources through improved interfaces and additional content, later offering web access as well as CD-ROM.[163] With the development of the internet and the substantial amount of freely available full text content on Europa, a new generation of web-based resources – EU Direct, EU Interactive and KnowEurope – appeared.[164] These made heavy use of hyperlinks to manage, and create pathways through, the overwhelming volume of material available. The key current awareness bulletin *European access,* containing valuable bibliographic reviews, moved from print to the web as *European access plus,* before transforming further into the largely full text source KnowEurope. Despite the pressure on commercial suppliers from free sources, they still had a role to provide reliable, added-value services. However, takeovers reduced the number of players in the field. The Spicers Centre for Europe database was developed into EU Interactive, as part of Lawtel; Thomson, owners of Westlaw, bought Ellis Publications; and LexisNexis acquired FT Profile.

Europe Direct was established as a one-stop contact point for questions about Europe from the general public.[165] Using a freephone telephone number people could ask for information in their own language. Discussion lists provided a self-help solution for information professionals. The groundbreaking Eurodoc, established in 1994, was aimed at EDCs worldwide, while the EIA's Eurotalk, launched in 1996, had a wider scope.[166]

Though the decade saw huge growth in – increasingly free – electronic provision, concerns remained over accessibility for all and the lack of archiving policies to ensure long-term availability of material.[167]

Notes

For information on developments in the UK official publications area it is worth consulting issues of *Refer*. Also, the British section of the 'Notable documents' issues of the *Journal of government information* and its predecessor *Government publications review* contain brief overviews of the state of official publishing.

1   David Butcher, 'British official publishing today: departmental publishing' in *Official publishing in the nineties*, ed. Valerie J. Nurcombe. London: Library Association Information Services Group, 1998, pp. 27–37.

2   Alastair Allan, *The myth of government information*. London: Library Association, 1990.

3   Alastair Allan, 'Government information and the winds of change' in *Official publishing in the nineties*, ed. Nurcombe, pp.108–16.

4   Cabinet Office, *Open government*. London: HMSO, 1993 (Cm 2290); For a reference copy of the Code of practice (later superseded by the FOI Act 2000) and annual reports from 1998, see the DCA website: <http://www.dca.gov.uk/foi/codpracgi.htm> (accessed 31/1/06).

5   Cabinet Office, *government.direct: a prospectus for the electronic delivery of government services*. London: TSO, 1996 (Cm 3438) (reviewed in 'SCOOP news', *Refer* **13** (1), 1997, 21–2).

6   House of Lords, Select Committee on Science and Technology (Session 1995–96), *Information society: agenda for action in the UK: fifth report*. London: HMSO, 1996 (HL 77) (reviewed in 'SCOOP news', *Refer* **13** (1), 1997, 22–3). The Government response appeared in Cm 3450 (Nov. 1996).

7   Cabinet Office, *Your right to know*. London: TSO, 1997.

8   *Freedom of Information Act 2000*. London: TSO, 2000.

9   *Data Protection Act 1998*. London: TSO, 1998.

10   Cabinet Office, *Modernising government*. London: TSO, 1999; Cabinet Office, *e-government: a strategic framework for public services in the information age*. London: Central IT Unit, 2000.

11   National Audit Office, *Government on the web*. London: TSO, 1999.

12   HM Treasury, *Cross-cutting review of the knowledge economy: review of government information: final report*. Available at: <http://www.hm-treasury.gov.uk./spending_review/spending_review_2000/associated_documents/spend_sr00_ad_ccrcontents.cfm> (accessed 1/2/06).

13   Cabinet Office, *Crown copyright in the information age* <http://www.opsi.gov.uk/advice/crown-copyright/crown-copyright-in-the-information-age.pdf> (accessed 1/2/06); Library Association, *Response to green paper on Crown copyright*. London: LA, 1998; Cabinet Office, *The future management of Crown copyright*. London: TSO, 1999 (Cm 4300). See also 'SCOOP news', *Refer* **15** (2), 1999, 22–5; Gordon Robbie, 'Crown copyright and HMSO', *Refer* **9** (2), 1993, 2–6.

14   'SCOOP news', *Refer* **15** (2), 1999, 24–5; 'SCOOP news', *Refer* **15** (3), 1999, 33.

15   John Pullinger, 'The creation of the Office for National Statistics', *Statistical news* **17**, 1997, 11–19; House of Commons, Treasury Committee (Session 1998–99), *First report: Office for National Statistics*. London: TSO, 1998 (HC 43–I–II) (reviewed in 'SCOOP news', *Refer* **15** (2), 1999, 20–2); Office for National Statistics, *Framework for national statistics*. London: TSO, 2000.

16   HM Treasury, *Statistics: a matter of trust: a consultation document*. London: TSO, 1998 (Cm 3882); HM Treasury, *Building trust in statistics*. London: TSO, 1999 (Cm 4412).

17   'SCOOP news', *Refer* **10** (1), 1994, 29; **10** (2), 1994, 30–1.

18   'SCOOP news', *Refer* **12** (1), 1996, 22–3.

19   Howard Picton, 'The privatisation of HMSO', *Refer* **12** (3), 1996, 2–14.

20   House of Commons, Committee of Public Accounts (Session 1997–98). *The sale of the Stationery Office: forty-ninth report*. London: TSO, 1998 (HC 599).

21   Alan Pawsey, 'HMSO: the residuary body' in *Official publishing in the nineties*, ed. Nurcombe, pp. 57–67; Alan Pawsey, 'Official publishing: the challenge of the internet and the HMSO approach' in *Official publishing: past present & future: SCOOP 30 years on anniversary seminar*, ed. Valerie Nurcombe. London: CILIP Information Services Group, 2002, pp. 43–51.

22   'SCOOP news', *Refer* **13** (1), 1997, 24–5; **13** (3), 1997, 25–6; **14** (2), 1998, 18; **15** (1) 1999, 26–7; David Rowell, 'From HMSO to TSO' in *Official publishing: past present & future*, ed. Nurcombe, pp. 21–7.

23   David Butcher, 'Official and legal information on CD-ROM', *Refer* **8** (1), 1992, 18–22.

24   David Butcher and Valerie Nurcombe, 'Two recent CD-ROMs: Hansard and Environmental Health', *Refer* **10** (1), 1994, 13–18, 25.

25   Gillian Evans and David Butcher, 'JUSTIS Parliament on CD-ROM', *Refer* **10** (3), 1994, 7–10.

26   'SCOOP news', *Refer* **11** (3), 1995, 29. Picton reviewed the situation in 1997: Howard Picton, 'The internet and official publishing' in *Official publishing in the nineties*, ed. Nurcombe, pp. 102–7.

27   *Guidelines for government websites.* For latest guidelines see:
      <http://www.cabinetoffice.gov.uk/e-
      government/resources/handbook/introduction.asp> (accessed 31/1/06).

28   Dan Jellinek, *Official UK: the essential guide to government websites.* London: TSO,
      1998 (reviewed in *Refer* **15** (3), 1999, 26–7).

29   House of Lords Hansard, 9/6/93, 546 no. 50, col. WA55; Howard Picton, 'The Statute
      Law Database and Statutes in Force: the current position', *Refer* **10** (1), 1994, 8–12.

30   Mark Barragry, 'Chadwyck-Healey: bibliographic control' in *Official publishing in
      the nineties,* ed. Nurcombe, pp. 68–71; Liz Marley, 'Chadwyck-Healey: COBOP and
      UKOP' in *Official publishing in the nineties,* ed. Nurcombe, pp. 72–5; 'SCOOP
      news', *Refer* **14** (2), 1998, 18.

31   'SCOOP news', *Refer* **14** (2), 1998, 18–19. This became available at
      <www.soton.ac.uk/~bopcas/feature.htm>. The emphasis was always on the social
      sciences. See also: B. Thackray, 'Survey reveals increasing importance of British
      Official Publications Current Awareness Service', *Managing information* **5** (9), 1998,
      28–9.

32   Simon Brackenbury, 'Tracking recent British official publications with BOPCAS',
      Refer **15** (1), 1999, 2–6.

33   'SCOOP news', *Refer* **11** (3), 1995, 27–8.

34   'SCOOP news', *Refer* **15** (3), 1999, 31.

35   The problems were touched upon in John Goodier, 'The green and the grey:
      government environmental publications', *Refer* **7** (2), 1991, 1–6, and in the
      introduction to their list of 'notable documents': Simon Brackenbury and Simon de
      Montfalcon, 'Great Britain and Northern Ireland', *Journal of government information*
      27 (6), 2000, 831–41.

36   Andrew Coburn, 'Issues in bibliographic control' in *Official publishing in the
      nineties,* ed. Nurcombe, pp. 15–26; Alastair Allan and Howard Picton, 'An open letter
      on the standards of service of HSE Books', *Refer* **12** (2), 1996, 13–18; 'SCOOP
      news', *Refer* **9** (3), 1993, 31; **10** (1), 1994, 29; **11** (3), 1995, 26; **13** (3), 1997, 26–7.

37   Generally, see David Menhennet, *The House of Commons Library: a history,* 2nd ed.,
      with additional material by Rob Clements and Chris Pond. Westminster: TSO, 2000,
      which contains a useful chapter (7) on developments of the 1990s.

38   See Chris Pond, 'British official publishing in the internet age', *Aslib proceedings* **52**
      (6), 2000, 200–6.

39   Papers (unpublished) in the files of the Journal Office, House of Commons.

40   *Electronic publication of House of Commons documents* (HC 328 1995–96), ix.

41   Pond, 'British official publishing', 201.

42   Menhennet, *House of Commons Library,* 160.

43   For a resumé of this from 1988, see House of Commons Internal Review Services,
      Department of the Library: review of the Reference and Reader Services Section,
      2000, 20–2 (unpublished).

44   Kim Greener, in *LHC* (*staff magazine of the HC Library*) **6** (1), Whitsun 1998, 31.

45   House of Commons, Information Committee, *Provision of a parliamentary data and
      video network: 1st report … .* London: HMSO, 1994 (HC 237 1993–94).

46   Quoted in Menhennet, *House of Commons Library,* p. 139.

47   This was especially relevant after 2000, but its origins were in the1990s. See House of
      Commons Internal Review Services, *Department of the Library*; and Chris Pond, 'The

House of Commons Library and the transfer of resources to user self-service 1979–2004', *Aslib proceedings* **57** (4), 2005, 318–32.

48 Menhennet, *House of Commons Library*, 141.

49 Michael Hopkins and Partners, *New Parliamentary Building, Portcullis House, Bridge Street Westminster*, November 1999.

50 For details of this see Pond, 'House of Commons Library and the transfer of resources', fig. 1 and Table IV.

51 David Butcher, *Official publications in Britain*. London: Bingley, 1991.

52 *Improving management in government: the next steps.* A report to the Prime Minister (Ibbs report). London: HMSO, 1988; *Next steps report* (*Executive agencies report*, 1999 on). London: HMSO/TSO. Annual.

53 *Public bodies.* London: HMSO/TSO. Annual.

54 Goodier, 'Green and the grey'; V. J. Nurcombe (ed.), *Environment & leisure: proceedings of two one-day seminars.* Winsford: ISG Publications, 1994.

55 SCOOP minutes, Nov. 1994, item 24/4.

56 SCOOP minutes, Nov. 1996, item 28/5.

57 SCOOP minutes through 1994 and letter 31 Jan. 1994 from D. Hunt at HSE to Ross Shimmon at the Library Association.

58 Stephen Hewett, 'SCOOP news', *Refer* **6** (1), 1990, 26; Howard Picton, 'SCOOP news', *Refer* **9** (1), 1993, 21.

59 Howard Picton, 'Electronic publishing from 1971–2001' in *Official publishing: past present & future*, ed. Nurcombe, p. 36.

60 SCOOP minutes, May 1991, item 17/9.

61 SCOOP, 'Code of practice for government department or agency documents issued to the public', *Refer* **9** (1), 1993, 4–6.

62 *Managing information* **4** (6), 1997, 14.

63 Pond, 'British official publishing'.

64 *Managing information* **4** (3), 1997, 5.

65 Howard Picton, 'SCOOP news – Office for National Statistics', *Refer* **15** (2), 1999, 20–2.

66 Howard Picton, 'SCOOP news', *Refer* **15** (1), 1999, 26.

67 Office of National Statistics, *Guide to official statistics*, ed. Elizabeth Purdie. London: HMSO, 1996 (there was also a floppy disk version); David Butcher, 'British official statistics reviewed', *Refer* **13** (1), 1997, 17–18.

68 Jean Clarke, 'Statistical sources of information for business', *Refer* **9** (2), 1993, 15–22.

69 Stephen Hewett, 'SCOOP news', *Refer* **6** (1), 1990, 27.

70 'SCOOP news', *Refer* **11** (1), 1995, 32; **11** (3), 1995, 27; **13** (2), 1997, 25.

71 'SCOOP news', *Refer* **14** (3), 1998, 27–8.

72 J. E. Rowley, 'The 1991 Census on CD-ROM: a challenge for libraries', *Aslib proceedings* **46** (1), 1994, 25–7.

73 'SCOOP news', *Refer* **15** (3), 1999, 31.

74 Martin Bennett, 'DTI and its agencies: an overview' in *Official publishing in business & industry*, ed. V. J. Nurcombe. Winsford: ISG Publications, 1997, p. 15.

75 David Butcher, 'Non-TSO official publishing' in *Official publishing: past present & future*, ed. Nurcombe, p. 31.

76 The following were all edited by Valerie J. Nurcombe, published by ISG Publications: *Publishing of the parliaments and assemblies of the British Isles*, 2000; *Official*

publishing in the nineties, 1998; *Official publishing in business and industry*, 1997; *Official publications and statistics in health and medicine*, 1996; *Official publications in education*, 1996; *Laws in the making*, 1994; *Environment & leisure*, 1994; *R & D and OPs: sources of publications on & resulting from officially funded research and development*, 1993; *Whitehall and Westminster reviewed*, 1992; *Who publishes what on the 1991 Census?*, 1991; *British official publications online*, 1990; *Brussels: Whitehall: Westminster*, 1989; *Who publishes official information on business & industry*, 1989; *Who publishes official information on statistics*, 1989; *Who publishes official information on health, safety & social services*, 1989.

77   *New Labour because Britain deserves better*. London: Labour Party, 1997.

78   Welsh Office, *A voice for Wales*. London: TSO, 1997 (Cm 3718); Scottish Office, *Scotland's Parliament*. London: TSO, 1997 (Cm 3658).

79   *Scotland Act 1998*. London: TSO, 1998; *Government of Wales Act 1998*. London: TSO, 1998.

80   Howard Picton, 'SCOOP news', *Refer* **16** (2), 2000, 28.

81   Howard Picton, 'Public access to information on the Scottish Parliament', *Refer* **15** (2), 1999, 1–7; Janet Seaton, 'The Scottish Parliament' in *Parliaments and assemblies of the British Isles*, ed. Valerie J. Nurcombe. Winsford: ISG Publications, 2000, pp. 17–30.

82   *The Scottish Parliament*: <http://www.scottish.parliament.uk> (accessed 28/1/06).

83   *Scotland legislation*: <http://www.opsi.gov.uk/legislation/scotland/about.htm> (accessed 28/1/06).

84   *Scottish Parliamentary and statutory publications May 1999–July 2000*. Edinburgh: TSO, 2000.

85   Janet Seaton, 'The Scottish Parliament's information strategy', *Refer* **15** (3), 1999, 9–14.

86   National Assembly for Wales, *Assembly information booklet/Llyfryn gwybodaeth y Cynulliad*. Cardiff: The Assembly, [*ca.* 1999].

87   Caren Fullerton, 'The Welsh Assembly' in *Parliaments and assemblies*, ed. Nurcombe, pp. 31–44.

88   *Publications lists*: <http://www.wales.gov.uk/keypubpublicationslists/index.htm> (accessed 28/1/06).

89   Howard Picton, 'SCOOP news – Wales', *Refer* **16** (3), 2000, 23–4.

90   George Woodman, 'The Northern Ireland Assembly' in *Parliaments and assemblies*, ed. Nurcombe, pp. 45–52.

91   *The Belfast Agreement*. London: TSO, 1998 (Cm 3883); *Northern Ireland Act 1998*. London: TSO, 1998.

92   *Acts of the Northern Ireland Assembly*: <http://www.opsi.gov.uk/legislation/northernireland/ni-acts.htm> (accessed 28/1/06).

93   *Northern Ireland Assembly. Committees of the Assembly*: <http://www.niassembly.gov.uk/io/5_2.htm> (accessed 28/1/06).

94   Department of the Environment, Transport and the Regions, *Building partnerships for prosperity: sustainable growth, competitiveness and employment in the English regions*. London: TSO, 1997 (Cm 3814).

95   *Regional Development Agencies Act 1998*. London: TSO, 1998.

96   Department of the Environment, Transport and the Regions, *A Mayor and Assembly for London*. London: TSO, 1998 (Cm 3897); *The Greater London Authority Act 1999*. London: TSO, 1999.

97   Annabelle Davies, 'The London Assembly: a brief preview' in *Parliaments and assemblies*, ed. Nurcombe, pp. 70–2.

98   London Assembly publications:
      <http://www.london.gov.uk/assembly/publications.jsp> (accessed 28/1/06).

99   The main sources of information for the period were *Refer: journal of the Information Services Group* and *ALGIS newsletter*, Institute of Information Scientists.

100   Acompline and Urbaline. Greater London Authority:
      <https://extranet.london.gov.uk/services.jsp> (accessed 21/02/06).

101   SCOOP, Local Authority Official Publications Working Party, *Guidelines on the preparation of local authority publications*. Winsford: SCOOP, 1989.

102   Valerie Nurcombe (ed.), *Local authority information sources: a guide to publications and databases*. Winsford: SCOOP, 1992.

103   ALGIS: <http://www.algis.org.uk> (accessed 10/02/06).

104   Jennie Grimshaw, 'The British Library: official publications and Social Sciences Reading Area,' *ALGIS newsletter* summer 1999, 2.

105   *Well connected? A snapshot of local authority web sites in 1999*. SOCITM, 1999.

106   *Better connected 2001: a snapshot of local authority web sites*. SOCITM, 2001.

107   *The internet and local authorities*. Bedford: Bedfordshire County Council, 1995 (LGIS briefing report; no. 1).

108   Alex Bax, *London local government in the information society*. London: London Research Centre, 1999.

109   LGCNet 1992: <http://www.lgcnet.com> (accessed 21/02/06).

110   *Freedom of Information Act 2000*. London: TSO, 2000.

111   Advisory Group on Openness in the Public Sector, *Report to the Home Secretary*, Dec. 1999:
      <http://www.nationalarchives.gov.uk/ERO/records/ho415/1/foi/foi08599.htm>
      (accessed 21/2/06).

112   Commission of the European Communities, *The internal market after 1992: meeting the challenge: report to the EEC Commission by the High Level Group on the Operation of the Single Market*. Brussels: EC, 1992. Chairman Peter Sutherland; Commission of the European Communities, *National implementing measures to give effect to the white paper of the Commission on the completion of the internal market: situation at 30.4.93*. Luxembourg: OOPEC, 1993; Commission of the European Communities, *Seventh report ... on the implementation of the Commission's white paper on completing the internal market*. Luxembourg: OOPEC, 1992 (COM (92) 383 final); *Single market review*. London: Kogan Page, 1997–98. 39 vols.; Ian Thomson, 'Bibliographic snapshot: the single market', *European access* 2, April 1997, 34–47.

113   Council and Commission of the European Communities, *Treaty on European Union*. Luxembourg: OOPEC, 1992; Finn Laursen and Sophie Vanhoonacker (eds.), *The ratification of the Maastricht Treaty: issues, debates and future implications*. Dordrecht: Nijhoff, 1994; Ian Thomson, 'Bibliographic snapshot: Maastricht', *European access* 3, June 1992, 11–13; 'Treaty on European Union', *Official journal of the European Communities, C* **191**, 1992, 1–112.

114   European Union, *Treaty of Amsterdam*. Luxembourg: OOPEC, 1997; House of Lords, Select Committee on the European Union, *How is the EU working: 18th report*. London: TSO, 2000 (HL 1999–2000 124); Ian Thomson, 'Bibliographic snapshot: EU

governance and institutional developments. Part 1', *European access* 5, Oct. 1998, 32–9.

115 Brian Ardy, 'Economic and monetary union: a review article', *Journal of Common Market studies* **38** (4), 2000, 667–76; European Commission, *Communication ... practical aspects of the euro: state of play and tasks ahead*. Luxembourg: OOPEC, 2000 (COM (2000) 443 final); European Commission, *Economic and monetary union: compilation of Community legislation*. Luxembourg, OOPEC, 1999; European Commission, *Euro 1999: 25 March 1998: report on progress towards convergence and recommendation with a view to the transition to the third stage of economic and monetary union*. Luxembourg: OOPEC, 1998 (COM (98) 1999 final); HM Treasury, *National changeover plan*. London: HM Treasury, 1999; HM Treasury, *Second outline national changeover plan*. London: HM Treasury, 2000.

116 *Bulletin of the European Communities*. Luxenbourg: OOPEC, 1968–1993. Monthly; continued as *Bulletin of the European Union*. Luxenbourg: OOPEC, 1994– . Monthly; Commission of the European Communities, *General report on the activities of the European Communities*. Luxembourg: OOPEC, 1967– ; *Directory of Community legislation in force and other acts of Community legislation*. Luxembourg: OOPEC. Six-monthly; Office of Official Publications of the European Communities, *General catalogue of publications 2000*. Luxembourg: OOPEC, 2000. Annual; *Official journal of the European Communities, L & C*, Luxembourg: OOPEC. Daily.

117 'Annual review of the activities of the European Community', *Journal of Common Market studies* (annual special issue); contains: 1993–1999, Ian Thomson, 'A guide to Community documentation', and 2000, Patrick Overy and Ian Mayfield, 'Documentation of the European Union in 1999'; Timothy Bainbridge and Anthony Teasdale, *The Penguin companion to European Union*. 2nd ed. London: Penguin, 1998; Desmond Dinan (ed.), *Encyclopedia of the European Union*. Basingstoke: Macmillan, 1998; Veerle Deckmyn, *Guide to official documentation of the European Union*. 3rd ed. Maastricht: EIPA, 1998; *The European Union encyclopedia and directory 1999*. 3rd ed. London: Europa Publications, 1999; *European voice*. The Economist Group, 1995– ; Foreign and Commonwealth Office, *Developments in the European Union*. London: TSO. Six-monthly in the command papers series; Stephen George, *An awkward partner: Britain in the European Community*. 3rd ed. Oxford: Oxford University Press, 1998; Pierre Mathijsen, *A guide to European Union law*. 7th ed. London: Sweet & Maxwell, 1999; Neill Nugent, *The government and politics of the European Union*. 4th ed. Basingstoke: Macmillan, 1999; Anne Ramsay (ed.), *Eurojargon: a dictionary of European Union acronyms, abbreviations and sobriquets*. 6th ed. Stamford: CPI, 2000; Tony Reid, *Guide to European Community grants and loans*. Newbury: Eurofi, 1992– (looseleaf); Alex Roney and Stanley Budd, *The European Union: a guide through the EC/EU maze*. 6th ed. London: Kogan Page, 1998; Ian Thomson, 'Bibliographic snapshot of the European Union in 1993', *European access* 1, Feb. 1994, 41–50 (annually in the first issue of the year, 1994–); *Vacher's European companion and consultant's register*. Berkhamstead: Vacher's Publications, 1975– . Quarterly; Douglas Yuill, John Bachtler and Fiona Wishlade (eds.), *European regional incentives 1999*. 18th ed. East Grinstead: Bowker-Saur, 1999.

118 Ian Thomson, 'Bibliographic snapshot: the information and communication policy of the European Union', *European access* 4, Aug. 1996, 37–45.

119   Commission of the European Communities, 'Lisbon European Council: conclusions of the Presidency: a Union closer to its citizens', *Bulletin of the European Communities* 6, June 1992, 11–12; Commission of the European Communities, 'Edinburgh European Council: Conclusions of the Presidency', *Bulletin of the European Communities* 12, Dec. 1992, 9–20.

120   Commission of the European Communities, 'Birmingham Declaration – a community close to its citizens', *Bulletin of the European Communities* 10, Oct. 1992, 9.

121   Commission of the European Communities, 'The subsidiarity principle', *Bulletin of the European Communities* 10, Oct. 1992, 116–26.

122   Ian Thomson, 'Bibliographic snapshot: transparency and openness', *European access* 6, Dec. 1997, 31–5.

123   Judith Barton, 'Reflection on information and communication policy of the European Community (commentary on the De Clercq report)', *EIS* 139, April 1993, 1–2; European Information Association, 'EIA submission to the EC Study Group on Information and Communication Policy', *EIA review* 2, July 1993, 9–13; Mission on Information and Communication Policy of the European Community, *Reflection on information and communication of the European Community: report by a group of experts chaired by Mr Willy De Clercq, MEP*. Brussels: EC, 1993. 2 vols.; Commission of the European Communities, *Information, communication, openness*. Luxembourg: OOPEC, 1994.

124   Eric Davies, 'Information and communication in the EU', *European information* 3, July 1998, 2–14; European Parliament Committee on Culture, Youth, Education and the Media, *Report on information and communication policy in the European Union* (*rapporteur Peter Pex*). Luxembourg: EP, 1998 (A4–0115/98).

125   European Commission, *Access to Commission documents: users' guide*. Luxembourg: EC, 1994; European Commission, *Access to Commission documents: a citizen's guide*. 2nd ed. Luxembourg: EC, 1997.

126   'Commission adopts proposed regulation on public access to EU documents', *European access* 1, Feb. 2000, 12–15; European Commission, *Proposal for a Regulation on public access to documents*. Luxembourg: OOPEC, 2000 (COM (2000) 30 final).

127   Mary Preston, 'Openness and the European Union institutions', *European access* 4, Aug. 1996, 7–10.

128   Mike Hopkins, 'National Consultative Conference, 7 to 8 January 1993, Stoke Rochford Hall: report of the breakout session for information specialists', *EIA review* 2, July 1993, 5–8; Jenny Lawson, 'Filling the European information gap', *European access* 1, Feb. 1993, 27–8.

129   Commission of the European Communities, London Office, 'Information deficit highlighted by EC survey'. Press release, ISEC/18/93 (10/11/93).

130   Michael Dolan, 'A public library network for European information', *European access* 1, Feb. 1994, 25–6; Rita Marcella, 'European Union information in public libraries', *European access* 5, Oct. 1995, 21–3; Rita Marcella, Graeme Baxter and Susan Parker, 'The provision of European information by public libraries in the UK: seminar held at the Representation of the European Commission in London on 25th June 1996', *European access* 5, Oct. 1996, 22–4.

131   European Commission, London Office, 'The European Union – serving the information needs of the general public', *European access* 4, Aug. 1994, 26–7; Rita Marcella, Susan Parker and Enrico Tortolano, 'The role of the Representation Offices

of the European Commission in EU member states', *European access* 3, June 1996, 20–2; Peter Barron, 'Relaying the message', *European access* 4, Aug. 1995, 19.

132   European Commission, DGX, *Europe info: directory of networks and other European Union information sources.* Luxembourg: OOPEC, 1995; National Co-ordinating Committee of the Network of European Relays, *European Union information: directory of UK sources.* 2nd ed. London: European Commission, 1998.

133   Peter Barron, 'The development of Europe.org.uk', *European information* 13, Jan. 2001, 20–1.

134   'European Information Association (EIA)', *European access* 1, Feb. 1991, 37–8; Anne Ramsay, 'From little acorns – the origins of the European Information Association', *EIA review* 9, Jan. 1997, 7–10.

135   *EIA information guides*; *EIA quick guides*; *EIA review.* EIA, 1993–1997; *European information*, EIA, 1998– .

136   Ian Thomson, 'Relay Europe', *European access* 4, Aug. 1991, 42–3.

137   Richard Caddel, 'European Documentation Centres: their role in the EC information chain', *European access* 5, Oct. 1991, 34–5; Ian Thomson, 'Challenges facing European Documentation Centres', *European access* 6, Dec. 1995, 16–19.

138   Brian Wilcox, 'The Euro Info Centre network – where now and whither?', *European access* 4, Aug. 1996, 25–6; Carl Wiper, 'Euro Info Centres after 10 years', *EIA review* 10, July 1997, 29–33.

139   Rob Cockburn, 'Rural society information and development needs: the role of the Carrefours', *European access* 5, Oct. 1993, 24–5; Eric Thain, 'Centres for rural information and promotion', *EIA review* 1, Jan. 1993, 13–16.

140   Bibiana Dantas, 'Innovation Relay Centres – links to technology and innovation across Europe', *European information* 2, April 1998, 9–11; Ian E. Traill, 'The VALUE relay service: a dissemination network for EC research', *European access* 5, Oct. 1993, 21–3.

141   David Morton, 'European Resources Centres for Schools and Colleges', *EIA review* 10, July 1997, 14–17.

142   Rachel Foster, 'DGX trains EDC representatives in Brussels', *EIA review* 7, Jan. 1996, 8–12.

143   Catherine Webb, 'The EDC exchange scheme: linking EDCs across Europe', *EIA review* 9, Jan. 1997, 25–33.

144   European Commission, *Who's who in the European Union? Interinstitutional directory.* Luxembourg: OOPEC, 1999 (and its online version, the IDEA database); Neville Keery, 'The European Commission's new approach to information and communication: access and information in a post-Maastricht context', *European access* 3, June 1994, 21–3.

145   Helen Browning and Suzanne White, 'Rethinking European Documentation Centres – is a regional network of repositories really the way forward?', *European information* 6, April 1999, 21–3; European Commission, DGX, *Re-thinking the European Documentation Centres: a DGX reflection paper.* Luxembourg: EC, 1998 (internal document).

146   Jean-Bernard Quicheron, 'EUROPA, EUROPAplus – future developments', *European information* 10, April 2000, 18–23; Grace Hudson, 'Europa usage continues to grow', *European access* 6, Dec. 2000, 23.

147   Commission of the European Communities, DG XXIII, 'Accessing information services: the network of National Awareness Partners', *Euro abstracts* **32** (8), 1994,

505–7; Julia Dickmann, 'Aslib and the National Awareness Partnership', *EIA review* 5, Jan. 1995, 24–8.

148 'A publisher for Europe: twenty five years of EUR-OP (Office for Official Publications of the European Communities)', *European access* 1, Feb. 1995, 23–4.

149 European Commission, 'Europe and the global information society: recommendations of the high-level group on the information society to the Corfu European Council (Bangemann group)', *Bulletin of the European Union. Supplement* 2, 1994, 5–39; European Commission, *Europe's way to the information society: an action plan.* Luxembourg: OOPEC, 1994 (COM (94) 347 final).

150 Antony Inglis and Keith Goodall, 'EC databases column', *European access* 4, Aug. 1992, 26–8; Antony Inglis, 'EC database column', *European access* 5, Oct. 1992, 18–19.

151 Antony Inglis and Keith Goodall, 'EU database column', *European access* 1, Feb. 1997, 21–2.

152 European Commission, *European Union database directory 1997*. Luxembourg: OOPEC, 1996; Grace Hudson, 'EU electronic information column', *European access* 6, Dec. 1998, 27–9; Grace Hudson, 'EU electronic information column', *European access* 5–6, Dec. 1999, 31–4.

153 *Butterworth's EC legislation implementator*. London: Butterworth, 1992– .

154 Grace Hudson, 'EU electronic information column', *European access* 3, June 1998, 22–3.

155 'Public register of Council documents', *European access* 1, Feb. 1999, 23.

156 Antony Inglis and Keith Goodall, 'EC database column', *European access* 4, Aug. 1992, 26–8.

157 Grace Hudson, 'EU electronic information column', *European access* 1, Feb. 1999, 26–8; OJ EUR-Lex L & C CD-ROM, EUR-OP, 1998– .

158 Freda Carroll, 'Eurotext – from project to service', *European information* 3, July 1998, 24–9.

159 Eurostat, *Eurostat publications and databases 1999*. Luxembourg: Statistical Office of the European Communities, 1999; Inger Nybrant, 'How to find out about European statistics', *EIA review* 9, Jan. 1997, 17–23.

160 Anne Ramsay, *Eurostat index*. 5th ed. Stamford: CPI, 1992.

161 Peter Littlewood, 'The Resource Centre for Access to Data on Europe (r.cade)', *EIA review* 10, July 1997, 44–50.

162 Christiane Mauwet (ed.), *The guide to EU information sources on the internet*. Brussels: Euroconfidentiel, 2000; Mafalda dos Santos (ed.), *The directory of online European information*. 3rd ed. Brussels: Landmarks, 2000.

163 Richard Hainbach, 'The role of the private sector in "adding value" to EU information', *European information* 2, April 1998, 19–23.

164 Eric Davies, 'A look at three new web-based services', *European information* 10, April 2000, 2–7.

165 Giancarlo Pau, 'Europe Direct: a one-stop shop for EU info', *EIS* 209, April 2000, 6–7.

166 Ian Thomson, 'Challenges facing European Documentation Centres', *European access* 6, Dec. 1995, 17; Antony Inglis and Keith Goodall, 'EU databases column', *European access* 5, Oct. 1996, 29.

167 Andrea Sevetson, 'The European Union on the internet: a vanishing record?', *European information* 1, Jan. 1998, 6–12.

18

Patents

Stephen Adams

Introduction

In the previous volume in this series, covering 1986-1990, the author of this chapter made the following comment:

> Each country traditionally has its own publications and legal procedures, which leads to difficulties in exerting bibliographic control over the material, and in assessing the results of a search.[1]

Despite many trends in harmonization and the general globalization of the information industry, this observation remained largely true throughout the subsequent ten years. Patent information is a unique mix of technical and legal documentation, and it is worth noting at the outset of this review that the majority of people who handle patent information on a daily basis do not work in libraries at all. The average public or government library was – and still is – unlikely to stock patent documents as a matter of course, and much of the basic knowledge on publication procedures and bibliographic sources is lacking in all but the most specialist establishment.

The major consumers for patent information during the 1990s were limited to research-based industries, supplemented by a moderate usage in financial broking and company strategy management. Since the techniques and services used by these organizations are seen as a means of obtaining competitive advantage, they are frequently not documented, and details about them are rarely published in the open literature. If published at all, news concerning innovative applications of patent data will tend to appear in journals which reflect the bias of the user; for example, using patent information to derive competitive intelligence (CI) is discussed in the CI literature, whilst discussions of the social, economic, legal or political impact of patent information and patent rights are scattered across the conventional economics or law literature.

Many of the developments in the patent information field are initiated by either the data producers (the patent offices) or within the private sector. Typically, these are not documented in the established library and information science literature, but are dispersed across a wide range of technical bulletins, newsletters and conference proceedings. Some information on technical and information science developments can appear in the formal journal literature such as *Journal of information science, Journal of chemical information and computer sciences, Online, E-content* or general industry newspapers such as *Information world review*. A notable contribution during the decade was the Nancy Lambert's 'Better mousetrap' column devoted to patents information, which appeared in the US *Searcher* magazine.[2] However, there is only one English-language periodical dedicated to the area, the Elsevier journal *World patent information* which has been published since 1979.[3] The table of contents and abstracts for this journal are included in the Elsevier Science Direct service. Legally-focused specialist periodicals such as the magazine *Patent world* sometimes carry articles of interest to the information professional.

Patent publication basics

A simple introduction to patent information is provided by the current author in chapter 11 of the handbook edited by Bradley, especially at Appendix 1.[4] More detailed books available during the period included the database survey published by Aslib (again with a useful summary of procedures), the British Library's extensive guide and a volume in the Bowker-Saur series 'Guides to information sources.'[5] A French-language guide was also published in the same period.[6] Many introductory texts exist in the field of intellectual property law, which provide a basic background for the librarian or information specialist operating in the field – one such example, published during this period, is from the LawCards® series.[7]

A patent for invention is essentially a legal instrument for controlling trade in a manufactured good or the processes for its production. The rights of a patent holder are often misunderstood, and assumed to include 'the right to make something'. In fact, the only rights conferred by the grant are negative ones – to *prevent other persons* manufacturing, selling, using or importing the product or process protected by the patent. The purpose of patent publication is to ensure that industry is made aware of the rights of patent holders, to enable third parties to avoid accidental infringement and to give due warning to potential deliberate infringers. The full definition of what constitutes patent infringement in the United Kingdom is outlined in section 60 of the Patents Act 1977.[8] It should be noted that: (*a*) act(s) of infringement must have taken place within the United Kingdom, and (*b*) the patent must have been in force within the United Kingdom at the time of the act(s) of infringement.

This means that, for example, United Kingdom patent holders cannot enforce their rights against actions carried out within France by a competitor company, since this fails criterion (*a*). Equally, a French company cannot exert its French patents against alleged infringing actions carried out in Britain, since this fails criterion (*b*). The French company would only be able to sue for infringement within the UK if it owns corresponding UK patents for the invention.

Corresponding national laws apply in other countries. As such, the rights conferred by a patent are limited by the territorial jurisdiction of the granting authority. The majority of national patent offices are still more or less a branch of government, often with strong links to the national Department of Trade and Industry or its equivalent.

Part of the procedure in granting a patent involves the publication of a description of the invention, also referred to as the 'specification'. These documents are available for examination by any member of the public, and serve two purposes. Firstly, they provide a public record of the nature of the protected invention, in order to assist innocent third parties who do not wish to accidentally infringe the patent holder's rights. Secondly, they provide a record of innovative progress through the years, which can be drawn upon for inspiration by other inventors. At the end of the patent's life, the invention becomes a part of the public domain and can be freely used by anyone else.

During the 1990s, between 750,000 and one million patent documents were published annually world-wide, and by the end of the decade the holdings at the British Library had risen to some 50 million items, ranging in date from 1617 to the present, from many different countries. They formed a vast scientific information resource, as well as a record of the legal rights of patent holders during the lifetime of the patent itself.

A distinct aspect of patent information since the mid-1960s has been the development of a 'double publication' regime. Many countries' patent laws now provide for a patent application to be laid open to public inspection within a relatively short period of filing (typically 18 months), before the case has been examined and granted. Provided that the applicant is successful, the definitive grant will appear some months or years later as a second document, which is frequently much more restricted in the subject matter discussed, and corresponding rights granted, than the original prospective application. In order to establish some control over these linked documents, various standards have been developed for the process of publication and citation. These are promulgated by the World Intellectual Property Organization (WIPO), a special agency of the United Nations based in Geneva. Typical bibliographic standards include ST.3 which provides for the identification of the publishing country or authority,[9] and ST.16, which defines the different publication stages for a given invention in each country.[10]

Patents and patent information in the United Kingdom

Any individual or corporate body, whether resident in the United Kingdom or elsewhere, is entitled to apply for a patent which will have effect within the United Kingdom. The reverse is equally true – other countries allow UK nationals or industrial organizations to obtain patents in their countries. As a result, a single invention is frequently protected by an entire 'family' of equivalent patent documents, each one issued by the national patent office of the country in which protection is sought. There is no such thing as a 'world patent', granting enforceable rights across national boundaries, at least as far as the United Kingdom is concerned.

There are only two types of patents which can enter into force in the United Kingdom – British national patents granted by the United Kingdom Patent Office, and European Patents granted by the European Patent Office (EPO). In the latter case, the patent applicant must indicate at the time of granting that they wish the United Kingdom to be included in the patent's coverage – a granted European Patent does not automatically have effect in all the member states of the system. This process is called 'designation'. Provided that the United Kingdom is duly designated, a European Patent is regarded as legally equivalent to a national one (section 77(1)(*a*) of the Act states that 'the proprietor of a European patent (UK) shall ... have the same rights and remedies ... as the proprietor of a [United Kingdom] patent ...'.).

This 'territorial' aspect of patents – one country, one patent – is an important distinction for the librarian or information specialist to remember, because it means that the *purpose* behind a patent enquiry will radically affect the range of information sources to be consulted. If a prospective patent holder is seeking to establish *patentability*, that is, whether their new invention is patentable in the United Kingdom, then world-wide sources must be used to try to establish that the invention is new. However, if the intention is to try to prove (or avoid) *infringement*, then the searcher need only consult the patent literature which is in force in the country or countries concerned. In the first case, searchers will find themselves using information sources which may originate, or be hosted, virtually anywhere in the world, whereas in the latter case, more 'home-grown' information products may fulfil the bulk of the search.

National and international legislative changes

In late 1990, a statutory instrument was issued which brought Part V of the Copyright, Designs and Patents Act 1988 into force.[11] This was amplified by a further set of Regulations the same year.[12] These effectively abolished the patent agents' monopoly on acting in application proceedings. From the effective date of these regulations (13 August 1990), any person was permitted to file a patent application in the United Kingdom, on their own behalf or for other people. They may not, however, style or advertise themselves as a 'patent agent' unless they have passed the qualifying examination and been entered on the official register.

A major change in patent documentation took place in 1987, and its effect was seen during the decade under review. A Statutory Instrument brought sections 77(6) and 78(7) of the Patents Act 1977 into force.[13] This meant that after the effective date (1 September 1987), the owner of any European Patent with a designation of the United Kingdom which had been granted in a non-English text was required to provide a translation into English. Failure to provide this text within the prescribed time limits led to the patent being declared void in the United Kingdom. This was not a retrospective provision, so all European Patents in German or French from the commencement of the European Patent Office up to 1 September 1987 automatically entered into force without translation. As a result of this change, many thousands of translated texts of European Patents were deposited at the UK Patent Office, with further copies being made available at the British Library. The impact can be seen in Table 1 (p. 315). The apparent trend in reducing numbers should not be taken as indicating that fewer European Patents are entering into force in the UK – it is more likely that a greater proportion are being published in English at grant, so that additional translations are not required.

The basic term of a United Kingdom patent, and of a European Patent designating the United Kingdom, is 20 years counting from the date of filing of the patent application. The previous volume in this series noted that EU regulations were being mooted at the time which would provide an extension of term for pharmaceuticals. These eventually bore fruit in the form of a Council Regulation in 1992 for pharmaceuticals and a further one in 1996 for agrochemical products.[14] These measures were brought into force within the United Kingdom by means of a series of Statutory Instruments.[15] A later Instrument revoked and substantially re-enacted the 1992 and 1996 Rules, and includes the text of the two European Regulations.[16]

The principal major change in patentable subject matter in the United Kingdom was effected by the publication of the European biotechnology directive[17] after protracted discussions (see, for example, the 1993 paper describing progress to that date).[18] However, the Directive did not enter into force in the United Kingdom until early in the following decade. An equally controversial area was that of patenting in the computer and software industries. Discussions raged on this for the whole period, and the United Kingdom (during its presidency of the EU) hosted a Europe-wide conference on software patents in March 1998 in the hope that this would lead to a more global approach to the issue.[19]

At the beginning of the decade, the European Patent Office had 13 members, including the United Kingdom. Between January 1990 and December 1999, a further 8 countries joined, of which 6 (Denmark, Monaco, Ireland, Portugal, Finland and Cyprus) were full members and the remaining two (Albania and Macedonia) were so-called extension states, which recognize European Patents on their territory. This meant that a British applicant could use a single application procedure to obtain protection in up to 21 countries.

The other international treaty in intellectual property to which the United Kingdom is party is the Patent Cooperation Treaty (PCT). This is administered by WIPO and provides a streamlined process for the early stages of patent application, but does not itself grant any patents.[20] Over the same period, PCT membership grew from 42 to 101, and its published application series became one of the most significant sources of patent information, in all technical areas.

One significant challenge for the patent information specialist during the period was the creation of the World Trade Organization (WTO), and the consequent harmonizing of many national patent laws. In order to ratify its membership of the WTO, a candidate country is obliged to sign a number of additional treaties, including the Agreement on Trade-Related Aspects of Intellectual Property (TRIPS). Since WIPO was already at work in some of the same areas, the two organizations had to work to clarify the future working relationships between them.[21] The TRIPS Agreement lays down certain minimum criteria for a member state's patent laws, such as on patent term. One consequence of this was that many candidate countries progressively amended their national laws to take account of TRIPS standards, as part of their WTO accession process. This makes tracking the legal status of granted patents a much more complicated process in these countries, since patents in force may have been granted under different legal conditions and (for example) have different periods of validity.

The British Patent Office

There were various changes in the administration and management of the UK Patent Office during the period. For the bulk of the decade, the Chief Executive was Paul Hartnack. On his retirement, he was succeeded by Alison Brimelow in March 1999. The Patent Office became an Executive Agency under the Department of Trade and Industry in 1990, and from 1 October 1991 was established as a trading fund.[22]

After a long period of slow decline, national filing rates began to recover during the mid-1990s, and in order to encourage this, various changes were made to the statutory fee structure. The initial fee for filing a patent application was completely abolished in 1998.[23] The same rules also abolished the fee associated with the lodging of the translation of a European Patent.

Statistics on the numbers of patents applied for, published, UK patents granted and EP translations deposited, are shown in Table 1.

Table 1 Grant statistics, 1990–2000

Calendar year	UK patent applications filed	UK patent applications published (GB-A)	UK patents granted (GB-B)	European Patent translations lodged in UK
1990	28,238	12,696	9,396	8,398
1991	27,587	12,202	9,346	8,921
1992	27,178	11,794	9,420	10,566
1993	26,648	10,980	8,330	10,999
1994	26,465	11,103	9,530	12,457
1995	26,739	11,142	9,475	12,427
1996	27,143	11,452	7,132	10,769
1997	27,203	12,474	7,945	10,928
1998	28,619	12,287	9,249	9,296
1999	30,467	12,043	7,995	9,017
2000	31,412	12,517	8,253	7,688

Computerization of the official Patent Office registers was carried out during the period. Preparation of the OPTICS system (the legal status register, initially for in-house use) was largely completed by 1990. The headquarters of the Patent Office was progressively moved to South Wales, with Concept House in Newport being opened in April 1991. The same year also saw the first utilization by the Office of a CD-ROM jukebox storage system, used to provide printed copies of British patent applications for sale to the general public. It was not until 1993 that the *de facto* standard for exchange of patent information on CD-ROM was fixed by WIPO as ST.40,[24] so this move was one of the earlier adoptions of the technology. Other uses of optical technology included the development of various training packages using large-format (30 cm) interactive disks. Some of these products migrated to CD format by 1995.

The Patent Office continued to make efforts to promote the IP system to industry and education, including the 'Be an Inventor' package for schools, which won the Library Association/T. C. Farries Public Relations and Publicity Award in 1994.

By 1996, the first steps were being made towards e-commerce, to provide for alternative methods of communication and payment of fees, in the form of the MIPEX (Message-based Industrial Property Information Exchange) project. The pilot project was completed in December 1998 and progressed to full implementation.[25] A description of the project was published in 1998.[26] The Patent Office's own website was launched in May 1997 and the OPTICS register was made available for public searching via this site in 1999.[27] By 1998, the first moves had been made to extend the website to bibliographic searching, as part of the esp@cenet® system, discussed later.

The Patent Office is required by statute to carry out searches on applications received for UK patents, as part of the granting process. However, by the mid-1980s, the volume of work was decreasing as a result of the United Kingdom's membership of the EPO: more cases were being filed, and searched, by this route than by the national route. Consequently, the Patent Office sought to leverage its expertise by offering a search broker service (the Search and Advisory Service, SAS) for non-applicants as well. This was started in the trade mark area in 1986, and extended to patents the following year. By 1995, it was reported that use of commercial search systems such as Dialog was 'routine'. The EPO's in-house search system (EPOQUE) was developed and shared with the patent offices of the member states, including Britain, and this formed the primary search tool for both statutory and SAS searches in the patents area.[28]

The Patent Office also sought to raise the profile of patent information by publishing the 'Patent information monograph series', designed to illustrate the breadth of technical knowledge contained in the documents. Subjects ranged from four-wheel drive to single-use syringes to microwaveable food containers; by 1994, there were eleven in the series.

British sources of patent information
Very few of the major sources of electronic patent information are truly 'home-grown'. For many years, virtually the sole representative of British excellence in database production was Derwent Information Ltd, based in London and

responsible for the production of the World Patents Index database, and a range of spin-off products from this. This company had been at the forefront of developing value-added databases in the patents field since 1948, initially as paper bulletins and subsequently on commercial host systems, starting with SDC-ORBIT in 1976. For many years, Derwent was partially owned by Thomson, the publishing group. In the early 1990s, Thomson took on 100% ownership, and the Derwent brand was gradually subsumed into Thomson Scientific.[29]

The only other major player dedicated to patent information based in the UK was Minesoft Ltd. This company was also London-based, and acted as UK agent for the French host Questel-Orbit for many years. Latterly, they collaborated with other companies to develop applications for text-mining tools in the patents field, and web-based patent document delivery applications (PatentOrder).

The British Library underwent significant changes in its services, many as a result of the move from Southampton Buildings, near Chancery Lane, to the new premises in St Pancras. In this context, it is worth noting that the Library continues to maintain some unique reference tools, including a full card index of patent assignees for British patents from 1971 and European Patents from 1978, British name indexes from 1617 and abridgements (allowing a classification-based subject search) from 1852. Texts of the judge's summing up in legal decisions from the Patent Office and the Patent Courts (including Court of Appeal, House of Lords and Patents County Court cases) are available from 1970, as well as the established legal periodicals such as *Reports of patent, trade mark and design cases* (RPC) and *Fleet Street reports* (FSR). More details on using the pre-1977 Act resources can be found in the book by van Dulken.[30] As well as British resources, the British Library holds name indexes for US patents from 1872; the earliest electronic sources do not provide access earlier than 1976.

Part of the British Library service was the dedicated Patent Express document delivery, based in London rather than at Boston Spa. It made extensive use of jukebox technology, providing access to over 1,000 CD-ROMs.[31] However, the first internet links were installed in 1998, before the move to St Pancras, and included one terminal in Chancery House for bibliographic searching, and two more in Southampton Buildings for access to the United Kingdom legal status register. The progressive migration to do-it-yourself document ordering from internet sites (which was accelerated by increased terminal availability in the St Pancras building) undermined the economics of Patent Express.[32]

Part of the CD-ROM collection held by Patent Express included the ESPACE-GB series, containing bibliographic data of United Kingdom patent applications, linked to facsimiles of the complete specification. The earliest disks in this series were received in 1994, and formed the first publicly available electronic bibliographic database dedicated to British patents.

For the bulk of the decade, ESPACE-GB and similar disk-based tools were the only means of electronic access to British patents. It was not until the launch of esp@cenet® in 1998 that a searcher could directly access a file containing only UK documents; prior to this, British data were subsumed into larger, multi-country family databases such as INPADOC and World Patents Index. At the initial launch, the so-called Level 1 servers, administered by the national patent offices of the EPO member states, only contained two years' worth of data, but many (including the British one) increased in size rapidly. By 2000, the British server could provide bibliographic details of all published applications under the 1977 Act (published from early 1979 onwards).

International sources of patent information
At the beginning of the decade, most industry-based users of electronic patent information would access it by means of one of the major online systems, most commonly Orbit, STN International or Questel. The reputation of the Dialog host in respect of scientific and technical information was less prominent, despite its widespread customer base. Following the take-over of Dialog by the Knight-Ridder publishing group, the company concentrated heavily on developing its news, financial and market information sources, and scientific and technical sources such as patents were relatively neglected. In 1993, Knight-Ridder also acquired DataStar, which had a biomedical focus. In 2000, the Thomson Corporation acquired from Knight-Ridder the operating group which included both online hosts, and incorporated them into the Thomson Scientific structure.[33]

During the same period, the Orbit host, which had had a chequered history through its involvement in the Maxwell publishing empire, was eventually bought by the French host, Questel, to form Questel-Orbit. At the time, Questel was still part government-owned under the France Telecom banner. A subsequent management buy-out resulted in a re-focusing of the company, to concentrate upon intellectual property information sources.

The third major player, STN International, started the decade as principal host to the *Chemical abstracts* file, but following an agreement in 1992, the first files from the Derwent stable appeared in 1994, and subsequently the host developed substantial strengths in intellectual property, including some exclusive file loadings.

Searchers engaged in patentability searching must ensure that their search is not limited to local information sources; the standard of 'universal novelty' requires that as many sources as possible are examined, irrespective of origin or language. In practice, relatively few files permit searching across multiple countries in a single operation. The Derwent World Patents Index covers some 40 countries, whilst INPADOC and the spin-off products using the same data cover approximately 70. Up to the year 2000, no one had succeeded in producing a genuinely global database, which could require coverage of the patent documentation from most of the 183 member states of WIPO (at the time of writing, a few still did not have their own patent laws). However, the smaller countries were not producing patent documents at a significant rate, and the existing multi-country sources claim that between 90% and 95% of all the patent documents published are accounted for by the current core countries. Nonetheless, the challenge remains for the searcher to maintain awareness of the launch of new searchable files, particularly for the more obscure countries, to fill in the remaining gaps.

A key player in the process of capturing this wide range of patent information was Univentio, a Dutch-based company.[34] They had a programme of obtaining historical paper records from national patent offices – many of which were being discarded – and capturing the data by OCR to create searchable databases. In the period under review, the product of this process was leased to established host services. The reason why Univentio features so prominently in the field is because of their parallel effort to provide machine translation into English of the original documents. It should be remembered that each country, in issuing a patent grant for the territory over which it has jurisdiction, is principally concerned with informing local industry, and will naturally use its own national language of publication. For the monoglot English-language searcher, this creates a considerable difficulty in ensuring that all the possible prior publications have in fact been located. The language barrier remains as one of the most significant hurdles to the establishment of universal novelty in a patent search.

Key changes in products and services
During the course of the decade, users saw a rapid change in the range of available media of distribution. The early years saw an expansion of many optical disk-based products, initially CD-ROMs of bibliographic (character-coded) data, followed by facsimiles of the entire documents. The US series of CASSIS disks, covering US patent data, was first received at the British Library in late 1993, and corresponding European data in the ESPACE-ACCESS disks by 1996. Facsimile disks of British, European and US specifications all arrived during 1994. A review of the tools available to a typical industry-based user was published by Lobeck at the beginning of the decade,[35] and it is interesting to compare this with a similar later article from 1995, by which time single platters had been largely overtaken by very large jukebox systems.[36] The volume of patent publication quickly overtook the storage capacity of the medium – by the mid-1990s, international patent applications under the PCT system were being issued at the rate of 3–4 new disks per week. This precipitated an early move to DVD-ROM technology which, together with the migration of the corresponding application software to 32-bit Windows standard, meant that patent information specialists were some of the earliest adopters of high-end technology in this field. The PATSOFT application software (DOS-based) had reached version 3.1 by 1992, when development of the Windows-compatible MIMOSA (MIxed MOde Software Application) started; it was launched in 1995.[37] Perhaps the last major product of significance in the optical disk area was GlobalPat, an ambitious database requiring over 140 disks and containing patent bibliographic data from 7 major patent publishing authorities, in some cases back to 1920. The intention was to provide a start-up tool for patent offices, particularly from less-developed countries, enabling them to attempt more comprehensive and sophisticated prior-art searches in-house.

However, optical disk technology had barely stabilized into a robust work application when it was challenged by the rise of the internet, which created a whole new method of handling patent information. Perhaps one of the earliest indications of the impact of this type of technology was provided at the EPO's annual user meeting in 1998, in Jena, where the use of satellite technology for distributing patent information across the Astra TV system was discussed,[38] although user interest in such a system had been expressed during surveys some years earlier.[39]

The earliest websites principally catered for document delivery, such as MicroPatent. This organization was initially founded as a joint venture between Opus Publications and Chadwyck-Healey, to distribute microfilm copies of patents. They expanded quickly to create the APS bibliographic database on CD, running DataWare software, by 1990; this permitted the almost unheard-of capability to search the complete texts of patent documents. By approximately 1995, MicroPatent had a presence on the internet, offering downloads of facsimile US patents using a customized plug-in application, 'PatentImage Viewer'. Around the same time, the US Patent & Trademark Office (USPTO) opened a website, allowing users to search the basic bibliographic data of US patents for the last 20 years, free of charge.

These developments posed an important challenge to the producers of the established databases mounted on hosts such as STN International, Questel-Orbit and Dialog, and practically destroyed the paper-based document delivery services of organizations such as the British Library. There were two types of response. Firstly, several of the hosts, including all three above, developed a browser-based interface to their existing collection of databases, in the form of tools like 'STN on the Web', QPAT and DialogWeb. This was an attempt to remodel the command-line interfaces into the increasingly popular 'point-and-click' style of searching, using pre-formatted search forms instead of field labels. The second response was from the database producers, who now found that their previous reliance upon the services of the hosts to distribute their data had been eroded, and that they could increase market share by loading their own databases on internet servers and supplying directly to the customer.

This response partly manifested itself in the form of new commercial products, such as the joint Optipat/IBM venture delivering bibliographic searching and full-text patent documents (later spun off from IBM as Delphion) and Derwent's Patent Explorer (a small range of full-text sources, including some European data). These products both appeared during 1997.[40] However, the principal reaction was from the public sector, seen in the actions of the patent offices themselves. By August 1996, some 11 patent offices had a website (Austria, Canada, EPO, Denmark, Hungary, Japan, Spain, Sweden, United Kingdom, United States and WIPO), a few of which included a rudimentary search tool. Within six months, this had doubled to approximately 24. In October 1998, the European Patent Office responded to the lead of the USPTO (now offering 20 years' worth of full-text free of charge) by launching the Distributed Internet Patent Service (DIPS), later re-christened esp@cenet®.

Perhaps the most contentious aspect of esp@cenet® was the inclusion of the so-called 'world-wide' database. Previous patent office offerings on the web had been limited to small files of bibliographic or full-text data from their own national patents. The EPO was the first to offer a dedicated search service able to retrieve information on patents from over 70 countries, in a single operation. In 1990, the EPO had taken over the operations of the International Patent Documentation Centre (INPADOC), an independent organization founded by WIPO and the Austrian government in 1972, which had created a highly-regarded multi-country patent family database. Much of the information in the INPADOC file overlapped with existing internal EPO search files. By 1998, the process of merging the two resources was effectively complete, and the combined tool – one of the biggest patent databases in existence – was laid open, free of charge to the public via the internet as the esp@cenet® world-wide file. This created a considerable challenge to the established database producers. Up to this time, accessing patent information had been a costly and complicated process. The processes of creating specially written bibliographic records, including enhanced indexing, and redistributing patent information through hosts offering sophisticated retrieval languages, involved considerable financial investment and took time to complete. The new services did not offer anything like the precision of retrieval required by industrial researchers, but for smaller businesses and casual users, they provide a rapid and user-friendly first attempt.

The 1990s also saw a significant development in the tools available for the chemical industry. One of the challenges in this field is the existence of so-called Markush patents. These are patents which protect not only a specific molecule or complex substance, but also a larger group of related products, which act as a kind of ring-fence to the most important one. Depending upon the method of definition, this surrounding group may encompass many thousands or millions of additional chemicals (Markush disclosures, or so-called 'prophetic' or 'paper' compounds), without specifically identifying any of them. However, these additional compounds constitute a valid prior disclosure, which act as a barrier to them being patented by anyone else. Search tools up to the late 1980s were not capable of providing systematic retrieval of these Markush disclosures. However, both Chemical Abstracts Service (CAS) and Derwent were researching in the field extensively, sometimes in collaboration with academia.[41] By the early 1990s, two competing solutions were launched: the Marpat file from CAS, which was a specialist extension of the CAS bibliographic file, and the Markush-DARC search system from Questel, which linked to the Derwent WPI bibliographic file. Various papers were published which discussed the relative merits of each system at the time.[42] The Questel system initially covered a larger range of searchable documents, but its first version was less flexible than Marpat, which had been tightly integrated into the specific compound searching features on STN from its launch. Markush-DARC was released as version 2, with enhanced software (allowing automatic 'translation' of chemical features) in 1994. A further revision and re-launch took place in August 1998, when the Merged Markush Service (MMS) was opened –

this provides a single search software across two bibliographies, the WPI file covering all areas of chemistry and a separate file covering pharmaceuticals only.

Up to 1993, the patent searcher was generally limited to text-only sources as interactive search files. If the search located a potentially useful candidate answer, a second step was required to go to the microfilm images of either the original document or a re-written abstract, to assess relevance in more detail. From around 1990, Derwent had produced scanned images of its abstracts, including a selection of the patent drawings, on CD-ROM as the Derpict product. However, by 1993, it became technically feasible for Derwent to link clipped images from each database record, for immediate viewing online. These were first released for the engineering sector on the STN and Dialog hosts, followed in 1994 by Orbit. At this time, dedicated terminal emulators such as ProComm Plus, were required to permit in-line viewing of pictures in the same session as text. As communications speeds increased rapidly, and most searchers began to use PCs rather than dumb terminals, it soon became routine to view both text and image data using a standard application package.

As noted above, it was not until 1998 that the law concerning patentability of microbiological inventions was clarified by the EU Directive.[43] However, the issue of searching of genetic sequences (descriptions of amino acid and protein com-position) was a live one throughout the period. To address the issue, Derwent created a specialist file (GeneSeq) from 1990, and also increased their coverage of specialist sources, creating *Biotechnology abstracts* on CD-ROM the following year, and launching *Conference fast-track* in 1993 to try to capture the non-patent literature disclosures from technical meetings and conferences. The EPO made substantial efforts to increase coverage of the non-patent literature in its statutory searches during the period, and adopted a policy of licensing in some of the commercial databases in the most important technical fields, such as biotechnology and engineering.

Patent libraries in the United Kingdom

Within the UK, during the 1990s there were only thirteen designated 'patent libraries' and they collaborated under the PIN (Patents Information Network) label.[44] The annual reports of the UK Patent Office show that there was at least some financial support for PIN libraries into the 1990s, and in 1996 the Europe-wide PATLIB conference was hosted in Aberdeen. However, the libraries in the network varied widely in the amount and sophistication of effort which they devoted to delivering patent information to their local communities. The most extensive members of the group were London (based at the British Library) and Leeds. It remains unfortunately true that the degree of involvement and support from the national patent office falls far short of the extensive co-operation provided by the USPTO in the form of its Patent & Trademark Depository Library (PTDL) Program.

User groups and professional development

The only UK professional body dedicated to patent searchers is the Patent and Trade Mark Group (PATMG), a special interest group of the Library Association, and a short history of this appeared in 1993.[45] It continued to publish a regular newsletter for communication.[46] During the decade its membership was usually in the range 200–250, mostly based in industrial research groups.

Some members of PATMG also belong to the Patent Information Users' Group (PIUG Inc.), which, although based in the United States, has a world-wide membership, drawn from patent search professionals in industry, law firms and independent searching organizations. The history of the PIUG was outlined in a paper by Lambert.[47] During the course of the 1990s, the activities of the group expanded considerably, to include a closed internet discussion list launched in 1995 (which had evolved from an earlier Dialog-Dialmail bulletin board started in 1991) and a well-established annual conference.

Notes

1 Stephen van Dulken, 'Patents' in *British librarianship and information work 1986–1990*, ed. David W. Bromley and Angela M. Allott. London: Library Association, 1992, v. 2, pp. 99–110.
2 *Searcher* (US). Medford, N.J.: Information Today Inc. ISSN 1070–4795. Monthly.
3 *World patent information*. Oxford: Elsevier. ISSN 0172–2190. Quarterly.
4 Stephen Adams, 'Patent information' in *The business and economy internet resource handbook*, ed. Phil Bradley. London: Library Association, 2000, pp. 200–24.
5 James F. Sibley, *Online patents, trade marks and service marks databases*. London: Aslib, 1992; Brenda Rimmer and Stephen van Dulken, *International guide to official industrial property publications*. 3rd ed. London: British Library, 1992; C. Peter Auger (ed.), *Information sources in patents*. London: Bowker-Saur, 1992.
6 François Jakobiak, *Les brevets: source d'information*. Paris: DUNOD, 1994.
7 *Intellectual property law*. 2nd ed. London: Cavendish, 2000 (Cavendish LawCards series).
8 *Patents Act 1977*. Public & General Acts 25 & 26 Eliz. 2 c. 37. London: HMSO, 1977.
9 *Recommended standard on two-letter codes for the representation of states, other entities and intergovernmental organizations*. WIPO Standard ST.3. Geneva: WIPO, 2003 (latest ed.).
10 *Recommended standard code for the identification of different kinds of patent documents*. WIPO Standard ST.16. Geneva: WIPO, 2001 (latest ed.).
11 *The Copyright, Designs and Patents Act 1988 (Commencement No. 5) Order 1990*, SI 1990 no. 1400.
12 *The Register of Patent Agents Rules 1990*, SI 1990 no. 1457.
13 *The Patents (Amendment) Rules 1987*, SI 1987 no. 288.
14 'Council Regulation (EEC) No. 1768/92 of 18th June 1992 concerning the creation of a supplementary protection certificate for medicinal products', *Official journal EEC, L* **182,** 2 July 1992, 1–5; 'Regulation (EC) No. 1610/96 of the European Parliament and the Council of 23 July 1996 concerning the creation of a supplementary protection

certificate for plant protection products', *Official journal EEC, L* **198**, 8 Aug. 1996, 30–5.

15 *The Patents (Supplementary Protection Certificate for Medicinal Products) Regulations 1992*, SI 1992 no. 3091 (in force 10 Dec. 1992); *The Patents (Supplementary Protection Certificate for Medicinal Products) Rules 1992*, SI 1992 no. 3162 (in force 2 January 1993); amended by *The Patents (Supplementary Protection Certificate for Medicinal Products) (Amendment) Rules 1993*, SI 1993 no. 947 (in force 21 April 1993); *The Patents (Supplementary Protection Certificate for Plant Protection Products) Regulations 1996*, SI 1996 no. 3120 (in force 2 Jan. 1997).

16 *The Patents (Supplementary Protection Certificates) Rules 1997*, SI 1997 no. 64.

17 'Directive 98/44/EC of the European Parliament and of the Council of 6 July 1998 on the legal protection of biotechnological inventions', *Official journal EEC* (L 213), 30 July 1998, 13–21.

18 N. Byrne, 'Patents for biological inventions in the European Communities', *World patent information* **15** (2), 1993, 77–80.

19 *Software patents in Europe: meeting the challenges of harmonisation and development in Europe: proceedings of a conference held in London, 23 March 1998* [CD-ROM]. London: Patent Office, 1998.

20 *Basic facts about the Patent Cooperation Treaty (PCT)*. Geneva: WIPO, 2002 (WIPO publication; no. 433(E)). Free of charge, also available at: <http://www.wipo.int/freepublications/en/patents/433/wipo_pub_433.pdf> (accessed 31/1/06).

21 *Implications of the TRIPS Agreement on treaties administered by WIPO*. Geneva: WIPO, 1996 (WIPO publication; no. 464(E)).

22 *The Patent Office Trading Fund Order 1991*, SI 1991 no. 1796.

23 *The Patents (Fees) Rules 1998*, SI 1998 no. 1778.

24 *Recommendation concerning making facsimile images of patent documents available on CD-ROM*. Geneva: WIPO, 1993 (WIPO standard ST.40).

25 *Annual report and accounts, 1998–1999*. Newport: Patent Office, 1999.

26 Robert Brookes, 'The MIPEX Project: furthering electronic commerce in the IP community,' *Patent world* July 1998, 25–30.

27 Patent Office website: <http://www.patent.gov.uk> (accessed 31/1/06).

28 C. Jonckheere, 'EPOQUE (EPO QUEry service) the inhouse host computer of the European Patent Office', *World patent information* **12** (3), 1990, 155–7; James F. Sibley, 'The EPOQUE suite of applications', *World patent information* **18** (3), 1996, 141–8.

29 Paul Blake, 'Thomson gets its act together', *Monitor* 161, 1994, 7–8.

30 Stephen van Dulken, *British patents of invention 1617–1977: a guide for researchers*. London: British Library, 1999.

31 Paul Blake, 'British Library's Patent Express adds jukebox system', *Information today* **10** (7), 1993, 36–7.

32 The service was to close in 2002.

33 'Thomson's Dialog bargain', *Information world review* 157, April 2000, 1.

34 From 2005 part of the Lexis Corporation.

35 Martin A. Lobeck, 'Patent information on CD-ROMs', *World patent information* **12** (4), 1990, 200–11.

36 Siegfried Hahnemann, 'Patent CD-ROMs: five years of experience and 2500 in jukeboxes', *World patent information* **17** (2), 1995, 106–11; Gert Frackenpohl, 'CD-

ROM jukeboxes and their use in local area networks', *World patent information* **15** (2), 1993, 75–6.

37 David J. Dickinson, 'MIMOSA: mixed-mode CD-ROM software', *World patent information* **17** (2), 1995, 112–14.

38 Alfred Wenzel, 'Data transmission by satellite' in *Proceedings of the EPIDOS Annual Conference 1998, Jena, Germany, 20–22 October 1998*. Vienna: European Patent Office, 1998, pp. 136–41.

39 Grayce Shomade and Tamara S. Eisenschitz, 'Advances in the delivery of patent information', *World patent information* **18** (2), 1996, 87–95.

40 Nancy Lambert, 'But what's in it for IBM? "Free" patents on the Net', *Searcher* (US) **5** (8), 1997, 33–7; Richard Poynder, 'Patent information for the masses', *Online and CD notes* Nov. 1997, 3–5.

41 William Fisanick, 'Storage and retrieval of generic chemical structure representations'. *U.S. 4642762-A*, granted 10 February 1987, assigned to Chemical Abstracts Service; Michael F. Lynch, Steven M. Welford and John M. Bernard, 'Computer storage and retrieval of generic chemical structures in patents. Part 1: Introduction and general strategy', *Journal of chemical information and computer sciences* **21**, 1981, 148–50. Part 1 of a series.

42 H. Tokuno, 'Comparison of Markush structure databases', *Journal of chemical information and computer sciences* **33** (6), 1993, 799–804; Norman R. Schmuff, 'A comparison of MARPAT and Markush DARC software', *Journal of chemical information and computer sciences* **31** (1), 1991, 53–9; Kathleen A. Cloutier, 'A comparison of three online Markush databases', *Journal of chemical information and computer sciences* **31** (1), 1991, 40–4.

43 'Directive 98/44/EC of the European Parliament and of the Council of 6 July 1998 on the legal protection of biotechnological inventions'. *Official journal EEC, L* **213**, 30 July 1998, 13–21.

44 In 2002 PIN was re-designated PATLIB UK, to bring it into line with other similar networks across Europe, supported by the European Patent Office. See <http://www.bl.uk/collections/patents/patentsnetork.html> (accessed 31/1/06).

45 Michael J. R. Blackman, 'The Patent and Trademark Group', *World patent information* **15** (3), 1993, 151–2.

46 *Searcher – the newsletter of the PATMG*. London: PATMG. ISSN 1467-2898. Published approximately quarterly. See also <http://www.patmg.org.uk>

47 Nancy Lambert, 'A succinct history of the Patent Information Users Group', *World patent information* **13** (3), 1991, 149–51.

19

The book trade

Keith Sambrook

The 1890s
During the last decade of the 19th century, the trading partners of the British book business established trade associations: the Booksellers Association of Great Britain and Ireland in 1895 and the Publishers Association in 1896. Publishers and booksellers wanted to bring some order into their respective businesses and into their commercial dealings with one another. For several decades a degree of *laissez-faire* anarchy had prevailed. Under the leadership of Frederick Macmillan, in 1901 the two associations jointly formed the Net Book Agreement (NBA) which required book retailers to sell each book at its publisher's list price, neither more nor less.[1] The consequence was to institutionalize the trade in a way bemoaned by the industry's freebooters but welcomed for the most part by authors and printers. An era of commercial stability extending throughout two world wars and beyond followed, during which most sales invoices, royalties and print-and-bind bills were paid on the due date and in full. Most publishing houses and bookshops remained in the hands of their 19th-century owners, and takeovers, mergers and bankruptcies were rare.

One hundred years on
At the beginning of the last decade of the 20th century, the two associations were firmly in place. The Booksellers Association represented the shared interests of over 2,000 bookshops, large and small, throughout the country. The Publishers Association could be said to be in a confident and assured mood after thirty and more years of successfully promoting the industry at home and abroad, with the encouragement of government often on a para-statal level. Its various working divisions, the Book Development Council, the Educational Publishers Council and, later, the Council of Academic and Professional Publishers, were each actively involved in government policies on the export and overseas trade and with the education and information industry at home. The mid-century maxim of 'trade follows the book' was still endorsed and upheld.

In 1991 just under 70,000 new titles and reprints were issued. By 1993 the total had risen to 82,322, an increase of 4.4% over 1992, which had shown a much larger increase of 16.4% over 1991. Half of the books in 1993 came from firms in consumer publishing within the entertainment and leisure industry. The other half was published by firms working as part of the overall education and information industry. For example, there were 8,013 adult fiction titles, 869 food and cookbooks, 1,990 on travel and 1,191 on various sports. There were 7,795 scientific and technical titles, making up 12,040 in STM (scientific, technical and medical) with 4,245 on medicine and related subjects. Legal books amounted to 1,881; over 7,000 new titles in history, politics and other branches of the social sciences were published as well as 3,128 on computer science and usage. Business management and finance was a growing category with 3,419 titles, and general economics totted up 3,461. Children's books, fiction, non-fiction and picture-playtime books were altogether 7,073. For pupils in school, there were 2,828 new textbooks. There were 2,257 titles classified as 'literature' as well as 1,430 books of poetry. A total of 46,377 titles were published in paperback at an average price overall of £13.40 and the remaining 35,000 or so in hardback at an average of £13.88.[2]

Publishers marketed these titles to retail and wholesale booksellers at a mutually accepted range of discounts which had been in force in principle and substantially in practice since early in the 20th century. They were, of course, graded by category and by order quantity, and higher rates applied to net books than to non-net titles.

Six years later, in 1999, 110,155 new titles and reprints were issued. As in 1991, 50% came from the entertainment and leisure wing of the industry and 50% from publishers of books for education, the professions, information and reference. There were 9,800 adult fiction titles, 1,318 food and cookbooks, 3,073 on travel and 1,421 on various sports. The grand total for STM titles was 12,753 of which 4,563 were medical and related and 8,170 scientific and technical. Business management had grown further during the period and now had 4,168 titles along with 4,670 on economics in general. History, politics and other branches of the social sciences had also become a major category with over 9,000 titles. Children's books had also leapt forward to over 9,000 titles. Schoolbooks overall were 3,963, an increase *in toto* over 1993 but the number of textbooks, as distinct from revision, testing and home learning titles, had dropped. 2,936 books were regarded as 'literature' and there were twice the number of poetry titles at 2,597. In paperback, 66,056 titles were published at an average price of £16.02, only 2p less than the average for the 70,000 or so in hardback at £16.04.[3]

Discounts in 1999 from publishers to retailers and wholesalers departed fundamentally from the established structures of 1993. Rates, particularly on paperbacks, were significantly higher, flexible, seasonal and both title- and customer-specific. High quantity orders for paperbacks and some new hardbacks had risen sharply accompanied by widespread sale-or-return facilities. Discounts given on smaller orders from independent bookshops, metropolitan and provincial, were almost universally lower than those enjoyed by all branches of the chainstore groups.

What had taken place in the intervening six years to account for these fundamental changes in commercial dealings between publisher and bookseller?

The abolition of the Net Book Agreement

The most decisive single event was the abolition in September 1995 of the NBA and the UK book trade's abandonment of retail (or resale) price maintenance (RPM). The PA and BA's agreement thus never scored a century and a condition reminiscent of what had prevailed prior to the 1890s returned to the business of books.

Much was written about the NBA both in attack and defence during the five years preceding its demise as well as in the years immediately following. Defendants pointed to the NBA's effectiveness in maintaining a mostly orderly market for nearly one hundred years. Once before in 1962 it had been challenged in the Restrictive Practices Court but, as is very well known, the Court ruled in its favour asserting that 'books are different', that is, different from other products not controlled by retail price maintenance.[4] In 1989, it was again proposed for referral to the Court by Pentos, at that time the owners of the Dillons and Hudsons groups of shops, but the Office of Fair Trading (OFT) rejected the appeal.

During the early 1990s, publishers and booksellers both carried out minor sorties against the fortress of RPM. In May 1991, the Reed Consumer Group extended non-net status to all its titles. In the same year Waterstones and Books Etc entered into a pre-Christmas price war with Dillons and in 1993 Cassell de-netted a full range of reference titles. These manoeuvres led to the OFT announcing in November 1993 that it would consider re-examining the NBA, and in April a survey of members by the PA showed general support for RPM but revealed significant exceptions amongst larger firms. In August 1994 the NBA was again referred back to the RPC and on Boxing Day the Hodder Headline Group withdrew from the Agreement.

Nonetheless some important players in the general consumer book trade supported the NBA's survival: for example, HarperCollins through its chairman, Eddie Bell, and W. H. Smith. Both changed sides at crucial moments later in the engagement.[5]

In May 1995, the supermarket chain, ASDA, instituted a price war by discounting Le Carré's *Our game* by 50% and in August W. H. Smith made a deal with Hodder Headline over low-priced or 'give-away' copies of Rosamunde Pilcher's *Coming home*. HarperCollins were now reported as being convinced the NBA had no future. The head of publishing at the BBC, Nicholas Chapman, currently president of the PA Council, predicted the downfall of the NBA as a 'millstone around the necks of publishers' and de-netted the BBC's children's list.[6] Further de-netting by HarperCollins and Random House followed with effect from 1 October 1995, accompanied by extensive discount promotions by both firms with W. H. Smith. Untidy ad hoc deals were then made by a wide range of competing publishers.

Expediency led the day in fearful expectation of savage competition ahead. Retailers were alarmed by the entry of the supermarkets into the mass book trade and publishers were fearful of one another. Fixed prices for books were effectively at an end.

The consequences

The chief predictions of the consequences of the abolition of the NBA were:

- bookshops would concentrate on high discount bestsellers and cut down the range of their shelf stock
- publishers would raise prices in order to compensate for handing out high price war discounts and to protect their margins
- reduction in margins would force publishers to be wary of risk-taking on new titles
- many small independent bookshops, unable to secure high discounts and enter price wars, would close
- in essence, the combined effect would be fewer bookshops, narrower stocks, fewer new titles and higher published prices.

Nigel Newton, Chairman of Bloomsbury Publishing, was quoted as believing that the maintenance of the NBA would have ensured that 'serious book buyers who comprise 70% of the UK book market' would not be 'forced to subsidize the occasional purchasers of bestsellers'.[7]

In the event, the sky did not fall in on the UK book trade. Nevertheless, a report on the abandonment of the NBA carried out by the Cranfield School of Management early in 1997 recorded higher published prices of up to 7.64% on hardbacks and 6.25% on paperbacks. The Booksellers Association reported that around 250 independent members had gone out of business but that this was offset by up to 200 or so new enrolments, especially branches of the chainstores.

As the decade progressed, it became clear that publishers of general fiction and high profile, celebrity-authored non-fiction were cutting into their margins on potential bestsellers and, at the same time, spending considerably more than hitherto on conspicuous promotion. Large posters of cover designs appeared on the walls of strategically located underground stations. Any subsequent bigger share of the mass market for some hugely publicized titles was acquired at the expense of net profit and heavy demands on cash flow.

At the Society of Authors there was growing concern that members would increasingly be offered contracts with royalties calculated on receipts (that is, on discounted revenues) instead of on published prices. This possible threat to earnings probably helped to bring about a sea change in the relationships between authors and publishers. What demonstrably happened was that authors turned to their agents not only to negotiate contracts but also to bargain at pre-acceptance auctions for the highest possible advances. Agents gradually assumed the role of commissioning editors. There began a steady migration of experienced editors from some of the best fiction and general houses to literary agencies. With years of working on authors' manuscripts behind them they were able to determine what new work was suitable for putting on offer to publishers and what scale of advance could be bargained for. In the current climate of wanting at almost any cost to have titles at the top of the mass market league table, publishers too often gave away only partially recoverable six-figure advances. Option clauses, binding authors to publishers for future works, disappeared from contracts.

In retrospect, ten years later, do we now see the abolition of the NBA as the catalyst for an emphatic shift in book marketing practices or as an inevitable response to evident shifts in the patterns of readership and social habits?

By the 1990s the number of 'occasional' buyers of bestsellers, whose shopping was generally done in supermarkets and department stores, was growing. They were accustomed to making purchases from a limited range of items pre-selected and governed by market forces using expensive and conspicuous publicity. Special customer orders for items currently out of stock were not the practice in high street stores and were unknown in supermarkets. In retail marketing, of course, there was nothing novel in this, but it was comparatively new in the book trade. In 1996, a senior spokesperson at W. H. Smith, however, defined their book marketing policy as being to deliver 'what our core customers want and our core customers are the mainstream people in this country'. Smiths believed these customers wanted 'a pre-selected range'. Hitherto, book buying had most often taken place in small or medium sized, privately owned shops servicing local markets. There were, indeed, large shops such as Foyles, Hatchards, Blackwells, Heffers, Thins, Sherratt and Hughes and so on, which existed in city centres before the arrival of the chains (Dillons, Waterstones). 'Serious' book buyers from country towns and the suburbs traditionally favoured their own local bookseller.

Chainstores and price wars
Awareness of the expanding 'mainstream people' market and of Smiths' priorities forced the burgeoning chainstore groups to go nationwide in preparation for a head-on price war. Smiths, after all, had for long been the only nationwide seller of books. Their stocking policy had been based on providing for the 'occasional' book buyer who had come in for newspapers, birthday cards or other stationery. Publishers of titles with bestseller mass market prospects were now alerted to the need for aggressive marketing to nationwide booksellers other than Smiths. With the 'millstone' of the NBA and RPM around their necks how would they be able to do this?

Defendants of the NBA had forecast that bookshops would 'pile 'em high and sell 'em cheap'. As plastic-covered binders' pallets of the latest paperbacks became a common sight on the floors of the larger stores, this prediction seemed to have been right. In practice, however, only about 2% of each year's new titles were deployed in the price wars: 2,000, say, out of 100,000. Was the fear that the other 98,000 or so would become increasingly unavailable from booksellers' shelves also to prove correct?

The 'pile 'em high and sell 'em cheap' policy was primarily aimed at customers who had rarely entered the bookshops regularly frequented by 'serious' book buyers. There were reports of customers in branches of the chains saying they had always been 'afraid of going into bookshops'. Post-NBA, larger bookshops especially made big efforts to draw them in with eye-catching window and floor displays, highlighting issues and celebrities familiar through TV and the popular media.

The price wars intensified. The main protagonists were initially Smiths, Waterstones and Dillons, joined later by Borders/Books Etc and, with less central fire power, Ottakars. Smiths was, of course, a Victorian foundation. Tim Waterstone had started up his shops over a century later in 1982. Dillons was founded after the Second World War by Una Dillon as an academic bookshop in Bloomsbury but by 1990 had been developed into a nationwide general chain owned by the Pentos company which had also bought up Hudsons, the small Midlands chain based in Birmingham. By 1994 Pentos was bankrupt and the entire Dillons chain was acquired by HMV Media through its subsidiary Thorn/EMI. Ottakars had been launched by James Heneage in 1988.[8]

In 1992, after a decade of good business, Tim Waterstone sold his shops to Smiths for what seemed to be a multiple of 50 victory for his original shareholders. Others saw it as capitulation. Its founder's optimism seemed justified by the evidence several years later that Waterstones was indeed performing better than other parts of the Smiths empire. Nevertheless the view persisted that it was only a matter of time before Smiths' commercially centralized, high street culture would overturn the more liberal, individualistic, eccentric Waterstone culture.

The sale of Dillons to Thorn/EMI in 1994 was attributed more to the failed ambitions of Pentos to rival Smiths in the non-book business (they had bought Rymans) than to a failure of Dillons within the book trade. Four years later, in 1998, HMV Media doubled its presence in the book business with the purchase of Waterstones from Smiths. At the time, Dillons employed nearly 2,000 people and Waterstones a hundred or so more. A Dillons branch manager was quoted a reflecting that they 'had been through worse before'. Tim Waterstone forecast the closure of three or four Dillons branches (which soon happened) but was confident the Dillons brand would survive in high streets outside London where the two chains had so far competed.[9] In the event, before the year was out, HMV announced the re-branding of 44 Dillons shops, including the flagship in London's Gower Street, and their intention to introduce the Waterstones management culture and business style into the overall running of the new company.

Out in the country, in heritage market towns away from the provincial city centres Ottakars had over 70 shops by 1998 when James Heneage identified a further 100 towns ripe for new Ottakars.[10] A recent stock market flotation seemed to promise sufficient resources for expansion on this scale. The purchase of four shops from Peter Bell in the commuting outer London suburbs and home counties towns moved the chain closer to the metropolitan centre. Nevertheless, they strenuously denied a plan to develop a strategic alliance with Barnes and Noble, the large old-established US bookstore group.

Speculation on Barnes and Noble's possible entry into the UK market inevitably followed the arrival in 1998 of their only same-size US rivals, Borders, who acquired Books Etc almost immediately after touchdown. Customers to Borders stores were straightaway invited to relax in the coffee shop before browsing the shelves for books, magazines and music. The Books Etc site gave them an entrée to Charing Cross Road confronting Foyles and they soon made plans to engage with the Oxford Street culture and compete against rival chains on a matching scale in Glasgow, Leeds and elsewhere.

An analysis of the estimated consumer book market share at the close of 1998 gave lead position to HMV's Waterstones/Dillons shops with 18%.[11] Smiths, even with their recent acquisition of John Menzies, had been overhauled at last and came second with 17%. Borders/Books Etc and Ottakars chalked up only 2% each, while Blackwells outperformed both with 3%, despite their concentration on the educational and academic sectors. Outside Oxford, Blackwells had bought Heffers in Cambridge to add to their other shops in Bristol, Liverpool and elsewhere, and moved into the Charing Cross Road alongside Borders/Books Etc. Smaller groups (e.g. Hammicks, Thins) jointly accounted for another 1%. Between them, therefore, the nationwide groups commanded 43% of the consumer book trade. CTNs (confectioners, tobacconists, newsagents) remained on 5% but a significant new entry to the league was made by supermarkets with 6%. Mail order firms and book clubs totted up a further 10%. Did these figures confirm predictions of a steady draining away of business from independent bookshops and the dominance of stores over shops?

The 'indies' were, in fact, holding their own. Altogether 36% of the consumer book business passed across their counters as they served their local and loyal customers with a degree of personal attention and professional know-how only rarely achieved in branches of the chains. Their most famous name did not appear individually in the analysis but Foyles must surely have accounted for a significant share of their overall percentage.

HMV had themselves envisaged a future with fewer 'indies' and a good number of those concentrating on specialist interests. Their assumption was that the consumer trade would go on expanding and belong to the nationwide chains, despite competition on the most popularly in-demand bestsellers from super-markets. In the 21st century, how accurate would this vision of book retailing prove to be?

The shifting ownership of the high street book business in the 1990s took place between a limited number of players. With the exception of HMV, they were already within the existing book industry; with the exception of Borders, they were British. During the decade was there a similar pattern of changing ownership in the fortunes of booksellers' suppliers, the leading consumer and general publishers?

Mass market publishing
The mass market for popular, easy leisure reading grew perceptibly from the 1990s onwards. The market for easy-to-watch viewing grew even more. Television, radio and newsprint companies scrambled to acquire control of copyright material which they could profitably recycle for big or small screens or, suitably adapted, feature in mass market full-colour magazines worldwide. Media corporations in the US and the UK such as Paramount, RCA, Thomson and Time Warner hoovered up

majority shareholdings in publishing firms holding valuable copyrights. This became fashionably known as the 'recapitalization' of the literary publishing industry. It kicked off the creation of corporate, multinational companies or conglomerates.

As an example, in the early 1990s Rupert Murdoch's News Corporation bought Collins from the Collins family including its 50% shareholding of Harper & Row in the USA. HarperCollins came into being. Hodder & Stoughton merged with Tim Hely-Hutchinson's Headline to form Hodder Headline. The renowned trio of Chatto & Windus, Jonathan Cape and Bodley Head, who had formed CVBC with Virago, were swept up into Random House's UK group and, two years later, were joined by Century Hutchinson. Reed IPC had acquired Hamlyn and then Octopus in the late 1980s and thereby the Heinemann Group as well as Methuen and other former ABP imprints. They jettisoned Hamlyn but retained the rest.

A number of distinguished general firms had been taken into the newly-formed Orion Group in 1991, including Weidenfeld and Gollancz. In the paperback world, Penguin had, of course, been in Pearson's possession since the 1970s. What turned out to be a foretaste of things to come was the absorption of Corgi and allied lists into the Bertelsmann media empire.

With the exception of the Random House and Bertelsmann purchases, these mergers and takeovers were essentially domestic. They were multinational only in the sense that the protagonists traded their products internationally and owned fully or in part branch companies worldwide. During the second half of the decade this pattern changed and foreign ownership grew.

Foreign ownership of British-based publishing houses was not unknown. The owners had almost always come from other English-medium firms in the US, Canada and Australia. Between the two world wars there had been, for instance, the buying up and buying back antics of Doubleday and Heinemann. Whoever were the owners, their publications were designed for readerships in the English-speaking world. By the 1990s, political, social, educational and cultural changes had extended the anglophone readerships globally. English had clearly and indisputably become the world's lingua franca. Books in English had for long enjoyed a far larger first language market than those in any other language; during the third quarter of the 20th century they were selling in ever-increasing millions in second language and non-anglophone markets.

Some publishers of books in other languages already had titles in English on their lists intended for specialist readers and scholars especially in STM and professional disciplines. Houses in the Netherlands, for example, with a limited domestic language market but with high standards and skills in the industry combined with a national assumption of English as a second working language, maintained a British association dating back to the earliest days of multiple-copy book publishing. Companies such as Elsevier enjoyed a renowned reputation worldwide as publishers of STM and professional material in books and journals. The acquisition of British and US firms of their own kind was a natural progression and in 1990 they merged with Reed IPC. In so doing they took on board the

Heinemann Group and Butterworth. Very soon, they disposed of those bits of the purchase which 'did not fit' and offloaded the Heinemann and Secker general lists to Random House along with Methuen and others from the old ABP group.

If the Dutch takeovers by Kluwer as well as Elsevier prolonged an old alliance, the buying into English language publishing by French language and German language companies was new. This second 'recapitalization' of British and US publishing was made in order to secure an essential foothold for the future in the global anglophone market. Titles from the buyers' own lists would be increasingly excluded. The solution was to buy companies whose titles would fit and prosper.

Bertelsmann began cautiously with mass market paperback lists brought together under the umbrella of their subsidiary, Transworld. Before long they made a decisive move towards the head of the ownership league with the purchase of Random House in the US and the UK. By the end of the 20th century they had taken over the top spots in both the ownership and revenue tables. Established imprints in British publishing which became labels in the Bertelsmann empire were Cape, Chatto, Bodley Head, William Heinemann and Secker (bought from Elsevier in 1997), Harvill, Vintage and Methuen, whilst in the US there were Doubleday, Dell, Knopf, Pantheon and Random House itself.

The German family firm of von Holtzbrinck, owners of fifty or so international companies, had in 1995 bought the British family firm of Macmillan including Pan and Picador as well as the distinguished Nature portfolio of science and reference books and journals. In the US they took over Macmillan's St Martin's Press.

At the head of the French language invasion was Hachette. They acquired the Orion group in 1997 and followed this up with Cassell in 1999. In their British group, therefore, they included Weidenfeld, Gollancz, Dent, Philip, Phoenix, Mitchell Beazley, Brimax and Franklin Watts. Into the 21st century they were to make further purchases of well-known names in British and US publishing, and moved very close to (and eventually overtook) Bertelsmann in both ownership and revenue leagues.

An interesting, eccentric and, in the event, short-lived change of domestic ownership occurred in 1999 when W. H. Smith bought Hodder Headline. The purchase by a bookselling chain of a leading consumer-title publisher was not welcomed by either its bookselling rivals or by publishers. In the 21st century it proved an easy victim for further predatory French expansion.

Education, information and the professions

Part of the book industry inhabits a different world. Educational, professional and academic publishing and bookselling belong to the education and information industry as distinct from the world of entertainment and the popular media. The smouldering tensions in the fiction and general business which fired the volcanic eruption of the NBA's break-up, and the tremors which followed, barely affected the publishing and marketing of school, college and professional textbooks or titles of scholarship, either monographic or for reference. Less newsworthy, even in the trade's own organ, *The bookseller*, the 'serious' part of the industry went about its business hardly troubled by price wars. Its title output rose year by year and also its prices which, although comparatively modest, nonetheless hit the pockets of students and scholars and the diminishing budgets of libraries.

Winds of change from other directions did affect it. For instance, the imposition of national curricula increasingly outdated some of the traditional practices of schoolbook publishers. When regional and national examination bodies under the supervision of the universities through the Oxford Board, the Cambridge Syndicate, the NUJMB, the Southern Universities Board and so on issued their own subject by subject curricula and syllabuses, publishers had played a central role in the creation of high quality competing textbooks. Editors in educational houses were closely involved with content as well as design and production. They sought out suitable authors and authorial teams and arranged the trialling of draft materials in workshops and classrooms as part of the editorial process. Freedom of choice in rigorously tested classroom texts was wide and individual firms became well-known for the reliability and often excellence of their subject specializations: Heinemann and Stanley Thornes for science, Heinemann also for English, Longman for history, languages and the social sciences, Cambridge University Press and Bell for mathematics, Oxford University Press across broad subject areas, and Edward Arnold and John Murray each for highly regarded texts in selected niches.

The supply chain to state schools through local authorities and to both state and independent schools through specialist firms such as Foyles Educational was well established. Discounts were standard and mostly unchallenged. Non-net status allowed suppliers to add to or subtract from publishers' list prices to meet their customers' requirements and compete for contracts.

Fewer names appeared on the title pages of textbooks at the end of the century. Heinemann Educational Books, Nelson Thornes (Thornes had acquired Nelson in 1999) and Hodder Arnold had outstripped their former main competitors by producing the most widely adopted texts to fit the national curricula. Even this achievement no longer put them at the head of the educational publishers' league table; this distinction had passed to Letts, the most successful publisher of revision, self-testing, home-learning and supplementary materials.

Moreover, as the vestiges of Empire receded and left behind independent countries either commercially sound and increasingly self-sufficient or impoverished and unstable, the export market for school books from the UK trickled away. The commercially independent produced their own essential needs either by originating new materials or by means of sub-licences from UK firms for local editions.

The poorer countries had to do without imports unless funded by the World Bank or other international organizations. Colleges and universities everywhere needed books and journals for both students and libraries. This also led to the steady flow of same-language reprint rights from UK firms to former imperial branches, now mostly in local ownership, for the production of impressions at economic prices. Otherwise the export business, though still buoyant in terms of demand, was conducted on long discounts and extended credits often in the face of threatened piracies of essential titles. Defence of copyright abroad replaced expansion of sales volumes as the prime preoccupation of the UK Publishers Association.

Native speakers of languages other than English had earlier in the century accepted the spread of English as the global lingua franca and set about learning it. Where the OUP and Longman had led, others, including Heinemann, Macmillan and Nelson, followed in the provision of ELT materials for use both in UK language schools and in the learners' own countries. Professional certificates testifying to the learners' proficiency at graded levels were issued by the Cambridge Examinations Syndicate and it was surprising that the CUP's own very successful entry into this market came comparatively late. The attraction to teachers and students of the 'authorized brand', once launched, knocked some competitors hard but throughout the 1990s the ELT market remained huge and there was plenty of room for several big players.

The arrival of Amazon

Traditional book-buyers, who had been used to entering bookshops knowing precisely what they wanted and expecting either to find it on the shelves or to have it promptly ordered for them, were provided from the mid-1990s with an alternative source of supply. The world wide web resources of Amazon became available.[12] For customers equipped to make use of it, Amazon could often offer quicker delivery of particular titles at lower prices than either an independent bookseller or chain store branch. The imperfections of the US-owned system proved, however, persistently irksome for both publishers and customers in the UK. Its prejudice in favour of the US edition of a co-published title breached market rights by frequently offering the US edition within a few days instead of the UK edition in several weeks. One reason for this was Amazon's speedy access to its US warehoused stocks. Without similar facilities in the UK, it was faced with supplying customers' often single copy/single title orders by indenting from publishers at discounts lower than it could afford. Eventually a partial remedy was reached by linking up for orders of this kind with the efficient medium of the UK wholesaler, Gardners, from their wide range of stockholdings in Eastbourne.

More books for leisure

A prominent feature of the consumer trade during the 1990s was the continuing steep rise in the publication and demand for travel and food books. The broadening out of the travelling classes of all ages produced a flood of titles giving guidance and directions on where to spend holidays, what to see and, above all, what to eat. Traditional Baedeker-type guides had given exhaustive and accurate information to travellers who knew where they wanted to go. Late 20th-century guides pointed the way for travellers to destinations worldwide, especially those previously out of the way or out of bounds. There was an accompanying (and lifestyle-related) mountain of 'foodie' literature. A wide range of cookbooks, often by celebrated TV and media chefs, was already on the market for improving and extending your home-cooking repertoire. The travel boom spawned, from both established and new imprints, guidance on the consumption of exotic foods in exotic lands. By the end of the 1990s, five out of the top ten titles in the annual, non-fiction, paperback league table were cookbooks.

Children

Heading up the league tables for children's books by a formidably large margin were titles about a memorable phenomenon of the 1990s, Harry Potter. The combined sales of hardback and paperback editions of J. K. Rowling's 700-page stories of Harry Potter's magical adventures had topped 6 million in the UK alone since 1997.[13] Harry shot his author to the top of all bestseller leagues by 2000 and rocketed his publisher, Bloomsbury, from the world of middle-range literary and general houses into the company of the top ten multinationals. Not even a recent update of the *Highway code* had quite chalked up seven-figure sales; neither could *Captain Corelli's mandolin* nor *The naked chef* despite very impressive performances.[14]

Gains and losses

What can be seen as the main features and achievements of the UK book trade in the 1990s? By the turn of the century, who had been benefited and who disadvantaged? Title output rose steadily by an average 5% per annum, so more authors got into print. Moreover, most categories of books increased year by year. Below average, surprisingly, was adult fiction. Adult non-fiction was, on the other hand, above the norm. Reality, as on television, preferred to the imagination? The costs of promoting new fiction in a period of price war prohibited expenditure on all but the most likely 5% or so of the 10,000-odd novels published. By comparison, children's fiction matched works for adults and, overall, notched up one of the highest category growths.

The industry's 5% average was more than doubled by educational, professional and STM titles. Over the decade there was a fall-off in school textbook output in the aftermath of the introduction of national curricula but in the world of further education and professional training previous records were exceeded.

Despite forebodings at the time of the assault on the NBA and its subsequent demise, the average price of books did not rise significantly over the ten-year period. This was clearly in part due, post-NBA, to the higher number of titles issued in paperback each year and the corresponding decline in hardback bindings. Published prices consequently evened out, although the prices for titles brought out in short hardback impressions, especially in the academic and reference categories, rose appreciably.

Another prediction that the overall number of bookshops would decrease, post-NBA, proved wrong.[15] An immediate fall-out did occur but, within five years, the number was restored. The accompanying fear that customers would find a reduced choice of titles on booksellers' shelves was, however, borne out. Branches of the four leading chains did demonstrably concentrate more and more on bestsellers. In attempts to gain market share from rivals, they over-ordered from publishers' overprinted stocks. Requests from shops to publishers for returns of mass market paperbacks grew alarmingly and were accompanied by requests for the disposal of other slow-moving titles from their shelves. The consequent wastage was immense. By the end of the 1990s, it was estimated that 300,000 books were shredded every week: one million a month from bookshop returns and binders' stocks.[16]

Over-production in the adult fiction and popular non-fiction market was to quite a large extent an own goal. Large advances extracted by agents from publishers often predicated quick sales of over 100,000 copies in order to recover the up-front outflow of cash. Many titles never approached this figure and as the advances went down the drain they were nearly matched by payments to the recycling companies.

Keeping up with the Corgis, the Bantams and the Penguins became an obsession in the consumer book trade. There was clear evidence that the potential sales of a select number of celebrated, accessible mass-readership titles were enormous. Creating bestsellers was the driven task of marketing departments: a task determined by the need to capitalize on the tendency of this readership to read only what other readers were fashionably reading.

A revealing venture by Persephone Books underlines the changes, especially in women's readership habits and authorship, over most of the 20th century. Persephone reprinted in paperback works by women writers originally published in hardback during the first fifty or so years of the century. These books were mostly read at the time by leisured and professional middle-class readers often borrowing from the flourishing circulating libraries. For late 20th-century readers there were no circulating libraries. Instead they could afford the quickly available paperback editions and, for the more popular titles, the opportunity to pop them into shopping baskets at supermarket check-outs.

No longer 'different'?
The British political empire had dissolved by the 1990s. An English language empire had succeeded it, worldwide. At home a popular, mainstream market for selected titles heavily promoted at cheap prices to a growing readership had emerged. This decade can, perhaps, be seen as one of accommodation by the British book trade to this shift in the nature of its markets home and away.

In some respects it clearly overreacted. There was huge wastage of investment and materials hand in hand with over-production and excessive discounting in pursuit of market share. The corresponding wastage of human talent and experience was agonizing, as takeovers and mergers 'rationalized' staff numbers and, in making one do what two had done before, jettisoned excellent publishing professionals into 'consultancies' or out of the book world altogether.

Overall, though, the industry responded dynamically and successfully; most confident, perhaps, in its traditional position within the educational and information worlds. Everywhere it experienced a decline in native ownership, particularly amongst its bigger and old-established members. This was offset by the healthy growth of new companies, small and specialist in many cases but flourishing on their own terms without the burden of chasing market share or handing out crippling advances. Some of these were in the sure professional hands and ownership of victims of corporate takeovers and mergers.

Some observers claimed that in these ten years the book trade shed its professional elitism, cast off its cultural blinkers and, variously recapitalized, threw itself into a world where books were not 'different'. Had it, perhaps, been more at ease, undercapitalized but austerely more creative, when they were?

Notes

1   Sir Frederick Macmillan, *The Net Book Agreement 1899 and the book war 1906–1908: two chapters in the history of the book trade.* Glasgow: Printed for the author by Maclehose, 1924.
2   *The bookseller* 18 Feb. 1994.
3   *The bookseller* 18 Feb. 2000.
4   R. E. Barker and G. R. Davies (eds.), *Books are different: an account of the dfeence of the Net Book Agreement before the Restrictive Practices Court in 1962.* London: Macmillan, 1966.
5   'NBA: the long road to oblivion', *The bookseller* 29 Sept. 1995, 8.
6   Ibid.
7   'Bookselling giants merge', *The bookseller* 20 Feb. 1998, 7.
8   Jenny Bell, 'Ottakars: a journey from designer concept to sound practice', *The bookseller* 8 April 1994, 10–11.
9   *The bookseller* 27 Feb. 1998.
10 *The bookseller* 30 Oct. 1998.
11 *Book publishing in Britain.* London: Bookseller Publications, July 1999.
12 M. Morouse, 'A cyberspace shopping trolley', *The bookseller* 18/25 Dec. 1998, 34–6; Mark Kerr, 'Bookselling and the internet', *Multimedia information and technology* **25** (1), 1999, 67–71.
13 J. K. Rowling, *Harry Potter and the philosopher's stone.* London: Bloomsbury, 1997; *Harry Potter and the chamber of secrets.* London: Bloomsbury, 1998; *Harry Potter and the prisoner of Azkaban.* London: Bloomsbury, 1999; *Harry Potter and the goblet of fire.* London: Bloomsbury, 2000.
14 Louis de Bernières, *Captain Corelli's mandolin.* London: Secker & Warburg, 1994, and later editions; Jamie Oliver, *The naked chef.* London: Michael Joseph, 1999; *The return of the naked chef.* London: Michael Joseph, 2000.
15 For reviews of the effects of the abolition of the NBA see: R. Knowles, 'Library book selling post-NBA', *Librarian's world* **5** (5), 1996, 2–6; *Taking stock* **6** (1), 1997 (special issue); Elaine Ansell, 'Some effects of the end of the Net Book Agreement', *New library world* **99** (114), 1998, 248–53; James Dearnley and John Feather, 'The UK bookselling trade without resale price maintenance: an overview of change 1995–2001', *Publishing research quarterly* **17** (4), 2002, 16–31.
16 Figures supplied by Paper Hub Recycling of Nottingham, October 1999.

20

The impact of the internet on libraries

Phil Bradley

The last decade of the 20th century was marked by a huge explosion in the rise and use of the internet, not only by academics and commercial organizations, but by individuals in their own homes, their libraries and cyber cafés. CD-ROM technology had become much more widely available and end-users were getting used to the idea that they could quickly and easily search for the information that they needed without a great deal of intervention from intermediaries. Easy access to the internet, and the wealth of good (and equally bad) information increased this awareness. The 'dot.com boom' led to the introduction of many new services, and an explosion in the number of search engines available to searchers. The decade can also be characterized by a lack of understanding about the medium; many companies (a lot of them owning search engines) did not really appreciate the power of the internet until at least half-way through the decade, and there was a pioneer feel about it. Libraries on the other hand were very quick to understand the importance of providing information using this new resource and UK libraries in particular were keen to embrace it. Equally, as we shall see, there was a lot of concern about how best to do this, with worries about the value of the information and how to make it available in the best way for the largest number of users – concerns that continued into the next decade. While there was a desire to utilize the internet, one of the major stumbling-blocks during the decade was a limitation of technology: computers were not networked, and access was provided using dial-up resources which proved less than ideal. Another barrier to widespread use of the internet within libraries, certainly public libraries, was the cost of providing a service. Telephone connections were expensive, much more so than they later became with widespread cheap access to broadband connections, and libraries often had to try and fund internet facilities from existing, limited resources. However, by the end of the decade it was clear that the internet was not some passing fad or phase and was turning into a major resource that libraries could use to provide a whole raft of information resources that they had never been able to do previously.

The early years
In the early 1990s the internet was a very different creation to that which became

familiar later. An early work, *Zen and the art of the internet,* described some of the facilities available to people using the internet for research.[1] It explained the connections between machines, how the domain system worked, made considerable reference to email and FTP (File Transfer Protocol), USENET (often referred to as newsgroups), and things such as Telnet and Archie. Early searchers needed to locate material that they wanted to refer to by telnetting to one of the 8 databases available (which between them contained about 50 gigabytes of information) to locate the information they needed, and then copy or FTP it to their own machines. All of this was done without the use of graphical interfaces, but by using a command line system that was cumbersome to say the least. Early developments included utilities such as Veronica and Jughead, but both of these were still command line driven and were not user-friendly. In order to use any of these services effectively it was necessary to have a good understanding of how computers worked and to be familiar with arcane computer languages and terminology.

That is not to say however that libraries were not already using the internet – very far from it. Libraries had started automating their catalogues in the 1960s, particularly in the United States. The Ohio College Library Center started networking library catalogues throughout that decade and the next, and in the 1970s more regional consortia added their catalogues to this collection to form a national, and later international, network. During the 1980s the system continued to develop with the addition of WAIS (Wide Area Information Server) which would index the full text of files in a database and allow searches of the files. Peter Scott of the University of Saskatchewan created his Hytelnet catalogue in 1990, which provided a single resource to obtain information on library catalogues, other telnet resources and how to get access to them. In 1991 the University of Minnesota created a simple to use interface to access files and data and created the gopher system (a term that referred to the fact that the utility could 'go fer this' or 'go fer that') and it took no knowledge of computer systems to use; it was simply necessary to click on a number to reach the specific resource the researcher wanted to make use of. However, this was still not an overly friendly system, and it still relied on a considerable understanding and appreciation of user computer systems.

The world wide web

Parallel with these early developments Tim Berners-Lee and others at CERN (the European Laboratory for Particle Physics) suggested a new system for distributing information, and in 1991 this protocol developed into what became known as the world wide web. It was based on the concept of hypertext – embedding links in text which pointed and led to other pages of information. It was however still very slow to develop, and did not receive a boost until 1993 when Marc Andreessen and his team at the NCSA (the National Center for Supercomputing Applications) created the first graphical browser Mosaic, which developed into Netscape. In these early developments different designers and developers tried to put their own stamp on the development of the internet; the threat being that it would descend into a mass of unrelated protocols that would require different software for different applications. This threat was countered by the establishment of the World Wide Web Consortium in 1994 to promote and develop agreed standards for the web.

While work was taking place in the technical developments of the internet at this time, it also started to expand in other ways as well – principally the user base. It was originally limited to users in the fields of education, research and government usage. Delphi, an American national commercial online service, offered email access in 1992 and then full access in 1995, when the National Science Foundation in the United States ended sponsorship of the internet backbone, and AOL, Prodigy and CompuServe came online and internet traffic began to rely on these commercial providers of networks.

Libraries in Britain
While many of the early developments of the internet took place in the United States British libraries and librarians were also becoming involved in the development of services that would play a significant role in the internet. In 1990 the Bulletin Board for Libraries (BUBL) was established.[2] It was created as part of Project Jupiter, a project based at Glasgow University which trained British librarians in the use of JANET (the Joint Academic Network). BUBL continued to develop (primarily in a voluntary capacity) until it was offered funding by JISC (the Joint Information Systems Committee) in 1994. JISC itself was established in 1993 to deal with networking and specialized information services.

As access to the internet developed, and more services became available, JISC produced its first five-year strategy plan in 1995, in particular the Electronic Libraries Programme (eLib) to develop access to electronic journals, improve access to bibliographic records, research materials and research data.

British librarians and information professionals took an early interest in the development of the internet and were keen to find ways in which they could take advantage of the resources that it was making available to them. On an anecdotal level, I ran one of the very first training sessions on the use of the internet in 1994 in conjunction with TFPL (a training and recruitment company specializing in the information profession) which was attended by over 40 librarians from the academic, public and commercial sectors. The delegates were enthused about the possibilities offered by the internet, although there was considerable mistrust about how it could be used and the effect it might have on their jobs and roles (something which continued for some years). Indeed a talk given to the Aslib Midlands Branch in March 1995 by Ian Winship focused in part on how librarians could take advantage of the internet and how it could enhance, rather than threaten, their positions.[3] I also recall reassuring librarians about how useful the internet could be by making reference to a posting in 1993 by Karen Schneider entitled '22 internet ref success stories'.[4] Some of the things that librarians were enthusing about were the abilities to find lyrics to a song from a rock band, the geographic coordinates of a town, biographies of astronauts, the text of the UN Declaration of Human Rights and average rents on farms. It seems strange that soon we would think nothing of obtaining this information via the internet, but at the time these were touted as major success stories of how useful it could be.

In the mid-1990s librarians were using the internet, but it was often simply as a way of disseminating information via email and mailing lists. The earliest edition of the *Internet resources newsletter*, dated October 1994, almost exclusively refers to using the internet for email purposes, listing many mailing lists and Mailbase lists.[5] There are a few references to specific websites that would be of interest to the academic community, but interestingly no reference at all to search engines, or how to actually search for information, despite the fact that the closing sentence of the first paragraph of the newsletter reads: 'We in the Library believe that there is a great deal of useful information to be found on the superhighways, but the problems are ... where is this information? ... and how can you get access to it?'

Search engines
This emphasis was shortly about to change, however, but in order to fully appreciate this it is necessary to revisit the United States to look at the development of certain resources that were starting to draw attention to themselves – search engines. As previously mentioned, early internet users needed to use tools such as Archie, a pre-web utility that could search for files, but this was unfriendly and limited. Both Archie and Veronica lacked any real ability to help a user find the information that they needed, since they could only index the title of a document, not the full text. As the web began to grow, these resources became less important; between 1993 and 1996 the web grew from 130 sites to more than 600,000.[6] Users needed to have an easy way of finding the information that was available on these sites, and the first real search engine that attempted to index this information was the WWW Wanderer, created by Matthew Gray from Massachusetts Institute of Technology. The Wanderer would, as the name suggests, wander around the web, span many sites for information and would then drill down into the site to index the data that it found. Shortly after this innovation another engine, WebCrawler, was introduced, going online in April 1994; this retrieved URLs in the same way as a browser does, indexed the full text of pages and made them available. It used a simple browser interface and full text search and would be recognized by searchers of today as a search engine, albeit a very simple one, with limited functionality.

The first search engine that many internet searchers will recall is AltaVista, produced by DEC (Digital Equipment Corporation) which went public on 15 December 1995 with access to over 16 million documents. During a similar time period Lycos was also introduced to the searching public. Lycos began life as a Carnegie Mellon University project, and it used mathematical algorithms and links to determine relevance in results, which of course is what Google also used slightly later. Both search engines were used widely by British librarians and an early article in *Ariadne* magazine compares the two of them.[7] This article is interesting for a number of reasons; there is a detailed explanation of how to use both search engines (indicating that although librarians were aware of the engines their understanding of how to use them was actually quite limited) and concerns were raised over their value. Criticisms included currency, relevance, accuracy and the limitations of the search interface – almost exactly the same criticisms that would continue to be made in years to come. Another question that arose at around the same time was articulated at the Infonortics conference in April 1996: 'Do we really need librarians?',[8] and this was certainly a concern that was very often voiced to me as I ran internet training courses in the mid 1990s. The rise of search engines, and the ease of access to information by end-users had been foreshadowed by the increase in availability of data provided by CD-ROM databases. As users found it easier to obtain information, librarians were beginning to have a concern about their future role in its provision, and many saw the rise of the internet as a challenge to the profession.

Subject gateways
However, British librarians were not slow to appreciate that access to good, high quality information was necessary if they were to utilize the resources available on the internet, and ROADS (Resource Organisation and Discovery in Subject-based services), part of eLib, was developed primarily to consider how metadata could be created, organized, searched and presented to the user.[9] Two early eLib projects, OMNI and SOSIG, were established.[10] Both were what I refer to as 'virtual libraries' or subject gateways, and their role was to identify and select high quality resources, review them and make them available to their end-users. Both of these, and indeed many other similar resources, were still in use at the time of writing, but these two, focusing on medicine and the social sciences respectively, were among the forerunners. They provided simple, quick and easy access to resources that librarians could trust in an academic environment, very similar in fact to what Yahoo! was doing in a more general way. Yahoo! made its debut in late 1994, and by the end of the year the site, with its simple structure and easy to user interface, had expanded to include many thousands of links, with traffic doubling every month. Its success was due to many different things, but predominantly because it made sense: at that point in time people did not automatically know what to do with a search box, but their hierarchical approach made sense to both technical people and new searchers. With resources such as Virtual Libraries and the Yahoo! approach to providing access to data, search was finally becoming much easier for librarians and the general public alike.

Public libraries
This shift towards an 'ease of use internet' is reflected in the way libraries in the UK were starting to use it, particularly in the public sector. While the eLib projects concentrated on a range of projects considering document delivery, digitization and on-demand publishing, public libraries were considering more fundamental questions, such as trying to incorporate access to the internet in the range of services that they provided. The major concerns of libraries in the mid-1990s were:

- how could the internet be used to answer queries from the public?

- how could public access be managed?
- how much was it going to cost?

A paper by Chris Batt delivered at the 61st IFLA General Conference in August 1995 entitled 'The library of the future: public libraries and the internet' started by explaining what the internet was, and then went on to explore how British libraries were starting to use it.[11] Three projects in particular were covered. ITPOINT, a project being run at Chelmsley Wood Library in Solihull, showed that there was a great deal of enthusiasm for public access to the internet and the resources were heavily used. Project EARL (Electronic Access to Resources in Libraries) was a collaborative project involving public libraries throughout the United Kingdom, providing a WWW server on which libraries could mount their own web pages. CLIP (Croydon Library Internet Project) was one of the forerunners in providing public access to internet-based material. Although we may smile at the limited technical resources available – CLIP ran on a 64kb internet connection (later it was not uncommon to find 8 megabyte connections) – at the time this was very fast access indeed. A major concern was the time that it would take to find information for a library user. The staff involved in CLIP made heavy use of a service called 'Stumpers', which was a mailing list for librarians to pose and answer difficult queries, so in this instance the internet was being used as a medium for the provision of information, rather than a repository in its own right. Subject guides were also widely used, including the British Library Portico information service. A major problem for CLIP was in the technical environment: connecting across the network, matching routers, getting browsers to work with different types of software and the costs of getting the service to work in conjunction with Croydon's existing network was, according to Batt, '... not trivial. In our experience the process will be both time-consuming, frustrating and will cost more than you expect'.

The CLIP project was not as discouraging to public libraries as that quote might lead one to believe, and many other libraries were looking to provide resources and access to the internet. The South Ayrshire Cyber Project aimed to make 15 internet workstations available to the general public by June 1996. CyberShack was set up by Hounslow library service, with four terminals being made available in an internet centre with the help of local computer companies.[12] However, while these were exciting initiatives it should be remembered that less than 1% of public libraries were offering internet access during the mid 1990s and this was due in great part to the cost of this provision.[13] It was estimated by Chris Batt in 1995 that it cost £11,500 to provide a state-of-the-art connection to the internet for a year – the cost of a library assistant. In the next decade, with fast internet access from home and subscriptions to internet providers costing a few pounds a month, it would seem almost inconceivable that libraries had to work in conjunction with local computer companies and could only offer access to the public at a price.

While not directly related to libraries, the role of city, local or county councils should not be overlooked; a great many libraries and library services maintain websites now as part of an overall council site, and were encouraged to do this during the mid 1990s. Several councils took an early lead in this area, and Surrey, Barnsley, Somerset, Liverpool, Manchester were quick to produce internet sites that acted as a local information resource. Indeed, both Leeds and Cambridge internet services were initially managed by librarians, although this did change over time.

Expanding uses

By this point librarians and information staff were starting to use the internet, although its primary use then (as it continued to be) was to transmit email from person to person. However, it was also beginning to have an effect in other areas. Although the following is anecdotal, it does illustrate the point well. Val Hamilton (research assistant, University of Glasgow) refers to a time just after the Kobe earthquake in Japan:

> I was a librarian at Stirling University, subject specialist for Japanese studies and had a Japanese-capable Toshiba laptop. The lists of those who had died in the earthquake were put on the web in Japanese script by volunteers – this may have been one of the first times the web was used in this way.
>
> We had a visiting Japanese student from Kobe, whom I knew slightly. Mine was the only computer on campus which could access the webpages so we spent a very, very long afternoon going through the lists with a connection that seemed to be able to break down at any number of different points in the process. She sat beside me silently in the basement store where the laptop was set up, scanning each page as it appeared and quietly breathing 'OK', as she got to the bottom without recognizing any names. I think we were both holding our breath as she read each page. Fortunately, her family was all OK.
>
> That is certainly when I became aware of the power and potential of the internet as a communication medium, and it was the spur I had needed to get to grips with the technicalities of connection.[14]

As librarians became more interested in using the internet, they also began to look at different ways that they could use it, both to supplement their existing work, but also to discover new ways of providing information. An interesting early project was the Treasure Island on the Web which was designed to introduce children to classic literature.[15] Interestingly, at the time of writing the site was still up and running, performing the same job. Also interesting to note is that even at that early stage, the designers of the site went to considerable trouble to ensure that it was produced in such a way as to appeal to the specific audience they had in mind. The point here of course is that librarians and information staff, being used to working with information, could quickly grasp the concept of displaying the correct information in the right way – something which sadly lacking on many corporate or commercial websites designed by technicians or graphic designers! Indeed, the launch of the UK Public Libraries website which was designed to compile a definitive listing of all UK public libraries on the web, paid particular attention to the needs of the blind and visually impaired.[16] Concern continued to be paid to the quality of information, and librarians were being guided to use resources that had been checked, such as Excite Web Reviews,[17] the Lycos Top 5% Sites, the Magellan Internet Guide, and resources created principally for the information community, such as Edinburgh Engineering Virtual Library (EEVL),[18] Organising Medical Networked Information (OMNI) and Social Science Information Gateway (SOSIG).

A bid for Millennium funding to help create a nationally networked internet resource for public libraries was turned down at the beginning of 1997, but individual library services continued to develop their own services. South Ayrshire took money from its book fund to create a public access internet service,[19] while Suffolk library service used their existing network to provide public access.[20]

The two years of 1997/98 were a period when British librarians were spending much of their available time looking at the internet, building on previous work, and finding new ways in which to use the resources that were quickly becoming available. *Ask a librarian* was started, which allowed anyone with an internet connection to fill in a short form detailing the question they needed the answer to, with the expectation of getting an answer within 48 hours.[21] The various training organizations, such as TFPL, Aslib, UkeIG, the Library Association, and Netskills were all starting to offer courses in the area of the internet, from basic to advanced search skills, internet resources for particular subject areas and writing and designing web pages and sites.[22]

New search engines
New search engines continued to be developed, such as Northern Light[23] which was an improvement on existing search engines, and provided more search facilities and an improved display of results, while Ask Jeeves introduced the concept of natural language questions.[24] This obviously proved to be of interest to the library community and while the service had its flaws it nonetheless received a glowing review from various quarters, such as Tracey Stanley, the search engine columnist for *Ariadne* magazine who was excited about the new range of possibilities available to end-users with a more sophisticated, easier to use interface.[25] However, the new engines faced stiff competition from the old favourites such as AltaVista, Yahoo! and Lycos, who were keen to keep their hold over the searching public, but which were also trying to work out how to make money out of the services that they provided. One approach was to begin to turn themselves into portal services to broaden their appeal and reach, although this idea was quite slow to take off, and never really fulfilled its potential, at least not in this period.

The 1998 UKOLOG conference drew many of these disparate strands together.[26] Sessions were held that welcomed the rise of the internet, and its role in a modern library setting, but lack of high-powered computers meant that libraries were struggling with little processing power, incomprehensible software and poor connectivity. Other papers questioned the lack of good, high-quality authoritative data, poor results from search engines, and the concern that disadvantaged groups would not be able to leverage the power of the internet, due to a lack of equipment. Concerns were also voiced about copyright issues, and legal implications; concerns that ironically we still have today. However, there were many positives to be taken from the internet: the way in which websites could be used to present information in new and dynamic ways, the ability for librarians to change the way in which they worked, and the availability of new software packages to assist librarians in improving services.

Hybrid libraries
The concept of 'hybrid libraries' was introduced – that is to say a library that was not just a traditional book-based library, nor a virtual library, but a combination of the two, utilizing the best of both approaches. While this later became common-place, at that period of time many librarians were uncertain about how to imple-ment such a service. Chris Rusbridge in his paper 'Towards the hybrid library' discusses the problems of integrating new resources into existing systems, authen-tication issues and the common theme of the role of the information professional and that of the technician.[27] It was becoming accepted that librarians would need to gain a much greater understanding of the technicalities of providing internet-based resources, but that equally this could be seen as a threat or at the very least a source of annoyance between the two different groups – an issue that in many cases remained unresolved in the next decade.

Google
Meanwhile, on the other side of the Atlantic work had been taking place throughout the whole of 1998 that was going to change the shape of the internet, in almost every way possible – with search engines, financial models, end-user experiences and perceptions and general acceptance of the internet. Two students, Larry Page and Sergey Brin, had been working on a project called Backrub, which utilized something called 'PageRank' – a method of ranking returned results via a new type of algorithm, which rewarded pages that had a lot of links going to them. Both men made the assumption that web authors would not want to link their pages or sites to bad or inferior ones, so a link was like a 'vote' for any particular page. While link data had been used for some time by other search engines Backrub took this to a new level, improving the relevance of results. This project was launched and incorporated in September 1998 as Google. Interestingly it was not seen at the time as being the megalith that it later became. Danny Sullivan wrote about it in 1998 and while not dismissing it out of hand merely gave it a passing nod in the piece that concentrated on other resources.[28] This was not uncommon; I certainly did not start writing about Google until 2000; it was not mentioned in *Ariadne* at all in 1999,[29] and in the *Internet resources newsletter* it gets a passing mention in January 1999 as a 'search engine aimed at researchers. Google crawls the Web, and analyzes hyperlinks to find out what is important and what people like'.[30]

Indeed, with hindsight, there was not that much to write about. It is certainly true that Google introduced a fresh new look to search engine interface design – the home page was uncluttered and results were presented in a format that was easy to understand, but it was unable to figure out a business model, and as Michael Moritz (a Google founder) said: 'As 1999 trickled by and we were burning cash without a clearly illuminated path to revenues, there was considerable concern.'[31] It was not until the end of 1999 that Google introduced the concept of paid advertising, and only in 2000 that their first paying customers appeared on the site.

Google was not the overnight success that we often think that it was, and throughout the rest of the decade concentration was focused in other areas and on other search engines. The major search engines continued to be the old warhorses of AltaVista and Yahoo! although a newcomer, AllTheWeb, was gaining attention.[32] The major search engine battleground continued to be fought out (as it would for several years to come) on the ground of the size of the indexes – AltaVista boasted what was then a huge 250,000,000 webpages indexed. However, one particular development is worthy of note (if only to mention it as a forerunning of Web 2.0-based applications not due for another five years), which is the personalization of search. Lycos, Excite and Yahoo! all introduced a limited level of personalization of the search experience. This allowed users to begin to configure search engines to match their own requirements for information, though only at the most basic level.

The end of the decade

UK-based virtual libraries or gateways such as SOSIG, OMNI and EEVL continued to develop apace as librarians were still in need of good, high quality resources. The problems that had plagued UK librarians continued to exist, and an interesting article from John Kirriemuir, talking specifically about internet provision within the Health Service, clearly highlighted some of these.[33] He paid particular attention to the cost of computing equipment, security and technical issues, poor support for librarians working with the internet, communication problems and access to good quality information – depressingly, many of the same problems continued to be experienced at the time of writing.

2000 proved to be something of a watershed for the internet as people at large became much more aware of it, and started to use it in larger numbers. In the first e-commerce survey of business from the Office of National Statistics (May 2001), it was found that nearly £57 billion worth of UK sales were made over the internet in 2000, which was about 2% of sales.[34] More internet service providers established services to provide affordable and fast connections to the internet. Approximately 60% of the population had access to affordable DSL or cable broadband services and approximately 40% of the population had a choice of service providers.[35] Ironically of course, 2000 was also the year of the 'dot.com bust' when many companies discovered that they could not make as much money as they were expecting, and folded. However, the growth in the information sector continued, building on easier and cheaper access to internet-based resources. In March 2000 for example the *Oxford English dictionary* went online in a format designed for maximum accessibility, with all the obvious advantages for the information community (other than the fact that it was a subscription-based product).[36] Other reference sources were also becoming more readily available, with Infoplease providing access to encyclopedias, almanacs, biographies, atlases and so on, the *Encyclopaedia Britannica*, and the *World book encyclopedia*.[37] An ever-increasing number of professional organizations created their own websites to provide information; in January alone the *Internet resources newsletter* alerted their readers to several dozen, and continued to add to an ever-growing list throughout the rest of the year.[38] The British Library introduced an online catalogue of its newspapers and periodical holdings at the end of 1999 and it quickly became a popular resource for information professionals. Schools began to embrace the internet in large numbers at this particular time; 80% of primary schools, 90% of special schools and almost 100% of secondary schools were connected to the internet by the end of 2000.[39]

The role of the internet was slowly but surely affecting every area of the provision of information – for example, a paper on the standards for university law libraries showed that all their member organizations provided access to the internet and 'in 2000, 77 per cent rated the part played by the Internet as substantial compared to 46 per cent in 1998'.[40]

On the search engine front, Google began to make headway as its advertising and business model began to bring money into the company, and it also struck a deal with Yahoo! to provide secondary results to their service, which is somewhat ironic given their subsequent competition with each other. Other search engines continued to develop, particularly in the area of multi- or meta-search engines (those that pull results from a variety of different search engines and display the results in a ranked order), providing even more variety for the information professional to use.

Without a doubt, the decade turned the information world on its head. While CD-ROM technology had raised the possibility of users running their own searches, access to information was still very much within the province of the information professional, acting as a gatekeeper, by taking queries, finding the answers and delivering them back to the original enquirer. By the end of the century this model was increasingly looking out of date as information professionals started to embrace the role of facilitator – not getting the information themselves, but by providing access via the technology in the form of networked computers, and by creating resources such as the aforementioned virtual libraries. Although there were many stumbling-blocks, the way was set; librarians and other information professionals could use the internet to help users in ways that had been undreamed of at the beginning of the decade, and rather than seeing the internet as a challenge to the profession could utilize it to provide better resources in the future.

Notes

1 Brendan P Kehoe, *Zen and the art of the internet: a beginner's guide to the internet*. 1992. Available from: <http://www.cs.indiana.edu/docproject/zen/zen-1.0_toc.html> (accessed 31/1/06). Later editions published by Prentice-Hall.

2 BUBL: <http://www.bubl.ac.uk>.

3 Ian Winship, 'Internet paper', 1995. Available from: <http://bubl.ac.uk/archive/lis/internet/intern3.htm>.

4 Karen Schneider, '22 internet ref success stories', 1993. Available from: <http://lists.webjunction.org/wjlists/publib/1993-September/063507.html>.

5 *Internet resources newsletter* 1, Oct. 1994: <http://www.hw.ac.uk/libWWW/irn/irn1old.html>.

6 John Battelle, *The search: how Google and its rivals rewrote the rules of business and transformed our culture*. London: Nicholas Brealey, 2005.

7 Tracey Stanley, 'Altavista vs. Lycos', *Ariadne* 2, March 1996: <http://www.ariadne.ac.uk/issue2/engines/intro.html>.

8 Nigel Ford, 'Anoraks and cardigans (2): New text search engines, Bath, April 1996', *Ariadne* 3, June 1996: <http://www.ariadne.ac.uk/issue3/bath/>.

9 Rachel Heery, 'ROADS: Resource Organisation and Discovery in Subject-based services', *Ariadne* 3, June 1996: <http://www.ariadne.ac.uk/issue3/roads/>.

10 Organising Medical Networked Information: <http://www.omni.ac.uk>; Social Sciences Information Gateway: <http://www.sosig.ac.uk>.

11 Chris Batt, 'The library of the future: public libraries and the internet'. Paper presented at the 61st IFLA Conference, Aug. 1995: <http://www.ifla.org/IV/ifla61/61-batc.htm>.

12 Ian Morson, Joy Harrison, David Cook, 'Boldly venturing into cyberspace', *Library Association record* **98** (3), 1996, 150–1.

13 Sarah Ormes, 'Internet activity in public libraries', *Ariadne* 3, June 1996: <http://www.ariadne.ac.uk/issue3/libraries/>.

14 Private communication, Jan. 2006.

15 Treasure Island on the Web: <http://www.ukoln.ac.uk/services/treasure>.

16 UK Public Libraries Website: <http://dspace.dial.pipex.com/town/square/ac940/ukpublib.html>.

17 Excite web reviews: <http://www.excite.com/>.

18 Edinburgh Engineering Virtual Library: <http://eevl.ac.uk/>.

19 South Ayrshire Council Online: <http://www.south-ayrshire.gov.uk>.

20 Suffolk County Council Suffolk Libraries: <http://www.suffolk.gov.uk/LeisureAndCulture/Libraries/>.

21 *Ask a librarian*: <http://www.peoplesnetwork.gov.uk>.

22 TFPL: <http://www.tfpl.com>; Aslib: <http://www.aslib.co.uk/>; UkeIG: <http://www.ukeig.org.uk/>; CILIP: <http://www.cilip.org.uk/>; Netskills: <http://www.netskills.ac.uk/>.

23 Northern Light: <http://www.northernlight.com/>.

24 Ask Jeeves (later Ask): <http://www.ask.com>.

25 Tracey Stanley, 'Ask Jeeves, the knowledge management search engine', *Ariadne* 17, Sept. 1998, <http://www.ariadne.ac.uk/issue17/search-engines/>.

26 UKOLUG Conference 1998: <http://lists.webjunction.org/wjlists/web4lib/1998-February/024133.html>.

27 Chris Rusbridge, 'Towards the hybrid library', *D-Lib magazine* July/Aug. 1998: <http://mirrored.ukoln.ac.uk/lis-journals/dlib/dlib/dlib/july98/rusbridge/07rusbridge.html>.

28 Danny Sullivan, 'Counting clicks and looking at links', *SearchEngineWatch* Aug. 1998: <http://searchenginewatch.com/sereport/article.php/2166431>.

29 *Ariadne*: <http://www.ariadne.ac.uk>.

30 *Internet resources newsletter* 52, 1999: <http://www.hw.ac.uk/libWWW/irn/irn52/irn52b.html>.

31 Battelle, *The search*.

32 AllTheWeb: <http://www.alltheweb.com/>.

33 John Kirriemuir, 'OMNI: accessing the internet, *Ariadne* 20, June 1999: <http://www.ariadne.ac.uk/issue20/omni/>.

34 Roger Darlington, 'What is electronic commerce and why is it so important?', 2001: <http://www.rogerdarlington.co.uk/ecommerce.html>.

35 Douglas Alexander, Speech to the Digital Content Forum, Dec. 2001: <http://www.dti.gov.uk/ministers/archived/alexander031201.html>.

36 *Oxford English dictionary*: <http://www.oed.com/>.

37 Infoplease: <http://www.infoplease.com/>; *Encyclopaedia Britannica*: <http://www.britannica.com/>; *World book encyclopedia*: <http://www.worldbook.com>.

38 *Internet resources newsletter* 64, Jan. 2000: <http://www.hw.ac.uk/libWWW/irn/irn64/irn64.html>.

39 Department for Education and Employment, *Statistics of education: survey of information and communications technology in schools, England, 2000* (Bulletin; no. 07/00, Oct. 2000): <www.dfes.gov.uk/rsgateway/DB/SBU/b000197/sb07-2000.pdf>.

40 Society of Legal Scholars, Libraries Committee, 'A library for the modern law school: a statement of standards for university law library provision in the United Kingdom: 2003 revision': <http://www.legalscholars.ac.uk/documents/standards2003.pdf>.

21

Education and training

Marion Huckle and Margaret Watson

Introduction

The period 1991–2000 proved to be one of great change and development, not only in professional education but also in higher and further education and in the emergence of vocational and work-based learning and its influence on the sector. In this chapter we will survey the principal changes and developments, and their impact on education and training. For an in-depth and comprehensive discussion of these issues, particularly during the first half of the decade, readers are advised to consult *The education of library and information professionals in the United Kingdom.*[1]

Higher education

The nature of higher education in the UK changed significantly over the period under review. The number of students studying at universities and colleges increased dramatically from approximately 1,200,000 in 1991 to over 1,800,000 in 2000, an increasing number of whom were mature (i.e. over 21) and part-time.[2] More students were recruited from overseas: in library and information studies (LIS) this recruitment was principally from the new and emerging nations rather than from Europe and our immediate neighbours.

These changes challenged universities to rethink all aspects of course content, structure and delivery to meet the needs of an increasingly customer-led, geographically dispersed student body. Many new students worked part-time. They brought a level of knowledge and understanding of professional issues and demands into the classroom: teaching staff had to respond appropriately both in terms of course content and in the development of flexible and accessible modes of study.

The passing of two Acts in 1992 abolished the so-called 'binary line' between the universities and the polytechnics and colleges, and established a unitary system of higher education.[3] The Acts awarded university status to former polytechnics, many of which had previously been providers of CNAA-accredited LIS under-graduate and postgraduate programmes.

The Acts created new funding councils for the UK: the Higher Education Funding Council for England (HEFCE); the Scottish Higher Education Funding

Council (SHEFC) and the Higher Education Funding Council for Wales (HEFCW), which together took over the funding of all higher education institutions in the UK from 1 April 1993.

Many of the 'new universities', including those offering degrees in librarianship, quickly established a reputation for excellence in both teaching and research. Both factors were important to funding as the funding bodies allocated most of their funds by formula for both teaching and research.

During the 1990s the process of teaching quality review was refined and developed. The purpose of the reviews was threefold:

- to secure value from public investment by using quality assessment judgements to inform funding
- to encourage improvements in the quality of education through the publication of assessment reports and subject overview reports and through the sharing of best practice
- to provide, through the publication of reports, effective and accessible public information on the quality of the education for which the HEFCE provided funding.

In 1997 the most influential and fundamental review of higher education since the Robbins report of 1963 was completed.[4] Known as the Dearing report it made a number of key recommendations including:

- changes in institutional and student funding
- further expansion of higher education
- development and implementation of a framework for qualifications
- support for an interdisciplinary arts and humanities research council.

The review led directly to the setting up of the Quality Assurance Agency for Higher Education (QAA), a body that became responsible for assessing academic quality and standards in higher education.[5]

QAA reviews provided students with an important additional element to help them select the most relevant courses for their interests and needs. The development of comprehensive quality audit mechanisms had a significant impact on the accreditation reviews conducted by the professional bodies, and influenced the subsequent review of LIS accreditation during the first years of the 21st century.

Research
The establishment of the 'new' universities created a more diverse research profile amongst higher education institutions. Many of the new universities had not previously had the strong commitment to research that characterized virtually all of the 'old' universities. However, a number of departments of library and information studies (DLIS)[6] had national and indeed international reputations for their research programmes.

A number of academic research units were established within DLIS, which made a significant contribution to professional understanding and practice. There were also some vitally important external sources of funding, including the British Library Research and Development Department, the Library and Information Commission (LIC) and the Arts and Humanities and Research Board.

Research was important to all higher education institutions as it had a direct impact on funding. The level of funding was dependent upon the outcomes of the HEFCE Research Assessment Exercise (RAE), a quinquennial survey first conducted in 1985/86.[7] The RAE ratings were used to determine the allocation of research funding for the subsequent five-year period and were allocated according to standards of international and national excellence. DLIS were not assessed in the first exercise, but in the second RAE the five schools in the 'old' universities were included and from 1992 all new universities, and hence all DLIS, were included.

During this period there were changes in both national and international topics of research. In the UK case research became more important with influence being exerted by technological change, funding bodies, and the changing nature of lifestyles and of library and information services.[8] In 1998 David Stoker argued that research was key to the future of the LIS profession and thus by implication to the future of LIS education.[9] In 1999 it was estimated that the majority of research funding for UK LIS was distributed via DLIS (£1,363,000 out of a total of £2,525,000).[10] A helpful survey of the LIS research landscape at end of the decade is provided in the report of an investigation conducted by the Centre for Information Research at the University of Central England.[11]

Further education

At the start of the decade around three-quarters of post-16 education took place in colleges of further education (FE), although it accounted for only one-third of the funding allocated through the funding councils. FE colleges were at the heart of vocational education and training, offering courses in full-time, part-time, day release and evening class mode. FE colleges also offered an alternative route into higher education for those who had originally been unsuccessful in the school system. During the 1990s a number of further education colleges started offering higher education courses, although none were developed for the library and information sector.

Increasingly the government and employers shifted the focus in education and training away from initial training for young people and towards the whole adult population. The emphasis was on creating a culture of lifelong learning, which was seen as crucial to sustaining and maintaining international competitiveness in an increasingly global economy. Investment in further education was identified as critical to addressing the skills shortage and to the creation of what came to be known as a 'learning society'. Government and employers agreed that in order to achieve a learning society there should also be a widening of participation in further education to bring more people into higher education and training from non-traditional backgrounds.

The Further Education Funding Council published a report that set out a national strategy for widening participation underpinned by a coherent funding strategy.[12] A subsequent green paper developed proposals for the expansion of further and higher education to improve the overall coherence and responsiveness of education and training provision for adults and to encourage adherence to the principles of lifelong learning across the community.[13]

Lifelong learning
In 1995 the newly formed Department for Education and Employment (DfEE) published a consultation document, building on the commitments made in an earlier paper[14] to raising the levels of participation in continuing education and training and on the acquisition and updating of skills, 'to explore how employers, individuals and providers of education and training can take further action to develop a culture of lifetime learning'.[15]

The government set ambitious targets for education and training to be achieved by 2000, highlighting particularly the role of technology in learning. Developments such as the increased access to computers and the spread of the internet made it possible for learning to be more flexible and accessible and for providers of education and training to attract new and increasing numbers of students.

Arguably, the emphasis on lifelong learning was more crucial in the dynamic and rapidly changing discipline of librarianship and information work than in almost any other domain. A number of DLIS started offering both Bachelors' and Masters' degrees by distance learning. The University of Wales, Aberystwyth and the Robert Gordon University were the first UK universities to offer library and information studies courses by distance learning, and were later joined by the University of Northumbria at Newcastle. However, the biggest change was in relation to the take-up of vocational qualifications by library and information workers.

Vocational qualifications
Until the late 1980s the best-known vocational awards within LIS were those offered by the City and Guilds of London Institute, in particular Certificate 737: the Library and Information Assistants' Certificate (LIAC). There were no prerequisites for entry, making it a very accessible qualification for library staff who had few or possibly no academic qualifications, and the syllabus placed considerable emphasis on work-based practical skills. Formal input was largely delivered by practitioners, with supporting evidence gained from practical tasks undertaken in the workplace. Those who gained their certificates were often rewarded by an increment on their salaries, and in some organizations they gained entry to additional training and development opportunities. From the late 1990s the LIAC came under increasing pressure from the new vocational awards established under the auspices of the National Council for Vocational Qualifications (NCVQ).

The NCVQ was a new national awarding body set up by the government in 1986. The organization was charged with developing a coherent national framework for vocational qualifications in England, Wales and Northern Ireland. The expectation was that vocational qualifications would range from technical, low level qualifications through to postgraduate level. Although never perceived as a threat to the traditional academic provision of professional vocational courses in universities they had a considerable impact on the higher education sector during the 1990s as an increasing number of students entering higher education arrived from a vocational qualifications route rather than traditional 'A' levels.[16]

In each of the areas for which vocational qualifications were developed a Lead Body was appointed. The task of the Lead Body was to compile an occupational 'map' and to match employers' requirements with the skills being taught.

The first set of standards for vocational qualifications in LIS were approved by the Lead Body for Information and Library Services in 1995. In areas where vocational qualifications were developed to level 4 or indeed level 5 (graduate level) they posed considerably more of a threat to traditional academic provision in the university sector. However, this was less evident in the LIS subject area as Scottish Vocational Qualifications/National Vocational Qualifications (S/NVQs) in LIS were initially restricted to Level 3. S/NVQs were recognized as entry-level qualifications that in some cases gained a student exemption from some parts of a taught course, but they never established full parity with LIS degrees.

S/NVQs provided a competence and work-based programme of learning and development, and were ideally suited to the continuing professional development (CPD) requirements of the LIS workforce. Although the administration and terminology varied in Scotland, a single system of qualifications operated throughout the UK: the awards were in effect interchangeable, regardless of where they were made. Many employers encouraged their employers to use S/NVQs to gain formal recognition of their work-based learning and achievements. In order to keep the qualifications relevant and up-to-date a revised set of standards was published in 1999. For some candidates the change caused difficulties, as it was not possible simply to transfer from the old to the new set of standards.[17] However, most students who were caught in the transition period were able to upgrade their units and achieve the new S/NVQs. By 2000 S/NVQs had become acknowledged as an essential component of the UK qualification system, in LIS and beyond.

In 1998 the government announced plans to establish a network of National Training Organizations (NTOs) covering all occupational sectors, replacing and augmenting the previous patchwork of Industry Training Organizations, Occupational Standards Councils and Lead Bodies. Employers were asked to pledge resources and to make other forms of contribution to ensure continuous delivery of a suite of relevant vocational qualifications for the whole sector.[18] Following the demise of the ILS Lead Body there was a considerable period of uncertainty before the Department for Education and Employment approved the new Information Services NTO in 2000.

Professional associations

In 1991 there were three leading professional associations for the library and information community in the UK: the Library Association (LA), the Institute of Information Scientists (IIS) and Aslib, the Association for Information Management.

The LA and the IIS were both membership organizations with a clear commonality of interests and activities supporting members engaged in library and information services across a wide range of settings. Aslib was primarily a corporate membership organization. It supported the sector by providing courses, conferences and publications, and was also involved in lobbying.

It was perhaps inevitable that there were calls to unify these organizations to provide a single powerful body to represent the whole LIS community. The first investigation conducted by Professor Wilfred Saunders considered the case for bringing the three bodies into a unified organization. Saunders concluded that:

> Collectively, the Institute, Aslib and the LA represent an extremely powerful combination of expertise in information science, information management and librarianship in all its varied manifestations. There is a high degree of interdependence between all three of these areas and the potential for mutually beneficial interaction is very strong indeed. The case for this potential being achieved more effectively via a single unified organization which includes the three organizations operating independently must be very strong.[19]

In 1991 both Aslib and the IIS decided not to proceed with discussions. However, a degree of collaboration continued between the LA and the IIS, principally in the area of the professional accreditation of courses. In 1996 the AGM of the IIS voted to commence discussions with the LA to explore a possible formal alliance. In September 1998 a joint publication was issued that set out the shared vision of an entirely new professional body which would represent the emerging information society in which the boundaries between librarians and information scientists were becoming increasingly blurred.[20] This report highlighted the clear commonality of interest between the two organizations. Both memberships were engaged in the provision of information services in a wide range of settings, and it was estimated that about 40% of IIS members were also members of the LA. Both organizations accredited programmes at universities, increasingly on a joint basis. Both awarded professional qualifications, maintained active publishing programmes, ran courses and conferences, and maintained a regional and special interest group structure.

The ensuing consultation revealed the extent to which members of both organizations valued both the accreditation role and qualifications. Many respondents acknowledged that Chartered status was an important benefit that should be retained in the new organization. One respondent wrote:

> ... the 'Gold Standard (i.e. Chartered membership) must be maintained meticulously as must be the strict accreditation of LIS courses in HE institutions ...

while another commented:

> The LA could learn from the IIS. In my opinion, for example, the IIS criteria for validating courses are more imaginative and relevant to the new information worker than those devised by the LA.[21]

The formal motion to unify in principle was put to the AGM of the IIS on 16 September 1999, and to the LA AGM a month later on 14 October 1999.[22] Members of both bodies voted overwhelmingly for unification. With a clear mandate secured from the memberships of both organizations the legal moves necessary to create the new body were set in motion. One of the most difficult matters to resolve, perhaps inevitably, was the name for the new body. Various permutations and combinations of words and phrases were considered at Council meetings of both the LA and the IIS. The IIS's final votes took place at an extraordinary general meeting held in July 2001, and the LA followed at its annual general meeting in October: the new body would be called CILIP (the Chartered Institute of Library and Information Professionals).

Both organizations saw unification as an opportunity to bring together and build on the best features of both the LA and the IIS and to create a strong platform for education and training for the profession in the early 21st century. From the outset it was acknowledged that CPD should form a crucial element of the qualifications and that any new qualifications structure should be hospitable to both informal and work-based learning.

During this period a number of smaller specialist professional associations were very active in the UK and many made a significant and valuable contribution to LIS education and training. They supplemented and extended formal academic education programmes by offering courses outwith the higher education environment. Some, like IAML (International Association of Music Libraries, Archives and Documentation Centres) campaigned vigorously for the reinstatement of specialist music librarianship modules on accredited courses. They were successful and in 2000 two specialist modules were delivered to students on the LA-accredited course at the University of Wales, Aberystwyth. Other organizations, such as BIALL (the British and Irish Association of Law Librarians) offered non-accredited professional development for new entrants to their sector through a series of specialist programmes.[23]

BAILER (the British Association for Information & Library Education and Research) was formed in 1992, superseding the Association of British Library and Information Schools (ABLISS). The new association included all teaching and research staff in the eighteen DLIS in the United Kingdom and Ireland. The association's main concerns were stated as: curriculum development, research issues and improving communication between those involved in LIS education, practitioners and the information profession at large.[24] It represented the academic community to practitioners and responded to policy and strategic issues within LIS education and research. Although accreditation was an activity that occurred primarily in individual institutions the dialogue and partnership between BAILER and the professional bodies was key to ensuring a smooth collaboration and partnership on matters of collective concern.

In 1999 FARMER, the Forum for Archives and Records Management Education and Research for the UK and Ireland, was formed for teaching and research staff in the area of archives and records management in universities in the United Kingdom and the Republic of Ireland. Although there was no formal collaboration with the LA the Forum made a useful contribution to LIS education and training in the broadest sense as it actively fostered the development and encouragement of teaching and research amongst staff in a number of LA- and IIS-accredited institutions.

Course accreditation and approval

The 1990s marked the shift to a graduate profession, which had been heralded in a Library Association's 1977 report.[25] The report signalled a major change in the relationship between the LA and DLIS, as the LA moved from being an examining body to an accrediting institution, developing its accreditation policies in partnership with the Council for National Academic Awards. The last LA examinations had been offered in 1985; admission to the professional Register for non-graduates was finally closed in 1990.

In 1990 there were 34 LA-accredited courses at 17 higher education institutions, and by 2000 this had increased to 60 accredited courses, the number of accredited institutions remaining static at 17.

In 1999 the IIS approved 93 courses at 20 institutions, awarding graduates up to 3 years' exemption from the normal 5-year work experience requirement for full membership of the IIS. In 1990 88% of LA-accredited courses retained the word library or librarianship in their course titles; by 2000 this had declined to 41% and there had also been a marked increase in the proportion of LIS courses offered at Masters' level. This mirrored the pattern of changing demand and development going on throughout higher education, referred to at the start of this chapter.

At the start of the period the lists of IIS-approved courses and LA-accredited courses demonstrated the philosophical differences perceived within the two communities. The IIS was perceived as the natural home for courses occupying the more technical and scientific area of the domain, whereas the LA operated in what was perceived as the traditional 'librarianship and information management' area. LA accreditation assessed courses against its Procedures for the Accreditation of Courses,[26] incorporating the Body of Professional Knowledge: the IIS applied its Criteria for Information Science to its assessment of the curriculum of courses presented for accreditation.[27] Despite their different approaches the underlying philosophy was that both organizations had in place effective mechanisms for ensuring the recruitment of quality-assured graduates into the profession, and eventually on to their professional Registers.[28]

By the end of the period the increasing recognition of the convergence of the more traditional domain of librarianship with the more technical areas of information science into a new and dynamic discipline had led to ever closer collaboration between the two bodies, which increasingly found themselves invited to accredit the same courses. Close links between the Library Association Accreditation Board and the Institute of Information Scientists Professional Development and Standards Committee already existed. It seemed sensible to rationalize this situation and in the autumn of 1999 this partnership was formalized through the preparation of a Joint Accreditation Instrument (JAI),[29] and the setting up of a Joint Accreditation Administration (JAA)[30] that brought the LA and the IIS Criteria for Information Science together in one coherent set of processes and procedures. Thus unification of accreditation preceded formal unification and the creation of the new professional body by almost three years!

The Dearing report had suggested that professional bodies should work in conjunction with the QAA in reviewing courses and subject areas.[31] One or two professional bodies fully delegated authority and responsibility for conducting reviews of professional courses to the QAA. The JAA, however, declined an invitation from the QAA to consider adopting this approach. The JAA considered that the aims and objectives of QAA subject review, while overlapping with accreditation in some areas, did not fully meet the needs of professional bodies, which viewed accreditation as an important indicator of the preparation for professional practice gained by students on professionally recognized courses.

The LA, the IIS and the Society of Archivists were invited to collaborate on the design and preparation of the subject benchmark statement for Librarianship and Information Management for Bachelors' degrees. The subject benchmark extended to both Archives and Records Management, neither of which was directly provided for at undergraduate level. A significant feature of the benchmark was the agreement from the participating organizations that the JAI should form the starting-point. The resulting benchmark statement, published in 2000, firmly embedded the professional bodies' requirements within course content and curriculum design.[32]

Curriculum change and development
Changes in funding, the development and expansion of information and communications technology (ICT), modularization and changing modes of delivery all had an impact on aspects of curriculum content and design. Some LIS programmes that were delivered solely as taught courses at the start of the period were studied entirely by distance learning at the end of the decade. The traditional experience of education which placed the teacher in a 'knowledge transmission' role was replaced by one in which the educator 'facilitated' learning through a range of activities, all of which were student-centred and in many cases self-directed by the learner.

Writing in 1997 Joan Day commented that:

The subject of librarianship or information science is not easy to define, it is a far from stable discipline ... The pervasive impact of technology on information handling has led to new knowledge and skills being needed, and consequent need to reshape the curriculum to make way for new topics.[33]

The combined impact of ICT, making technology affordable and accessible, and the changing needs and expectations of students posed both a challenge and an opportunity to the LIS academic community. The rapid expansion in access to ICT across society established new roles for library and information professionals that required them to support and enable end-users to make effective use of information, whether for home or for business. Employers expected new graduates to be equipped to deal with changing demands. Many universities, and indeed DLIS, found they had to invest considerable resources in bringing both UK and international students up to an acceptable level of ICT skills in order for them to participate effectively in learning and find posts on graduating.

Students and employers demanded greater flexibility in course structures and an ever-increasing range of knowledge and skills to equip them for the demands of a complex and rapidly changing environment. Information-handling skills were no longer the prerogative of the traditional library and information sector: they were becoming recognized as essential skills across the whole workforce. At the same time there was a decline in the job market in the traditional first destination sector of many LIS graduates as jobs in the public sector declined. Many DLIS responded by developing courses specifically targeted at the new and emerging markets, such as health informatics and business information. New courses and curricula were developed in response to detailed market research amongst employers and recent graduates, and the results were reflected in the titles of the courses offered.[34] Undergraduate and postgraduate degrees in Librarianship and Library and Information Studies were still available but a study of course titles in 2000 shows an increasing number of specialist awards such as: Electronic Information Management (the Robert Gordon University), Electronic Communication and Publishing (University College London) and Chemoinformatics (University of Sheffield).

Alongside the need for new information-handling and -managing skills all graduates were expected to develop a range of transferable skills, such as interpersonal skills, team working, research and report writing.[35] As numbers of LIS students increased and the student profile became predominantly postgraduate and part-time the challenge of incorporating ever more topics into the curriculum became acute.

The introduction of modularization presented a partial solution. Modularization described the process of standardizing module size and weighting, i.e., the credit awarded at the successful conclusion of a particular unit of study, so that, for example, all students on a Bachelors' course would gain equal credit for any single module and would undertake equal amounts of study. Introducing a credit-based system introduced flexibility into education, allowing students to study at their own pace to suit personal and financial constraints.[36] Modularization emphasized explicit outcomes in relation to each element of a degree rather than the more broadly defined course, enabling students to pick an individual course of study rather than following a closely prescribed curriculum.

One consequence of modularization became increasingly apparent during the regular interactions with professional bodies such as the Library Association and the Institute of Information Scientists. Although the core requirements for accredited courses were never directly equated to a curriculum, the opportunity for students to follow individual programmes of study that might have relatively little relationship to the overarching named award became an increasing challenge for accreditation visiting parties.[37] In 1996 it was claimed that over 90% of universities had adopted a modular curriculum with 80% claiming to have established credit frameworks.[38] The development of credit-based curriculum also facilitated the move towards harmonization of credit transfer within the European Union.

At the start of the decade the emphasis was on the preparation of students for work in the expanding information sector and a typical curriculum covered the core areas of the collection and organization of information, an appreciation of the social and other contexts within which information services are provided and a broad range of management (transferable) skills. In addition to the core subjects many DLIS offered specialist options that addressed the library and information needs of specialist sectors such as children, health and music. However, as the range of what were deemed core subjects increased, the number and range of specialist options decreased. The nature and direction of courses also varied, depending on the overall orientation of the institution, so that the LIS curriculum within a business school was inevitably different in its orientation from that of a standalone LIS department.

In a letter to the *Library Association record* in 1992 Professor John Feather stated:

> The alternative to the loss of specialisms is to sacrifice the knowledge and skills which lie at the heart of professional practice … It seems to me wholly logical that the schools should be concerned with initial professional education (as well as with research) and the profession itself, through its various representative bodies, should accept responsibility for continuing professional development.[39]

By the end of the decade many courses had all but abandoned a number of the core subjects and indeed core courses associated with traditional librarianship, in favour of far more specialist provision as universities attempted to meet the increasingly diverse needs for information skills.[40] The range and diversity of courses developed significantly as cognate disciplines such as records management, and health and legal information, influenced formal academic LIS education.

Continuing professional development
By the 1990s the importance of training and development throughout a career, or continuing professional development, was becoming embedded across the sector. In order for students to be equipped with the essential range of practical and

professional skills, employers realized that a properly planned programme of top-up training was essential if library and information workers, and the services they offered, were to survive and thrive in the modern environment. The LA was one of the earliest non-statutory professional bodies to recognize the need for a structured programme of personal development. In 1992 it published a toolkit, the Framework of Continuing Professional Development, which offered advice, guidance and practical exercises to help members assess and plan their training and development.[41] There was an increasing understanding of the crucial need for information professionals to be able to respond to the changing demands of a rapidly changing discipline, which could not be satisfied by traditional academic programmes of study.

Both the LA and the IIS based their professional qualifications on evidence of successful professional development. Applicants for professional qualifications were expected to demonstrate that they had built upon the formal underpinning provided in an academic course of study and had become well-rounded professionals with a good understanding of the wider profession and their own role within that profession. However, the application processes and procedures of the LA remained closely linked to academic practice. Applications were considered against carefully specified criteria and feedback was offered to those whose applications were unsuccessful.[42] Additional formats were added in 1995 as the LA attempted to keep up with trends for assessment in further and higher education.[43]

Information and communications technology and skills
Library and information services experienced a period of rapid technological change and an increasingly demanding clientele, both factors that had enormous influence on education and training, both in formal academic environments and in workplace learning. During the late 1990s the government funded a number of projects to identify the skills challenge that ICT presented to the library and information community, resulting in a number of influential reports.[44]

The SKIP Project (SKills for new Information Professionals) described the emerging roles within academic libraries.[45] Two Library and Information Commission (LIC) reports identified and articulated the need to update the knowledge and skills of all staff working in public libraries, in particular in the area of ICT skills. In 1997 LIC set down a vision of a new breed of librarian:

> Investment in the training of librarians creates a human resource with talents that benefit all sections of the community. The skilled librarian will be confident in providing enlightened support in navigating the information maze, advocating accessible routes to learning for all, and welcoming citizens into the People's Network.[46]

The following year the *Building the new library* report recommended two levels of training to help people become familiar and comfortable with the role and use of ICT in libraries, both for themselves as staff and on behalf of users.[47] The new roles identified in the public library sector included advising, training, learner support, managing change and acting as an intermediary.[48] These recommendations had great impact on training in the sector. One of the most influential projects was the allocation of £20 million from the National Lottery New Opportunities Fund (NOF) for training public library staff to help them meet the challenge of *Building the new library*.

The European Union

In 1991 a European Union *Directive on the mutual recognition of professional qualifications* (89/48/EEC) was implemented in UK law.[49] Under this legislation the LA and the IIS had to accept any qualification recognized in another EU country for the purposes of admission to their Registers, as long as the required period of academic study was at least three years at higher education level. This established equivalence between the qualifications of any graduate of a department/school of librarianship/information studies from elsewhere in the EU with degree courses obtained in the UK. The LA had a statutory duty to deal with enquiries from EU citizens wishing to establish the equivalence of their qualifications, and thus advised many on the additional education and training that might be required for them to be able to practise and gain professional recognition in the UK.

In a move designed both to enhance the employability and mobility of European citizens and to increase the international competitiveness of European higher education the then twenty-nine European heads of government signed the EU Bologna Declaration in June 1999.[50] The principal aim was to create a 'European Higher Education Area' by 2010. By signing the agreement each signatory country pledged to reform its own higher education system to create overall convergence at European level. The Declaration recognized that despite strong national educational systems all European higher education systems were facing similar challenges, many of which have been referred to elsewhere in this chapter. The Declaration did not enforce reform on national governments. The hope was that the various national education systems would recognize the benefits of establishing a common platform: the process aimed at creating convergence and not standardization. The Declaration was principally an invitation to the higher education community to contribute to the reform process, overseen in the UK by the Department for Education and Employment.

Conclusion

The closing decade of the 20th century was a period of great change in all areas of library and information work in the United Kingdom and nowhere was this more evident than in education and training. The boundaries between formal academic provision and training became increasingly blurred. Employers' expectations of new entrants expanded and they looked for new solutions to help their workforce keep pace with the demands of a dynamic and rapidly changing discipline. Changes in higher and further education also impacted on the sector. In 2000 it seemed clear that employers and the LIS community could no longer rely on initial education and occasional training to remain competitive. The challenge of the 21st century was to make opportunities for learning available to all in the most appropriate and accessible formats and to encourage all those working in the sector to commit themselves to becoming lifelong learners.

Notes

1   Judith Elkin and Tom Wilson (eds.), *The education and training of library and information professionals in the United Kingdom*. London: Mansell, 1997.
2   Higher Education Statistics Agency: <http://www.hesa.ac.uk> (accessed 10/2/06).
3   *Further and Higher Education Act 1992*; *Further and Higher Education (Scotland) Act 1992*.
4   National Committee of Inquiry into Higher Education, *Higher education in the learning society*. London: HMSO, 1997. Chairman Sir Ron Dearing. (The 'Dearing report'.)
5   Quality Assurance Agency for Higher Education: <http://www.qaa.ac.uk> (accessed 27/1/06).
6   For consistency the term Department of Library and Information Studies (DLIS) is used throughout this chapter.
7   Higher education and Research Opportunities in the United Kingdom: <http://www.hero.ac.uk/rae> (accessed 27/2/06).
8   Maxine Rochester and Pertti Vakkar, 'International LIS research: a comparison of national trends', *IFLA journal* **24** (3), 1998, 166–75.
9   David Stoker, 'A strategy for LIS research in the next century', *Journal of librarianship and information science* **30** (1), 1998, 3–5.
10 David Haynes, David Streatfield and Noeleen Cookman, *Review of research funding for LIS*. [London]: Library and Information Commission, 2000 (LIC research report; 40).
11 Sarah McNicol and Clare Nankivell, *The LIS research landscape: a review and prognosis*. Birmingham: Centre for Information and Research, 2002.
12 Further Education Funding Council, *Learning works: widening participation in further education*. Coventry: FEFC, 1997.
13 Department for Education and Employment, *The learning age: a renaissance for a new Britain*. London: HMSO, 1998 (Cm 2790).
14 Board of Trade, *Competitiveness: forging ahead*. London: HMSO, 1995 (Cm 2687).
15 Department for Education and Employment, *Lifetime learning: a consultation document*. London: DfEE, 1995, p. 7.
16 Alan Smithers and Pamela Robinson, *Post-18 education: growth, change, prospect*. London: Council for Industry and Higher Education, 1995 (Executive briefing).
17 Justin Arundale. *Getting your S/NVQ*. London: Library Association in association with the Information and Library Services Lead Body, 1999.
18 Information and Library Services Lead Body, Letter to all Heads of Service in archives, libraries, records management offices and tourist information centres, about the formation of the Information Services NTO. October 1998.
19 Wilfred L. Saunders, *Towards a unified professional organisation for library and information science and services: a personal view*. London: Library Association, 1989.
20 *Our professional future: a proposal for a new organisation for the library and information profession: a consultative document* .... London: IIS; LA, 1998.

21 Analysis of consultation document responses presented to the UPG March 1999. (Restricted circulation).

22 *Our professional future: revised proposals for a new organisation for the library and information profession.* Issued to the memberships of the IIS and the LA August 1999.

23 BIALL: <http://www.biall.org.uk>.

24 BAILER: <http://www.bailer.ac.uk>.

25 Library Association, Working Party on the Future of Professional Qualifications, *Report.* London: Library Association, 1977. (The 'Paulin report'.)

26 Library Association, *Procedures for the accreditation of courses.* London: LA, 1990.

27 Institute of Information Scientists, *Criteria for information science.* London: IIS, 1988.

28 Marion Huckle, 'Professional accreditation of library and information courses in the United Kingdom', *Cadernos BAD* **1**, 2003, 74–86. Paper presented to a joint BAD/ EBLIDA seminar, Estoril.

29 *Joint Accreditation Instrument.* London: LA/IIS Joint Accreditation Administration, 1999.

30 JAA – the governance group formed from the LA Accreditation Board and the IIS Professional Standards and Development Committee, which oversaw the application of the JAI.

31 National Committee of Inquiry into Higher Education. *Higher education in the learning society.*

32 Quality Assurance Agency for Higher Education: <http://www.qaa.ac.uk> (accessed 27/2/06).

33 Joan Day, 'Curriculum change and development' in *The education and training of library and information professionals in the United Kingdom,* ed. Elkin and Wilson, pp. 31–52.

34 Kate Wood, 'UK higher education and qualifications'. Paper delivered to the British Council conference 'The Higher service at German Libraries – the future of education and professional qualification in the European context', Leipzig, 2000.

35 *Skills for graduates in the 21st century.* Cambridge: Association of Graduate Recruiters, 1995.

36 *Learning works,* p. 86.

37 Mick Betts and Robin Smith, *Developing the credit-based modular curriculum in higher education.* London: Falmer Press. 1998.

38 Higher Education Quality Council, *Understanding academic standards in modular frameworks.* London: HEQC, 1996; Higher Education Quality Council, *Regulatory framework for academic standards in credit-based modular curricular higher education – graduate standards programme.* London: HEQC, 1997.

39 John Feather, 'Schools are aiming for well-educated generalists' (letter), *Library Association record* **94** (7), 1992, 449.

40 A detailed comparison of the changes in course content and direction can be undertaken through examination of the unique archive of course materials relating to accredited courses held at CILIP.

41 Library Association, *Framework for continuing professional development.* London: LA, 1992.

42 Library Association, *Routes to Associateship.* London: LA, 1988, rev. 1990.

43 Library Association, *Associateship regulations and notes of guidance.* London: LA, 1995.

44 Margaret Watson, 'Education and training of library and information professionals'. Paper delivered to an international conference, University of Parma, November 2003.
45 Penny Garrod and Ivan Sidgreaves, *Skills for new information professionals: the SKIP project*. London: Library Information Technology Centre, 1997.
46 Library and Information Commission, *New library: the people's network*. London: LIC, 1997, p. 43.
47 Library and Information Commission, *Building the new library*. London: LIC, 1998.
48 Bronwen Jones *et al.*, *Staff in the new library: skill needs and learning choices*. [Boston Spa]: British Library Research and Innovation Centre, 1999 (British Library research and innovation report; 152).
49 *Professional qualifications, the European Communities (recognition of professional qualifications) regulations 1991*. (Statutory Instrument 1991 no. 824).
50 Bologna Secretariat website: <http://www.dfes.gov.uk/bologna/> (accessed 24/3/06).

22

Research

David Nicholas

Introduction

The intention of this chapter is twofold: (1) to describe the essential features of the research landscape during the period 1991–2000; and (2) to highlight the most important events that took place during that time.

It was a period which was characterized by research of an international and lasting character, especially in the areas of information retrieval, information seeking and information technology. The major researchers of this period (e.g., David Ellis, Tom Wilson, Peter Willett, Stephen Robertson, Charles Oppenheim) are well-known names, and continued to be the most highly cited authors well into the next decade.

This was also a watershed period, which, arguably, witnessed the complete transformation of the Library and Information Science (LIS) research environment. After a couple of decades of relative growth, the LIS research community was in for a decade of continuous and sometimes confusing change. The major agents of change were: (*a*) a wholesale overhaul of the funding environment, signalled largely by the end of large-scale British Library involvement in research during the decade; (*b*) the Research Assessment Exercise (RAE), first introduced in 1986 but really impacting only heavily in the LIS field during this decade, whose purpose was to improve the quality of research being conducted by UK higher education institutions; (*c*) last, but by no means least, the internet, which began to redefine the boundaries of research throughout the 1990s. Each of these 'agents' will be dealt with in turn and then the outcomes, in terms of the major research projects and researchers that featured during this decade, will be critically examined.

Despite the undoubted achievements of the decade and the major developments that took place, most of which were going to have an impact well into the next decade, there are no comprehensive research reviews of this seminal decade. The closest we get are works by Meadows (on the early years of the decade) and McNicol and Nankivell (on the later years).[1] For the closely allied archives field there is a good account by Shepherd.[2]

The funding environment

This would probably be the really big research story for the decade, if it were not for the arrival of the internet on the scene. During the period fundamental changes took place in the funding environment, something which, of course, changed the very nature of the research and its outputs. We shall therefore spend some time looking at the nature and consequence of this change. Roberts, in the research chapter of the previous volume of *British librarianship and information work*, talked about 'a centrally funded research culture emanating from the British Library Research and Development Department (BLR&DD)'.[3] And according to East this 'centrally funded culture' accounted for 44% of the LIS grant awards in the years 1978, 1982, and 1985.[4] This explains why Roberts mentioned BLR&DD more than two dozen times in his chapter, which was mostly devoted to its good work. During the first half of the decade the BLR&DD was still the pre-eminent research force in the field. Undoubtedly, the BLR&DD 'has been influential in the direction in [which] research in library and information has developed; has incorporated and indeed trailblazed new technology in both management and service delivery; and has had a positive effect on the public's perception of libraries'.[5] Meadows provides a review of the work of the BLR&DD in promoting and financing research in the library and information science field, over a 20-year period (1975–1994).[6] It was certainly unusual for a relatively small field, like LIS, to have its very own government funding 'council' and this situation was not going to last.

1996 marked the demise of the BLR&DD, and the beginning of the end of special funding (and pleading) for the field. For a short period of time the BLR&DD metamorphosed into the British Library Research and Innovation Centre (BLRIC). In 1999, the research-funding activities and resources of BLRIC were transferred to the Library and Information Commission (LIC). This led to an increase in strategic (policy) research and, more controversially, consultancy.[7] According to McNicol and Nankivell:

> During its short existence, the LIC underwent considerable organisational change, culminating in its functions being transferred to a new body, the Museums, Libraries and Archives Commission [*sic, recte* Council] (MLAC) in April 2000. MLAC almost immediately changed its name to Re:source: the Council for Museums, Archives and Libraries. This was seen by many as a negative development; the change from the LIC to Resource 'appears to have caused an unwelcome vacuum in the area of LIS research'.[8]

If anything, Resource was even more focused on consultancy than its predecessors.

During the middle of the decade another research funder of consequence entered the field – the Joint Information Systems Committee (JISC), a strategic advisory committee working on behalf of the funding bodies for further and higher education (FE and HE) in England, Scotland, Wales and Northern Ireland. Its work was of a much more developmental and, of course, academic nature. JISC tended to fund projects to trial, pilot, develop or evaluate new technologies and techniques.

Relevant programmes funded by JISC during the decade included: the

Electronic Libraries (eLib) Programme, the Technologies Application Programme, Information Strategies, Non-formula funding of Specialised Research Collections, the Pilot Site Licence Initiative, the National Electronic Site Licensing Initiative, Development of Network Efficiency Mechanisms and the New Technologies Initiative. The eLib programme began in 1995; its third phase was completed at the end of 2001.[9] We can add to that list digital preservation and subject-based information gateways.

JISC was not the only new entrant. For much of the decade the European Commission was very active in the field, funding two Framework Programmes for Research and Technological Development: the 'Libraries Programme' and the 'Telematics for Libraries' programme. The UK provided the largest number of participants from one country, namely 134. The types of projects included: computerized bibliographies; international interconnection of systems and related international standards; provision of new library services using ICT; stimulation of a European market in telematic products and services specific to libraries; network-orientated internal library systems; telematic applications for interconnected library services; and library services for access to network information resources.[10] We shall refer to this work later when we describe the research of Peter Brophy.

As Wilson noted, the situation by the end of the decade was now one where 'the research upon which international reputation now depends is funded entirely by the research councils'.[11] This was especially true of the Arts and Humanities Research Board, which was given the responsibility for LIS research funding during this period. However, it has to be said that the impact of the AHRB at the end of the decade was still relatively light, with fewer than five grants awarded. Wilson goes on to point the significance of the shift which was: '(1) that it became much more difficult to obtain funds because of the increased vigour of the selection process; (2) the kinds of projects funded where different, less future of library orientated and more academically relevant'.

The impact of the demise of the British Library involvement in research on the LIS research environment towards the end of the decade was enormous, something best illustrated by Elliott's analysis of who funded research in 2000.[12] According to data received by *Information research watch international*, the research in progress research register, the key funders were now, in rank order: the European Commission, the Library and Information Commission (LIC), DCMS/Wolfson Public libraries Fund, the Arts and Humanities Research Board and the Joint Information Systems Committee (JISC). Many of these organizations did not even exist at the beginning of the decade and the others were largely insignificant players. Other organizations funding LIS research included Resource: the Council for Museums, Archives and Libraries; the BNB Research Fund; and the Library Association.

Towards the end of the decade, in 1999, LIS research, development and related activities were estimated to be worth more than £20 million per year, including grants for the development of LIS products or services, such as those of JISC, and funding for the implementation of specific services, such as digitization, cataloguing and access programmes.[13] The list of funding bodies ended the decade as looking like this: 'Resource, the Library Association, OCLC Office of Research, Ulverscroft, John Campbell Trust, JISC, Wolfson Foundation, Anderson Committee's Research Support Libraries Programme, the Follett Committee's Non-Formula Funding for Research Collections in the Humanities, AHRB, BECTA, Daiwa Anglo–Japanese Foundation, DfES, DoH, ESRC, European Parliament, LSDA, HSE, Joseph Rowntree Foundation, Leverhulme, Mental Health Foundation, NHS R&D Division, Nuffield Foundation, Royal Irish Academy, Save & Prosper'.[14]

The Research Assessment Exercise (RAE)

The RAE was intended to control significant flows of HEFCE research funding to individual institutions that could demonstrate that they could conduct quality research and thus were 'safe hands'. With RAE money institutions could fund their research infrastructure, and provide staff with space and time to research and experiment. In this respect, therefore, we are still talking about the funding environment. However, the RAE was to do much more than this because, with its establishment of a range of research metrics and outputs, it changed the focus of research and its outputs, putting a much greater emphasis on the merits of funded research (as opposed to individual scholarly research), team/centre research and peer-reviewed journal publication dissemination.

Two RAEs took place in the eighties (1986 and 1989) but they were rough and ready exercises (not mentioned by Roberts in the 1985–1990 volume) and the RAE did not really impact upon the sector until 1992. This was followed by another RAE in 1996, which was itself more elaborate and formal, and this was to be the pattern for the future. The key results of the two RAEs are given in Table 1. This lists the higher education institutions which engaged in LIS research and essentially confirmed the pre-eminence of two library schools during this period – those of City University and the University of Sheffield, which both recorded the maximum rating for each of the two assessments (which was a 5 in 1992 and a 5* in 1996). Elkin and Law, both members of the Library and Information Management (LIM) panels, have left us with a description of the working of the panels and the outcomes.[15] Wilson made a comparison of the results of the two assessments, to demonstrate the ways in which research funding in the fields of librarianship and information management had changed and what the effect was.[16]

The internet

This was the decade when the internet began to have a really big impact on the LIS profession for which it presented many challenges, changes and research opportunities. It created the means by which disintermediation could happen and it created a world in which search engines would become dominant (and the subject of party conversation). From a research point of view it widened the research boundaries considerably, moving LIS research away from libraries and taking it into the home and office. Surprisingly, this was not fully acknowledged by commentators, either then or at the time of writing. Thus the CILIP-funded LIS report *Research landscape: a review and prognosis*[17] barely considered the internet as a major research driver or influence on the research landscape, despite the evidence provided by Table 2. The internet was regarded as another field of study rather than an agent which created a paradigm shift. JISC perhaps was the first funder to recognize its potential impact in their Electronics Library Programme (eLib). The British Library Research and Innovation Centre was also involved with projects like *The changing information environment: the impact of the Internet on information seeking.*[18]

Table 1 Outcome of RAE 1996 and 1992: unit of assessment 61: Library and Information Management

Name of institution	Institution rating		Proportion of staff selected
	1996	*1992*	
University of Bath	2	3	A
Bath College of HE	1	–	E
University of Brighton	3b	3	C
University of Central England	3b	–	A
University of Central Lancashire	2	2	A
City University	5*	5	A
De Montfort University	3b	3	C
La Sainte Union College of HE	1	–	A
Leeds Metropolitan University	2	–	E
Liverpool John Moores University	2	1	E
Loughborough University	5	4	C
Manchester Metropolitan University	3b	2	C
University of Northumbria	3a	2	C
University of Salford	4	2	A
University of Sheffield	5*	5	A
Thames Valley University	1	1	E
University College London	2	2	B
University of West of England	3b	2	C
Queen Margaret College	3b		B
Robert Gordon University	3a	2	B
University of Strathclyde	4	4	A
University of Wales, Aberystwyth	3b	4	B
The Queens University of Belfast	3a	2	A

(A = 95–100%; B = 80–94%; C = 60–79%; D = 40–59%; E = 20–39% 'research active' staff)

Characteristics of the research

Describing and evaluating the individual characteristics and features of the research conducted over a decade, given the sheer volume of research conducted, would be a thankless task and one that would not provide a great deal of illumination for the reader. Fortunately, there are a number of publications which can be consulted to obtain some of the necessary detail.[19]

Here we shall concern ourselves with pointing to the key research characteristics of the decade, the main changes that had occurred since the previous decade and identifying the key players and projects.

By pulling together the work of a number of commentators we can identify the broad features of research during this period:

- The broad focus of work was on the 'fundamental issues of information management, especially information retrieval, information-seeking behaviour, organisational impact of information systems'.[20]
- There was a great interest in new technologies: 'research has been, and is likely to continue to be, subject to the forces of both technological change and of organisational change within the major funding bodies.'[21]
- It was influenced by the emergence of the information society.[22]
- The economic, social, educational, community and lifestyle impacts of library services on individuals and communities, were a major concern.[23]
- There was an increase in short-term, consultancy-based projects and also in large scale demonstrator projects, in many cases in response to calls for proposals issued by government-funded agencies.
- The focus of LIS research moved from an emphasis on libraries themselves and their management to a consideration of the needs of information users.

Table 2 Research concerns in the period 1991–2000 as indicated by the index terms used by scholarly journal authors to describe their research

Term	Rank	Number
Document supply	1	28
Electronic publishing	2	19
Information technology	3	18
Internet	4	18
Interlending	5	17
Libraries	6	17
Information systems	7	16
Information retrieval	8	12
Copyright	9	9
Information services	10	8
Journal publishing	11	6
Library services	12	6

Another (more quantitative) approach to establishing what interested researchers during this period is to examine the most common index terms used in articles by British LIS researchers appearing in journals indexed in the ISI databases. The Table 2 shows the result of such an analysis, and certainly IT terms dominate the top of the table, but the interest in document supply and interlending shows the internet appearing on the scene rather late in the decade.

It was not just the subject of research that was changing; the methods were changing too. Thus Rochester and Vakkari pointed out that research methods in 1985 at the international level were: conceptual, survey, and system design.[24] In the UK system design was not as common, but literature reviews were more common. Ten years later case or action research was increasingly being used in the UK, and towards the end of the decade transactional log analysis was coming into its own.

In picking out the most important features, projects and players, we have adopted a systematic and two-pronged approach by (*a*) concentrating on those academic departments that shone in the RAE; (*b*) utilizing citation analysis.

(*a*)   The departments were City University, University of Sheffield and Loughborough University.

(*b*)   The citation approach adopted was that utilized by Holmes and Oppenheim, which sought to establish a correlation between scores achieved by UK academic departments in the 1996 Research Assessment Exercise and the number of citations received by academics in those departments for articles published in the period 1994–2000, using the Institute for Scientific Information's (ISI) citation databases.[25]

The Holmes and Oppenheim citation study was carried out on all 338 academics who taught in the UK library and information science schools. These authors between them received 2,301 citations for articles they had published between 1994 and 2000. The results were ranked by department and compared to the ratings awarded to the departments in the 1996 RAE. Details are shown in Table 3 (overleaf). Stephen Robertson and Peter Willett were clearly the leading lights and we shall feature their work later.

The big names and projects

This section looks at the big research names and projects that were the key research milestones for the decade. This period was characterized by the work of a number research colossuses, amongst whom can be counted Stephen Robertson (information retrieval), Peter Willett (information retrieval), Tom Wilson (information seeking), David Ellis (information seeking) and Peter Brophy (e-libraries). The work of these five researchers will be highlighted, to provide a close acquaintance with the range and quality of work that was being conducted during the nineties. The text which follows was provided by the researchers and edited by the author.

Table 3 The top thirty most heavily cited library school authors, 1994–2000

Rank	Name	Institution	Number of citations
1	S. E. Robertson	City University, London	439
2	P. Willett	University of Sheffield	410
3	D. Ellis	University of Wales, Aberystwyth (at Sheffield during this period)	117
4	M. Hancock-Beaulieu	University of Sheffield (at City during this period)	114
5	C. Oppenheim	University of Loughborough	102
6	T. D. Wilson	University of Sheffield	80
7	D. Bawden	City University, London	78
8	E. Davenport	Queen Margaret College, Edinburgh (later moved)	47
9	M. Lynch	University of Sheffield	46
10	G. McMurdo	Queen Margaret College, Edinburgh	41
11	A. J. Meadows	University of Loughborough	38
12	G. Philip	Queen's University, Belfast	37
13	J. Feather	University of Loughborough	37
14	E. M. Keen	University of Wales, Aberystwyth	36
15	D. Nicholas	City University, London	34
16	M. H. Heine	Northumbria at Newcastle	33
17	P. Brophy	Manchester Metropolitan University	27
18	S. Jones	City University, London	26
19	N. Ford	University of Sheffield	25
=20	S. Walker	Leeds Metropolitan University	24
=20	A. Morris	University of Loughborough	24
22	F. Gibb	University of Strathclyde	23
23	P. F. Burton	University of Strathclyde	22
24	C. McKnight	University of Loughborough	23
25	B. Usherwood	University of Sheffield	22
26	B. Loughbridge	University of Sheffield	18
27	J. Harrison	University of Loughborough	17
=28	I. Rowlands	City University, London	16
=28	A. Goulding	University of Loughborough	16
=28	L. A. Tedd	University of Wales, Aberystwyth	16

Stephen Robertson

Robertson's work was very much involved with the Okapi project which moved to City University from the then Polytechnic of Central London in the late '80s. Okapi was then an experimental OPAC (Online Public Access Catalogue), allowing a subject search on library catalogues. At City it became a general-purpose text retrieval system, both for projects on real-user interactive searching and for TREC-style offline laboratory experiments. The basic principle of any Okapi user interface was one that became very familiar in later years, but was quite unusual at the time: a text box into which the user typed an unformatted free-text query. The system was expected to be able to produce something at least sensible in response to a query in this format. One of the requirements of a system like that was that it should allowed approximate matching ('best match') between the query and the document, which in turn implied ranking the output references: documents which matched well should be ranked before those which matched less well, but the latter should not be excluded entirely.

The Okapi team conducted a series of live-user experiments on offering relevance feedback options to users. After an initial search, users were invited to make relevance judgements on a few of the top-ranked references, and the system would then attempt to improve the formulation of the query and reiterate the search. Although relevance feedback did not really become commonplace, it was later well established that it can help some users very significantly. The team also took part in the annual (from 1991/92) TREC (Text REtrieval Conference) competitions. This large international collaboration was masterminded by the National Institute of Standards and Technology in the United States, but based in large measure on work done in the UK, first in the Cranfield projects of the 1950s and 1960s, and then in the Ideal Test Collection project of the 1970s. Each round of the competition involved a series of retrieval tasks, on a common set of test materials, using a common set of effectiveness measures. The Okapi group was the first UK group to take part, and entered every competition in the 1990s. The single most evident outcome of this work was the Okapi BM25 ranking function.[26] This might broadly be described as a form of tf–idf (term frequency–inverse document frequency) function, but with some features which made it particularly successful, to the extent that it became one of the commonest ranking algorithms in current use, and the one which every researcher would like to beat. The Okapi team also contributed extensively to the interactive tasks at TREC, and to the routing/filtering tasks, where the work on relevance feedback was significant.

The team at City University was partially disbanded in 1998, when two members joined the new Microsoft Research Laboratory in Cambridge and continued the work there. In 2000, Stephen Robertson, the leader of the group, was awarded the prestigious Gerard Salton award of ACM SIGIR for his work. Robertson and his team published widely.[27]

Peter Willett

Computerized methods for the storage and retrieval of both textual and chemical-structural information were studied under the direction of Peter Willett at the Department of Information Studies in the University of Sheffield during the decade. Much of the work focused on expanding natural language queries for text searching. One way in which this can be done is to use co-occurrence information: if a query word X co-occurs frequently with another word Y, then X and Y may have related meanings and Y might thus usefully be added to a query containing X. This approach had been studied for many years, albeit with variable results: Peat and Willett provide a simple quantitative analysis that explains much of this variation.[28] An alternative approach involves adding morphological variants of existing query terms, either by enumerating the variants or by conflating them by means of a stemming algorithm, and Ekmekçioglu and others report a detailed comparison of these morphological approaches with the co-occurrence approach.[29] There had been several reports of the use of stemming for conflating morphological variants in modern English; work at Sheffield looked at approaches that could be used to identify historical forms of modern English (so as to enable end-user searching of historical text-databases without the need to be familiar with ancient spelling)[30] and to search databases of Slovene, Latin and Turkish text.[31] Finally in the text area, studies were carried out on the extent to which the linkage structure in hypertext representations of full-text documents was a controlling factor in the effectiveness of subsequent searches of those documents, with the work showing that there were often considerable variations in the linkage structures devised by different people.[32]

Library and information science research has traditionally focused on textual information, but there are many academic disciplines that have developed databases containing very specific types of information. One such discipline is chemistry, where there is a need to search and to process very large databases of chemical molecules, and this was the subject of continuing interest in Sheffield for many years. Systems for the representation and searching of two-dimensional (2D) chemical structure diagrams had been under active development since the 1960s; work in Sheffield during the period under review extended these systems to permit the searching of three-dimensional (3D) representation of molecular structure, where XYZ atomic coordinate information is available. The work developed novel 3D techniques for both substructure searching and similarity searching (these are the chemical equivalents of Boolean and best-match text searching, respectively).[33] Later studies, in collaboration with colleagues in the Department of Molecular Biology and Biotechnology in Sheffield, extended these techniques to enable the searching of the 3D structures of protein molecules.[34] Considerations of cost-effectiveness in modern pharmaceutical research mean that there is a significant need to select some small subset of the millions of molecules that might be synthesized and tested for biological activity, so that attention can be focused on just this subset. Work in Sheffield on the calculation of molecular similarity and dissimilarity resulted in a body of selection techniques that were to be widely used in operational systems for pharmaceutical research.[35]

Textual and chemical information processing may appear to be very different but it is often the case that analogous algorithmic techniques can be applied to the different types of information. This observation spurred a continuing study of the use of evolutionary computing techniques, in particular genetic algorithms, for a range of combinatorial problems in textual and chemical database-processing.[36]

Tom Wilson

Tom Wilson was very active on a wide number of research fronts during this period. These interests included:

- the information needs of university heads of department[37]
- business information needs, especially with regard to the web[38]
- re-establishing previous interests in information-seeking behaviour[39]
- information strategies and strategic information[40]
- scholarly communication and digital information: a general interest rather than funded research[41]
- professional education.[42]

Wilson is probably best known during this decade for his continuous work in the information-seeking field, especially in revisiting and developing a model of information-seeking behaviour that first appeared in 1981. 'The model suggests that information-seeking behaviour arises as a consequence of a need perceived by an information user, who, in order to satisfy that need, makes demands upon formal or informal information sources or services, which result in success or failure to find relevant information.'[43] The 1996 variant of the general model benefited from information-seeking research conducted by Wilson into a diverse range of disciplines. However, according to Wilson, the 1999 rewrite of the 1981 model sparked quite a lot of activity in exploring some of the theoretical ideas he drew attention to. The paper in *Journal of documentation* which outlined the ideas proved particularly influential, and by 2005 it had attracted 123 citations.[44] Another major piece of information-seeking related research conducted was the 'Uncertainty project', which explored ideas developed through qualitative research by applying quantitative techniques.[45]

Peter Brophy

The future library, operating in complex networked environments remote from its users, was the focus of studies by Peter Brophy at the Centre for Research in Library and Information Management (CERLIM), initially at the University of Central Lancashire and from 1998 at Manchester Metropolitan University.

This work took place against a background of massive change in higher education at a time when direct end-user access to digital information, within ever more complex learning and research environments, had become the accepted norm.

CERLIM was one of the first UK research centres to become extensively involved in both the European Commission's Libraries Programme (later Information Society Technologies Programme), and JISC's Electronic Libraries (eLib) Programme (later Information Environment (IE) Programme). Both supported critical investigations into the nature of the library in networked space.[46]

In 1993, when the world wide web was emerging as a delivery platform, CERLIM started working on the concept of the 'Library without walls', work reported at the biannual conference of that name.[47] Within the UK context, the focus on hybrid libraries which emerged as the key theme of the final phase of the eLib programme was an important contributor to emerging models of information environments.[48] In the European context, work encompassed electronic library performance measurement, building on prior work on quality management, the integration of libraries into the lifelong learning and the development of self-service libraries.[49] In addition, concerns over social exclusion led to work on accessibility, seeking to ensure that the move to electronic services did not result in the exclusion of users with disabilities.[50]

David Ellis
In the 1980s David Ellis, of the University of Sheffield, established that amongst the complex patterns of information-seeking behaviour was a relatively small number of different types of activity. These were initially characterized as:

- starting (activities characteristic of the initial search for information)
- chaining (following chains of citations or other forms of referential connection between material)
- browsing (semi-directed searching in an area of potential interest)
- differentiating (using differences between sources as a filter on the nature and quality of material examined)
- monitoring (maintaining awareness of developments in a field through the monitoring of particular sources)
- extracting (systematically working through a particular source to locate material of interest).

During the 1990s the original model was extended and developed in studies of the information-seeking behaviour of other groups of researchers, including physicists and chemists, and engineers and research scientists in an industrial environment.[51] In each case, the derivation of the categories and properties was inductive and followed the grounded theory approach.[52] Despite the differing disciplinary backgrounds of the groups of researchers studied, there was considerable similarity both in general and in detail between them.

The study of the chemists identified activities consistent with starting, chaining, browsing, differentiating, monitoring and extracting as well as two other characteristics not highlighted in the study of the social scientists:

- verifying (checking that information is correct)
- ending (characteristics of information-seeking at the end of a project).

The study of the physicists employed different terminology to that of the social scientists but it was clear that the activities themselves could be closely mapped to the characteristics of the original model:

- initial familiarization (activities undertaken at the earliest stages of information-seeking)
- chasing (following up citation links between material)
- source prioritization (ranking sources based on perceptions of their relative importance)
- maintaining awareness (activities involved in keeping up to date)
- locating (activities engaged in to actually find the information).

Finally, the study of the engineers and researchers identified activities consistent with surveying, chaining, monitoring, browsing, extracting, and ending, as well as:

- distinguishing (activities undertaken when information sources are ranked according to their perceived relative importance)
- filtering (characterized by the use of criteria or mechanisms to make the information as relevant and precize as possible).

The model was widely cited in the information behaviour literature, perhaps particularly, and most pertinently, in papers in the Information Seeking in Context Conferences (ISIC), including papers by Spink, Vakkarri, Wilson, Limberg, Solomon, Toms, Lomax *et al.*, Spink *et al.*, and Johnston in the second ISIC Conference held in Sheffield, UK, in 1998,[53] and in the third ISIC conference held in Gotenborg, Sweden, in 2000, which included papers by Wilson *et al.*, and Fulton and McKechin *et al.*, Thomas & Nyce, and Renecker, Jacobson & Spink.[54]

The behavioural approach to user modelling outlined did not address cognitive or affective aspects of information-seeking. However, the range of different groups studied, and the employment of a consistent methodological approach across the different studies, indicate that the approach represents a broadly based, robust and widely applicable way of modelling the information-seeking behaviour of researchers in both academic and industrial research environments.

Conclusion
The research community at the end of the decade was faced with a more dispersed, diverse and more difficult funding environment. Some researchers were finding it difficult as the old familiar funding lines began to disappear or simply became more difficult to obtain. LIS research was now being judged in a much wider subject context and much, but not all, of it was found wanting. This would not have

surprised Haynes, Streatfield and Cookman who contended that traditionally LIS had lacked research culture and research credibility.[55]

There was another important change: consultancy was replacing research and even the 'research' that was being funded was increasingly being directed, as a consequence of the increase in tendering, something which JISC was very fond of, or programme-directed or thematic research (in other words, research topics which funders actively encourage researchers to investigate). What was happening was that research freedom was becoming more constricted.

BLR&DD started the decade as the most influential research organization, and JISC and the EU were proving to be the most influential organizations at the end of the decade.

Nevertheless the same organizations and same individuals that had proved so successful in the previous decade were also largely those that dominated this decade: probably a case of the survival of the fittest. Sheffield and City were the leading institutional lights and the big names were very much the same – Robertson, Brophy, Ellis, Willett and Wilson.

Notes

1   Jack Meadows, *Innovation in information: twenty years of the British Library Research and Development Department*. London: Bowker-Saur, 1994; Jack Meadows, 'PROSPECTS: a strategy for action: review article', *Library and information research news* **22** (72), 1998, 11–14; Sarah McNicol and Clare Nankivell, *The LIS research landscape: a review and prognosis*. [Birmingham]: Centre for Information Research, [2003]. Available from: <http://www.ebase.uce.ac.uk/cirtarchive/projects/past/LISlandscape_final%20report.pdf > (accessed 31/1/06).

2   John Shepherd, *Review of research priorities and practice for the Museums, Libraries and Archives Council (MLAC)*. [London]: South East Regional Research Laboratory, 1999.

3   Stephen Roberts, 'Research' in *British librarianship and information work 1986–1990*, ed. David W. Bromley and Angela M. Allott. London: Library Association, 1992, v. 1, pp. 220–35.

4   Harry East, 'Funded research in the United Kingdom. Part 1: Sources and distribution of grants', *Library Association record* **90** (1), 1988, 29–31.

5   Patrick Conway, 'Information and library research 1975–1994: a review article', *Journal of librarianship and information science* **27** (1), 1995, 47–50.

6   Meadows, *Innovation in information*.

7   McNicol and Nankivell, *LIS research landscape*, 15.

8   McNicol and Nankivell, *LIS research landscape*, 23, with quotation from Linda Ashcroft and Stephanie McIvor, 'LIS research and publishing: the forces of change', *Library review* **49** (9), 2000, 461–9.

9   McNicol and Nankivell, *LIS research landscape*, 27.

10 McNicol and Nankivell, *LIS research landscape*, 26.

11 Tom Wilson, 'Research in librarianship and information science in the UK: the Research Assessment Exercises', *Information research watch international* Feb. 2002, 3.

12 Pirkko Elliot, 'Who funded research in 2000?', *Information research watch international* Aug. 2001, 1.

13 David Haynes, David Streatfield and Noeleen Cookman, *Review of research funding for LIS*. [London]: Library and Information Commission, 2000 (LIC research report; 40).

14 McNicol and Nankivell, *LIS research landscape*, 19.

15 Judith Elkin and Derek Law, 'Research Assessment Exercise 1992: Library and Information Management and Communications and Media Studies panel', *Journal of librarianship and information science* **26** (3), 1994, 141–7; Judith Elkin and Derek Law, 'The 1996 Research Assessment Exercise: the Library and Information Management panel', *Journal of librarianship and information science* **29** (3), 1997, 131–41.

16 Wilson, 'Research in librarianship and information science in the UK', 2–4.

17 McNicol and Nankivell, *LIS research landscape*.

18 David Nicholas and Peter Williams, 'Journalists and the internet', *Research bulletin of the British Library Research and Innovation Centre* 20, 1998, 9–10.

19 Meadows, *Innovation in information*.

20 BAILER, Heads of Schools and Departments Committee, 'Academic research in information science and librarianship: a position statement', *Library and information research news* **23** (73), 1999, 7–18.

21 Ashcroft and McIvor, 'LIS research and publishing'.

22 BAILER Heads of Schools and Departments Committee, 'Academic research'.

23 John Pluse and Ray Prytherch, *Research in public libraries: final report of the project on research in public libraries*. [London]: British Library Research and Innovation Centre, 1996 (BLRIC report; 8).

24 Maxine Rochester and Pertti Vakkari, 'International LIS research: a comparison of national trends', *IFLA journal* **24** (3), 1998, 166–75.

25 Alison Holmes and Charles Oppenheim, 'Use of citation analysis to predict the outcome of the 2001 Research Assessment Exercise for unit of assessment (UoA) 61: Library and Information Management', *Information research* **6** (2), 2001. Available from: <http://informationr.net/ir/6-2/paper103.html> (accessed 31/1/06).

26 S. E. Robertson and Stephen Walker, 'Some simple effective approximations to the 2-Poisson model for probabilistic weighted retrieval' in *SIGIR '94*, ed. W. B. Croft and C. J. van Rijsbergen. London: Springer, 1994, pp. 232–41. Reprinted in: Karen Sparck Jones and Peter Willett (eds.), *Readings in information retrieval*. San Francisco: Morgan Kaufmann, 1997, pp. 345–54.

27 S. E. Robertson, 'Overview of the Okapi projects', *Journal of documentation* **53** (1), 1997, 3–7 and other papers in this issue; Stephen Robertson and Stephen Walker, 'Threshold setting in adaptive filtering', *Journal of documentation* **56** (3), 2000, 312–31; S. E. Robertson, S. Walker and M. Beaulieu, 'Experimentation as a way of life: Okapi at TREC', *Information processing and management* **36** (1), 2000, 95–108.

28 Helen J. Peat and Peter Willett, 'The limitations of term co-occurrence data for query expansion in document retrieval systems', *Journal of the American Society for Information Science* **42** (5), 1991, 378–83.

29 F. Çuna Ekmekçioglu, Alexander M. Robertson and Peter Willett, 'Effectiveness of query expansion in ranked-output document retrieval systems', *Journal of information science* **18**, 1992, 139–47.

30 Heather J. Rogers and Peter Willett, 'Searching for historical word forms in text databases using spelling-correction methods: reverse error and phonetic coding methods', *Journal of documentation* **47** (4), 1991, 333–53.

31 Mirko Popovič and Peter Willett, 'The effectiveness of stemming for natural-language access to Slovene textual data', *Journal of the American Society for Information Science* **43** (5), 1992, 384–90; Robyn Schinke *et al.*, 'A stemming algorithm for Latin text databases', *Journal of documentation* **52** (2), 1996, 172–87; Robyn Schinke *et al.*, 'Retrieval of morphological variants in searches of Latin text databases', *Computers and the humanities* **31** (5), 1997, 409–32; F. Ç. Ekmekçioglu and Peter Willett, 'Effectiveness of stemming for Turkish text retrieval', *Program* **34** (2), 2000, 195–200.

32 David Ellis, Jonathan Furner-Hines and Peter Willett, 'On the creation of hypertext links in full-text documents: measurement of inter-linker consistency', *Journal of documentation* **50** (2), 1994, 67–98; David Ellis, Jonathan Furner and Peter Willett, 'On the creation of hypertext links in full-text documents: measurement of retrieval effectiveness' *Journal of the American Society for Information Science* **47** (4), 1996, 287–300.

33 D. E. Clark *et al.*, 'Pharmacophoric pattern matching in files of three-dimensional chemical structures: comparison of conformational-searching algorithms for flexible searching', *Journal of chemical information and computer sciences* **34** (1), 1994, 197–206; D. E. Clark, Peter Willett and P. J. Kenny, 'Pharmacophoric pattern matching in files of three-dimensional chemical structures: use of smoothed bounded-distance matrices for the representation and searching of conformationally-flexible molecules', *Journal of molecular graphics* **10** (4), 1992, 194–204; David A. Thorner *et al.*, 'Calculation of structural similarity by the alignment of molecular electrostatic potentials', *Perspectives in drug discovery and design* **9/10/11**, 1998, 301–20.

34 H. M. Grindley *et al.*, 'Identification of tertiary structure resemblance in proteins using a maximal common subgraph isomorphism algorithm', *Journal of molecular biology* **229** (3), 1993, 707–21; P. J. Artymiuk *et al.*, 'A graph-theoretic approach to the identification of three-dimensional patterns of amino acid side-chains in protein structures', *Journal of molecular biology* **243** (2), 1994, 327–44.

35 J. D. Holliday, S. S. Ranade and Peter Willett, 'A fast algorithm for selecting sets of dissimilar structures from large chemical databases', *Quantitative structure-activity relationships* **14** (6), 1995, 501–6; M. Snarey *et al.*, 'Comparison of algorithms for dissimilarity-based compound selection', *Journal of molecular graphics and modelling* **15** (6), 1997, 372–85; V. J. Gillet, Peter Willett and J. Bradshaw, 'The effectiveness of reactant pools for generating structurally diverse combinatorial libraries', *Journal of chemical information and computer sciences* **37** (4), 1997, 731–40; V. J. Gillet *et al.*, 'Selecting combinatorial libraries to optimize diversity and physical properties', *Journal of chemical information and computer sciences* **39** (1), 1999, 169–77.

36 Textual: A. M. Robertson and Peter Willett, 'Generation of equifrequent groups of words using a genetic algorithm', *Journal of documentation* **50** (3), 1994, 213–32; A. M. Robertson and Peter Willett, 'An upperbound to the performance of ranked-output searching: optimal weighting of query terms using a genetic algorithm' *Journal of documentation* **52** (4), 1996, 405–20. Chemical: G. Jones, Peter Willett, and R. C. Glen, 'Molecular recognition of receptor sites using a genetic algorithm with a description of desolvation', *Journal of molecular biology* **245** (1), 1995, 43–53.

37 A. Pellow and T. D. Wilson, 'The management information needs of heads of university departments: a critical success factors approach', *Journal of information science* **19**, 1993, 425–37.

38 T. D. Wilson, 'Tools for the analysis of business information needs', *Aslib proceedings* **46** (1), 1994, 19–23; C. Cockburn and T. D. Wilson, 'Business use of the world-wide web', *International journal of information management* **16** (2), 1996, 83–102.

39 T. D. Wilson, 'Models in information behaviour research', *Journal of documentation*, **55** (3), 1999, 249–70.

40 T. D. Wilson, 'Information system strategies and the logistics of information service delivery' in *Infomationslogistik: proceedings 6. Internationale Fachkonferenz, Garmisch-Partenkirchen*, ed. K. A. Stroetmann. Frankfurt: Deutsche Gesellschaft für Dokumentation, 1992.

41 T. D. Wilson, 'Redesigning the university library in the digital age', *Journal of documentation* **54** (1), 1998, 15–27.

42 T. D. Wilson, 'Departmental responses to the UK Research Assessment Exercises: the emergence of strategic thinking in research planning' in *Proceedings: the 1st British–Nordic Conference on Library and Information Studies, 22–24 May 1995*, ed. M. Hancock-Beaulieu and N. O. Pors. Copenhagen: Royal School of Librarianship, 1995, pp. 259–64.

43 T. D. Wilson, 'On user studies and information needs', *Journal of documentation* **37** (1), 1981, 3–15, at p. 14.

44 T. D. Wilson, 'Models in information behaviour research', *Journal of documentation* **55** (3), 1999, 249–70.

45 T. D. Wilson, 'Exploring models of information behaviour: the "Uncertainty" Project' in *Exploring the contexts of information behaviour: proceedings of the Second International Conference on Research in Information Needs, Seeking and Use in Different Contexts, Sheffield, UK, 13–15 August 1998*, ed. T. D. Wilson and D. K. Allen. London: Taylor Graham, 1999, pp. 55–66.

46 Peter Brophy, 'Towards a generic model of information and library services in the information age', *Journal of documentation* **56** (2), 2000, 161–84.

47 Ann Irving and Geoff Butters (eds.), *Proceedings of the first 'Libraries Without Walls' Conference, Mytilene, Greece, 9–10 September 1995*. Preston: CERLIM, 1996; Peter Brophy, Shelagh Fisher and Zoe Clarke (eds.), *Libraries Without Walls 2: the delivery of library services to distant users*. London: Library Association, 1998; Peter Brophy, Shelagh Fisher and Zoe Clarke (eds.), *Libraries Without Walls 3: the delivery of library services to distant users*. London: Library Association, 2000.

48 Stephen Pinfield *et al.*, 'Realizing the hybrid library', *D-lib magazine*, Oct. 1998. Available from: <http://www.dlib.org/dlib/october98/10pinfield.html> (accessed 26/1/06); Peter Brophy and Shelagh Fisher, 'The hybrid library', *New review of information and library research* **4**, 1998, 3–15.

49 Monica Brinkley, 'The EQUINOX Project: library performance measurement and quality management system', *Exploit interactive* 3, Oct. 1999; available from: <http://www.exploit-lib.org/issue3/equinox/> (accessed 26/1/06); Peter Brophy and Kate Coulling, *Quality management for information and library managers*. Aldershot: Gower, 1996; Peter Brophy and Alan MacDougall, 'Lifelong learning and libraries', *New review of libraries and lifelong learning* **1**, 2000, 3–17; Peter Brophy, 'The SELF Project: an investigation into the provision of self-service facilities for library users', *Vine* 105, 1997, 8–13.

50 Jenny Craven, 'Good design principles for the library website: a study of accessibility issues in UK university libraries', *New review of information and library research* **6**, 2000, 25–51.

51 David Ellis, Deborah Cox and Katherine Hall, 'A comparison of the information seeking patterns of researchers in the physical and social sciences, *Journal of documentation* **49** (4), 1993, 356–69; David Ellis and Merete Haugan, 'Modelling the information seeking patterns of engineers and research scientists in an industrial environment', *Journal of documentation* **53** (4), 1997, 384–403.

52 David Ellis, 'Modelling the information-seeking patterns of academic researchers: a grounded theory approach', *Library quarterly* **63** (4), 1993, 469–86.

53 Thomas D. Wilson and David K. Allen (eds.), *Exploring the contexts of information behaviour: proceedings of the Second International Conference on Research in Information Needs, Seeking and Use in Different Contexts, August 1998, Sheffield, UK.* London: Taylor Graham, 1999.

54 Lars Höglund and T. D. Wilson (eds.), *The new review of information behaviour research* **2**, 2001. Contains papers from ISIC III, the Third International Conference on Research in Information Needs, Seeking and Use in Different Contexts, August 2000, Goteborg, Sweden.

55 David Haynes, David Streatfield and Noeleen Cookman, *Review of research funding for LIS.* [London]: Library and Information Commission, 2000 (LIC research report; 40).

23

Cooperation

Frances Hendrix

Introduction

In *Co-operation in action*, the editors Stella Pilling and Stephanie Kenna state: 'because of its all pervading influence ... co-operation is difficult to define precisely – it can mean different things to different people at different times'.[1]

The authors of the Apt Partnership report suggest that cooperation might simply be regarded as an agreement to work together to share available resources to create cost-effective common services which benefit from economies of scale, but they continue: 'Within the library and information community not all agreements to work together to share resources or to create services are universally regarded as examples of true co-operation.'[2] They suggest that 'there is a widely held view within the library profession that true co-operation contains an element of altruism – a willingness to contribute resources to the general good of providing access to library and information materials'.

Did all the activity, discussions, projects, committees and debates, publications and definitions make a real difference? What actually happened in the 1990s in the name of cooperation? This cannot be a complete overview of such a wide and possibly ill-defined topic, and whatever is mentioned or excluded will be open to argument and disagreement, but I write from a particular perspective and experience of that era: how it looked and seemed to me, and what remain in my mind as the big issues, the major events.

I start with what immediately sprang to my mind when the idea of this volume and chapter was floated. The overwhelming memory was of two aspects: first, the on-going – and as it seems in retrospect, incessant – argument about the definition of cooperation; second, would it in practice actually prove to be a cost-saving tool?

In retrospect it seems that although most people subscribed to the concept of cooperation and liked the idea, they were not always so keen to participate in cooperative activities, even when there was an incentive to do so, such as grants and earmarked funds to develop specific activities. For instance, when Viscount (the automated inter-library loan system developed by LASER, the London and South Eastern Library Region) acquired funds to assist Regional Library Bureaux to automate their holdings and location files, some did not take advantage of those funds.

During the decade many reports and enquiries looked at what cooperation actually took place, and between whom, and examined the real costs involved. Most cooperative activity revolved around the Regional Library Systems, the majority of which were concerned with interlending and the transport schemes that existed for delivering the items. For many this was the extent of cooperation. In some regions there were also subject specialization schemes, but these were not universally maintained and they were very much seen as only a public library activity.

In the latter part of the decade, however, interesting work began to surface on the then emerging internet. Innovative ideas developed into service provision, some of which continued or were to be transmogrified into other services. Some providers started to seek novel applications of the rapidly emerging new technologies and the activity across all library sectors laid the foundations for much of what was to occur after this decade. This included in higher education (HE) the JANET network and the start of cooperative licensing for online resources, and in public libraries the automation of interlending and the launch of Viscount. Pressure, particularly from LASER working with HE institutions, led to public libraries getting interested in and then using the internet, along with some of the first discussions about a national electronic network for public libraries.

What was notable in this decade were the breadth of available funds and the opportunities for funded experimentation, innovation and research, on both a large and a small scale. A range of significant funding opportunities were available for the library sector, from a variety of sources. These included the British Library, the Department for Culture, Media and Sport (DCMS), and European Community funds, as well as many other general and specific sources. The university and the public library sectors took great advantage of these monies with successful bids, and many innovative projects were funded; many of them led to real services, real benefit and real progress, pushing the sector to make changes and develop new ideas and services. Many of the projects also brought together groupings of people who had not had close ties before, and it is recognized that in the university sector the 'Follett' money led to a breed of university staff with proven project management skills.

The funding also enabled cross-sector working, and often this was a requirement of its provision. In order to encourage public libraries to embrace the internet, for example, JANET was cited as a vehicle to emulate. Many senior colleagues in the HE sector were very supportive and a move was made (unsuccessfully) to change the rules of JANET to allow access to the network for public libraries.

Towards the end of the decade the changes occurring in the political, economic and cultural landscape pointed to a more strategic and regional focus for the library sector, and especially for the Regional Library Systems.[3] This was the era of the Comprehensive Spending Reviews (CSR), which highlighted the roles of the regions and encouraged a more formal regional structure with the new strategic and developmental cultural bodies. In particular the creation in 2000 of Resource, the Council for Museums, Archives and Libraries, was significant in the further development of the regional role and the change of emphasis of the Regional Library Systems, henceforward to be based on the boundaries of the regional Government Offices.[4]

A cooperative landscape?

Writing in 1995, Brian Burch, chair of LINC (the Library and Information Co-operation Council) said:

> but that IT will, sooner or later, revolutionise information services seems to many of us beyond question, predicating new forms of library and information co-operation. Perhaps above all we are uncomfortable with this notion because it clearly further erodes the virtual monopoly that libraries and information services have enjoyed in the provision of information. What price library and information co-operation when users have the means and the incentive to tap information sources direct from their homes or office desk?[5]

Moore and Carpenter divide the UK's library cooperatives into three categories:

- the well-established solid core of consortia with origins in the 1920s and 1930s
- those established in the 1990s, of which they identify five, some originating in development or experimental projects
- those established since 1997, all but one of which depended on external and time-limited funds.[6]

The authors suggest that the period from 1997 onwards was one where three political shifts were conducive to cooperative activity: regionalism, joined-up government, and a willingness to finance change and development. The authors predicted a bright future for cooperation, providing a powerful means of meeting service objectives in cost-effective ways, and they highlighted the growing importance of technology and networking in shaping the future of cooperation.

Several themes reflect the sorts of activity and development that represented cooperation during the period covered by this volume.

Organizations

The one major organization for cooperation was LINC, established in 1989 as a successor to the former National Committee for Regional Library Cooperation. Among its general aims were to manage cooperative activity between libraries and information services, to offer advice to government on library cooperation issues, and to exercise influence over government on issues which affected cooperative activities. Subsequently the activities of LINC were subsumed under Resource, the Council for Museums, Archives and Libraries.

In addition there were FIL (Forum for Interlending), CONARLS (Circle of Officers of National and Regional Library Systems), and each of the individual

Regional Library Systems (ten in all), as well as bodies such as SINTO, HATRICS, etc., and a number of LIPS (Library and Information Plans), CURL, and others.

Technology

The trend for larger libraries to move from their organizational computer services to stand-alone specialized systems continued apace during the decade. There was a wide range, from large minicomputer-based systems supporting multiple terminals in public libraries, to single-user PC-based systems in small specialist libraries.[7]

The number of suppliers of computer systems remained fairly static until the end of the decade, when mergers and takeovers began to occur, sometimes by companies which were not necessarily specialists in the field. The systems being provided had not changed or developed significantly, and interoperability was still at an early stage. However, those who had been in at the early stage of offering MARC-based record systems, such as BLCMP, Dynix and OCLC, continued to be major players. The type, design and functionality of computer systems were factors in the development of cooperative activity and exchange of data.

CD-ROMs still featured quite heavily and had a range of uses, and it was only late in the decade that their use, once predicted to be unlikely to last for more than a few years, began to decline, though for some specialist libraries and purposes they continued to fulfil an important role. Again, CD-ROM had uses for cooperative activity, especially where participants did not have suitable computer systems.

Library management systems (LMS), which had originally developed mainly for circulation control, had increased in functionality over the period and began to be developed and refined with serials control, report generation, online public access catalogues, and towards the end of the decade for external web access.

Standards were still central to much of the functionality of systems, but new standards based on ISO, Z39.50, ARTTel and others, were being explored and developed for the more immediate exchange of data. During the decade in question, though it was subsequently overtaken by other major ICT-related standards, MARC was probably the most significant.

MARC records

The use of MARC records for record supply and retrospective conversion was at its height during this decade, both supply and conversion being components of cooperative services and activity. MARC records were still being sought from a variety of places to use within both single and union catalogues and for acquisition data. Many book suppliers had by now started to offer them (sometimes of variable quality) to those purchasing their stock. These records were often available weeks in advance of records from the British Library, and could always be updated with a full quality BL record later. A significant amount of retrospective conversion was still going on, especially as libraries updated their LMS and wanted to upgrade their basic bibliographic records from older systems. Towards the end of the 1990s interoperability, metadata and other more specialized operations and standards began assume greater prominence. BLCMP converted to Talis and continued to offer a range of services to its member libraries.

Interlending

This was generally considered to be the main cooperative activity, especially between public libraries, university libraries tending to go direct to BLDSC (the British Library Document Supply Centre). The first interlending system had appeared in the 1930s, and many of the Regional Library Systems still had interlending as their core function. Until the 1980s, however, and the introduction by LASER of the Viscount automated interlending and messaging system, this activity was a manual one.

Towards the end of the decade the major emphasis, and cooperative activity, was on interconnection of systems, networked services and interoperability.[8]

BLDSC was still a central, almost universally used, system for sourcing items for inter-library loans, especially serials. However, as a result of European funding and experimentation on systems such as ION (Interlending OSI Network) and the ILL protocol, the linking of inter-library loans both between individual libraries and with the BLDSC system became a major feature, with messaging a standard aspect. LASER developed the software to link all but one of the Regional Library Systems (one very small RLS, Information North, would not cooperate with what was seen as the most technically developed RLS), revolutionizing the process of automated interlending.

Electronic resource-sharing

Electronic resource-sharing became a very significant feature during this decade as can be seen in the selection of projects mentioned below, and significant sums of money were earmarked to support experimentation in this field.

Writing in 1988, Fred Friend asked why resource-sharing (or 'access', as it was now called) was generating so much interest.[9] He suggested that libraries had been sharing their resources for centuries, to a far greater extent than users realized, but that because the emphasis had always been on holdings, resource-sharing had never formed the major component of any library service. Nevertheless:

> the value of resource-sharing has always been greater than statistics would indicate ... that one visit to request an item from another library may make such a difference to the user's research. ... For the librarian ... resource-sharing may have political value out of all proportion to its quantity in showing that librarians do co-operate, and ... to be actively involved in resource-sharing may increase the librarian's chances of getting an increase in the book buying budget.

However, 'expensive resource sharing is perceived to be a contradiction in terms'.

Network/communication projects

The improvements in telecommunications, including the use of email, the introduction of the Integrated Services Digital Network (ISDN) and widening access to
the internet had a significant impact on developments and services in the document
delivery area. Although electronic document transmission was possible some years
prior to 2000, it was a very slow process. With the advent of the new high speed
networks, such as SuperJANET, the transmission of documents and other media
became a reality. There were a number of groups and institutions working on networking projects aiming to link and achieve interconnectivity between different
document delivery users and suppliers. Further projects and bodies, such as the
Group on Electronic Document Interchange (GEDI), investigated technical
development and standards in the network area.

Many of the new systems being developed were based on the ANSI/NISO
Z39.50 specification, a search and retrieve protocol. The standard allowed users of
different software products to communicate with each other and exchange data.
The facility to use local user interfaces for searching other databases was also
made possible. The International Organization for Standardization (ISO) also had a
search and retrieval standard known as SR or ISO 10162/3. These developments in
networking and communication systems now enabled electronic resource-sharing
on both a national and international basis.

Electronic document delivery systems

A number of projects aimed to develop integrated electronic document delivery
software/systems and to incorporate many aspects of resource-sharing networks,
communications and scanning technologies. The increased availability of large
quantities of bibliographic information with restricted access to the material on site
increased the need for a document delivery service. The main benefit of an integrated electronic document delivery system was that the whole process from initial
searching for information, checking of local holding information, through to the
ordering and receiving of documents, could be performed in one continuous
process from the end-user's workstation. Early work in this area had to overcome
technological barriers to provide this. With the high-speed communication networks and technological advances in this area, the number of services was
expected to grow, and thus the extent of cooperation was increased.

During times of financial constraint, with increasing pressures to provide access
to a wider variety of materials, libraries have, over the years, had to consider
various options. Depending upon geographic location, resource-sharing could offer
one solution to the problem and enable collections to be used more effectively. The
following projects highlight research work that was aimed at providing shared
document delivery services. Some projects such as the Journal Articles Sent on
Demand (JASON NRW) and OhioLink were further developed into successful
services.[10] The technology and standards enabled cooperative activity across
geographical boundaries and technological barriers, and lessons were learnt and
transferred internationally.

There was a move from activities such as interlending, location of material, collaborative acquisition, information and advice services, Library and Information Plans, and cooperative activity in training and development to services and systems based on the 'new technologies'. This can be illustrated by looking at the following examples of developments, prototypes and services that were launched. The era saw the launch of the JISC Electronic Libraries Project (eLib), which stimulated a flurry of activity in university libraries. In public libraries EARL (started in 1995) did much to bring together libraries in cooperative activity which was internet-based and much of its work was later to be encompassed in the People's Network.

LASER continued to fund and develop significant ICT systems for resource-sharing and interlending, and pushed the move to interoperability and use of standards. The enhanced automated inter-library loan system, V3, launched in the 1990s, led the way.

V3.Online

Launched at the beginning of 2000, V3.Online was a client-server service for resource-sharing and interlending requesting.[11] Within the first 12 months of going live it was upgraded to V3.Web which offered superior functionality via internet web access. It was the first and only totally integrated search, message and loan management service in the United Kingdom, and was developed by LASER in conjunction with LIBPAC (later V3FM Ltd). It was the largest and most advanced of the regional library interlending systems and over 100 libraries made daily use of it.

It consisted of:

- a comprehensive database of relevant bibliographic information of some 5 million titles
- a unique location service giving access to over 40 million copies held in public libraries.

It provided:

- full transaction management facilities for lending and borrowing resources
- full management information and accounting for use
- internet access via the latest 'thin-client' web technology.

It was backed by UK public libraries, national, academic and special libraries and international partners.

V3.Online followed on from the Viscount system which LASER had run suc-cessfully for many years. It was the pinnacle of what had been since the 1930s the major cooperative activity arranged via the RLSs for book lending between public libraries, and is a good example of the internationalism of cooperation. It continued LASER's long history of regional and inter-regional resource-sharing activities started in 1926.

Whether the library materials required were held by public libraries, the British Library or other specialized libraries, V3 allowed them to be found via the web interface and immediately requested for loan through a local library. V3 allowed library staff to manage the whole process of lending and returning items as appropriate to the type of material.

Across the UK, but also in Europe and the United States, significant progress was being made on networking libraries and library systems from a wide range of funding sources. Many groups and organizations developed cooperative-type systems for resource-sharing and document delivery, which were the key activity at the time, and some of the more interesting, successful and long-standing are highlighted below. Also highlighted is the wide geographical range of similar projects to share systems and services across boundaries of country and type of library.

The Electronic Libraries Programme (eLib)
eLib was created in 1994 to provide access to networked resources, and to fund projects which 'transform the use and storage of knowledge in higher education institutions'.[12] From 1995 to 1997, subject-based information gateways were the focus. Projects were conducted in mainly untouched areas and resulted in OMNI (Organising Medical Networked Information), ADAM (Art, Design, Architecture & Media) and RUDI (Resource for Urban Design Information), all building databases of internet resources in their subject areas from scratch.

1997–1999 saw the birth of the Resource Discovery Network (RDN), which came about as a result of planning a future for eLib with a development programme of translating successful projects into services. It was the UK's free national gateway to internet resources for the learning, teaching and research community, linking to more than 100,000 resources via a series of subject-based information gateways. JISC funds were limited and this was the way to continue the work started in 1993. Collaboration was the key, and RDN collaborated with about 70 organizations.

LAMDA
The LAMDA (London and Manchester Document Access) project funded by the eLib Programme involved the development of a cooperative document delivery service between academic libraries in London and Manchester.[13] Requests for items not available in the home library's stock were routed first to local libraries, then to libraries in the other city, and finally to BLDSC if they were not available. The service aimed to provide electronic delivery of material over the academic network where possible. The libraries involved with supplying material throughout the project were: in London: King's College, University College London, the British Library of Political and Economic Science (BLPES), and the University of Westminster, and in Manchester: the John Rylands University Library, Manchester Business School, Manchester Metropolitan University, the University of Salford and UMIST.

BLDSC

The British Library Document Supply Centre (BLDSC) was involved with many electronic document delivery projects. These included trials with standard service fax, delivery of scanned images in cooperation with the University of East Anglia, SuperJANET and the Electronic Document Interchange between Libraries (EDIL).[14] In 1995 BLDSC was also involved with a project called DISCovery, aimed at providing fast access to scientific, medical and technical documents directly to the end-user. A weekly CD-ROM containing the last six months of the *Inside contents* database was provided. Requests could be placed during a search and articles would be delivered by fax within two hours.

ION

Project ION was initiated and part funded by the Commission of the European Communities DG XIII under the Information Market Policy Actions (IMPACT) Programme. The project commenced in 1990 and involved a consortium of international library organizations comprising: LASER, using the Viscount interlending network service, in the UK; Pica in the Netherlands; and the SUNIST network host in France.[15]

Project ION was a pilot/demonstration project using the interlending open system interconnection (OSI) network. The overall objectives of the project were to achieve interconnection between the three different computerized networks; improve the efficiency of international interlending services; and demonstrate the use of OSI network communication. During November 1993, ION began a live service that involved 50 test site libraries. The technical aspects of the connections were hidden from the end-user. The ILL messages were converted into the ISO ILL standard. End-users had easy access to the different service infrastructures and systems at the receiving library, including international databases, and could also specify a service within a country to which they wished to direct the ILL request.

De Montfort University

During 1991–1995 De Montfort University was working, in collaboration with other partners including Tilburg University and Elsevier Science, on several research projects funded under the Commission of the European Communities DG XIII/E Telematics for Libraries Programme. The Electronic Libraries Image Server for Europe (ELISE) project investigated image retrieval and quality, and aimed to develop a system for the interconnection of full colour image banks in libraries from member countries.[16] A further project, the European Libraries SGML Application (ELSA), was funded for two years from 1994.[17] The project aimed to develop a system to deliver SGML documents from publisher to library. The British Library Research and Development Department, with IBM UK Scientific Centre, funded the Electronic Library Information Online Retrieval (ELINOR) project at De Montfort University until May 1996. This project aimed to provide a large collection of material in text and image form direct to end-users' workstations. A number of publishers gave permission for their works to be scanned and held in electronic form. The ELINOR system also included facilities to monitor copyright and usage statistics.[18]

EARL

The EARL Consortium for Public Library Networking, which began as Project EARL (Electronic Access to Resources in Libraries) revolutionized the library landscape by offering public libraries a web presence, as well as models for national networked services. It preceded the People's Network, and stimulated the move by public libraries to internet and web activity. The original idea and the cooperative concept of EARL were developed by LASER.

EARL was established in 1995 to enhance the role of public libraries in providing library and information services over the internet. It had over 130 partners in local authorities, and associate partners in government, the profession, higher education, and the commercial sector. It was a collaborative approach to establishing a national information and resource-sharing service for public libraries in the UK. It began with a pilot phase in 1994 that included a scoping study and a pilot demonstration service being launched. By 1995 there were 120 library authorities involved, using EARL to provide email facilities (their only method of emailing then), web page creation, access to a range of databases and the development of Earlweb which provided a gateway to a number of internet resources. Other activities included a project called Readiness, a range of specific Task Groups and collaboration with a number of European partners.[19]

Through collaboration, EARL aimed to demonstrate and extend the ability of public libraries to deliver networked information and knowledge-based services. These were developed primarily through EARL's seventeen Task Groups working on new ways to deliver shared services over the network.

The EARL Consortium provided public libraries with very successful demonstrators such as *Familia, Ask a librarian, Euroguide* and others. More importantly it gave public libraries a higher technical profile, through advocacy and research, and offered them support and guidance to enhance their own services. It laid the groundwork for such initiatives as the People's Network.

To raise the profile of public libraries on the web EARL developed the EARL Awards for the best UK public library web pages, celebrating the best of what public libraries were doing on the world wide web.[20] Awards were made in four categories to reflect the features that make a library site informative, interesting, useful and a pleasure to visit. By highlighting the best, EARL hoped to establish a benchmark to which other public libraries could aspire.

Many of the winners and runners-up were leading the process of information networking in their localities and councils. Nationally that was a role that the public library service not only could but had a duty to fulfil. The 'information society' needed public libraries to commit themselves to networking. These websites were among the more visible signs that the commitment was being made.

The Awards were for:

- best information content
- best interactive features
- best collection of internet resources
- best design and usability.

In 1997, EARL held a major conference 'EARL and the New Public Library'. Over 200 delegates from public library authorities and other organizations from England, Scotland, Wales, Northern Ireland and the Channel Islands attended. The conference set out to define the collective strategy of public libraries in response to recent government policy initiatives, addressing in particular *New library: the people's network*, the report commissioned from the Library and Information Commission (LIC) by the DCMS, which placed public libraries at the heart of the information society.

A number of strategic initiatives were agreed at the conference:

- Public libraries must act quickly to advocate implementation of the People's Network in each authority.
- EARL would coordinate information and advice across the UK in support of local needs.
- EARL would prepare proposals for the policy and development of *New library* to harness libraries' resources on a national scale.
- EARL must persuade the DCMS and LIC of the benefits of central funding for new national services.
- Public libraries must collaborate on a national and regional basis to negotiate licensing agreements for commercially available information.

EARL provided libraries with the support they needed, encouraged an expanding base of information, and developed the structures for advanced public and technical services. More broadly it aimed to foster development and initiatives among all participants across the network, collaboration being considered the key. The project was developed by a preliminary planning team, all active in the development of library networking, and from the views of early contributing members. Project EARL published an online newsletter free of charge, which reported on the progress of its various endeavours and kept informed the institutions that were affiliated with it.

It could be said that EARL was a major, if not *the* major, cooperative activity for public libraries of the decade in the UK, bridging the gap between paper-based cooperation and the internet age, bringing the internet into focus for public libraries, and giving many (almost all) the opportunity to experiment with web services without risk, and being very much the precursor and instigator for the People's Network. It also facilitated significant cross-sector and cross-domain cooperation, with close working and excellent support form the HE sector.

All of the above projects advanced the concept, idea and reality of cooperation, as well as shaping the systems, services and ideals of the following decade. Much of what was 'discovered' then continued to play a part in early 21st-century technologies, processes and structures but by then they were no longer referred to as being part of an ethos of cooperation.

In retrospect
As mentioned earlier, one of the major reports that came midway into the decade was *The Apt review*, commissioned by LINC, whose members were predominantly the Regional Library Systems. In the foreword the then chair of LINC, Brian Burch, Librarian of Leicester University, described the background to the commissioning of the report. He stated that library and information cooperation was facing an unprecedented series of major upheavals, including the effects of local government reorganization, the Department of National Heritage's review of public libraries and Library and information Plans, and the proposed establishment of a national Library and Information Commission. He continued:

> Library and information co-operation is the essential reason for LINC's existence, but we can no longer assume either that existing forms of co-operation are appropriate or, more fundamentally, that there will be unquestioning and universal support for any acti-vity with the co-operation label.

These words would soon seem prophetic, as LINC was to disappear, LIC to become part of Resource, and the word cooperation to cease to be centre stage.

The Apt study had several highly relevant conclusions:

- Cooperative activity was small and, though vitally important, perhaps overstated.
- IT had reached a threshold which would fundamentally alter the context of the provision of library services, though the imminence of those changes was not generally fully understood in public libraries.
- The Follett report had focused academic libraries on access, especially remote access to information and resources, and the concept of the virtual library.[21]
- Formal cooperative structures were less well developed between libraries and other agencies except through the Library and Information Plans (LIPs), the effectiveness of which had been questioned.
- The costs and benefits of cooperation did not lend themselves to any accurate 'objective' evaluation by application of mathematical formulae.

The first recommendation of the Apt report was that the new environment should give much greater priority to the development of practical cooperative arrange-ments and less attention to promoting the ideal of cooperation.

> Although co-operation is an important integral part of the ethos of library and information work, actual co-operative activity is generally most evident where the need for co-operation is most obvious, ... the review has confirmed the existence of a

widespread view that the practice of co-operation falls far short of the extent of the enthusiasm for co-operation in theory within the library and information services community.

A number of other reports debating cooperation were also published, including the Aslib report of 1995 and the BroadVision report of 1996.[22] These give a flavour of the debate on cooperation at the middle of the decade under review.

The Department of National Heritage held its own seminar in 1996 examining where Regional Library Systems might develop further, and many of the seminar papers touched upon or focused on cooperative activity.[23] This was one of the first airings of the then developing project EARL.

However, in the presentation on EARL at this seminar Peter Stone introduced the move to the global as opposed to the regional. He quoted Paul Evans Peters of the Coalition for Networked Information describing the impact of the internet as 'the biggest migration in history'. How right they both were. Likewise the Apt authors noted that 'the level of support for the concept of co-operation, in principle, and the actual level of co-operative activity, in practice, can be largely attributed to the limited extent to which co-operative activity is actually imperative to satisfy the needs of the great majority of actual users, as opposed to potential end-users, at the present time'.

Conclusion

Looking back it all seems 'much ado about nothing', a plethora of navel-gazing reports, the justification of what we were doing and how good it was to cooperate. Much of the debate was on how the Regional Library Systems should develop, and of course they continued to exist in large part in the following decade, as regional Museums, Libraries and Archives Councils (MLACs). They would no longer depend on offering services as their core activity and *raison d'être* but were to become joint organizations, of libraries, archives and museums, aiming to achieve the ultimate cooperative activity of working together and deciding policy and strategy for those sectors and domains on a regional basis.

However, in the period under review, developments that did shape the future were also launched, many via the Electronic Libraries Programme, for academic libraries in particular, many by LASER via ION, Viscount and V3, and a range of other projects, and significantly the inheritance left via EARL. Some of us saw the future then, and some of it was to be realized, though there would be less talk of the importance or relevance of cooperation. In the excellent OCLC publication *The 2003 OCLC environmental scan: pattern recognition* there is a paragraph on collaboration:

If the last few decades of library and information developments have taught us anything, then it is surely that the really significant advances, and the most meaningful and lasting solutions, are cooperative ones. And more than that, they are tending to be global ones. MARC, AACR2 and even the internet itself, are obvious examples of this, and there are many others; and the rise of consortia of every kind is testimony to the growing recognition of the value – the necessity even – of institutional co-operation, at both local and international levels. ... I hope we can all agree that, even where we are in competition, we also have a mutual self-interest in helping to build systems and processes and models of service-delivery solutions that are based on cooperatively-agreed solutions and standards.[24]

Cooperation did continue after this period, but often in another guise. Perhaps the reason is that suggested by Fred Friend in 2000:

Now that the geographical barriers to the flow of information are breaking down and disappearing how can we use the new internationalism to provide users with a better service? ... This is not a question of technology but of structures. Our co-operative structures were shaped in an age of geographical barriers to information. Should they or can they be re-shaped in a truly international way?[25]

Notes

1 Stella Pilling and Stephanie Kenna (eds.), *Co-operation in action: collaborative initiatives in the world of information*. London: Facet, 2002, ix.

2 Apt Partnership, *The Apt review: a review of library and information co-operation in the UK and Republic of Ireland*. Sheffield: Library and Information Co-operation Council, 1995 (British Library R&D report; 6216).

3 Department for Culture, Media and Sport, *Libraries and the regions: a discussion paper*. London: DCMS, 1999.

4 Later there was a further change in the shape of Resource, which changed its name to the Museums, Libraries and Archives Council in 2004. The regional MLAs (MLACs) were been drawn into the main body of MLA and became regional divisions of that main body, with the Chairs of the regional MLACs sitting on the board of MLA.

5 Apt Partnership, *Apt review*, Preface.

6 Nick Moore and Julie Carpenter, 'Mapping the British co-operative landscape' in *Co-operation in action*, ed. Pilling and Kenna, pp. 13–28, at p. 15.

7 Juliet Leeves, *Library systems: a buyers' guide*. 2nd ed. Aldershot: Gower, 1989.

8 Peter Stubley, 'Interoperability: Z39.50, ISO ILL and the UK National Union Catalogue feasibility study', *Information management report* Sept. 2000, 11–14.

9 Frederick J. Friend, 'LAMDA: so what is so exciting about LAMDA?', *Ariadne* 14, March 1998: available at: <http://www.ariadne.ac.uk/issue14/> (accessed 2/06).

10 Peter Smith, 'Different organisational forms for interlibrary loans and electronic document delivery: the examples of ION and the North-Rhine Westfalian Urgent Order System (JASON)', *Libri* **44** (4), 1994, 381–7; K. W. Neubauer, 'Express ordering and delivering system of journal articles. JASON NRW', *Libri* **44** (4), 1994, 388–92; F. Summann, 'JASON NRW: express ordering and delivery system of journal articles', *Vine* 96, Sept. 1994, 11–13.

11 Jennifer Cox *et al.*, 'V3.Online: past, present and future', *Interlending & document supply* **28** (4), 2000, 169–77.

12 Resource Discovery Network, *About RDN*: <http://www.rdn.ac.uk/about/> (accessed 2/06).

13 John Blunden-Ellis, 'LAMDA: a new venture in document delivery', *Law librarian* **27** (2), 1996, 97–8; S. Taylor, 'Document delivery in practice: the LAMDA project' in *Document delivery beyond 2000: proceedings of a conference held at the British Library, September 1998*, ed. Anne Morris, Neil Jacobs and Eric Davies. London: Taylor Graham, 1999, pp.102–7. LAMDA finished after ten years in 2005.

14 Andrew Braid, 'Standardization in electronic document delivery: a practical example', *Interlending & document supply* **24** (4), 1996, 12–18.

15 C. Deschamps, 'The ION and EDIL projects', *INSPEL* **29** (2), 1995, 133–44; Jean Plaister, 'Project ION: OSI pilot/demonstration project between library networks in Europe for interlending services', *Vine* 82, April 1991, 11–17.

16 K. Black, 'ELISE – an online image retrieval system', *Aslib information* **21** (7/8), 1993, 293–5

17 R. J. Adams, 'Electronic libraries SGML applications: background to project ELSA', *Program* **29** (4), 1995, 397–406.

18 D. G. Zhoa and A. Ramsden, 'Report on the ELINOR electronic library pilot (user aspect, system architecture, copyright management)', *Information services & use* **15** (3), 1995, 199–212.

19 Peter Smith *et al.*, 'EARL: collaboration in networked information and resource sharing services for public libraries in the UK', *Program* **31** (4), 1997, 347–63.

20 See for example 'The EARL awards for the best UK public library web pages', *Program* **32** (2), 1998.

21 Joint Funding Councils' Libraries Review Group, *Report*. Bristol: HEFCE, 1993. Chairman Sir Brian Follett. (The 'Follett report'.)

22 Aslib Consultancy, *Review of the public library service in England and Wales: final report*. London: Aslib, 1995; BroadVision Consultancy, *Library and Information Plans: review and further initiatives. Final report*. Newcastle upon Tyne: Information North for the Department of National Heritage, 1995.

23 Department of National Heritage, *Regional library development: where next? Proceedings of the Regional Issues Seminar organised for the Department of National Heritage by the Library and Information Co-operation Council (LINC) 9th and 10th February 1966, Viking Hotel, York*. Bruton: LINC, 1996.

24 OCLC, *The 2003 OCLC environmental scan: pattern recognition: a report to the OCLC membership*. Dublin, Ohio: OCLC, 2004.

25 Frederick J. Friend, 'Libraries of one world: librarians look across the oceans', *Collection management* **24** (3/4), 2000, 281–7.

24

Publicity and promotion

Linda M. Smith

The remit of this publication is to record the history of library and information services during the 1990s. However, to appreciate the progress of the development of promotion and marketing as practised by library and information services during this period, it is important to realize that it was only in the late 1980s that library and information services began to realize that public relations and marketing were a core activity if they were to survive and flourish. Prior to this, libraries had always been regarded as 'pillars of society'. Now, they were finding themselves in the position of proving their value and benefit to the communities that they served in order to compete with other departments for their share of the budget and resources.

The economic background

The early 1990s were a period that saw dramatic cuts in public library service provision as local authorities were forced to make cuts in their budgets. If ever there was a time when it was essential to market the value and importance of library services it was then. This economic climate of cutbacks and budget restraints exerted pressures on the library services and public libraries became cost centres with their own financial targets. Libraries were forced to look at other ways of income generation: these included sponsorship, grants, friends of libraries, donations and joint ventures. All of these had an impact on marketing and promotion of services and again the need for libraries to take marketing seriously was highlighted. In 1996, Pots and Roper undertook a study to compare sponsorship and fundraising in the United Kingdom and the United States.[1] They found that the problems that created the need for sponsorship and fundraising were similar in both countries but that the United States was more aggressive in marketing and obtaining sponsorship. They concluded that libraries in the United Kingdom could learn much from their activities.

Tom Featherstone (President of the Library Association in 1991) remarked on the irony of presenting the Carnegie Medal (a medal which bears the name of the greatest library benefactor, Andrew Carnegie) at a time when so many cuts were being made. Indeed the recipient of the award, Gillian Cross made an impassioned speech urging library staff to market and promote the value of their services.[2]

Education for publicity

Owing to the level of sophistication that had been achieved in the advertising, media and print industries, it is understandable that the public now had very high expectations of any form of promotional activity presented by any business or organization. In their eyes, sophistication meant professionalism, which in turn generated trust and confidence in the product or service. Sadly, on the whole, the standard of professionalism in PR and marketing did not match the standards of professional excellence offered by library services themselves. There were huge gaps in skills and resources that needed to be addressed if a high standard of promotion and marketing activity was to be achieved.

One of the obvious ways to encourage PR and marketing in libraries is to ensure that it is an integral part of professional education. However, the inclusion of this in the syllabus of departments of library and information science was piecemeal, which was very unfortunate. Only by having its importance emphasized in professional education could new graduates entering the profession work with confidence to influence senior management to provide the essential resources and expertise for this type of activity. Although Elkin and Wilson highlighted the need for changes to be made in the syllabus to embrace the social, political and economic changes that were affecting libraries, no mention was made of the inclusion of marketing.[3]

Although publicity for libraries was covered in the City and Guilds' syllabus for library assistants, staff undertaking these courses often found, as did library and information science graduates, that resources to develop this type of activity were lacking. They were not in a position of seniority to secure the resources, and so any new-found enthusiasm was dampened. The result was that publicity material was designed and printed by in-house reprographic units, which were frequently unable to guarantee deadlines or which produced material that lacked quality owing to the lack of resources.

Of course, it is one thing to secure budget and resources, but this type of work requires hands-on practical knowledge, most of which could be gained by talking to professionals operating in the commercial world of design and print, copy writing, signage and display. Hands-on courses were essential to provide this experience. The Publicity and Public Relations Group (PPRG) of the Library Association, and other Groups, organized day courses and conferences on various aspects of PR and marketing. More often than not, delegates would comment on the lack of funds and resources to undertake PR and marketing activity on a sustained basis. This being the case, it is not surprising that promotional activity was limited to one-off events. (These courses did go some way to bridge the skills gap. Indeed, they highlighted the importance and value of this work to library services, but in no way could it match the ideal situation of marketing being included in the professional syllabus.)

The Library Association

Undoubtedly, the appointment of a marketing officer at the Library Association in 1990 was a significant milestone in the history of PR and marketing and had a significant impact in this decade. The role of the marketing officer was to promote the value of membership to existing members, lapsed members and potential members. The first post-holder, Virginia Smith, commented that 'marketing an organisation of some 25,000 members to themselves was an interesting and unusual concept'.[4] She identified that there was a gap between Library Association headquarters and the membership; she therefore argued strongly that this gap needed to be bridged by a communication strategy and a clear understanding of each other's needs if the organization was to fulfil its role and grow. The profession needed to pull together and become a force to be reckoned with. By doing this, librarians would influence the role that library and information services could play within their communities, the United Kingdom and indeed the world.

During this period, the commercial world was becoming very much aware of the importance of commercial image and branding. As a professional marketing person Virginia Smith acknowledged the significance of this, and therefore she presented a case to the Library Association Council to consider commissioning a new logo and brand to be applied to all of its printed material and merchandise. The creative brief for the design stated that it should be 'modern, simple and flexible'.[5] When the new corporate style was launched, it was described as the first step to market the Library Association's assets, the greatest of which was its members. It wanted its members, employers and the public to know what librarians and library services stood for. The new corporate identity displayed a modern free-style typeface that was presented in a subdued purple. Undoubtedly, the typeface did give the Library Association a more appealing and personable image but the colour could not be described as in any way dynamic. Successfully executed, the new image did much to raise the profile of the Association amongst its members. It could also be argued that the new corporate identity for the Association acted as a driver for individuals to be more conscious of their institution's image. Many librarians began to realize the importance of clearly branded publicity material with the library authority's name; but it has to be said that the adoption of this idea was slow. Only in the late 1990s when many promotional projects began to involve substantial sponsorship was there real progress in the consistent application of the corporate brand.

There were many who said that the role of the marketing officer for the Library Association should have incorporated the national promotion of libraries. This was partly achieved by the introduction of major awards and the raising of the profile of the Public Relations and Publicity Awards, together with the planning and involvement in National Libraries Week.

National Libraries Week

During the 1990s the Library Association's Marketing Department took a pivotal role in the development and promotion of National Libraries Week. The theme for

1993 was 'Everybody Needs Libraries'. Branded, printed template publicity material was produced centrally under the aegis of the Library Association to enable libraries to purchase items on which they could overprint details of their individual events. This of course helped to minimize costs for participating libraries. The event was launched in the House of Commons and was sponsored by Mark Fisher (the Labour Party's library spokesman at that time) with an early day motion deploring the cuts affecting the nation's library services, and parliamentary questions. The many events that took place across the country and the national and regional media coverage are outlined in the November issue of the *Library Association record* for that year.

In 1999 the Marketing Department set up the Marketing Group. It was developed as a networking group for qualified marketing professionals working within library authorities. These people were often working in isolation and this network provided the opportunity for them to communicate with people facing similar challenges and issues. The membership consisted predominantly of public librarians. There were two aspects to the group: email discussion lists and a quarterly information network meeting hosted by volunteers.

Desktop publishing, software and print technologies made rapid advances in the 1990s. These offered the potential for library and information services to design and produce their own publicity material. However, these technological advances were only just becoming available to libraries, and, as mentioned earlier in this chapter, they highlighted a skills gap. Any item of publicity produced on a PC (few libraries had access to Apple Macintoshes with the appropriate software) inevitably would look sharper than a hand-written notice, of which there were many in libraries. However, the lack of design skills and appropriate software made a large proportion of desktop published material look amateurish in appearance. A poster or leaflet can only communicate a message if the copy is relevant to the audience and the principles of typography, layout and design are applied.

The Publicity and Public Relations Group
Whilst strides were being made within the Library Association with internal marketing, the Publicity & Public Relations Group continued to promote the value of a planned and sustained approach to public relations, promotion and marketing. The Group's involvement in the Public Relations and Publicity Awards undoubtedly did much to help this work and will be discussed fully later in this chapter.

There still seemed to be reluctance within the profession to learn from the commercial world. This probably stemmed from the realization that the majority would not be able to secure the budget and resources to achieve campaigns comparable to commercial standards. Nevertheless, much could be learnt from their techniques and methodology. The PPRG realized that it was in a unique position to encourage and promote excellence in PR and promotional campaigns in all types of library and information service. The Group maintained its commitment to excellence and innovation through the provision of conferences and courses that covered every aspect of public relations and marketing, giving practical information on writing effective copy and using the media and its quarterly newsletter *Public eye.*[6]

Wherever possible, the Group engaged presenters for their conferences and courses who were professionals within their own fields, be it copywriting, design and print, image promotion, media, display or signing and guiding. This enabled delegates to gain first-hand knowledge and to benefit from their ideas and experience. Of course, this was not always easy to achieve; such professionals could command high fees which the Group was not in a position to pay. In the majority of cases the PPRG benefited from good will and personal contacts.

The PPRG also worked with the Library Association in the production of promotional artwork for Library Promotion Fortnight. This took place in November 1990. The idea was that individual libraries could obtain artwork to apply to their own printed material. However, the PPRG was concerned about the lack of funds available from the Library Association for this major event. Representatives were invited to join a steering group and give the benefit of their time and expertise but there was no money available for administration costs. There was concern that if a major project such as this was to be launched, PR advice, reasonable off-the shelf publicity and guidance on media coverage were essential if libraries were to recognize that promotion was essential their future.

Public perceptions

The Consumers' Association published a report on public libraries in 1990.[7] It surveyed 400 *Which?* members and revealed that in general public libraries were used and valued. 51% rated the services as 'good', and 7% as 'excellent'. Interestingly, these findings were the same for adults and children. However, the survey showed that 41% of the people who participated thought that libraries were 'not good' or 'not good at all' at marketing and promoting there services. It could be argued that the readers of *Which?* were likely to be articulate, and able to find out about the services they need. However, their comments underline that there was a severe lack of this type of activity in libraries at this time. It is ironic that during this period, libraries were expanding their services and facilities beyond the core free services that they were obliged to provide. These included sale of publications, video and tape loans and events which were intended as income-generating activities and therefore it was important that they were promoted in order for them to be successful.

The *Which?* survey also pointed out that the aesthetic aspects of library buildings and their accessibility can affect marketing of library services: inconvenient opening hours, unattractive buildings, the lack of books and the poor condition of stock. These all deterred people from using libraries. In marketing terms, these factors relate to understanding the customer and gearing the service to satisfy their needs. Indeed, the *Which?* survey played its own part in promoting the public library service. It brought about a greater awareness of the statutory duty of local authorities to provide free of charge a comprehensive and efficient library service comprising free reference and book lending services to the people who live, work and study within the local authority boundary. In a section about libraries serving the community, the key services that the public could expect were outlined. (It is fair to say that the public could question why public libraries did not take on the responsibility to inform their communities more widely of both core and extended service activities. This argument also opens up a further debate in that if libraries of all kinds had been more vocal in their marketing and promotional activities, they might not have been in a position where they had to fight so hard for their share of resources.)

Alongside the *Which?* survey, the Library and Information Commission recognized the importance of promoting public library services in response to the Department of National Heritage Public Library Review. They commented that the range and depth of services offered by public libraries were not widely understood by the general public.

As public libraries examined their market sectors, they began to recognized the need to promote their services and facilities to multi-cultural groups whose first language was not English. Birmingham Libraries provide us with an example of strategic marketing to black and ethnic minority children. Their campaign focused on the under-fives, with the community librarians working with a small number of organizations representing the predominantly black and ethnic minority population rather than marketing indiscriminately.

Loughborough University Department of Library and Information Studies together with the Department of Management Studies and the Department of Physical Education investigated the marketing practices of leisure facilities and public library services. They aimed to identify the marketing strategies of local authorities. A report of their findings covered the role of marketing, services and planning, the marketing mix and training.[8] Each topic was analysed and the survey concluded that few authorities included marketing in their strategic planning or employed marketing professionals, and that there was little evidence of marketing training for staff. The pressing need for a professional approach to marketing was emphasized in the report. In the few authorities where marketing professionals were employed, they were on a grade that did not enable them to influence policy.

Commercial sponsorship

A noticeable development in public library marketing became more apparent in the late 1990s and that was the increased use of large media advertising boards and bus shelter advertising in town and city centres. These examples of strategic marketing were enabled by much larger marketing budgets and of course marketing expertise. One such example was the Birmingham Library Campaign of 1997.[9]

Another innovative approach was the flagship scheme developed by the Boots Company of Nottingham who were instrumental in the promotion of books and reading aimed at parents of very young children.[10] In 1998 Boots began a three-year pilot project costing £150,000 in partnership with Nottingham City Council and Nottinghamshire County Council to promote the value of books for babies.

Each parent was given a bag of books and information about Nottinghamshire's Libraries. The libraries provided a key role in the provision of suitable meeting places and for families to have access to a wide range of books. Research during the project provided the evidence of the value of exposing children to books at a very young age. The project was so successful that the three partner organizations provided a further million pounds to allow the project to continue for a further five years. Many other library authorities started to develop similar schemes of their own to encourage and promote library use and the value of reading.

A revolutionary idea was used to market the value of all types of library in Sunderland. This came under the strap-line of 'Sunderland the Learning City' and in a truly cross-sectoral approach all the libraries in Sunderland opened their doors to people who lived, worked or studied in the city.[11] It presented them with the unique opportunity to study in any of the 29 libraries in the city, whether public or academic.

Academic libraries

To many librarians, marketing was an activity for public libraries, but by the mid-1990s academic libraries were being encouraged to market their services. In July 1996, Brewerton argued that academic librarians had a responsibility to market their services and facilities.[12] Academic librarians tended to think that any form of marketing would belittle their standing in academia. They held the belief that they had a captive market, and any form of promotion was therefore limited to user guides for freshers, publicity of opening hours and information sheets. It also has to be said that the majority of these were produced in an amateurish fashion. Brewerton urged them to become involved in National Libraries Week as this event was designed to raise public awareness of all types of library – marketing was not just the domain of public libraries. The Library Association's own planning for National Libraries Week made it clear that the encouragement of academic librarians to become involved in marketing activities was a key issue. Of course, it was at this time that new competition was emerging in the field of information provision: the development of the internet which was both an opportunity and a threat to libraries. This type of competition meant that it became even more important for academic librarians to market and promote their professional skills and library services.

Brewerton's article obviously had impact, because as part of National Libraries Week in 1997 twenty academic libraries across the United Kingdom opened their doors for 24-hour access for one night during the week.[13] (At that time 24-hour access was very unusual.) In addition to this, Bath University Library hosted an Internet Day and Staffordshire University held a Visual Resources Seminar to promote their special collections. Similar diverse events happened in all types of library across the United Kingdom. The National Libraries Week events were designed to appeal to all age groups and in the case of special libraries the appropriate occupations. There is clear evidence that the number of events taking place in all types of library had shown a significant increase since the previous National Libraries Week.

At this time, there were only a handful of people involved in marketing and publicity in academic libraries. Most of them had marketing and publicity written into their job descriptions but few, if any, were marketing professionals. Nottingham Trent University and Oxford Brookes University where amongst the few universities which had such posts and the post-holders were often asked to run practical courses to share their knowledge and experience with colleagues in other universities, colleges and to the public library sector.

Sponsorship

In 1999, another significant development in academic library marketing came on the scene. Youth Media Ltd., a Scottish company, began work with six Scottish universities. The idea was simple: the libraries were asked to display posters that carried approved commercial advertising in return for income from the sponsors. This became a successful venture with a great many higher education institutions participating. The portfolio of products soon extended to bookmarks that carried a library message on one side and a commercial message on the reverse. There was a tangible benefit to both the universities and the commercial sponsor. The commercial sponsor communicated its message to a captive audience and the university library was able to use high quality full colour printing to promote specific aspects of the service. Typically, libraries used this medium to promote opening hours, websites, new services, student behaviour policies, etc. In some cases, such as Times Newspapers, the bookmark was also a discount voucher, which was of course an extremely attractive proposition to students.

It is interesting to note that Youth Media Ltd. was developed by someone who was undertaking a Master's degree in entrepreneurship at the time. He noticed that posters communicating information relating to health and welfare, anti-binge drinking and graduate recruitment were being displayed in the Student Union. His immediate reaction was that this type of poster might have greater impact if displayed in university libraries.

At about the same time, another company, ScreenTime, was founded. This company aimed to provide a screen-saver communication system to universities. They began work with the University of East London and eventually expanded their portfolio of participating academic institutions. Again, there were mutual benefits for both the sponsor and the university. In contrast to Youth Media, the scope of their medium is limited to screen-savers but they do work with other organizations such as business, media agencies and sports organizations.

Health service libraries

Health service libraries were also forced to market their value extensively in the mid-1990s as management and financing of the health service became a major political issue.[14] Along with this came massive changes in professional health education and initiatives such as the Patient's Charter and the Health of the Nation which of course affected library provision. Health librarians realized that these changes and initiatives meant that they needed to raise their profile. Through lobbying and networking with National Health Service officials at a high level, they achieved the appointment of the first ever NHS library adviser in 1995. They also obtained a strong voice within the NHS, which helped to secure the survival of health libraries at a time of rapid change within the Health Service.

Awards

It is interesting to note that library suppliers were integral to the development of the promotion of libraries. The late Tom Farries, President of T. C. Farries & Co. Ltd. library suppliers, did a tremendous amount of work throughout his career to encourage librarians to promote their services. Although outside the time-frame of this publication, it is worth noting that this work began in the mid-1980s when he enabled the Library Association through sponsorship to embark on an annual Public Relations and Publicity Awards Programme. This programme also involved the Publicity and Public Relations Group (PPRG) of the Library Association. However, it was in the 1990s that these awards gained their credibility. In 1994 the tenth year of the Awards.[15] The PPRG became more involved in the planning, organization and judging of the awards and the chairperson of the PPRG became chairperson of the panel of judges. The venue for the Awards was indeed prestigious, the Churchill Room at the House of Commons; but this alone was not enough to make the Awards recognizable in their own right, they required their own quality marketing. The combined efforts of the Library Association, the PPRG and T. C. Farries & Co. Ltd. made it possible to design a brand for the Awards that was applied to promotional leaflets, bespoke stationery, entry forms, invitations and certificates, thus establishing a credible identity within the library and information profession.

Once more widely promoted bearing its own brand, the award programme attracted a greater number of entries from all sectors of the library and information profession. Prior to this, entries had been largely from the public library sector. There was also a substantial improvement in the standards of presentation of each entry, and this was another pointer that the Awards were gaining professional recognition.[16]

The organizers recognized that it was important that the awards programme reflected marketing and promotional activities within libraries. Consequently, the categories were revised. They now comprised:

- promotional campaign with a budget under £500
- promotional campaign with a budget over £500
- printed publicity material
- sponsorship and partnership projects
- audio-visual and multi-media
- the Tom Farries Award for Personal PR Achievement.

Entries submitted to the Awards programme were wide-ranging, representing every type of library activity: the promotion of new buildings, local studies projects, the benefits of buying into school library services, academic induction programmes, reading schemes and much more. The only category which despite promotion suffered from an extremely low number of entries was the Tom Farries Award for Personal PR Achievement. Those that were received, however, proved to be of a very high calibre. (Both the Library Association and the PPRG were of the opinion that this reflected the fact that on the whole, librarians are a self-effacing profession.) Many of the winning entries were documented in articles published in *Public eye*, the quarterly newsletter of the PPRG. The entries also demonstrated the commitment, hard work and professionalism of many dedicated library staff and their ability to engage the support of others. These attributes made a very powerful statement that there was across the United Kingdom the will to promote library services. Such determination and effort needed underpinning by the adequate provision of resources to facilitate planned and sustained promotional and marketing activity on a sound professional basis; libraries needed and deserved nothing less.

The Library Association and the PPRG always underlined the importance of using success in the Awards to further promote the library service. Success provides a wonderful opportunity to boost staff morale and develop press and media contacts. It also provides the opportunity for professional networking as other library authorities used winning initiatives to benchmark their own services. The organizers also encouraged those who did not win to use this as a tool to secure the necessary resources to bring projects to fruition.

The Awards reflect well the development of promotion in libraries. This period saw the execution of many excellent and innovative projects that involved partnerships between several library authorities or partnerships between libraries and commercial organizations. In the late 1990s, some of these projects commanded huge resources. It was interesting to note that this had a significant impact on the standards of PR and marketing. The fact that a large number of organizations was involved meant that there was access to greater resources, both financial and in terms of expertise which in turn meant a greater perception of the need for quality.

Another development originating from T. C. Farries & Co. Ltd. at this time was the Great Ideas Network.[17] The company recognized that across the United Kingdom librarians were actively engaged in a wide variety of stock promotion. Obviously, it would be to the benefit of everyone if staff undertaking this type of work could be brought together to share experience. T. C. Farries & Co. Ltd. facilitated this through a series of well-attended seminars. The participants were either staff who were new to this type of work or those who had greater experience that they could share with others. The programme covered planning a promotion (budget, publicity resources, ideas); a framework on which to develop a promotion; networking and useful contacts. From this emerged the Great Ideas Network, with the company acting as a clearing house for ideas, contacts and examples of good practice.

The early 1990s also saw a downturn in public library issues and libraries were forced to look at the ways that they could promote their stock in order to increase issues and secure their existence. Reader development initiatives that were in the first instance primarily led by library suppliers helped to address this problem. Books for Students was a pioneer in this field, encouraging librarians to look at the positive mass market value of paperbacks, which at this time were not considered as 'core' stock by many library authorities. Paperbacks have the appeal of attractive covers, portability, quick reads and the potential for eye-catching display. Display was considered paramount in this marketing initiative and eventually the paperback display bin became an accepted feature in public libraries. Stock promotion and marketing became an integral part of reader development and this activity was further helped by the partnership of Books for Students with Opening the Book. The promotional activity of this kind extended well beyond the best-seller lists to include books in translation and books for people who had basic reading skills.

National Year of Reading
1998 was designated the National Year of Reading and the Arts Council funded a great number of reading promotions in libraries during that year. As with the National Libraries Week promotions, guidance was also available from the Library Association. The National Year of Reading was another huge campaign to encourage reading for pleasure and the use of libraries. Examples of individual reader development projects, too numerous to mention, were featured in the entries for the Library Association & T. C. Farries' Public Relations and Publicity Awards and others were documented in the *Library Association record*. Undoubtedly, this type of retail style stock promotion was innovative for its time.

It is fair to say that the importance of marketing and promotion became more apparent during the 1990s as library and information services of all kinds realized that if they were to survive and develop they had to make their customers and stakeholders aware of their value, worth and potential to the public, education, business and commercial sectors. They began to work in partnership with other organizations and departments and in commercial partnerships with business. These are some of the chief factors that brought about huge steps forward in quality and innovation towards the close of the decade as the library partners and sponsors had a right to expect high standards of presentation for the projects in which they were involved.

Acknowledgements
This chapter has given a broad overview of the progress of publicity and marketing as practised in libraries in the United Kingdom. Much of the information is based on the first-hand experience of the author in her capacity as Chairperson of the Publicity & Public Relations Group and Chairperson of the panel of judges for the

Library Association & T. C. Farries Public Relations & Publicity Awards. She also acknowledges the help of her personal contacts engaged or formerly engaged in publicity and marketing activities in libraries, namely: Louisa Myatt (Marketing Manager, CILIP); William Jenkins (Youth Media Ltd.); Anthony Brewerton (Oxford Brookes University); Geoffrey Smith (former Deputy Chairman, T. C. Farries & Co Ltd.) and David Lindley (former Director of Books for Students).

Notes

1   Janet Christine Pots and Vincent de P. Roper, 'Sponsorship and fundraising in public libraries: American and British perceptions', *New library world* **96** (1118), 1995, 13–22.

2   'Shout now', *Public eye* Aug. 1991.

3   Judith Elkin and Tom Wilson (eds.), *The education of library and information professionals in the United Kingdom.* London: Mansell, 1999.

4   Virginia Smith, 'Getting to know you', *Public eye* Aug. 1990, 1–2.

5   'The new look', *Library Association record* **93** (1/2), 1991, 14.

6   Paul Black, *Manipulating the media: a handbook for librarians.* London: PPRG, 1997; Patrick Quinn, *Effective copywriting for librarians.* [London]: PPRG, 1992.

7   'Public libraries', *Which?* Feb. 1990, 108–10.

8   Margaret Kinnell and Jennifer McDougall, *Meeting the marketing challenge: strategies for public libraries and leisure services.* London: Taylor Graham, 1994.

9   Felicity Rock, 'To raise your profile, raise the roof', *Library Association record* **100** (4), 1998, 188–9.

10 Books for Babies: <www.nottinghamcity.gov.uk/arrow/arrow_books_for_babies_.htm> (accessed 11/01/06).

11 'Sunderland breaks barriers', *Library Association record* **99** (9), 1997, 459.

12 Anthony Brewerton, 'It's not just public (library) relations', *Library Association record* **98** (7), 340.

13 *Library Association record* **99** (11), 1997, 600.

14 Michael Carmel, 'Thriving amid chaos: healthcare and library services in the 1990s', *New library world* **96** (1120), 1995, 28–34.

15 A. White, 'Putting the name in the frame: ten years of the LA/T. C. Farries Public Relations and Publicity Awards', *Library Association record* **96** (5), 1994, 257–60.

16 Linda Ashcroft, 'Awards celebrate public relations excellence', *New library world* **98** (1137), 1997, 238–9.

17 Liz Wilson, 'Why borrow, why buy, why promote? and the Great Ideas network', *Public eye* spring 1994.

25

User education and user studies

Philippa Dolphin

USER EDUCATION

In his chapter on user education and user studies in the last *British librarianship and information work* Colin Harris reported that work on user education during the period 1986–1990 was thin, except perhaps in schools, but he made some fairly accurate forecasts for the future.[1] He noted that the government's intention to expand higher education would change its character, and that increased computer ownership and the growth of electronic information resources would have an impact on the value and use of information. These changes did have an enormous effect on education and on libraries, as did the growth of part-time education and lifelong learning, distance education, changes in nurse education, the emergence of evidence-based medicine, and the Follett report which was published in 1993.[2] All these initiatives brought fresh challenges for staff in library and information services who spent much of their time ensuring that users and potential users were able to gain maximum benefit from the increasing amount of information available: finding and using information effectively, evaluating their sources, and organizing and presenting information. The language these staff used to describe their work in this area began to change too. At the beginning of the decade the literature reported work on 'user education', but towards the end of the 1990s there was more emphasis on 'information literacy', 'information skills' and 'information handling skills'. There were numerous local studies published by librarians in individual educational establishments, but much of the work of surveying activity, identifying best practice and influencing policy, particularly in schools and further education, was funded by the British Library.

Although the great majority of reported work in this area is concerned with schools and further and higher education, there was also some interest in how the general public would learn to handle the increased amount of networked information which was becoming available. In 1997, Streatfield discussed the government's plans to get everyone on to the internet.[3] He argued that investment in technology, and emphasis on resource-based learning and evidence-based healthcare, had not been matched by the development of training to equip people to become effective information users. Information problem-solving skills must be better taught at primary, secondary and tertiary levels so that people were able to find, select and evaluate information. The following year, an interesting attempt to provide information skills in a public library context in Scotland was described by Newton, Sutton and McConnell.[4] The project was funded by the British Library Research and Innovation Centre to develop public library support for library users engaged in open or distance learning. A web-based directory of open learning materials was created, and the team collaborated with Robert Gordon University to develop information skills training to be run at the public library. The project was designed to respond to a variety of learners including business people, school, college and university students, people needing new skills for employment, retired people wishing to learn something new, and women wanting to update in order to return to work.

Schools

Harris observed that during the second half of the 1980s it was 'only in schools that user education has ceased to be regarded as something separate from the mainstream activity of the institution'.[5] This trend continued in schools with well resourced and properly staffed libraries. Rogers published a useful review of information skills teaching in schools and the further education sector in 1994, although 90% of the references are from the 1980s.[6] He covered the various definitions of information skills by previous researchers and practitioners, the progress made in the field and the impact of information technology. CD-ROMs became widely used in schools in the early 1990s and were popular with pupils. A number of authors highlighted the erosion of the traditional roles of pupils and teachers as a result of this increased use of technology. Butterworth looked at the requirement for more sophisticated information skills amongst pupils and staff as a result of the growth of relevant information sources, such as newspapers, on CD-ROM.[7] In the same year, Irving considered what information was needed for assignments set by schools, where students could find it, and what skills they required.[8]

The British Library sponsored useful research into the implications of curriculum and teaching changes. A major project on Information Skills in GCSE and the Role of the Librarian was undertaken 1989–1990, but reported in 1991.[9] The report suggested that GCSE called for students to have sophisticated information skills and access to a wide range of resources. Examples of good practice were found mainly in Local Education Authorities where there was a school library service and advisory service supporting teachers, librarians and schools in the implementation of information skills. In 1992 a further British Library sponsored project was set up to disseminate the findings of the Library Use, Information Skills and GCSE Project conducted between 1989 and 1991. The main conclusion of the project, reported by Phtiaka, was that school libraries were often organized by young, inexperienced and untrained staff.[10] Teachers should attend structured library courses, and there should be more training opportunities for library staff. The report also called for external validation of library services.

Several authors credit the new National Curriculum with having a major impact on the need for improved information skills in schools. Brown produced a useful review of the national situation in the early 1990s.[11] She claimed that the National Curriculum and the Technical and Vocational Education Initiative (TVEI) had resulted in recognition of the benefits of information skills and the importance of the role of the librarian. However, she quoted an unpublished survey for the National Council for Educational Technology which reported that 80% of the school librarians questioned ran inductions for students, but only 29% had put on sessions for teachers.[12] Relevant case studies by Gooderham, Small and Drury describe the implementation of information skills policies and programmes in individual schools, prompted by the demands of the National Curriculum.[13]

A great deal of research and original thinking in the area of information skills in schools was undertaken by Herring. In 1994, he explored the demands of information technology in schools, and emphasized the importance of the involvement of the librarian in both the planning and implementation of information skills teaching.[14] In his book on teaching information skills, published in 1996, he discussed the range of interrelated skills which comprise information skills and looked at examples of good practice around the UK.[15] There is also a chapter on whole school policies on information skills. Herring advocated the PLUS model. The initials stand for: purpose – identifying the purpose of an investigation or assignment; location – finding relevant information resources related to the purpose; use – selecting and rejecting information and ideas, reading for information, note taking and presentation; and self-evaluation – reflection on performance. In 1997, he argued that information skills are key learning skills which students should acquire in school but which they will use throughout their lives.[16]

Further education
It was encouraging to observe a growth in user education activity in colleges of further education. A very high percentage of the work reported from this sector during the 1990s was initiated by the British Library. The Information Skills in Further Education Project, funded by the British Library Research and Development Department and the National Foundation for Educational Research (NFER) was completed in December 1990. It resulted in a range of recommendations and strategy proposals for colleges which were published in the early 1990s. A report by Morrison, published in 1991, looked at information skills teaching in five colleges to discover where and by whom these skills were taught, and to make recommendations.[17] A fundamental factor was the way in which the library was perceived within the institution and the cultural climate in which collaboration between the library and academic work took place. Markless and Streatfield reported on case studies of information skills teaching in eleven colleges.[18] The factors which tended to support success were found to be: understanding the nature of information skills and the processes involved in developing them, resources to support student research and assignments, staff

development, a policy framework for the introduction of information skills, and embedding the skills in a particular initiative such as Open Learning or Technical and Vocational Education. Morrison and Markless presented a number of strategy proposals based on the outcomes of the same project.[19] These included: stressing information skills in the college development plan, performance indicators, course planning and staff development, and a shift in teaching towards a more student centred approach. The authors explored the implications of the project for librarians and their input and involvement in college development.

In 1993 Robertson and Williams surveyed business studies students in further education in Scotland, with particular reference to their ability to identify keywords to search for information for their project work.[20] Their poor information skills hindered their work on independent assessments. College teaching staff tended to ignore these issues because of time and financial constraints. Following the survey, a flexible computer assisted learning package was created to investigate the potential of hypertext in developing students' project thinking skills.[21]

A comprehensive survey of user education in further education was funded by the British Library in 1995.[22] A questionnaire was sent to all further education libraries in the UK, followed by visits to selected colleges. The report highlighted different approaches and common difficulties. The conclusions were that: (1) there was a high level of commitment to user education despite staffing levels; (2) there were big differences between different categories of user (for example, only 9% of part-time evening students got any user education); (3) there was little done beyond induction; (4) librarians were rarely involved in course planning or assessment; (5) little evaluation was undertaken; (6) developments in IT were identified as creating a greater need for user education.

Few local studies were reported, but two papers by Atkinson and Scott in 1995 reviewed the development of information skills teaching within an access programme at Hackney Community College in London.[23] The authors investigated problems with previous teaching in this area at the College, using experiential learning theory. Success factors included: close liaison with teaching staff, the use of a range of teaching strategies, the proper identification of information skills, and its inclusion in assessment. Basu and Duigan described further developments in the programme in 1997, including the integration of presentation skills.[24]

The Effective College Library research project ran from 1995 to 1999, funded jointly by the British Library Research and Development Department and the Further Education Development Agency. In 2000, Markless and Streatfield described a number of lessons which emerged from the project.[25] With regard to information skills initiatives, they found that those focused on a major assignment or on one course often tended to provide an important impetus for development. Concrete examples with before and after information were more powerful arguments than papers or discussions.

Higher education

The 1990s saw a big growth in student numbers. The Joint Funding Councils'

Libraries Review Group which was set up to recommend how libraries might cope with the resulting pressure on space, staff and resources, reported that 'Between 1988–89 and 1992–93 the number of full-time equivalent (FTE) Home and EC undergraduate students rose by 57 per cent from 517,000 to 811,000 (not counting 43,000 students in former DFE funded institutions). Although the extent of this growth has varied widely between institutions, all parts of the UK have experienced growth at a similar rate.'[26] Different kinds of student were now benefiting from higher education, including more overseas students. The sector turned to new teaching methods such as resource-based learning, e-learning, and distance learning. Face to face contact hours were reduced. The publication of the Follett report in 1993 resulted in the release of funding for the Electronic Libraries Programme and other initiatives, intended to help higher education libraries cope with these extra pressures. A high percentage of the writing on user education during the decade described possible solutions to educating a larger and more diverse student body. Project funding was frequently dependent upon staff working together with other institutions to find sector-wide, and usually electronic, solutions.

Prior to the impact of the Follett report there were many excellent local initiatives in response to rapid changes in higher education. The specific problems of providing user education for the increasing numbers of overseas students were highlighted in a 1992 article by Robertson, who surveyed 20 higher education libraries in Scotland.[27] Goodall looked at library support for students on higher education courses which were franchised to further education colleges in Lancashire and Cumbria, and commented on the difficulties of providing appropriate library resources and information skills teaching for higher education students in a further education context.[28] Projected increases in student numbers and the desire to maintain quality were the main drivers behind changes in information skills teaching at the University of Hertfordshire at the start of the 1992/93 academic year.[29] Nene College developed an interactive hypertext guide, described as a labour intensive solution.[30] Bailey and Jenkins described changes in approaches to information skills at Cheltenham and Gloucester College of Higher Education in response to college mergers, a doubling of student numbers between 1990 and 1994, the introduction of a modular structure, a compulsory workshop programme, and the College's commitment to the development of independent learning.[31] Martin described changes made at the University of Plymouth Institute of Health Studies library when the introduction of diploma level education for nurses resulted in a big demand for a wide range of information resources.[32]

The web began to be seen as a way in which institutions might share the burden of educating users. The Electronic Libraries Programme (eLib) projects included several on this theme which had a huge national impact.[33] The very large scale Netskills project,[34] established in 1995, produced an internet tutorial, TONIC, in addition to face to face workshops and seminars to library staff and the wider higher education community. NetLinkS, also funded via eLib from 1995 and based at the University of Sheffield, was designed to support, encourage and train librarians involved in providing reference help and user education for networked learners.[35] This new breed of network learner support (NLS) professionals is described by Levy, Fowell and Worsfold as providing user education and creating training tools for students using electronic libraries and, increasingly, on online and distance learner courses.[36] Finally, the EduLib project was designed to provide training and development for librarians involved in teaching students.[37]

Few university libraries were unaffected by the Follett report and subsequent developments. One example was the University of Aberdeen, which saw a 70% increase in student numbers during the first half of the decade. Spurred on by this change and by the Follett and Fielden reports[38] and the EduLib project, the library initiated a major research study to assess the quality of library and information skills teaching. Academic and library staff and students were surveyed about the current situation and possibilities for the future. Steele and Stewart described the range of far-reaching changes which was proposed.[39] A useful review was provided by Mendelsohn, who looked at the effectiveness of librarians in teaching, and reviewed the various initiatives designed to help, including EduLib, Netskills and NetLinkS.[40]

A number of other major national initiatives were established during the decade to encourage the use of electronic networks and collaboration between institutions. The Higher Education Funding Councils' Teaching and Learning Technology Programme funded a number of interesting projects. Glasgow University's Teaching with Independent Learning Technology (TILT)[41] project began in 1993, with the intention of demonstrating how information technology could be successfully incorporated into university teaching. Library staff were very involved with this campus-wide exercise to produce and evaluate various types of computer-assisted learning, and library guides were transformed to toolbooks and then made available online. Five hypertext packages were produced: how to choose books and journals, library search skills (general), library search skills (business), computer sources, and study skills. By 1996 these packages were being used in more than 130 institutions in the UK and overseas.

Project EDUCATE (End-user courses in information access through communication technology) was funded by the Commission of the European Communities between 1994 and 1997.[42] Six libraries were involved, including Imperial College and Plymouth University in the UK. Its initial target groups were students of science and engineering. Model self-paced user education courses with detailed information about the selection and use of information tools were developed and made available via a website.[43] By the end of the project nine subject modules had been produced. The courses were designed for use by both librarians and academics in their own education and training programmes. In 2000, Fjällbrant described the major outcome of EDUCATE as being the production of the INTO INFO programmes, which provided a means for learning about and accessing relevant information resources.[44] Programmes included sections on the evaluation of search results and constructing personal reference databases. The author argued that the project was designed to fit with the trend in education to facilitate learning rather than to teach a certain set of material. EDUCATE led on to a number of spin-off projects, including DEDICATE (Distance Education Information Courses Through Networks)[45] in 1998–99. Although DEDICATE was tested outside the UK it drew heavily on the experience gained through NetLinkS.

Wood and colleagues from the Department of Information Studies at the University of Sheffield studied students' use of networked resources which they felt could play a major role in student-centred learning.[46] They described this work at the first ELVIRA Conference, together with their plans to develop instruction packages to help students make more effective use of these resources. Further work on this project reported in 1997 indicated a significant correlation between undergraduates' cognitive and learning styles and their searching behaviour.[47]

The IMPEL (Impact on People of Electronic Libraries) project, based at the University of Northumbria and funded through eLib, looked at a range of social, organizational and cultural issues associated with working in an increasingly electronic library environment. IMPEL comprised five linked strands, one of which looked at the impact of resource-based learning on subject librarians.[48] Amongst the conclusions of the project was that 'the importance of user instruction for both academic staff and students will be increased with the implementation of resource based learning, with subject librarians using a variety of methods of instruction including presentations, seminars, workshops etc.' The need for 'training for subject librarians in teaching and learning methods and skills to improve user education' was stressed.

Towards the end of the 1990s SCONUL (the Standing Conference of National and University Libraries) became more active in the field of information skills. A task force was set up, and a briefing paper was distributed to SCONUL members which outlined seven stages (or 'pillars') of information literacy.[49] These progressed from the most basic (the ability to recognize a need for information) to the most sophisticated (the ability to synthesize and build on existing information, thus contributing to the creation of new knowledge). The earlier stages would be appropriate for undergraduates, and the later ones for postgraduates. This work helped SCONUL lobby the Quality Assurance Agency (QAA) over the skills required by students in different subject areas. The QAA produced 14 benchmarking statements, all of which made some reference to students needing to obtain information, to use it critically, and in some cases to synthesize from reading. An analysis by Peters concluded that many of this first batch of statements were very vague, and that there was very little indication of the need for students to identify and locate information for themselves.[50] She highlighted examples of good practice, for example that the QAA would expect history students to demonstrate that they have 'bibliographic skills; the ability to gather, sift, select, organize and synthesize large quantities of evidence; the ability to formulate appropriate questions and to provide answers to them using valid and relevant evidence and argument'.

Although coined in the early 1970s, the term 'information literacy' was increasingly used during the 1990s. Weber and Johnston defined the term in their paper written in 2000, and offered some alternative approaches.[51] They described the design and implementation of and students' response to an information literacy class at the University of Strathclyde and the University of Sheffield. Further work by Johnston looked at the thorny issue of assessment of information literacy, and considered a number of methods: transcripts of test results, portfolios of work, learning diaries, and expert, self and peer assessment.[52]

By the end of the decade the use of the web for teaching, including the teaching of information skills, was becoming mainstream. A questionnaire survey by Rhodes and Chelin investigated the extent to which the internet was employed for user education by 68 UK universities in 1998.[53] They found that the web was mainly used as a supplement to face to face teaching, in order to support independent student-centred learning and to reach part-time and distance learners. Although only 10% of user education was delivered solely via the web in 1998, responses to the questionnaire indicated that this percentage would increase in the future.

Finally, very few articles were concerned with the needs of academic staff and support staff. Price, at the Institute of Education in London, looked at these groups and how they could be encouraged to learn and share the skills of librarians.[54] She stressed that 'we should not be surprised that academics do not know the secrets of our profession'.

USER STUDIES

The user studies literature increased enormously over the decade. The types of user being studied varied, although certain groups such as nurses continued to feature strongly. Towards the end of the 1990s there was an increasing focus on public libraries, with particular emphasis on reading, lifelong learning and disadvantaged groups such as the disabled and refugees. Researchers were also very interested in how and why people used the internet, online catalogues and electronic journals.

Public libraries and the voluntary sector
In 1993, the CIPFA Public Library Statistics Working Party carried out a large scale pilot survey to test a possible standardized national questionnaire for public library users, which might be adopted as a measure of quality.[55] However, public libraries continued to use a variety of mechanisms for studying their communities.

In 1992 a project in Solihull looked at residents' attitudes to and awareness of local public library and information services, and the factors involved in non-use of libraries.[56] Two years later a much bigger study, which formed part of the public library review, was reported by Myers.[57] This involved in-depth interviews with 850 people in eight English boroughs, metropolitan districts and counties, to ascertain their views on the types of services which should be offered and whether charges should be levied. Interestingly, although professional librarians felt that the service had deteriorated over the past five years, those surveyed felt that it had improved. More than two fifths of the sample saw public libraries as an 'asset to the community'. Although interviewees gave high ratings to functions that public libraries have always performed, there was also a rising interest in innovative services. In the same year, a questionnaire survey commissioned by the Library Association and Dawson UK found generally positive attitudes to libraries, despite what was perceived as a generally narrow range of services.[58] The survey indicated that libraries were important to all age and social groups, with 49% of all respondents using libraries at least once a month. A survey of Hackney residents reported in 1996 indicated that they would prefer quality over quantity.[59] This led to an improvement plan to reduce the number of branch libraries. In the same year, Brent Libraries used focus groups to find out more about customer needs and to monitor the performance of contractors.[60]

Several studies investigated the value of public libraries to specific age groups. A survey conducted in 1992 looked at the use of public libraries by old people, and sought their opinions of the services they used.[61] In 1995 the Library Power Campaign was launched by the Library Association. The campaign was designed to advertise the opportunities open to young people in both public and school libraries in 100 UK locations. Part of this work involved surveys and library power ratings for libraries.[62] A pilot survey of children in 18 public library authorities was undertaken in 1996 to explore their use and non-use of libraries. A paper by Gordon and Griffiths described the development of the methodology for surveying children from 0 to 16.[63] A survey of the use of the internet by old people reported in 1998 looked at the types of information needed and the contribution which the internet can make to people's lives.[64] It concluded that old people would benefit from greater provision of computers for internet use in the public library. Concern that the internet was too male-dominated led to a survey by Williams, Huntington and Nicholas in 2000 into the reasons why women are discouraged from using it.[65] They explored the gender differences between the way information technology and the internet are employed.

There was some interest in looking at the use made of libraries and information services provided by the voluntary sector. An extensive survey funded by the British Library was undertaken into enquiries dealt with by UK national voluntary organizations working in the environmental sector.[66] The results showed that general enquiry services in 111 such organizations were responsible for answering 590,000 queries during 1994. Such services were seen as an aspect of marketing the organization, but coordination could prove profitable. In 1996, Nicholas and Colgrave reported on a study into how local government councillors kept up to date, and what information providers were available to them.[67] The role played by the Citizens Advice Bureau (CAB) in providing information to rural communities in the Shetlands was the subject of a study reported in 1998.[68] Interviews revealed that community leaders tended to be used for advice, rather than CAB staff whose training and access to resources made them better suited to this work. The report concluded that CAB services should be better publicized and more accessible. The information needs of rural communities were also covered by two reports for the British Library in 1993 and 1998.[69] There was increasing awareness of the needs of rural users, with great reliance being placed on the benefits of information technology.

A continuous survey ran between 1989 and 1996, examining the book-buying habits and library use patterns of British adults. A final report and extension to the survey was published in 1997.[70] Funded by the British Library, the survey focused on: levels of use of public and specialist libraries; use of specific services within libraries; and reasons for non-use. The British Library also funded a questionnaire survey from Book Marketing Ltd in 1998 which looked into household use of and attitudes to public libraries, with the aim of helping public libraries understand their users and plan their services.[71]

The Centre for Research in Library and Information Management (CERLIM) at Manchester Metropolitan University was granted funding by Resource (the Council for Museums, Archives and Libraries) to look at the value and impact IT access in public libraries (the VITAL Project). They undertook a questionnaire survey of users of services in Birmingham, Cheshire and Cumbria to determine whether these facilities were considered as vital, useful add-ons or not necessary in these regions.[72]

The National Year of Reading (September 1998 to August 1999) was the focus for much activity in libraries. An evaluation of the use of UK public libraries for reading was funded by the Library and Information Commission and the National Literacy Trust.[73] Amongst the many objectives of the evaluation was the need to assess the impact of the Year on children, adults and those who were not in formal education. Yu and O'Brien developed a typology of adult fiction readers, following a survey they reported in 1999.[74] They looked at adult fiction borrowers in two medium sized public libraries, and mapped their reading habits.

Two of the more important documents to emerge during this time period were collections of published and unpublished research undertaken between 1990 and 1998 entitled *Perspectives of public library use.*[75] Information was gathered from government reports, public library authorities, academic departments, and student dissertations. They contain a vast amount of information about public libraries and their use, including information about users: demographic information, book borrowing and reading habits, the use they made of non-public libraries and non-book borrowing facilities. The earlier report, published in 1995, noted the big increase in students using public libraries following the expansion of universities in the early 1990s. Amongst the survey topics covered in the second report, published in 1999, were:

- methods of user consultation used by all UK public libraries
- user satisfaction surveys by 125 authorities
- information about users of Birmingham Central Library, including age, sex, occupation, ethnic origin and other aspects in 1995
- the extent of library use amongst children aged 5–11 in Birmingham and their opinions of the services
- non-use by lapsed borrowers from Sandwell Community Libraries

- use and non-use by Asians in Hounslow
- the social and economic impact of public library activities in Newcastle upon Tyne and Somerset
- the impact of temporary library closure, as a result of a strike in Sheffield, on user behaviour and attitudes
- significant census data elements which are predictors of UK public lending branch usage
- user preferences for a range of proposed new, particularly IT based, services in Bromley
- the frequency of borrowing by members in Westminster's public libraries
- the provision and use of periodicals in central libraries in Leicester, Nottingham and Coventry
- the nature and extent of need for citizenship information by the general public.

Increased numbers of refugees during the 1990s had an impact on public services, and public librarians in the large urban centres attempted to reach out to these groups. The main countries of origin were Nigeria, Somalia, India, Pakistan, Turkey, and Sri Lanka. Raddon and Smith attempted to identify and assess the information needs of refugee groups in the UK and to develop strategies to meet these needs.[76] They found little coherence in the collection, publication and dissemination of relevant information, and a need for greater coordination between voluntary and statutory bodies. Olden looked at the experiences of Somalis in London.[77] Since they came from a largely urban culture, Somalis tended to get information via word of mouth, often via the mobile telephone and satellite TV. Professionals tended to use the internet extensively, and there were few Somali language publications.

British Library
The new British Library building at St Pancras was formally opened in 1998, and a number of surveys were undertaken during the planning stages. Cranfield and Hellowell reported in 1992 on a questionnaire survey of readers.[78] This looked at usage of the library by different groups and nationalities. 65% of users were students and academic staff, and 35% of readers lived outside the UK. Surveys of usage of the Science Reference and Information Service reported by Reid and Leigh in 1995 were used in planning admissions procedures, stock arrangements and the deployment of staff for when the service moved into the new British Library building.[79]

Education
The expansion of student numbers, increased diversity, different modes of study, the development of new electronic services, the rise of quality audit, and the availability of sophisticated survey software were all factors behind the many user studies undertaken in the higher education sector. The mid-1990s, for example,

saw increased use of software such as Priority Search to manage library satisfaction surveys in larger academic libraries.[80] Wu and others described user reaction to the ELINOR (Electronic Library and Information Electronic Retrieval) pilot project at De Montfort University, based on a study undertaken in 1993.[81] In 1995 a further study looked at users and non-users throughout all departments at the Milton Keynes campus.[82] As a result of the survey a number of improvements were made to the system, including increased end-user support and improved liaison with academic staff via focus group meetings. Two surveys undertaken at Aston University in 1996 looked at attitudes to and use of current awareness services and individual article supply (CASIAS) by academics.[83] Some useful research at the University of Sussex described by Jacobs investigated the background behind often puzzling responses to book availability surveys.[84] Semi-structured interviews revealed the background and user attitudes behind responses. Focus groups and a questionnaire survey at Glasgow Caledonian University demonstrated the difficulty of providing services to many different types of user, particularly part-timers, who tended to be less satisfied than other user groups.[85]

Librarians in academic libraries were particularly concerned about usage of electronic journals and datasets which were taking up an increasing percentage of their budgets. One of the most important datasets in use in university libraries in the 1990s was BIDS ISI. Pinfold reported the results of an analysis of usage by staff and students at the University of Birmingham between 1991 and 1997.[86] The trend was for a steady increase in usage during this period, with heaviest use by staff and postgraduates in the sciences. Tomney and Burton looked at the perceived advantages and disadvantages of electronic journals amongst users and non-users at the University of Strathclyde.[87] Again, usage was much higher in science and engineering. The majority of academics were interested in using electronic journals but often just needed the time to locate and learn how to use them. Arts and humanities academics appeared to be the slowest to adjust, but the acceptance of electronic journals as part of the Electronic Libraries Programme and their inclusion in the Research Assessment Exercise were welcomed as important steps in helping to change attitudes. McKnight and others investigated usage of electronic journals amongst academics, researchers and masters students in six different disciplines at Loughborough University.[88] The Follett-funded SuperJournal Project enabled detailed research into usage of and satisfaction with a number of experimental electronic journals, giving academics, librarians and publishers useful experience of sophisticated new resources. In 1999, Eason, Ku and Harker reported on the use and usefulness of the core and peripheral functions of the journals included in the project.[89]

The Centre for Research into Quality at the University of Central England undertook a very extensive annual student satisfaction survey.[90] About 30% of all UCE students were surveyed in 1994–95. It focused on the total learning experience of students, covering all aspects of the institution, including the library. Regular student satisfaction surveys were conducted at Nene College in

Northampton during the 1990s. Johnson reported on the development of the methodology and the results obtained over a five-year period.[91]

Universities and colleges began to experiment with different means of library and information support for the increased numbers of distance learners, and to ask these students what they wanted. Unwin, Stephens and Bolton produced a useful British Library funded report, containing the results of a series of questionnaire surveys undertaken between 1994 and 1996.[92] These covered the experiences of postgraduate distance learning students, arrangements made for library use by the various course providers, and support given by university and public libraries. Open University (OU) students are mainly taught via distance learning, and a survey reported by Bremner in 2000 looked at how these students used OU, public and other academic library services.[93] The author concluded that there should be wider promotion of the OU library services available to its students.

There was an increasing emphasis during the decade on the importance of lifelong learners and their needs, together with concern about social exclusion. Research into the role of libraries in provision for lifelong learners was funded by the Library and Information Commission in answer to their call on the 'The Value and Impact of Library and Information Services'.[94] Gender, social class, ethnic origin, previous experience of library use and access to a PC were all found to influence attitudes to and use of libraries. Some of the more significant findings were that females reported greater barriers in accessing information than males, those from blue collar backgrounds relied more heavily on institutional learning resources, and those under 21 demanded greater electronic access than did older students.

Healthcare professionals
Changes in nursing education over the decade prompted a number of major local and national studies. A questionnaire survey of nursing libraries in the Northern Region published in 1994, indicated low standards in nursing libraries, with the majority failing to meet CoFHE (Colleges of Further and Higher Education Group) standards.[95] Crane and Urquhart surveyed trained nursing staff in Plymouth in 1992–93 to discover their preferences with regard to professional development, with particular reference to their choice of journals.[96] Funding became a more than usually contentious issue as higher education took on the education of increasing numbers of nurses, often sharing libraries with doctors and other health professionals. Gove and others investigated the activity of users of a multi-disciplinary library at St George's Hospital, in order to help establish a formula for funding.[97] Nurses, midwives and health visitors on pre-registration courses at Kingston University were surveyed to discover which libraries they used and how much assistance they required; the implications for library services and collection development at St George's Hospital where these students were registered were assessed in an article by Yeoh and Morrissey.[98] Wakeham found that nursing researchers generally had a positive attitude towards nursing libraries and that

library staff were felt to be more approachable and helpful than the staff of medical and hospital libraries.[99]

In 1995, a British Library funded study of nursing researchers throughout the UK indicated that the library was the primary source of research information, and although CD-ROM databases were popular, little use was being made of networked and online information.[100] The researchers also highlighted important issues connected with access to libraries and information for qualified nurses, and the inclusion of information costs in research proposals. Further research into the information needs of and possible service developments for nurses was undertaken as part of the UNNDERPIN project (University of Northumbria at Newcastle Development of and Research into the Provision of Information to Nurses and nurse educators).[101] The EVINCE (Establishing the Value of Information to Nursing Continuing Education) project looked at the use of information from National Health Service (NHS) and higher education libraries by nurses, midwives and health visitors in 1995/96.[102]

Midwives were particularly information-conscious, needing a wide variety of general and specialized information resources, according to research by Bawden and Robinson reported in 1997.[103] Semi-structured interviews with midwives and psychiatric nurses and their information providers revealed psychiatric nurses to be less well served and less demanding of library services. Hughes looked at ward managers' perceptions of their clinical and resource management information needs and found that research literature and information technology were not regarded as valuable sources.[104] The ward managers interviewed were more likely to use informal methods to obtain information. By the end of the decade healthcare professionals were becoming skilled and discerning internet users. Nurses, midwives and health visitors were surveyed by Ward in 2000 to discover what they might want from an information service delivered over the internet. Speciality information, peer reviewed articles, and bibliographic databases were considered the most important areas.[105]

Changes in the NHS and the increasing emphasis on evidence-based medicine were two of the factors which prompted studies of GPs' information-related behaviour in the Trent Region and the Anglia and Oxford Region. As a result of the studies described by Wood and others in 1995, best information practice guidelines and recommendations for library and information services were drawn up.[106] In the same year, the Value project, funded by the British Library Research and Development Department, examined the effectiveness of NHS libraries.[107] As a result of the project, a quality assurance kit was produced to help improve information provision and delivery to clinicians.

Scientists
The enormous costs of information provision for academic and industrial scientists prompted a number of studies. Williams looked at the information needs of chemical researchers in UK academic institutions, in the light of increased journal costs, the existence of increasingly sophisticated document delivery systems, and

pressure on library budgets.[108] Philip reported the results of a British Library funded research project in 1996 into 26 universities which showed that academic chemists in departments with high research ratings were more likely to use leading edge or advanced structure based information systems.[109] Also, interestingly, organic and inorganic chemists were more likely to use these systems than physical chemists.

A large-scale study of biologists published by Rolinson and others in 1995 looked at the use of information sources by biologists in different types of institution, and compared them with scientists as a whole.[110] Biologists had a very wide range of information needs compared with scientists as a whole, and changes in information handling were occurring, but at different paces according to the location and specialism of the biologist.

Librarians

A number of studies looked at users' perceptions of library and information professionals. Fleck and Bawden used questionnaires, interviews and case studies to establish how library service users in a law firm and a medical school viewed the library staff compared with law and medical professionals.[111] Although library and information staff were generally highly regarded they were seen as having a service and reactive function rather than being dynamic and proactive.

The information-gathering behaviour of librarians came under scrutiny as part of the Electronic Libraries Programme-funded Newsagent project. Secker, Stoker and Tedd undertook a user needs assessment during 1996.[112] They sent out email questionnaires and held focus groups to assist in the design of an electronic current awareness service for information professionals. Lack of time, information overload, irrelevant or inappropriate information, not knowing what is available, and lack of resources were some of the issues facing library and information staff.

Business and management

There was surprisingly little interest in this sector. A study of the information needs of management researchers published in 1995 resulted in a profile of the UK management researcher: relying heavily on periodicals, tending to read little non-English language material and placing little significance on continental literature.[113] A survey by Hall, Oppenheim and Sheen looked at the use of and attitudes to patent information in small and medium sized enterprises (SMEs) in the UK.[114] The initial questionnaire survey suggested that there is no correlation between educational level or the nature of the business, and use of patent information. The use of patent agents as intermediaries was found to be problematic. In-depth interviews explored issues such as the level of research and development, the way the patent information is obtained and used, and the impact of the internet.

Law

The heavy use of expensive printed and online information by lawyers was the subject of several studies. Willis reported on a survey of nearly 1,000 solicitors and their use of the Law Society's library in London, and alternative sources of information.[115] Eisenschitz and others surveyed law firms in England and Scotland in order to examine their take up of Lexis, the online legal database, and factors which inhibited its use.[116] Other surveys of the use of electronic legal databases were reported by Pedley and by Wall and Johnstone, both in 1997.[117]

The media

Oppenheim and Walker evaluated library services at BBC Scotland in 1996, raising awareness and providing useful guidelines for development.[118] Surprisingly, the internet was still not a major source of information for traditional journalists at the end of the decade. A survey of over 300 journalists by Nicholas and others reported that poor access to the internet and good access to other information resources were the main reasons for this.[119] The older, more senior and the new media journalists were found to be the main users.

Use of catalogues and electronic libraries

Numerous surveys of the use of online catalogue and information retrieval systems were undertaken, in order to improve design and plan future development and help for users. A few examples are included here. Balaam reported on an investigation into use of catalogues at Liverpool Public Libraries and Liverpool John Moores University, and found enthusiasm for the online catalogue.[120] Bryant looked at use of the various catalogues in Cambridge University Library in order to discover whether the age of the item sought had any marked influence on the level of detail required by users.[121] The use of a touch-screen public health information system was investigated by Jones and others, in order to assess the demand for easily accessible medical information in Scotland.[122] Users of the Micro Gallery of Western European Paintings at the National Gallery were surveyed before and after they used the system to assess ease of use and approaches to searching.[123]

Notes

1   Colin Harris, 'User education and user studies' in *British librarianship and information work 1986–1990*, ed. David M. Bromley and Angela M. Allott. London: Library Association, 1993, v. 2, pp. 170–91.

2   Joint Funding Councils' Libraries Review Group, *Report*. Bristol: Higher Education Funding Council for England, 1993. Chairman: Sir Brian Follett.

3   David Streatfield, 'Towards information empowerment?', *Assignation* **14** (2), 1997, 1–5.

4   Robert Newton, Audrey Sutton and Mike McConnell, 'Information skills for open learning', *Library review* **47** (1–2), 1998, 125–34.

5   Harris, 'User education', p. 170.

6   Rick Rogers, *Teaching information skills: a review of the research and its impact on education*. London: Bowker-Saur, 1994 (British Library research series).

7   Margaret Butterworth, 'Online searching and CD-ROM in British schools', *Education for information* **10** (1), 1992, 35–48.

8   Ann Irving, 'Information skills across the school curriculum', *Inspel* **26** (3), 1992, 224–33.

9   Julie Howard, *Information skills and the secondary curriculum: some practical approaches*. London: British Library, 1991 (Library and information research report; 84).

10   Helen Phtiaka, *Library use, information skills and GCSE development project*. London: British Library, 1992 (Research and development report; 6082).

11   Jenny Brown, 'Developing information skills' in *Managing library resources in schools*, ed. Margaret Kinnell. London: Library Association, 1994, pp. 189–203.

12   National Council for Educational Technology, *Survey of school libraries*. NCET, 1992 (unpublished).

13   Jo Gooderham, 'Information skills across the curriculum: a chronology' in *School libraries in action*, ed. Margaret Kinnell. London: British Library, 1994 (Research and development report; 6130); Graham Small, 'Integrating information skills into the mainstream curriculum: the evolution of a model', *School librarian* **41** (4), 1993, 142–4; Claire Drury, 'Keeping the customer satisfied: customer relations in a learning resource centre', *School librarian* **44** (2), 1996, 48–9.

14   James E. Herring, 'Information technology developments in secondary schools: implications for school librarians', *International review of children's literature and librarianship* **9** (1), 1994, 24.

15   James E. Herring, *Teaching information skills in schools*. London: Library Association, 1996.

16   James Herring, 'Enabling students to search and find', *Library Association record* **99** (5), 1997, 258–9.

17   Marlene Morrison, *Information skills in further education: the development report*. London: British Library, 1991 (Research and development report; 6058).

18   Sharon Markless and David Streatfield, *Cultivating information skills in further education: eleven case studies*. London: British Library, 1992 (Library and information research report; 86).

19   Marlene Morrison and Sharon Markless, *Enhancing information skills in further education: some strategies for senior managers, lecturers and librarians*. London: British Library, 1992 (Research paper; 99).

20   Joan E. Robertson and Dorothy A. Williams, 'Information skills in further education: a business studies perspective', *Education for information*, **11** (4), 1993, 289–96.

21   Joan E. Robertson and Dorothy A. Williams, 'Information skills development in further education: the impact of a students-centred computer-aided learning approach in business studies', *International forum on information and documentation* **18** (3–4), 1993, 48–55.

22   Margaret Chapman, *User education in further education college libraries*. London: British Library, 1996 (Research and innovation report; 5).

23   Judy Atkinson and Nicola Scott, 'Rethinking information skills teaching', *Learning resources journal* **11** (2), 1995, 45; Judy Atkinson and Nicola Scott, 'Rethinking information skills teaching: conclusion', *Learning resources journal* **11** (3), 1995, 52.

24   Ann Basu and Michael Duigan, 'From concept to practice: collaborative work in information/presentation skills', *Learning resources journal* **13** (3), 1997, 9–14.

25   Sharon Markless and David Streatfield, 'Becoming more effective: some choices', *Education libraries journal* **43** (3), 2000, 5–18.

26   Joint Funding Councils' Libraries Review Group, *Report*.

27   Joan E. Robertson, 'User education for overseas students in higher education in Scotland', *Journal of librarianship and information science* **24** (1), 1992, 31–50.

28   Deborah Goodall, 'Franchised courses in higher education: implications for the library manager', *Library management* **15** (2), 1994, 27–33.

29   Di Martin, 'Towards Kaizen: the quest for quality improvement', *Library management* **14** (4), 1993, 4–12.

30   Michael Aynsworth, Brelda Baum and Andrew Martin, 'Establishing hypertext for user education: one library's experience', *Vine* 91, 1993, 16–18.

31   Lynette Bailey and Martin Jenkins, 'Evolution of a workbook as part of an information skills programme', *Library review* **44** (4), 1995, 13–20.

32   Susan Martin, 'Reflections on a user education session with nursing students', *Health libraries review* 15 (2), 1998, 111–16.

33   Electronic Libraries Programme (eLib), *The projects*, 2001, available from <http://www.ukoln.ac.uk/services/elib/projects/> (accessed 29/12/05).

34   *Netskills: quality internet training*. University of Newcastle, 2005 <http://www.netskills.ac.uk/> (accessed 29/12/05).

35   'NetLinkS: collaborative professional development for networked learner support' (eLib: the projects, 1997) <http://www.ukoln.ac.uk/services/elib/projects/netlinks/> (accessed 29/12/05).

36   Philippa Levy, S. Fowell and Emma Worsfold, 'Electronic Libraries Programme: networked learner support', *Library Association record* **98** (1), 1996, 34–5.

37   'EduLib: educational development for higher education library staff' (eLib: the projects, 1998) <http://www.ukoln.ac.uk/services/elib/projects/edulib/> (accessed 29/12/05).

38   John Fielden Consultancy, *Supporting expansion: a study of human resource management in academic libraries.* (Report for the Management Sub-group of the Library Review). Bristol: HEFCE, 1994. (The 'Fielden report').

39   Michael Steele and Allan Stewart, 'Enabling access: implementing library and information skills (LIS) at the University of Aberdeen', *Education libraries journal* **41** (2), 1998, 5–12.

40   Susan Mendelsohn, 'Keeping up with expectations', *Library manager* **18**, 1996, 19–21.

41   Linda Creanor, Helen Durndell and Carol Primrose, 'Library and study skills using hypertext: the TILT experience', *New review of hypermedia and multimedia* **2**, 1996, 121–47.

42   Nancy Fjallbrant, 'EDUCATE: a networked user education project in Europe', *IFLA journal* **22** (1), 1996, 31–4.

43   *Into info*. Educate Consortium, 2001 <http://educate.lib.chalmers.se/> (accessed 29/12/05).

44   Nancy Fjallbrant, 'Information literacy for scientists and engineers: experiences of EDUCATE and DEDICATE', *Program* **34** (3), 2000, 257–68.

45   Nancy Fjallbrant, 'Networked information literacy – the European EDUCATE and DEDICATE projects', *New review of information networking* **6**, 2000, 53–60.

46   Frances Wood *et al.*, 'Information skills for student centred learning' in *Electronic library and visual information research: proceedings of the first ELVIRA conference*, ed. Mel Collier and Kathryn Arnold. London: Aslib, 1995, pp. 134–48.

47   Frances Wood *et al.*, *Information skills for student centred learning: a computer-assisted learning approach*. London: British Library, 1997 (Research and innovation report; 37).

48   Sandra Parker and Maureen Jackson, 'The importance of the subject librarian in resource based learning: some findings of the IMPEL 2 project', *Education libraries journal* **41** (2), 1998, 21–6.

49   SCONUL Task Force on Information Skills, *Information skills in higher education*. London: SCONUL, 1999 (Briefing paper).

50   Janet Peters, 'Information skills and the QAA benchmarking statements', *SCONUL newsletter* (21), 2000, 23–4.

51   Sheila Webber and Bill Johnston, 'Conceptions of information literacy: new perspectives and implications', *Journal of information science* **26** (6), 2000, 381–97.

52   Bill Johnston, 'How can you tell that you are information literate?' in *Online 2000*. Oxford: Learned Information Europe, 2000, pp. 45–53.

53   Helen Rhodes and Jacqueline Chelin, 'Web-based user education in UK university libraries: results of a survey', *Program* **34** (1), 2000, 59–73.

54   Gwyneth Price, 'User education in higher education: helping academics join the learning environment', *IATUL proceedings* new ser. **9**, 1999 <http://www.iatul.org/conference/proceedings/vol09/papers/abs/price.html> (accessed 18/10/05).

55   David Fuegi, 'Towards a national standard for a public library user survey', *Public library journal* **9** (2), 1994, 49–51.

56   Clare Nankivell, 'A mutually enriching partnership', *Library and information research news* **15** (54), 1992, 22–4.

57   John Myers, 'Stable, quiet retreats, or bustling with innovation?' *Library Association record* **96** (8), 1994, 426–7.

58   'Positive opinion poll', *Library Association record* **96** (1), 1994, 34–6; Guy Daines, 'Wide impact overall', *Library Association record* **96** (1), 1994, 37.

59   John Pateman, 'More or less in Hackney', *Library Association record* **98** (11), 1996, 582–3.

60   Karen Tyerman, 'Getting things in focus: the use of focus groups in Brent Libraries', *Library management* **17** (2), 1996, 36–9.

61   P. Lucas, 'Library use by elderly people', *Public library journal* **8** (3), 1993, 61–4.

62   David Streatfield and Rob Davies, *The Library Power survey report on libraries and young people*. London: British Library, 1995 (Research and development report; 6217).

63   Jonathan Gordon and Vivien Griffiths, 'A national poll for children', *Library Association record* **99** (7), 1997, 372–4.

64   Monica Blake, *The internet and older people*. London: British Library, 1998 (Research and innovation report; 97).

65   Peter Williams, Paul Huntington and Dave Nicholas, 'Women on the web: why the internet may still be male dominated', *Online and CD notes* **13** (9), 2000, 5–9.

66   Derek Stephens and Paul Eden, *General enquiry services in national voluntary environmental organizations*. London: British Library, 1995 (Research and development report; 6190).

67 David Nicholas and Kate Colgrave, 'Councillors and information: a study of information needs and information provision', *Aslib proceedings* **48** (2), 1996, 37–46.

68 Susan F. Beer, Rita Marcella and Graeme Baxter, 'Rural citizens' information needs: a survey undertaken on behalf of the Shetland Islands Citizens Advice Bureau', *Journal of librarianship and information science* **30** (4), 1998, 223–40.

69 David Barton, *Library and information provision in rural areas*. Stamford: Capital Planning Information, 1993; Penelope Yates-Mercer and Gillian Wotherspoon, *Information needs of rural users: an update*. London: British Library, 1998 (Research and innovation report; 116).

70 British Library Research and Innovation Centre, *Libraries and the consumer 1994–1996: a comprehensive guide to the library market*. Book Marketing, 1997 (Research and innovation report; 66).

71 British Library Research and Innovation Centre, *Household library use survey 1998*. London: British Library, 1998 (Research and innovation report; 144).

72 Juliet Eve, 'Vital measurements', *Library technology* **5** (4), 2000, 49, 51.

73 David Streatfield *et al.*, *Rediscovering reading: public libraries and the National Year of Reading*. London: British Library, 2000 (Library and Information Commission research report; 30).

74 Liangzhi Yu and Ann O'Brien, 'A practical typology of adult fiction borrowers based on their reading habits', *Journal of information science* **25** (1), 1999, 35–49.

75 Len England and John Sumsion, *Perspectives of public library use: a compendium of survey information*. Loughborough: Library and Information Statistics Unit and Book Marketing, 1995; Steve Bohme and David Spiller, *Perspectives of public library use 2: a compendium of survey information*. London: British Library for LISU and Book Marketing, 1999 (Research and innovation report; 166).

76 Rosemary Raddon and Christine Smith, *Information needs of refugee groups*. London: British Library, 1998 (Research and innovation report; 71).

77 Anthony Olden, 'Somali refugees in London: oral culture in a Western information environment', *Libri* **49** (4), 1999, 212–24.

78 G. Cranfield and J. Hellowell, 'Use of a national library: a survey of readers in the Humanities and Social Sciences Reading Rooms of the British Library', *Alexandria* **4** (3), 1992, 197–211.

79 A. Reid and B. Leigh, 'The science reading rooms of the British Library: the user community and patterns of use', *Alexandria* **7** (1), 1995, 61–70.

80 Anne Bell, 'User satisfaction surveys: experience at Leicester', *New review of academic librarianship* **1**, 1995, 175–8; Emma Robinson, 'Studying user satisfaction: why do it? how to do it? where next? One library's experience', *New review of academic librarianship* **1**, 1995, 179–85; Angela Horrocks, 'What do users want? Using Priority Search surveys to determine user satisfaction with library services', *SCONUL newsletter* (15), 1998, 21–4.

81 Ziman Wu, Anne Ramsden and Dianguo Zhao, 'The user perspective of the Elinor electronic library' in *ELVIRA 1: proceedings of the first ELVIRA conference*, ed. Mel Collier and Kathryn Arnold. Milton Keynes: De Montfort University, 1994.

82 Clare Davies, 'User issues' in *ELINOR: Electronic Library Project*. London: Bowker Saur, 1998 (Research and Innovation Centre report; 22).

83 Kate Brunskill, *CASIAS services: a critical evaluation of the functionality, costs, impact and value*. London: British Library, 1996 (Research and innovation report; 4).

84　N. A. Jacobs, 'Students' perceptions of the library service at the University of Sussex: practical quantitative and qualitative research in an academic library', *Journal of documentation* **52** (2), 1996, 139–62.

85　John C. Crawford, 'Report on the general satisfaction survey conducted at Glasgow Caledonian University Library, February/March 1997 and a linked focus group investigation', *SCONUL newsletter* **11**, 1997, 11–16.

86　Stephen Pinfold, 'The use of BIDS ISI in a research university: a case study of the University of Birmingham', *Program* **32** (3), 1998, 225–40.

87　Hilary Tomney and Paul F. Burton, 'Electronic journals: a case study of usage and attitudes among academics', *Journal of information science* **24** (6), 1998, 419–29.

88　Cliff McKnight *et al.*, 'User studies of commercial and free electronic journals', in *Electronic publishing '97: new models and opportunities: proceedings of an ICC/IFIP conference held at the University of Kent at Canterbury, 14–16 April 1997*, ed. Fytton Rowland and Jack Meadows. Washington, D.C.: ICC Press, 1997.

89　Ken Eason, Liangzhi Yu and Susan Harker, 'The use and usefulness of functions in electronic journals: the experience of the SuperJournal Project', *Program* **34** (1), 2000, 1–28.

90　Lee Harvey, 'Student satisfaction', *New review of academic librarianship* **1**, 1995, 161–73.

91　Hilary Johnson, 'User satisfaction surveys over 5 years: a college of higher education experience' in *Academic library surveys and statistics in practice*. London: British Library, 1998 (Research and innovation report; 92).

92　Lorna Unwin, Kate Stephens and Neil Bolton, *The role of the library in distance learning*. London: Bowker-Saur, 1998. (Research and innovation report; 96).

93　Alison Bremner, 'Open University students and libraries project 1999', *Library and information research news* **24** (76), 2000, 26–38.

94　Barbara Hull, *Barriers to libraries as agents of life-long learning*. London: British Library, 2000 (Library and Information Commission research report; 31); Barbara Hull, 'Identifying the barriers to libraries as agents of lifelong learning', *Library and information research news* **24** (77), 2000, 16–22.

95　Susan M. Childs, 'A survey of nursing libraries in the northern region', *Health libraries review* **11** (1), 1994, 3–28.

96　Sophie Crane and Christine Urquhart, 'Preparing for PREP: the impact of changes in continuing education for nurses on library provision of journals and current awareness services; a case study', *Health libraries review* **11** (1), 1994, 29–38.

97　Susan Gove, Susan Gilbert and Jean Yeoh, 'Reader activity in a multidisciplinary health sciences library: a case study at St George's library', *Health libraries review* **10** (2), 1993, 75–84.

98　J. Yeoh and C. Morrissey, 'Selection of library services by post registration nursing, midwifery and health visiting students', *Health libraries review* **13** (2), 1996, 97–107.

99　Maurice Wakeham, 'What nursing researchers think about librarians', *Health libraries review* **13** (2), 1996, 109–12.

100　Elaine Blair and Maurice Wakeham, *The use of libraries by nursing researchers*. London: British Library, 1995 (Research and development report; 6207).

101　Linda Banwell *et al.*, 'Implications of the UNNDERPIN Study at St George's Hospital, Morpeth, Northumberland', *Health libraries review* **12** (4), 1995, 279–93.

102   Christine J. Urquhart and Rebecca Davies, 'EVINCE: the value of information in developing nursing knowledge and competence', *Health libraries review* **14** (2), 1997, 61–72.

103   David Bawden and Kay Robinson, 'Information behaviour in nursing specialities: a case study of midwifery', *Journal of information science* **23** (6), 1997, 407–21.

104   M. Hughes, 'Information in resource management: ward managers' perceptions', *Health informatics journal* **5** (1), 1999, 20–9.

105   R. Ward, 'Nurses' Net needs', *Health informatics journal* **6** (4), 2000, 196–203.

106   Frances Wood *et al.*, 'Information in primary health care', *Health libraries review* **12** (4), 1995, 295–308; Frances Wood *et al.*, *Information in general medical practice: a qualitative approach*. London: British Library, 1995 (Research and development report; 6191).

107   Christine J. Urquhart and John B. Hepworth, *The value to clinical decision making of information supplied by NHS library and information services*. London: British Library, 1995 (Research and development report; 6205).

108   Ivor Williams, 'How chemists use the literature', *Learned publishing* **6** (2), 1993, 7–14.

109   G. Philip, 'Use of "leading-edge" information systems by academic chemists in the UK. Part 1: The results of a preliminary investigation', *Journal of information science* **21** (3), 1995, 187–99; G. Philip and F. P. Cunningham, *Availability and use of automated chemical information systems by academic chemists in the United Kingdom*. London: British Library, 1995 (Research and development report; 6184); G. Philip, 'Use of "leading-edge" information systems by academic chemists in the UK. Part 2: Constraints and the need for usability engineering'. *Journal of information science* **22** (2), 1996, 93–106.

110   Janet Rolinson, A. J. Meadows and H. Smith, 'Use of information technology by biological researchers', *Journal of information science* **21** (2), 1995, 133–9; Janet Rolinson, H. Al-Shanbari and A. J. Meadows, 'Information usage by biological researchers', *Journal of information science* **22** (1), 1996, 47–53.

111   I. Fleck and D. Bawden, 'The information professional: attitudes and images: examples from information services in law and medicine', *Journal of librarianship and information science* **27** (4), 1995, 215–26.

112   Jane Secker, David Stoker and Lucy Tedd, 'Attitudes of library and information professionals to current awareness services: results from a user needs survey, using focus groups, for the Newsagent project' in *Proceedings of the Second British–Nordic Conference on Library and Information Studies, Edinburgh*, 1997. London: Taylor Graham, 1997, pp. 249–58.

113   John Symons, *Information needs of management researchers*. London: British Library, 1995. (Research and development report; 6213).

114   Matthew Hall, Charles Oppenheim and Margaret Sheen, 'Barriers to the use of patent information in UK small and medium-sized enterprises. Part 1: Questionnaire survey', *Journal of information science* **25** (5), 1999, 335–50; 'Part 2 (1): Results of in-depth interviews', *Journal of information science* **26** (2), 2000, 87–99.

115   Carole F. Willis, 'Solicitors' legal research and use of libraries', *Law librarian* **23** (4), 1992, 171–4.

116   Tamara Eisenschitz, 'Use and importance of Lexis in England and Scotland', *Law librarian* **25** (4), 1994, 219–26.

117 Paul Pedley, 'The use of online databases and CD-ROM in law libraries', *Business information review* **14** (1), 1997, 19–26; David S. Wall and Jennifer Johnstone, 'Lawyers, information technology and legal practice: the use of information technology by provincial lawyers', *International review of law, computers and technology* **11** (1), 1997, 117–27.

118 Charles Oppenheim and V. Walker, 'Evaluation of BBC Scotland library services', *Aslib proceedings* **48** (3), 1996, 60–6.

119 Dave Nicholas *et al.*, 'The impact of the internet on information seeking in the media', *Aslib proceedings* **52** (3), 2000, 98–114.

120 Amanda Balaam, 'Approaches to library catalogues', *Library management* **14** (5), 1993, 9–12.

121 Philip Bryant, *Use and understanding of the library catalogues in Cambridge University Library: a survey*. London: British Library, 1993 (Research and development report; 6124).

122 Ray Jones, L. M. Navin and K. J. Murray, 'Use of a community-based touch-screen public-access health information system', *Health bulletin* **51** (1), 1993, 34–42.

123 Micheline Beaulieu and Victoria Mellor, 'The Micro Gallery: an evaluation of the hypertext system in the National Gallery, London', *New review of hypermedia and multimedia* **1**, 1995, 233–60.

26

Reference and information services

Bob Duckett

In an issue of *Reference reviews* Stuart James wondered if 'Bob Duckett might not be the last UK reference librarian actually called that ...'.[1] That nomination was incorrect as Bob Duckett has retired and there are still a number of 'reference librarians' in post, but the designation has become pretty rare. The same goes for 'reference libraries'. In 1992, I wrote an article entitled 'Paradise lost? The retreat from reference', in which I waxed lyrical about the glorious tradition of the large reference libraries that grew up in our major, and not so major, cities, and mourned their loss.[2] The 1970s were very much a decade of experimentation in developing new services in response to, and using the increased resources of, the larger library authorities that were created in the 1974 local government (England and Wales) reorganization. Specialized information services replaced the earlier bookish environments. In the 1980s we moved into new areas of community information and responded to the newly identified needs of minority populations, ethnic and disadvantaged people, who were being excluded from our perceived elitist and outdated services. We were also experiencing 'Cuts and computers', to use the title of the penultimate chapter in Alistair Black's ground-breaking social history of the twentieth century public library.[3]

Financially, the eighties were hard years in libraries, and from this time we see many economies that had a disproportionate effect on traditional reference services. Expensive reference books and serials were cut, as well as staff, and even whole departments. It was not only the social environment that was changing fast: the computer had come, and reference/information professionals were busy being trained on how to access and use Dialog, BLAISE, IRS and other online services.

The 1990s, the decade which is the focus of this work, saw the rapid development of ICT (information and communication technology) which threatened to vanquish print-based information sources. We saw, too, greater involvement of government in providing the agenda for public libraries. The traditional reference library, and librarian, continued to be marginalized, to be replaced by new concepts of service such as the virtual reference desk and one-stop shops. 'Information' replaced 'reference', and only towards the end of the decade, with the development of 'knowledge management' and 'value-added' services, was a personal service element re-asserted. Stuart James continued: 'but whatever the post or title (or even without a specific post) the function of answering questions remains basic in every library, large or small, whether geared to a specific reference of information service or fielded by whoever happens to be on duty'.

Collections

The 1990s opened with much attention and angst focused on the bookstock, still the major resource for information and enquiry work. An early model for public libraries was that of the British Museum Library and other libraries of national renown such as the historic university libraries of the time. Broadly custodial policies were adopted whereby the 'best' literature was collected and preserved as a resource for research and study in 'reading' rooms. With the 'retreat from the book', hastened by the 'culture of the cost accountant' (to use the term from an editorial in the *Journal of librarianship and information science*), widescale stock disposal took place.[4] A spirited debate took place in the June–December 1990 letter columns of the *Library Association record* with headlines such as 'Where have all Brent's books gone?' and 'If in doubt, chuck it out'. One correspondent commented that 'books are a commodity like tins of beans'. Richard Hoggart, an eminent upholder of quality reading, attacked the popularization of the public library service and scorn was poured on libraries in the polemical book by W. J. West in *The strange rise of semi-literate England: the dissolution of the libraries*.[5] West identified 273 titles of worth which he had purchased cheaply from secondhand bookshops and which had been discarded by libraries. The libraries were identified. The debate was picked up in the national press: 'Should libraries sell their books? Many libraries have been quietly selling off their stock'[6]; 'Librarians who deny us our conversations with the past' about the disposal of books from the Royal Commonwealth Society library and 'the new Dark Age descending over the land'.[7] Reaction from librarians was to point out the realities of the cost of maintenance, the poor use made of such collections, and the need to develop other services more in tune with public need and demand.[8] But the public disquiet led the British National Bibliography Research Fund to commission Capital Planning Information 'to look at the problem of retention and disposal which might lead to the establishment of a national policy for the optimum use of printed materials being considered for disposal from libraries'. The report was published in July 1994.[9] Seminars were held at the British Library and at Stamford (the latter organized by CPI) the following year, but nothing tangible emerged; no one was prepared to take a lead. The British Library did not consider the problem to be within their remit. Indeed, the responsible disposal of library bookstock was made more difficult by the closure of the British Library's BookNet department (the earlier 'Gifts and Exchange Section') shortly afterwards. Through this agency, lists of unwanted books had been circulated to libraries, which could select any titles they wanted for just the cost of their postage.

However, the greater consciousness of the problems of collection management resulted in a number of stock policies, principally at an individual library level – to inform stock purchase and disposal. Academic libraries had been aware of the problem at least since the Atkinson report in 1976, and the British Library had set up its own internal review in 1989.[10] The wider picture was also attempted, notably in the Library and Information Plans (LIPs), but very few of these survived the incorporation of institutions of further and higher education, the lack of funds, and the diverse governance of potential partners. Information North; Co-Book, a Midlands libraries' reserve collections cooperative scheme; and the work of ARLIS (Art Libraries Society) were notable exceptions.[11] Against these shrinking or 'steady state' collections, there was now beginning a greater knowledge of other libraries' stocks through the inter-availability of library catalogues.

Collection policies became standard, and stock revision and disposal better planned. In 2000, IFLA's *Draft guidelines for public libraries* contained sections on Collection development, Reserve stocks and Standards for book and electronic information facilities.[12] Even so, it is a sobering exercise to compare the quality and level of non-fiction stocks of public libraries at the end of the nineteenth century with those at the end of the twentieth. As a look into the surviving stacks of the long-established municipal libraries will testify, valuable collections of quality were built up. The universities, colleges and special libraries were subject to the same pressures. That the book was taking an ever-decreasing share in public library activity is reflected in the Apt review of library and information cooperation in 1995, which 'takes the view that a public library system which remains predominantly based on printed text is likely to become more a museum of an obsolescent culture than the core of an information system which addresses the emerging needs of the general public'.[13]

There were also new ideas of how best to provide information to these new constituencies. 'Community information' became increasingly fashionable and operated on quite different lines: leaflets and pre-packaged 'info' rather than monographs and serials; community 'drop-in' centres rather than hushed and intimidating reading rooms; street-wise information advisers with CAB (Citizens Advice Bureau) training rather than the academically literate subject specialist. Indeed, the role of librarians as community advocates and activists was seriously debated. No longer did subject specialists with their roots in traditional academic disciplines seem appropriate to the modern-day community-orientated library service. Many reference libraries and reference sections disappeared, with reference and lending stock being integrated. Expenditure on bookstock and journals was reduced, reserve stocks were weeded and the space vacated used for new services. Attention was now paid to identifying collections on a regional level, and beyond, where knowledge of the location of material was more important than having the material itself. Up to a point this was a development of the union catalogue principle, but with the added bite of planned cooperation. But even so, access to expensive monographs and journal runs became ever more difficult, especially for people some distance from London and the copyright libraries. In some cases a protectionist culture developed. A 1990 *Which?* report gave a thumbs-down to the reference stock at local libraries: 'Only 40 per cent rated the reference collection as anything better than "fair" and 18 per cent considered the range and currency of the reference stock "very poor" or "poor".[14] In 1995, the Department for National Heritage estimated there were some 19 million reference books in UK public libraries.[15] This sounds a lot, but in a 1994 survey of twenty of the UK's larger municipal libraries, reference librarians and collection managers were worried about the future of these collections, built up over a century or more, and containing great bibliographic wealth.[16]

Books

Yet there was no let-up in the quantity and quality of information and reference books being published. Gavin Higgins' *Printed reference sources* of 1980 became *The reference sources handbook* in 1990 under the editorship of Peter Lea and Alan Day, with a fourth edition in 1996.[17] In these, specialists contributed chapters on the standard categories into which reference work is often divided. In the 1996 edition, the chapters were headed: bibliographies; dictionaries; encyclopedias; biographical sources; geographical sources; local history; community information; business and company information; news and current affairs; periodicals; government publications; official publications of international organizations; statistical sources; grey literature, standards and patents; audio-visual materials. Contributors included many of the acknowledged authorities such as Stephen Willis, A. J. Walford, Chris Makepeace, Allan Bunch, Christine Reid, Valerie Nurcombe, David Mort and Anthony Thompson. John Walford's name reminds us that volumes of his own long-running work, *Guide to reference material*, continued to be revised throughout the decade. *Refer*, the journal of the Information Services Group of the Library Association, continued to feature the wide-ranging and critical surveys of reference sources by the veteran Charles Toase, and under the energetic editorship of Stuart James *Reference reviews* went from four to eight issues a year, and went electronic as well. The Walford, McColvin and Besterman Awards (for, respectively, sustained and continual contribution to bibliography, a guide to the literature, and an outstanding reference work) continued to attract worthy candidates.

Traditional reference publishing continued unabated with revisions to a number of the multi-volume standards such as the *Oxford English dictionary*, *Cambridge bibliography of English literature*, and the *Grove dictionary of music and musicians*. New large-scale works such as the *Dictionary of art* (41,000 articles by 6,700 scholars in 34 volumes), and medium-range works such as *World encyclopedia of theatre* (6 volumes) and the *International dictionary of historic places* (5 volumes) made their appearance. There were, however, a number of new developments. The quality of reference book publishing improved with better colour and inventive layouts. There was a plethora of 'factbooks' and reference trivia published for the popular market – the term 'listomania' was coined. Bloomsbury and Fitzroy Dearborn were two of the welcome newcomers to reference publishing producing high quality work, while some of the established reference publishers received 'makeovers' or suffered amalgamations. One of these was Facts On File, which extended its activities, and another was HMSO, most of whose publications were re-branded as TSO publications. HMSO, once reliably drab and dowdy, now rivalled the popular market leaders in quality, attractiveness and appeal: the 50-plus titles in the *Aspects of Britain* series were particularly good. Another development that caused librarians problems was works published in multiple formats. Titles such as *Books in print* and *Ulrich's international periodicals directory* were available in print, CD-ROM, microfiche and online versions. In the case of *Ulrich's plus*, the CD-ROM was offered on both Windows and Macintosh versions, and Ulrich even had a magnetic tape version. Changing formats was another problem: the *Times* newspaper annoyingly switched from microfilm to microfiche in 1990, though microfiche had, thankfully, became the preferred microform, the singular *International genealogical index* having led the way.

These new formats also provided new challenges to the skills of selection and use, particularly as websites became a further option. The problems of pricing, licensing and archiving were further problems to be faced, not to mention fighting the sales hype. Many of the electronic products were not, in fact, as complete as their print versions – newspapers and some government material in particular – although they scored better on flexibility. Publisher pressure was, I suspect, fiercer than ever, with a variety of special offers, pre-publication discounts, limited offers, payments by instalment and standing order discounts being just a few that tested our administrative skills.[18]

In 1991 the Minister for the Arts asked the Registrar of the Public Lending Right Advisory Committee to look into the possibility of extending PLR to books held in local authority library reference collections. A discussion paper was issued in November 1991. The complexities and administrative burdens were outlined and little further was heard![19]

In 1998, the Library Association published a new edition of *Basic reference stock for the public library*.[20]

New formats

The importation of new media formats and the harnessing of new information and communication technologies in the 1990s, was plain for all to see.[21]

The decline in book purchase and journal subscriptions is, in part, related to the increase in the number of formats in which information and literature could be acquired or accessed. Microform resources continued to be purchased, particularly for newspapers and for preservation purposes, but the 1990s saw the introduction of CD-ROMs to add to databases which could be accessed electronically from distant suppliers. Computer technology was developing, though teletext and the old Prestel system featured prominently at the start of the decade. In 1991 the *Directory of online databases* noted 4,465 electronic databases which were accessible from 645 hosts and 88 gateways.[22] Examples were *FLORA*, a 'computerized key' to 786 species of wild plants with multi-access approach (colour, leaf-design, etc.); the Cetedoc *Library of Christian Latin texts* on CD-ROM of some 21 million words from almost 250 large volumes; and Chadwyck-Healey's *The reference station*, a CD-ROM suite covering four daily papers and the weekly *Economist* and *Hansard* (Parliamentary debates). Chadwyck-Healey was another publisher active in this decade, developing a large range of documentary and archive resources in microform and CD-ROM.

Technological obsolescence became a problem, with Betamax videos, ultafiche, microcards and cassetted microfilm being just some of the now-forgotten casualties. Librarians of the time who coped with computer-assisted services will recall the laborious call-up and logging-in procedures, fickle modems, lengthy response times, online costs and the frequent loss of contact. We agonized, too, about how to charge for these high status services. The reference library at the end of the twentieth century needed, some claimed, to be little more than a computer terminal mediated by the computer-literate, person-friendly, information officer. The holdings strategy of the nineteenth-century librarian–custodian was giving way to the virtual library, the library without walls, 'the joined-up library'. And this was even before the more accessible internet, with its world wide web and email text delivery was commonplace in libraries. Books about IT tended to be more about the technicalities of IT rather than finding information in a public service context. Books with titles such as *Making information available in digital format* and *Knowledge-based systems for general reference work – applications, problems, and progress* were not for front-line staff.[23] A historical development was seen in the titles of Phil Bradley's corpus: *CD-ROMs* of 1994 becoming *Going online and CD-ROM* (1994), then *Going online, CD-ROM and the internet* in 1997.[24] It was only with the end-of-decade roll-out of the People's Network that use of the internet for enquiry work become widespread, with a consequent proliferation of searchers' guides, though Andy Dawson's *The internet for library and information service professionals* was first published in 1995.[25]

Information technology
The nineties were very much a decade of re-skilling for information staff. Computers spread everywhere and re-wiring our reading rooms was a constant and noisy activity. The development of OPACs and online services continued, but a £50 million grant from the National Lottery in the late 1990s to set up the National Grid for Learning (NGfL) distributed by the New Opportunities Fund presaged a massive shake-up of library information services in the public sector. The NGfL envisaged public access to computers in every library to participate in this national network: 'A mosaic of inter-connecting networks and education services based on the Internet which will support teaching, learning, training and administration in schools, colleges, universities, libraries, the workplace and homes'.[26] All library staff were to be trained to a high level of competence in ICT. The massive and rapid development of the world wide web raised the stakes and as the millennium closed, library staff were busy studying for their ECDLs (European Computer Driving Licences), reorganizing reading rooms, and 'getting their heads round' the

new information environment. Information services would never be the same again. Digital technology and the virtual library had arrived. With it came all sorts of organizational and behavioural problems such as booking procedures, assisting users, machine maintenance, limiting access to pornography, chat lines, playing games, and noise. Particularly difficult was the problem of how we should plan for the future of information work; 'Why have a library when everybody uses Google?' There was the challenge for the next decade!

An early leader in the 'cyberspace' culture was the new library at Croydon, opened in 1993. This library boasted the largest public-access CD-ROM network in any UK public library; public access personal computers for private hire; CD-ROMs for loan; internet access, including email facilities: a database linking resources in the local studies library and the borough's museum; and the networking of electronic services to schools and other libraries.[27] The much-heralded re-opening of the British Library on its new site at St Pancras in 1998 in was another massive step in making knowledge resources available to the public.

A new development was the virtual reference library which was already developing in the United States. In the UK we had Project EARL (Electronic Access to Resources in Libraries). Founded in 1995, services included *Magnet* (library journal holdings), *Familia* (directory of family history resources) and *Ask a librarian*. The latter was a free public access website for anyone to ask a question.[28] Some sixty public libraries participated in *Ask a librarian*, each taking a 24-hour stint of duty to do their best to answer the questions received within 48 hours. In May 2000, *Ask* received 785 questions, averaging some 25 a day. Unanswered questions were sent system-wide to all participants for help. Enquiries came from all over the world. The service was particularly impressive for the degree of altruism shown since rarely did an enquiry come from one's own home patch. Interestingly, the majority of enquiries were answered using the world wide web itself, which says something about the lack of skill of many internet users and the continued need for the mediating role of the librarian.

Email became a fact of life and new procedures were needed to cope with enquiries received electronically. Electronic discussion groups enabled librarians to discuss and promote ideas, while web-based services, not to mention website development and maintenance, became new roles taken on by reference and information staff. Finally, digitization of resources was added to the activities and challenges of library staff. Truly had the print-based library taken a back seat!

Information matters

Anyone reading this will be aware of the semantic and cognitive problems caused by the words 'reference' and 'information'. The frequent and unconsidered conflation of 'reference' and 'information' was a cause of concern and engendered much confusion and damage. Thus 'reference' came to mean 'reference libraries', and the sexier 'information' an information *service*, though 'information' often came to be treated as if it were a commodity.[29] It was clear, however, that throughout the decade there was a self-conscious push to promote the 'information' label and dispose of the olde worlde 'reference library' tag. Libraries themselves were being re-branded as 'library and information' services. This was, after all, the 'Information Age'. Labels apart, what, in fact, were we reference/information people doing? In 1992, a survey was commissioned by the Information Services Group of the Library Association into 'The Provision of Information Services in the Public Libraries of the United Kingdom'.[30] This snapshot, amusingly titled with the double pun *Information matters*, looked at libraries, both general libraries and those with reference *and* lending departments; staffing; enquiry desks; unstaffed reference collections; training; enquiries; enquirers; independent users; readers crossing authorities' borders; online computer terminals; and staff views on the function of the public library. The lack of data relating to information/enquiry work was lamented, with a dangerous focusing on 'business information' leading to erroneous assumptions about the possibilities of fee-charging (semantics again!). Rather amusingly, after disbanding its subject-departmentalized central library service in 1985, Bradford established separate 'reference' and 'information' libraries, but neither staff nor public understood the difference and the latter library was re-branded as Business Information!

Cuts and charging

> Cuts in public spending over the last twenty years have affected library services. Small branch libraries have closed and others are open for shorter hours on fewer days. Therefore it is less easy for people like myself who are in employment and working long hours to use the facilities.[31]

If libraries are not open, their information and reference facilities cannot be used. By 1992, only 18 public libraries were open for more 60 hours or more, whereas there had been 229 in 1974. In early 1999 the *Sunday times* reported that at least fifty libraries were at risk of being shut, thereby 'adding to the 500 ... which have been closed over the last 10 years'. It was predicted that by March 1999 only 21 libraries would be open for 60 hours or more a week.[32] Reported one librarian, who wished to remain anonymous: 'Clearly the budget will represent the largest single challenge to our ability to continue to deliver the comprehensive reference and information services currently available. It would not be overtly pessimistic to say that no improvement, and probably significant deterioration in the budget, is likely over the next three years.'[33] Outside the public library sector, it was reported that the ITV News Service was staffed by only one librarian per shift and only one daily national newspaper was being filed;[34] that the Royal Commonwealth Society commenced sales of its library collections, 'due to unresolved internal financial pressures';[35] and the British Architectural Library halved its spending on reference books in 1992 'to reduce annual expenditure by £½m'.[36] In 1997 the Audit Commission found that although expenditure on public libraries was increasing it was not being channelled into books and other materials.[37]

There were other factors at work. The continued expansion in higher education reduced academic demands made on public libraries, while government policies to involve more people in education from infants (e.g., Sure Start) to the retired (e.g., University of the Third Age) diverted many resources away from the traditional quality non-fiction stock and services into basic literacy and leisure-based facilities.

Related to costs was the enterprise economy of the late '80s and '90s, when privatization and commercialization were standard. In 1988, a government green paper advocated a charging for services or contracting them out.[38] Charging for the use of reference facilities and contracting out specialized services were suggested. Two years earlier, the Adam Smith Institute had suggested that charging in public libraries would provide the income needed for renewal.[39]

Partly as a consequence of government policy, charging became a big issue in the '90s. There was strong pressure to recoup costs. Simple cost recovery, such as for photocopying and printing from microfilm and fiche, was sanctioned under the 1964 Public Libraries Act, but charging for non-local users, online searches, handling enquiries and undertaking research, opened up new areas of debate. Subtle distinctions were made between 'core' (free) and 'value-added' (charged) services. Local politicians became involved and there were wide variations in practice. Information and reference services were not exempt. Some libraries charged for internet access, others for using the St Catherine's House index of births, marriages and deaths. Some services were put out to tender, and there were experiments with in-house genealogists and other specialists who charged for their services, charging the client either directly or via the library. Charging for 'research' enquiries was also tried. Income, though, was rarely sufficient to be worth the effort and such arrangements seldom lasted long. Private enterprise was not interested. There were some exceptions and successes, notably in the case of Westminster. Here an internal market was created. In 1992 five library business units were established, of which the Westminster Reference Library, the Schools Information Service, and 'Information for Business' were three.[40] Charging for business information was an exception and many libraries were active in this domain. Examples were Glasgow's Business User Services, Sheffield's Science Park Information Service, and Birmingham's Information Direct. In 1990, some fifty libraries came together to form the national Business Information Network, while a number of libraries in West Yorkshire circulated their superseded yearbooks and directories to partner libraries. The situation varied from authority to authority, with the overall national picture becoming confused.

Opposition to charging for basic services was robust and in the 1995 review of public libraries sponsored by the Department of National Heritage charging was 'shelved' and a rather different policy introduced whereby core services, including use of the internet, were to be free at the point of delivery.[41] Two years later, the DNH suggested that libraries should make more use of volunteer staff, open longer hours and use references libraries as homework centres (much to librarian derision!).[42]

Services

With the changing nature of reference service came a changing nomenclature for the staff. The obsolete title 'reference librarian', noted at the beginning of this article, was changing into all manner of hybrids, with 'information' and 'manager' emerging as the dominant elements: Information Services Manager, Information Resources Officer, and Library and Information Services Manager being just three to be seen in job advertisements. This diversity, some might say, reflected the uncertainty and confusion about exactly what 'business' we were in. Knowledge Manager and Electronic Resources Officer, seen towards the end of the decade, furthered the confusion. The de-professionalization of information and enquiry work was also apparent as a cost reduction strategy.

> The situation today is even more confusing as reference libraries are transmuted into resource centres, information centers, one-stop-shops and street corner universities. Now it is the case of reference librarians battling to keep their services going in the face of diminishing resources, new politically-driven agendas, and the naïve assertion that 'everything's on the Net anyway, so why worry?'.[43]

A review of 16 UK reference/information services appeared in the 1994 *Encyclopedia of reference work*.[44] These included Berkshire, Birmingham, Bradford, Cheshire, Cleveland, Dublin, East Sussex, Glasgow, Leicestershire, Newcastle and Sheffield. The range of services, and their organization, showed a wide diversity, ranging from Glasgow's ten specialized departments centralized within the Mitchell (reference) Library, to distributed countywide networks.

Answering questions

One of the hallmarks of a modern library service had been that members of the public (or an institution's students or employees) could go to a library and expect to find the answer to their information needs. Traditionally, the answer had lain in the bookstock.

Given the impossibility of having large traditional reference libraries in the majority of authorities, most opted for a more focused 'information service', that is, the provision of answers to enquiries not needing a prolonged search into a variety of sources. Thus a 'quick reference service', such as the provision of directories, annuals, guides, and so on, for the use of the casual enquirer, was distinguished from a 'research service' which, in some cases was charged for, but in others, languishing.

It is a moot point how successful reference work had been. A rash of studies using unobtrusive testing techniques were not impressed with the success rate, generally about 55%.[45] These studies did the cause of reference and information work no favours and probably contributed to the reluctance of management to continue funding such 'losers'. But enquiries continued to be a staple of public library service. In 1997 the Department of National Heritage estimated 53 million requests were made for information in public libraries a year.[46] In the Library

Association report *Information matters* (1993), the authors ask 'why it is that when the majority of chief librarians claim that answering enquiries is one of the main functions of their library services, so little attention is paid to it?'[47] The report quotes the County Librarian of Somerset writing in *The bookseller*: 'the fastest growth area in public libraries is the provision of information. In the past four years enquiries in Somerset rose by some 60% and show no signs of dropping off. This pattern of increase is common to many library authorities'.[48] Questions abound at this point over the definition of an enquiry, and indeed, the *Information matters* report observed that 'a quarter of the enquiry figures submitted to CIPFA [Chartered Institute of Public Finance and Accountancy] appear to be invented'.[49] CIPFA, which organized the collection of annual statistics from public libraries, carried out its own survey and found that figures fluctuated wildly between similar-sized or adjacent authorities. It concluded that the recording procedures were not being observed.[50] CIPFA later abandoned counting enquiries because of the lack of consistency. The problem remained unresolved at the time of writing. A total of 71% of the libraries surveyed for the *Information matters* report believed that enquiries had become more complex.

'Information work now [2000] features a less educated clientele less willing to seek out information for themselves. From the schoolchild wanting "Everything on X", more concerned to fill a project folder than to understand what goes in it, to the pub quizzer, competition groupie and trivia addict, today's reference librarian reaches for the *Guinness Book of Records*, lists of collective nouns and *The Top Ten of Everything*.' Such was the cynicism engendered in one nineties librarian, yet also, '... a day's work on the enquiry counter is a veritable roller coaster around the universe of knowledge: Government White Papers and literary quotations; circuit diagrams and OS maps; astrological ephemerides and tide tables; Dead Sea Scrolls and *Index Islamicus*; *Which?* reports and house prices.'[51]

The widespread use of the internet for enquiry work and the accessing of remote databases and websites did not really develop till after this period, but the decade saw a rapid development of IT from online access to remote databases, through CD-ROMs, to web-based services. EARL's *Ask a librarian* service has already been mentioned. Another development was public library provision of free public access internet terminals. In 1997, the Library and Information Commission (LIC) published *New library: the people's network*, setting out a strategy for a radical transformation of the public library service. It proposed that public libraries should be connected to a national digital network. This would give them 'a fundamentally new role as managers of electronic content and gateways to a vast wealth of online information'.[52] Among the issues treated were the electronic library, networked environment and performance evaluation. In 1998, the LIC proposed 'to develop a New Library Network which will initially be based on the Internet but which is capable of evolving into a dedicated broadband network ... [and] is compatible with the process being developed by the UK education departments for the National Grid for Learning'.[53] A number of strategies were developed for providing this, ranging from widespread distribution of terminals networked throughout a library system, to channelling requests to a central sources as in the 'Leeds Direct' model.

One problem related to enquiries concerned library policy. Who do you accept enquiries from? How many? In what form? How long do you spend on the answer? With the rising awareness of costs (staff time and materials) and charging options, the nineties saw a more cautious and, regrettably, more restrictive view on what questions to accept. Public access to university and college libraries for non-students had become difficult; licensing agreements with suppliers were another barrier; while the abolition of the Library Licence (with Retail Price Maintenance on books) whereby publishers give discounts on the understanding that the public could have access, closed another door. Another issue was performance measurement, where the administrator was less well disposed to 'extra-territorials' using a library's services (to use the phrase from the COCRIL survey of regional libraries mentioned below).[54] Even in the public library situation, where all comers had a legal right of unfettered access, restrictions were often placed on quizzes and open-ended research-type questions. 'Three quickies or 10 mins max', I recall telling my staff. Finally, of course, the creeping de-professionalization and loss of specialist staff affected the availability of staff and their competency to handle complex enquiries.

Management and cooperation

The Library Association provided standards for reference and information services in public libraries, a new edition of which was produced in 1999.[55] These were designed 'to enable each local authority to set service standards appropriately tailored to the needs of their own communities within the national framework'. They covered the topics of users, services, resources, ICT, accommodation, management, quality of service and performance assessment, publicity, promotion and relationships. In 2000, the government produced its own standards for public libraries, though very little related to reference and information services.[56]

It was a pity that the flurry of activity in the late 1980s that went into local LIPs (Library and Information Plans) and sector LIPs (such as VALIP – visual arts, and LAWLIP) subsided so quickly. At a time when the government was encouraging partnerships, the money was not available, and libraries became less willing to allow non-members to use their (expensive) services. Staffing cuts everywhere made it more difficult to cooperate. However, LINC, the Library and Information Co-operation Council, the body involved in cooperative matters, had as one of its objectives for the year 2000, 'to further resource discovery and resource sharing, and particularly to support retrospective cataloguing conversion'.

The concept of the Regional Reference Library cropped up from time to time, and in 1996, Capital Planning Information (CPI) produced a report as a follow-up to the 1983 study commissioned by COCRIL (Council of City Reference and Information Libraries) and carried out by CRUS (Centre for Research on User Studies).[57] CPI made various recommendations. 'Regionalism' was then part of government policy and the regional reference library surfaced briefly in the government's public library review and LINC's Apt review.[58] The issue was still under discussion and the success of Information North as regional information agency was commended at a seminar in 1999.[59]

The need for basic training in reference and information work continued. Christine Huett produced her *Reference work* in 1990, Denis Grogan updated his *Practical reference work* in 1992, and Tim Buckley Owen's *Success at the enquiry desk*, appeared in 1996, was reprinted a year later, and was already in its third edition by 2000. *The internet public library handbook* by Joseph Janes and others was another to appear towards the end of the decade.[60]

And so we entered the new millennium, a mouse in one hand and a book in the other!

Notes

1 Stuart James, review of *Know it all, find it fast*, *Reference reviews* **16** (8), 2002, 6.
2 Bob Duckett, 'Paradise lost? The retreat from reference', *Library review* **41** (1), 1992, 4–24.
3 Alistair Black, *The public library in Britain, 1914–2000*. London: British Library, 2000.
4 David Stoker, 'Libraries at bursting point' (editorial), *Journal of librarianship and information science* **24** (2), 1992, 67–9.
5 Richard Hoggart, 'A library is not a burger bar', *Independent on Sunday* 30 June 1991; W. J. West, *The strange rise of semi-literate England: the dissolution of the libraries*. London: Duckworth, 1991.
6 Nicholas Bagnall, 'Should libraries sell their books? Many libraries have been quietly selling off their stock', *Sunday telegraph* 22 Dec. 1991.
7 Chrisopher Howse, 'Librarians who deny us our conversations with the past', *Daily telegraph* 16 Jan. 1992.
8 For a bullish view see John Pateman, 'Keeping live stock and disposing of the remains: what is good husbandry?', *Library Association record* **94** (2), 1992, 104–5.
9 Capital Planning Information, *Disposal of printed material from libraries: report to the British National Bibliography Research Fund*. [Boston Spa]: British National Bibliography Research Fund, 1995.
10 Brian Enright *et al.*, *Selection for survival: a review of acquisition and retention policies*. London: British Library, 1989.
11 ARLIS/UK & Ireland, *Guidelines on stock disposal*. Bromsgrove: ARLIS, 2000.
12 International Federation of Library Associations and Institutions, *Revision of IFLA's guidelines for public libraries*. IFLA, 2000. Available at: <http://www.ifla.org/VII/s8/proj/gpl.htm> (accessed 31/1/06).
13 Apt Partnership, *The Apt review: a review of library and information co-operation in the UK and Republic of Ireland*. Sheffield: Library and Information Co-operation Council, 1995.
14 'Public libraries', *Which?* Feb. 1990, 108–10.
15 Department of National Heritage, *Reading the future: a review of public libraries in England*. London: DNH, 1997.
16 R. J. Duckett, 'Reference libraries today' in *Encyclopedia of library and information science*, v. 54, ed. Allen Kent. New York: Dekker, 1994, pp. 305–35.

17 Peter W. Lea and Alan Day (eds.), *The reference sources handbook*. 3rd ed. London: Library Association, 1990; 4th ed., 1996.

18 For more on 1990s reference publishing see Bob Duckett, 'Reference publishing' in Lea and Day (eds.), *Reference sources handbook*. 4th ed., pp. 1–18.

19 Public Lending Right Reference Books Working Party, *Discussion paper*. PLR, 1991.

20 Library Association, Information Services Group, *Basic reference stock for the public library*. 5th ed. London: Library Association, 1998.

21 Black, *Public library in Britain*, p. 131.

22 *Directory of online databases*. Amsterdam: Cuadra/Elsevier, 1991.

23 Terry Coppock (ed.), *Making information available in digital format: perspectives from practitioners*. Edinburgh: Stationery Office, 1999; John V. Richardson, *Knowledge-based systems for general reference work: applications, problems, and progress*. London: Academic Press, 1995.

24 Phil Bradley, *CD-ROMs: how to set up your work station*. London: Aslib, 1994; Phil Bradley and Terry Hanson, *Going online and CD-ROM*. 9th ed. London: Aslib, 1994; Phil Bradley, *Going online, CD-ROM and the internet*. 10th ed. London: Aslib, 1997.

25 Andy Dawson, *The internet for library and information service professionals*. London: Aslib, 1995.

26 Department for Education and Employment, *Connecting the learning society: National Grid for Learning: the government's consultation paper*. London: DfEE, 1997.

27 E.g. H. G. Kirby, 'Public libraries and the information society: case study of Croydon Library Service' in *Public libraries and the information society*, ed. J. Thorhauge *et al.* Luxembourg: European Commission, 1997.

28 Formerly at <http://www.earl.org.uk/ask>, subsequently re-branded as <http://www.peoplesnetwork.gov.uk/enquire> (accessed 31/1/06).

29 See, for example, Patricia Glass Schuman, 'Reclaiming our technological future', *Library journal* **115** (4), 1990, 34–8 ('our business is not information. Our mission is to facilitate understanding through knowledge'). The historical distinction between 'reference' and 'information' is aired in: Bob Duckett, 'From reference library to information service: services in danger', *Library review* **53** (6), 2004, 301–8.

30 J. R. A. Walker, *Information matters: the provision of information services in the public libraries of the United Kingdom*. London: Library Association, Information Services Group, 1993.

31 Mass Observation Archive, 'The public library', 1999, G2089. Quoted in Black, *Public library in Britain*, p. 144.

32 'Fifty libraries face closure', *Sunday times*, 31 Jan. 2000. Quoted in Black, *Public library in Britain*, p. 144.

33 Quoted in Duckett, 'Reference libraries today'.

34 *Library Association record* **93** (10), 1991, 647.

35 *Library Association record* **94** (1), 1992, 23.

36 *Library Association record* **94** (1), 1992, 19.

37 Quoted in D. Watson, 'A positive weapon for renewal?', *Library Association record* **99** (11), 1997, 580–1, at p. 580.

38 Office of Arts and Libraries, *Financing our public library service: four subjects for debate: a consultative paper*. London: HMSO, 1988 (Cm 324).

39 Adam Smith Institute, *Ex libris*. London: The Institute, 1986.

40 P. Cox, 'The Westminster experience' in *Competitive tendering and libraries: proceedings of seminars held in Stamford, Lincolnshire*, ed. Maggie Ashcroft and Alex Wilson. Stamford: Capital Planning Information, 1992.

41 Aslib, *Review of the public library service in England and Wales for the Department of National Heritage*. London: Aslib, 1995.

42 Department of National Heritage, *Reading the future*.

43 Bob Duckett, 'Reference and information services', *Library review* **49** (9), 2000, 454–60.

44 Duckett, 'Reference libraries today'.

45 For example P. Hernon and G. R. McClure (eds.), *Unobtrusive testing and library reference services*. Norwood, N.J.: Ablex, 1987; K. Whittaker, 'Unobtrusive testing of reference enquiry work', *Library review* **39** (6), 1990, 50–4.

46 Department of National Heritage, *Reading the future*.

47 Walker, *Information matters*.

48 *The bookseller*, 12 June 1992, quoted in Walker, *Information matters*.

49 Walker, *Information matters*, p. 44.

50 John Sumsion, Richard Marriott, Helen Pickering, *The CIPFA enquiry count*. Loughborough: Library and Information Statistics Unit, 1994 (LISU occasional paper; no. 7); Naomi Blake, *Enquiry statistics: an analysis of enquiries asked at selected public and special libraries in the UK*. Loughborough: Library and Information Statistics Unit, 1995 (LISU occasional paper; no. 11).

51 Duckett, 'Reference and information services'.

52 Library and Information Commission, *New Library: the people's network*. [London: LIC], 1997.

53 Library and Information Commission, *Building the new library network: a report to government*. London: LIC, 1998.

54 Colin Harris, *The use of reference services in public libraries: a study of large city libraries*. Sheffield: University of Sheffield, Centre for Research on User Studies, 1983 (CRUS occasional paper; no. 8); Capital Planning Information, *Regional reference libraries: a position statement*. Bruton: CPI, 1996.

55 Library Association, Information Services Group, *Guidelines for reference and information services in public libraries*. London: Library Association, 1999.

56 Department for Culture, Media and Sport, *Comprehensive and efficient: standards for modern public libraries: a consultation paper*. London: DCMS, 2000.

57 Capital Planning Information, *Regional reference libraries*.

58 Aslib, *Review of public library service*; Apt Partnership, *Apt review*.

59 Anne Sugg (ed.), *Planning a regional future: the library and information services context: proceedings of a seminar held at Stamford, Lincolnshire on 10th February 1999*. Bruton: Capital Planning Information, 1999.

60 Christine Huett, *Reference work*. Newcastle-under-Lyme: Association of Assistant Librarians, 1990; Denis Grogan, *Practical reference work*. 2nd ed. London: Library Association, 1992; Tim Buckley Owen, *Success at the enquiry desk*. London: Library Association, 1996. 3rd ed., 2000. Joseph Janes *et al.*, *The internet public library handbook*. New York; London: Neal-Schuman, 1999.

27

Library management systems

Lucy A. Tedd

General overview

In one of the first papers on library management systems (LMS) in the UK to be published during the review period of 1991–2000, Arfield describes how the changing economics of computing resulted in staff at Reading University Library wishing to move away from a system shared between various libraries to an integrated library management system under local control.[1] Reading had been a member of the SWALCAP (originally standing for the South Western Academic Libraries Co-operative Automation Project) which had provided shared cataloguing and circulation services to a number of academic libraries in the UK since 1979. However, ageing equipment was becoming increasingly unreliable and staff at Reading felt that the SWALCAP service was unable to cope with the increasing number of terminals that were required for the users. This situation was replicated in other academic and public libraries at the start of the 1990s and many moved over, or migrated, to integrated library management systems (in Reading's case the LIBS 100 system from CLSI was chosen). Jones, of the House of Lords Library, describes how the decline in the number of customers of the shared services resulted in the decision by SLS (SWALCAP Library Services) to withdraw them.[2] Following a study undertaken by an external consultant (when it was recommended that a multi-user integrated LMS be chosen) a decision was made to implement the ADVANCE system from the company Geac in the House of Lords. Another reason for libraries choosing to replace their LMS during this period was the fact that some LMSs were not designed to cope with dates in the 2000s – i.e., they were not Year 2000 (or Y2K) compliant.

Many of the integrated LMSs, such as CLSI's LIBS 100 and Geac's ADVANCE, were developed during the 1980s so that by the 1990s these comprised a number of modules to cover the general library housekeeping functions of:

- cataloguing: creating records for material held in the collection
- circulation: keeping track of who has what item from the collection on loan
- providing access to the catalogue: via an Online Public Access Catalogue (OPAC)
- acquisitions: selecting and ordering items for the collection and maintaining the accounts

- serials control: managing the acquisition of serial publications and so dealing with challenges such as claiming for missing issues
- inter-library lending: to enable books and serials to be borrowed from different libraries.

Most LMSs are now integrated, i.e., data is held only once by the system and is then used by all the modules and functions. This has an obvious benefit as a search of an OPAC can inform the user as to the number of copies of the title are held, where they are housed, as well as whether or not they are out on loan, and if so when they are likely to be returned.

The libraries of the early 1990s, be they public, university, college, medical, government, legal, industrial, or school, dealt primarily with printed materials such as books, reports, scholarly journals and so on, as well as what were referred to as non-book materials, such as films, videos, tape-slide productions, CD-ROMs and so on. However, by the end of the 1990s the huge impact of the internet and the world wide web meant that staff in libraries increasingly were involved in not just managing the collections housed physically within the four walls of their library building but were also involved in providing access to a vast range of digital information sources of potential relevance to their users which were housed outwith the library building. This mixture of providing access to print and digital collections caused some writers, such as Oppenheim and Smithson, to refer to the development of the hybrid library.[3]

For many of the staff working in libraries in the early 1990s the LMSs were their first experiences in using computers. By the end of the 1990s though, following much training in information and communications technology (ICT) as part of the Electronic Libraries Programme (eLib) in the UK's academic libraries, and the People's Network in public libraries, staff became much more familiar with using computer systems.[4] The functionality required by LMSs inevitably evolved during the 1990s and some suppliers kept pace with technological developments whereas others failed. Another development of the 1990s was that many smaller libraries were able to afford to buy LMSs as systems began to cost thousands (or in some cases hundreds) of pounds rather than hundreds of thousands of pounds.

A number of books appeared during the decade providing, *inter alia*, advice to librarians involved in selecting and managing LMSs.[5] *Managing the electronic library* covers a wider area than LMS with 40 contributors, mainly from the UK academic community.[6] The main theme of this book is change and how staff in university libraries were responding in the 1990s to the rapidly changing higher education system in the UK with its increasing student numbers and greater diversity and requirement for flexibility of access to information. For many libraries the challenge relating to LMS was not necessarily choosing a new system 'from scratch' but migrating from one system to another as described earlier. Muirhead's book includes a number of case studies written by library staff from a range of different types of library describing their experiences in migration.[7]

Muirhead also edited the British version of a book on planning for library automation which was written in the US.[8]

Brief descriptions of some of the library management systems available
In this section brief descriptions will be given of some of the LMSs used in UK libraries between 1991 and 2000. Further details are provided in the excellent directory of 30 LMSs compiled by Leeves with Russell through funding from the British Library Research and Development Department (BLR&DD) under the auspices of the Library Information Technology Centre (LITC) at South Bank University in London.[9] The LITC was a centre which, in 1991, moved from its former base at the Polytechnic of Central London to the South Bank Polytechnic. LITC was funded by the BLR&DD to offer impartial advice on LMSs and general automation projects to librarians and information professionals. Staff at LITC were involved in a number of activities related to LMSs including the production of briefing documents, guides,[10] introductory packs (e.g., for special sectors, such as school libraries),[11] providing consultancy advice to individual libraries choosing a new LMS, being involved in funded research work and publishing the journal *Vine*. The Leeves with Russell directory was based, in part, on an earlier directory of some 29 LMS in Europe;[12] of these over 50% referred to LMS used in UK libraries at that time. Other references to case studies describing particular implementations have, in the main, been taken from the journals *Program* and *Vine*.

ADLIB
This LMS was initially developed in the 1980s by Lipman Management Resources of Maidenhead and in the 1990s was supplied by Adlib Information Systems. Leeves with Russell record 11 users of ADLIB in the mid-1990s, of which 10 were special libraries. An example of a library and information service implementing ADLIB is provided by Wilsher who describes the decision made by the Advisory, Conciliation and Arbitration Service (ACAS) to choose the catalogue, OPAC and acquisitions modules of this system to replace the previous BookshelF system used when ACAS was part of the UK government's Department of Employment.[13]

ALEPH 500
Ex Libris developed its first LMS, the forerunner of the ALEPH 500 system, for the Hebrew University in Jerusalem in the 1980s and it became a popular system in Europe. The first customer for ALEPH 500 in the UK was King's College London (KCL) which, in 1996, was looking for a new LMS to replace the soon to be defunct LIBERTAS system. Sudell and Robinson describe that procurement process and explain how its use of industry standards (Unix, Oracle, Windows, SQL etc.) was one of the major reasons for its being chosen for King's.[14] Many other academic libraries followed KCL in choosing ALEPH 500 including Bristol, as described by King.[15]

ALICE

This LMS originated in Australia and was introduced into the UK market in 1992. It is primarily aimed at school libraries and proved to be popular, Leeves with Russell recording some 320 users in special, college and prison libraries as well as in schools. Darroch provides a brief description of the place of ALICE in the LMS marketplace in the late 1990s.[16]

ALS

Automated Library Systems (ALS), a British company, had been involved with computer-based library systems since the late 1960s when it developed a special device based on punched paper-tape for automatically recording details of books and borrowers at a library's issue desk. During the 1990s the suppliers developed a version of the ALS System 900 which would run on open systems platforms (as opposed to the previous proprietary hardware and software solution) as well as dealing with Electronic Data Interchange (EDI) developments in the acquisitions module. Ashton describes how EDI with ALS was used at Hertfordshire Libraries Arts and Information Service.[17]

BookshelF/Genesis

BookshelF originated as a microcomputer-based software package developed in the 1980s for the Cairns Library at the John Radcliffe Hospital in Oxford. However, by the 1990s the multi-user system of BookshelF became known as Genesis and was marketed by the Specialist Computer Group (SCG). Rowley describes how this LMS was one of the first to run as a Windows product with a graphical user interface (GUI).[18] Further details of BookshelF are provided by Fisher and Rowley.[19] Leeves with Russell report that take-up of this new LMS had been quite rapid during the early 1990s with there being 37 customers (mainly college or small academic), including both previous BookshelF customers which had upgraded to the new improved system as well as new customers.

CAIRS-LMS

The Computer Assisted Information Retrieval System (CAIRS) was initially developed as an in-house information retrieval system for the Leatherhead Food Research Association in the mid-1970s. CAIRS-LMS was developed to complement this and was used by those libraries in the 1990s which typically had sophisticated information retrieval requirements and comparatively low numbers of loans. Perrow describes the upgrade from the microcomputer version of CAIRS (MicroCAIRS) to CAIRS-LMS at Templeton College.[20] Leeves with Russell record 218 users of CAIRS-LMS, the vast majority of whom were special libraries. Bennett and Tomlinson describe the use of the inter-library loans module of CAIRS-LMS at the library of the Institution of Electrical Engineers.[21]

DataTrek

This LMS originated from software developed in the US but by the 1990s some UK special libraries were using it. Hoey, for instance, describes its implementation at the Royal Society of Chemistry (RSC).[22] Like similar learned societies, the RSC had been using online information retrieval system since the 1980s and by the 1990s realized the need for a complementary LMS. In 1996 DataTrek, by then part of the Dawson Holdings group, acquired Information Management and Engineering (IME) the producers of the TINLib software.

Dynix/Horizon

The history of Dynix up to the early 1990s is provided by Gilmartin with Beavan who were responsible for implementing this LMS at Glasgow Caledonian University.[23] The original Dynix LMS was developed in the US in the 1980s and Leeves with Russell state that there were 68 users of this LMS in the UK in public, university, small academic/college and special libraries. During the 1990s a client-server LMS, Horizon, was marketed by the firm Ameritech Library Services, which had merged with Dynix during the 1990s. Hackett and Geddes describe the Horizon LMS, noting that it was truly scaleable with installations in small special libraries as well as large multi-site academic libraries.[24] They also note however that it might have been argued that Horizon was marketed too early in the UK in 1995, when the product lacked depth of functionality required to deal with the needs of large multi-site universities. However, by 1998, when universities including Huddersfield, Middlesex, Staffordshire, Strathclyde and Birkbeck College, University of London had implemented Horizon the feeling was that customers were 'beginning to reap the benefits of its fully graphical, client/server construction'. In 2000 Ameritech Library Services became known as epixtech Inc. and continued to supply existing products as well as web-based solutions and services.

Galaxy

The Galaxy 2000 LMS, from the British firm DS Ltd proved to be a popular system, particularly in public libraries, during the 1990s. Neary describes how Birmingham Library service, the biggest metropolitan library authority in the UK with 40 community libraries and the busiest lending library in Europe, installed the Galaxy 2000 LMS in 1994 and then upgraded it to a newer version in 1999.[25] Galaxy 2000 offered the usual LMS modules but also had a separate issuing function for use of the Birmingham's housebound service. Some 230 terminals for ViewPoint, the OPAC module of Galaxy, had been installed throughout Birmingham by 1999.

Geac

The Canadian firm Geac first installed its Geac Library Information System in a UK library in 1979 and this software ran on proprietary hardware and was used in several UK libraries in the 1980s. In 1988 Geac acquired an American company,

Advanced Libraries, and developed its software, ADVANCE, to run under the Unix operating system and this became its main LMS offering in the 1990s. For instance, in the mid-1990s Edinburgh University upgraded its previous Geac (Geac 9000) system to ADVANCE, Newcastle University chose this system as did the public library at Hamilton District Libraries in Scotland, the National Library of Wales and the Bodleian Library at the University of Oxford. A history of library automation at the Bodleian, including the implementation of the DOBIS/LIBIS system in the late 1980s is provided by Crawshaw.[26] Burnett describes the 1995 decision to migrate to ADVANCE, along with an assessment of the impact of automation on such a large organization with a catalogue of some eight million items.[27] Geac ADVANCE was the basis for the Oxford Libraries Information System (OLIS) that provided library housekeeping services for many of the Oxford colleges, academic libraries within the university as well as the copyright library. During the 1990s Geac also acquired CLSI and its LIBs 100 system and marketed this for some time.

Heritage

Heritage, like Genesis, was developed from the original BookshelF software although Heritage was initially a single-user system, and was marketed by Logical Choice (which became known as Inheritance Systems during the 1990s) in Oxford. Alper describes the implementation of Heritage in a small one-librarian medical service and concluded that this LMS had proved to be a great time-saver in issuing and claiming books and had excellent statistical reporting facilities.[28] In 1997 the library at the Central School of Speech and Drama, having outgrown its previous LMS, needed a new system. Edwards describes the selection process for this new system which resulted in a short list of four LMSs ranging in price from £3,000 to £27,400.[29] Heritage was chosen (at a cost of £11,350) and the paper describes some of the innovative features of this LMS.

INNOPAC/Millennium

The American company Innovative Interfaces Inc. (III) started to market the INNOPAC system in the UK in the early 1990s, the first customer being the library at the University of Wales, Bangor. In 1995 staff at the University of Hull chose INNOPAC to replace the previous Geac 9000 as it had improved functionality.[30] In 1997 III acquired the UK company SLS and its LIBERTAS software. Towards the end of the 1990s III started to develop its Millennium system which, *inter alia*, provided a web-based interface for each module. Users of Millennium in the UK included Sheffield Hallam University, St Andrew's University, and St Mary's University College at Twickenham. The School of Oriental and African Studies at the University of London chose Millennium because of its proven ability to deal with Chinese, Japanese and Korean material. Myhill provides a personal insight into the challenges faced at the University of Exeter in migrating from LIBERTAS to Millennium.[31]

LIBERTAS

The stand-alone LMS LIBERTAS, of SLS, was designed with assistance from many of the systems librarians who were working in the libraries of member universities of the SWALCAP cooperative. LIBERTAS was launched in 1986 and initially incorporated modules for cataloguing, OPAC, and circulation control. Leeves with Russell report 46 users of LIBERTAS in UK libraries by the mid-1990s. Bradford utlines the advantages and disadvantages of using the ILL module of LIBERTAS at Bristol University, which was an original member of SWALCAP. In 1997 SLS was sold to III and support for the LIBERTAS system declined.[32]

OLIB

Smith describes how the Bar Library in Belfast which serves all practising barristers in Northern Ireland implemented the OLIB LMS from the British firm Fretwell-Downing in 1996.[33] The requirements for this special library included the need to provide a document management/delivery service for members as well as an efficient system for managing the library. Initially the Bar Library used the cataloguing, circulation and OPAC modules of OLIB with the intention of implementing the acquisitions and serials modules at a later date.

Talis

The other early cooperative for library automation in the UK was BLCMP – originally Birmingham Libraries Co-operative Mechanisation Project. Like SWALCAP it had developed stand-alone software for its members which, in the early 1990s, was known as BLS – BLCMP Library System – and included modules for acquisitions, cataloguing, OPAC, circulation and serials control. In 1992 BLCMP announced a new Unix-based system known as Talis. Like LIBERTAS, Talis had been designed in conjunction with the cooperative's member libraries. It was based on a modular principles using computing industry standards for an open systems design. Among the early users of Talis were the John Rylands University Library of Manchester and the public library of the Royal Borough of Kingston upon Thames. Leeves with Russell report 30 users of Talis in the mid-1990s, most of whom were university or public libraries in the UK. Wilson describes the experiences of migrating from BLS to Talis at Nene College, the first institution to undertake this migration, and produced a lengthy list of 'morals of migration'.[34] In 1999 BLCMP changed its name to Talis and became a commercial company. This decision followed much consultation with the members of the cooperative and the new company stated that strong customer relationships and customer focus would remain central to the culture of the business.

TINLib

TINLib, also known as The Information Navigator, was developed by the British firm IME in the 1980s. It was one of the earliest systems to offer a navigational facility and to make use of Windows for display and selection of data. Leeves with

Russell report that there were 315 users of TINLib in the mid-1990s in the UK although a full customer list was not supplied. Chappell and Thackeray outline the need for an automated system to replace the existing manual systems at the library of the Arts Council of Great Britain and how the use of TINLib had increased the effectiveness and efficiency of the library and made its collections much more accessible.[35]

Unicorn

Haines describes her experiences during 1990 in attempting to negotiate the acquisition of an American system, Unicorn, from the Sirsi Corporation, which was previously not available in Europe, for use in a British independent health fund, the King's Fund.[36] Sirsi was determined not to enter the European market without a partner with expertise in library software support and with the necessary technical skills in Unix systems. This was finally achieved and the system was successfully launched in the UK in 1991. Leeves with Russell reported some 37 users of Unicorn most of which were medical, legal or government libraries. Scott Cree, for instance, outlines how Unicorn was introduced into the UK government's Department of Health library where it needed to be integrated with the Department's office information system and added to a large network with multiple applications.[37] By the end of the 1990s Unicorn was used in a variety of libraries including the Cheltenham and Gloucester College of Higher Education, the London School of Economics, the Royal College of Nursing, the Royal Veterinary College, and the library at the Natural History Museum.

Voyager

Endeavor Information Systems was formed in the US in 1994 and its first product was its Voyager LMS. The WebVoyage module of Voyager allowed web browsers to query the Voyager database, which was based on the Oracle relational database management system. Voyager became the LMS of choice for a number of libraries looking for new systems following the demise of LIBERTAS. In Wales, for instance, the university libraries of Aberystwyth, Cardiff, Lampeter and Swansea as well as the Welsh College of Music and Drama were all faced with choosing a new system and they decided to approach the selection process in a consortial way, as described by West.[38] Each institution was free to choose its own system following the selection process. In the event all chose Voyager from Endeavor and these systems were implemented, with differing OPAC interfaces, in 1999. Knights outlines the procurement and migration experiences at Hertfordshire University Library in moving also from LIBERTAS to Voyager.[39]

Functionality

Inevitably not all the LMSs offered all modules in a way that satisfied all staff in libraries. In the 1990s there were some examples of libraries which had one LMS for most of its applications but used another for a specific function. For instance, Edwards describes that although Croydon Libraries had automated its circulation and stock control procedures for many years a decision had been made to delay the automation of the acquisitions processes as the LMS in place (CLSI's LIBS 100) did not satisfy the needs of the acquisitions staff.[40] In 1997 the acquisitions module from ALS's Meritus system was adopted, which in conjunction with a network solution allowed EDI ordering and invoicing to be implemented. The requirements for inter-library loans (ILL) which for many libraries in the UK involves the use of the centralized British Library Document Supply Centre have not always been met by LMSs, particularly those developed outside the UK. Leeves describes solutions for automating ILL in the early part of the 1990s and Prowse describes the process of developing an ILL module for the ALEPH 500 LMS that had been installed at KCL.[41]

System overviews in the literature, 1991–2000

Apart from the Leeves with Russell directory which includes details of users of the different LMS, other studies and surveys were also undertaken during the period. In 1991 Blunden-Ellis reported on an update to a previous survey and aimed to provide an analysis of the UK market for LMS in a form that complemented the US annual LMS marketplace survey.[42] The data for this market analysis was retrieved from questionnaires sent to LMS suppliers including ALS, BLS, CLSI, DS, Dynix, Fretwell-Downing, Geac, IME and SLS. He concluded that DS was the overall market leader and that there was plenty of evidence of suppliers enhancing their products. In conclusion he stated that

> This market will become increasingly competitive on economic, geographic and techno-logical levels and so no vendor, even with a good current share, can confidently expect a 'blue skies' future. Investment in research and development and customer satisfaction remain the key activities for the immediate future.

By 1992 Blunden-Ellis reported that BLS had the market share with SLS as second.[43] These were established major forces, and newer suppliers in the market at that time, such as Dynix and IME, were performing well. In the final survey in this series Blunden-Ellis and Graham extended the coverage of their questionnaire as it was sent to 38 suppliers identified by the LITC and 29 responses were received.[44] Previous surveys had concentrated on larger LMS suppliers and since this survey included many smaller LMS suppliers a total of nine market segments was identified. The web was just beginning to impact on libraries at the time of this last survey and the final point made was that library housekeeping systems would become just one of a suite of services designed to deliver packaged information quickly and effortlessly.

A different perspective on the use and growth of LMS in public libraries in the UK was provided in other surveys. In 1991 Dover reported on a survey undertaken through funding from the Office of Arts and Libraries through the BLR&DD.[45] Questionnaires were sent to 109 public library authorities and 95 responses were analysed. Of these only 15 had no computer-based system in their library and some

23 had been using computers for over 15 years. The four main service objectives identified for using computers in libraries at that time were:

- better stock utilization
- improved throughput
- better management information
- better access to services.

Batt, then of the London Borough of Croydon, carried out a series of six surveys of information technology in public libraries between 1984 and 1997. Comparisons year on year though are problematic given various local government reorganizations, such as that in 1997. In the sixth edition he reported that 95% of the 168 authorities surveyed had some form of automated circulation system in at least one service point.[46] This compared with 82% in the previous survey of 1993. He also found that 38% had an automated circulation system in all their libraries. Table 1 shows some of the LMSs used.

Table 1 LMS used in public libraries as reported by Batt

	1993	1997
ALS	9	13
BLS	15	32
CLSI/GEAC PLUS	11	9
DS	28	36
Dynix	15	20
Genesis	–	8
Unicorn	–	1

Availability of an OPAC had featured on Batt's questionnaire since 1985 and his report shows the shift from 7 authorities with some form of OPAC in 1985 to 143 in 1997: a considerable change. Automated acquisitions were reported in 76% of the authorities and 26% (44 of the 168) were also using EDI to communicate with a range of suppliers.

An intriguing view of LMS in the 1990s is provided by Heseltine, who outlines the history and current state of the LMS market using the stages through which Christian passes in *Pilgrim's progress*.[47] The 'delights' to be found at the end of the journey were described as:

- improvements in the user interface; he noted that many of the LMSs were developed from systems of the 1970s and 1980s which had rudimentary user interfaces
- access to a wider range of information
- improved management information

- systems designed for end-users and not library staff
- implementation of standards.

Yeates also wrote about how the LMSs of the 1990s reflected a conservative view of the library as a passive repository which took little account of the needs of users and of the possibility of dynamic interaction.[48]

However, in a study of ten libraries from the academic, public and special sectors which had purchased library management systems in the mid-1990s Murray found that some of Heseltine's 'delights' had come to pass.[49] He noted the following:

- New generation LMSs were more flexible (portable and easier to use, more powerful in terms of connectivity) and incorporated industry standards.
- New LMSs were less staff-intensive (in terms of support and backup).
- More suppliers now offered software-only packages.
- Client/server systems and Windows-based LMSs had yet to become a mandatory requirement in the procurement process.
- Some of the libraries had taken the views of their end-users into account when having systems demonstrated.
- The production of management information remained an area of difficulty for some systems.
- There was unanimity in the belief that web developments in terms of software being provided by suppliers and the ability to link from the LMS to the internet would dominate the marketplace.

Raven provides a very general review of the LMS marketplace for academic libraries in 2000 and notes: 'Deciding on a new library management system has become much more difficult for universities in the UK in the last two years. The range continues to expand rapidly and if you've grown with your present system for the last ten years or so, change can be a frightening prospect.'[50]

Some developments between 1991 and 2000
Akeroyd provides an overview of integrated LMS towards the end of the decade in his introductory paper to a special issue of *Vine* on LMS in 1999.[51] His developments have been used as a basis for this section although other aspects have also been added.

Technological developments
Many of the early LMSs used their own specially developed operating systems. However, during the 1990s many suppliers moved to developing systems that ran on the Unix operating system. Similarly many of the early LMSs were designed around specially developed database management systems. During the 1990s there was a move away from these to industry standard relational database management systems such as Ingres (used by Galaxy 2000), Informix (used by Unicorn), Oracle

(used by ALEPH and Olib) and Sybase (used by Horizon and Talis). Another technological development of the 1990s was the adoption of the client-server architecture. In this model a split is made between the applications software (which runs on a computer known as the client) and the database software (which runs on a computer known as the server). The two communicate with each other over a network using a communications protocol (or set of rules). Processing which involves data manipulation or aspects of screen display can be carried out on the client computer and only database queries from the client and responses from the server need to be communicated across the network.

Self-service

An important development during the 1990s was the installation of self-issue machines in libraries so that users could issue and return their own books. The library at the University of Sunderland was one of the first to use machines from the 3M company for this purpose. Stafford describes this service and highlights the four Ps (preparation, publicity, position and persuasion) necessary for a successful implementation.[52] In 1996 a conference was held at Sunderland on self-issue systems and its proceedings contain a number of case studies.[53] A special issue of *Vine* was published in 1997 on self-service in libraries and Cookman describes the introduction of a 3M self-issue terminal at Maidenhead public library.[54] The general experience was that library staff accepted the benefits of the new terminal and that on busy days queues had reduced noticeably. However, when the issue desk was quiet it appeared that users preferred the human approach to issuing and returning materials.

Messages to users by email or text

With many users having access to email and/or mobile telephones some LMS incorporated the facility to use these technologies for sending overdue notices, alerts for reserved items or other communications. Sudell and Robinson noted that the reader record in the ALEPH 500 system at KCL could hold a variety of addresses.[55] If an email address was entered then that would be first in line, otherwise the system could handle multiple postal addresses so that an appropriate address could be used depending on whether it is term time or vacation.

Improved accessibility via the OPAC and use of the Z39.50 protocol

OPACs have always been designed with end-users in mind and so the interfaces that developed over the years from the command-driven and menu-based systems at the start of the decade to the form-filling on web pages were all intended to be straightforward to use. However, the information being searched, i.e. the records in the catalogue database, was often stored in MARC format, containing little information to support elaborate subject searching. The 856 field of MARC allowed the inclusion of a URL in the bibliographic record and by the end of the 1990s some OPACs were using this to provide links to digital objects.

A further development of the 1990s related to OPACs was the Z39.50 standard.

As defined by Dempsey *et al.* Z39.50 is 'a retrieval protocol which allows client programs to query databases on remote servers, to retrieve results and to carry out some other retrieval-related functions.'[56] The main impact of this was that it enabled users to search, say, the OPAC of a neighbouring library (which might perhaps use Horizon) using the same user interface as the local library (which might be based on Talis). For this to happen the relevant LMSs needed to have appropriate software to make them Z39.50 compatible. A list of LMS with this capability is provided by Dempsey *et al.* and includes: ADVANCE, ALEPH, DataTrek, Dynix, Horizon, INNOPAC, LIBERTAS, OLIB, Talis, TINLib and Unicorn. Brack describes the RIDING Project which resulted from one of the eLib Programme's large scale resource discovery (clumps) projects and which provided a Z39.50 Search and Retrieve facility for all the Yorkshire and Humberside university OPACs, plus the British Library Document Supply Centre databases and the Leeds Library and Information Service OPAC.[57]

Catalogue record provision
Most LMSs allowed for original cataloguing of bibliographic records as well as for allowing the import of, usually MARC, records from external sources. Although not all LMSs were using the MARC record for internal processing of records they usually did include the ability to input or output records in this format. The early UK cooperatives of BLCMP and SWALCAP developed large databases of MARC records which proved valuable to the cataloguers of their member libraries. Many of these records were subsequently incorporated into the OCLC database in the US and made available internationally. Retrospective cataloguing of materials held in libraries continued and Bryant's report outlined the issues, opportunities and need for a national strategy in this area.[58]

Examples of consortial working
Although the BLCMP and SWALCAP cooperatives had disappeared by the end of the 1990s there were several examples of other consortial projects and systems related to LMSs. Some of these consortia were formed as part of the eLib Programme, others, such as the Welsh academic libraries already mentioned, were linked with the sharing of resources for the procurement of a new LMS.

COPAC
COPAC, the OPAC of the Consortium of University Research Libraries, was by the end of the decade providing free access to the merged catalogues of twenty major university research libraries in the UK and Ireland. Cousins describes the development of COPAC and its launch in the mid-1990s.[59] COPAC is an example of a physical merged catalogue, the records from all the libraries being combined into one database, with checks to identify duplicate records. During the 1990s COPAC was available via a text interface as well as a web interface.

M25 Consortium

The M25 Consortium of Academic Libraries was formed in 1993 with the aim of fostering cooperation amongst its London-based, higher education member libraries in order to improve services to users. In 1998 the M25 Link project was funded as part of the eLib Programme and aimed to establish a pilot virtual clump to provide single search access to the library catalogues of six members of the M25 Consortium. The project consisted of a seamless search tool, using the Z39.50 protocol, to the OPACs of the six pilot partners which between them had a range of LMSs including: Horizon, INNOPAC, Libertas, Talis and Unicorn. An overview of the work undertaken by the M25 Consortium is provided by Enright.[60]

Foursite consortium

Froud describes the Foursite consortium of four public libraries in the South West of England which came together to identify replacement computer requirements and which subsequently went on to share a single LMS operated by one of its members, Somerset.[61] The Foursite consortium demonstrated that significant cost savings could be achieved at all stages in the process of specifying, selecting and implementing an LMS under the following circumstances:

- political support and enthusiasm by members of the consortium
- flexible management in all authorities who were prepared to make sacrifices in the interest of the consortium's objectives, coupled with an openness that precluded any hidden agendas
- tight project management
- clear terms of reference for individual groups and clear ground rules
- good communication systems
- expert technical advice.

Use of project management methodologies

There was some evidence during the 1990s of project management methodologies being used for the procurement and implementation of LMSs. Lewis describes the use of PRINCE (Projects IN Controlled Environments: a methodology used in government departments) at the University of Wales Bangor for the procurement, in conjunction with the North East Wales Institute, of a replacement LMS.[62] Chambers and Perrow reported on a questionnaire carried out as part of a study on the use of project management methodologies generally in university libraries in the UK.[63] Of the 80 university librarians who responded, 28% had used project management software – and the most popular software was Microsoft Project.

Closer links between LMSs and archives

Suffolk County Council's Libraries and Heritage is an example of an organization covering public libraries, record offices, arts and museums. Suffolk had installed its first LMS (a batch system to deal with circulation in conjunction with a microfiche catalogue) in 1980. By 1987 this had been replaced with an LMS using proprietary hardware, software and communications which managed circulation, acquisitions, cataloguing, community information, the OPAC, email, dial-in facilities and management information. In 1995, when the time came to replace this LMS, the aim was to provide a system which would use generic hardware, software and communications which would provide a networking infrastructure to bring internet access to all branches and which would also serve the needs of Suffolk's archives and museums. Pachent describes the procurement process which resulted in the acquisition of DS Ltd's Galaxy 2000 and the CALM 2000 systems.[64] Closer links between LMSs and archives in the public sector were enhanced by the formation of Resource, the Council for Museums, Archives and Libraries in 2000 as the strategic body working with, and for, museums, archives and libraries.[65]

Fitzgerald and Flanagan describe the implementation of the Unicorn system at the Royal Botanic Gardens, Kew for managing its collections of archives as well as books.[66]

Human aspects

One of the core texts related to the human aspects of the use of computers in libraries is that by Morris and Dyer.[67] In the introduction to this work the authors note that there are many pitfalls on the road to the successful implementation of any computer system, such as an LMS, in a library and that if people respond badly to the introduction of the new system, the anticipated effectiveness will not be achieved. They also note that poor workstation and job design can result in poor health and can induce, or increase, stress and that poorly designed user interfaces can result in under-used systems and a decrease in accuracy. The book provides much advice as to how to overcome such challenges and to design systems that are human-friendly.

The role of the systems librarian developed during the 1990s. Following research funded in the early 1990s by the BLR&DD Muirhead reported on the result of a questionnaire aimed at identifying the education, qualifications, previous experience etc. of staff who were involved in the day-to-day running of LMSs in libraries in the UK and also edited a book containing a series of case studies.[68]

Stress related to technology, or 'technostress', emerged as an identifiable condition during the 1990s. Harper noted that with UK libraries undergoing increasingly rapid technological change at the end of the 1990s this change would have consequences at every level of an organization, all of which must be managed.[69] He advised that managers needed to adopt solutions ranging from addressing technical and health issues to being prepared to review job descriptions and roles. Further information on how the implementation of an LMS affected job design and staffing structures was provided by Dyer *et al.*, while Daniels looked at the effect of the implementation of an LMS on non-professional staff in three college libraries.[70]

Some final thoughts

Inevitably there were many changes and developments related to the provision and availability of library management systems during the 1990s. Much appeared in the literature on experiences of libraries in choosing and implementing particular LMSs. One aspect that was promised but probably not greatly used during the 1990s was the management information delivered from LMS. By the end of the 1990s some LMSs incorporated interfaces to standard tools such as Microsoft's Excel for the presentation of statistical data.

During the 1990s there was an almost total lack of reporting on ways of evaluating LMSs once they had been installed. Given the large amounts of resources, in terms of time and money, invested in procuring LMSs it is perhaps surprising that libraries did not carry out a post-implementation review, although there may well be reasons for this including, for instance:

- no one requested it
- not enough time
- no money
- no suitable staff to carry out the evaluation
- fear of drawing attention to an LMS's defects soon after large amounts of time, money and collective energy had been expended
- lack of a baseline for comparison of improved service.

However, there are many reasons why a post-implementation evaluation of an LMS should take place. Such reasons include to:

- determine if the broader goals of the library are being met by the LMS
- determine if the particular goals of implementing the LMS have been met
- determine if the system as delivered satisfies the contract
- enable others to learn from the experience
- provide an account to the funding body of the money spent on the LMS
- investigate complaints from the staff or users about the system
- establish a benchmark showing at what level of performance the LMS is operating.

Akeroyd concluded his overview of LMSs with a description of some of the functionality required by future systems and which were beginning to be investigated in some research projects at the end of the 1990s.[71] These included:

- the integration of multiple sources and systems, both of bibliographic information and the full-text of documents
- the simplification of access to sources
- the personalization of systems
- a change in the way that software is created and maintained.

Only a review of the next years would provide an overview of such future developments.

Notes

1   J. A. Arfield, 'CLSI's LIBS-100 at Reading University', *Program* **25** (1), 1991, 51–7.

2   David Lewis Jones, 'The Geac ADVANCE system in the House of Lords Library', *Program* **27** (2), 1993, 123–34.

3   Charles Oppenheim and Daniel Smithson, 'What is the hybrid library?', *Journal of information science* **25** (2), 1999, 97–112.

4   Chris Rusbridge, 'Towards the hybrid library', *DLib magazine* **7** (7/8), 1998. Available at: <http://www.dlib.org/dlib/july98/rusbridge/07rusbridge.html> (accessed 14/1/06); Library and Information Commission, *New library: the people's network*. London: Library and Information Commission, 1997.

5   Marlene Clayton with Chris Batt, *Managing library automation*. 2nd ed. Aldershot: Ashgate, 1992; Robin T. Harbour, *Managing library automation*. London: Aslib, 1994; Jennifer Rowley, *Computers for libraries*. 3rd ed. London: Library Association, 1993; Jennifer Rowley, *The electronic library*. London: Library Association, 1997; Lucy A. Tedd, *An introduction to computer-based library systems* 3rd ed. Chichester: Wiley, 1993.

6   Terry Hanson and Joan Day (eds.), *Managing the electronic library*. London: Bowker-Saur, 1998.

7   Graeme Muirhead (ed.), *Planning and implementing successful system migrations*. London: Library Association, 1997.

8   Graeme Muirhead (ed.), *Planning for library automation: a practical handbook*. London: Library Association, 1998.

9   Juliet Leeves with Rosemary Russell, *libsys.uk: a directory of library systems in the United Kingdom*. London: LITC, 1995.

10   Library Information Technology Centre, *Guide to choosing an automated library system*. London: LITC, 1992; *Library housekeeping systems for MS-DOS and Windows*. London: LITC, 1996.

11   Library Information Technology Centre, *Introductory pack on library systems for schools*. London: LITC, 1993.

12   Juliet Leeves, John Baker, Alice Keefer and Gitte Larsen. *Library systems in Europe: a directory and guide*. London: TFPL, 1994.

13   Richard Wilsher, 'A new system for new circumstances: ADLIB at ACAS', *Vine* 108, 1998, 37–40.

14   Peter Sudell and Margaret Robinson, 'ALEPH 500 at King's College London', *Vine* 115, 1999, 33–56.

15   Peter King, 'Implementing a new library management system at Bristol University: experiences with Aleph 500', *Program* **34** (4), 2000, 385–96.

16   A. Darroch, 'Alice through the looking glass', *Electronic library* **17** (3), 1999, 159–60.

17   J. Ashton, 'Development of EDI acquisitions facilities in the ALS system', *Vine* 94, 1994, 22–8.

18   Jennifer Rowley, 'GENESIS: a new beginning or a new generation', *Electronic library* **12** (5), 1994, 277–83.

19   Shelagh Fisher and Jenny Rowley, *Bookshelf: a guide for librarians and system managers*. Aldershot: Ashgate, 1992.

20 David Perrow, 'Implementing CAIRS-LMS in a small academic library: experience at Templeton College Oxford', *Program* **25** (3), 1991, 207–21.

21 G. Bennett and J. Tomlinson, 'Interlibrary loans management with CAIRS at the Institution of Electrical Engineers', *Vine* 96, 1994, 19–23.

22 Peter Hoey, 'The DataTrek automated library management system in the Library of the Royal Society of Chemistry', *Program* **26** (1), 1992, 19–28.

23 Jacqueline Gilmartin with Anne Beavan, *Dynix: a guide for librarians and systems managers*. Aldershot: Ashgate, 1992.

24 Brian Hackett and George Geddes, 'Towards a new HORIZON', *Vine* 108,1998, 7–14.

25 Mandy Neary, 'DS Galaxy 200 at Birmingham', *Vine* 115, 1999, 18–23.

26 Tom Crawshaw, 'Library automation at Oxford', *Program* **25** (4), 1991, 291–301.

27 Peter Burnett, 'Emerging from the bibliographic wilderness: catalogue automation in the Bodleian Library, University of Oxford', *Cataloging and classification quarterly* **30** (1), 2000, 51–72.

28 Helen Alper, 'Selecting Heritage/Bookshelf-PC for the District Library, Queen Mary's University Hospital, Roehampton', *Program* **27** (2), 1993, 173–82.

29 J. Adam Edwards, 'Heritage IV: new system installation at Central School of Speech and Drama', *Vine* 115, 1999, 24–33.

30 Diane Leeson, 'The INNOPAC library system at the University of Hull', *Vine* 115, 1999, 11–17.

31 Martin R Myhill, 'Time for change: a personal insight into library systems' implementation: experiences at Exeter University Library', *Program* **34** (1), 2000, 89–101.

32 J. Bradford, 'The LIBERTAS ILL module', *Vine* 95, 1994, 36–43.

33 David Smith, 'Laying down the law with OLIB at the Bar Library, Belfast', *Vine* 108, 1998, 24–30.

34 Maurice Wilson, 'Talis at Nene: an experience in migration in a college library', *Program* **28** (3), 1994, 239–51.

35 Stephen Chappell and Annie Thackeray, 'TINLib: why and how the Arts Council chose this integrated software system to run its library', *Program* **26** (4), 1992, 387–92.

36 Margaret Haines, 'The year of the UNICORN: a review of the first year's experience with the UNICORN collection management system at the King's Fund Centre', *Program* **26** (2), 1992, 165–76.

37 John Scott Cree, 'UNICORN at the Department of Health', *Catalogue and index* 119, 1996, 6–8.

38 Chris M. West, 'Scrum Five: the Welsh universities' library system consortium', *SCONUL newsletter* 16, 1999, 11–15.

39 H. Knights, 'Our voyage into the future', *Vine* 116, 1999, 49–54.

40 Frank Edwards, 'Acquiring an acquisitions module: Croydon Libraries' solution', *Program* **32** (2), 1998, 95–105.

41 Juliet Leeves, 'Automation of ILL management system', *Interlending and document supply* **21** (3), 1993, 18–25; Stephen Prowse, 'Development of the interlibrary loans module for Aleph 500 at King's College London', *Program*, **34** (1), 2000, 75–87.

42 John Blunden-Ellis, 'A UK market survey of library automation vendors (January 1989–January1990)', *Program* **25** (2), 1991, 133–49. The comparable US survey was Frank R. Bridge, 'Automated system marketplace 1992', *Library journal* **117** (6), 1992, 58–72.

43   John Blunden-Ellis, 'A UK market survey of library automation vendors (1990–1991)', *Program* **26** (3), 1992, 291–305.

44   John Blunden-Ellis and Margaret E. Graham, 'A UK market survey of library automation vendors (1992–1993)', *Program* **28** (2), 1994, 109–24.

45   Marilyn Dover, *Issues in the use of library automation*. London: Library Information and Technology Centre, 1991.

46   Chris Batt, *Information technology in public libraries*. London: Library Association, 1998.

47   Richard Heseltine, 'New perspectives on library management systems: a Pilgrim's Progress', *Program* **28** (1), 1994, 53–61.

48   Robin Yeates, Library automation: the way forward, *Program* **30** (3), 1996, 239–53.

49   Ian R. Murray, 'Assessing the effect of new generation library management systems', *Program* **31** (4), 1997, 313–27.

50   Debby Raven, 'Library systems marketplace 2000', *Library Association record* **102** (1), 2000, 32–3.

51   John Akeroyd, 'Integrated library management systems: overview', *Vine* 115, 1999, 3–10.

52   Janet Stafford, 'Self issue – the management implications: the introduction of self-service at the University of Sunderland', *Program* **30** (4), 1996, 375–83.

53   Andrew McDonald and Janet Stafford (eds.), *Self-service in academic libraries: future or fallacy? Proceedings of of a conference organised by Information Services, University of Sunderland, in conjunction with SCONUL, held at St Peter's Campus, University of Sunderland, 24/26 June 1996.* Sunderland: University of Sunderland Press, 1997.

54   Noeleen Cookman, '3M self-issue terminal at Maidenhead Library', *Vine* 105, 1997, 20–3.

55   Sudell and Robinson, 'ALEPH 500'.

56   Lorcan Dempsey, Rosemary Russell and John Kirriemuir, 'Towards distributed library systems: Z39.50 in a European context', *Program* **30** (1), 1996, 1–22.

57   Verity Brack, 'Service developments at the RIDING Z39.50 gateway', *New review of information and library research* **5,** 1999, 135–44.

58   Philip Bryant, *Making the most of our libraries: the report of two studies on the retrospective conversion of library catalogues in the United Kingdom, and the need for a national strategy*. Boston Spa: British Library Research and Innovation Centre, 1997. Also available at <http://www.ukoln.ac.uk/services/papers/bl/blri053/> (accessed 5/7/05).

59   Shirley Cousins, 'COPAC: the new national OPAC service based on the CURL database', *Program* **31** (1), 1997, 1–21.

60   S. Enright, 'Update on the M25 consortium', *SCONUL newsletter* 16, 1999, 16–18.

61   Rob Froud, 'The benefit of Foursite: a public library consortium for library management systems', *Program* **33** (1), 1999, 1–14.

62   Ainsley C. Lewis, 'The use of PRINCE project management methodology in choosing a new library system at the University of Wales Bangor', *Program* **29** (3), 1995, 231–40.

63   Shirley Chambers and David Perrow, 'Introducing project management techniques at the Robinson Library, University of Newcastle', *Journal of librarianship and information science* **30** (4), 1998, 249–58.

64   Guenever Pachent, 'Network 95: choosing a third generation automated information system for Suffolk Libraries and Heritage', *Program* **30** (3), 1996, 213–28.

65   It changed its name to the Museums, Libraries and Archives Council in February 2004.

66   S. Fitzgerald and J. Flanagan, 'UNICORN at Kew: computerising the libraries and archives at the Royal Botanic Gardens Kew', *Program* **27** (4), 1993, 331–40.

67   Anne Morris and Hilary Dyer, *Human aspects of library automation.* 2nd ed. Aldershot: Gower, 1998.

68   Graeme A. Muirhead, 'Current requirements and future prospects for systems librarians', *Electronic library*, **12** (2), 1994, 97–107; Graeme Muirhead (ed.), *The systems librarian: the role of the systems manager.* London: Library Association, 1994.

69   Stephen Harper, 'Managing technostress in UK libraries: a realistic guide', *Ariadne* **25,** 2000. Available at <http://www.ariadne.ac.uk/issue25/technostress/> (accessed 14/1/06).

70   Hilary Dyer, Deborah Fossey and Kathryn McKee, 'The impact of automated library systems on job design and staffing structures', *Program,* **27** (1), 1993, 1–16; Rachel Daniels, 'Effects on non-professional staff of the implementation of computer-based library systems in college libraries: some case studies', *Program* **29** (1), 1995, 1–13.

71   Akeroyd, 'Integrated library management systems'.

28

Cataloguing

J. H. Bowman

The rules

At the start of the decade the 1988 edition of the *Anglo-American cataloguing rules*, 2nd edition (*AACR2*) was in use.[1] Amendments issued in late 1993 included various minor changes, among them a slight redefinition of the chief source of information, and the welcome abolition of the anomalous capitalization of the first word following an article in title main entries and series statements.[2] A further consolidated edition was issued in 1998 (actually 1999), incorporating changes which had occurred meanwhile.[3] Changes were made to prescribed sources of information for some materials, and the specification of particular kinds of illustration in printed books was made optional. An electronic hypertext version, known as *AACR2R-e*, became available on CD-ROM for the first time. As usual, Michael Gorman prepared a revised edition of his *Concise AACR2*.[4] Throughout the period the Library Association/British Library Committee on AACR2 continued to contribute to the revision process.[5]

As a result of the International Conference on the Principles and Future of Development of *AACR2* held at Toronto in 1997, Tom Delsey of the National Library of Canada used data modelling to provide a logical analysis of the principles of the code. This was reported in Britain in 1998.[6]

Special materials

In 1991 the results of a survey into rare book cataloguing were published.[7] They revealed a wide variety of practice regarding the MARC fields used for special information and in the ability of different systems to hold the information at all. Some new fields were introduced into the UKMARC format (see below, p. 473), and in 1997 the Rare Books Group of the Library Association published guidelines for cataloguing rare books.[8] The problems of cataloguing off-air videorecordings were discussed, with recommendations, by Turp in 1992.[9] In 2000 the Cataloguing and Classification Committee of ARLIS/UK & Ireland produced its *Art exhibition documentation in libraries*.[10]

The MARC format

At the start of the decade 71% of British libraries responding to a survey had a database of records in machine-readable form; this figure ranged from only 50% in colleges of further education to 100% in universities. The most widely used version of the MARC format was UKMARC, which was in use in about 50% of the libraries that had machine-readable records.[11] The British Library was the largest supplier of records, with 64 libraries of those surveyed, followed by BLCMP with 52. Sixteen libraries acquired records in USMARC format, and these were presumably chiefly those that had chosen American library management systems. One such was the National Library of Scotland, which had adopted the VTLS system and opted to have UKMARC records converted.[12] Many libraries, especially public, still felt that MARC was too detailed for their needs, and there was a fairly strong view that it was unsuitable for certain non-book materials.

The British Library expressed a desire to involve the user community more closely in the development of the MARC format, and issued a consultative paper on the future management and maintenance of the format; a report on the responses was published in 1992.[13] In October 1992, as a result of the survey of rare book cataloguing mentioned above, new fields, including 561 Provenance note, 563 Binding information note, 756 Fingerprint, and various others, were introduced. The National Bibliographic Service (NBS) also started a series of short pieces in its newsletter *Select*, giving examples of the ways in which different libraries used its records.[14] In 1993 the NBS published a free booklet, *Setting the record straight*, which was intended to explain the background, structure and uses of the MARC format, with particular reference to UKMARC. It went into a second and later a third edition.[15] Also in May 1993, at the request of the book trade, yet more fields were introduced, including 355 UK price, 358 Product information and 512 Detailed summary note, and certain other clarifications were made.[16] In 1996 the NBS issued a new (fourth) edition of the UKMARC manual, replacing that of 1990.[17]

The major question which occupied many years of the decade was that of 'harmonization', that is, the potential reconciliation of the differences between UKMARC and the North American versions of MARC. This began to be publicly discussed in 1995, when the British Library produced a background paper 'Towards a common MARC format' in preparation for an open meeting held at the Library Association.[18] It was recognized that the difference in formats was an obstacle to record-sharing, which was otherwise being made easier by advances in technology. Moreover, much of the complexity of the UKMARC format was no longer felt to be justifiable. The general feeling of the meeting was that harmonization should proceed.[19] Proposals for format amendment and for harmonization were issued in 1996, giving details of the changes that the British Library intended to make, and accompanied by a report from Richard Christophers on the features unique to UKMARC.[20] The response was extremely low (40 responses to 1,600 copies of the paper); most respondents were in favour of adopting most of the proposals, but there was a strong desire to retain the system-generated punctuation of UKMARC, and some unease at moving uniform title main entry to the 130 field and at the loss of the 248 field.[21] In late 1997 it was announced that the Library of Congress and the National Library of Canada had agreed on full harmonization (the format was renamed MARC 21 from 1999), and that agreement had been reached that no further divergence between them and UKMARC should be allowed, but it was recognized that it would not be possible for UKMARC to harmonize with them completely in the short term.[22] The British Library made minor changes to UKMARC to make it more compatible with MARC 21, and there matters rested until 1999, when Book Industry Communication presented a report on the subject.[23] It suggested three possible options: to continue using UKMARC, adopting MARC 21 fields where they did not conflict; to adopt a partially harmonized format, retaining some UKMARC features such as automatic generation of punctuation; or to abandon UKMARC and adopt MARC 21 entirely. Following this, the British Library started a new round of consultation, with the result to be announced in 2001. Meanwhile it published MARC conversion tables on CD-ROM to assist companies which needed to convert UKMARC to MARC 21 format.[24] Many libraries, seeing which way the wind was blowing, began to switch to MARC 21.

Some began to question the future of MARC altogether, particularly in view of other metadata schemas (see below, p. 485), and to ask whether it should be replaced by something else. Oddy, in her excellent book on the context of cataloguing, noted that MARC was used only within the library world, and that other systems were cut off from it.[25] She suggested that in the future SGML (standard generalized markup language) might take its place, but in fact this did not happen in the period under review. Hopkinson stressed the advantages of MARC, namely that it was based on an international standard, so that system designers knew what the expect; that it was not proprietary; that it allowed for variable-length fields; and not least that a very large number of MARC records were in existence.[26] He felt that it was at least secure for the foreseeable future.

The British national bibliography

From the end of 1991 responsibility for Cataloguing-in-Publication (CIP) records was passed from Book Data to J. Whitaker & Sons, and the British Library relinquished its remaining contribution. Although the records adhered to *AACR2* level 1, they were created in Whitakers' own format and converted. There were some differences in forms of name, and titles were capitalized according to Whitakers' own practice.[27] Capitalization was raised as a problem the following year, but certain other improvements were agreed on.[28] From 1991 a separate 'Forthcoming titles' sequence was introduced in *BNB*.[29] Some librarians were concerned about the deficiencies in CIP records in *BNB*, and others about the declining number of new books that actually contained a CIP record printed inside; the response from the British Library, that records for the latter continued to be available in the printed *BNB*, could hardly have been satisfactory.[30] In 1993 a survey of users' opinions of the CIP programme was undertaken, which revealed that the chief sources of irritation with the records were capitalization, names of publishers, and forms of name in headings.[31] These problems were solved in 1995 when the contract was moved from Whitakers to Bibliographic Data Services Limited of Dumfries. Records were then created to *AACR2* level 2 standard, with current Dewey numbers and LCSH; this contract was renewed in 1998.[32]

In 1992 a major consultative exercise began, to obtain customers' views on various aspects of the *BNB*.[33] Various other initiatives occurred. The publication of *BNB on CD-ROM* changed from quarterly to monthly from January 1993 with a view to improving its use as a selection tool.[34] A list of categories of publications excluded from *BNB* was published in 1993, and this was followed the next year by a code of service for the National Bibliographic Service.[35] In 1994 a new service, Catalogue Bridge, was started, which made it easier to transfer records into local systems.[36] One of the omissions introduced in 1988 in catalogue records for certain classes of material had been Place of publication, and this was finally restored from September 1993.[37] In celebratory mood, the British Library published a history of the *BNB* to 1973 (the year in which it had become part of the newly formed British Library).[38]

By the latter half of the decade a review of the nature and purpose of the national bibliography was being called for. National publishing output was continuing to rise yearly; publication was very much easier; and publication was taking place in a greater variety of formats, not least online. In 1997 a seminar was held to discuss these matters.[39] It was felt that a national bibliography was important, and that its production was one of the British Library's key responsibilities. It should continue to be available in printed form, but there was scope for cooperation with other libraries in producing supplementary listings, which might be available electronically. As a result of the seminar the British Library launched another consultation exercise.

An important aspect of MARC records in the national bibliography was their timeliness, and UKOLN (the UK Office for Library Networking, previously the Centre for Bibliographic Management) had been monitoring the availability of *BNB* MARC records since 1980. A rolling survey, involving academic and public libraries, reported the percentage of the UK imprint for which libraries were likely to find a *BNB* MARC record at the cataloguing stage and at ordering.[40] The 'hit rate' increased from an average of 84% in 1991 to 91% in 2000.[41] From 1996 to 1998 the survey was extended to examine records from other suppliers also: those included were Bibliographic Data Services, BLCMP, CURL, LASER, OCLC, SLS and Unity, as well as two CD-ROM services, Book Data's BookFind and Whitakers' BookBank. This survey was conducted at the ordering stage only. In most cases there was little difference between the academic and public library sectors. BLCMP and SLS had the highest hit rates, at 97% and 96% respectively, and this was accounted for by the fact that their databases contained records from a wide variety of sources.[42]

Cooperation

The Shared Cataloguing project, which had been running as a pilot since 1989, became permanent from the start of 1993. A collaborative project, it had been started as a result of the British Library's *Currency with coverage* proposals. The British Library was reluctantly forced to concede that the other copyright deposit libraries could contribute to its cataloguing and help meet its targets. The aim was to share the cataloguing of copyright deposit material between the British Library and the other deposit libraries on a 70 : 30 basis. The individual libraries set up 'fast cataloguing streams', to ensure the rapid processing of their legal deposit titles, with the intention that a record could appear in *BNB* as soon as the book was received at the British Library. Allocation of material was initially based on publishers' names but was subsequently changed to title.[43]

CILLA (the Co-operative of Indic Language Library Authorities) continued to be active, and in 1993 arranged for its database to be mounted by BLCMP.[44] Later it was the subject of a short historical review by its coordinator.[45]

In 1997 BLCMP launched a new service using EDI (electronic data interchange) whereby catalogue records could be transmitted at the same time as orders were fulfilled, so that when the new stock arrived a catalogue record would already be present in the local system. This was later named the Talis Cataloguing Service.[46]

A concern that arose in cooperative systems was that of quality and consistency. BLCMP commissioned the Centre for Bibliographic Management to perform a survey of its union catalogue, in order to establish what percentage of records found in the database was being edited, and to find out which were the main fields that needed editing, and the kinds of changes being made.[47] It was found that about 8 out of 10 records were used without editing, and that 19% of the edits concerned spelling and punctuation errors, transliteration differences, and mistakes in publication date, collation and title. Many of the edits were of Whitakers' records, to upgrade them to full *AACR2* standard. Some edits affected other libraries adversely. At LASER a specially written software package was implemented in 1994 in order to monitor the headings in the Viscount database, and henceforward all newly imported records would be automatically checked.[48] The QUALCAT project attempted to devise an expert system to select the best record from duplicates, and to develop a fully automated quality control package.[49]

By 1996 BLCMP was able to take advantage of the increasing use of the internet in libraries by allowing members to gain access to its central database via the internet instead of the previous dedicated line; twelve members were reported as having taken this up.[50] In a similar way the British Library offered web access to BLAISE-LINE.[51]

Occasionally there was a move away from cooperatives as libraries switched systems. Birmingham Libraries, for example, left BLCMP in 1993 and chose DS Galaxy 2000 as their management system.[52]

OPACs (online public access catalogues)

At the beginning of the decade, academic libraries far outpassed public in their provision of OPACs for users. A survey of the former in 1992 found that 82 out of 104 respondents had an OPAC of some kind; 75 of these were using commercial systems, and 7 in-house software.[53] A survey of public libraries in 1991 revealed a variety of physical formats for catalogues, the majority being either microfiche or microfilm. Out of 167 library authorities 56 had OPACs available to the public, with a further 71 having online catalogues available to staff only.[54] Contrasting this with the situation in academic libraries, Batt noted the differing priorities of the two sectors, but predicted that the number of authorities with OPACs would inevitably increase. By 1997 his results had indeed changed, and not merely in this respect.[55] Interest had shifted from catalogues to the internet, and the major concern was how to make the catalogue available via the web, rather than about the nature of its search engine. The number of OPACs had risen to 143, with still a further 40 for staff use only. Fiche and film had fallen from 85 to 46, and hard copy from 31 to 16 (these were presumably chiefly card catalogues, but the survey does not differentiate between these and possible printed catalogues or computer print-outs). A more extensive survey by the British Library in 1993 showed that out of 3,007 libraries only 318 had catalogues on microfiche, of which 194 were public and 57 university libraries.[56]

Throughout the decade, there were many discussions of OPACs and attempts to predict their future.[57] Batt reported on a conference entitled OPAC 2000 which had been held in November 1990.[58] Generally it was felt that development since the mid-1980s had been disappointing, and there was no reason to believe that it would be any more rapid in the years to come. This view was to a great extent borne out by reality.

The early user interface was based on text and menus, from which the user chose by entering a letter or number, but in the early 1990s some work was done towards introducing a graphical user interface. At the University of Huddersfield a prototype interface was developed for an Apple Macintosh.[59] Sirsi introduced a 'ring menu' on their Unicorn system, which allowed users to use the Tab key to circulate round a list of options before pressing Enter to choose one.[60] INNOPAC, from Innovative Interfaces Inc., was noteworthy for not requiring the user to press Enter; pressing the appropriate letter or number from the menu sufficed. On the whole, though, there was little progress or change in interface until the arrival of the web OPAC.

The search options were fairly standard across different systems, most providing searching by author, title, keyword, class-number and control number; the author/title combination was also quite widespread.[61] Some systems provided specific searches for series, corporate name, and conference name, and occasionally even publisher was found. Special formats required special access points. Maps, for example, would ideally be provided with the facility for searching by geographic coordinates, though this was not envisaged as being feasible at the British Library.[62]

The exact meaning of keyword access was not always clear, but in many cases it provided the first attempt at any kind of subject access apart from using the classification scheme. If subject access was provided specifically it was mainly by the use of subject headings. In the early years of the decade there was considerable interest in development, following on from the Okapi project at the Polytechnic of Central London. SLS (Information Systems) Ltd was probably the only supplier to incorporate any features from that project, and its system LIBERTAS employed quite sophisticated ranking systems.[63] There was little sign that the project had much effect elsewhere. Another early feature was the tendency to mount locally-produced subject indexes on commercial OPAC systems. Many libraries had computerized their subject indexes long before having OPACs, and were reluctant to discard them. A survey in early 1990 found that nine academic libraries had in-house subject indexes on their OPACs, and it is likely that many more still had quite independent indexes.[64] Ratcliffe, while admitting the great value of subject access to undergraduates, questioned its utility among academics, who were usually looking for works that they already knew about.[65]

As use of OPACs increased, new ways were sought to increase the amount of information given to users. One of these was table of contents information, which, because it was not compulsory in *AACR2*, did not appear as part of the catalogue record. From 1995 Blackwells' BookTOC (book table-of-contents) service became available via BLCMP; the information provided could be included in Keyword indexes to improve retrieval.[66] Nevertheless this did not seem to be taken up by many libraries. On the other hand, the facility to restrict searches by specifying date of publication, or physical format, became widespread.

Self-service assumed considerable importance in the face of increasing pressure on staff and, in academic libraries, increasing student numbers. From quite early on, provided that the OPAC was linked to an online circulation system, as was usually the case, it was possible for borrowers to examine their own records to see what they had on loan. The first addition to this was the facility to place reservations on items that were on loan, and this, first introduced by Geac in the 1980s, became common during the early 1990s. Nevertheless it was by no means universal, partly because libraries feared that they would be overwhelmed with reservations. Matters requiring policy decisions included: whether to issue every borrower with a PIN (personal identification number); whether to permit a reservation if some copies were purportedly not on loan; whether to allow borrowers to have items recalled. At multi-site libraries there were further questions, relating to inter-site requests and transit.[67] Occasionally a library would try to implement some other self-service function via the OPAC: Bradford University Library, for example, allowed self-service issue and renewal on a URICA system, but this was very unusual.[68]

Most OPACs in academic libraries offered so-called 'reading lists', by tagging records so as to allow users to search by course code or lecturer's name. What was never stated at the time, though acknowledged later, was that these lists could only ever include individually catalogued items. They therefore did not include periodical articles, or any works which were not in stock. It was not till the end of the decade that this problem began to be solved by the introduction of new systems. At Loughborough, for example, a special project began, which used open source software to develop something that could properly be called a reading list system.[69]

Prior to the general development of institutional and library websites, some institutions used their library OPACs to include some basic elements of campus information. Sometimes a library included non-standard material in the OPAC. It was unusual to include individual periodical articles, or cuttings, but this became possible with some systems, for example CAIRS, used at the Chartered Insurance Institute.[70] At Sandwell Community Library the OPAC was used to publish creative writing.[71]

A recurrent problem throughout most of the decade was that of the effect of using an OPAC externally, rather than within the library, and with the increasing use of the internet this became more acute. Thomas drew attention to the problems, which related particularly to terminal emulation and the resultant discrepancy between the key that the user pressed and its effect on the host system.[72] Difficulties with the backspace key and the function keys were frequent, with the result that some OPACs were almost unusable outside their own library. Many systems also required passwords, but gave no information about how to obtain them; others made it impossible to disconnect at the end of a session. These problems were not wholly resolved until the appearance of the web OPAC.

Research into OPACs continued, and the Okapi project, which had moved to City University in 1989, was developed further. It instituted a GUI project, which it was hoped would allow the partial superimposition of successive screens of information in windows, so that users would be able to see the steps of their search.[73] Robertson summarized the various projects which were active in 1997, all designed as search systems for users who were not expert searchers.[74] There is no evidence that the outcomes of these projects had any further effect on OPACs. As Hancock-Beaulieu pointed out in 1993, further development was dependent on collaboration with system suppliers, and they would act only if pressed to do so by information professionals.[75] Further development seems to have been cut short by the arrival of the web OPAC. Hancock-Beaulieu used transaction log analysis to examine subject-searching behaviour in public and academic libraries and recommended improved integration between the pre-coordinate and post-coordinate approaches.[76] The Bradford OPAC Project (BOPAC) tested a hierarchical record structure in order to display relationships between different manifestations of works.[77] Bowman looked at the ways in which seemingly minor features such as punctuation marks could drastically affect retrieval, and at the way in which the structure of personal and corporate headings could present difficulties.[78]

From the mid-1990s the world wide web became a very obvious presence, and users started to realize that they could find all kinds of information on it. It was therefore not long before web-accessible OPACs began to appear. Loughborough University was an early developer of such a system, in conjunction with their system supplier, BLCMP.[79] It was seen that in future it would be possible to provide hypertext links not only to other records within the catalogue but also to external sites. In 1996 six members of BLCMP were among the first university libraries to have their OPACs mounted on the world wide web.[80] By 1997 fifty members were either using or had chosen BLCMP's TalisWeb; these included ten public libraries using it on local intranets.[81] At the John Rylands University Library the normal terminals continued to be provided for users within the library, with the web catalogue available only to those outside, and this was the general pattern elsewhere also. The systems librarian there saw the web catalogue as 'the biggest breakthrough in library computing' and he was to be proved right.[82] Web catalogues started with all the functionality of terminal-based OPACs, but provided the added advantages of being to 'cut and paste' information from the OPAC into other applications, and being able to 'bookmark' favourite pages. It was also easier to integrate the OPAC into the institution's general website, including its corporate identity, and it became possible to provide links to external resources of all kinds. The Royal Postgraduate Medical School Library launched its web catalogue using Sirsi's Unicorn system in April 1997.[83] Links were provided to electronic journals, which were very important, and to external sources. Among public libraries the first authority to have a web catalogue was Hertfordshire, and this was followed in late 1997 by Suffolk, which, unlike Hertfordshire, allowed users to find out when material was due back, and to reserve it if desired.[84] Babu and O'Brien examined web catalogues from six major system suppliers and provide a useful summary of the state of affairs towards the end of the 1990s, including the range of access points.[85]

During the following years the web interface spread rapidly, so that by the end of the decade it was in the majority. Figures taken from the lists of higher education institutions having OPACs available via the internet are as follows:[86]

	1998	1999	2000
Telnet access	70	58	46
Web access	29	53	71

The spread of web catalogues facilitated, though it did not necessarily begin, the cataloguing of materials that were accessible only via the internet. Napier University was an early exponent of this, and recognized that it would have to be done using *AACR2* and MARC.[87] Questions to be resolved related to the level at which material was be catalogued ('granularity'), seriality, currency, and restrictions on access. Another project was CATRIONA (Cataloguing and Retrieval of Information Over Networks Applications), which was carried out at Strathclyde University Library.[88] Later many 'gateways' were developed, which provided access to full catalogue records for selected electronic resources. The advent of the internet also provided cataloguers with many more sources of information when cataloguing.[89]

The British Library's own OPAC became available in the reading rooms in autumn 1993, and on a trial basis to those libraries which were part of JANET (the Joint Academic Network) from April 1994. Special client software was required, and this gave users the same interface as they would see in the reading rooms.[90] The initial one-year trial was extended for a second year.[91] A report, however, indicated that it was not being as widely used as hoped, and questioned its continued economic viability. It was suggested that the special features might be removed, and the OPAC made available via JANET in the normal way.[92] In the event this is what happened, for in 1997 it was superseded by the release of a web version, entitled OPAC 97. This was a free service available to all, and had a quite different interface.[93] Development of the interface took account of users' comments on the previous one, in particular the cumbersome nature of the menu-driven system.[94] In 2000 OPAC 97 was in turn replaced by a new version called the British Library Public Catalogue, and this obtained sponsorship from the internet book company Amazon.[95]

In the latter part of the decade, much began to be heard about the ANSI/NISO information retrieval standard Z39.50-1995. This was a set of rules governing the ways in which two computers could interact with each other to exchange data. In effect, it allowed a user to perform a search without having to understand the search syntax that might be required by the system being searched. A second phase of the BOPAC project (BOPAC2) looked at the problems of handling sets of records from different databases.[96] In due course Z39.50 allowed the simultaneous searching of several different catalogues, and many such groupings grew up.[97] An early example of a Z39.50-compliant system was TINLib from IME, which had a Z39.50 interface from 1996.[98] By the end of the decade most systems would advertise that they were Z39.50-compliant. Nevertheless it was sometimes more effective to create a combined database, and this is what the Consortium of University Research Libraries (CURL) did when it launched its union catalogue, COPAC.[99] Anyone using the catalogue would have been struck by the number of duplicate records, and would have queried the effectiveness of the means described by Cousins to reduce them.[100] By the end of 2000 live links had enabled circulation data for seven of the member libraries to be incorporated.[101]

Some systems made efforts to make their OPACs more accessible to visually impaired people, and publicity was given to this in 1994, because the President of the Library Association, Gill Burrington, was herself partially sighted. The catalogue at the Royal National Institute for the Blind provided large print display on the screen, a voice synthesizer, a tape recorder, and the facility to print results out in braille.[102] Islington believed itself to be the first public library to offer screen magnification with speech enhancement on its OPACs in 1997.[103]

Non-roman scripts were a further problem, which needed to be tackled if libraries were to serve the whole of their local communities. At Liverpool Libraries an experimental Chinese OPAC was developed, but this remained separate from the main system, which could not handle Chinese characters.[104]

Retrospective conversion

To make the best use of OPACs it was necessary to convert old catalogues to electronic form, and a great deal of retrospective conversion, and in some cases recataloguing, therefore occurred throughout the period. The Library Information Technology Centre (LITC) published a very useful outline of the options available and the procedures involved, the choice being chiefly between in-house keyboarding and buying in machine-readable records.[105] A variety of keyboarding agencies existed, as did suppliers of records. The third possibility, scanning and conversion using optical character recognition (OCR) software, remained unsatisfactory and unproved until late in the period. Costs of conversion were always difficult to estimate because of the different methods and the number of variables, but in the late 1980s it was reckoned that the average cost per record could be about £2.[106] Ratcliffe questioned whether academic libraries were right to place so much emphasis on retrospective conversion; at Cambridge it was estimated that 80% of reader requirements rarely went back beyond twenty years.[107]

At the Ministry of Defence map library a project which seems to have consisted of recataloguing began in 1988 and by 1992 had covered about 40% of the maps.[108] Unlike most conversion projects, this involved examining each map anew, and entering 69 data elements for each map, to assist retrieval later. A team of 40 data entry staff was employed, in two shifts of 20 people, with two managers. Such a method was unusual.

At Lancaster University Library the cost of buying in records was felt to be unacceptable, and in 1990 the library therefore began a retrospective conversion project using *BNB* on CD-ROM; in 1993 the Library of Congress CDMARC was added. Unusually, the work was done by the ordinary staff, and the opportunity taken to improve their keyboarding competence. Experience related from other institutions convinced them that they should download only as many records as they could immediately edit, so as not to be left with a major tidying-up exercise later. By 1994 72% of the stock had a machine-readable record.[109]

At the National Library of Scotland conversion started in 1991 with serials, in order to integrate with the Scottish Academic Libraries Serials (SALSER) project; this included creation of check-in patterns for current subscriptions. By the end of 1993 almost 17,000 bibliographic records had been converted, and work then proceeded with records for books published from 1968. Legal deposit material was dealt with first, and 227,000 items had *BNB* cards, for which conversion was contracted out to North West Data Services, where records were matched against the British Library databases.[110] In due course the Union Catalogue of Books at the British Library's Document Supply Centre started to be converted, using Catalogue Bridge.[111] Funding was always a problem in achieving retrospective conversion, and Trinity College Dublin was lucky in twice securing large sums from an anonymous donor, which from 1992 onwards enabled them to convert some of their many catalogues. The records that required keyboarding were dealt with by Saztec of Ardrossan.[112] At the Tate Gallery Library, cards were divided between two companies, one of which operated on a double-keying principle.[113] Some libraries opted to send their records to OCLC Online Computer Library Center in Dublin, Ohio, whose database could be used as a source of records.[114] OCLC also dealt with the post-1920 catalogue from the Bodleian Library; this project lasted from July 1994 to May 1998.[115] Newman and Westhill Colleges in Birmingham proved the benefits of joining BLCMP by achieving a conversion rate of 41 items per hour and a hit rate of over 90% in the BLCMP database.[116]

Turning to the national scene, the *Report* of the Joint Funding Councils' Libraries Review Group (the 'Follett report') in 1993 included a recommendation that a study should be commissioned to establish whether a national retrospective conversion programme was justified.[117] In the event two studies were undertaken: one into higher education libraries by Russell Sweeney and Steven Prowse, and the other commissioned by the British Library Research and Innovation Centre and looking at a range of other kinds of library; the results of the two were published together.[118] An estimated 50 million catalogue records were awaiting conversion, but these represented a very much smaller number of actual titles. It was recommended that there should be a national strategy for converting them, and this view was supported by others.[119] Chapman summarized the reports, considered the local and national benefits of retrospective conversion and reviewed the literature on it to that point.[120] However, no strategy had been adopted by the time the Library and Information Commission published a further report, *Full disclosure*, in 1999.[121] This found that retrospective conversion was fragmented, and again included a recommendation for a national strategy; it was reckoned that a ten-year programme would convert 80% of the records in libraries and archives. This would assist with various government initiatives such as Lifelong Learning and the National Grid for Learning, which could not work effectively unless the contents of collections (including archives) were recorded. By this time it was estimated that about 28 million records remained to be converted in higher education libraries, 12 million in public and 9 million in other libraries; as before, the number of titles represented was far fewer.[122] The report's recommendations were discussed at a major conference, 'Under Development', which was held at the British Library in May 1999, with over 140 participants. The British Library then set up an initiative entitled Full Disclosure, with the intention of supporting and encouraging retrospective conversion.[123] Chapman put the problem of retrospective conversion into a broader cultural and international context, emphasizing its importance in relation to the nation's collective memory.[124]

Despite the lack of a national strategy, retrospective conversion projects continued to take place, usually with special short-term funding. Many of these involved special collections, such as the Durning-Lawrence collection at the University of London Library.[125] By the mid-1990s projects were often receiving funding from the Heritage Lottery Fund; one of the these was the Society of Genealogists.[126] In 1998 the Linen Hall Library in Belfast received funding for the computerization of its catalogues.[127]

Within the British Library itself, the conversion of the *British Library catalogue of printed books* (to 1975) was completed in 1991.[128] It had started in 1987 and was the third such attempt. The project had several unique features, including the many hierarchically structured headings, which, because it was a printed catalogue, were not repeated before each entry. Initially no one knew exactly how many records were in the catalogue, but after conversion it was discovered that there were over 100 different languages and that only 53% of the records were in English. It was decided to work from the published version of the catalogue, and not to attempt to incorporate corrections even when it was known that these were necessary. The contract was awarded to Saztec Europe and the work done in Scotland over a period of four years. A particular problem following the keyboarding was that of combining main and added entries: in the printed catalogue these could only be seen separately and they therefore had to be converted separately. Matching was done by computer, using shelfmarks, and this reduced the number of records by three million; nevertheless, 100,000 records still needed manual editing. Because they did not conform to *AACR2*, the converted catalogue records were left unintegrated into the British Library's other online catalogues. Initially the catalogue was made available via BLAISE-LINE.[129]

The British Library's map catalogues were also converted by keyboarding, this time by Access Innovations of New Mexico, under contract to Research Publications International (later Primary Source Media).[130] It was felt to be impossible to eradicate the inconsistencies present in the existing catalogues, though some could be solved by program afterwards. Although originally planned for 1994 the release of this catalogue on CD-ROM did not take place until 1999. It was intended that geographic area codes, taken from the Dewey Decimal Classification, could later be automatically inserted into each record in order to facilitate hierarchical searching.

In 2000 the conversion of the British Library's manuscripts catalogues was completed, following a three-year programme. This was one of the first retrospective conversion projects where optical scanning formed a significant part of the process.[131]

Authority control

Writing in 1993, Ní Chinnéide claimed to perceive a steady move away from authority control.[132] This was evidenced by the fact that the British Library's CIP records used headings which did not necessarily agree with those in the Library's Name Authority List. Further inconsistency was being introduced by many libraries' use of OCLC records. Tidying the records up became pointless, as new inconsistencies would keep appearing. Quite tellingly, Ní Chinnéide cites examples of four headings for the same author, where in every case if the cataloguer had simply used the form of name on the title-page there would have been no difficulty. The inconsistencies arose from adding full names and dates in a variety of different ways.

Hers was an isolated view, however, and authority control, which had never been very high on the agenda previously, began to assume considerable significance during the decade. In 1992 Pat Oddy presented a paper on authority control at the British Library,[133] and in 1993 the British Library and the Library of Congress agreed to work towards having a joint authority file, the Anglo-American Authority File. In the first instance this involved planning for the convergence of the British Library Name Authority List and the United States National Authority File, but it was recognized that full convergence would take many years.[134] Speaking in 1996, Danskin predicted that the final phase of creating the Anglo-American Authority File would be complete in 1999, but this proved not to be the case.[135] The British Library's Name Authority File, however, did become available by FTP in 1999.[136]

The demand for cataloguers

There was a perceived decline in the number of professional staff employed in libraries, and this had particularly affected cataloguers.[137] A survey conducted in 1994/95 found 160 cataloguing posts, offering a reasonable job market for cataloguers, though about 42% of posts were temporary.[138] A further survey compared the British situation with that of the United States and found some decline in both countries.[139] Nevertheless there was still a reasonable demand, and it would be premature to abandon teaching cataloguing. Indeed, the need for retrospective conversion revealed an apparent shortage of cataloguers towards the end of the decade.[140] Ratcliffe seemed to regret the passing of the days when academic cataloguers were all graduates, as he saw their replacement by technical staff.[141]

The perennial debate about whether cataloguing and classification should be taught was revived by Paul Burton, who felt that they were unnecessary. Naturally this provoked contradiction.[142] One correspondent pointed out that nowadays he was lucky if an applicant for a cataloguing job had spent as much as one afternoon studying *AACR*. A survey undertaken by the Cataloguing and Indexing Group in Scotland showed (erroneously) that only two departments were teaching cataloguing and classification as a compulsory course.[143] For those needing to learn, a revised edition of Hunter and Bakewell's standard textbook appeared.[144]

Metadata

By the middle of the decade, with the growth of material available on the world wide web, concerns were raised about its retrieval, and there was an increasing belief that existing cataloguing standards were inadequate for it. A possible solution was to incorporate metadata into the resource when it was created, so that search engines could more easily pick it up. Following a workshop which took place at Dublin, Ohio in 1995, a metadata element set called Dublin Core achieved widespread use. This provided for a core set of fifteen elements, mostly corresponding to elements of a catalogue record, which could be attached to electronic resources.[145] Despite hopeful prospects, there was no evidence that libraries were using such metadata either to create traditional catalogue records or to incorporate descriptions of electronic resources into their catalogues.

CIG activities

The Cataloguing & Indexing Group of the Library Association began to question its identity and name, but no change took place.[146] In 1993 it published a celebration of its existence and of its contribution to cataloguing and classification, and in 1999 Hunter reviewed its history.[147] It continued to hold an annual conference, alternately on its own or as part of the UmbrelLA conference of the parent body.

A user's view

It is rare for users to write about their experiences of catalogues, and an article by a university lecturer, dealing with the use of catalogues by students and academics studying English literature at Edinburgh University, was therefore noteworthy. 'Whatever the sophistication today of the catalogue which replaced the black guardbook volumes of the 1960s, it remains the single greatest challenge and stimulus to the student in English today at the outset of a reading career at University.'[148] Would he have said the same at the end of the decade?

Notes

1   *Anglo-American cataloguing rules*, 2nd ed., 1988 revision, ed. Michael Gorman and Paul W. Winkler. London: Library Association, 1988.

2   *Anglo-American cataloguing rules*, 2nd ed., 1988 revision. *Amendments 1993*. London: Library Association, 1993.

3   *Anglo-American cataloguing rules*, 2nd ed., 1998 revision. London: Library Association, 1998. Electronic version announced in *Library Association record* **100** (11), 1998, 572.

4   Michael Gorman, *The concise Anglo-American cataloguing rules 2nd edition: 1998 revision*. London: Library Association, 1999.

5   Lists of the members appear at the front of each edition of *AACR2*. A brief account of the committee's work also appears in *Catalogue & index* 130, winter 1998, 4–5.

6   Michael Heaney, 'Models, materials and moments: the model of AACR', *Catalogue & index* 129, autumn 1998, 1–3.

7   Ann Lennon and David Pearson, *Rare book cataloguing in the British Isles: results of a survey carried out on behalf of the Rare Books Group of the Library Association*. London: British Library, 1991 (British Library research paper; 94).

8   Library Association, Rare Books Group, *Guidelines for the cataloguing of rare books*. London: Rare Books Group, 1997.

9   Stephen Turp, 'Guidelines for cataloguing off-air videorecordings', *Audiovisual librarian* **18** (2), 1992, 94–112.

10   *Art exhibition documentation in libraries: cataloguing guidelines* compiled by the ARLIS/UK & Ireland Cataloguing and Classification Committee. [Bromsgrove]: ARLIS/UK & Ireland, 2000. There had been a previous edition in 1987 in draft form.

11   Russell Sweeney, *Survey on the use of UKMARC, 1991*, under the aegis of the Centre for Bibliographic Management, University of Bath. London: UBIS, [1991?].

12   Fred Guy, 'Record supply: experiences at the National Library of Scotland', *Catalogue & index* 108, summer 1993, 1 and 4–6.

13   'The UKMARC format', *Select* (*National Bibliographic Service newsletter*) 5, winter 1991, 3–4; Ross Bourne, 'UKMARC format: management and maintenance', *Select* 8, autumn/winter 1992, 6–7.

14   *Select* 8, autumn/winter 1992, 5 (Napier University); 10, summer 1993 (Staffordshire

County); 12, spring 1994 (Tameside); 13, autumn 1994 (Bury); 14, winter 1994/5, 6 (Lancashire County); 17, spring 1996, 6–7 (Birmingham).

15 British Library, National Bibliographic Service, *Setting the record straight: understanding the MARC format*. Boston Spa: British Library, 1993. 2nd ed., with subtitle *a guide to the MARC format*, by R. W. Hill, 1994. 3rd ed., by R. W. Hill, 1999. The 3rd ed. was also available electronically.

16 *UK MARC manual: amendments, changes and additions to the 3rd edition*. [Boston Spa: British Library, 1993].

17 *The UKMARC manual: a cataloguer's guide to the bibliographic format*, ed. A. E. Cunningham & B. P. Holt. Boston Spa: British Library, 1996.

18 *Towards a common MARC format: background paper for the open meeting being held at Library Association headquarters, Friday 21 July 1995*. [London?: British Library, 1995].

19 *Towards a common MARC format: proceedings of an open meeting held at the Library Association headquarters, London, 21 July 1995*. [Boston Spa?: British Library?, 1995].

20 British Library, National Bibliographic Service, *UKMARC format: format amendment proposals and harmonisation proposals*. Boston Spa: British Library, 1996; R. A. Christophers, *Report on the use of content designators in the UKMARC bibliographic format*. October 1995.

21 *MARC harmonisation: responses to the propositions outlined in the UKMARC consultative paper of 9 February 2006*. [Boston Spa]: British Library, 1996.

22 'Major milestone achieved towards MARC harmonisation', *Program* **31** (4), 1997, 383–4; Stuart Ede, 'LandMARC decision', *Select* 20, summer 1997, 3.

23 Book Industry Communication, Bibliographic Standards Technical Subgroup, *MARC harmonisation: a report to the British Library*. [London?: BCI], 1999; *Select* 28, summer 2000, 1–2; 29, winter 2000, 4.

24 *Library technology* **4** (3), 1999, 45.

25 Pat Oddy, *Future libraries, future catalogues*. London: Library Association, 1996, p. 165.

26 Alan Hopkinson, 'Traditional communication formats: MARC is far from dead', *International cataloguing and bibliographic control* **28** (1), 1999, 17–21.

27 *Select* 3, spring 1991; 4, summer 1991; 5, winter 1991.

28 Arthur Cunningham, 'Cataloguing-in-Publication: major review of progress', *Select* 8, autumn/winter 1992, 8–9.

29 Ibid.

30 M. R. Stallion, 'Cataloguing-in-Publication' (letter), *Library Association record* **93** (8), 1991, 517; Judy Powles, 'Cataloguing not in publication' (letter), *Library Association record* **94** (6), 1992, 381; response from Stuart Ede, *Library Association record* **94** (7), 1992, 449.

31 James Elliot, 'The British Library CIP programme: the 1993 survey results', *Select* 12, spring 1994, 10–11.

32 *Select* 16, autumn 1995, 3; *Select* 23, winter 1998, 6. A profile of BDS appeared in *Select* 28, summer 2000, 3–4.

33 *Select* 6, spring/summer 1992, 3.

34 *Select* 9, spring 1993, 1.

35 Ibid., 4–5; 12, spring 1994, 7.

36 *Select* 11, winter 1993, 3.

37   Ibid.
38   Andy Stephens, *The history of the British National Bibliography: 1950–1973.* Boston Spa: British Library, 1994.
39   Cynthia McKinley and Peter Robinson (eds.), *The future of the national bibliography: proceedings of a seminar held in June 1997.* Boston Spa: British Library, 1997.
40   Ann Chapman, 'Why MARC surveys are still a hot bibliographic currency', *Library Association record* **94** (4), 1992, 248–9, 253; Ann Chapman, 'National library bibliographic record availability: a long term survey', *Library resources and technical services* **39** (4), 1995, 345–57; Ann Chapman, '1994 revisited: a year in the life of the BNBMARC currency survey', *International cataloguing and bibliographic control* **26** (2), 1997, 41–6; Ann Chapman, 'Availability of bibliographic records for the UK imprint', *Journal of documentation* **55** (1), 1999, 6–15.
41   *BNB currency survey* [website]. Bath: UKOLN, 2005, <http://www.ukoln.ac.uk/bib-man/surveys/bnbmarc/> (accessed 10/8/05).
42   Ann Chapman, *Bibliographic record provision in the UK: measuring availability against demand.* Bath: UKOLN, 1998; Ann Chapman, 'Record supply for UK imprint', *Library Association record* **100** (7), 1998, 364–5.
43   Frederick Ratcliffe, 'Sharing the burden, cataloguing legal deposit: a British project', *European research libraries cooperation* **1**, 1991, 2–14; *Select* 6, spring/summer 1992, 6; 8, autumn/winter 1992, 9; James Elliot, 'A decade of working together', *Select* 27, spring 2000, 2–4.
44   'CILLA joins forces with BLCMP', *Program* **27** (2), 1993, 204.
45   Ewa Lipniacka, 'Cilla', *Public library journal* **9** (2), 1994, 52–4.
46   *Program* **32** (4), 1997, 417; **34** (1), 105.
47   Ann Chapman, *Quality of bibliographic records in a shared cataloguing database: a case study using the BLCMP database.* [Bath]: Centre for Bibliographic Management, 1993; Ann Chapman, 'Up to standard? A study of the quality of records in a shared cataloguing database', *Journal of librarianship and information science* **26** (4), 1994, 201–10.
48   Martin Harrison, Frances Hendrix, Ewa Lipniacka, 'Quality and standards on the LASER database and use of a specially designed authority file', *Catalogue & index* 122, winter 1996, 6–7.
49   F. H. Ayres *et al.*, *QUALCAT: automation of quality control in cataloguing.* [London]: British Library Research and Development Department, 1994 (British Library research and development report; 6068).
50   *Program* **30** (3), 1996, 292.
51   *Program* **30** (4), 1996, 391.
52   Brian R. Gambles, 'Catalogue Bridge in Birmingham', *Select* 17, spring 1996, 6–7.
53   John C. Crawford, Linda C. Thom, John A. Powles, 'A survey of subject access in academic library catalogues in Great Britain', *Journal of librarianship and information science* **25** (2), 1993, 85–93.
54   Chris Batt, *Information technology in public libraries*, 4th ed. London: Library Association Publishing, 1992, p. 11.
55   Chris Batt, *Information technology in public libraries*, 6th ed. London: Library Association Publishing, 1998, p. 6.
56   *Select (National Bibliographic Service newsletter)* 14, winter 1994/5, 9.
57   See for example: 'Fourth OPAC forum', *Catalogue & index* 101/102, autumn/winter 1991, 9; 'OPAC forum 5', *Catalogue & index* 105/106, autumn/winter 1992, 12–13;

'OPAC forum 6', *Catalogue & index* 112, summer 1994, 10–11.

58   Chris Batt, 'OPAC 2000, or, The thoughts of chairman Batt', *ITs news* 23, Feb. 1991, 32–5. See also Mary Feeney, 'OPAC 2000', *Vine* 81, Dec. 1990, 4–14.

59   F. J. Murphy, A. S. Pollitt, P. R. White, *Matching OPAC user interfaces to user needs*. [Huddersfield]: Polytechnic of Huddersfield, 1991. (British Library R & D report; 6041).

60   'News from Sirsi', *Program* 25 (4), 1991, 383.

61   Crawford *et al.*, 'Survey of subject access', p. 88, list various options, but it is obvious that not all of them appeared as specific choices in as many cases as stated.

62   James D. Elliot, 'The use of OPACs (Online Public Access Catalogues) in map libraries', *European research libraries cooperation* 1, 1991, 169–74.

63   Leo Favret, 'OPACs today: the story so far', *ITs news* 31, March 1995, 22–9; Janet Kinsella, 'Classification and the OPAC', *Catalogue & index* 105/106, autumn/winter 1992, 1 and 3–10.

64   John C. Crawford and John A. Powles, 'In-house (locally generated) subject indexes mounted on academic OPACs', *Library review* 40 (1), 1991, 29–36.

65   Frederick W. Ratcliffe, 'Retrospective cataloguing: some afterthoughts', *Alexandria* 4 (1), 1992, 69–78, at p. 74.

66   *Program* 29 (4), 1995, 462. For a description of the system's operation in the US see Robert P. Holley, 'Blackwell North America's Table of Contents service', *ISBN review* 15, 1994, 55–66.

67   Jill Lambert, Judith Andrews, John McMullan, 'The implementation of a public reservation service in a multi-site academic library', *Program* 28 (4), Oct. 1994, 367–77.

68   Peter Ketley, 'Circulation functions within OPAC: self-issue and self-renewal at Bradford University Library', *Vine* 92, Sept. 1993, 7–11.

69   Gary Brewerton and Jon Knight, 'From local project to open source: a brief history of the Loughborough Online Reading List System (LORLS)', *Vine* 33 (4), 2003, 189–95.

70   Robert Cunnew, 'The analytic OPAC: incorporating a journal index in an online catalogue using CAIRS and AACR2', *Catalogue & index* 118, winter 1995, 1–5.

71   *Library Association record* 98 (4), 1996, 173.

72   David Thomas, 'Beyond the PAD>: a critical look at making OPACs accessible to end users', *UC&R newsletter* 33, 1991, 6–13.

73   Margaret Fieldhouse, 'OKAPI opens a new window on the world of OPACs', *ITs news* 28, Nov. 1993, 25–30.

74   S. E. Robertson, 'Overview of the Okapi projects', *Journal of documentation* 53 (1), 1997, 3–7.

75   Micheline Hancock-Beaulieu, 'Online catalogues: a review of the research programme in the UK', *ITs news* 26, 1993, 16–20.

76   Micheline Hancock-Beaulieu, Stephen Robertson, Colin Neilson, 'Evaluation of online catalogues: eliciting information from the user', *Information processing & management* 27 (5), 1991, 523–32; Micheline Hancock-Beaulieu, 'A comparative transaction log analysis of browsing and search formulation in online catalogues', *Program* 27 (3), 1993, 269–80.

77   F. H. Ayres, L. P. S. Nielsen, M. J. Ridley, 'Bibliographic management: a new approach using the manifestations concept and the Bradford OPAC', *Cataloging & classification quarterly* 22 (1), 1996, 3–28; F. H. Ayres, L. P. S. Nielsen, M. J. Ridley,

'Design and display issues for a manifestation-based catalogue at Bradford', *Program* **31** (2), 1997, 95–113.

78   J. H. Bowman, 'The catalog as barrier to retrieval. Part 1: Hyphens and ampersands in titles', *Cataloging & classification quarterly* **29** (4), 2000, 39–60; 'The catalog as barrier to retrieval. Part 2: Forms of name', *Cataloging & classification quarterly* **30** (4), 2000, 51–73.

79   John Arfield *et al.*, 'Developing a world-wide web OPAC', *Vine* 99, June 1995, 32–7.

80   *Program* **30** (3), 1996, 294.

81   *Program* **31** (3), 1997, 288.

82   Charlie Hulme, 'Implementing a world wide web OPAC: TalisWeb at the John Rylands University Library of Manchester', *ITs news* 34, Dec. 1996, 25–31.

83   Elizabeth Davis and Judith Stone, 'A painless route on to the web', *Library technology* **2** (4), 1997, 77–8; Elizabeth Davis and Judith Stone, 'From A to Z: automated catalogue to web OPAC and Z39.50', *Health libraries review* **15** (2), 1998, 128–32.

84   *Library Association record* **100** (1), 1998, 16.

85   B. Ramesh Babu and Ann O'Brien, 'Web OPAC interfaces: an overview', *Electronic library* **18** (5), 2000, 316–27.

86   These figures are based on the lists formerly shown on the NISS website at <http://www.niss.ac.uk> (accessed at various dates during those years). The variation in totals is due to increasing numbers of OPACs becoming available each year.

87   Paul Cunnea, 'Cataloguing the web or blowing in the wind? One library's experience', *Catalogue & index* 137, autumn 2000, 1–4.

88   Gordon Dunsire, 'CATRIONA: netting the cat and PACing the Net', *Catalogue & index* 115, spring 1995, 1–3; Dennis Nicholson *et al.*, *Cataloguing the internet: CATRIONA feasibility study*. London: British Library, Research & Development Dept., 1995; Mary Fletcher, 'The CATRIONA project: feasibility study and outcomes', *Program* **30** (2), 1996, 99–109.

89   Alan Poulter, 'The internet as a tool for descriptive cataloguing', *Cataloging & classification quarterly* **24** (1/2), 1997, 187–94; Gordon Dunsire, 'The internet as a tool for cataloguing and classification: a view from the UK', *Journal of internet cataloging* **2** (3/4), 2000, 187–95.

90   *Select (National Bibliographic Service newsletter)* 12, spring 1994, 1–2; 13, autumn 1994, 6–7.

91   *Select* 15, spring 1995, 1–2.

92   Margaret E. Graham, *Evaluation of the British Library Network OPAC in selected academic libraries*. [Newcastle-upon-Tyne: University of Northumbria], 1995.

93   John Lowery, 'OPAC 97 to be launched in May!', *Select* 19, spring 1997, 1; 'OPAC 97 hits the big time at Internet World', *Select* 20, summer 1997, 1–2.

94   Jan Ashton, 'Development of the British Library's OPAC 97: the value of a user-centred approach', *Program* **32** (1), 1998, 1–24.

95   *Select* 28, summer 2000, 5; *Program* **34** (3), 2000, 309.

96   F. H. Ayres, L. P. S. Nielsen, M. J. Ridley, 'BOPAC2: a new concept in OPAC design and bibliographic control', *Cataloging & classification quarterly* **28** (2), 1999, 17–44.

97   Robin Yeates, 'ZNavigator for information retrieval', *ITs news* 35, May 1997, 24–7; Margaret Merrick, 'Z39.50 and the virtual distributed catalogue', *Catalogue & index* 130, winter 1998, 1–4.

98   *Program* **30** (1), 1996, 76.

99   Shirley Cousins, 'COPAC: the new national OPAC service based on the CURL database', *Program* **31** (1), 1997, 1–21; Shirley Cousins, 'Virtual OPACs versus union database: two models of union catalogue provision', *Electronic library* **17** (2), 1999, 97–103.

100 Shirley Anne Cousins, 'Duplicate detection and record consolidation in large bibliographic databases: the COPAC database experience', *Journal of information science* **24** (4), 1998, 231–40.

101 *Curlnews*, Dec. 2000 <http://www.curl.ac.uk/members/curlnews/curlnews4.htm> (accessed 28/10/05).

102 Bernard Fleming, 'An accessible service', *Library Association record* **96** (12), 1994, 671.

103 *Library Association record* **99** (12), 1997, 637.

104 Alan Seatwo, 'Chinese OPAC in Liverpool public libraries', *New library world* **100** (1151), 1999, 254–64.

105 *Retrospective conversion and sources of bibliographic record supply: a review of the options.* London: LITC, 1992.

106 Ann Chapman, 'Retrospective catalogue conversion: a national study and a discussion based on selected literature', *Libri* **46** (1), 1996, 16–24, at p. 21.

107 Ratcliffe, 'Retrospective conversion', pp. 73, 76.

108 Murray Parkin, 'MODMAP: the automation of the UK Ministry of Defence Map Library card catalogue', *European research libraries cooperation* **3**, 1997, 67–75.

109 Ken Harrison and David Summers, 'Retrospective catalogue conversion at Lancaster University Library', *Program* **29** (2), April 1995, 107–22.

110 Anne Matheson, 'Scotland converted', *Select* (*National Bibliographic Service newsletter*) 12, spring 1994, 9.

111 Richard Thurlow, 'The state of the Union Catalogue', *Select* 22, spring 1998, 3–4.

112 Barbara McDonald, 'The Stella project: retrospective conversion at Trinity College Dublin', *Catalogue & index* 127, spring 1998, 1–5.

113 'Retrospective conversion at the Tate Gallery Library', *Catalogue & index* 136, summer 2000, 1–3.

114 For example, Guildhall Library, and Wellcome Institute, 'News from OCLC', *Program* **25** (2), 1991, 164–5; Queen's University Belfast, *Program* **26** (1), 1992, 80–1; Royal Botanic Gardens, Kew, *Program* **27** (2), 1993, 213; also the University of Essex and several institutions of the University of London, *OCLC newsletter* 222, July/Aug. 1996, 16.

115 *Library technology* **3** (3), 1998, 42.

116 'News from BLCMP', *Program* **27** (3), 1993, 295.

117 Joint Funding Councils' Libraries Review Group, *Report*. Bristol: HEFCE, 1993. Chairman Sir Brian Follett, p. 74.

118 Philip Bryant, *Making the most of our libraries: the report of two studies on the retrospective conversion of library catalogues in the United Kingdom, and the need for a national strategy*. Boston Spa: British Library Research and Innovation Centre, 1997. Also available at <http://www.ukoln.ac.uk/services/papers/bl/blri053/> (accessed 5/7/05).

119 Philip Bryant, Barry Bloomfield, Bernard Naylor, 'Sour grapes and cherry picking?', *Library Association record* **99** (7), 378, 380.

120 Ann Chapman, 'Retrospective catalogue conversion: a national study and a discussion based on selected literature', *Libri* **46** (1), 1996, 16–24.

121   Ann Chapman, Nicholas Kingsley, Lorcan Dempsey, *Full disclosure: releasing the value of library and archive collections* ... [London]: Library & Information Commission, 1999 (Library and Information Commission report; 10). Also available at: http://www.ukoln.ac.uk/services/lic/fulldisclosure/ (accessed 5/7/05).

122   Ibid., 4.

123   See British Library, *Full Disclosure* [website], [2004], at <http://www.bl.uk/about/cooperation/fdhome.html> (accessed 5/7/05).

124   Ann Chapman, 'Revealing the invisible: the need for retrospective conversion in the virtual future', *Alexandria* **12** (1), 2000, 33–43.

125   K. E. Attar, 'Durning-Lawrence online: benefits of a retrospective catalogue conversion project', *Libri* **53** (2), 2003, 142–8.

126   'Cataloguing the winners', *Library Association record* **98** (11), 549.

127   *Library Association record* **100** (10), 505.

128   See Pat Oddy, 'Managing retrospective catalogue conversion', *European research libraries cooperation* **1**, 1991, 15–24; Alan Danskin, 'The retrospective conversion of the British Library catalogue of printed books', *International cataloguing and bibliographic control* **26** (4), 1997, 90–1.

129   John Westmancoat, 'The British Library Catalogue goes live', *Select* (*National Bibliographic Service newsletter*) 8, autumn/winter 1992, 9.

130   Tony Campbell, 'Retroconversion of the British Library's map catalogues: the art of the possible', *European research libraries cooperation* **3**, 1993, 1–6; Tony Campbell, 'Conversion of the British Library's map catalogues: the keys to success', *INSPEL* **28** (1), 1994, 67–79.

131   'British Library manuscripts catalogues go online', *Program* **34** (3), 2000, 310–11; Rachel Stockdale, 'The retrospective conversion of the British Library manuscripts' catalogues: a description of the project', *Journal of the Society of Archivists* **21** (2), 2000, 199–213.

132   Caitríona Ní Chinnéide, '"A foolish consistency – ": the obsolescence of authority control in the online catalogue', *An leabharlann* 2nd ser. **9** (4), 1993, 99–117.

133   Pat Oddy, 'British Library catalogues: out of control?', *Catalogue & index* 107, spring 1993, 1, 3–5.

134   Alan Danskin, 'Better, faster, cheaper cataloguing!', *Select* 16, autumn 1995, 11; Alan Danskin, 'The Anglo-American Authority File: completion of phase 1', *Select* 17, spring 1996, 11; Alan Danskin, 'The Anglo-American Authority File: completion of phase 2', *Select* 20, summer 1997, 13.

135   Alan Danskin, 'International standards in authority data control: costs and benefits', paper delivered at 62nd IFLA General Conference, 1996. Available from: <http://www.ifla.org/IV/ifla62/62-dana.htm> (accessed 18/8/05).

136   *Select* 25, summer 1999, 4.

137   Melvyn Barnes, 'Will the last cataloguer to leave please turn out the light?, *Catalogue & index* 116, summer 1995, 4.

138   Mike Towsey, 'Does anyone out there want a cataloguer?', *Catalogue & index* 117, autmn 1995, 4–5.

139   Michael Towsey, 'Nice work if you can get it? A study of patterns and trends in cataloguing employment in the USA and the UK in the mid-1990s', *Cataloging & classification quarterly* **24** (1/2), 61–79.

140   'Cataloguing skills shortage: the next management consultants?', *Catalogue & index* 131, summer 1999, 11.

141 Ratcliffe, 'Retrospective conversion', p. 71.

142 Paul Burton, 'The decline and fall of "Cat. & Class."', *Catalogue & index* 124, summer 1997, 9; responses in *Catalogue & index* 125, autumn 1997, 8–9, and 126, winter 1997, 5.

143 Anne Ward, 'Cataloguing education' (letter), *Catalogue & index* 137, autumn 2000, 5. The departments were at Robert Gordon University and Liverpool John Moores; University College London should also have been included.

144 Eric J. Hunter and K. G. B. Bakewell, *Cataloguing*. 3rd ed. London: Library Association Publishing, 1991.

145 See *Dublin Core Metadata Initiative* <http://dublincore.org/> (accessed 7/10/05); Andy Powell, 'An idiot's guide to the Dublin Core', *New review of information networking* **3**, 1997, 157–64; Lorcan Dempsey and Rachel Heery, 'Metadata: a current view of practice and issues', *Journal of documentation* **54** (2), 1998, 145–72; Michael Gorman, 'Metadata or cataloguing? A false choice', *Journal of internet cataloging* **2** (1), 1999, 5–22.

146 Keith V. Trickey, 'The future of CIG', *Catalogue & index* 105/106, autumn/winter 1992, 2.

147 John Byford, Keith V. Trickey, Susi Woodhouse (eds.), *AACR, DDC, MARC and friends: the role of CIG in bibliographic control*. London: Library Association, 1993; Eric Hunter, 'The man with the oily rag meets the millen[n]ium: the life and times of CIG', *Catalogue & index* 134, winter 1999, 1–6.

148 Ian Campbell, 'A reader looks at the catalogue', *European research libraries cooperation* **1**, 1991, 86–98, p. 97.

29

Classification and subject organization and retrieval

Vanda Broughton

It is always difficult to paint a comprehensive picture of the state of classification and subject organization and retrieval in the United Kingdom because of the great variation in practice and in the range of tools and methods used. In comparison with descriptive cataloguing, where the standards of AACR and MARC are widely adhered to, there are any number of local, in-house and special classifications, thesauri and keyword lists, systems of subject headings, and, particularly in the corporate sector, locally devised taxonomies and other subject access tools. Nor is there any place where the classifications in use by UK institutions are systematically recorded, although, with the spread of web OPACs, it is becoming easier to determine what these are on an individual basis.

Nevertheless, it is possible to detect some general trends in the 1990s, and a number of the initiatives and projects described below reflect a desire to work towards common standards in the interest of more efficient information exchange. There was a tendency, led by the British Library, to move away from minority systems and to adopt one of the general schemes in wider use.

As a consequence, the UK's own systems of classification and subject indexing were increasingly abandoned in favour of the big US subject tools, namely Library of Congress Subject Headings, the Library of Congress Classification, and the Dewey Decimal Classification. It would be foolish to pretend that these were not already the dominant systems in the UK, but through the 1990s attempts to retain smaller (and possibly superior) British tools were regarded as counter-productive.

Given the enormous progress made in the theory of classification and subject indexing by British librarians over the preceding forty years this must be regretted, although much of the body of theory would later be taken up by other communities concerned with retrieval, particularly within the context of the world wide web.

Moves to bring the general systems of subject access closer together are also part of the trend towards uniformity, with some of the schemes looking to parallel content. Towards the end of the decade, the concept of mapping of systems on to each other, or on to a central control language, with a view to automatic switching between headings and classmarks, found much favour.

Paralleling the spread of automation in libraries, another discernible trend is the increase in the use of word-based tools, such as thesauri and subject headings. With the burden of retrieval very much on the electronic catalogue with its easy keyword search facilities, the need for detailed shelf arrangement may be seen as less pressing than in the past, and the inadequacies of traditional bibliographic classifications more easily overlooked.

Beyond the confines of the managed electronic environment, concern was shown for the control and organization of digital resources on the world wide web. From a position early on, where classification was regarded as a suitable, and even a necessary, tool, the tendency was to favour other types of controlled vocabulary, primarily the thesaurus.

Classification at the British Library and National Bibliographic Service, and in collections generally

The 1990s saw a number of changes in the arrangements for subject access at the BL in all of the three relevant areas: the physical organization of open access collections; subject description on BNBMARC records; and subject indexing of the *British national bibliography*.

In 1991 a decision was made to replace PRECIS in the *BNB* with a new system of subject headings, COMPASS (COMPuter Aided Subject System), 'a simplified restructuring of PRECIS designed to provide cost-effective subject collocation ...'.[1] The increase in the use of online bibliographic services, where all parts of a record could be searched simultaneously, reduced the need to duplicate information in the descriptive and subject fields (as was necessary in the hard copy *BNB* with its separate author/title and subject indexes). Consequently, subject strings were made much shorter, some of the conceptual categories of PRECIS were abandoned, and geographic elements of the description were treated independently, as were the names of persons as subjects.[2] COMPASS remained in place in the *BNB* until the end of 1996 when it was abandoned in favour of LCSH.[3]

LCSH had been included on BNBMARC records from 1971, but the practice ceased in 1987 as part of wider measures to reduce the cost of record creation. The decision was unpopular and there were 'persistent demands for the reinstatement of Library of Congress Subject Headings'.[4] They were reintroduced after a detailed customer survey of subject systems, and from October 1994 were added to all BNBMARC records except those for serials, juvenile material, fiction and short stories, all of these categories except fiction being added by late 1995.[5] From January 1997, genre fiction headings were added to fiction records, using the *Guidelines on subject access to individual works of fiction, drama, etc.*[6] The expectation was that the BL would become more involved in the development of the headings as a partner in the Subject Authority Cooperative Program (SACO Program) and be able to exert influence on their future direction. The first heading contributed by BL to the LCSH file was 'Luminescent probes', and the first specifically British heading was for the Ring ouzel, a bird unknown in America.[7]

In January 1997, LCSH replaced COMPASS as the controlled vocabulary for the *BNB*. It is clear that there was some opposition to this move. MacEwan states: 'It has been suggested that following this path effectively means the end of our involvement in development work on the principles and practice of subject indexing.'[8] Nevertheless, economic factors and a strategic commitment to greater cooperation combined to make the adoption of LCSH advantageous to the Library. Not least of these advantages was the potential for retrospective addition of LCSH to BL records to fill the gap left from 1987 to 1995.[9] The need for a shared subject cataloguing standard seems to have been primary. MacEwan says that 'Precis or COMPASS or some other alternative might have been (or have become) better systems, but they are not in wide enough use to be the basis for a shared standard in the developing context of cooperation'.[10]

Research carried out at the Department of Information and Library Studies at Aberystwyth into subject access in OPACs suggested that PRECIS would indeed outperform LCSH.[11] A large number of search queries collected from a public library and a polytechnic library were matched against DDC, PRECIS and LCSH to determine the extent to which the natural language could be matched by the indexing language. DDC was generally too broad to match the subjects of enquiries, achieving only 33% correspondence; LCSH doubled this at 68% matching, but PRECIS was able to represent 88% of the enquiries exactly,[12] and 'if the language [PRECIS] had been applied to its fullest potential, it would have been possible to achieve an exact match between practically every enquiry and its indexed surrogate'.[13] However, the strong claims of LCSH are recognized and 'given the dominance of LCSH for subject indexing in libraries it seems likely that this will be seen as the most appropriate mechanism ...'.[14]

Another major factor was undoubtedly the spread of LCSH in UK academic libraries during the previous ten years. A survey conducted by the BL in 1992 to assess the need for LCSH data showed that 25% of respondents used LCSH, compared to 13% using COMPASS; 60% of university libraries used LCSH, and 35% of polytechnics.[15] When, in 1993, the National Bibliographic Service carried out a survey of subject access to BNBMARC records, 91 library systems were known to be using LCSH, 'and the majority of these were larger academic/research libraries'.[16] A survey of subject access to academic library catalogues in the same year suggests that usage of LCSH was rather lower, with only 17 out of 86 libraries surveyed applying it, although admittedly this may be misleading, as 'Thirty-two libraries achieve subject access by using the MARC fields 645–691 on published bibliographic records', and it seems likely that at least some of these data were LCSH.[17]

Although a number of projects examined various aspects of the OPAC, few of these considered subject searching. In addition to those already mentioned which looked at use of particular controlled languages in indexing, one exercise used search logs to determine user strategies and evaluated the provision of online help for subject searches.[18] It appears that despite the widespread application of subject headings, their use was far from intuitive. The author concluded that:

Use of subject headings is quite difficult for the user. They are not used to framing their requests in the controlled vocabulary required to match with subject headings. Very few OPACs have online subject indexes, and, as yet, no British OPAC has an online thesaurus, so users do not have access to the correct subject terminology while online.[19]

A workshop organized by the National Bibliographic Service in November 1992 looked at the use of various standards in libraries and bibliographic work, including those for subject access. A keynote paper addressed problems of usability, reviewed the subject standards currently in use, and made recommendations for the future.[20] It was proposed that various simplified systems of subject organization had failed the user, and that classification in conjunction with new technology, particularly intelligent OPACs, would help to improve subject retrieval. Faceted systems were an appropriate tool for this, as they had the potential to advance subject searching, and the speaker hoped that UDC and BC2 data could be added to BNBMARC records, and that DDC would continue to develop its analytico-synthetic features. The Library of Congress Classification and LCSH were regarded as inappropriate for online searching.

The speaker concluded his presentation with the observation that:

> The FID International Study Conference on Classification Research for Knowledge Representation and Organisation in Toronto in 1991 included 54 delegates from ten countries. It appears that only seven of the participants were not North American. Given the strength of interest in classification and the scale of knowledge about it in the UK, it was sad to see how little of that knowledge was presented at the conference.[21]

Working groups at the workshop considered this keynote paper, and their responses were interesting. They generally were of the opinion that the existing standards were sufficient, and that work should concentrate on the development of technology to support advanced searching. One group felt that future cataloguing codes should include guidelines for the structure of subject data as well as for description and access points. They were agreed that 'classification still has an important part to play, both as a switching language to enable interrogation ... in a range of languages, and also for use in more sophisticated OPACs such as Okapi where it is an invaluable element in relevancy feedback'.[22]

However, the notion that LCSH might be quietly abandoned did not meet with approval. One group thought that LCSH might be 'a *terrible* system', but it was too widespread to ignore, while another reported that 'a survey of users had shown that for sound economic reasons, alternatives could simply not be entertained'.[23]

With the now almost universal use of automation, a desire for standardization and uniformity in the interests of bibliographic data exchange was evident. While this could never approach the consistency of practice of descriptive cataloguing (because of the proliferation of different controlled vocabularies for subject description) the domination of a few large international systems of subject access was to be the norm from the mid-1990s onwards.

Hence, at least part of the purpose of adopting LCSH was to enable greater cooperation with international partners in addition to the Library of Congress. The British Library was a partner in CoBRA (Computerised Bibliographic Record Actions) funded by the European Commission from 1996 to 1999.[24] Among other activities, the BL worked in cooperation with other European national libraries through the Multilingual Subject Access Working Group to investigate the mapping of LCSH on to European systems of subject headings.[25] Using Theatre and Sport as the test areas, the group demonstrated that a high level of equivalence links could be established between LCSH and the French RAMEAU (*Répertoire d'autorité-matière encyclopédique et alphabétique unifié*) and German SWD (*Schlagwortnormdatei*) systems of headings.[26]

It had been decided to use Dewey in the open access collections at St Pancras more than twenty years before the reading rooms there opened.[27] A working party set up in 1972 to look at how the different classification and indexing systems in use throughout the various parts of the British Library could be rationalized recommended that 'the PRECIS system can adequately provide for the continuation of the Subject Index' and that 'the Dewey Classification should be accepted as the favoured classification scheme, insofar as a single scheme proves to be necessary'.[28] In 1990, Russell Sweeney, then the British representative on the DDC Editorial Policy Committee and chair of the Library Association DDC Committee (LADDCC), was asked to investigate how DDC might be implemented, with particular reference to the level of application, the choice between options, and the need for any local modifications.[29]

The report was discussed by the Library's Committee of Directors in April 1991 and they 'endorsed the report and accepted Dewey as a suitable system for the relevant open access collections at St Pancras', although it does not seem as if there were any other candidate classifications.[30] It was agreed that DDC numbers should be restricted to six digits, and that the option of collocating bibliographies with the subject should be adopted. Making Great Britain first in the filing sequence of places was an option not taken up. The books in the General Humanities Reading Room, as well as those in the Rare Books and Music Reading Rooms, were reclassified to DDC for the opening of the new building.[31]

The 21st edition of DDC was published in July 1996, and was implemented at the British Library in December of that year, appearing in the *BNB* in January of 1997.[32] Workshops on the new edition were run by members of the LADDCC at several places in the UK, and as a consequence a number of comments and responses were passed back to the Editors and the EPC.[33] 1996 also saw the publication of *Dewey for Windows*, the CD-ROM version of the 21st edition, which introduced such features as multiple views and drag and drop facilities for number building.[34] By 2000 *Dewey for Windows* had incorporated a number of additional features including mapping of LCSH on to DC21 numbers, a mechanism for building Cutter numbers, and the inclusion of synthesized classmarks based on the 1,000 most frequently used built numbers on WorldCat.[35]

Throughout the 1990s the LADDCC continued to receive and comment on proposed changes to the DDC. A more substantial contribution to the development of the scheme occurred in the radical revision of the life sciences schedules for the 21st edition, when Ross Trotter of the British Library was invited to be guest editor.[36] The life sciences schedules had been seen to be in need of radical revision as far back as the 1970s when the distinction between process biology and descriptive biology was so far advanced that the subordination of all documents to the organism studied created substantial difficulties in the application of the scheme.[37] A revision of process biology submitted to the EPC in 1974 was rejected by the LADDCC on the grounds that it did not go far enough. Subsequent independent work by the groups on each side of the Atlantic produced two drafts with 'huge and irreconcilable differences between them', too great to be addressed in time for the 20th edition.[38] In 1993 the newly appointed Editor, Joan Mitchell, visited the UK to speak about the scheme and to establish connections with interested UK parties. Out of this visit came the idea to invite Ross Trotter to guest edit the revision of life sciences, and to ensure the input of the UK DDC community. The reconciliation of differences required much detailed work, both in Washington and in the UK, in establishing literary warrant, drafting versions, and in comparing the notation of DDC20 and the proposed DDC21. 'The life sciences were discussed at the May 1994 EPC meeting ... It was an historic moment when the Committee unanimously agreed to accept the new schedules for inclusion in the 21st edition.'[39] Other work included revision of the taxonomic schedules, during which specific numbers were newly created for lions, tigers and wolves, there were 'spot expansions' for birds, bats and monkeys, and worms and worm-like animals were relocated to a more comfortable position.

Otherwise, British involvement in the general schemes was with the second edition of the *Bliss bibliographic classification*, and, from 1993 onwards, with the *Universal decimal classification*, when Dr I. C. McIlwaine became the Editor-in-chief of that scheme.

The Bliss bibliographic classification 2nd edition
The excellence of the schedules so far developed was testified to when BC2 was a contender for the classification of the stock at the new Bibliothèque nationale de France, although ultimately DDC was the chosen scheme.[40]

Work continued on further new schedules for BC2, and the 1990s were a particularly productive period, with a number of important main classes being published. These included:

A/AL	Philosophy and logic (1991)[41]
AM/AX	Mathematics, Statistics and probability (1993)[42]
Q	Social welfare 3rd edition (1994)[43]
R	Politics and public administration (1996)[44]
S	Law (1996)[45]
AY/B	General science and physics (1999)[46]

The classification of Mathematics, which was developed under a grant from the John C. Cohen Foundation, presented some interesting and previously unencountered problems of analysis, requiring innovative solutions. These largely arose from the complexity and abstract nature of the subject's terminology, and also from the radical nature of the mathematical classification in BC2.

> All existing classifications of mathematics plunge straight into an enumeration of branches and disciplines, to which all concepts are subordinated. ... BC2, on the other hand, has extracted from the various branches and disciplines a more or less complete vocabulary of mathematical operations, processes, properties, elements, etc. and organized them as rigorously as possible into reasonably well-defined categories.[47]

Difficulties relate to the structure of the subject, for example 'In most subjects, there is a substantial body of literature relating to all the facets independently ... This is not the case in mathematics',[48] and to the use of terminology, 'The verbal form may give a misleading impression of the hierarchical relations', and 'the terminology often leaves a key term unstated'.[49]

Nevertheless the facet-analytical methodology proved equal to the task and a fully faceted classification was constructed. Of interest is the introduction of a fundamental category unique to Class AM/AX, that of 'Relations' which is used to accommodate concepts such as functions, equations, homomorphisms, and so on, which conceptually lie somewhere between 'processes' and 'properties'.

On a more practical level, a number of libraries adopted BC2 during this period.[50] Of some significance for the development of the classification was its take-up by several Cambridge libraries, and the formation of a Cambridge Bliss user group, CamBUG, which met for the first time on the 23 March 1995.[51]

BC had been used in a small number of Cambridge collections for some years: Fitzwilliam and Queens' were already using BC2, Queens' having begun reclassification in 1988.[52] The Haddon Library (the Faculty library for Archaeology and Anthropology) used Bliss's original scheme, but also began to convert to BC2 at an early stage, the anthropology part of the collection being completed in 1988.[53] The second edition was now to be adopted by more college libraries, including the Sidney Sussex College library, and the Quincentenary Library at Jesus College, where work began on reclassification in January 1996.[54] One advantage of the larger user base in Cambridge was the availability of online BC2 data, since 'All Bliss libraries contribute[d] to the Cambridge Union', the first time that anyone had been able to access records with BC2 classmarks attached.[55]

CamBUG worked actively on schedule development producing a number of advanced draft schedules for subjects such as history and literature, archaeology, and the earth sciences.[56]

Outside Cambridge, BC2 was adopted by the National Society for the Prevention of Cruelty to Children library in 1994, the Merseyside Probation Service library in 1995, Alcohol Concern's library in 1997, and the National Autistic Society library in 1998.[57] Libraries which had used BC1 but which abandoned it in favour of another scheme during this period included Homerton College, Cambridge and Birkbeck College, London.[58] The Radzinowicz Library of criminology in Cambridge had used BC1 from its inception, but chose, for various reasons, not to reclassify to BC2.[59]

One major aspect of the work on BC2 was its influence on other systems, both in terms of the theoretical and structural principles underlying the scheme, and the detail and richness of the vocabulary.

The use of BC2 schedules and drafts as quarries for designers of other classifications and thesauri seems to be gaining ground. This is partly due to the invaluable publicity they receive from Jean Aitchison's excellent papers and books on problems of structured vocabularies. One example of this was a request for copies of schedules relevant to agriculture, biochemistry, etc., from the National Agricultural Library in the USA. The NAL is cooperating with FAO and CAB International (Commonwealth Agricultural Bureaux) in developing a classified structure for two major thesauri – CAB thesaurus and AGROVOC.[60]

The suitability of BC2 as a basis for conversion to a thesaurus was already established,[61] and during this time further BC2-based thesauri were developed, notably the Royal Institute of International Affairs thesaurus, which was built on the penultimate draft schedules for Class R Politics.[62]

A pilot project to investigate the use of the BC2 vocabularies in creating a fully faceted UDC is documented in a number of sources, and leads naturally into a discussion of that scheme.[63]

The Universal Decimal Classification

It should be emphasized that the UDC is very much an international classification, and its ruling body consists of members from across the world. Users from many different countries contribute to the ongoing development of the scheme, and the work described here represents the British contribution, and is only a part of the overall activity associated with UDC.

During the 1990s some major changes to the management of the UDC occurred. Responsibility for the scheme moved away from FID (Fédération internationale de documentation) and passed into the hands of the UDC Consortium, a body formed from the publishers of the scheme in Dutch, English, French, Japanese and Spanish, and which came into existence on 1st January 1992.[64] The British Standards Institution, publisher of the English Edition of UDC, was a founder member of the Consortium.[65] A separate editorial board was set up, replacing the existing Revision Advisory Group, and on which there were three UK representatives, including the editor of the English edition, Geoffrey Robinson.[66] Dr I. C. McIlwaine, of University College London, was invited to become the Editor-in-chief, thus paving the way for a major UK input into the development and future direction of the scheme.[67] In 1997 a part-time research assistant was appointed to work on the revision of the scheme, and in 1999 this post became full-time.[68]

A move towards a fully faceted structure for UDC had already been embarked upon with the revision of Class 8 Literature, and now the new Editor-in-chief made this policy explicit.[69] 'We are hoping to eliminate the spelling out of compound concepts and instead create a fully faceted classification, where every concept is expressed in simple terms ...'.[70] Plans were made for a radical re-structuring of the scheme using BC2 vocabularies as a basis for a faceted UDC accompanied by a thesaurus, the suitability of BC2 as a starting-point for such a venture having been already well demonstrated.

A proposal had already been aired as to how this might be carried out, using BC2 Class T (Economics) as the source vocabulary.[71] Discussions with the Editor of BC2, Jack Mills, led to the decision, at his suggestion, to base a pilot project on the recently revised Health sciences instead.[72] In May and June 1993 a preliminary investigation was carried out, in which the schedules were compared for content, schedule order and citation order, and notational problems were examined. The sub-discipline Dentistry was converted from BC2 to UDC format, and a thesaurus derived from the resulting schedule.[73] It was decided that the BC2 structure and citation order should be followed, but that the level of detail should remain at that currently used in UDC, and that the notation should be retained.[74] The outcome of the pilot was 'sufficiently promising to lead the UDC Consortium to enter into a formal agreement with the Bliss Classification Association',[75] and results were soon disseminated, including examples of the preliminary drafts of the new faceted schedules for Class 61.[76]

More limited, but nonetheless significant, arrangements were made with the Editor of Dewey with a view to achieving conformity of UDC and DDC, for example in the geographical tables.[77]

Revisions of a number of UDC classes were produced during the 1990s, including a substantial number of parts of Class 61, Medicine. Between 1993 and 1999 progress reports, proposals, amended drafts and finalized schedules were published for physiology, diseases and pathology of the gastro-intestinal, respiratory and cardiovascular systems (1995), curative medicine, pathology general, urogenital system (1996), health sciences, medical sciences general, health, hygiene and preventive medicine (1998), and clinical sciences and pathology (1999).[78]

Other substantial revisions published during the period include schedules for vertebrates in 1996, and the taxonomic classes of botany, navigation (which was revised and relocated in 629), the physiographic regions in the Area Table, and the Area Table for Germany in 1997.[79] An extended classification for the United Kingdom Area Table, reflecting changes in administrative divisions since 1983, was published in 1998,[80] and revised schedules for Religion, Tourism, Environmental Science, and Cinema appeared in 1999.[81] Further Area Table expansions were made for the USA in 2000, concerning which, 'part of its purpose was to render the notation for the USA fully hierarchic and searchable by truncation'.[82] Astronomy was also brought to an advanced state during this time,[83] under the direction Dr G. A. Wilkins, at the University of Exeter, with the help of a number of interested parties who constituted the 'Friends of UDC52'.[84]

The need for a new schedule for Class 2 Religion had been recognized for some time, and a draft revision had been developed. However, the Revision Advisory Group, although pleased with the general approach (which did much to address the criticisms of Christian bias in the scheme), were not happy with the notation, which made extensive use of apostrophe auxiliaries:[85]

> the proposal reduces Class 2 to a main table of religions, supplemented by two special auxiliaries, which themselves, at a number of junctures, are supplemented by special auxiliaries.[86]

Further work on the class, implementing the policy of a more faceted UDC, culminated in the publication of a completely faceted schedule in 1999.[87]

In addition to work on the main tables of UDC, much effort was put into the revision and development of the Auxiliary Tables. It had been noted in 1997 that 'The move towards a fully faceted UDC that resulted in the introduction of new common auxiliary tables for materials, –03, and personal characteristics, –05, in the 1970s, seems to have lost its momentum'.[88] The following year, the Editor-in-chief was able to report that 'work has concentrated on the auxiliary tables, and various approaches have been adopted to make their application more logical and standardized'.[89] An examination of the 'point-of-view' auxiliary, Table 1i, had revealed many anomalies in it, and a disparate collection of concepts embracing forms, persons, operations, and other categories. There was also 'a residue of terms which appear to belong to a general category of *properties*. This suggests that a systematic auxiliary needs to be provided for these, along the lines of those already existing for persons and materials'.[90] A draft proposal for such an auxiliary table was published in 1998,[91] and was immediately applied to the schedules for medicine, where 'the implementation improves the tables considerably, and some additional terms were discovered that are possible candidates for the properties table'.[92] The common auxiliary for time, Table 1g, was also the object of revision in order to remove a number of illogicalities in the table, and to address the odd notation used there.[93]

In addition to the production of new schedules, a major event in 1999 was the publication by the BSI of a new compact edition of UDC, the old Abridged Edition being long out of print.

> In 1997, acting on evidence of a certain demand for UDC in a cheaper and more concise form, BSI decided to produce a highly abridged version of UDC in the range 3–5,000 entries, with an introduction addressing those unfamiliar with classification, to be issued in paperback format and called the 'Pocket Edition'.[94]

This it was hoped to market to first-time users, and those who would find it helpful in non-traditional uses of classification, such as the organization of personal libraries, computer files, and object collections. A preliminary list of classes was mechanically extracted from the Master Reference File, based on notational length (3 digits for auxiliary tables, and 4 digits for main table numbers) but some substantial modification of this was necessary to correct unevenness, and provide an appropriate level of detail: 'enough to be serviceable but not so much as to be intimidating'.[95] Ultimately:

> Although to some extent one distorts the scheme to produce an abridgement at all, the basis of a sophisticated and very flexible indexing and retrieval language is still there, and its character and distinctive features still inform this abridged and simplified version.[96]

Having used the Pocket Edition for teaching during the last six years, I can testify to the fact that it has all the functionality of its progenitor, and that students are able to produce very complex and detailed classmarks for documents across the whole spectrum of subjects. Although sometimes the classmark lacks specificity, because of the highly synthetic nature of UDC exhaustivity presents no problems. Perhaps because of its limited size, which makes navigation of the vocabulary much easier, they seem to actively enjoy using it and testing the limits of its capacity to express complex subject content.

Classification research
The Classification Research Group (CRG) continued to meet, a highlight being the visit of Eric de Grolier to the meeting on 21 February 1992.[97] Most of its ongoing work centred on discussion of draft schedules of BC2.[98] The contribution of the CRG to the development of BC2 is testified to in the introduction to the newly revised class for general science and physics, published in 1999:

> we are pleased to acknowledge the valuable contribution made by friends and colleagues in the Classification Research Group. CRG discussions have been a constant help and stimulus in designing the schedules.[99]

It could be said that the emphasis on BC2 impeded the work of the Group in other directions. Undoubtedly, BC2 occupies the place of the new British classification which failed to come to fruition under the NATO grant in the 1960s, and this is one reason why it plays such a major part in the work of the CRG. The CRG had always sought to locate its work firmly within the realm of practical classification, and there can be no better focus for this than an actual scheme. But there was little effort to address the wider questions of subject organization and information retrieval encountered in a wired world, and at the end of 2000 the Group held a meeting devoted to defining its aims and objectives.[100] A particular concern was the lack of knowledge of classification theory, and the level of sophistication achieved by the LIS community, in the wider information world:

> It was agreed that there was a need to disseminate information about classification, and in particular faceted classification, to people who are now facing the problems of

knowledge organization, particularly those developing computerized systems.[101]

Although, as noted above, little attention was paid to subject searching in managed systems, one area of OPAC research that would prove fruitful, and which showed the influence of CRG methodology on computerized systems, was that conducted by Steven Pollitt and his colleagues at the Polytechnic of Huddersfield. In what was a very thorough piece initial piece of work, one of the OPAC functions investigated was that of Boolean searching.[102] The researchers tried several different approaches, and found them too complicated to deal with a search involving more than two terms. 'In looking for a simpler method that could nevertheless meet users' needs, [they] eventually adopted the approach used by Pollitt in MenUSE'.[103] The MenUSE system involved a graphical user interface in which all choices were made from menus, and that would later be adapted by Pollitt for his 'view-based searching' in which subject search terms would be selected and combined in the same way.

View-based searching used a system of successive filtering of searches, in which search terms could be added by the searcher to modify or refine searches. The innovative aspect of view-based searching was that terms, rather than being chosen by the searcher on an ad hoc basis, were selected from a controlled vocabulary displayed in a series of windows; each window represented a facet of the subject and consisted of all the concepts in that facet. Windows could be opened in any order and the search manipulated in an interactive manner. The interface devised was called HIBROWSE,[104] and it was first applied to an ORACLE held database of UK hotel information,[105] and later to European Community information.[106] The first substantial implementation and testing of the methodology was carried out under a British Library Research and Innovation Centre grant, using a HIBROWSE interface developed for searching the medical database EMBASE.[107]

In HIBROWSE systems the combination of faceted classification and relational databases provided a powerful retrieval tool that required no detailed knowledge on the part of the end-user of either the information architecture or the controlled vocabulary. By 1997 Pollitt was looking forward to its application in pre-coordinate mode, where it would retain 'the flexibility and retrieval power for the user to refer to values in facets without needing to be aware of facet sequencing', i.e. citation order.[108] He also envisaged the potential of view-based searching for OPACs:

> The OPAC will provide a superior means for browsing than could be provided in a physical arrangement of items on shelves. The arrangement can be dynamic and selective to suit the changing needs of the user. The role for classification remains, but its application can now be focused on issues of presentation at the user interface and mechanisms for searching the databases beneath it.[109]

In June 1997 University College London hosted the Sixth International Study Conference on Classification Research.[110] Forty years on from the enormously influential 'Dorking conference',[111] the 1997 conference was in part a celebration of classification research over that period, and the conference proceedings proper were accompanied by a published volume of seminal papers.[112] Thirty-five speakers from fourteen different countries gave a selection of papers on theoretical aspects of classification, indexing, the thesaurus, and information retrieval. The keynote address was given by Jack Mills, who spoke on the development of faceted classification, the continuing work of the Classification Research Group, and its contribution to the evolving methodology of schedule construction in BC2.

Classification and the internet
The question of how to respond to the increasing number of digital resources available through the world wide web became pressing in the mid 1990s. From a subject point of view, there were two aspects to the problem: the subject element of cataloguing web-published material for inclusion in catalogues, and the use of controlled vocabularies as organizing and retrieval tools for web resources in managed and unmanaged environments. The second of the two generated rather more discussion and investigation than the first.

The 1990s witnessed the first subject portals designed and managed for the UK higher education community under central government funding. At that time there was no question of organizing web-based resources other than with a conventional classification system, and nearly all of these early portals used some established system of subject access.

> Quality controlled subject services ... also understood that a browsing structure based on subject classification would be a desirable compliment [*sic*] to a search engine type service. Most subject services of this type, and almost all of the Electronic Libraries (eLib) Programme access to network resources service ... currently use a classification scheme which can be browsed.[113]

There were a number of British contributors to the DESIRE project deliverable which looked at the role of classification schemes in internet organization, including representatives of UKOLN and the Social Science Information Gateway, SOSIG. British internet services specifically examined in the study included BUBL (BUlletin Board for Libraries),[114] NISS (National Information Systems and Services),[115] OMNI (Online Medical Networked Information),[116] and SOSIG,[117] all of which used UDC (although BUBL later adopted Dewey instead), Biz/ed,[118] which used DDC, and EEVL (Edinburgh Engineering Virtual Library),[119] which employed an in-house system based on the Engineering Information (Ei) Classification Codes.

The linearity of the traditional bibliographic scheme was not thought to be a handicap. Staff at SOSIG, which employed a modified form of UDC, felt that 'One advantage of classifying internet resources is that you can assign more than one number to a resource, since they do not need to be put in numerical order on a shelf – they can be kept in two place[s] at once'. It was normally the case that only the broad structure of the classification was used (some systems opting just to use the first three digits of classes in the decimal schemes), and the classmarks or other classification codes were usually not evident to the end-user.

A survey of cataloguing and classification of internet material carried out in 1996 concluded that:

> ... subject access is nearly always preferable to keyword access. ... anyone who actually has to do research, especially in unfamiliar subject areas or languages, would be considerably more successful with subject rather than word-based search strategies.[120]

The survey, which considered a number of British initiatives including CATRIONA, BUBL, ROADS, OMNI, NISS and SOSIG, commented on the fact that, while 'the British projects are also attractive because of their relatively low cost',[121] the cataloguing of items was often not MARC-based, and, because 'one need not be a professional cataloguer to complete a NISS descriptive template ... the input is quite varied'.[122]

This was recognized by researchers on the CATRIONA project, who agreed that reliance on volunteer staff was a drawback.[123] Set up to consider how best to approach the cataloguing of internet resources, CATRIONA assumed that a library-style approach using established cataloguing standards was the only accept-able method. For reasons of economy and manageability it is clear that any attempt at good coverage of the internet must presuppose a distributed model of catalogue, with many contributors.

> ... it is assumed that the best solution to the problem is not one or several large central OPACs, but a distributed catalogue of internet resources based on a range of regional or other building blocks, and that the way forward is to design a mechanism and a set of protocols and procedures which will allow any library (or other group) to participate.[124]

Much of the literature from CATRIONA and other projects in this area is con-cerned with the machine aspects of information exchange and interoperability, although descriptive cataloguing standards are fairly fully covered. In such a collaborative environment, it is hardly feasible not to require MARC as a starting point, and CATRIONA recommended the use of USMARC. The problem of cross-searching the inevitable variety of locally employed subject indexing tools was really not addressed, although the specification of client requirements for version 4 of the CATRIONA model includes the 'ability of server to use a thesaurus to iden-tify general subject terms appropriate to more specific terms entered by user, and to use the general terms to identify appropriate subject catalogues', which suggests that some sort of central switching language or mapping tool is envisaged.[125]

With reference to the BUBL Subject Tree, the CATRIONA team recognized its limitations, suggesting that the simple hierarchical tree structure would not cope with the collections of a medium sized library, let alone the vast resources of the internet.[126] They knew that:

> Libraries will consider that cataloguing and indexing by professional cataloguers on a world-wide basis is essential in order to accurately place a resource within the universe of knowledge in a retrievable way. Natural language will not be considered adequate.[127]

In this, however, they may have been mistaken. As the 1990s progressed there was a move away from dependence on search engines alone, in favour of alternative retrieval tools. Many of the commercial search engine providers now adopted a more classificatory approach to their material with the creation of browsing structures, or subject trees, the largest and best known of which was probably the Yahoo directory. The hierarchical structure of the subject tree was intuitive for most untrained users, and 'even large scale, complex and deep hierarchies having seven or more levels of headings' could be 'explored simply and successfully by users who have had no instruction, and who probably want no instruction'.[128] This can be explained by the fact that the vocabulary of the subject tree was simpler, briefer and more easily understood than that of controlled vocabularies 'because vendors take care that their headings employ popular and easily understood terms, and usually represent topics from the perspective of everyday life'.[129] By the end of the decade the subject tree was a normal part of general web organization, with search engines such as Lycos, Excite, Infoseek and LookSmart providing sub-stantial 'classified' directories.[130]

There was a tendency as the 1990s progressed for even the managed gateways to abandon close classification with a conventional library scheme, and instead to adopt an alphabetico-classed approach using locally created subject headings in similar directory based structures, although these were often flatter than the commercial equivalents because of the more specific nature of the content.

A number of British librarians wrote enthusiastically of the potential of faceted classification as a tool for the organization of the web. Given that the constraints imposed on traditional classifications by the need for linear arrangement are not present in the online environment

> the electronic manipulation of documents or their surrogates should allow a more organic approach to allocation of new subjects and appropriate linkage between subject hierarchies. Hypertextual links can replace conventional references and the cross-classification of documents can be seen as a positive benefit ... What is required is a much more rigorous approach to consistently implementing faceted principles which promise to provide the flexibility to achieve automatic hypertextual linking of related concepts.[131]

The use of facet analysis as a basis for different types of tool was also seen as advantageous in indexing and searching the web, where, because of its 'bottom-up' approach, it can form a bridge between the concept based systems of conventional classification, and the word-based systems preferred by most internet services.[132]

Despite these speculations, there was little practical investigation of how facet analysis might be applied, although the work of Elizabeth Duncan in the immediately preceding period had shown that it worked well in conjunction with hypertext.[133]

The web was an important source of tools for cataloguing, as well as resources to be catalogued, and now much of the work of classification would be carried out using tools accessed electronically. *Dewey for Windows* has already been mentioned, and in 1995 the Library of Congress Classification and LCSH also became available electronically in the form of *Classification plus*, which, like *Dewey for Windows*, was a commercial product based on the Library's own machine-readable classification data.[134] With the spread of web OPACs there was much more visible classification data on bibliographic records to be had, and alongside these specific resources, there sprang up a large number of discussion groups, email lists and other fora dedicated to the exchange of professional views and experience.[135]

Towards the end of the 1990s some concern was expressed about the multiplicity of systems used for subject access across the various information sectors, and the problems of cross-sectoral subject searching were finally recognized. The HILT (High Level Thesaurus) Project was set up in 2000 as a one-year project jointly funded by the RSLP (Research Support Libraries Group) and JISC (Joint Information Systems Committee).[136] Its purpose was to study and report on the situation with regard to cross-searching and browsing by subject across a range of communities, services and resource types, including archives, libraries, museums and heritage, the Distributed National Electronic Resource, the Resource Discovery Network, bibliographic databases, and data sets, and with both further and higher education in mind.

At last there was 'evidence of growing agreement that interoperability in respect of subject schemes in a distributed environment is recognized as an issue and that a standards based approach is the answer, but no evidence that one particular scheme or single approach will provide the whole answer'.[137] It was also clear that there was very little information available about the needs and behaviour of users when subject searching. The work of the HILT project was carried over into 2001, but the preliminary stages revealed the extent of the diversity of practice in subject description.

Among the 42 stakeholders in the survey 14 different published schemes were in operation, the most popular being LCSH, followed by DDC and the Unesco thesaurus. Most organizations used more than one tool (a classification plus a subject heading list for example), and 21 used an in-house system of some sort, making a grand total of 35 different schemes. Even where a published standard was employed, 64% of stakeholders had modified it in some way or another.[138] It is hardly surprising therefore that there was considerable resistance to the idea that a single controlled vocabulary (DDC for choice) could, and should, be voluntarily adopted by all concerned.

One solution was the High Level Thesaurus itself, a broad overarching subject structure from which subject descriptors could be assigned to items more specifically described in the locally applied indexing language. This mirrored the situation in government departments, where the Government Category List was being developed as a broad level thesaurus for e-government metadata, to which departmentally generated subject data would also be mapped upwards.

It was also clear that, outside conventional libraries, the thesaurus, rather than the classification, was the preferred indexing tool, for archives, museums, and digital libraries, and for the corporate and government sectors. As the new millennium began, the tool that had been described only in 1960 as 'thesaurus – a new word in documentation' looked set to take centre stage.[139]

Notes

1   Neil Wilson, 'COMPASS: news from the front', *Select* (*National Bibliographic Service newsletter*) 4, summer 1991, [6–7].
2   Ibid.
3   *Select* 18, winter 1996, 11.
4   James Elliot, 'Library of Congress Subject Headings: is the case to be altered?', *Select* 6, spring/summer 1992, 7.
5   'Subject information in BNBMARC records', *Interface* (*National Bibliographic Service technical bulletin*) 13, Feb. 1996, 2–3.
6   'New heading for fiction', *Interface* 17, Oct. 1996, 7.
7   James Elliot, 'Subject headings come home to roost', *Select* 14, winter 1994/95, 7.
8   Andrew MacEwan, *Working with LCSH: the cost of cooperation and the acheivement of success: a perspective from the British Library*. Paper presented at the 64th IFLA General Conference Amsterdam August 16–21 1998. Available at: <http://www.ifla.org/IV/ifla64/033-99e.htm> (accessed 1/06). Also reproduced in *International cataloguing and bibliographic control* **28** (4), 1999, 94–7.
9   Ibid.
10   Andrew MacEwan, 'LCSH and the British Library: an international subject authority database', *Catalogue & index* 120, summer 1996, 1–6, at p. 2. Paper also given at a CIG seminar entitled 'LCSH: the future for subject access', Libtech, University of Hatfield, Sept. 1995.
11   Shirley Anne Cousins, 'Enhancing subject access to OPACs: controlled vocabulary vs. natural language', *Journal of documentation* **48** (3), 1992, 291–309.
12   'The subject enhancement of OPAC records and the need for multilingual access', *Vine* 90, 1993, 33–5.
13   Cousins, 'Enhancing subject access to OPACs', 294.
14   'Subject enhancement of OPAC records', 34.
15   Unpublished information from the Copyright Libraries Shared Cataloguing Programme Steering Group reported in I. C. McIlwaine, 'Subject control: the British viewpoint' in *Subject indexing: principles and practice in the 90s*, ed. R. P. Holley. Munich: Saur, 1995 (UBCIM publications. New series; v. 15), pp. 166–80.
16   MacEwan, 'LCSH and the British Library', 1.

17 John C. Crawford, Linda C. Thom and John A. Powles, 'A survey of subject access to academic library catalogues in Great Britain', *Journal of librarianship and information science* **25** (2), 1993, 85–93.

18 Fran Slack, 'Subject searching on OPACs: problems and help provision', *Vine* 83, 1991, 4–9.

19 Ibid., 5.

20 Rodney Brunt, 'Subject access standards' in *Standards – back to the future: proceedings of a workshop on the future of bibliographic standards*. Boston Spa: British Library, 1993 (NBS occasional publications; 2), pp. 23–38.

21 Ibid., 36.

22 *Standards – back to the future: proceedings of a workshop on the future of bibliographic standards*. Boston Spa : British Library, 1993 (NBS occasional publications; 2), p. 40.

23 Ibid., 42.

24 Peter Dale, 'Key CoBRA event promises continued co-operation', *Select* 24, spring 1999, 1–3.

25 Patrice Landry, 'Multilingual subject access: the linking approach of MACS' in *The thesaurus: review renaissance and revision*, ed. Sandra K. Roe and Alan R. Thomas. Binghamton, N.Y.: Haworth, 2004, pp. 177–91. Also published as *Cataloging & classification quarterly* **37** (3/4), 2004.

26 Andrew MacEwan, 'Crossing language barriers in Europe: Linking LCSH to other subject heading languages', *Cataloging & classification quarterly* **29** (1/2), 2000, 199–207.

27 John Byford, 'The British Library, DDC and the new building', *Catalogue & index* 103/104, spring/summer 1992, 1–5.

28 British Library, Working Party on Classification and Indexing, *Final report*. Boston Spa: British Library Lending Division, 1975 (BL research and development report; 5233), as quoted in Byford, 'British Library, DDC ', 3.

29 Byford, 'British Library, DDC', 4.

30 Byford, 'British Library, DDC', 4; the report itself was unpublished: Russell Sweeney, 'Classification of St Pancras open access material: a study undertaken for the British Library', 1990.

31 Alan Day, *The new British Library*. London: Library Association, 1994, 35.

32 Ross Trotter, 'Dewey 21 – a personal view', *Select* 20, summer 1997, 4–5.

33 Ibid., 5.

34 'Dewey 21: a classification for the 21st century', *Interface* 16, Aug. 1996, 2–3.

35 Joan Mitchell, 'The Dewey system in the twenty-first century' in *The future of classification*, ed. Arthur Maltby and Rita Marcella. Aldershot: Gower, 2000, pp. 81–92.

36 Gregory New and Ross Trotter, 'Revising the life sciences for Dewey 21', *Catalogue & index* 121, autumn 1996, 1–6, at p. 3.

37 Ibid., 1.

38 Ibid., 2.

39 Ibid., 4.

40 'Classification Research Group/Bliss Classification Association', *Library Association record* **93** (8), 1991, 534.

41 J. Mills and Kenneth Bell, *Bliss bibliographic classification. 2nd ed. Class A/AL Philosophy and logic*. London: Bowker-Saur, 1991.

42   J. Mills and Vanda Broughton, *Bliss bibliographic classification. 2nd ed. Class AM/AX Mathematics, statistics and probability.* London: Bowker-Saur, 1993.

43   J. Mills and Vanda Broughton, *Bliss Bibliographic Classification. 2nd ed. Class Q Social welfare.* London: Bowker-Saur, 1994.

44   J. Mills and Vanda Broughton, *Bliss Bibliographic Classification. 2nd ed. Class R Politics and Public administration.* London: Bowker-Saur, 1996.

45   J. Mills and Vanda Broughton, *Bliss Bibliographic Classification. 2nd ed. Class S Law.* London: Bowker-Saur, 1996.

46   J. Mills and Vanda Broughton, *Bliss Bibliographic Classification. 2nd ed. Class AY/B General Science and Physics.* London: Bowker-Saur, 1999.

47   J. Mills and Vanda Broughton, *Bliss bibliographic classification. 2nd ed. Class AM/AX Mathematics, statistics and probability.* London: Bowker-Saur, 1993, xxxviii.

48   Ibid., xxxix.

49   Ibid., xli.

50   Alan R. Thomas, 'Bliss classification update', *Cataloging & classification quarterly* **19** (3/4), 1995, 105–17.

51   *Bliss classification bulletin* 37, 1995, 28.

52   Clare Sargent, 'Classifying the undergraduate collection at Queens' College, Cambridge', *Bliss classification bulletin* 32, 1990, 10–12.

53   Elizabeth Russell and Heather Lane, 'Working towards an archaeology schedule at the Haddon Library', *Bliss classification bulletin* 41, 1999, 17.

54   Karen E. Attar, 'The application of the Bliss Bibliographic Classification in Cambridge College Libraries', *New review of academic librarianship* **6**, 2000, 35–49; Heather Lane, 'Managing organizational change: perspectives on conversion', *Bulletin of the Association of British Theological and Philosophical Libraries* **6** (2), 1999, 5–10; Rhona Watson, 'Quincentenary Library, Jesus College, Cambridge', *Bliss classification bulletin* 39, 1997, 14–16.

55   Karen E. Attar, 'Blissful perceptions: BC2 or not in Cambridge', *Bliss classification bulletin* 42, 2000, 12–15, at p. 12.

56   *Bliss classification bulletin* 41, 1999, 5–6; Elizabeth Russell and Heather Lane, 'Working towards an archaeology schedule at the Haddon Library', *Bliss classification bulletin* 41, 1999, 17–26; Heather Lane and Sarah Butler, 'Notes on the implementation of Classes DG/DY (Earth sciences) draft schedule in the library of Sidney Sussex College, Cambridge', *Bliss classification bulletin* 40, 1998, 18–22.

57   Sue Mitchell and Gerry Power, 'Bliss bibliographic classification at NSPCC library', *Bliss classification bulletin* 38, 1996, 8–12; Kathleen Wright, 'Using Q in MPS', *Bliss classification bulletin* 37, 1995, 24–7; Roy Johnson, 'Alcohol Concern's library and information service – a history', *Bliss classification bulletin* 39, 1997, 12–14; *Bliss classification bulletin* 40, 1998, 2.

58   *Bliss classification bulletin* 37, 1995, 28; 39, 1997, 20.

59   Helen Kraup, 'Radzinowicz Library', *Bliss classification bulletin* 41, 1999, 15–16.

60   *Bliss classification bulletin* 34, 1992, 6.

61   Jean Aitchison, 'Bliss and the thesaurus: the Bibliographic Classification of H. E. Bliss as a source of thesaurus terms and structure', *Journal of documentation* **42** (3), 1986, 160–81.

62   Jean Aitchison in association with Nicole Gallimore, Susan Boyde *et al.*, *Royal Institute of International Affairs Library Thesaurus.* London: RIIA, 1992. 2 vols.;

Jean Aitchison, 'Class R: Politics and public administration', *Bliss classification bulletin* 37, 1995, 10–23.

63   *Bliss classification bulletin* 36, 1994; I. C. McIlwaine, 'UDC centenary: the present state and future prospects', *Knowledge organization* **22** (2), 1995, 64–9.

64   P. David Strachan and Frits M. H. Oomes, 'Universal Decimal Classification update', *Cataloging & classification quarterly* **19** (3/4), 1995, 119–31; McIlwaine, 'UDC centenary', 65.

65   Ben G. Goedegebuure, 'The UDC Consortium', *Extensions and corrections to the UDC* 15, 1993, 7–9.

66   I. C. McIlwaine, 'Report of the Editor in chief', *Extensions and corrections to the UDC* 16, 1994, 9–18.

67   I. C. McIlwaine, 'Preparing traditional classifications for the future: Universal Decimal Classification', *Cataloging & classification quarterly* **21** (2), 1995, 49–58, at p. 49.

68   Alan Stevens, 'A time of change and challenge', *Extensions and corrections to the UDC* 20, 1998, 3–4; I. C. McIlwaine, 'Report of the Editor in chief', *Extensions and corrections to the UDC* 21, 1999, 5–6.

69   McIlwaine, 'Preparing traditional classifications', 51.

70   McIlwaine, 'UDC centenary', 66.

71   N. J. Williamson, 'Restructuring UDC: problems and possibilities' in *Classification research for knowledge representation and organization: proceedings of the 5th International Study Conference on Classification Research*, ed. N. J. Williamson and M. Hudon. Amsterdam; London: Elsevier, 1992 (FID 698), pp. 381–7.

72   McIlwaine, 'Preparing traditional classifications'.

73   I. C. McIlwaine and N. J. Williamson, 'Future revision of UDC', *Extensions and corrections to the UDC* 15, 1993, 11–17.

74   Ibid., 14; ibid., 17.

75   McIlwaine, 'Preparing traditional classifications', 53; I. C. McIlwaine, 'Classification schemes: consultation with users and cooperation between editors', *Cataloging & classification quarterly* **24** (1/2), 1997, 87–90.

76   I. C. McIlwaine and N. J. Williamson, 'A feasibility study on the restructuring of the Universal Decimal Classification into a fully faceted classification system' in *Knowledge organization and quality management: proceedings of the Third International ISKO Conference, 20–24 June 1994, Copenhagen, Denmark*, ed. Hanne Albrechtsen and Susanne Oernager. Frankfurt/Main: Indeks, 1994, pp. 406–13; I. C. McIlwaine and N. J. Williamson, 'Future revision of UDC: progress report on a feasibility study for restructuring' *Extensions & corrections to the UDC* 15, 1993, 11–17.

77   McIlwaine, 'Classification schemes: consultation with users', 91–2.

78   I. C. McIlwaine and N. J. Williamson, 'Class 61 – Medicine: restructuring progress 2000', *Extensions and corrections to the UDC* 22, 2000, 49–50.

79   I. C. McIlwaine, 'Report of the UDC Editor in chief', *Extensions and corrections to the UDC* 19, 1997, 3–4.

80   Geoffrey Robinson, 'Annex 1. United Kingdom: administrative divisions. An extended classification', *Extensions and corrections to the UDC* 20, 1998, 109–20.

81   I. C. McIlwaine, 'Report of the Editor in chief', *Extensions and corrections to the UDC* 21, 1999, 5–6.

82   Geoffrey Robinson 'USA – an extended classification', *Extensions and corrections to the UDC* 22, 2000, 185–224.
83   G. A. Wilkins, 'Revision project Class 52 – Astronomy', *Extensions and corrections to the UDC* 17, 1995, 67–9.
84   'Report on the revision of UDC 52', *Extensions and corrections to the UDC* 19, 1997, 5.
85   I. C. McIlwaine, 'A proposal for the revision of UDC Class 2 Religion with general observations on the introduction of greater facet analysis into the UDC', *Extensions and corrections to the UDC* 15, 1993, 31–44.
86   Ibid., 44.
87   Vanda Broughton, 'A new classification for the literature of religion', *International cataloguing and bibliographic control* **29** (4), 2000, 59–61. Also presented as a paper at the 64th IFLA Conference, Jerusalem 2000, and available at: <http://www.ifla.org/IV/ifla66/papers/034-130e.htm> (accessed 31/1/06).
88   Geoffrey Robinson, 'An odd point of view: some reflections on Table 1i in the UDC common auxiliaries', *Extensions and corrections to the UDC* 19, 1997, 29–31.
89   I. C. McIlwaine, 'Report of the Editor in chief', *Extensions and corrections to the UDC* 20, 1998, 5–6.
90   Vanda Broughton, 'The revision process in UDC: an examination of the systematic auxiliary of point-of-view using facet-analytical methods', *Extensions and corrections to the UDC* 20, 1998, 17–20. Also delivered as a paper at the workshop 'UDC in the next millennium', IFLA Conference, Amsterdam, 20 Aug. 1998.
91   Vanda Broughton, 'The development of a common auxiliary schedule of property: a preliminary survey and proposal for its development', *Extensions and corrections to the UDC* 20, 1998, 37–42.
92   McIlwaine and Williamson, 'Class 61 – Medicine', 50.
93   Geoffrey Robinson, 'Time out of mind: a critical consideration of Table 1g', *Extensions and corrections to the UDC* 22, 2000, 28–31.
94   Geoffrey Robinson, 'Abridging the UDC: the compiling of the Pocket Edition', *Knowledge organization* **26** (3), 1999, 149–56.
95   Ibid., 150.
96   Ibid., 155.
97   Minutes of the 280th meeting of the Classification Research Group, 21 Feb. 1991.
98   I. C. McIlwaine and Vanda Broughton, 'The Classification Research Group – then and now', *Knowledge organization* **27** (4), 2000, 195–9.
99   J. Mills and Vanda Broughton, *Bliss bibliographic classification. 2nd ed. Class AY/B General science and physics.* London: Bowker-Saur, 1999, xv.
100   Minutes of the 326th meeting of the Classification Research Group held at University College London, 10 Nov. 2000.
101   Ibid., minute 2837.
102   F. J. Murphy, A. S. Pollitt and P. R. White, *Matching OPAC user interfaces to user needs.* Huddersfield: Polytechnic of Huddersfield, 1991 (British Library research and development report; 6041).
103   Ibid., p. 81. The reference is to A. S. Pollitt, 'A common query interface using MenUSE – a Menu-based User Search Engine' in *Online Information 88: 12th International Online Information Meeting, London, 6-8 December 1988: proceedings.* Oxford: Learned Information, [1989], v. 2, pp. 445–57.

104 A. Steven Pollitt, Martin P. Smith and Patrick A. J. Braekevelt, 'View-based searching systems – a new paradigm for information retrieval based on faceted classification and indexing using mutually constraining knowledge-based views', available at: <http://www.view-based-systems.com/papers/bcshci.htm> (accessed 1/06).

105 Geoffrey P. Ellis, Janet E. Finlay and A. Steven Pollitt, 'HIBROWSE for hotels: bridging the gap between user and system views of a database' in *Proceedings of the 2nd International Workshop on User Interfaces to Databases; Lake District Conference Centre, Ambleside, UK July 1994*. Berlin: Springer, 1994, pp. 45–58.

106 A. Steven Pollitt *et al.*, 'A common query interface for multilingual document retrieval from databases of the European Community Institutions' in *Proceedings of the 17th International Online Information Meeting London December 1993*. London: Learned Information, 1993, pp. 47–61.

107 Mark Treglown *et al.*, *HIBROWSE for bibliographic databases: a study of the application of usability techniques*. Boston Spa: British Library; University of Huddersfield, 1997 (British Library research and innovation report; 52).

108 A. Steven Pollitt, 'Interactive information retrieval based on faceted classification using views' in *Knowledge organization for information retrieval: proceedings of the Sixth International Study Conference on Classification Research held at University College London 16–18 June 1997*. The Hague: FID, 1997 (FID 710), pp. 51–6, at p. 55.

109 A. Steven Pollitt, *The key role of classification and indexing in view-based searching*. Paper read at the 63rd IFLA General Conference Copenhagen 31 Aug.–3 Sept. 1997, available at: <http://www.ifla.org/IV/ifla63/63polst.pdf> (accessed 1/06).

110 *Knowledge organization for information retrieval: proceedings of the Sixth International Study Conference on Classification Research held at University College London 16–18 June 1997*. The Hague: FID, 1997 (FID 710).

111 *Proceedings of the International Study Conference on Classification for Information Retrieval*. London: Aslib, 1997.

112 Alan Gilchrist (ed.), *From classification to knowledge organization: Dorking revisited, or 'Past is prelude'*. The Hague: FID, 1997 (FID 714).

113 Traugott Koch and Michael Day, *DESIRE (Development of a European service for information on research and education) Deliverable D3.2: Specification for resource description methods, Part 3. The role of classification schemes in internet resource description and discovery* February 1997, p. 6. Available at: <http://www.ukoln.ac.uk/metadata/desire/classification/classification.pdf> (accessed 1/06).

114 <http://www.bubl.ac.uk> (accessed 1/06).

115 NISS no longer exists, having been replaced by HERO (*Higher education research opportunities*): <http://www.hero.ac.uk> (accessed 1/06).

116 <http://www.omni.ac.uk> (accessed 1/06)

117 <http://www.sosig.ac.uk> (accessed 1/06)

118 <http://www.bized.ac.uk> (accessed 1/06)

119 <http://www.eevl.ac.uk> (accessed 1/06)

120 J. Woodward, 'Cataloguing and classifying information resources on the internet', *Annual review of information science and technology* **31**, 1996, 189–219.

121 Ibid., 211.

122 Ibid., 211.

123   Dennis Nicholson and Mary Steele, 'CATRIONA: a distributed locally-oriented, Z39.50 OPAC-based approach to cataloguing the internet', *Cataloging & classification quarterly* **22** (3/4), 1996, 127–41.

124   Dennis Nicholson *et al.*, *Cataloguing the internet: CATRIONA feasibility study.* London: British Library Research and Development Department, 1995 (Library and information research report; 105), p. 5.

125   Ibid., 17.

126   Nicholson and Steele, 'CATRIONA', 129.

127   Ibid., 138.

128   Alan Wheatley, 'Subject trees on the internet: a new role for bibliographic classification' in *Internet searching and indexing: the subject approach*, ed. Alan R. Thomas and James R. Shearer. Binghamton, N.Y.: Haworth, 2000, pp. 115–41, at p. 134.

129   Ibid., 132.

130   Ibid., 137.

131   Robert Newton, 'Information technology and new directions' in *The future of classification*, ed. Arthur Maltby and Rita Marcella. Aldershot: Gower, 2000, pp. 43–57, at pp. 50–1.

132   David Ellis and Ana Vasconcelos, 'The relevance of facet analysis for world wide web subject organization and searching' in *Internet searching and indexing: the subject approach*, ed. Alan R. Thomas and James R. Shearer. Binghamton, N.Y.: Haworth, 2000, pp. 97–114. Also published as *Journal of internet cataloging* **2** (3/4), 2000.

133   Elizabeth Duncan, 'A faceted approach to hypertext' in *Hypertext: theory into practice*, ed. R. McAleese. London: Intellect, 1989, pp. 157–63; Elizabeth Duncan, 'A concept map thesaurus as a knowledge-based hypertext interface to a bibliographic database' in *Informatics 10: prospects for intelligent retrieval.* London: Aslib, 1990, pp. 43–52.

134   Lois Mai Chan and Theodora L. Hodges, 'The Library of Congress Classification' in *The future of classification*, ed. Arthur Maltby and Rita Marcella. Aldershot: Gower, 2000, pp. 105–27, at p. 107.

135   Gordon Dunsire, 'The internet as a tool for cataloguing and classification, a view from the UK' in *Internet searching and indexing: the subject approach*, ed. Alan R. Thomas and James R. Shearer. Binghamton, N.Y.: Haworth, 2000, pp. 187–96.

136   Dennis Nicholson *et al.*, *HILT: High-level thesaurus project. Final report to RSLP & JISC* December 2001. Available at: <http://hilt.cdlr.strath.ac.uk/Reports/FinalReport.html> (accessed 1/06).

137   Ibid., 17.

138   Ibid., 25.

139   Brian Vickery, 'Thesaurus – a new word in documentation', *Journal of documentation* **16** (4), 1960, 181–9.

30

Indexing and abstracting

J. H. Bowman

General aspects of indexes

Mary Piggott considered the merits of authors' being their own indexers, and expressed surprise that authors did not always know of the existence of indexers.[1] The author was undoubtedly the person best informed about the content of the book, but on the other hand the indexer might be better able to adopt the position of a total stranger looking for information. Bell examined the question of bias in indexes and discussed ways in which the indexer could maintain impartiality.[2]

One of the hardest aspects of indexing is identifying concepts, or 'aboutness', as it came to be called. Several articles referred to it, but a definition always proved elusive. Farrow suggested that an existing model of text comprehension could be followed, and suggested ways in which this might be tested.[3] Bell examined the intriguing difference between 'hard' and 'soft' indexing, which related both to the nature of the subject content and to the extent to which indexers should follow rules and adhere to standards.[4] These were felt to be most appropriate in dealing with technical material, where subjects could be more clearly defined. Likewise the rigid following of a rule on every occasion, in order to create consistency, might lead to less satisfactory results than would be produced by sometimes being inconsistent. She felt that there were now so many indexing specialisms that people like her might be left out on a limb, and she championed the cause of the ordinary back-of-the-book indexer.

The process of indexing can be as varied as the subject being indexed, and a collection of brief descriptions of six experienced indexers' ways of working revealed great diversity.[5] Some marked up the proofs beforehand, others went straight into the indexing. Some were still using entirely manual methods, but most used a computer, either with an indexing program or simply for word-processing.

Some indexing projects

Several articles dealt with problems of specific indexes, especially indexes to periodicals. An index to *The Athenaeum* was compiled at City University using relational database software, TINman from IME.[6] Howat described the difficulties of preparing an index to some early nineteenth-century newspapers in Perth.[7] Symondson outlined the process undertaken by the Incorporated Society of Law

Reporting for England and Wales in compiling the ten-year consolidated indexes to the *Law reports*.[8] Richard Jones described his procedure for indexing the *British medical journal*, something he had at the time been doing for a couple of years.[9] The weekly publication necessitated rapid work; entries were input using MACREX and then output as a word-processor file, which was then made available on the editorial office network. Different sections of the journal were indexed in different ways, depending on their subject content. Multiple authorship, so common in medicine, bulked out the index greatly, to doubtful purpose. Hall described the difficulties of indexing a 23-volume series of economics books.[10] In particular, it had been important to allow enough time to work on the index without losing ordinary customers.

A rather different task was that of producing a consolidated index to *The Oxford history of England*; this was done by starting with the indexes to the existing sixteen volumes, and merging them using MACREX.[11] The 13-volume edition of Gladstone's diaries was to some extent indexed during publication, as the editors had compiled a card index as they went along. This was later computerized by the creation of a database in several sections, and a subject index was compiled from scratch.[12]

Some other major indexes published during the decade included:
Who was who: a cumulated index 1897–1990. London: A. & C. Black, 1991
Index to Domesday Book. Chichester: Phillimore, 1992. 3 vols.
The Gilbert and Sullivan journal 56-year index. By Geoffrey Dixon. Ayr: Rhosearn Press, 1996
Index to the Gilbert and Sullivan Society magazine nos. 1–40, 1977–1995. By Geoffrey Dixon. Ayr: Rhosearn Press, 1996
Index to book reviews in England 1775–1800. By Antonia Forster. London: British Library, 1997

Wheatley Medal
The Wheatley Medal had been set up by the Library Association in 1961, to be awarded annually for an 'outstanding' index published in the United Kingdom; its history after thirty years was reviewed by Jill Ford in 1993.[13] Typically about twenty nominations were received, and from these a winner, runner-up and third place were usually selected, though sometimes there was no award. Ford made some suggestions to improve the process: that in future there should be a cash prize to accompany the medal; that a submission document should be required, outlining the problems that the indexer had encountered in making the index; and that publicity should be improved, with a specific call for nominations. All these recommendations were implemented, and from 1992 a cash prize of £200 was instituted.

The following were the winners of the medal during the decade (in each case the year is that to which the award relates; the actual presentation took place the following year):

1991   Elizabeth Moys: index to *British tax encyclopedia*. London: Sweet and Maxwell, 1991

1992   Paul Nash: index to *The world environment 1972–1992: two decades of challenge*, ed. Mostafa K. Tolba and Osama A. El-Kholy. London: Chapman & Hall on behalf of the United Nations Environment Programme, 1992

1993   Janine Ross: index to R. Macrae, R. K. Robinson, M. J. Sadler, *Encyclopaedia of food science, food technology and nutrition*. 8 vols. London: Academic Press, 1993

1994   H. C. G. Matthew: index to *The Gladstone diaries: with cabinet minutes and prime-ministerial correspondence*. Oxford: Clarendon Press, 1994

1995   Ruth Richardson and Robert Thorne: *The Builder illustrations index 1843–1883*. London: Builder Group and Hutton & Rostron in association with the Institute of Historical Research, 1994

1996   Gillian Northcott and Ruth Levitt: index to *Dictionary of art*, ed. Jane Turner. 34 vols. London: Macmillan, 1996

1997   Janine Ross: index to *Rheumatology*, ed. John H. Klippel and Paul A. Dieppe. 2 vols. London: Mosby, 1994

1998   Caroline Sheard: index to *Rook/Wilkinson/Ebling textbook of dermatology*, 6th ed. London: Blackwell Science, 1998

1999   Barbara Hird: index to *The Cambridge history of English medieval literature*. Cambridge: Cambridge University Press, 1999

2000   David Crystal and Hilary Crystal: index to their *Words on words: quotations about language and languages*. London: Penguin, 2000

Bibliography

The current awareness bibliography started by Hans H. Wellisch was continued in instalments by Jean Wheeler in *The indexer*.[14]

Standards

In 1991 the Society of Indexers had representatives on two British Standards Institution Committees: DOT/– and DOT/2 (Mary Piggott) and DOT/8 (Valerie Chandler), and this continued for several years. The major publication during the decade was ISO 999.[15] In advance of publication Calvert provided an outline of the chief differences between this and BS3700:1988, which it superseded, and following publication Booth summarized it.[16] It was the only indexing standard which had had contributions from all over the world. A difference from the British Standard was in the presentation of runs of locators, the recommendation being that none of the digits should be elided. Word-by-word alphabetization was preferred to letter-by-letter, though the latter was admitted if necessary.

Indexing special subjects

Bell discussed the various types of fiction that might benefit from indexes, and described some unpublished indexes that she had undertaken for pleasure.[17] It was not clear whether any works of fiction had ever had indexes published. In some cases an index could be a work of fiction in itself.[18] For her own interest she had produced a complete index to the novels of Angela Thirkell.[19] Vickers too had indexed the work of S. L. Bensusan for his own enjoyment.[20]

Certain specialisms began to develop their own interest groups. For example, in 1992 a special newsletter for archaeological indexers, *Trial trench*, was started, edited by Cherry Lavell.[21] In 1993 the Society of Indexers formed a Genealogical Group.[22] Moys described the difficulties of legal vocabulary, and the indexing of loose-leaf supplements.[23] In 1996 under her editorship an international newsletter for law indexers was launched.[24]

Leonard Will discussed the principles of indexing museum objects; these were the same as for printed publications, but fresh problems arose, particularly in the relationship between description and access points.[25] The indexing of images always presents special problems, and in 1993 the British Library issued a review of the literature of the subject, containing almost a hundred books and articles.[26] On a very specific topic, a great challenge was presented by the design of tartans. The Scottish Tartans Society had set up the Register of All Publicly Known Tartans in 1963, and their method of indexing them was described by Lumsden.[27] Crystal discussed the indexing principles and procedures which he and his wife followed when compiling *Words on words*, which was an anthology of quotations about language and languages.[28]

When the Scottish Parliament was established in 1999 it was necessary to devise ways of indexing its published proceedings.[29] It was decided that thesaurus control was essential, and POLIS (the Parliamentary On Line Indexing Service, already used by the British Parliament) was adopted, with indexers employed locally in Edinburgh. In 2000 the library of the Royal Institute of British Architects included in its re-released online catalogue an index to over 300 architecture periodicals.

Index arrangement

Bowman examined the little-considered question of interfiled Greek and roman alphabets in indexes to Greek texts and found that there were several ways of doing this, all of them being in contravention of the general recommendation that alphabets should be kept separate.[30] Another filing problem, that of word-by-word *vs* letter-by-letter, was discussed by Crystal in relation to *The Cambridge encyclopedia*, which actually changed its filing system from the former to the latter between editions because so many readers had been confused.[31] Mulvany stated that when using the word-by-word system all punctuation should be ignored, even if this acted as a separator of surname and forename, for example. This, not surprisingly, was roundly condemned by John Vickers, who secured the support of Geoffrey Dixon, the indexer of *The indexer*.[32] The correspondence continued through several more issues and at least three continents, but experiments involving non-indexers seemed to support Mulvany's view.

Another old 'rule', about not using classified arrangements in indexes but instead being as specific as possible, was examined by Moys.[33] In law book indexing it was common to have classified indexes, but she detected a trend towards the more specific, which she welcomed. In another examination of changing practice, Booth looked at how capitalization, alphabetization, cross-references and other topics had changed over the years since the publication of Knight's textbook.[34] In Knight's day, for example, it was still normal to give each entry an initial capital, whereas ISO 999:1996 recommended lower case except for proper names. Likewise, Knight had used five different types of cross-reference (*see, see also, see under, see also under* and *q.v.*), but these had now been merged into just two (*see* and *see also*). The filing of abbreviations such as *St* as if spelt out had also ceased to be recommended (though still widely practised).

A European perspective was provided by Michael Robertson, who had lived in Germany for fourteen years and worked in publishing there for seven. He provided examples of the many differences from British practice.[35] In Germany the combination *Sch* was frequently treated as a separate letter of the alphabet and therefore filed after *Sz*. The en-dash was frequently used to repeat the main heading. In France it was common for books (if they had indexes at all) to have several separate indexes, and for there to be many occurrences of undifferentiated strings of page locators.

Computers in indexing
With the advance of computers in indexing, *The indexer* ran a short series on members' experiences. Although the computer helped with the input and was invaluable in sorting, it did not eliminate the time-consuming task of editing the index.[36] Bell found that she could use a word-processing package in conjunction with a specially written sorting program.[37]

The indexing of computer databases was also a problem. As Adams pointed out, the idea that providing full text eliminated the need for indexes at all was false.[38] She had developed a system entitled SIGNPOSTS, which included a dictionary matrix, a recording matrix, and indexing/recording manual, a user manual and a printed thesaurus, and had applied it to a database of London archaeology. Galbraith also wrote on the practicalities of indexing electronic documents.[39]

The Society of Indexers' publication *Microindexer* continued through the first half of the decade, keeping abreast of new developments both in computers and in indexing software. MACREX and CINDEX continued to be very popular packages. In 1995, however, *Microindexer* ceased publication because it was felt that so many indexers were now using computers that there was no longer a need for a special publication, and any appropriate material would be published in the main *Newsletter*.

At the end of the decade Ross summarized the effect that new technology had had on indexing since the early 1980s.[40] Automatic indexing packages, however much disapproved of by indexers, were essential if it was to be possible to provide any kind of index to the internet. Machine-aided indexing programs scanned the text and matched words against a pre-existing thesaurus of terms within the subject. Indexes to printed books were not immune from change either: indexes would now normally be provided to publishers electronically, and sent by email for immediate typesetting.

Automatic indexing
Some feared that as it became increasingly possible to search full text, there would no longer be any need for indexers at all.[41] In any case if indexes were necessary surely they could be created automatically? In fact, despite several attempts, it was recognized among professional indexers that automatic indexing could never be satisfactory, chiefly because it had to rely on words in the text, and it could not deal with synonyms, homographs or relationships.[42] Bell bemoaned the inter-ference by the author of a book which she had indexed, who had added all kinds of unnecessary entries, mostly extracted automatically from the text.[43]

Ryan described the changes that were affecting archivists now that so many producers of records created them electronically.[44] It was essential that appropriate indexing methods were used from the start when dealing with electronic records, and because the records themselves were physically invisible the archivist was dependent on the good will of their creator.

The Society of Indexers
Membership remained fairly stable throughout the decade, rising from 926 in 1991 to 931 in 2000, though dipping somewhat below this in some of the intervening years. Initially the Society continued to have evening meetings about six times a year at the Library Association in London, and papers based on many of these subsequently appeared in *The indexer*. From about 1994 these began to be referred to as meetings of the 'London Group' and they became less frequent. Regional groups also continued to hold meetings. Annual conferences likewise continued, in a variety of places. In 1991 members of the Council held a meeting to discuss the future of the Society, applying a SWOT analysis to it.[45] This was followed by an open meeting for members in October 1992, and in due course led to a new constitution in 1994 and subsequently to the appointment of a paid administrator. The question of fees for indexing was debated in correspondence throughout the decade, and from time to time the Society issued revised recommendations, and surveys of current practice.[46]

In 1992 the Society launched a series of 'Occasional papers on indexing', of which the first three dealt with biographies, legal materials, and medical and biological sciences.[47] These were followed a few years later by others covering newspapers, magazines and periodicals, and children's books, the latter based on the research mentioned below.[48] At the end of the decade the Society published a celebratory anthology of past writings.[49] In 1996 an office in Southwark was acquired, and in 1999 it was moved to Sheffield. Also in 1996 the name of the *Newsletter* was changed to *SIdelights*. Sadly, in the same year Hazel K. Bell relinquished the editorship of *The indexer*, and an editorial team was established in her stead; the page size was changed to A4, and henceforward the journal acquired an even more international flavour. Bell looked back on her years as editor and upon the transformations which had occurred during that time.[50] She compiled a classified list of contents covering 1958 to 1995, and also wrote a history of the Society, its predecessors, and related bodies overseas.[51] The fortieth anniversary of the Society was celebrated at the Leeds annual conference in 1997. Piggott wrote a brief history of one of the remoter antecedents, the Index Society, which lasted from 1877 to 1879, and whose object was to create indexes to standard works and special subjects which lacked them.[52]

In 1998 the Society started a website. In October of the same year representatives from the Society of Indexers, the American Society of Indexers, the Australian Society of Indexers and the Indexing and Abstracting Society of Canada came to an agreement regarding international cooperation.[53] This involved them all being in an equal relationship, rather than the overseas associations being separately in a direct relationship with the Society of Indexers.

Education and training

The Society of Indexers' open learning course continued to be revised, and replacement units were issued. Throughout the decade the Society continued to run one-day workshops at various different levels, to suit beginners and experienced indexers.[54] Book Indexing Postal Tutorials, run by Ann Hall from Moffat, continued to offer practical training in indexing. Hall briefly described some of the problems that her students encountered in the arrangement of their practice indexes.[55] Booth looked at possibilities of continuing professional development.[56] The relevance of the Society of Indexers' two qualifications, Accreditation and Registration, began to be questioned, particularly in relation to their perception by publishers. Following considerable correspondence on the merits of Registration, the system of applying for admission to the Register was changed from September 1998 with a view to making it more rigorous.

The indexing profession

Wallis considered the question of whether indexing is a professional activity.[57] In the light of a list of characteristics said by the Monopolies and Mergers Commission to distinguish professionals, she examined the Society's guidelines on recommended practice, and considered the qualifications offered by the Society, and in particular the process of applying for Registration. Her conclusion was that indexers could not regard themselves as professionals.

Halliday, a former Chair of the Society, examined the ways in which people came into indexing, and the paths available for them to progress.[58] *The indexer* included a series giving brief biographies of several 'Index makers of today'.[59]

Should indexers be named? was a question which often exercised the minds of indexers. Following some correspondence by others, Wallis and Lavell summarized the points of view of the major authorities, most of whom favoured naming, and they recommended that indexers should work together to ensure this.[60] Difficulty might arise if the publisher subsequently altered the index, and it might need a test case under the Copyright Act to secure protection for the indexer. The question of copyright had already given cause for concern, as some publishers had tried to force indexers to waive their moral rights under the Copyright, Designs and Patents Act 1988.[61] Graham Cornish spoke on the subject at a one-day conference, stating that an index is copyright in the same way as a database.[62] Nevertheless this did not protect the indexer if the publisher wished to use a different indexer for a revised edition.[63]

A constant challenge for those involved in indexing is that it is taken for granted or ignored, resulting in a continuing struggle to raise its status with publishers, and it was therefore useful that a short article about it appeared in *Learned publishing*.[64] Two other rare events occurred during the decade under review: in 1993 Ann Hall attended the Woman of the Year luncheon because of her indexing work, and in 1999 the BBC broadcast a short series of radio programmes about indexes and indexing.[65]

Carey Award
The Carey Award is presented by the Society of Indexers for outstanding services to indexing and to the Society. During the decade it was presented as follows:
1991   Professor Ken Bakewell, who retired after three years as President of the Society
1994   Barbara Britton, Treasurer 1980–1992
1997   Hazel Bell, editor of *The indexer* 1979–1995
2000   Mary Piggott, President of the Society 1995–1997, for services to indexing.

Research
Bakewell drew attention to the need for more research in indexing, and suggested some possible topics, which included length of indexes, alphabetization, presentation (e.g., set-out *vs* run-on subheadings), and user reactions.[66] At his instigation the Society of Indexers submitted a research proposal to the British Library, the outcome of which is mentioned in the next section. The Society itself established a Research Committee under Bakewell's chairmanship in 1994.

Andrea Frame conducted research into the views of publishers and indexers on indexing.[67] This had a 15% response rate from indexers and 49% from commissioning editors who had been suggested by the indexers. The mean length of time that people had worked as indexers was 12.9 years, and they spent an average of 22.4 hours a week doing it. Two-thirds of them had other work as well. A wide range of rates of pay was reported. Qualifications were good, most of the indexers having at least one degree; in indexing, 34.7% were Registered Indexers and 18.1% Accredited. Generally, editors were positive about the benefits of employing indexers, and many were loyal to their regular indexers. It appeared that indexers were more self-critical, as many of them expressed lesser degrees of satisfaction with their work than their editors did. The level of satisfaction tended to increase with the complexity of the index.

There has never been much research involving index users, and the following, although conducted in India, is included here because it was published in a British journal.[68] The study looked at users' reactions to the indexes to philosophy books, but it was conducted entirely at a theoretical level, no specific books being referred to. A slight majority (54%) preferred a single index to multiple sequences, though 61.7% felt that transliterated words ought to be put in a separate sequence. 71% thought that footnotes should indexed along with the text.

Indexing for children

A major interest of research was in the indexing of children's books. Yvonne Dixon had been asked to compile simple indexes to a series for young children, and she sought the views of several publishers and librarians.[69] It was felt to be important that children should succeed on their first attempt, otherwise they might not try again. One librarian thought that all children should be taught to use indexes between the ages of eight and eleven. Most publishers, on the other hand, had little interest in the subject. Dixon devised a simple questionnaire to use with children, and asked them how they used indexes. Their main problems were with cross-references, terms appearing in the index that did not appear on the page, and with the basics of alphabetical order.

Following Bakewell's suggestion, the British Library awarded a grant of £23,800 to Liverpool John Moores University to carry out research in indexing children's books. The research sought, among other things, to assess the quality of indexes in children's books, to investigate the views of librarians, teachers and publishers, and to identify the most useful entries and styles for such indexes. Questionnaires were sent to indexers, librarians, parents and teachers, and a total of 98 were returned. Work was also done with 154 children in four schools, focusing on Key Stage 2, age 7–11. The results were published as a report and summarized in *The indexer*.[70] Most children were aware of the nature of an index, though they tended to ignore subheadings, and found cross-references hard to understand. It could also sometimes be difficult actually to find the information on the designated page. Younger children in particular had difficulty with ranges of locators. All the participating publishers felt that an index was important in a children's book, but fewer than a third of them always provided one. There was generally felt to be considerable room for improvement. The report concluded with 21 recommendations, the prime one being that all children's information books should contain indexes.

Abstracting and indexing services

The decade started grimly for abstracting and indexing journals, with Grimwood-Jones bemoaning the number of cancellations which were being forced on libraries by rising prices.[71] She outlined some factors which should assist in deciding which such journals to take.

A new music indexing service, *MusBib*, was launched in 1991, covering 100 journals and newspapers.[72] A new legal index, *European legal journals index*, was started in 1993.[73] An important trend during the decade was that gradually abstracting and indexing services which had hitherto appeared in printed form began to be published also on CD-ROM.[74] For example, in 1994 a cumulative edition of *Film index international* from 1930 to the end of 1993 was issued on CD-ROM jointly by Chadwyck-Healey and the British Film Institute.[75] This was followed by *ARTbibliographies modern*, *Historical abstracts on disc* and others from ABC-CLIO.[76]

CD-ROMs

Throughout the decade there was discussion over the long-term future of CD-ROM as a publication format, and its relationship to online publishing. *The indexer* contained many summaries of new CD-ROM publications and started a specific section in 1995.[77] Newspapers began to appear as full text on CD-ROM, complete with indexes: the *Times* from 1990 and the *Independent* retrospectively to 1988. In 1991 the *Guardian* made the whole of its 1990 text available on a CD-ROM.[78] Research Publications issued *British news index on CD-ROM*, giving access to nine British newspapers.[79] Chadwyck-Healey issued a catalogue of all their CD-ROMs in 1992.[80] In 1993 the British Library started a new CD-ROM service known as *Inside information*, which contained details of the contents pages of over 10,000 journals held at the Document Supply Centre.[81] The well-known Clover indexes to newspapers and magazines first appeared on CD-ROM in 1996, and in 1998 an internet version was launched.[82]

In the early years of the decade, citation indexes were beginning to become available on CD-ROM.[83] By the end of the decade they would be easily accessible (at a price) via the world wide web.

Newspaper indexes

In 1992 it was announced that *The independent* was to have a monthly index, cumulating into an annual volume, prepared by Research Publications International, of Reading.[84] *Palmer's index to the Times* covering 1790 to 1850 was issued on CD-ROM by Chadwyck-Healey in 1994.[85] This was followed in 1998 by the *Official index to the Times, 1906–1980* from the same publisher.[86]

Steemson, of Express Newspapers plc, wrote about indexing a large clippings library.[87] Cuttings from newspapers were scanned and stored on optical disks, and then indexed. Vocabulary was chosen on the basis of what journalists were likely to look for, and this was very different from what the library had done before. The value of images of cuttings, as opposed to plain text, is discussed. At the Atomic Weapons Research Establishment it was found possible to replace a KWOC index to newspaper cuttings, which had been produced on a mainframe computer, with a microcomputer-based system, enabling the index to be distributed on floppy disk.[88]

The process of abstracting

Wheatley and Armstrong surveyed the abstracts found in three types of database: online databases of printed sources, internet subject trees and internet gateways.[89] The former tended to have the longest abstracts, but did not perform well in readability tests. The shortest and most readable abstracts were found in the internet subject trees. In all cases it was found that coverage of subsidiary features such as bibliographies, figures and tables was low. They also noted the steep rise in the use of abstracts by searchers who were not information workers, and the fact that abstracts did not pay attention to their needs. Later the same authors examined the guidelines issued by database producers for their own abstractors.[90] The survey was based on 14 responses from an initial request to 20 publishers; some others were unable to help because they used only authors' own abstracts. It found little agreement between the various abstracting services. Guidelines tended to be most prescriptive when dealing with measurable aspects such as length, broad content, grammar and paragraph structure. Nevertheless many of the guidelines gave no very specific advice as to length. Most recommended not repeating information from the title.

Following suggestions that structured abstracts in medical journals did not always accurately reflect the text, Hartley considered psychological literature to examine whether structured abstracts were better than traditional ones.[91] He looked at thirty articles with traditional abstracts and compared them with structured ones that were required when the articles were accepted for publication. Few inaccuracies were found, and there was no evidence of a significant difference.

Notes

1   Mary Piggott, 'Authors as their own indexers', *The indexer* **17** (3), 1991, 161–6.
2   Hazel K. Bell, 'Bias in indexing and loaded language', *The indexer* **17** (3), 1991, 173–7.
3   John Farrow, 'All in the mind: concept analysis in indexing', *The indexer* **19** (4), 1995, 243–7.
4   Hazel K. Bell, '*Vive la différence!* The survival of the softest', *The indexer* **18** (4), 1993, 231–6.
5   Pat F. Booth (ed.), 'How we index: six ways to work', *The indexer* **20** (2), 1996, 89–92.
6   Micheline Hancock-Beaulieu and Susan Holland, 'Indexing *The Athenaeum*: aims and difficulties', *The indexer* **17** (3), 167–72.
7   Marjory M. Howat, '19th-century Perth newspapers indexed and abstracted', *The indexer* **18** (1), 1992, 16–18.
8   Brian Symondson, 'The consolidated index to Law Reports', *The indexer* **18** (2), 1992, 79–82.
9   Richard Jones, 'Indexing the *British Medical Journal*', *The indexer* **19** (1), 13–18.
10 Gary Hall, 'Multi-volume indexing of an economics series', *The indexer* **18** (3), 1993, 153–5.

11   Richard Raper, 'Making the consolidated index to *The Oxford history of England*', *The indexer* **18** (1), 1992, 31–2.

12   H. C. G. Matthew, 'Indexing Gladstone: from 5 × 3" cards to computer and database', *The indexer* **19** (4), 1995, 257–64.

13   Jill Ford, 'The Wheatley Medal – thirty years old: past, present and future', *The indexer* **18** (3), 1993, 189–91.

14   *The indexer* **18** (3), 1993, 173–86; **18** (4), 1993, 247–58; **19** (1), 1994, 37–44; index in **19** (2), 1994, 111–22; **19** (3), 1995, 193–200; **19** (4), 1995, 279–82; **20** (1), 1996, 25–30; index in **20** (2), 1996, 81–6; **20** (3), 1997, 137–40, 149–52; **20** (4), 1997, 201–7; **21** (1), 1998, 25–32; index in **21** (2), 1998, 77–84.

15   *ISO 999:1996 Information and documentation: guidelines for the content, organization and presentation of indexes*. Geneva: International Organization for Standardization, 1996.

16   Drusilla Calvert, 'Deconstructing indexing standards', *The indexer* **20** (2), 1996, 74–8; Pat F. Booth, 'Good practice in indexing: the new edition of International Standard ISO 999', *The indexer* **20** (3), 1997, 114.

17   Hazel K. Bell, 'Indexing fiction: a story of complexity', *The indexer* **17** (4), 1991, 251–6; Hazel K. Bell, 'Should fiction be indexed? The indexability of text', *The indexer* **18** (2), 1992, 83–6. See also Hazel Bell, 'On the indexability of butterflies', *Logos* **3** (3), 1992, 149–52.

18   Hazel K. Bell, 'Indexes as fiction and fiction as paper-chase', *The indexer* **20** (4), 1997, 209–11.

19   Hazel K. Bell, 'Thirty-nine to one: indexing the novels of Angela Thirkell', *The indexer* **21** (1), 1998, 6–10.

20   John A. Vickers, 'A Marshland index, or "Indexing for the hell of it"', *The indexer* **19** (4), 1995, 276–8.

21   *Society of Indexers newsletter* 1992/3, 2.

22   A brief outline of its history was given by Colin Mills in *Society of Indexers newsletter* fourth quarter 1995, 3.

23   Elizabeth M. Moys, 'Legal vocabulary and the indexer', *The indexer* **18** (2), 1992, 75–8; 'Computer-assisted indexing of looseleaf supplements', *The indexer* **19** (4), 1995, 283–6.

24   *Brief entry: a newsletter for law indexers*. Sevenoaks: E. M. Moys. Reviewed in *The indexer* **20** (3), 1997, 174.

25   Leonard Will, 'The indexing of museum objects', *The indexer* **18** (3), 1993, 157–60.

26   A. E. Cawkell, *Indexing collections of electronic images: a review*. Boston Spa: British Library, 1993. (British Library research review; 15).

27   Keith Lumsden, 'Scottish tartans: an indexing challenge', *The indexer* **22** (2), 2000, 69–71.

28   David Crystal, 'Quote index unquote', *The indexer* **22** (1), 2000, 14–20.

29   Tori Spratt and Shona Skakle, 'Indexing the proceedings and publications of the Scottish Parliament', *The indexer* **22** (2), 2000, 65–8.

30   J. H. Bowman, 'One index or two? Some observations on integrated indexes to classical Greek texts', *The indexer* **18** (4), 1993, 225–30.

31   David Crystal, 'Some indexing decisions in the Cambridge encyclopedia family', *The indexer* **19** (3), 1995, 177–83.

32   Nancy C. Mulvany, *Indexing books*. Chicago; London: University of Chicago Press, 1994. Letter, with further response from Mulvany: *The indexer* **19** (3), 1995, 213–15;

letter from Dixon: **19** (4), 1995, 297; further letters: **20** (1), 1996, 31; **20** (2), 1996, 87–8; **20** (4), 1997, 216–17; **21** (4), 1999, 189.

33   Elizabeth M. Moys, 'Classified v. specific indexing: a re-examination in principle', *The indexer* **20** (3), 1997, 135–6, 153–5.

34   Pat F. Booth, 'Lifelong indexing: freelancing and CPD', *The indexer* **21** (1), 1998, 2–6. G. Norman Knight, *Indexing, the art of: a guide to the indexing of books and periodicals.* London: Allen & Unwin, 1979.

35   Michael Robertson, 'Foreign concepts: indexing and indexes on the Continent', *The indexer* **19** (3), 1995, 160–72.

36   'How indexers operate', *The indexer* **17** (4), 1991, 280–2.

37   Hazel K. Bell, 'Technological hominid', *The indexer* **18** (2), 1992, 120–1.

38   Audrey M. Adams, 'Putting the horse before the cart: rapid access to data banks by the "SIGNPOSTS" method', *The indexer* **18** (1), 1992, 3–9.

39   Ian Galbraith, 'The practicalities of document conversion', *The indexer* **18** (2), 1992, 118–19.

40   Jan Ross, 'The impact of technology on indexing', *The indexer* **22** (1), 2000, 25–6.

41   Lesley and Roy Adkins, 'Is the writing on the pall? Will indexing survive the end of the millennium?', *The indexer* **19** (4), 1995, 248.

42   Hans H. Wellisch, 'The art of indexing and some fallacies of its automation', *Logos* **3** (2), 1992, 69–76.

43   Hazel K. Bell, 'Perilous powers in authorial hands', *The indexer* **21** (93), 1999, 122–3.

44   David Ryan, 'From 5 by 3 to CEA: archival indexing at the millennium's end', *The indexer* **21** (4), 164–8.

45   *SI newsletter*, 1991/3, 5.

46   *SI newsletter, passim.*

47   Hazel K. Bell, *Indexing biographies and other stories of human lives*, 1992; 2nd ed.: 1998; Elizabeth M. Moys *et al.*, *Indexing legal materials*, 1993; Doreen Blake *et al.*, *Indexing the medical and biological sciences*, 1995.

48   Geraldine Beare, *Indexing newspapers, magazines and other periodicals*, 1999; K. G. B. Bakewell and Paula L. Williams, *Indexing children's books.* 2000.

49   Doreen Blake *et al.* (eds.), *Anthology for the millennium.* Sheffield: Society of Indexers, 1999.

50   Hazel K. Bell, 'The evolution of an editorial office in a small society', *Learned publishing* **9** (1), 1996, 23–7.

51   Hazel K. Bell, 'Classified contents of The Indexer, 1958–1995', *The indexer* **20** (3), 1997, 141–8; followed with 1996–97, *The indexer* **21** (1), 1998, viii; 'History of indexing societies. Part 1: SI: the first ten years', *The indexer* **20** (3), 1997, 160–4; 'Part 2: Three affiliations', *The indexer* **20** (4), 1997, 212–15; 'Part 3: Society of Indexers 1968–1977', *The indexer* **21** (1), 1998, 33–6; 'Part 4: 1978–82', *The indexer* **21** (2), 1998, 70–2; 'Part 5: 1983–87', *The indexer* **21** (3), 1999, 134–5; 'Part 6: 1988–91', *The indexer* **22** (1), 2000, 34–8; 'Part 7: 1992–5', *The indexer* **22** (2), 2000, 81–3.

52   Mary Piggott, 'How the Index Society began – and ended', *The indexer* **22** (1), 2000, 33–5.

53   *The indexer* **21** (3), 1999, 132; *The indexer* **21** (4), 1999, 154.

54   *SI newsletter, passim.*

55   Ann Hall, 'Problems, some unusual (marking Book Indexing Postal Tutorials', *The indexer* **20** (4), 1997, 182–4.

56   Pat F. Booth, 'Lifelong indexing: freelancing and CPD', *The indexer* **21** (1), 1998, 2–6.

57   Elizabeth Wallis, 'Indexing as a professional activity', *The indexer* **20** (4), 1997, 189–91.

58   Jill Halliday, 'Indexing as a career: development issues', *The indexer* **21** (2), 1998, 64–6.

59   'Index makers of today', *The indexer* **18** (4), 1993, 244–6 (Elizabeth Wallis, Mary Piggott, John Vickers); **19** (1), 1994, 51 (Bella Hass Weinberg); **19** (2), 1994, 129–31 (Geraldine Beare, David Lee); **19** (3), 1995, 208–9 (Michael Robertson, Michèle Clarke); **19** (4), 1995, 288–9 (Drusilla Calvert, Frances Lennie); **20** (1), 1996, 23–4 (Ann Hall, Nancy Mulvany); **20** (2), 1996 106–7 (Laurence Errington, Linda Fetters); **20** (3), 1997, 165–6 (Hazel K. Bell, Douglas Matthews). Later this was continued in *SIdelights*: summer 2000, 1–3 (Richard Raper); winter 2000, 17–19 (Geoffrey Dixon).

60   Elizabeth Wallis and Cherry Lavell, 'Naming the indexer: where credit is due', *The indexer* **19** (4), 1995, 266–8.

61   Letter to members from Elizabeth Wallis, Registrar of Society of Indexers, March 1992.

62   Graham Cornish, 'Copyright, indexes and indexers in the electronic world', *SIdelights* autumn 1997, 11–15.

63   Letter from Charles Oppenheim, *Library Association record* **100** (9), 1998, 461.

64   Lesley Adkins and Roy Adkins, 'First catch your indexer', *Learned publishing* **6** (3), 1993, 30–1.

65   *The indexer* **19** (1), 1994, 50; Douglas Matthews, 'Broadcasting on indexing', *The indexer* **21** (4), 1999, 172–3.

66   K. G. B. Bakewell, 'Research in indexing: more needed?', *The indexer* **18** (3), 1993, 147–51.

67   Andrea Frame, 'Indexers and publishers: their views on indexers and indexing', *The indexer* **20** (2), 1996, 58–64; 'Part 2', *The indexer* **20** (3), 1997, 131–4.

68   B. Ramesh Babu, 'User preferences for indexes in philosophical books: a survey', *Library review* **41** (1), 1992, 47–55.

69   Yvonne Dixon, 'Indexing for children', *The indexer* **20** (1), 1996, 8–10, 15.

70   Paula L. Williams and K. G. B. Bakewell, *Indexes to children's information books: a study of the provision and quality of book indexes for children at National Curriculum Key Stage 2*. Wetherby: British Library Research and Innovation Centre, 1997 (British Library research and innovation report; 129); Paula L. Mathews and K. G. B. Bakewell, 'Indexes to children's information books', *The indexer* **20** (4), 1997, 193–4; Paula L. Mathews and K. G. B. Bakewell, 'Indexing children's information books', *The indexer* **21** (4), 1999, 174–9; Paula L. Mathews and K. G. B. Bakewell, 'Children and indexes', *New library world* **100** (1150), 1999, 201–6.

71   Diana Grimwood-Jones, 'Abstracting and indexing journals: the unkindest cut?', *Serials* **4** (1), 1991, 12–13.

72   *Library Association record* **93** (6), 1991, 349.

73   *European legal journals index*. Hebden Bridge: Legal Information Resources, Jan. 1993–.

74   E.g. *British humanities index plus*, *Current technology index plus* and others from Bowker-Saur, advertised in *Library Association record* **94** (4), 1992, 234.

75   *Library Association record* **96** (1), 1994, 16.

76   *Library Association record* **96** (11), 1994, 608.

77   *The indexer* **17** (3), 1991, 192–3; **19** (3), 1995 and later.

78   *Library Association record* **93** (3), 97.

79   *The indexer* **17** (4), 1991, 249.

80   *Library Association record* **94** (6), 1992, 419.

81   Advertised in *Library Association record* **95** (6), 1993, 365.

82   *Library Association record* **98** (6), 1996, 321; *Library technology* **3** (4), 1998, 54.

83   Helen E. Chandler and Vincent de P. Roper, 'Citation indexing: uses and limitations', *The indexer* **17** (4), 1991, 243–9.

84   *The indexer* **18** (2), 1992, 107.

85   *The indexer* **19** (2), 1994, 87; *Library Association record* **97** (2), 1995, 109.

86   *Library Association record* **100** (6), 1998, 309.

87   Michael Steemson, 'Direct electronic access to a large clippings library', *The indexer* **19** (1), 1994, 19–21.

88   Julian R. Brock, 'A microcomputer-based alternative to a printed KWOC index', *Program* **25** (4), 1991, 367–72.

89   A. Wheatley and C. J. Armstrong, 'Metadata, recall and abstracts: can abstracts ever be reliable indicators of document value?', *Aslib proceedings* **49** (8), 1997, 206–13.

90   C. J. Armstrong and A. Wheatley, 'Writing abstracts for online databases: results of an investigation of database producers' guidelines', *Program* **32** (4), 1998, 359–71.

91   James Hartley, 'Are structured abstracts more or less accurate than traditional ones? A study in the psychological literature', *Journal of information science* **26** (4), 2000, 273–7.

31

Preservation

Alison Walker

Introduction: redefining preservation

Preservation was first included as a separate chapter in *British librarianship and information work 1981–1985*. At that point some explanation of the scope of the concept was necessary. By the time of the next volume in the series covering 1986–1990, preservation was felt to be well-established within the library discipline. The main themes of preservation had remained fairly constant: the need to provide good storage, appropriate environmental conditions, protective enclosures, risk assessment and control, interventive conservation, and a relevant financial and policy regime.

Although there was growing awareness of the interdependence of preservation and other aspects of library management, the need to promote and champion preservation had not been superseded, and there was a continuing need to ensure organizational and financial commitment to the support of collections.

There was, however, a perceived dichotomy between preservation (seen as restrictive) and public access to collections. This had to be overcome. Preservation had to be seen as facilitating access rather than impeding it. 'No access without preservation' became the watchword. But even this came to seem simplistic in the late 1990s as competition for resources became more intense. Collaboration, selection, resource-sharing, multipurposing became critical as means of integrating preservation into an increasingly project-based landscape.

The scale and speed of progress in digitization and the use of digital resources was the single most significant development in libraries in this decade, with a very significant impact on preservation policy and practice. The need to develop means and technologies for the preservation of electronic media created a new dimension for preservation.

These changes in focus are exemplified in some of the general literature on preservation over the ten-year period. At the start of the decade John Feather produced the first British general summary of preservation practice, *Preservation and the management of library collections*.[1] The National Preservation Office's 1991 *A reading guide to the preservation of library materials* similarly gave a simple thematic introduction to the core elements of preservation.[2] Ross Harvey's 1993 textbook and reader for students and practitioners were more comprehensive and thought-provoking.[3] Feather and others provided a much more developed analysis of preservation in UK libraries in 1996, based on research funded by the Leverhulme Foundation.[4] The development of more complex approaches to preservation was becoming more apparent. To some extent, as in the previous decade, new thinking came from overseas: a great deal from the United States, through the Research Libraries Group and the Commission on Preservation and Access (from 1997 the Council on Library and Information Resources), a constant publisher of innovative work, but also from its European counterpart, the European Commission on Preservation and Access. Of particular note are *Choosing to preserve* and *Preservation management: between policy and practice*.[5] The work of the National Library of Australia was influential. As in the UK, a National Preservation Office (NPO) was hosted by the National Library, with a remit for the coordination of activity across the country, and for the formulation of a national preservation strategy for the documentary heritage. The National Library of Australia was quick to realize the impact of digital material in libraries: a working group on Preserving Access to Digital Information, set up in 1993, has carried forward a comprehensive collection of resources on its website.[6]

Research and development
The British Library Research and Innovation Centre (BLRIC) funded and managed a number of research projects under its strand Preservation of Library and Archive Materials (later Preservation of and Access to the Recorded Heritage) which had critical impact in preservation.[7] The quantity and nature of past and current research were examined by Graham Matthews in 1996.[8] Some widely used tools for preservation management emerged from BLRIC's programme. *A model for assessing preservation needs in libraries* analysed a number of existing methodologies for preservation surveys and provided a model which was later further developed, with database functionality and modifications to incorporate archive materials, by the NPO.[9] Within the same strand *Cooperative activities in preservation* was completed in 1999.[10] Matthews and Eden continued and consolidated awareness of the need to plan for emergencies and disasters.[11]

The research functions of BLRIC were taken forward by the Library and Information Commission (LIC) from 1999. Further important work was undertaken under a new programme Preservation of the Recorded Heritage, mostly completed after 2000.[12] Within our period were completed a project to define needs for a national strategy for preservation surrogates, and *Benchmarks in collections care for libraries*, a system for assessing levels of collection care in libraries, as a parallel to the Museums and Galleries Commission's *Levels of collection care* for museums.[13] Also funded by LIC was *Review of preservation management training* described below under Education and training. BLRIC, in collaboration with JISC and the NPO, managed the series of reports on digital preservation referred to below under digital preservation.

The first stage of Shared Preservation in Scotland (SPIS), a project to examine the sharing of preservation responsibilities, initiated by the Scottish Federation of

University and Research Libraries (SCURL) and funded by the Scottish Higher Education Funding Council (SHEFC), commissioned Janet Gertz of Columbia University Library to define the elements that should form part of a shared preservation scheme and to make recommendations.[14] The second stage was funded by LIC, beginning in 2000. Gertz identified features of a shared programme which were considered mandatory, strongly recommended or highly desirable. The second stage examined how the recommendations could be applied. The suggestion of shared storage was supported by the great majority of participants.

Surrogacy

Surrogacy, or substitution, meaning the use of microfilm to provide substitute copies for fragile or heavily used material, was featured strongly in both 1981–85 and 1986–1990. The Mellon Microfilming Project ran from 1998 to 1997, using the generous funding from the Andrew W. Mellon Foundation, to film material at Oxford and Cambridge Universities, and for a national programme of grants administered by the British Library.[15] The Mellon Project officer was based at the National Preservation Office for the duration of the project, and organized the NPO's 1992 annual conference 'Microforms in libraries'.[16] Grants totalling over £1 million were awarded to filming programmes in 13 institutions and 12,500 reels of preservation quality film were produced. The definition and application of the highest standards in image creation, processing, recording and storing the film was a key element in the project. *The Mellon microfilming manual* was used by all grantees.[17] Based on the standards described in the Research Libraries Group *Preservation microfilming handbook*, it became a *de facto* UK quality standard for preservation microfilming.[18] After the project had finished, the manual was redeveloped by members of the former technical advisory group to form the *NPO guide to preservation microfilming*, and included technical specifications for the creation of film which would subsequently be digitized.[19] The need for a specially designed store for the master films created under the project was recognized, and a store was set up at the National Library of Wales. One of the most significant legacies of the Mellon Project was the pump-priming given the Scottish Newspapers Microfilming Unit in Edinburgh.[20]

Disaster and emergency planning

The fire at Norwich Central Library in 1994 concentrated minds wonderfully: a flood at the Fawcett Library in 1995 also had impact in the profession.[21] A great deal of literature was published on disaster planning throughout the decade, and generally speaking the number of libraries with effective disaster plans was rising. Apart from the work by Matthews and Eden mentioned above, perhaps the most useful UK materials were John Ashman's *Disaster planning for library and information services*, the Society of Archivists Scottish Region guidelines and the website begun in 1997 by the M25 Consortium of Academic Libraries to provide a model and background information for members or for other libraries seeking to develop a plan.[22] The framework of Prevention, Preparedness, Reaction and Recovery was widely adopted.

The potential for cooperation in disaster management was always strong: sharing facilities, equipment and skills could spread costs, provide economies of scale and encourage joint working between institutions. REDS, the (East Midlands) Regional Emergency and Disaster Support Service, was set up by the East Midlands Museums Service in 1991, providing reaction and recovery services to museums, archives and libraries in the region.[23] This was seen as a useful model for the English regions. Other cooperative agreements were set up in Scotland, and the M25 group developed a mutual support agreement. An alternative model adopted by many libraries was subscription to companies offering recovery services, which also sometimes offered assistance with planning and preparation. Harwell Drying and Restoration Services, the Disaster and Damage Control Centre, Document SOS, and a few of the large commercial conservation and binding companies offered such services. A broader, international perspective was provided by the proceedings of a symposium organized by the International Group of the Library Association in 1998, which presented the direct experience of professionals in dealing with service continuity in times of war and major catastrophe, emphasizing the global and political dimension of emergency planning and the need to protect cultural artefacts in time of war.[24]

Mass deacidification

The search for a mass process which would deal with the mass problem of deteriorating nineteenth- and twentieth-century paper continued. In 1990, the paper strengthening and deacidification process developed by the British Library (graft co-polymerization) had reached the stage of seeking commercial partnership for the development of a pilot plant. However, it did not prove possible to move the process from research to commercial implementation. The continuing desire in the library and archive community to address the perceived issue of acidic paper gave support to the British Library Co-operation and Partnerships-funded research into the feasibility of mass deacidification in the UK, which began in 1999.[25] Meanwhile, in Europe, mass deacidication facilities using a variety of processes were set up in the Netherlands, Switzerland, Germany and France, but UK libraries did not appear inclined to send material to these providers.

Education and training

The education of librarians had been an important area of activity in the previous decade, and continued to be so between 1991 and 2000. The inclusion of preservation in undergraduate and postgraduate courses was pressed for. Despite this, the number of courses offering a preservation option diminished. A review of current provision was undertaken with funding from the Library and Information Commission in 1999.[26] The results were featured at the NPO annual conference 1999.[27] For libraries, the picture emerged of schools where pressure on the curriculum was intense, and preservation management was rarely taught as a subject in itself, but did figure in modules which covered general collection management, collection development, or special collection management. Encouragingly, the preservation of electronic data was beginning to be taught, but not apparently in great depth. The provision of mid-career training was adequate in some areas but there were gaps, and the need for a national preservation training strategy was identified. The research elicited responses indicating some resistance to training in preservation management unless it was coordinated with other management needs.

The conservation profession
Awareness of what preservation meant, and what it included, was strengthened by the publication of Stefan Michalski's description of the nine agents of deterioration.[28] The agents defined were: direct physical forces; thieves, vandals and displacers; fire; water; pests; contaminants; light; incorrect relative humidity; and incorrect temperature. Together with Rob Waller's analysis of risk assessment as applied to preservation the definition provided a systematic framework for the consolidation of preservation practice in collections.[29] These and other concepts originally promulgated within the conservation profession influenced library preservation managers. The continuing professionalization of conservation meant that the role of conservators within a library became more managerial than in the past.[30] Librarians generally deal with preventive measures. Conservators deal with both preventive and interventive conservation: mutual understanding between the librarian and the conservator is needed. The changes were highlighted by a strengthening of the professional associations in conservation, an upgrading of conservation courses often to first or postgraduate degree standard, introduction of a professional accreditation (qualification) scheme[31] and continuing professional development requirements, and the adoption of a common (European) code of ethics.[32]

Standards
The compilation and use of standards, both formal and informal, was a feature of preservation during this period. British Standard 5454 *Storage and exhibition of archival documents* was first issued in 1989.[33] Although formally a standard for archival documents, it was used as a *de facto* standard in libraries throughout the 1990s. The 2000 revision made this explicit and the text was altered to reflect this wider applicability.[34] The existence and use of this standard was a major factor in the improvement of storage for libraries, particularly rare book, historic and special collections, in formulating criteria which were widely used in grant-aided projects. Funding bodies expected and required that new storage would comply with the standard. Perhaps most significant was the emphasis on control of the environment. It was recommended that buildings should be constructed so as to allow accurate monitoring and control for the storage of paper and parchment to a constant temperature within the range 13 °C and 18 °C, and a constant relative humidity within the range 55–65%. The 2000 revision offered new parameters, making a

distinction between frequently-used material, which was to be kept at a fixed point between 16 °C and 19 °C with a tolerance of 1 °C on either side in order to minimize the need for acclimatization. Little-used material should be kept at a fixed point between 13 °C and 16 °C with a tolerance of 1 °C on either side. Relative humidity should be at a fixed point between 45% and 60% with a tolerance of 5% on either side. The emphasis on storage and packaging was significant and influential: the boxing of library materials, and the use of acid-free materials for boxing and packaging, were an important feature of preservation in the 1990s as part of the move to protection and non-interventive processes which gave large-scale preservation benefit to collections.

The Museums and Galleries Commission's series of *Standards in collection care* was both authoritative and accessible. Of particular interest to librarians was the volume on photographic collections.[35] The International Federation of Library Associations and Institutions (IFLA) published the comprehensive *IFLA principles for the care and handling of library material.*[36]

The promotion of permanent paper became less urgent as paper manufacturers moved to more alkaline output, partly as a result of environmental legislation on production effluent. However, the use of recycled paper, championed for laudable environmental reasons, was seen as a threat to longevity and a possible future conservation problem.[37]

Funding

The impact of funding available for preservation and conservation through the Heritage Lottery Fund (HLF) was very significant. From its inception in 1994 the HLF gave many millions of pounds for heritage projects, including the acquisition, preservation and conservation of library materials and the physical improvement of premises. Precisely how much was spent on library preservation and conservation between 1994 and 2000 is quite difficult to pinpoint as conservation was often part of larger projects, and building improvements with a focus on access might also have preservation benefits. Examples of major library projects which included preservation in the early years of HLF were for the Ruskin Library at the University of Lancaster (£2.3 million), the Wordsworth Trust (£2.25 million), and Chetham's Library (£1.8 million). The largest single library preservation grant was for NEWSPLAN 2000, for the microfilming of local newspapers, which was given a grant for the development stage in 2000, to be followed by the full award of £5 million from 2001.

Smaller grant schemes which provided funding for preservation and conservation were the British Library Grants for Cataloguing and Preservation, funded through the British Library Research and Innovation Centre from 1993 to 2000, and the National Manuscripts Conservation Trust (from 1990). Both schemes provided extremely useful small grants. Library conservation continued to be represented in the programmes of the Esmée Fairbairn Foundation and the Pilgrim Trust.

In concluding the Preservation chapter for 1986–1990, the author felt that money would be key to the 1990s preservation effort. Looking back on the decade the issue now seems to be more about the way in which funding was distributed and deployed. The project culture – funding for specific aims over a limited period of time – became a deciding factor in the way preservation was managed. It was rarely possible to obtain external funding for long-term work. Preservation could be funded but the public context of increased access and educational benefit became an essential dimension of any preservation project. Equally, preservation was able to take its place as an element of access-driven projects.

In the UK wide-ranging reviews of higher education library provision such as the Follett and Anderson reports had implications for preservation in the building of a new cooperative landscape for the shared long-term retention of resources.[38] These reports can be seen as stepping-stones on a path that the profession was still following at the time of writing. The Higher Education Funding Councils' non-formula funding (NFF) competitions for 1994/95 and 1995/96 (following the Follett review 1993) were focused on conservation, cataloguing and preservation. *Accessing our humanities collections* lists the projects supported, most of which included an element of conservation or preservation.[39] The total funding given for preservation (as opposed to cataloguing) is not given but the amounts granted to each institution can be found on the HEFCE website.[40] A significant amount of preservation microfilming (the largest project was the London School of Economics pamphlet collection) was accomplished under this scheme. The University of Dundee received funding to set up a library conservation unit, supplying subsidized, high-quality services to Scottish universities.[41] The Unit continued in operation after 2000 providing services to higher education and other libraries and collections, although without the subsidy element provided by NFF. Leeds University also received funding for a workshop to support the conservation of special collections, and Southampton University a significant amount for the conservation of archive collections.

Digitization

Between 1991 and 2000, the impact of digital media on preservation came in two ways: through the investigation of the potential of digitization for preserving text and intellectual content, and through the perceived need and urgency of ensuring that digital content could itself be preserved. The terminology was a little confused: 'digital preservation' and 'digital archiving' were both used, with both meanings, and frequently to the irritation of archivists. As the decade progressed the quantity and complexity of 'born-digital' material increased, whether websites, databases or other formats. Being complex and interactive, these manifestations had no viable existence outside the digital format and their preservation became an increasingly pressing issue.

In the late 1980s there was early discussion centring on the longevity of media (optical disks and CD-ROMs).[42] Digital imaging technology was also developing fast. It was in the early 1990s, however, that intensive work began to develop techniques and methodologies, and the two aspects of digitization as preservation and preservation of digital content progressed rapidly, in parallel and in concert. Much research and innovative practice originated in the US, and had immense impact in the UK. The Commission on Preservation and Access (later the Council on Library and Information Resources), the Research Libraries Group, Yale and Cornell University Libraries, the Digital Library Federation – all were at the forefront. The British experience cannot be described without some exploration of the US background.

Impetus for large-scale digitization for preservation in the US sprang essentially from the Brittle Books project to microfilm large numbers of books threatened by brittle paper, which had received funding from the National Endowment for the Humanities from 1983 on. Digital technology appeared to offer the chance of wider and easier distribution of text and images. Yale University Library's Project Open Book 1994–96 aimed to explore the feasibility of large-scale conversion of preservation microfilm to digital imagery by modelling the process in an in-house laboratory.[43] In parallel, the digital to microfilm conversion project at Cornell examined methods of preserving digital content on preservation microfilm.[44] The concept of the 'hybrid' approach to imaging and preservation, discussed by Don Willis in 1992, informed both these projects.[45] The concept was based on defining options for the reciprocal use of digitization and microfilming: scan first then transfer to computer output microfilm (COM), or film first and digitize from film. The project did conclude some benefits in image quality from scanning as the primary form of image capture. In the UK, however, there was no large-scale use of the scan-first/COM option.

Indeed, by 1995, Valerie Ferris was able to point to only a handful of UK digitization projects, most of which had focused on manuscript material.[46] However, many of these were significant steps forward for digital technology. The British Library's Initiatives for Access programme was the showcase for a number of projects. Of relevance to preservation were the Electronic Beowulf project, Turning the Pages, and DAMP (Digitization of ageing microfilm project).[47] The first two were examples of the way in which digitization can allow access for research and enjoyment while avoiding handling of the original. For the Electronic Beowulf the manuscript was scanned at high resolution (2000 × 3000 pixels in 24-bit colour). Backlighting with fibre-optic cable allowed the capture of images from sections of the manuscript covered by nineteenth-century paper frames. The resulting images revealed more than could be seen by the naked eye and provided a significant research resource. Turning the Pages, a process which involved scanning material and presenting it in an interactive 'page-turning' format, was a new project at that stage: following re-engineering it subsequently became more widely available. Many texts can be viewed on the British Library's website.[48] The DAMP project focused on digitizing microfilm of eighteenth-century newspapers from the Burney collection. The film had been made in the early 1980s from original material which in itself was not always completely legible and had been difficult to film because of variable print quality. At this stage, the main difficulty was the need for extensive manipulation of the image to ensure legibility and to economize on disk storage. The processes used in the project were the forerunners of more successful later ventures which benefited from cheaper and more efficient storage media and the further development of image manipulation software.

By the end of the decade digitization and the need to be aware of the implications of digital media had become facts of library life. From 1996 the annual conferences on Digital Research in the Humanities brought together a wide variety of interests, mainly from UK higher education institutions.[49] In Europe, 1996 also saw the first event of the DLM Forum, organized under the auspices of the European Union, which aimed to address the problems of the management, storage, conservation and retrieval of machine-readable data.[50]

There was still some scepticism about the preservation value of digitization. Certainly there was benefit in providing a copy of a text which could be easily viewed, transmitted, even manipulated, without handling the original. In contrast, there was awareness that the availability of images in some cases brought more scholars and visitors to see the original documents. *Digitisation as a form of preservation?* posed a question which many would say had still not been answered conclusively at the time of writing.[51] Digitization seemed to provide many benefits: ease of access and distribution, relative ease of creation, and apparent safe storage. 'Yet', said the authors, 'for preservation managers digitization is in a way a wolf in sheep's clothing. How to deal, from a preservation point of view, with a medium that is notoriously unstable, for which 10 years is a long term?' The digital object created for the preservation benefit of an original document would itself need long-term preservation.

Digital preservation

Opportunities for the digitization of library materials, and the incorporation of 'born-digital' materials into library collections were a major feature of British librarianship in this period. The need to consider and implement the preservation of these materials followed naturally if not always immediately. There was a considerable period of awareness-raising during which those involved in preservation had to become aware themselves of what would be required to sustain digital collections, and to influence funders and creators to the need to implement preservation strategies from the point of creation since it is rarely possible to preserve retrospectively.

The National Preservation Office's seminar for 1988, *Preservation and technology*, while discussing various media and technologies which could be used in preservation, did not focus on the need to preserve digital media.[52] By the early 1990s, awareness of the need to develop ways of ensuring the longevity of digital content was emerging. Again, the most innovative work was done initially in the US. Michael Lesk's *Preservation of new technology* concluded that copying and media refreshment could ensure preservation of data.[53] Willis proposed the hybrid approach in 1992.[54] In 1996, Don Waters and John Garrett summarized previous work and reported the findings and recommendations of the Task Force on preserving digital information.[55] They considered the key problems in technology refreshment as a means of preservation, and considered alternatives to refreshment. They concluded that migration was an essential component of digital preservation, and that a national system of certified repositories with a fail-safe mechanism to protect culturally significant material should be instituted. They called for further investigation into hardware and software emulation systems, authentication and IPR, requirements and standards for the description and management of digital data and emphasis on the design of systems that would facilitate archiving at the creation stage. Effectively, this was the agenda for the second half of the decade.

Digital preservation was very much an international arena, and major work already done elsewhere was not repeated in the UK, but its applicability was examined. The UK library context was analysed primarily under the auspices of higher education. The Joint Information Systems Committee of the Higher Education Funding Councils (JISC) and the British Library held a conference at Warwick in 1995 at which a number of action points were agreed.[56] Firstly, an analysis of the Waters and Garrett CPA/RLG report to identify recommendations which were relevant to the UK situation, and subsequently a series of reports funded by JISC under the Electronic Libraries (eLib) programme, as a collaboration between JISC and the National Preservation Office.[57] The JISC/NPO studies on the preservation of electronic materials covered data types and formats, costing models for preservation, the needs of data creators, responsibility for data archiving, strategic policy framework, and post-hoc rescue.[58] A synthesis of the studies was published in 1999.[59] These short-term studies were an essential forerunner to later work such as CEDARS.

The NPO had extended its focus to digital information and presented *Preservation and digitisation* as its conference theme in 1996 and *Guidelines for digital imaging* in 1998, jointly presented with the Research Libraries Group.[60] The 1998 conference attracted an international audience and proved a very fruitful interchange of experience and practice.

The significance of digital resources for the higher education community was further reflected in the CEDARS project, again funded under eLib.[61] CEDARS began in April 1998 and ended in March 2002. Its broad objective was to address strategic, methodological and practical issues and provide guidance in best practice for digital preservation. These issues ranged through acquiring digital objects, their long-term retention, sufficient description, and eventual access.[62] Closely associated with CEDARS was the CAMiLEON project between the universities of Leeds and Michigan and funded by JISC and the US National Science Foundation (NSF). CAMiLEON stands for Creative Archiving at Michigan and Leeds: Emulating the Old on the New. This collaboration examined emulation as a digital preservation strategy and became particularly well-known for its pioneering work in rescuing the BBC Domesday.[63]

There was a general move from investigation and experiment to practice, from theory to the development of agreed models and tools for the management of digital materials. Jones and Beagrie's *Preservation management of digital materials: a handbook* was developed under funding from the Library and Information Commission and aimed to provide an authoritative guide to current best practice and life-cycle approaches to digital preservation.[64] *Moving theory into practice: digital imaging for libraries and achives,* by Kenney and Rieger, was the outcome of much international collaboration and advocated an integrated approach to digital imaging programs, from selection to access to preservation and management.[65] The Northeast Documentation Center published its *Handbook for digital projects: a management tool for preservation and access.*[66] In the UK, the Arts and Humanities Data Service and the Technical Advisory Service for Images were set up within the higher education arena both to safeguard digital content and to provide advisory services on creating content.

The JISC/NPO Digital Preservation Workshop held in March 1999 at the University of Warwick was an invitation-only workshop funded jointly by JISC and the British Library. It was organized by UKOLN in conjunction with the National Preservation Office. It aimed to build on the first Warwick workshop held in 1995 and set out an agenda and recommendations for the next five years. Notably these led to the establishment of the JISC Digital Preservation Focus, the JISC Digital Preservation and Continuing Access Strategy, and the Digital Preservation Coalition.[67]

Preservation 2000: An International Conference on the Preservation and Long Term Accessibility of Digital Materials, a meeting held at York in December 2000, sponsored by CEDARS, RLG, UKOLN and OCLC, major players in digital preservation with significant impact on UK practice, summed up the achievements of the decade.[68] There was general awareness that even more in the digital world than with traditional material there would be no access without preservation.

But still in 1998 Jeff Rothenberg was able to say: 'There is as yet no viable long-term strategy to ensure that digital information will be readable in the future.'[69] Research continued into emulation (for example Rothenberg), the implementation of the Reference Model for Open Archival Information Systems issued by NASA as a draft recommendation for space data system standards[70] and the Universal Virtual Computer:[71] the Internet Archive's Wayback Machine offered alternative means of access to web materials captured since 1996 by the Internet Archive.[72]

Although many digital preservation challenges remained, it is important to recognize that substantial progress had been made in the period between 1991 and 2000. This allowed the emergence of new practical and collaborative initiatives such as the Digital Preservation Coalition, the Digital Curation Centre, the Digital Archive at the National Archives, and the UK Web Archiving Consortium in the next few years after 2000.

Organizations

The National Preservation Office, set up by the British Library in 1984 following the Ratcliffe report, continued to serve libraries and archives throughout the UK and Ireland by providing leadership, information services, seminars and conferences, and guidance publications. The new emphasis on security begun in 1988 bore further fruit in collaboration with the Home Office Police Research Group's *Theft and loss from UK libraries: a national survey.*[73] From 1995, responsibility for the funding of the Office became a joint venture, with the British Library providing the majority funding, but in partnership with the other UK and Ireland legal deposit libraries and national libraries, and national archive institutions. The Office's 1997 annual conference launched this new format with the enthusiastic support of the new partners.[74] With this diversification of funding came a widening of perspective. Digital preservation was a very active part of the Office's work between 1996 and 1999 and formed the theme of two of its annual conferences. The JISC/NPO studies mentioned above and their summary volume, *Digital culture*, were concrete and influential outcomes.[75]

The new British Library building at St Pancras, so long in the planning and construction, was formally opened by the Queen in 1998.[76] Improved storage and environmental conditions for the collections had been a major driver for the project and its successful completion achieved this. The collections' move from Blooms-bury and other locations in London was the largest ever undertaken in the UK.[77] The move of the conservation studios for manuscript and Oriental material from their previous accommodation was an opportunity for modernization and a review of management structures. It was significant that on the retirement of Dr Mirjam Foot the post of Head of Collection Care was taken by a conservation professional.[78]

In April 2000 the Library and Information Commission joined the Museums and Galleries Commission and the British Library Research and Innovation Centre to form a new agency, funded by DCMS, to be the strategic body working with and for museums, archives and libraries. It was christened Resource.[79] In a cross-domain arena preservation clearly had a useful role: many of the concerns, techniques and processes are similar whether one is dealing with books, archives or objects, and naturally there is a common sense of stewardship for the collections in an institution's care. The Resource *Manifesto* included an expression of core values stating that 'the care, maintenance and enrichment of collections provides an essential starting point for the development of the sector'.[80] From the outset the organization had the potential to be a major influence on libraries, with a particular focus on collections.

National preservation strategy
The period saw efforts to define the components of a national preservation strategy. The development of a strategy was an objective of the NPO, and the subject of its 1995 annual conference.[81] The work accomplished under the BLRIC and LIC research programmes incorporated many of the necessary strategic elements: structured analysis of preservation need, benchmarks for levels of collection care, analysis of training and education needs, a national strategy for surrogates. As part of its coordinating role, the NPO developed, and tested in CURL libraries, the Register of Collection Strengths, which together with the

assessment of preservation needs would have mapped collection strengths, retention intention and preservation status.[82] The information maintained on the Register's database would inform policy decisions and appropriate distribution of resources. The Register was not added to after the pilot testing but the concept of a centralized collection description service was taken forward within the Distributed National Electronic Resource (DNER).[83]

At the end of the decade, Resource emerged with a remit for a strategic role which included collection stewardship. The desire in the library community to tackle preservation issues on a national scale and at a national level was demonstrated, and the new body was looked to for leadership. Clearly, though, preservation was only one of many issues on its agenda. Raising awareness of the need for preservation would now take place at a different, national and strategic level.

Notes

1   John Feather, *Preservation and the management of library collections*. London: Library Association, 1991.
2   Geraldine Kenny (ed.), *A reading guide to the preservation of library materials*. London: Library Association, 1991.
3   Ross Harvey, *Preservation in libraries: principles, strategies and practices for librarian*. London: Bowker-Saur, 1993 (Topics in library and information studies); Ross Harvey, *Preservation in libraries: a reader*. London: Bowker-Saur, 1993 (Topics in library and information studies).
4   John Feather, Graham Matthews and Paul Eden, *Preservation management: policies and practices in British libraries*. Aldershot: Gower, 1996.
5   Yola de Lusenet (ed.), *Choosing to preserve: towards a cooperative strategy for long-term access to the intellectual heritage*. Amsterdam: ECPA, 1997; Yola de Lusenet (ed.), *Preservation management: between policy and practice*. Amsterdam: ECPA, 2000.
6   National Library of Australia, Preserving Access to Digital Information: <http://www.nla.gov.au/padi/index.html> (accessed 31/1/06).
7   Stephanie Kenna, 'Preserving our heritage', *Research bulletin* (*British Library Research and Innovation Centre*) 19, spring 1998, 12–13.
8   Graham Matthews, *Research in preservation management*. London: British Library Research and Innovation Centre, 1996 (British Library research and innovation report; 30).
9   Paul Eden *et al.*, *A model for assessing preservation needs*. London: British Library Research and Innovation Centre, 1998 (British Library research and innovation report; 125).
10 Paul Eden and Elizabeth Gadd, *Cooperative preservation activities in libraries and archives: project report with guidelines*. Boston Spa: British Library Research and Innovation Centre, 1999 (British Library research and innovation report; 161).
11 Graham Matthews and Paul Eden, *Disaster management in British Libraries: project report with guidelines for library managers*. London: British Library, 1996 (Library and information research report; 109).

12 Adrienne Muir, 'New research in preservation management', *Library and Information Commission research bulletin* summer 1999, 14–15.

13 April Edwards, Graham Matthews, Clare Nankivell, *Developing a national strategy for preservation surrogates.* London: Library and Information Commission, 2000 (Library and Information Commission report; 54); Nancy Bell and Helen Lindsay, *Benchmarks in collections care for libraries: pre-publication distributed to delegates at the NPO seminar 'Caring for collections'* November 2000; *Levels of collection care: a self-assessment checklist for UK museums.* London: Museums and Galleries Commission, 1998.

14 Janet Gertz and Paul Byrne, *Shared preservation in Scotland.* London: Resource, 2001 (Library and Information Commission report; 108).

15 National Preservation Office, *Mellon Microfilming Project: final report 1988–1997.* London: NPO, [1998].

16 *Microforms in libraries: the untapped resource?* London: National Preservation Office, 1992.

17 *Mellon microfilming manual.* London: Mellon Microfilming Project, 1992.

18 Nancy Elkington, *Preservation microfilming handbook.* Mountain View: Research Libraries Group, 1992.

19 *Guide to preservation microfilming.* London: National Preservation Office, 2000.

20 This later became UKArchiving: see <http://www.ukarchiving.co.uk> (accessed 31/1/06).

21 B. P. Person, *An inquiry into the fire at the Norwich Central Library on the 1st August 1994.* Norwich: Norfolk County Council, 1995; Christine Wise, 'The flood and afterwards: a new beginning for the Fawcett Library', *Library conservation news* 48, autumn 1995, 102.

22 John Ashman, *Disaster planning for library and information services.* London: Aslib, 1995; Society of Archivists, Scottish Region, Disaster Preparedness Working Group, *Disaster preparedness: guidelines for archives and libraries.* London: Society of Archivists, 1996; M25 Consortium of Academic Libraries disaster control plan site: <http://www.m25lib.ac.uk/m25dcp/plan/> (accessed 31/1/06).

23 East Midlands Museums Service, Regional Emergencies & Disaster Support (REDS) service: <http://emms.org.uk/reds.htm> (accessed 31/1/06).

24 Paul Sturges and Diana Rosenberg, *Disaster and after: the practicalities of information service in times of war and other catastrophes.* London: Taylor Graham, 1999.

25 Jonathan Rhys-Lewis, *The enemy within! Acid deterioration of our written heritage.* London: British Library, 2001.

26 Stella Thebridge and Graham Matthews, *Review of preservation management training in the UK and abroad.* London: British Library, 2000 (Library and Information Commission report; 48).

27 *Training for preservation management: the next step. Proceedings of the NPO annual seminar 1999.* London: National Preservation Office, 2000.

28 S. Michalski, 'A systematic approach to preservation: description and integration with other museum activities' in *Preventive conservation: practice, theory and research*, ed. Ashok Roy and Perry Smith. London: International Institute for Conservation, 1994.

29 Robert Waller, 'Conservation risk assessment: a strategy for managing resources for preventive conservation' in *Preventive conservation*, ed. Roy and Smith.

30 Stan Lester, 'Becoming a profession: conservation in the UK', *Journal of the Society of Archivists* **23** (1), 2002, 87–94.

31 Through the National Council of Conservator-Restorers.

32 European Confederation of Conservator-Restorers' Organizations, *Professional guidelines*. Brussels, 1994.

33 *British Standard recommendations for storage and exhibition of archival documents*. London: British Standards Institution, 1989 (BS 5454:1989).

34 *Recommendations for the storage and exhibition of archival documents*, London: British Standards Institution, 2000 (BS 5454:2000).

35 *Standards in the museum care of photographic collections*. London: Museums and Galleries Commission, 1996.

36 Edward P. Adcock (ed.), *IFLA principles for the care and handling of library material*. Paris: IFLA-PAC, 1998.

37 See for example Library of Congress, *Final report to Congress on the Joint Resolution to Establish a National Policy on Permanent Papers* December 31 1995, section on Environmental issues: <http://www.loc.gov/preserv/pub/perm/pp_9.html> (accessed 31/1/06).

38 Joint Funding Councils' Libraries Review Group, *Report*. Bristol: HEFCE, 1993. Chairman Sir Brian Follett. (The 'Follett report'); Joint Funding Councils Libraries Review, *Report of the group on a national/regional strategy for library provision for researchers*. Bristol: HEFCE, 1995. (The 'Anderson report').

39 *Accessing our humanities collections: a guide to specialised collections for humanities researchers*. London: JISC, 1996.

40 Higher Education Funding Council for England, *C14/95 Libraries Review: non-formula funding of specialised research collections in the humanities. 1995–96 recurring allocations*, available at: <http://www.hefce.ac.uk/pubs/hefce/1995/c14_95.htm> (accessed 31/1/06).

41 Dundee University Library, Book & Paper Conservation Studio: <http://www.dundee.ac.uk/library/lib_cons.html> (accessed 31/1/06).

42 For example, in papers given at the NPO seminar 20–21 July 1988, in *Preservation and technology*. London: British Library, 1989; D. R. Winterbottom and R. G. Fiddes, *Life expectancy of Write Once Digital Optical Discs*. London: British Library, 1989 (British Library research paper; 66).

43 Paul Conway, 'Preliminary research findings', *D-Lib magazine* Feb. 1996.

44 Anne R. Kenney, *Digital to microfilm conversion: a demonstration project 1994–6*. Ithaca, N.Y.: Cornell University Library, 1996.

45 Don Willis, *A hybrid systems approach to preservation of printed materials*. Washington: Commission on Preservation and Access, 1992.

46 Valerie Ferris, 'Digital initiatives in the UK' in *Selecting library and archive collections for digital reformatting*. Mountain View: Research Libraries Group, 1996.

47 The Beowulf project is described at: <http://www.uky.edu/~kiernan/eBeowulf/guide.htm> (accessed 31/1/06).

48 British Library, *Turning the pages*: <http://www.bl.uk/onlinegallery/ttp/ttpbooks.html> (accessed 31/1/06).

49 Digital Resources for the Humanities: <www.drh.org.uk> (accessed 31/1/06).

50 DLM stands for 'Données Lisibles par Machine'. See DLM-Forum: <http://europa.eu.int/ISPO/dlm/> (accessed 31/1/06).

51 Hartmut Weber and Marianne Dörr, *Digitisation as a method of preservation?* Amsterdam: European Commission on Preservation and Access, 1997.

52 *Preservation and technology: proceedings of a seminar held at York University 20–21 July 1988*. London: National Preservation Office, 1989.

53 Michael Lesk, *Preservation of new technology: a report of the Technology Assessment Advisory Committee to the Commission on Preservation and Access*. Washington: Commission on Preservation and Access, 1992.

54 Willis, *Hybrid systems approach*.

55 Donald Waters and John Garrett, *Preserving digital information: report of the Task Force on Archiving of Digital Information*. Washington: Commission on Preservation and Access, 1996.

56 Marc Fresko, *Long term preservation of electronic materials: report of a JISC/British Library workshop 27–28 November 1995*. London: British Library, 1995 (British Library research and development report; 6328).

57 Graham Matthews, Alan Poulter, Emma Blagg, *Preservation of digital materials policy and strategy issues for the UK*. London: British Library, 1997 (British Library research and innovation report; 41).

58 John C. Bennett, *A framework of data tapes and formats, and issues affecting the longterm preservation of digital material*. London: British Library, 1997 (British Library research and innovation report; 50); Tony Hendley, *Comparison of methods & costs of digital preservation*. London: British Library, 1998 (British Library research and innovation report; 106); Data Archive, University of Essex, *An investigation into the digital preservation need of universities and research funders: the future of unpublished research materials*. London: British Library, 1998 (British Library research and innovation report; 109); David Haynes *et al.*, *Responsibility for digital archiving and longterm access to digital data*. London: British Library, 1997 (British Library research and innovation report; 67); Neil Beagrie and Daniel Greenstein, *A strategic policy framework for creating and preserving digital collections*. London: British Library, 1998 (British Library research and innovation report; 107); Seamus Ross and Ann Gow, *Digital archaeology: rescuing neglected and damaged data resources*. London: British Library, 1999 (British Library research and development report; 108).

59 Mary Feeney (ed.), *Digital culture: a synthesis of JISC/NPO studies on the preservation of electronic materials*. London: National Preservation Office, 1999.

60 *Preservation and digitisation: principles, practice and policies. Papers given at the NPO 1996 Annual Conference University of York 3–5 September*. London: National Preservation Office, 1997; *Guidelines for digital imaging: papers given at the joint NPO and RLG preservation conference in Warwick, 28–30 September 1998*, London: National Preservation Office, 1998.

61 CURL Exemplars in Digital Archives.

62 Kelly Russell, 'CEDARS: long-term access and usability of digital resources: the digital preservation conundrum', *Ariadne* 18, Dec. 1998, available from: <http://www.ariadne.ac.uk/issue18/cedars/intro.html> (accessed 31/1/06).

63 CAMiLEON Project: <http://www.si.umich.edu/CAMILEON/> (accessed 31/1/06).

64 Maggie Jones and Neil Beagrie, *Preservation management of digital materials workbook*. London: Resource, 2000; *Preservation management of digital materials: a handbook*. London: British Library, 2001.

65 Anne R. Kenney and Oya Y. Rieger, *Moving theory into practice: digital imaging for libraries and archives*. Mountain View: RLG, 2000.

66 Maxine K. Sitts (ed.), *Handbook for digital projects: a management tool for preservation and access*. Andover, Mass.: NEDCC, 2000.

67 *Joint JISC/NPO Digital Preservation Workshop, 3/4 March 1999*, organized by University of Warwick: <http://www.leeds.ac.uk/cedars/OTHER/warwick2.htm> (accessed 31/1/06).

68 Michael Day, 'Preservation 2000', *Ariadne* 26, Dec. 2000: <http://www.ariadne.ac.uk/issue26/metadata/> (accessed 31/1/06).

69 Jeff Rothenberg, *Avoiding technological quicksand: finding a viable technical foundation for digital preservation*. Washington: Council on Library and Information Resources, 1998.

70 Consultative Committee for Space Data Systems, *Reference model for an open archival information system (OAIS): red book*. Washington, D.C.: DDSDS Secretariat, 1999, available from: <http://ssdoo.gsfc.nasa.gov/nost/wwwclassic/documents/p2/CCSDS-650.0-R-1.pdf> (accessed 31/1/06).

71 Raymond A. Lorie, of the IBM Research Division, proposed strategies for maintaining accessibility to both archived data files and archived program behaviours, based on the use of a Universal Virtual Computer. See his 'Long-term archiving of digital information' (IBM research report; RJ 10185 (95059)), May 2000, available from: <http://domino.watson.ibm.com/library/CyberDig.nsf/7d11afdf5c7cda948525 66de006b4127/be2a2b188544df2c8525690d00517082> (accessed 31/1/06)

72 Internet Archive: <http://www.archive.org> (accessed 31/1/06).

73 John Burrows and Diane Cooper, *Theft and loss from UK libraries*. London: Home Office Police Research Group, 1992 (Crime prevention unit series paper; no. 37).

74 *Towards the 21st century*. London: National Preservation Office, 1997.

75 Feeney (ed.), *Digital culture*.

76 Sir Anthony Kenny, *The British Library and the St Pancras building*. London: British Library, 1994.

77 Mirjam Foot, 'Moving the British national collections', *LIBER quarterly* **10**, 2000, 387–92.

78 Helen Shenton was appointed in 1998.

79 In February 2004 it changed its name to the Museums, Libraries and Archives Council (MLA).

80 Resource, *Manifesto*. London: Resource, 2000.

81 Vanessa Marshall, 'The National Preservation Office: raising awareness in the UK now: planning for the future of our past', *Alexandria* **11** (3), 1999, 191–201; *Piecing together the jigsaw: the framework for a national preservation strategy for libraries and archives*. London: National Preservation Office, 1997.

82 The National Preservation Office Register can be viewed at: <http://npo.sequence.co.uk/> (accessed 31/1/06).

83 Stephen Pinfield and Lorcan Dempsey, 'The Distributed National Electronic Resource (DNER) and the hybrid library', *Ariadne* 26, Dec. 2000: <http://www.ariadne.ac.uk/issue26/dner/> (accessed 31/1/06).

Index

Arrangement is word by word; references are to pages. Because everything in the book concerns libraries in some way, more specific entry points are used wherever possible. Entries for organizations should be assumed to be for their *libraries* unless otherwise stated.

Groups and other subordinate bodies of the Library Association are entered under *Library Association*. Individual universities are entered under the distinctive word, or the personal name, in their title, rather than under 'University of ...'.

Synonyms: There is a particular problem in this volume with use of *internet/world wide web*, *automation/computers*, *information technology*, etc., and with *digital/electronic*. On the whole, terms have been indexed as used by the contributors, and readers are urged to try the various possibilities. Some cross-references have been provided.

The endnotes are not indexed, neither are the contributors' names.